Hungary in World War II

WORLD WAR II: THE GLOBAL, HUMAN, AND ETHICAL DIMENSION

G. Kurt Piehler, series editor

Hungary in World War II

Caught in the Cauldron

Deborah S. Cornelius

Fordham University Press | New York 2011

Library of Congress Cataloging-in-Publication Data

Cornelius, Deborah S.
Hungary in World War II : caught in the cauldron / Deborah S. Cornelius.—1st ed.
    p.   cm.— (World War II: the global, human, and ethical dimension)
    Includes bibliographical references and index.
    ISBN 978-0-8232-3343-4 (cloth : alk. paper)
    ISBN 978-0-8232-3344-1 (pbk. : alk. paper)
    ISBN 978-0-8232-3345-8 (ebook)
    1. World War, 1939–1945—Hungary. 2. Hungary—History—1918–1945. I. Title.
D765.56.C67   2011
940.53'439—dc22
2010039622

Printed in the United States of America
13 12 11   5 4 3 2 1
First edition

Contents

Maps

Acknowledgments

I am indebted to many people who have helped me over the years to research and write this manuscript. Although I could not begin to name them all, there are a few I would like to thank personally: first of all, my friend and editor, G. Kurt Piehler, who persuaded me to embark on this project and maintained his support throughout. From the beginning Attila and Andrea Pók, Zsuzsa L. Nagy, and Pál Péter Tóth encouraged me in my endeavor. My friend and fellow author Joan Gimlin commented on many versions of the chapters. I am especially thankful to György Molnar, who was my constant adviser and guide on all things military. I owe special thanks to Emöke Tomsics for her assistance in the Historical Photo-Archive of the Hungarian National Museum in finding suitable illustrative photographs. I am also grateful to scholars in the United States who read the manuscript and offered invaluable suggestions and corrections, in particular Gerhard L. Weinberg and Nándor Dreisziger, and also to the helpful staff at Fordham University Press. My profound gratitude goes to those many individuals who granted me interviews, often reliving painful experiences. And finally, my thanks to my children, Krisztina Fehérváry and András Fehérváry, who supported me throughout.

The maps for the manuscript are the creation of cartographer Béla Nagy from the Institute of History of the Hungarian Academy of Sciences, who prepared them in consultation with me.

All translations from the original Hungarian sources are my own unless otherwise noted. In the end, responsibility for what has been written is entirely my own.

Hungary in World War II

Introduction

Public interest in Hungary's role in World War II has perhaps never been greater than in the years since the change of regime in 1989–90. The full story of Hungary in World War II could not be told until the collapse of the Communist system, forty-five years after the end of the war. Hungary was occupied by the Red Army in 1945, and since the Soviets considered Hungary's participation in the war a crime against the Soviet Union the war was not commemorated. Memorials were raised to the heroic Soviet dead, with memorial speeches and parades, but there were no Hungarian war memorials, no tributes to the fallen Hungarian soldiers. During the following forty years of Communist rule, history was presented from the Soviet point of view. As historian Domokos Kosáry explained: "The situation that facts are just now coming to light is not just that the detailed research was missing, but—much more—that in the service of the Stalinist type of history, the tendency was to select the data which supported that viewpoint, and to pass over or omit other data which did not. . . ."[1]

After forty years of censorship, most people knew only the version of history they had learned in school; that the disastrous war had been brought on by the "fascist reactionary" wartime regime; that all political and military leaders of the period were war criminals, and that Hungary had been liberated by the Soviet Army on April 4, 1945—celebrated every year as Liberation Day. Other key elements of the official version included the assertion that only Communists had been participants in the resistance against the German occupation and the profascist Arrow Cross rule, and that all families that had fled to the West before the Russian invasion had been tainted with fascism. Even prisoners of war who returned from Soviet labor camps were sworn to silence, treated as second-class citizens, and prevented from speaking about their experiences.

It is only in recent years that historians in Hungary have been free to examine and reevaluate their country's role in the war. One by one former taboo questions have been addressed and a new generation of historians has begun to re-examine the period, but forty years of controlled propaganda and education cannot be eliminated easily, and there are still topics that are discussed only hesitantly or not addressed at all.

My first contact with Hungarians came in 1957. As a recent college graduate on an extended tour of Europe, I met with young Hungarian refugees at the University of Edinburgh and again at the University of Vienna. Impressed with their patriotism and idealism, I returned to Yale and wrote my master's thesis on the 1956 Hungarian Revolution. In the 1970s and 1980s I visited Hungary, taking my children to visit their paternal grandparents and to learn a bit of the language and culture, but it was in 1984 that, as a PhD candidate at Rutgers University, I decided to study and write about Hungary. I had realized how little was known about Hungary by the English-speaking public, and how misleading the few references in the European history textbooks from which I had been teaching were.

I arrived in Hungary on a Fulbright Fellowship in 1987, at a time of dramatic change, with the anticipation of greater changes to come. One rushed out every day to get the newspaper and read about the latest happenings. Censorship was loosening; dormant civic societies were being revived. People were suddenly willing—even eager—to tell their stories to an American historian or share their unpublished manuscripts, in hopes that their long-banned history would reach the American public.

Two groundbreaking events, seemingly innocuous to the Western world, give an indication of the changing times. In 1988, an exhibit of the history of Hungarian scouting was allowed to be displayed in the provincial town of Szeged, much to the surprise of newspaper reporters and former scouts. Scouting, a vibrant movement in Hungary from the time the first scout troop was founded in 1911, had been condemned as a fascist organization and the Hungarian Scout Association disbanded in 1948, incorporated into the state-controlled Communist Pioneer youth movement.

The second event was the opening in 1988 of an exhibit on the folk high school movement at the Belvarosi (Central City) Roman Catholic church in Budapest. Begun in the late 1930s, the movement was intended to educate peasant youth in order to create a new village leadership; it was dissolved in 1948 along with the Communist elimination of all autonomous groups of civil society. In 1988, the exhibit was considered daring, and those attending were surprised that the opening was allowed at all.

The pace of change accelerated, and a turning point came with the dramatic reburial of Imre Nagy on June 16, 1989. Three hundred thousand gathered at Heroes Square in silence before the black-draped coffins while the names of the victims of the 1956 Revolution were solemnly read out, and a student leader, Victor Orban, was the first to make the stunning demand—that the Russian Army "go home."

With the end of the Hungarian socialist regime and departure of Soviet occupation troops a year later on June 16, 1990, Hungarians experienced a sudden blossoming of interest in subjects that had been suppressed under Communist rule. Streetside booths were bursting with maps in the Hungarian colors, red, white, and green, displaying the boundaries of the thousand-year-old Kingdom of Hungary, superimposed with the borders of the truncated state after the Treaty of Trianon in 1920—a taboo subject under the socialist regime, since the lost territories had been granted to the neighboring states, the socialist countries of Czechoslovakia, Romania, and Yugoslavia.

Gradually, in the 1990s, more and more forbidden topics found their way into public discourse, and some political and military figures, condemned and executed after the war as war criminals, were rehabilitated. On May 8, 1993, local inhabitants of Dunapentele were allowed to dedicate their war memorial to local soldiers who had fallen in the war or been deported. The private reburial of Admiral Miklós Horthy was allowed, despite vigorous debate. Some resistance fighters, who were not Communists, gained recognition, dispelling the myth that only Communists had participated in the resistance. Even the subject of the hundreds of thousands of Hungarians taken as forced labor to the Soviet Union as prisoners of war was broached, albeit not without hesitation.

In 2001 when I started research for this project, I searched the used bookstores in Budapest for out-of-print copies of memoirs and publications from the 1970s and 1980s, as well as the archives for materials remaining from the war period, much of which had been destroyed. Yet within a few years, I was eagerly awaiting the next work to be published by one of the new generation of historians who had begun to research and re-evaluate Hungary's role in World War II.

I have consulted with numerous historians who have written on the period, and I have also been fortunate in being able to conduct interviews with Hungarians who lived through those difficult days and were generous in sharing their experiences with me. Since most consultations and interviews were conducted in Hungarian, all translations are my own unless otherwise noted.

My objective in this work is to reveal the story of Hungary in World War II and to understand why people involved in the war's turmoil acted as they did under the pressure of unprecedented developments. But in order to view Hungary's role in a clear light, it is first necessary to set the stage by going back to the recent history of the Kingdom of Hungary and the events leading up to Hungary's participation in the war.

At the end of World War I, the Habsburg Empire, and within it the Kingdom of Hungary, had disintegrated. The Treaty of Trianon, the peace treaty signed at Versailles after World War I, granted two-thirds of the kingdom to the neighbor countries, along with three-fifths of its people. The northern part, the Uplands [Felvidék], ceded to the newly created state of Czechoslovakia, had been an integral part of the kingdom, with the historic city of Pressburg (or Pozsony or Bratislava), the former seat of the Hungarian Diet and site of the crowning of Habsburg rulers as sovereigns of Hungary. Transylvania, which had been part of the Hungarian realm since the arrival of the Hungarians and was considered the heartland of the nation, was granted to Romania. The newly created Yugoslavia received the rich fertile lands of the southern part of the kingdom, while a small piece in the west was offered to Austria.

Hungarians were hard pressed to believe that the thousand-year-old Kingdom of Hungary could disintegrate; it had survived the Tatar invasion, one hundred fifty years of Turkish occupation, the rule by the Habsburgs, and the Revolution for Independence in 1848 (see Map 1). The new states were to have been nation states in the spirit of President Wilson's doctrine of self-determination of nations, but each was multiethnic. Three million ethnic Hungarians still lived in those territories, most of them on the borders of the new truncated Hungarian state. Hungarians never recovered from their sense of injustice at the dismemberment of the kingdom, and their belief that the Treaty of Trianon had been a dreadful mistake, which the architects of the treaty would eventually rectify. Understanding of this point is key to deciphering the Hungarian behavior in World War II.

From the end of World War I and the Treaty of Trianon, Hungary had never given up the hope that it would be able to reclaim its lost territories, or at the very least the areas inhabited mainly by ethnic Hungarians. During the interwar years the small, impoverished, and politically isolated state had struggled to establish a government and stabilize the economy, but its lost lands were never forgotten.

Map 1. The Austro-Hungarian Monarchy in Europe 1914.

With the outbreak of World War II it was clear that Hungary would not be able to avoid being involved in the war. Despite efforts to maintain her neutrality, her geopolitical situation in Central Europe—surrounded by countries either allied with or occupied by Germany—predetermined her participation. The question was whether this participation would take shape as a German ally or an occupied country.

The lure of regaining Hungary's lost territories combined with Germany's stunning early successes persuaded many that the restoration of the territories might be won through a German alliance. This belief was strengthened by the fact that Hungarian life maintained a surprising amount of normalcy, even though limited for its Jewish citizens, until the German occupation in March 1944. Political institutions remained relatively unchanged, cultural life flourished, and reformers planned for the postwar restructuring of Hungary's anachronistic political and social system, as well as the system of landed estates, which virtually all parties recognized as unavoidable.

For Hungarians the tragedy of Trianon repeated itself in World War II. In contrast to their earlier experience, the last year of the war brought brutal devastation and a crushing defeat—the German occupation, Jewish deportations, the fascist rule of the Arrow Cross Party, the unparallel, long six months of frontline battles, which blanketed the whole country, followed by further devastation wrought by the Soviet occupying forces. Hungary paid a bitter price for the brief recovery of its lost territories. Of grave consequence for the nation was the destruction of its traditional leadership and of the very structure of society. Few could have imagined the nature of the system, which was to replace the regency of Admiral Miklós Horthy.

1   The Legacy of World War I

To understand Hungary's role in World War II, one must go back to World War I and the defeat of the Central Powers (Germany, Austria-Hungary, and Bulgaria) by the Triple Entente (Great Britain, France, and Russia), the collapse of the Austro-Hungarian Monarchy, and the tumultuous years between 1918 and 1920. During this brief period, the thousand-year-old Kingdom of Hungary disintegrated, the Habsburg monarch, Charles I, abdicated in favor of a republic, Hungary's neighbors occupied much of the country, and a short-lived Bolshevik regime took control. As a final blow to the devastated and demoralized Hungarian people, the peace treaty signed at the Grand Trianon Palace in Versailles confirmed the loss of two-thirds of Hungary's territory and three-fifths of its people, reducing the population from 18.2 million to 7.9 million. Hungarians felt a deep sense of injustice at the dismemberment of their kingdom and believed that the Treaty of Trianon had been a dreadful mistake that would eventually be rectified.

Once a part of the Austro-Hungarian Monarchy, the largest state in Europe, Hungary had become a small country in Central Europe, cut off from the sea and the outside world, and surrounded by antagonistic neighbor states. The territories lost had been integral parts of the Kingdom of Hungary and carried great symbolic value. Transylvania, ceded to Romania, had been considered the Hungarian homeland from the time of the entrance of the first Magyar tribes. Northern Hungary, ceded to Czechoslovakia, was the only part of the kingdom that had maintained Hungary's independence during the Turkish occupation. Its main city, Pozsony/Bratislava, had been the site of the Hungarian parliament until 1848 and the crowning of Hungarian kings (see Map 2).

The losses were so drastic that Hungarians struggled to understand the reasons for this catastrophe. Although many of those who lived in the territories lost to the neighbor states were non-Magyar—not ethnic Hungarians—over three million considered themselves Magyar.[1] One and one-half million of these lived in solidly Hungarian-inhabited belts near

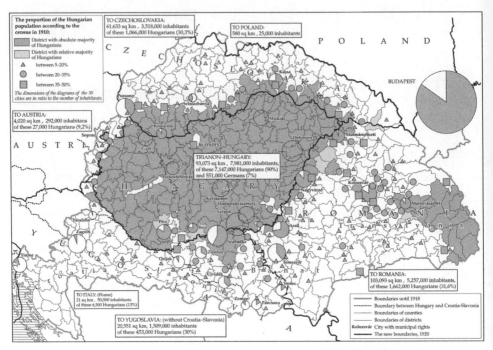

The proportion of the Hungarian population according to the census in 1910:
District with absolute majority of Hungarians
District with relative majority of Hungarians
△ between 5-20%
● between 20-35%
■ between 35-50%
The dimensions of the diagrams of the 30 cities are in ratio to the number of inhabitants.

TO CZECHOSLOVAKIA: 61,633 sq km , 3,518,000 inhabitants of these 1,066,000 Hungarians (30,3%)

TO POLAND: 580 sq km , 25,000 inhabitants

TO AUSTRIA: 4,020 sq km , 292,000 inhabitans of these 27,000 Hungarians (9,2%)

TRIANON–HUNGARY: 93,073 sq km , 7,981,000 inhabitants, of these 7,147,000 Hungarians (90%) and 551,000 Germans (7%)

TO ROMANIA: 103,093 sq km , 5,257,000 inhabitants, of these 1,662,000 Hungarians (31,6%)

TO ITALY: (Fiume) 21 sq km , 50,000 inhabitants of these 6,500 Hungarians (13%)

TO YUGOSLAVIA: (without Croatia–Slavonia) 20,551 sq km, 1,509,000 inhabitants of these 453,000 Hungarians (30%)

Boundaries until 1918
Boundary between Hungary and Croatia-Slavonia
Boundaries of counties
Boundaries of districts
Kolozsvár City with municipal rights
The new boundaries, 1920

Map 2. Trianon-Hungary, after the Peace Treaty of Trianon, 1920.

the new borders. Even though the treaty in principle had been based on self-determination, the areas populated by a majority of Hungarian speakers were granted to the neighbor states without plebiscites.[2] Viewed by Hungarian citizens as a grave injustice, the cutting off of the Hungarian-inhabited territories blinded the population to the claims of non-Hungarians for self-determination. The result was a complete denial of the peace treaty and widespread demands for *mindent vissza* (everything back), an attitude that was to persist throughout World War II.

During the final weeks of World War I the Habsburg Monarchy began to disintegrate. On October 28, 1918, the Czechs seceded from the Austrian Empire, announcing the formation of an independent Czechoslovak Republic. Two days later, a Slovak national council proclaimed their independence from the Hungarian Kingdom and union with the Czech state. In Zagreb, on October 29, the Croatian National Council of Croats, Serbs, and Slovenes declared their independence from Austria-Hungary. Romanians living in Transylvania proclaimed their secession on October 27, although they did not give up the idea of autonomy until December, and Ukrainians (Ruthenians) announced secession on October 31. On October

30 the Austrian National Assembly adopted a provisional constitution, and finally, on October 31, a democratic revolution broke out in Hungary. By the time an armistice was signed on November 3, 1918, the monarchy had ceased to exist.

The Hungarian Revolutions of 1918 and 1919

In the fall of 1918, as it became clear that the war had been lost, revolutionary forces began gathering in Budapest. Tensions among the population had been rising, with food riots, strikes, and increasing desertions from the army—a result of the terrible losses during the war, rising prices and growing shortages. The revolutionary spirit of the October Revolution of 1917 was spreading, fueled by the returning Hungarian prisoners of war from Russia with demonstrations expressing sympathy with the Bolsheviks and demanding peace. On the evening of October 30 news came of a revolution in Vienna and the crowds grew larger. The revolution began with the troops, which had been brought to Budapest in order to crush the popular movement. Officers and soldiers tore the imperial ensigns from their caps and replaced the emblem with the red and white aster flowers on sale to celebrate All Souls' Day, launching the so-called Aster Revolution.

Count Mihály Károlyi, a pacifist and idealist, emerged as the symbol of the revolution. Despite his aristocratic heritage he had become the most popular politician in Hungary. During worker strikes in June 1918, which were put down brutally by the military, the party led by Károlyi took on the role of speaking for the striking workers in Parliament.[3] The revolutionaries united around him as head of the recently formed revolutionary National Council, and he became prime minister in November 1918. The Social Democrats, who had never been represented in Parliament, became the main support of the government because of their popular appeal, along with an efficient centralized machinery and affiliation with labor unions.[4] People were tired of war and wanted reforms. Colonel Linder, minister of war, in a move that soon proved to be a mistake, dismissed the army on November 2 with the slogan, "I never want to see a soldier again."[5]

In the early weeks of his ministry, Károlyi enjoyed countrywide popularity. The revolution was accomplished with little bloodshed, accompanied by great optimism that order would be restored and peace made with the Entente powers, especially since it was known that Károlyi had good relations with the principal members of the Entente. During the war he had made covert contacts with British and French diplomats in

Switzerland and proclaimed himself a follower of Woodrow Wilson's Fourteen Points. Many welcomed Károlyi's liberal reform program, designed to deal with the political issues that the former conservative government had failed to address. Károlyi, one of the richest landowners in Hungary, aimed to liquidate the semi-feudal remnants of an outmoded order, and promised land reform, autonomy to the national minorities, and universal suffrage including women. Liberals, the younger clergy and the members of the feminist movement enthusiastically supported his plans for reform.[6] Károlyi was confirmed by the Habsburg Emperor and King of Hungary, Charles IV, who abdicated on November 13, and on November 16 the National Council announced the People's Republic of Hungary before Parliament. Hungary had finally regained its independence, but as a defeated nation.[7]

The surrender of the Austro-Hungarian Monarchy on November 3 in the Padua Armistice had virtually ignored Hungary. Károlyi, alarmed at the imminent invasion of Hungary from the south by the Serbs and French, decided to send a delegation to Belgrade to discuss the application of the Padua armistice agreement to Hungary. On November 7 Károlyi led the delegation to negotiate with French General Louis Franchet d'Esperey, Allied Commander of the Balkan armies in Belgrade. The delegation was full of optimism, believing that the establishment of a democratic republic would meet Wilson's conditions for peace. In an effort to indicate the democratic nature of the new Hungary, the delegation included a Social Democrat as well as a representative of the Soldiers' and Workers' councils. Their expectations were disappointed. The Entente powers were suspicious of the liberal revolution, and the French particularly were concerned for their own security. They greatly feared the spread of the Russian Revolution to Central and Western Europe, and the Hungarian Soldiers' and Workers' councils appeared much too similar to those established in Russia by the Bolsheviks.

General d'Esperey dashed their hopes, greeting them coldly and speaking as conqueror to the conquered. One of the participants noted that General d'Esperey "identified himself more with the despised Austro-Hungarian generals than with the democratic military organization that was responsible for the revolution among the belligerents."[8] When Károlyi asked for fair treatment of his government as the true representative of the Hungarian people, d'Esperey interrupted him saying that he was only a representative of the Magyars. "I know your history," he said. "In your country you have oppressed those who are not Magyar. Now you have the Czechs, Slovaks, Rumanians, Yugoslavs as enemies; I hold these people in the hollow of my hand. I have only to make a sign and you will be destroyed."[9]

General d'Esperey was rude to the representative of the National Council, Jewish Baron Lajos Hatvany, humiliating him, and sarcastic to the soldier-worker representative who appeared in a revolutionary uniform which he had designed himself. D'Esperey exclaimed: "*Vous êtes tombés si bas!*" (You have fallen so low!) He said that he had agreed to talk with them only out of respect for Károlyi and urged them to support Károlyi as Hungary's only hope. His cold tone softened only when he asked about the "unfortunate young king."[10] Károlyi tactfully avoided explaining that the government was about to dethrone King Charles and declare a people's republic. But despite d'Esperey's hectoring and insults, the Hungarians were offered reasonably fair terms at the time.

Károlyi continued his attempt to establish diplomatic relations with the victors, but without success. He hoped to gain the support of President Wilson whose Fourteen Points speech had been greeted enthusiastically by the Hungarian population, but Wilson as well as the British had adopted a wait-and-see attitude, leaving military decisions in the area to the French. The Allies had decided that Hungary, like Germany, was to be treated as an enemy state. In their fear of revolution and Bolshevism, they gave way to the French policy, which was intended to create a chain of strong successor states—Czecho-Slovakia, Romania, and the South Slav states—as a protective belt against Germany and Soviet Russia. The protective belt was to cover as much of the territory of the former monarchy as possible, regardless of ethnic considerations.[11]

The liberal revolution, rather than gaining their favor, only increased their fears of the spread of Bolshevism. They suspected that the Károlyi government was a possible carrier of Bolshevism and refused to recognize the new government. During the next months, the government's primary concern—along with the attempt to establish diplomatic relations with the Entente powers—was to hold the country together.

In November 1918, Oszkár Jászi, head of the new ministry for nationality affairs, began to negotiate with leaders of the non-Hungarian nationalities. A proponent of a federal solution to the question of nationalities within the monarchy, Jászi offered the non-Hungarian nationalities maximum autonomy within the borders of Hungary, but these offers came much too late. For a time, negotiations with the Slovak representative, Milan Hodža, appeared to be positive, but Hodža was abruptly withdrawn by the new Czech government; autonomy for the Slovaks would destroy their plans for a Czecho-Slovak state. Only the Ruthenians, the

Ukrainian population of Hungary, agreed to the terms. The Transylvanian Romanians at first had aimed for autonomy, fearing that Transylvania would be swallowed up by the more backward and conservative Romanian Old Kingdom, but in December they voted to join Greater Romania.[12]

The military convention signed on November 13 had established a demarcation line between Hungary and those territories that had seceded from the Monarchy. However, the new Czecho-Slovak republic, Romania, and the South Slav states, eager to be in possession of the lands they claimed by the time the peace conference began, ignored the agreement. The refusal by the Entente to prevent Hungary's neighbors from occupying Hungarian territory before the conclusion of the peace treaty came in direct violation of the Belgrade military convention.[13] Hungary's neighbors were encouraged by the French who aimed to strengthen these countries against Bolshevik Russia. France's earlier concern to build a united defense against Germany had changed after the Bolshevik revolution and the defeat of the Central powers. Now the planned barrier of East European countries against Germany was to be anti-Russian. The Czech Legion, which had been organized in Russia and involved in fighting the Reds in Siberia, had been under nominal French command since December 1917. Poland and Romania both had territorial claims against Communist Russia.[14]

Supported by the French, Serbian, and Romanian troops occupied southern Hungary, Czech troops began to invade northern Hungary, and Romanian troops moved west to take Transylvania. The Entente powers ordered Hungarian troops to evacuate Slovakia and the Romanian army entered Kolozsvár, the capital of Transylvania. By January, Hungary had lost more than half of its former territory. Authorized by the Entente, the neighbor countries sent in troops as well as civil authorities to the Hungarian territories that they claimed. The territory they occupied corresponded roughly to what was to become the new Hungarian frontier.

The occupation came as a tremendous shock to the Hungarian inhabitants; it was incomprehensible to them that they should be under a foreign rule. Rezső Peery, then a small boy of nine, recalled his amazement when Czech troops occupied his city in northern Hungary: "I gaped in astonishment at . . . the long long procession of armed troops marching toward the Market square."[15] Italian Alpine troops accompanied the Czech forces invading Pozsony/Bratislava. "The occupation of the city in 1919 was accompanied by such brutality that it aroused the spirit of opposition in even the most tolerant. . . . The barbarities of the occupation remained before our eyes. . . . Respect for the interests of honor, truth, spirit and culture, were thus interwoven in our eyes with the matter of national loyalty. As it was said in the case of Alsace-Lorraine: 'Jamais en parler, toujours y penser' [Never talk about it, always think about it]—that was our attitude in national matters, just like the Alsacians."[16]

Erzsébet Arvay told of the bitter night in 1918 when her family debated whether to leave their village in Transylvania where her father was the teacher: "My father paced the room during the whole night trying to decide whether we should flee or stay." The family traveled in chaotic conditions by train with seven-year-old Erzsébet and her two-week-old baby sister to the home of her mother's parents in Transdanubia.[17]

In this difficult situation, the Károlyi government's position became more and more tenuous as the population lost faith in its ability to deal with the Entente. On November 24, led by Béla Kun, revolutionary soldiers who had returned from Soviet prisoner of war camps established the Communist Party of Hungary, and the peacemakers became more and more convinced hat Hungary was rapidly becoming a hotbed of Bolshevism and anarchy.[18]

In mid-December the British war cabinet debated the Hungarian government's request to send a mission to Paris, and agreed with the French that Hungary as a defeated country had no right to send a mission. In addition to the breakdown of civil administration, the collapse of the transport system, and inflation, the economic blockade by the Entente prevented the entry of food and coal. The coal blockade by the Czech government caused economic havoc in Hungary. The mayor of Budapest appealed to President Wilson to have the Czechs lift the blockade, but Beneš frankly admitted that the Czechs expected to exploit the coal situation to hold Hungary in check.[19] Since Hungary had signed an armistice and not a peace treaty the Allied blockade continued. People cut down their trees for heat; trains cut their schedules, and city lighting was reduced.

Enthusiasm for the regime was fading. Károlyi began to implement his reform program, but progress was slow. With the increase of discontent the number of social democrats in the government was increased. Aristocrats, who had always been suspicious of Károlyi's idealism and had never trusted him to defend their class interests, tried to discredit him with Entente missions as not capable of stopping Bolshevism.[20] The industrial workers, small farmers, poor peasantry, and the many prisoners of war who had returned from Soviet Russia regarded his program as only a prelude to a more radical revolution. The administration announced the eight-hour day but there was no work, and the returned soldiers contributed to the huge numbers of unemployed. Small farmers and agrarian workers slowed down farm production as they waited for the expected land reform. Workers on the estates went on strike and it was necessary to introduce forced labor. Inflation continued unabated; expenses of the state were huge while its income was greatly reduced.

The Opening of the Paris Peace Conference

Meanwhile, on January 18, 1919, the peace conference opened in Paris, with twenty-seven nations assembled to discuss the terms for the defeated nations. The smaller nations soon realized that the plenary sessions were only ritual occasions; matters were decided by conferences among the Big Four—President Woodrow Wilson, David Lloyd George for Great Britain, Georges Clemenceau for France, and Vittorio Orlando for Italy.

From the outset the peace conference suffered from confusion over its organization, purpose, and procedure. The Big Four had originally planned a preliminary conference to hammer out the terms to be offered—terms of military and naval disarmament and the main outlines of future territorial settlement. A subsequent congress was planned at which the enemy would be represented and would have occasion to advance counter proposals. However, as the months went by what had been a preliminary conference became the real thing. The Germans, who originally asked for the armistice in the belief that peace would be made according to Wilson's Fourteen Points, were denied representation, as were the Hungarians.

A major task facing the conference was the drawing of new borders. The old political structures had been dismantled; the multinational Habsburg monarchy had disintegrated, the Russian Empire was no more, the German Empire had been defeated and a new democratic republic formed. Borders supposedly were to be drawn based on the principle of the nation-state and of self-determination. Yet the general feeling was that the defeated countries, Austria-Hungary, Bulgaria, but especially Germany, had to be punished and that the small allied countries should be rewarded. Here the problem was the multiethnic nature of the whole region of Central and Eastern Europe and the competing nationalisms. There were also the political and economic interests of the Entente powers. The French demanded security from Germany, the British were interested in colonies, President Wilson fought hard for his League of Nations.

The victors had no organized plan of procedure. They realized that it made no sense to have a discussion among all twenty-seven states, so in order to give the smaller allied states some feeling of participation, they asked the delegates to put into writing territorial or other concessions they desired to obtain from the treaty. They then invited the delegates to expound their claims before the Supreme Council. Instead of dealing successively with each of the enemy states in the order of importance—making a treaty first with Germany, then with Austria, Hungary, Turkey, and Bulgaria—they dissipated their forces by listening to the long, drawn-out presentations.

By this time the states neighboring Hungary had occupied much of the land they claimed. The question was how much more land they would be able to gain and where the borders would be drawn. "In the heady atmosphere of 1919, it was madness not to grab as much as possible."[21] The smaller powers made claims far in excess of their real expectations, also demanding land solidly inhabited by ethnic Hungarians. When Czech troops marched into his village in northern Hungary, Zoltán Boross, a Hungarian boy of twelve, remembered that no one could speak Czech or Slovak; his mother, who spoke German, became the translator.[22]

Inevitably in multiethnic Central and Eastern Europe claims overlapped. Various rationales were used in the demands. The Czech claims rested upon "two radically different, indeed mutually incompatible, principles."[23] They claimed the lands of Bohemia and Moravia on historic grounds, but based their claim to Slovakia, which had been historically part of the thousand-year-old Kingdom of Hungary, on ethnic grounds, asserting that Czechs and Slovaks were two branches of the same nation. They also claimed Ruthenia, with a primarily Ukrainian population, in order to have a common border with Romania. The Romanians had exorbitant demands, claiming much of the Hungarian kingdom—Transylvania, the Bánát, Bessarabia, and Bukovina—and also a wide band of the Hungarian lowlands, all of which they argued were historically and ethnically part of Romania. Yugoslavia, which already possessed much of what it wanted by the time the peace conference opened—Bosnia-Herzegovina, the Slovene heartland, much of Dalmatia, the old Kingdom of Croatia—demanded territories conflicting with territories claimed by Romania, including the Bácska, which was part of the rich southern Hungarian plain, and all of the Bánát, with 28,500 square kilometers (about 11,000 square miles) of rich black soil and abundant rivers and streams.[24]

Finally, the Supreme Council, which found Romania's demands excessive, had become tired of the wrangling with Yugoslavia over the Bánát. Lloyd George recommended referring the claims to a subcommittee of experts for a just settlement. He believed that after the committee had studied the matter and found the "truth," only a few issues would need to come back to the Supreme Council. Thus, the special territorial commission, the Commission on Romanian and Yugoslav Affairs, the first of several such commissions, was established to determine the future of the Bánát and other pieces of territory in south-central Europe.[25]

Each territorial commission consisted of two delegates from each of the five great powers, ten delegates in all, one of whom was termed a *technical expert*, although in many cases these so-called specialists had little or no first-hand knowledge of the countries involved. The main task of each territorial commission was not to recommend a general territorial settlement but to pronounce on the particular claims of the various states. Although it was not realized at the time, the recommendations of the delegates were to go into the peace treaties unchanged since the leaders had no time to consider them in detail. In the end, the members of the Romanian commission determined the future shapes of Yugoslavia, Romania, Greece, and Bulgaria, as well as the balance of power in the Balkans between Hungary and its neighbors, and between the Soviet Union and south-central Europe.[26]

The Birth of the Hungarian Soviet Republic

In Hungary living conditions continued to deteriorate. The lack of medicine, a result of the blockade, was particularly devastating because the Spanish flu pandemic—today estimated to have killed at least twenty-five million worldwide—had struck with frightening speed.[27] On Christmas and New Year's Eve authorities in Budapest forbade or restricted the opening of places of amusement because of the danger of contagion, although village celebrations and balls were held in the countryside. In February the administration introduced meatless and fatless days, and people joked about the coarse bread, made of pearl barley with bran. Refugees were living in railroad cars; soldiers were without clothing or shoes. In Budapest it was ordered that anyone with more than five suits or pairs of shoes should turn them in to be redistributed.[28]

In January a government crisis led to Károlyi's resignation as prime minister. However, since the Socialists decided to continue to support him, Károlyi continued to lead the government, now as president of the republic. By February 1919 the domestic situation had deteriorated to a state of chaos. The newly formed Communist Party under the leadership of Béla Kun presented a major threat; although unable to convert many of the prewar Socialists and trade unionists, it succeeded in recruiting a new generation, including returning, demoralized soldiers and younger intelligentsia. The government decided to quell the Bolshevik movement and after a demonstration on February 21 arrested Béla Kun and about one hundred other Communists. The arrests only aroused sympathy for the Communists and the movement continued to thrive. The party now had approximately ten to fifteen thousand members in Budapest and another twenty-some thousand in the provincial towns. The arrests also upset the Socialists who believed the government should not interfere in the internal problems of the workers' movements.[29]

Land reform had been one of the driving forces of the revolution, and the Károlyi government finally passed a land reform act on February 16, 1919. However, failing to realize the impatience of the agrarian population and the urgency of reform, the government decided to wait until the spring work season to carry it out. The only actual land distribution Károlyi made was when he symbolically distributed lands from his own estate. Universal suffrage was enacted, including suffrage for women, but the elections were postponed until April in the hope that elections could also be held in the occupied territories.[30]

The government was already on the verge of collapse when, on March 20, 1919, an order came for Hungarian troops to evacuate a new neutral zone which the Supreme Council had decided to create along the Hungarian-Romanian border to facilitate a plan for military intervention against Russia.[31] The head of the French military mission in Budapest, Lt. Col. Ferdinand Vix, presented Károlyi with this decision as an ultimatum—later known as the Vix note—in which Hungary was given ten days to evacuate the neutral region. Károlyi protested that if he agreed to the neutral zone there would be revolution and his government would fall; the Hungarians were being asked to withdraw from almost exactly the territory claimed by Romania, while the Romanian troops were allowed to move westward by 100 kilometers. Vix, who had been continually frustrated by the conflicting orders he received from his French superiors and the Supreme Council, simply stated that Hungary must accept the ultimatum from Paris, and that the Allies would keep Romania in check.[32]

The following day, March 21, mass hysteria erupted. The populace greeted the news of the ultimatum with defiance and spontaneous demonstrations. They now believed that the Károlyi government had been mistaken in its efforts to cooperate with the Entente powers. The government hastily decided to reject the Vix note and to hand over power to the Socialists. Although the Social Democratic Party had previously refused to work with the Communists, now the more radical Socialist leaders announced that only with communist collaboration would they take power. The government was so eager to hand over power that the ministers did not even question why the respected moderate Socialist leader, Ernő Garami, resigned from the party. Károlyi, who believed he would continue as president, learned by accident that the Workers' and Soldiers' councils of Budapest had proclaimed the dictatorship of the proletariat. The population now placed its hopes in a Russian alliance to save the integrity of the country and accepted as its emblem the red proletarian fist smashing the peace table in Paris.[33]

On March 21 the new cabinet, the Revolutionary Governing Council, proclaimed the Hungarian Soviet Republic and dismissed President Károlyi. Although a Social Democrat, Sándor Garbai, was given the post of president of the council, real power was in the hands of Béla Kun as People's Commissar for Foreign Affairs. Initially this government consisted of a Socialist-Communist coalition with two-thirds of the people's commissars from the former Social Democratic Party, but the Communists acted quickly and managed to dismiss the Socialist ministers within days. At first the transition went quite smoothly, supported by the patriotism of the population. Many of the more conservative citizens, if they had not already left the country, had withdrawn from public life. Officials, the peasantry, even the officers hoped the Soviet Republic would establish order and that its pro-Russian policy could preserve prewar Hungary against the decisions of the peace conference.

The peaceful transition to the Soviet Republic surprised everyone, including the Communists, who had believed that it would take an armed uprising to gain power. Their leadership was composed primarily of Hungarian Bolsheviks, the majority Jewish, who had returned from Russian POW camps full of revolutionary fervor. They believed that the Hungarian revolution was only the first of the great socialist revolutions that would break out throughout Central Europe and spread throughout the world, leading to the World Revolution. Their goal was socialism and the spread of world revolution, but since it had been a wave of patriotism that had brought the new government into power, Kun modified much of his earlier dogmatic rhetoric.[34] A number of young progressive intellectuals gained positions in the government, including the movie director Sándor Korda, and the sociologist Karl Mannheim was named a university professor.[35] Life in the cities was relatively peaceful, but the optimistic mood lasted only a month.

During the first weeks the Kun government issued dozens of decrees intended to transform society by introducing socialism, equality, and public ownership of industry, trade, agriculture, and finances. The state nationalized factories, decreed the abolition of aristocratic titles and privileges, guaranteed freedom of speech and assembly, and abolished alcohol. Some of the more extreme measures intruded on private life, such as the compulsory reallocation of housing and furniture, taking over bank deposits and jewelry of individuals, and even the order for compulsory baths and sex education for schoolchildren.[36]

Since the new regime regarded religion as superstition, it advocated complete separation of church and state. It secularized all denominational, regional, and private schools, and eliminated the twice-daily prayers. The churches were forbidden to participate in public life and Catholics were horrified by plans to turn churches into cinemas. Religious orders of both sexes were dissolved, churches were desecrated, and priests and nuns were physically attacked.[37]

The real problem for the regime was the countryside. Hungary was still primarily an agricultural country and the urban revolutionaries had little understanding of the peasantry. Suspicious of peasant landowners, they planned to skip the Russian example of distributing land and move immediately to collectivized agriculture. Land reform, planned by the Károlyi government, was enacted on April 5 but there was no actual land distribution; instead estates were transformed into state farms and cooperatives, often retaining the same overseers, which further alienated the deeply religious peasants, who were already upset by the regime's atheistic policies. In reaction, much of the peasantry turned against the proletarian dictatorship.[38]

Mobile detachments to combat counterrevolutionary activities were organized under the command of the people's commissar for military affairs, Tibor Szamuely. Known as the Lenin Boys, the brigades were deployed at various locations around the country where counterrevolutionary movements were suspected to operate. The brigades instituted what became known as the Red Terror with ruthless and brutal recriminations against people in the countryside whom they accused of being involved in so-called counterrevolutionary activity. Sometimes, the brigades carried out executions without any concrete charge for purposes of intimidation. Szamuely personally killed and tortured many Hungarians.

Free and secret elections were held as planned on April 7. However, because of regulations a large part of the population was excluded. All men and women who had reached eighteen years of age, with the exception of the "exploiters and priests," could vote. Anyone who had hired workers or received income without work, especially those in commerce, priests, ministers, and those in holy orders, were barred from casting a vote. In Budapest the vote was held by secret ballot, but generally in the villages the vote was open. Of the four to four and a half million who were eligible, about half did not vote, a number that was especially high in the countryside. Many women, especially in the villages, did not dare to vote for fear of social censure.[39]

Ironically, it was only with the establishment of a Bolshevik regime that Wilson and Lloyd George began to question the harsh policy toward Hungary promulgated by the French. The idea of the neutral zone had originated from the French, and increasingly the British, the Americans, and the Italians came to blame the unreasonably rigid anticommunist policy of France for the revolution. At the meeting on March 31 they condemned the way the peace conference participants had treated the Hungarians. Wilson admitted that perhaps it had been unwise to establish the neutral zone. Lloyd George expressed doubts whether the Vix note had made clear that the neutral zone would have no effect on the definition of new frontiers. While Clemenceau continued to say that "the Hungarians are not our friends but our enemies," Lloyd George noted that it was dangerous to leave millions of Hungarians outside their country—just as it was to leave Germans under Polish rule. It was decided to send the widely admired South African General Jan Smuts to Hungary to assess the situation and persuade the Kun regime to accept a slightly modified neutral zone.[40]

The Smuts delegation arrived on April 4 and was greeted with great excitement by the population in Budapest who believed that it implied recognition of the regime by the Entente. However, Smuts had not been sent to negotiate, but to collect information and inform Kun of the Entente's insistence on a neutral zone. Smuts met with Kun several times, and Kun made a good impression on him.[41] Smuts presented the proposal to Kun concerning the neutral zone which was slightly different from the Vix note, with borders that shifted to the favor of Hungary to the extent of eight to ten kilometers, and at some places twenty kilometers. It also provided that the Romanians would not be allowed to advance further than their current positions, and that the neutral zone was to be occupied by British, French, Italian, and possibly American troops.[42]

The Hungarian negotiators, in the expectation that there would be further negotiations, responded to the concessions offered by Smuts with counterproposals, failing to understand that Smuts was not empowered to negotiate. Smuts made a final appeal for the acceptance of the conditions as proposed, but when unsuccessful he decided to break off discussions and gave the word for his train to leave. The Kun delegation, still expecting further negotiations, stood waiting on the platform. Harold Nicolson, a member of the Smuts delegation, described their departure: "And as they stand the train gradually begins to move. Smuts brings his hand to the salute. We glide out into the night, retaining on the retinas of our eyes the picture of four bewildered faces looking up in blank amazement."[43]

In his report Smuts supported Kun's idea of a meeting of states concerned over disputed borders, and also suggested that the wartime blockade be lifted once the Hungarians accepted the demarcation line. Those in Paris ignored his recommendations; they were more concerned with his conclusion that the new government in Hungary was essentially Bolshevik. They hoped that the Soviet Russian system was about to collapse, and were not willing to tolerate another Bolshevik regime in the center of Europe. The French General d'Esperey had been organizing a joint Romanian, Serbian, and Czechoslovak attack on the Hungarian Soviet Republic with tacit support from military quarters. On April 16 the Royal Romanian Army crossed the demarcation line, aiming at the overthrow of the Kun regime. Toward the end of the month they were joined by Czechoslovak forces, but the Yugoslav government declined to take part in the intervention. By the end of April the Romanian army was near Budapest.

The question of the intervention was raised at the peace conference on April 26 in connection with the peace treaties with Austria and Hungary, and Wilson succeeded in having his proposal adopted to call upon Romania to stop its advance. But the letter with the appeal was not forwarded until days later.[44]

Settlement of Peace Terms

In the meantime in Paris the work of the peace conference continued. Since the territorial commissions were instructed only to make judgments on particular claims of the small states rather than a more general settlement, there were unfortunate results: "The Committee on Romanian Claims, for instance, thought only in terms of Transylvania, the Committee on Czech claims concentrated upon the southern frontier of Slovakia."[45] The technical experts understood that their recommendations would be subject to a final discussion in which the interested parties would have their say, but pressed for time the Supreme Council accepted their recommendations with virtually no change. In effect the committees constituted the final court of appeal.

Harold Nicolson, who represented Britain on both committees, admitted: "It was only too late that it was realized that these two separate Committees had between them imposed upon Hungary a loss of territory and population which, when combined, was very serious indeed. . . . Had the work been concentrated in the hands of a 'Hungarian' Committee, not only would a wider area of frontier been open for the give and take of discussion, but it would have been seen that the total cessions imposed placed more Magyars under alien rule than was consonant with the doctrine of Self-Determination."[46]

On May 8 the Council of Four was presented with the recommendations on Hungary's borders with Romania, Czechoslovakia, Austria, and Yugoslavia, and approved them with scarcely any discussion. Nicolson described the scene at the Quai d'Orsay:

There in that heavy tapestried room, under the simper of Marie de Medicis, (with the windows open upon the garden and the sound of water sprinkling from a fountain and from a lawn-hose)—the fate of the Austro-Hungarian Empire is finally settled. Hungary is partitioned by these five distinguished gentlemen— indolently, irresponsibly partitioned—while the water sprinkles on the lilac outside—while the experts watch anxiously. . . . They begin with Transylvania, and after some insults flung like tennis balls between Tardieu and Lansing, Hungary loses her South. Then Czecho-Slovakia, and while the flies drone in and out of the open windows Hungary loses her North and East. . . . Then the Jugo-Slav frontier, where the Committee's report is adopted without change. Then tea and macaroons.[47]

In Hungary the Romanian and Czech invasions created a new situation in which the survival of the revolution was at stake. The regime dropped the language of proletarian revolution and appealed simply to patriotism. Half the working population of Budapest enlisted in the newly formed Hungarian Red Army, which was staffed mainly by former Imperial and Royal Army officers. Even conservative army officers found Kun better than the Romanians. Many who joined the Red Army were later to serve as high-ranking officers in World War II. Géza Lakatos, then a young career officer, explained: "That was the time when—with the support of the victorious Entente powers—and hungry for new territory—Czech and Romanian neighbors crossed the so-called demarcation line . . . and forced their way into the territory of the truncated country. . . . In the first days of May, the Red Army Command ordered all of the general staff officers who were in Budapest to Gödöllö. What could I do? I was a professional officer, accustomed to obey." Lakatos was made aide-de-camp for the Red Army Commander, Vilmos Böhm, "the former typewriter salesman, who had absolutely no military training."[48]

In the meantime, two counterrevolutionary Hungarian groups were forming. In Vienna an anti-Bolshevist committee, including the future prime ministers Pál Teleki and István Bethlen, established contact with representatives of the British, United States, and Italian governments and sent appeals to the peace conference protesting the invasion of Hungary. On May 5 a second group formed in Romanian-occupied Arad, and then moved to French-occupied Szeged. Its location and French occupation made it a natural focus for refugees from Transylvania, including many former military officers, one of whom, Captain Gyula Gömbös, began to organize the National Army. On his suggestion Miklós Horthy, former admiral of the Imperial and Royal Navy, was asked to accept the position of minister of war. At the end of the war, Horthy, at age fifty-one, had gone into retirement, expecting to end his days managing his estate in Kenderes. Instead, he began a new career. The majority of the force of about four thousand in the National Army were radical young officers, many refugees from Transylvania, who were ready to punish those who had supported the revolution. The French supported the counter-revolutionary government without giving it official recognition.[49]

A Hungarian counterattack on May 30 pushed back the Czechs, driving a wedge between them and the Romanians. Within a few days the Hungarian forces occupied most of central and northwestern Slovakia. The Hungarian-populated areas welcomed the Red Army as liberators and hundreds joined the Hungarian army, while in eastern Slovakia a Slovak Soviet Republic was proclaimed. The Allies found it difficult to agree on how to proceed. The Czechs made additional claims but the Allies, by now worried about the conflict, rejected most of them. "We must be fair even to the Hungarians," said Lloyd George, "they are only defending their country."[50]

On June 13 the Council of Four sent a telegram informing the Hungarians that the future borders with Czechoslovakia and Romania had been settled, and ordering that they withdraw their troops into their own territory within five days. Telegrams were also sent to Czechoslovakia and Romania, announcing that immediately following the withdrawal the Romanians would also retreat. This was the first official notice that the future borders of the Hungarian state had been decided. After a short delay, the government, faced with an exhausted army, ordered the retreat. By doing so it lost the support of the nationalist officers, and in the following weeks it was clear that the Soviets and the Communist Party had lost much of their prestige.

Despite the Hungarian withdrawal the Romanians refused to retreat. The situation looked bleak for the future of the international Bolshevik revolution. The Bavarian Soviet Republic had been overthrown and a life and death struggle was taking place between the Soviets and the Russian counterrevolutionary forces. In a last desperate effort the Hungarians attempted to drive the Romanians back across the Tisza River but failed and their lines collapsed.

On August 1 the Hungarian Governing Council resigned and escaped to Vienna. Chaos followed the collapse of the Kun regime. Ignoring the peace conference on August 3, the Romanian army marched into Budapest. They demanded the surrender of Hungary's entire supply of arms and ammunition, 50 percent of the rolling stock, 30 percent of agricultural machinery and cattle stock, 30,000 wagonloads of wheat and maize, and payment of all costs of the occupation.[51] As a condition for any agreement, the Romanians demanded the right to annex the entire Hungarian territory east of the Tisza River. The Czech army, reorganized with French assistance, also launched an offensive.

In the fall of 1919, in reaction to the revolutions of 1918 and 1919, a nationalist and anti-Semitic hysteria swept the country. Blame for the defeat and dismemberment of the nation was placed on communists and the Jews who had played an important role in the 1918 revolution and made up more than half of the people's commissars in the Bolshevik government. With French permission, the National Army, headed by Horthy, moved to Siófok in Transdanubia, the western part of the country not occupied by Romanian troops. The National Army moved through the area with orders to reestablish law and order and execute ringleaders of the Soviet Republic. Intent on exacting revenge for the revolution, paramilitary detachments carried out what came to be called the White Terror, with a total disregard for the law. Hundreds of Jews, poor peasants, and workers were murdered. It is not known how many people fell victim to the White Terror; estimates range anywhere from one thousand to five thousand, including those killed by the Romanian occupying troops.[52]

With the final acceptance of the Treaty of Versailles by the German representatives on June 28, the international power situation changed. German representatives had been summoned to France to receive their treaty in its final form without discussion, a "break with diplomatic precedent that infuriated the Germans."[53] Wilson sailed for home and Lloyd

George left Paris. In July, the Council of Four was replaced by the Council of Plenipotentiaries, and control passed into the hands of Clemenceau and other French leaders. The situation was further complicated by rivalry between the French and British. The French, eager to strengthen their position in Central Europe, supported Romanian demands, while the British were uneasy with the increase of French influence in Central Europe. The British demanded the termination of Romanian occupation of Hungary with growing decisiveness.

It was only with the help of the British diplomat Sir George Clark, who came to establish order, and the four generals of the Inter-Allied Military Mission, sent by the Supreme Council to superintend the disarmament and the withdrawal of the Romanian troops, that the Romanian troops could finally be persuaded to withdraw in mid-November.[54] The United States representative, Brigadier General Harry Hill Bandholtz, earned the gratitude of the Hungarian population by preventing a group of Romanian soldiers from looting the Transylvanian collection of the Hungarian National Museum on the night of October 5, 1919.[55] On December 1 the statesmen in Paris recognized a new coalition government in Hungary, and elections for a one-chamber national assembly were announced for January 25 and 26.

Presentation of the Treaty of Trianon

With the new more stable coalition government in office, the Council of Four decided they could now offer Hungary peace terms. A Hungarian delegation was invited to Paris and arrived on January 7. The delegation, headed by Count Albert Apponyi, received a cold but correct welcome from the French and was given the peace terms in a brief ceremony at the Quai d'Orsay. Clemenceau curtly informed Apponyi that he would be allowed to make a statement the following day but that there would be no verbal negotiations—only written ones.[56]

The treaty reduced the area of Hungary, discounting the semi-autonomous Croatia, from 282,000 square kilometers to 93,000 square kilometers. The largest portion, some 103,000 square kilometers, including Transylvania, was ceded to Romania, although the area called Transylvania took in not only historic Transylvania but also the eastern part of the Great Hungarian Plain and the eastern Bánát. Czechoslovakia received 61,000 square kilometers, Yugoslavia 20,000, and Austria 4,300. Poland and Italy were also ceded small areas. Out of the total number of 10.6 million people transferred to the neighbor states, 30.2 percent (3.2 million) were Magyar or ethnic Hungarian; 1.6 million transferred to Greater

Romania, close to one million to Czechoslovakia, and almost half a million to the Kingdom of Serbs, Croats, and Slovenes.[57]

In the face of the devastating loss Apponyi argued that Hungary was being punished more severely than any other of the defeated nations. Besides losing two thirds of its territory and its population, and being cut off from its markets and sources of raw materials, it was expected to pay heavy reparations. Three and a half million Hungarians would end up outside of Hungary. Citing the principle of self-determination pronounced by President Wilson, he pointed out that if the principle was a fair one it should apply to Hungarians as well. At the very least plebiscites should be held in territories taken from Hungary. Apponyi's presentation, displaying his fluency in many languages, was impressive; however he weakened his case by complaining that Hungarians were being condemned to live under the rule of inferior civilizations—a widely held Hungarian view.[58]

Apponyi and the other members of the delegation returned to Budapest on January 20. They had been granted ten days which they were able to extend by another ten days to prepare their answer. Although the peace conditions had been known since June the coalition government considered them unacceptable. They had been under the illusion that they would be able to receive more favorable terms than had the Soviet Republic. The Hungarian answer to the great powers on February 12 was essentially unchanged from that of Apponyi: if Hungary would not be allowed to retain its former borders, at the very least there should be plebiscites held in Hungarian-inhabited territories. However, the Czechs, South Slavs, and Romanians—determined to retain their newly acquired territories—sent a joint memorandum to the great powers rejecting any change to the newly established borders, and also firmly rejecting any possible plebiscites. In Paris none of the great powers were ready to upset the existing arrangement.[59]

Between February and June 4, 1920, negotiations with a new French government suggested that the treaty might be modified. A regent, Admiral Miklós Horthy, was elected in March, and the new government under Prime Minister Count Pál Teleki conducted negotiations with the French who were interested in economic concessions. In return the Hungarians requested revision of the frontiers and plebiscites. But in the end the British and the French were not prepared to revise the treaties. On May 6, 1920, French Prime Minister Alexandre Millerand handed the text of the definitive peace conditions to the head of the Hungarian peace delegation. The Hungarian claims were disregarded in every respect.[60] A letter of explanation accompanying the treaty raised unfounded hopes that possible border rectifications might be subjects of discussion in the future. On June 4, 1920, in a brief ceremony at Trianon Palace near Versailles, Hungarian representatives had no alternative but to sign the treaty.[61]

On November 13, 1920, the Hungarian National Assembly, discussing the question of the ratification of the treaty, resolved that the Hungarian flag before the Parliament should be flown at half-mast as a sign of national mourning until such time that the "Kingdom of the Holy Crown of St. Stephen" be once again made whole. It soon became the custom throughout the country that the flag be flown at half-mast on public buildings.[62]

For Hungarians the peace treaty came as an inexplicable miscarriage of justice. Not only had they not been permitted to participate in treaty discussions, contrary to established diplomatic procedure, they also had been refused the right of the Wilson doctrine of self-determination. No plebiscites had been permitted in the solidly Hungarian-inhabited territories contiguous with the new frontiers, with the exception of that with Austria. With the signing of the treaty they felt cheated and humiliated.

"'Trianon' became shorthand for Great Power cruelty and its memory fueled an almost universal desire among Hungarians to undo its provisions."[63] The population maintained its conviction that the treaty had been inexplicably harsh and fully expected it to be revised. It was considered to be an arbitrary act of the victors, and it was believed that the restoration of Hungary's pre-1918 borders depended only on a change in power relations.[64] In Hungarian schoolrooms geography was taught according to the map of the former kingdom, and school children grew up with the belief that Trianon Hungary was simply a temporary phenomenon.[65] Twice a day they recited:

I believe in one God
I believe in one homeland
I believe in God's eternal truth
I believe in the resurrection of Hungary.

For the next twenty years the main goal of foreign policy was to achieve some form of revision of the treaty. It was unfortunate that although several of the most prominent leaders did not expect complete revision of the treaty, the propaganda of the period—*Mindent vissza!* (Everything back!) and *Nem, nem, soha!* (No, no never!)—created in the population the belief that total revision was the only possibility.[66]

Aftermath

Although the Treaty of Trianon had been based on the premise that the "successor states"[67] would be nation-states on the Western model, the newly formed states were all multiethnic. Czechoslovakia was ethnically the least homogeneous, with the Czech population of approximately six and a half million augmented by close to two million Slovaks in order to balance the minority populations of three and a quarter million Germans, close to one million Magyars, as well as Polish and Ruthenian minorities.[68] Greater Romania, which had more than doubled in size through the treaty, contained numerous minorities, the largest being Magyar, German, and Jewish; the majority lived in the newly gained provinces, while the population of the old kingdom was more than 90 percent Romanian. The Kingdom of Serbs, Croats, and Slovenes, the most ethnically complex, included German, Magyar, Romanian, Albanian, Turkish, and others. The success of the new or enlarged states depended on the formation of new national identities and loyalty to the new state.

The great powers had been well aware that the successor states would contain large minority populations, but they believed this was the only alternative in order to make the states economically viable. They insisted on internationally guaranteed protection of minority rights in order to promote the loyalty of these populations to the sovereign states. The Commission on New States and Minorities drew up specific clauses for the protection of minorities. These clauses were included in each of the individual treaties. The granting of minority rights was to be the international obligation of the given state and compliance with these rights was to be guaranteed through the League of Nations. Yet the system of international guarantees, even if wholly embraced by the successor states—which it was not—could not by itself have solved minority problems in such an ethnically diverse region.[69]

Hopes of the Entente powers that the successor states would become strong independent nation-states on the western model proved unfounded. Instead, the dissolution of the Austro-Hungarian Monarchy established a group of small, insecure and antagonistic states isolated from each other. The treaties disrupted the region of east central Europe, which from the mid–nineteenth century under the monarchy had an especially well-functioning free market. The pace of economic modernization and growth had been formidable, almost as rapid as in Germany or Sweden. The peace treaties sliced up this efficient economic unit, blocked centuries-old commercial routes, and broke off time-tested and fruitful economic relations. Raw materials were separated from industries, workers from their work places, and economic, political, and military barriers were erected between the states. Conflicting political interests prevented economic cooperation.

If the newly formed states had followed a policy of cooperation the consequences might not have been so grave; instead they adopted a policy of isolation to achieve complete economic self-sufficiency. They imposed bans on exports and imports, high protectionist customs tariffs, and, from 1931, strict state controls on foreign exchange transactions. The concern for military security diverted attention from domestic and social problems. Contrary to Entente expectations the region as a whole became susceptible to the influence of the great powers and eventually dependent on Germany.

The psychological impact of the Treaty of Trianon was so pervasive that it produced a syndrome akin to a national disease. The loss of the territories was "tantamount to the death of the nation," only to be prevented by the return of Greater Hungary.[1] The trauma of defeat shook the nation's foundations and made it almost impossible to accept the new situation and to acknowledge the rights of other nationalities. The emergence of a cult of Trianon was marked with the erection of four heroic statues on Freedom Square, representing the lost territories. On the day of the unveiling tens of thousands filled the square as the Catholic Bishop István Zadravecz called as witnesses "the Hungarian God, the sacred flag, and the Hungarian spirit . . . that we shall not rest until we are united with North, South, East, and West."[2] The Holy Crown, popularly known to be a gift from the Pope for the coronation of St. Stephen in A.D. 1001, became the symbol of the dismembered kingdom, often spoken of as a living person or organism; "the lopped off limbs . . . faint with the loss of blood; in a swoon, they await death or resurrection."[3]

Ultra-patriotic societies sprang up, both civilian and military, supported especially by young radical-right officers, which blamed international Bolshevism and the forces of world Jewry for Hungary's losses and agitated for revision of the treaty throughout the 1920s and 1930s. Students learned geography in interwar Hungary as if the Treaty Trianon had never taken place. "Whole generations of youngsters grew up having only historic Hungary's borders etched into their minds and fully convinced that Trianon Hungary was but a temporary situation that was bound to disappear like an evil nightmare."[4]

Conditions in the country were chaotic. In the years from 1918 to 1920 refugees from the cut-off territories flooded the country, leaving their possessions behind. Those more fortunate moved in with relatives or friends, but thousands lived for years in railroad boxcars in Budapest railway stations. The refugees did not consider the remnants of the state their homeland; the lands from which they came had long traditions as part of the thousand-year-old kingdom; they felt themselves strangers in truncated Hungary. Budapest, a multiethnic city with a large German and Jewish population, carried none of the symbolism attached to Kolozsvar (Cluj) in Transylvania or Pozsony (Bratislava), now in Czechoslovakia.[5] Many refugees landed in the cities of Szeged or Debrecen, close to the new border with Romania. The young Viola Tomori from Transylvania never felt at home on the flat lands around Szeged; she missed the mountains of her homeland, and as a Protestant, felt herself a stranger in the largely Catholic city.[6]

Refugee students swarmed into Budapest from the former Hungarian universities of Kolozsvár (Cluj) and Pozsony (Bratislava). Penniless and without family support they registered at the University of Budapest. In the fall of 1919, overcrowding led to campus violence, fueled by radical students who blamed the Treaty of Trianon on the communist government of Béla Kun with its heavily Jewish make-up, and the wave of anti-Semitism forced the government to suspend university classes.[7]

By the middle of 1920 anti-Semitism had become a societal issue with many demanding that the civil rights of Jews be curtailed, citing the participation of Jews in the revolution and the high incidence of Jews among war speculators. Already in the fall of 1919, the overburdened medical faculty and faculties of law and theology had raised the necessity of establishing a quota system for students. In August 1920, Minister of Culture and Education István Haller submitted a bill to the National Assembly to limit the admission of Jewish students to the universities. After several weeks of debate, on September 22, the National Assembly endorsed Act XXV: 1920, which came to be known as the anti-Jewish *numerus clausus* law. The ailing Prime Minister Teleki did not participate in the debate, but in a speech to the Szeged electorate in October he defended the act, although condemning generalizations about the Jews. In his arguments he distinguished between the integrated Jewry who identified themselves with national goals and the newly immigrated and not assimilated *Galicians*, who in his view were responsible for the revolution and thus justified the discrimination.[8]

The law restricted the number of any ethnic group admitted to the university to the percentage of that group within the population, but it was aimed at Jewish students who constituted only 6 percent of the population but composed 30 percent of law students and 50 percent of medical students. A thriving community before the war, Hungarian Jews were now subject to discriminatory legislation severely limiting the access of

Jews to institutions of higher learning and, by extension, the academic professions.[9]

The defeat of the monarchy brought dire economic consequences. The population, reeling from the effects of the war and the treaty, was struck with a wave of inflation, which hit the country in 1920. Many in the middle class had already lost their savings by investing in government bonds during the war which were now worthless. At the peak of inflation in 1924, one gold crown was equivalent in value to 18,000 paper crowns. The cost of living rose eightfold between 1921 and 1924 while pay increased only three and a half times.[10] The unprecedented surge of inflation resulted in grave impoverishment of workers and employees and was especially destructive to the middle class, particularly those on fixed incomes.

The Problems of the New State

The truncated Hungarian state in 1920 was not only the smallest country in Central Europe but also the weakest in terms of economic resources and military strength. The country was isolated politically, surrounded by enemy countries, with a greatly reduced army. A new government had to be established, including new ministries of defense, foreign affairs, and finance, functions that had been carried out as common affairs under the dual monarchy. The government was unable to offer employment for the large middle class and the growing surplus of educated youth, not to mention the refugees from the lost territories. The social and economic problems of the large agrarian population and calls for land reform, which had been a major demand of the peasantry during the revolutions of 1918 and 1919, remained unsolved. One former problem no longer remained—that of the non-Hungarian nationalities. While the former Hungarian kingdom had been multiethnic, Trianon Hungary was almost ethnically homogeneous. The only significant non-Hungarian ethnic group that remained was the Hungarian-German population, known as Swabians, who were not as yet consciously nationalistic or united.[11]

Impoverished, flooded by refugees, and forced to pay war indemnities, the country struggled to come to terms with the new economic situation. The new boundaries cut across traditional cultural and economic communities, separating major cities from their hinterlands, factories from sources of raw material, markets from sources of transportation. The loss of territories had drastically reduced supplies of raw materials as well as markets. Most of Hungary's external trade had been conducted within the monarchy, with 80 percent of its agricultural exports going to

Austria and the Czech lands. The mountainous territories now in Czechoslovakia and Romania had provided most of country's raw materials. Only 11 percent of iron ore and less than 16 percent of the forests remained. One of the two black coalfields was lost, all of the salt mines, and all deposits of other ores discovered until then—gold, silver, copper, mercury, and manganese.[12]

On the other hand, industrial capacity, especially manufacturing capacity, was located in and around Budapest, including the processing plants for the oil wells of Nyitra, Transylvania, and the Mura Valley. Most of the flour mills, engineering works, printing presses—accounting for one-third of the country's industrial production—were also around Budapest. Hungary now had to import raw materials and machinery for almost every industry, while the agriculture and alimentary industry could not exist without exports. Thus the country became extraordinarily dependent on foreign trade, and as a result reacted to every change in the world economy.[13]

The Hungarian military had inherited a reputation as an excellent fighting force from the time of the Austro-Hungarian Monarchy, but the losses of population and territory after World War I and the extreme limitations placed on the military by the Treaty of Trianon changed the situation completely. Under the treaty Hungary's military was limited to 35,000 officers and men, to be used solely to maintain order and guard the frontier. Hungary was forbidden to mobilize or to establish a general staff; it was prohibited from having an air force or armored units; even the quantity and quality of armaments were restricted. Despite the stringent limitations imposed by the treaty, the successor states continued to consider Hungary a threat, even though they were militarily immensely more powerful. In the early 1920s Czechoslovakia, Romania and Yugoslavia formed a pact of alliance, known as the Little Entente, to oppose any Hungarian efforts to win revision of the peace treaty.

In light of the threat from the neighboring countries the state needed to make some kind of military preparation, but supervision by the Allied Supervisory Committee made it necessary to carry out all planning in secret. According to Géza Lakatos, a young officer at the time, a tremendous amount of energy went into the extremely complicated maneuvers to hide preparations. The new reduced army had seven so-called mixed brigades, each with two infantry regiments, one artillery division, and one cavalry company disguised as a gendarme cavalry company. Border guards were established under the cover name of customs guard. An intelligence and counter-intelligence division was established under the cover name of VI-2 Division, which developed close ties with the German military leadership. A general staff was disguised under the title Ministry of Defense VI Group, and a new Hungarian Academy of War was established to train staff officers.[14] Still, the military remained a small, insignificant force.

In 1920 the newly elected National Assembly faced the question of the form of government for the new state. The failure of the reform measures of the Károlyi government and the disastrous policies of the Béla Kun regime had created a general aversion to the Left in any form, and thousands of liberals and leftist-thinking individuals had been forced to emigrate. Public opinion was largely united in favoring a restoration of the monarchy as a way to establish historical continuity and the country's claims to the lands of the historic kingdom. Many so-called legitimists looked to a restoration of a Habsburg ruler, despite the fact that the great powers and the successor states refused to permit the return of a Habsburg king. Their fears that it would lead to an effort to restore the Habsburg Monarchy were confirmed by the two royal coups d'état attempted by the former Habsburg Emperor and King of Hungary, Charles IV, after the war.

In this situation the assembly passed Law I, declaring Hungary to be a kingdom but, following a medieval precedent, established the position of regent to hold the office of head of state until such time as a monarch could replace him. On March 1, 1920, the deputies voted overwhelmingly to elect the head of the National Army, fifty-two-year-old Miklós Horthy, as regent, a position that was expected to be temporary. The elections took place under the shadow of the February 17 murder of two social-democratic journalists who had openly criticized the White Terror. In the confused circumstances on the day of the election the military occupied the square in front of the parliament building and several officers accompanied Horthy into the parliament, although Horthy would probably have been elected without the show of force, since there was no other viable candidate.[15]

In some ways Horthy had unique qualifications for the position. A member of the Protestant gentry and an admiral in the Imperial and Royal Navy, he was accustomed to command. He had traveled the world with the fleet, visiting every continent except America; he was fluent in German, and also spoke English and French as well as Italian and Croatian. In his naval career and service as aide-de-camp to Emperor Franz Josef he had become a man of the world, familiar with court life, comfortable in diplomatic circles, and able to move gracefully in society.[16] He had married the attractive Magdolna Purgly, a Catholic, and his family life was exemplary; he was a popular figure at social gatherings as he played the piano well and was an excellent dancer. His appearance was splendid, and along with his informal manner and winning presence he was also a genuine military hero. During the war at the Battle of Otranto, the greatest sea engagement in the Adriatic, although wounded and on a stretcher, he continued directing operations from his ship for hours. The Italians considered him a hero, the British respected him. Even Roosevelt had heard of his exploits during the war.[17]

But nothing in his training or earlier career had prepared him for his new role. Horthy was no diplomat and understood little about politics. Impulsive and prone to hasty decisions he was easily swayed by the last person he had spoken with. He followed the code of honor of a nineteenth century gentleman, was conservative, rabidly anti-Bolshevik, and overconfident in the abilities of his military leaders. According to the respected Hungarian diplomat, György Barcza, who knew him well, he believed that in the end the military would be able to lead the country. If ever he could not find a suitable prime minister he would just name a military government that would put the country in order. He was completely and openly honest and found it impossible to dissemble. He himself was aware that he had no interest in theoretical reasoning.[18]

As regent, Horthy was given powers almost equal to those of the monarch. He chose the prime minister who was responsible to him in fact if not in law, and he had the right to convene, prorogue, and dissolve Parliament. Although he had no veto right, he had the right of initiative and could return a bill twice for consideration. Most important to Horthy, he was also Supreme War Lord, solely responsible for the command, training, and organization of the armed forces. Officers swore their oath of allegiance to him as they had done earlier to the emperor in the Austro-Hungarian Monarchy. Yet, despite the powers granted him he was careful not to exceed his constitutional authority, and for the first years of his reign he left political decisions to his prime minister. Since his election was considered a temporary solution the law did not stipulate how long the regent could serve and no thought was given to his successor. In the spring and summer of 1920, few would have expected his tenure to last more than a few months, possibly a year. It was expected that the question of the monarch would be solved, with no need to continue the position of regent. No one could have imagined that Horthy would remain in power for more than twenty years.[19]

Society in the Truncated State

Society remained highly stratified and, if anything, more resistant to change than during the dual monarchy. Long, festering social and economic problems, which had touched off the revolutions of 1918 and 1919, remained unsolved. Aristocrats, who had lost estates in the territories, clung all the more tenaciously to their estates in Hungary. Remnants of the old feudalism, which allotted status and prestige according to birth and feudal rank, survived through World War II in a system often termed semifeudal. Although serfdom had been abolished in 1848, as in England, during the enclosure movements there had been no land reform. Large estates remained and an agrarian proletariat emerged, each dependent on the other—the large estates depended on the agrarian proletariat for cheap manpower and the proletariat depended on the estates for employment. Half of the country remained in the hands of a small number of landlords, which included impersonal institutions such as the state or church, while the vast majority of the agrarian population owned little or no land.[20] A land reform passed in 1920 was extremely modest, distributing only around 5 percent of agricultural land to 400,000 peasants. The government's dependence on the support of conservative landowners prevented a more serious reform.

Hungary, like Poland, had a large nobility divided into two groups—the upper nobility or aristocracy and the common nobility or gentry. However, many aristocrats and even more gentry owned very small estates or no land at all. The census of 1925 showed one-half (49.8 percent) of the total agricultural area was in the hands of 10,760 owners of large and medium estates, while the other half was shared by 840,000 small landholders.[21] Owners of the largest estates came almost exclusively from the aristocracy, but they received their income more from their positions in large banks or large industrial firms, or as chairmen or members of boards of directors. With the end of the monarchy they had lost some of their special political position, but the traditions and conservatism which they retained became one of the most effective brakes against the ambitions of the extreme Right.

The large capitalists—both finance capitalists and owners of the largest banks and industries—formed a small but extremely powerful group, consisting of about fifty Jewish families tied to each other through various connections—business, family, or social. Because of the situation caused by the Treaty of Trianon, their effect on economic life and policies became even greater but their role in public life remained small. The large landowners and large capitalists at the top of the social pyramid were estimated to make up 2 to 3 percent of the population in 1940.[22]

Hungary had no middle class in the American or western European sense of the term. The so-called Christian middle class consisted of civil servants, officers in the army, the landed gentry, and other owners of medium-sized estates. The gentry who made up much of this class possessed the greatest social prestige and formed the foundation of government support, considering themselves to be the bearers of national values. Their economic influence had been gradually declining, especially after the agricultural crises of the 1880s and 1890s, and many had moved into the city and taken up positions in the civil service, the state bureaucracy, and the corps of higher military officers. After the war the reduction of the army and the public administrative apparatus, as well as the wave of inflation, had further reduced their economic position. Reduced to existence on meager salaries, they still felt it necessary to keep up appearances. Status and prestige, as well as a system of values that centered on the honor of gentlemen, became all the more important and made them cling fast to all of their privileges. Since their code of behavior prohibited them from indulging in any kind of manual work, even carrying a shopping bag, no middle-class family could be without a servant, regardless of economic circumstances.[23]

The professions and occupations in commerce and industry—the other element of a Western middle class—had historically been considered unworthy of a Hungarian gentleman, and by default these positions came to be filled mainly by Jews. Jewish assimilation had been encouraged in the latter part of the nineteenth century, and those who had immigrated in the late eighteenth and nineteenth centuries had become well assimilated, although a wave of immigration at the end of the nineteenth century from Galicia, a result of persecution in Romania and Russia, brought a new and different Jewish population which did not assimilate.

A bill passed by Parliament in the late nineteenth century made Judaism an accepted religion, and allowed civil marriage as well as freedom of religious choice. Many Jews had become prosperous; some were granted titles and became landowners, mixing and intermarrying with gentry families and the aristocracy. The modern capitalistic economy was almost entirely their creation, and the overwhelming majority of banking, industrial and commercial establishments, and small businesses were in their hands. They also occupied the majority of better-paid positions in the so-called free professions—medicine, law, journalism, and acting.[24]

Status and prestige were allotted according to feudal rank, and perpetuated by the obligatory forms of address: Excellency, Dignity, Greatness, or Authority. Even at informal parties, unless strictly within the family, the seating order of guests had to follow the official list of titles and ranks. In Hungary, everyone had his class and status imprinted on his appearance, revealed by his general behavior, his clothing, housing, nutrition, manners, etiquette, and speech; the middle and ruling classes with their well-tailored suits and manicured hands. Through such external traits, class position could be sized up at first glance, and unknown persons could address each other with the proper titles and ranks.[25] The painter, Gyula Lőrincz, who had grown up in the more democratic Czechoslovakia, lost his chance of entering the University of Budapest because he failed to give the interviewing professor the proper title. He addressed him as "Mr. Professor" (*Professor úr*) instead of "Honorable Ministerial Councillor" (*méltóságos kormányfő tanácsos úr*) and was thrown out of the office.[26]

Lack of positions for the children of the middle classes became a matter of great concern. Positions in the civil service were limited and the influx of refugees had inflated the population seeking "gentlemanly" jobs. Since a university education was one of the primary qualifications for a middle-class career, ever greater numbers of youth entered the universities. Less stringent admission standards and the transfer of the two universities from the lost territories led to a glut of young intellectuals, all competing for positions already overfilled with qualified adults. This oversupply of intellectuals led to an increase in anti-Semitism, and although open and virulent anti-Semitism died with stability and an improvement of the economy, the generation raised after the war was indoctrinated with the notion that Jewish control of industry and capital and the heavy Jewish percentages in certain occupations restricted their own advancement.

The peasantry, a term that denoted an occupational group rather than a social class, were divided into different classes and much more stratified than the farming class in America. A small number of rich peasants, those who owned more than thirty yokes or forty-two acres, were present in almost every village and enjoyed great local authority. The medium peasantry or smallholders, landowners with ten to thirty yokes, were an independent group, often considered to represent the backbone of the nation and a possible source for a new rural middle class; they often supported political parties of the opposition. The poor peasantry, estimated at about three million persons, consisted of the dwarf-holders (those who owned some land but not enough to support a family) as well as the landless proletariat, estimated at one-sixth the total population of the country. They made their living as agricultural laborers, the majority working on the large estates. This group was virtually separated in society by their appearance and way of life, unknown and ignored by the rest of the nation. Together the rural poor combined with the great mass of unskilled workers in the cities made up about 60 percent of the population.[27]

The Bethlen Era

Appointed as prime minister in April 1921, Count István Bethlen was to become the key figure during the ten years of his ministry, and to remain one of the most influential men throughout the rest of the interwar period and the war years, acting as Horthy's most trusted advisor. A scion of an old Transylvanian family, strongly conservative, highly intelligent, Bethlen was a visionary statesman, an excellent tactician, and a true diplomat. He had studied in Vienna, Budapest, and England, and spoke German, English, French, and Romanian. Although he had a reserved manner and was never personally popular, he was extremely persuasive and skilled in handling men. Horthy trusted him implicitly, leaving most government and administrative decisions in his hands.[28]

With his appointment Bethlen began the process of consolidation. The previous government of Count Teleki had been forced to resign after the first attempted royalist coup d'état. The country was politically divided and forces of the extreme Right were still active. Bethlen's first priority was to create order and deal with the economic situation for which he needed the large capitalists in order to stabilize the economy. The financiers, although of Jewish origin, had long since assimilated and considered themselves loyal Hungarians. Bethlen won their confidence by protecting their financial interests, rejecting the views of the right-wing counterrevolutionary officers, led by Gyula Gömbös, who opposed collaboration with so-called Jewish capitalists. Somewhat reluctantly, Horthy had finally distanced himself from his former compatriots in the National Army, thus weakening their position.

One of the first steps in the Bethlen government was to apply for admission to membership in the League of Nations on May 23, 1921. However, the ministry requested that the question of the Austro-Hungarian border be settled before consideration of its application. There was disagreement over the Burgenland, a region—mostly German inhabited but including the town of Sopron and its environs—which had been awarded to Austria. Through Italian intervention the governments of

Austria and Hungary, meeting in Venice in October 1921, reached a compromise by which a plebiscite should decide the status of Sopron and environs. The plebiscite was held in mid-December and on December 31, 1921, the Entente commission announced that Sopron and the environs belonged to Hungary. Contrary to the provisions of the peace treaty, a compromise solution had been reached on a territorial issue. This was the first success of the Bethlen government and the new Austro-Hungarian frontier became the calmest section of the Trianon frontiers.[29]

After the failure of a second putsch attempt by the former king, Charles IV, the question of a Habsburg restoration, which the Little Entente countries had opposed so bitterly, was dropped. Under the improved international situation the Bethlen government now aimed to achieve Hungary's admission to the League of Nations. This was all the more necessary since the countries of the Little Entente were making efforts to expand their alliance system through agreements with Poland and Austria.[30]

In August the representatives of the Little Entente states decided not to oppose Hungarian admission. The League committee concerned with the matter took up the question of Hungary on September 11, 1922, and admission passed practically without debate. On a motion from Poland, Hungarian accession to membership of the League was adopted by acclamation. Hungary became an equal member, at least formally.

Membership in the League of Nations was also necessary in order to secure the loans, which Hungary desperately needed, but the question of a loan was tied to reparations payments, the amount of which was still not decided. The whole question of reparations was connected with the rivalry between Great Britain and France and the larger problem of the postwar European settlement. France, with its ambitions for European hegemony and desire for security, demanded an enormous indemnity from Germany, while Great Britain endeavored to secure a balance of power on the Continent. With United States support the British were able to restrain French aspirations and secure a reduced amount of reparations for Germany, along with large investment credits and access to wider markets.

In the case of Hungarian reparations the French supported members of the Little Entente in insisting on high reparations, and also that any loan should come under the supervision of the Reparations Commission to which the Little Entente states belonged. The Hungarian government could expect help only from London, since Anglo-American capital played the most significant role in the Hungarian economy. Hungarian delegates began negotiations in London in March 1923. The British were not against granting the loan but wanted to secure the deal under the supervision of the League, a condition that the Council of Ministers accepted. Opposition by the Little Entente was finally broken when the British made public that Czechoslovakia—also applying for loans—could only hope for support if they stopped obstructing the Hungarian request.

According to the conditions of the British government, the loan to Hungary was made through mediation of the League of Nations with control entrusted to a neutral body appointed by the League. In a relatively favorable agreement in December 1923, the Reparations Commission decided that Hungary was to pay two hundred million gold crowns over twenty years. The loan, under auspices of the League, was floated in July 1924 for two hundred fifty million gold crowns, half from Britain and the other half from six other powers, primarily the United States, Switzerland, and Italy.[31] To supervise the fulfillment of the loan terms and conduct of public finances the League sent a chief delegate, the American jurist Jeremiah Smith, to Hungary. This was also an important political gesture, showing that the British financial circles trusted in the Hungarian political regime, and by strengthening the economic situation intended to strengthen Bethlen in the struggle against the isolation of the country.[32]

The National Bank of Hungary, established in 1924, was formally separate from the state and run by a supreme council of prominent Hungarian business figures, primarily of Jewish origin. With an inflation-related business recovery much of the earlier debt simply disappeared. Despite its human cost, inflation benefited the economy by sharply reducing production costs and increasing competitiveness.

Intent on creating a powerful but manageable governing party, Bethlen formed the Party of Unity, a political alliance not only of large landowners, financiers, and industrialists, but also the gentry, army officers, and middle-class civil servants. In elections for the National Assembly of 1922, the party received 143 out of 245 seats, which gave the government a solid base for its activities. From that time on the government always had a majority in Parliament, partly because of the practice in the countryside of open voting—as opposed to the secret ballot. It was said that the good Hungarian peasants are too honest to need a secret ballot. Since the prime minister was also the head of the party and determined the candidates on the party list for election, in essence the prime minister controlled the Parliament.

Bethlen maintained the support of the liberal middle class by allowing the small opposition parties, supported primarily from Budapest and the urban Jewish middle class, to operate freely in Parliament. Yet despite the active participation of the opposition, the government party ruled throughout the whole period. Anyone who wanted to play an effective role in politics had to belong to the government party, although he might start out by attracting attention in the opposition. Bethlen brokered an agreement with the Social Democratic Party that was to have a major impact on political life throughout the interwar period. The agreement allowed the party to participate in Parliament for the first time, but it stipulated that they not engage in any political activity in the countryside. The Social Democrats had been much weakened by their role in the revolutions of 1918 and 1919, so they agreed. Thus the agrarian population remained without effective political representation.

As a counter balance to possible extremism in the popularly elected National Assembly, Bethlen restored the *Felsőház*, the upper house of Parliament in 1926. The composition of the membership was designed to recognize significant public interest groups, but to avoid the influence of political parties. Although conservative, it differed greatly from the aristocratic preserve of the pre-1918 house, since the majority of the members achieved their positions through their education and professional careers. The five classifications of membership included elected aristocrats; two groups composed of those with high positions in the legal profession; the church, including the high rabbi; and representatives of the universities and other institutions. A fourth group consisted of elected representatives from the various administrative districts of the country, and a fifth of those appointed by Horthy. Their relatively long terms of ten years meant that members were under much less political pressure than the lower house. Subject to intense criticism throughout the interwar years for its representation of vested interests, the upper house was to become a guardian of Hungary's liberal heritage during World War II, opposing anti-Semitism and National Socialism.[33]

This system created a manageable governing party which controlled the National Assembly, a conservative upper house, an economy heavily influenced by the large capitalists and landowners, which was to remain in effect with little change until the occupation of the country by the Germans in March 1944.

The Impact of Refugees from the Ceded Territories

The influx of refugees from the ceded territories exacerbated existing social and economic tensions. Between 1918 and 1924 an estimated

426,000 ethnic Hungarians fled from the cut-off territories into truncated Hungary.[34] The great majority of refugees were members of the upper and middle classes, including large numbers of government officials and members of the intelligentsia. The first wave of refugees at the end of 1918 and beginning of 1919 were fleeing for their lives, leaving all their possessions behind. A second wave was the result of the wholesale dismissal of Hungarians from administrative positions and educational institutions, including the large group of officials and workers in state enterprises such as the postal service and the railroad. Subsequent purges forced many professionals and members of the managerial strata to leave. The land reforms, which confiscated the lands of German and Hungarian landowners who had fled—as well as greatly reducing the estates of those who remained—destroyed the economic power of Hungarian landowners. Also affected were a large number of estate employees, managers, even agricultural workers, whose existence was tied to large-scale agriculture.[35]

In its determination to maintain the nation's claims to the ceded lands, the government committed itself to supporting the refugees and assimilating them into the country, but in the economic chaos of truncated Hungary the flood of refugees overwhelmed the government. The attempt to provide them with jobs similar to the posts they left behind strained the budget and slowed down the economic recovery of the whole country. The financial burden imposed on the state treasury strained the country's economic resources to the utmost.

By July 1921 the government had decided to discourage the flight of the Hungarian population, issuing entry permits only in special cases. Those who wished to flee were told that it was unpatriotic; to leave would weaken the Hungarian minority and thus the cause of the whole Hungarian nation. The government decision was based not only on economic considerations but also on the fear that a diminished minority would weaken the case for revision of the treaty, and possibly hasten assimilation of those left in the successor states. Even so the total number of Hungarians remaining in the lost territories sharply declined; in Czechoslovakia, when compared with the 1910 census, the Hungarian population was decreased by 13.7 percent, in Romania by 13.4 percent and in Yugoslavia by 9.5 percent.[36]

Yet no government dared to alienate the refugees. Their position in the country and their influence—not only on foreign policy but also on domestic affairs—was to have tremendous consequences for the future. Refugees held a number of prominent positions in the government. These included two extremely influential prime ministers: István Bethlen and Pál Teleki. Refugees became a major power in the National Assembly; although they represented only 6.9 percent of the total population they captured 33.1 percent of the seats in the First National Assembly, and their strength remained remarkably constant throughout the 1920s. They enjoyed a privileged position both in state employment and in receiving pensions. The proportion of refugees employed by the state steadily increased at the expense of employees born in inner Hungary and was concentrated in the most prestigious positions. Their numbers were proportionally greatest in the judiciary, among government officials, and in the field of education.[37]

Their influence permeated all public institutions, the greatly expanded law enforcement agencies, and especially the army officers corps. In a study of four hundred officers of the military elite who had entered military service under the Austro-Hungarian Monarchy before World War I, more than half (209) had been born in areas later ceded to the successor states.[38] They were to exercise an exceptionally strong influence on public opinion, especially on Hungarian foreign policy. In education the refugee influence was of crucial importance. Refugee teachers made up about a quarter of primary school teachers and about a third of secondary school and university faculties. The exodus of a large number of liberal and socialist intellectuals who emigrated from Hungary after 1919, and the dismissals of many suspected of leftist sympathies, increased their relative influence.

Refugee students were given entry permits even when others were restricted, and they filled the universities, contributing to the problem of the unemployed intelligentsia. Their presence radically altered the social composition of the student body, increasing the proportion of students from families of officials or officers.[39] Because of the scarcity of civil service jobs, they were more inclined to prepare for the free professions, which had earlier been avoided by this class as not fit for gentlemen and thus left to Jewish students—law, medicine, engineering. They became part of the new generation of youth, and were wooed by the older generation who looked to them to resurrect Hungary. *Youth* became such an influential concept that those in their thirties and even in their forties would define themselves as members of the new youth.

The assimilation of refugees into society was successful but the cost was high. Although they gradually became more moderate as their lives became more secure, they did not give up the dream of returning to their old homes. Many still had parents, siblings, and relatives living in the ceded territories. Tibor Petrusz, the son of a refugee from Czechoslovakia, told how his family traveled every summer to his father's birthplace of Csetnek (Stitnik) in Czechoslovakia to visit his grandparents. On crossing the border between the two countries, his father would point and say: "'There is the demarcation line.' He refused to recognize the border as permanent, considering it simply the line established by the Allied powers before the treaty."[40] Refugee families like that of Tibor were convinced that they would eventually return to their homes. They continued to visit their relatives across the new national borders and to lay wreaths on family graves on All Saints' Day, waiting for the time when they would return.

The Hungarian Population in the Ceded Territories

Although the Paris peace treaty had been based on the premise that the successor states would be nation-states, the newly formed states were all multiethnic. Since the new states claimed to be national states, their success depended on the formation of new national identities and loyalty to the new state. In this situation the large Hungarian populations were considered a threat and governments introduced policies to eliminate or neutralize the danger they posed.

CZECHOSLOVAKIA

The Hungarian community that remained in Czechoslovakia was radically changed after the refugee exodus. The Hungarian-speaking area, former northern Hungary, the Felvidék, had no independent history as a region. Many of the former political and cultural leaders had fled, and the remaining population—divided by class, status, and religion—had no political or cultural tradition to unite them. Sixty-four percent of those remaining were made up of agrarian and forestry workers. The potential political strength of the Hungarian-speaking population was weakened by the census of 1921, which included a separate national category for Hebrew/Yiddish. Many of those who were both Hungarian speakers and Jewish declared their nationality as Hebrew, reducing the census figures for Hungarians to 745,431. Under Czechoslovak regulations this number was considered too few to qualify for the minority rights granted the German minority, including the right to a separate university. Measures by the state authorities to dissolve or suspend the activities of Hungarian cultural and educational organizations paralyzed Hungarian cultural life. Aside from the officially recognized Hungarian political parties, no form of Hungarian organization was allowed.[41]

Hungarian political life developed according to the interests of the various classes. Rather than cooperating with the government the two Hungarian parties represented in Parliament formed an opposition bloc. The conservative National Christian Socialist Party, led by Géza Szüllő, represented the landowning classes and the clergy, while the National Hungarian Party of Smallholders, Farm Hands, and Craftsmen of Jószef Szent-Ivány represented the farmers and tradesmen. The Christian Socialist Party, which stood for a return to historical Hungary and the power of the former ruling classes, continually emphasized in Parliament that they had been forcibly cut off from Hungary, and their negative attitude, made primarily for propaganda reasons, eliminated any possibility of working cooperatively with the Czechoslovak government. The National Hungarian Party of Szent-Ivány was more progressive, flexible, and realistic, and more interested in accomplishing positive measures to help the Hungarian minority.[42]

Szent-Iványi, who reorganized and renamed his party, the Hungarian National Party, left the Hungarian opposition bloc in time for the 1925 elections, hoping to make an agreement with the Czechoslovak Agrarian Party to improve the economic situation of the Hungarian minority. But his plans came to naught, partly because of the extreme negativism of the conservative party as well as the shortsightedness and nationalist rigidity of the Czechoslovak government party.[43]

By the second half of the 1920s the situation of the Hungarian population began to improve. The consolidation of Czechoslovakia had progressed to the point that Czech and Slovak politicians no longer feared that the national minorities would cause the disintegration of the state. For the first time they considered the possibility of including national minority parties in the government, and the government lifted its ban on Hungarian cultural organizations. A new generation of Hungarian youth began to attend Czechoslovak universities rather than leaving for Budapest as their older brothers had done, but despite the necessity to continue their studies in the Czech language they continued to remain strongly conscious of maintaining their Hungarian identity.[44]

GREATER ROMANIA AND TRANSYLVANIA

The situation for the Hungarian population remaining in Transylvania was quite different from that of northern Hungary. Transylvania formed a geographical unit separated from surrounding areas by high plateau and mountain ranges, and it also had a long tradition of political autonomy and separate corporate identity. From medieval times the three historic peoples of Transylvania—the German Saxons, Hungarians, and

Székely Hungarians—had maintained their separate identities, including religious freedom and the special privileges of the Saxons and Székelys. Over the years, more and more Romanians moved into the area but had not been included as one of the historic peoples. Both Hungarian and Romanian nationalists viewed the area as the birthplace of their respective nations, and many Transylvanians believed in the idea of a unique Transylvanian identity.[45] In 1918 members of both groups had considered the possibility of an autonomous Transylvania, with multiethnic rule by Saxons, Hungarians, and Romanians.[46]

The Romanians, separated from their neighbors by their orthodox religion, considered the Romanian nation to be unique. They regarded the ethnic minorities in Greater Romania as foreigners and were particularly antagonistic to the Magyars—the former ruling nation—and Jews. Measures were taken to eliminate the potential influence of both Hungarians and Jews in the new state, although neither posed a serious threat.[47]

Voluntary flight and the expulsion of prominent Hungarian citizens and their families by Romanian officials sharply reduced the number of Hungarians who were to remain in Transylvania.[48] The great majority of refugees were members of the upper and middle classes, including large numbers of government officials, members of the intelligentsia, and the professors and majority of the students of the University of Kolozsvár. After the initial exodus the remaining Hungarian intellectual community floundered. The landed gentry gradually came to terms with the existing situation and the condition of the peasantry was largely unchanged; the middle classes, on the other hand, had lost their function in society.

After 1920 attempts by the Transylvanian Hungarians to unite were marred by political conflicts between conservative former officials, mainly concerned to influence outside opinion for revision of the Paris peace treaty, and others, who believed it necessary to accommodate and perhaps achieve Transylvanian autonomy. The historical Hungarian churches—Unitarian, Reformed, and Catholic—stepped in to fill the leadership vacuum, and for the next ten years became leaders of the Hungarian population.[49] Not until 1929 did a new generation of Hungarian youth begin to attend Romanian universities. Their situation was quite different from that of the Hungarian students in Czechoslovak universities. Czechoslovakia was a democracy and poor students with Czech diplomas had many opportunities for financial aid; Hungarian university students founded a student organization, the Czechoslovakian Hungarian Academic Organization, in 1925. Romania in 1925 was under martial law with a limited right of association; little student aid was available and a state law expressly prohibited the establishment of any university organization based on nationality.[50]

SOUTHERN HUNGARY

The territories from the Hungarian kingdom ceded to the new state of the Southern Slavs had no historical antecedent as a separate entity; the population was highly mixed but Hungarian and German minorities formed an absolute majority. After the war the Serbians gave the combined territories—the Bánát, the Bácska, and parts of Baranya County—the name of the Voivodina. The primary motivating force for the flight of the Hungarian population from the areas later called Voivodina was fear for their lives. In the last two months of 1918 at least five thousand Hungarians fled, and in the first three months of 1919 perhaps three times that many or more.

The firing of Hungarian administrative personnel in the Voivodina took place rapidly and with fewer protestations from officials than in Transylvania or Czechoslovakia. The population of about 500,000 Hungarians consisted of an extremely thin stratum of the middle class and an overwhelming majority of peasants. Historical attachments to the area were slight, since the territory had always been considered a border area and, unlike the Bánát with its German population, it had no Hungarian culture or tradition of its own. The politically active middle class, consisting of former members of the state administration, landowners, and professionals, was greatly weakened and there was no strong peasant burgher/citizenry. During the 1920s the peasants and workers were more interested in the social equality advocated by the Communists, Socialists, and trade union movements, than in retaining their Hungarian culture.[51]

The Hungarian Party of Yugoslavia was formed in 1922, with encouragement and material support from the Hungarian government but its room for maneuver was extremely limited, and the new political leadership of lawyers, middle landowners, and doctors had no historical experience in dealing with peasants and workers. Eventually, measures by the royal dictatorship—primarily aiming to resolve Serbian-Croatian differences—led to the loss of the Hungarian party's modest achievements. The relatively small number of Hungarians in Yugoslavia, their lack of charismatic leaders, the nature of Yugoslavian internal political life, and the virulent nationalism of the governing parties greatly hindered the political activities of the Hungarians of Voivodina.

Moderate Recovery

In the second half of the 1920s Hungary broke out of its diplomatic isolation and enjoyed a moderate economic recovery as foreign loans produced a modest economic boom. The first significant breakthrough from Hungary's diplomatic isolation came with Bethlen's visit to Benito Mussolini in 1927 and the signing of a treaty of friendship between Italy and Hungary. Mussolini was much admired in Hungary, as he was in countries of the West, for the progress he had made in modernizing Italy. The two countries, with a certain mutual sympathy through history, also shared dissatisfaction with the peace treaties. Italy believed it had been wronged for not receiving the lands promised during the war by the English and French, and Mussolini looked to Hungary to support his drive to extend Italian influence in southeastern Europe, while Budapest looked to Italy for support in re-arming and the revision of the Treaty of Trianon. Bethlen's earlier silence on the question of revision had led the Allies to believe that he accepted the limitations of the Treaty of Trianon, but after his Italian visit he began to speak publicly on the need for revision of the treaty.

With the government's solid majority Bethlen was able to achieve certain of his planned reforms, although his scope for action was limited by lack of funds and the government's conservative base. He made modest social welfare reforms, and supported educational reform. Bethlen encouraged Jewish participation in public life, and in 1927 the *numerus clausus* law was amended in the National Assembly: the racial discrimination section was removed and more emphasis was placed on social composition.[52]

Bethlen had already instituted a program to develop centralized medical insurance for the industrial population in 1927, raising the proportion benefiting from a prewar 30 percent to 80 percent, and additional social welfare measures of 1927–28 extended health insurance to new social classes. Sick pay was raised from 50 percent of wages and salaries to 60–75 percent. Accident insurance benefits were also raised. The government made old age, disability, widow, and waif insurance obligatory. The next step should have come in 1929 with health and accident insurance for agricultural workers, but the impact of the Great Depression—already felt in Hungary in 1929—forced Bethlen to abandon the plan.[53]

Education was to play an important part in the drive for revision of the treaty. Minister of Education Count Kuno Klebelsberg, a member of an old Transylvanian family, based his educational reform on two fundamental principles; to raise the educational standard of the masses and to produce professional men in all fields of science to solve the great cultural, economic, technical, and health problems of the country.[54] Klebelsberg often stressed Hungarian "cultural superiority" as the basis to justify revision of the Treaty of Trianon, and he believed that educated Hungarian intellectuals would persuade the western countries of the justice of Hungary's claims. His educational policies were backed by Bethlen, despite the expense of the reforms.

Klebelsberg firmly believed that Hungary in its weakened state and reduced size must reestablish and maintain its universities. Hungary was known for its excellent denominational schools, the historic Protestant and Catholic *gymnázia*, but because the University of Budapest was inadequate for the large number of postwar students, he reestablished the former universities of Kolozsvár, Transylvania, and Pozsony, northern Hungary, to towns in the countryside—Szeged and Pécs, respectively. At the new university in Debrecen he expanded the medical facilities and also built new facilities for the College of Humanities and Social Sciences. The relocations aimed to decentralize higher education and form regional cultural centers away from Budapest. Many students who were not able to gain admission to the overcrowded university in Budapest studied at these smaller universities. The system of state scholarships for study abroad which Klebelsberg established in Berlin, Vienna, and Rome, enabled several hundred Hungarian students to study and become known in foreign universities each year.

The condition of elementary education in the countryside was a much greater challenge. Despite the requirement for six years of elementary education, there were great problems in bringing education to the agrarian population, particularly those in the Alföld, the Great Hungarian Plain, where roads were often nonexistent and the population was widely scattered on isolated farms known as *tanya*. The strongly Calvinist peasantry[55] were said to live in the *tanya* world: "A half a million souls live far from city and village in the Alföld like cultural exiles. These are the people of the Alföld tanya world. Living in areas with no roads—without schools, churches, doctors, pharmacies or any of the facilities of community life . . . with no one to help them or protect them."[56]

Klebelsberg aimed to end the situation in which these children received an inferior education. Under his ministry 3,500 new elementary school classrooms were constructed and 1,500 new homes for elementary teachers were completed by 1930; the number of grade school pupils allowed per classroom was reduced from sixty to forty, and teacher-student ratios improved. The rate of literacy increased to 90 percent, close to Austrian and Czech levels.[57] Unfortunately the state had limited funds and the project moved slowly.

The Effects of the Depression

As an agricultural country Hungary suffered severely from the economic crisis of the depression, which struck all of society. Hungary could no longer sell its produce, foreign sources of loans dried up, factories and workshops closed while others laid off workers, and living standards were drastically reduced as prices declined and unemployment grew. The depression was particularly hard on youth, as young skilled workers and university graduates remained unemployed. A report of 1928 stated that 2,500 university graduates left the universities every year with no hope of placement. By 1931 the situation had deteriorated to such an extent that the administration saw the necessity of creating the National Commission for Unemployed Degree-Holders in order to provide a modicum of support for the unemployed intelligentsia. It was not unusual to see unemployed graduates clearing snow or eating in soup kitchens. This generation had become a new cultural proletariat.[58]

The crisis affected agricultural workers more than any other social group, salaries dropping by as much as 50 to 60 percent. Prices for agrarian goods fell 54 percent between 1929 and 1933, which was especially hard on the small farmers who were unable to pay their debts and faced the auctioning off of their farms. Sándor Kiss, son of a small farmer, remembered that in 1932, at the deepest point of the depression, the family raised crops in vain; they could not sell their wheat, potatoes, even their animals. There was no money, not only for clothing, but often none for sugar or salt.[59] Production on large estates declined, the result being that agrarian workers were only able to work 150 days a year instead of 200, and the day worker's salary was cut by half. The Independent Smallholders Party was reestablished in 1930 to represent the more prosperous peasants, but the majority of the agrarian population remained without political representation.

THE GÖMBÖS ERA

In Hungary, as elsewhere in Europe, the drastic economic situation created conditions conducive to the growth of new political extremes. The fate of Europe hung in the balance, leading to a willingness to experiment with radical solutions to the urgent economic and political questions. Unemployment, strikes, and social unrest led Prime Minister Bethlen to resign in August 1931, and an interim government under Prime Minister Count Gyula Károlyi instituted martial law. By 1932, the conservative government party, as well as the liberals and Social Democrats, were ready to accept any government that promised to restore order. Attention turned to Gyula Gömbös, who had been instrumental in organizing the National Army at Szeged. In the early 1920s he advocated making Hungary a one-party state and led the radical group of anti-Semitic officers known as *race protectors*, but by the end of the decade he had moderated his rhetoric and in 1929 he joined the government party as minister of defense.

Political and economic leaders believed that Gömbös would establish a strong government and restore law and order, and in 1932 Horthy appointed him prime minister. However, former Prime Minister Bethlen, among others, was concerned that Gömbös would attempt to establish a fascist state. Before Gömbös's appointment Bethlen set secret conditions to limit his room to maneuver. To meet these conditions Gömbös agreed to work within the existing parliament of the government party, which was still largely loyal to Bethlen and to refrain from propagating racist ideas.

Gömbös and his followers represented a new era in Hungarian politics and society. The leading figures of the Bethlen period had grown up during the Austro-Hungarian Monarchy and carried with them its values and culture. The higher officers had begun their careers in the Habsburg army and seen their active service with that army in World War I. All looked on the existing situation as temporary, expecting that when the time was right Hungary would be returned to its old borders. The prime ministers—Bethlen, Teleki, and Károlyi—were all counts, and the political leaders had been the great landowners and finance magnates, representatives of the old order who looked down on Gömbös, the son of a Lutheran teacher of German extraction.

Gömbös represented a new middle class and intelligentsia. This generation had grown up in the Christian-nationalist spirit of truncated Hungary of the 1920s and lacked the nostalgia of the older generation; they included a new group of technocrats, who had achieved success through their education rather than their heritage. Among his supporters were the strata of gentry, army officers, and civil servants who had not succeeded in realizing their career goals in the 1920s. Gömbös himself was a man of the people with a genuine affection for workers and peasants. He enjoyed making speeches to working class audiences extolling the blessings of honest work. An outspoken Hungarian nationalist who loved public applause, Gömbös had no respect for titles and was the first premier on record whose cabinet did not contain a single count. He knew that he was unlettered and inexperienced—his speeches had to be largely written for him—but he was ambitious and hard working, and had practical ability and a remarkable political vision.[60]

Gömbös, who was nicknamed Gombolini, modeled himself on Mussolini and planned to bring about a transformation of society similar to that of Mussolini in Italy. He delivered his maiden speech by radio to the nation at large—an unheard of event—and vowed to transform the soul of the nation, with a promise to create a state that would work for national goals with far-reaching social and economic measures to benefit all classes and social strata.

The regent's appointment of Gömbös as prime minister in October 1932 coincided with the spectacular electoral victories of the Nazi party in Germany. On January 30, 1933, Hitler came to power, radically changing the international climate in Central Europe. One month after his appointment Gömbös traveled to Italy, Hungary's most important foreign ally, where Mussolini confirmed his friendship for Hungary, and Gömbös praised fascism in glowing terms. On his return he staged an enormous procession of the patriotic associations; when he appeared to address the members from a balcony, Mussolini fashion, they hailed him with shouts of "Long live our Leader!"[61]

In June 1933 Gömbös became the first European leader to meet with Hitler, but his high hopes for his visit were unfulfilled. Like most other European politicians, Gömbös did not realize that Hitler wanted absolute power. Hitler was indifferent to Gömbös's goals of regaining former Hungarian territory, offering support only through his intention to destroy Czechoslovakia. In the matter of Austria the interests of the two countries were opposed, since Hungary and Italy both wanted Austria to maintain its independence. Public opinion in Hungary had also been upset by the brutal actions of the Nazi government against the opposition and the attitude to Austria.[62] Gömbös then turned to Italy and together with Austria signed the March 17, 1934, treaty whose undeclared aim was to prevent the annexation of Austria. During his administration he continued to find cooperation with Mussolini of primary importance.

At first Gömbös's program of national unity raised high hopes throughout the population. Even young reformers greeted his ninety-five-point program of reform with enthusiasm, hoping that his government had a realistic plan to address the complaints about the Bethlen era and institute the badly needed economic and social reforms. Gömbös did make progress in taking the country out of the depression through cooperative trade agreements with Italy, Austria, and the Little Entente countries, Czechoslovakia and Romania. A trade agreement was made with Germany in 1934, and by 1936 Germany had become Hungary's main trading partner. The Germans had begun using the bilateral clearing system, which at the time seemed favorable to Hungary; the disadvantages of the agreement, which made possible the accumulation of large debts, only became evident later on.[63] But although the Gömbös government tried to improve the situation of the agrarian population, placing a moratorium on the debt payments which had led to the selling of land at public auction, and introducing the forty-eight-hour work week and minimum wage for workers, his spectacular ninety-five-point program remained largely unfulfilled.[64]

One of Gömbös's primary aims was to strengthen and rejuvenate the military, which had been so severely limited by the Paris peace treaty. The Hungarian army had taken on many of the features of the former Habsburg armed forces, including regulations, training methods, the code of honor, even the cut of the uniforms, as well as the basic principle that the army should be completely apolitical. During the Gömbös administration the apolitical mentality of the army changed to one in which many officers supported the Germans and National Socialism. Germany was considered a model in organization and training and a number of the young Hungarian officers spent a year of service in German military units before they began their training for the officers corps. Gömbös retired a large part of the corps of generals and promoted younger officers who held his political views; then, in 1934, he took advantage of military resignations to replace several higher officers with his own people. The number of younger radicalized men in political life and in the military accelerated the turn to the extreme Right.

The appearance of Ferenc Szálasi—later to become leader of the extreme Right—on the political scene marked the beginning of the politicization of the military. During his life as an active officer Szálasi had sympathized with the ordinary foot soldiers, often walking and chatting with them rather than riding on horseback. Szálasi resigned his office after Gömbös forbade him to be involved in politics, but as a parting gift to his fellow officers he presented them with a silver cigarette case engraved with the words, *"Találkozunk a barrikádokon!"* (We shall meet on the barricades!) Many of his followers left the general staff, and those who were interested in social problems turned to the new ideology of the extreme Right.[65]

In 1935 Gömbös made a surprise move to increase his political power. He had earlier started to reorganize the government party, which he re-named the Party of National Unity, and began a nationwide campaign to establish a modern mass party network, but he had encountered opposition to his dictatorial ambitions. Under pressure he had been forced to abandon his plan to transform the club-like government party into a fascist-type mass organization.[66] Now he devised a plan to escape from the secret conditions imposed by Bethlen and secure the election of many of his rightist supporters. After resigning and persuading the regent to reappoint him, he adjourned the parliamentary session and called for early elections. The Party of National Unity gained 170 of 245 seats; ninety-eight of the deputies had never been elected before and most belonged to the extreme Right. The counter-revolutionaries of 1919, Gömbös's military comrades and extreme-right activists, now dominated Parliament.

Yet Gömbös's victory was short-lived. The victory itself and his attempts to set up corporate institutions to replace the trade unions increased opposition to him. Not only the conservative establishment but also the trade unions blocked his plans to establish a corporatist state. Moderates in Hungarian society clearly recognized the dangers of the rightward trend, and although it was never publicly acknowledged, a working agreement was gradually established between the conservative wing of the government party and the left opposition. The new group, made up of Bethlen's followers, the Christian and Independent Smallholders parties, the Social Democrats, and various others, included the most conservative as well as the most progressive elements in society.[67]

By 1936 Gömbös had become isolated. Italy's Ethiopian campaign had pushed it closer to Germany, and Mussolini agreed to an alignment with Germany, in effect giving up its protection of an independent Austria. Political groups began moving away from Gömbös, including even the extreme Right, which found him not fascist enough. He had lost the regent's support by his treatment of the military officers, old friends of Horthy's, who had resigned in 1934. Resistance against him had grown to such an extent that he would have been removed, but his serious kidney disease and premature death on October 6, 1936, made such a move unnecessary.

After his death, Gömbös's domestic reforms were reversed, but his ministry had brought a change in the political atmosphere with serious consequences for the future. For the first time in politics demagogic methods were used and the state became more authoritarian. After the elections of 1935, the new members of Parliament constituted a new guard and changed the tenor of politics. But most important was the changing of the guard in the civil service and the army, especially in the general staff. The number of younger radicalized men in political life and in the military strengthened the turn to the extreme Right.[68]

THE VILLAGE RESEARCH MOVEMENT

Loss of hope in Gömbös and his failure to carry out reform strengthened the movement of a new generation of critical young reformers, who had become concerned with the social and economic conditions of the peasantry, generally agreed to be the most serious problem facing Hungarian society. Formerly, peasant problems had been seen as social problems, blamed on the disintegration of the traditional village and declining peasant morality, but in the 1930s they were beginning to be seen as political problems. The one million dwarf-holders and 1.2 million agrarian workers were dependent for work on the large estates or seasonal work in the cities, while the 600,000 farm laborers lived and worked on the large estates. Only a small percentage of the peasantry owned enough land to be independent farmers.[69] The reformers looked to these independent farmers as the basis to form a new progressive peasant leadership for the modernization of Hungary.

The leaders of the official churches showed little interest in social problems. The Roman Catholic Church was the largest among the large estate owners, and the high Catholic clergy were understandably reluctant to address the question of land reform.[70] Church estates were divided among several hundred persons or institutions, but the largest part of the 862,704 cadastral hold were held as large estates, many located in socially sensitive areas of the country.[71] The Protestant churches were no better; their leadership firmly controlled by the landowning gentry, who often showed less social awareness than members of the high aristocracy. The alarming spread of radical sects among the agrarian proletariat dramatically demonstrated the failure of the traditional churches.

In the early 1930s groups of university students began to carry out village research among the peasantry. They had been influenced by *népi* (or populist) writers who believed that after the massive 1919 defeat of the proletariat it would be the peasants, who—following a radical land reform—would provide the mass strength for national renewal and the base for a new middle-class intellectual leadership.[72] Hungary's urban population was strongly influenced by German culture, and recently assimilated elements were especially dominant among the urban middle class. Urban dwellers had little knowledge or understanding of the actual conditions of the peasantry, holding the general misconception encouraged by the romantic literature of the nineteenth century that the peasantry lived an idyllic life of plenty. Yet a major part of the agrarian population formed the most backward and poorly educated layer of society. Despite the efforts of Minister of Education Klebelsberg, village isolation and poverty still prevented many agrarian youth from completing even the six years of required elementary education. The village researchers aimed to influence public opinion on behalf of this politically powerless population through objective scientific research, which would document the hopeless conditions of the countryside.[73]

One of the earliest groups of village explorers, the Szeged Youth, thought to find the source of true Hungarian identity among the so-called *pure* Hungarian peasantry on the Alföld. They developed a plan to provide services for the scattered agrarian families living on isolated homesteads on the Great Hungarian Plain and organized series of educational seminars. Although the seminars dealt with subjects such as modern methods of agriculture, the lectures also featured controversial writers addressing contemporary problems. Government fears of potential peasant unrest were revived by a massive worker demonstration in Budapest in September of 1930, and in 1931 the authorities ended the lecture series, charging that the students were inciting the peasantry to rebellion. Yet the later sociographic publications of the Szeged Youth on the problems of the agrarian proletariat motivated groups such as the Protestant Pro Christo Diákok college and the Catholic group, Young Hungary.[74]

The movement gained momentum throughout the 1930s as university youth in a variety of organizations—including Senior Scouts, YMCA, and Catholic and Protestant youth groups—took part in *village exploring*. In 1935 university students from the Protestant Pro Christo Diákok college in Budapest began research in the small Protestant village of Kemse in order to examine Hungary's declining birth rate, considered by many to be one of the most serious problems facing Hungary at the time. They were influenced by the work of the populist writer Gyula Illyés, *Pusztulás* (Destruction), which documented the decline of the Protestant Hungarian population and the accompanying increase of prosperous Swabian settlements in western Hungary.[75] The students were appalled to find what they deemed to be a society in physical and moral disintegration. Their study, *Elsüllyedt falu a Dunántúlon* (A Sinking Village in Transdanubia), revealed in graphic terms the problem of abortion, a practice begun in the nineteenth century to prevent further division of the land. The students found that the practice, which resulted in the so-called only child syndrome, not only crippled the women but affected the whole way of thinking and morality of the villagers. But the community, especially the women, defended the practice of family limitation as their way of dealing with a lack of available land.[76]

In 1936 Zoltán Szabó, a leading member of the Catholic youth group Young Hungary, examined the poverty of the inhabitants of the small village of Tard in northern Hungary because of the system of entailed estates. The villagers had no way to increase their small holdings since their lands were surrounded by the Coburg entailed estate, thus preventing the growth of a class of independent farmers. The head of the family farmed his small plots of land, but the sons had no choice but to work at low-paid seasonal labor on the entailed estates. Even young children were sent out to earn something. One little girl of seven explained: "I worked seven and a half days from four in the morning to six at night. My meals: in the morning a glass of milk, at noon noodle soup, in the evening milk. I could hardly wait for breakfast."[77]

The lowly status of peasant youth led to a self-image of inferiority and subservience. In an interview with one of the young villagers, Szabó asked him to sit down, but the youth was uncomfortable sitting down in the presence of the young gentleman. He had become accustomed to "taking orders from the 'gentleman in trousers' . . . standing dutifully, with cap in hand, ..."[78]

Gyula Illyés, who had grown up on one of the great estates, described the lives of the farm servants who worked and lived on the estates west of the Danube. In his work, *People of the Puszta*, he explained that *puszta* referred to the conglomeration of farm servants' dwellings, stables, sheds, and granaries built in the middle of a large estate. The farm servants "live under one roof in long, low, single-storey houses like slum tenements on the outskirts of a city. . . . In morals, customs, outlook on life, and even in the way they walk and move their arms, they differ sharply from all other social strata. They live in utter isolation, more hidden away and cut off than any villagers. They work all day, Sundays included, and in consequence hardly ever stir from the puszta. . . . It is a world apart; . . ."[79]

In the summer of 1936 university student Imre Kovács traveled through the southeastern region of the Great Plain, documenting the hopeless situation of the peasantry. In his work, *The Silent Revolution*, he described the failure of the traditional churches to address social problems, leading to a flight of the peasantry into radical sects; hundreds of thousands had emigrated from their earthly unhappiness to salvation in the other world, a silent revolution. "The one-child syndrome, the sects and the extreme muddled political movements are the hopeless experiments of an oppressed people." Although revolutions are often a sign of vitality, Kovács explained that this revolution was an enervated people's last cry: "Sects are the harbingers of revolution, but good gentlemen, you don't have to fear: there will be no more peasant revolution in Hungary."[80]

THE MARCH FRONT

March 15, 1937, marked the beginning of a movement known as the March Front to bring about widespread democratic reform. A small group of populist writers and village researchers, meeting weekly at the Budapest Central Café, decided to assemble a program with proposals to answer the most burning domestic questions; land reform, political reform, and the renewal of the middle-class from the peasantry. Their program offered a democratic alternative proposed by no other organized movement. On the anniversary of the 1848 War for Hungarian Independence in front of the National Museum, the site where Sándor Petőfi had read out the original twelve points which started the revolution, Imre Kovács read out their twelve-point program to the crowd of five thousand students, workers and intellectuals.[81]

Among the twelve points were demands for freedom of speech, press, and assembly, universal suffrage with the secret ballot, the division of estates over 500 hold (700 acres), the forty-hour workweek, and a minimum wage. The twelfth point carried international significance by challenging the doctrine of revision. It proposed revision of the Trianon borders not by recreating the former Hungarian kingdom but through the exercise of self-determination based on the decisions of all the people of the Danube basin. It also challenged the expansionist aims of Nazi Germany and Soviet Bolshevism by demanding independence from "Pan-Slavism and Pan-Germanic imperialist aims."[82] As Kovács recalled, when he had finished reading out the twelve points at first the crowd was silent; then, as if catching their breath, they applauded, shouting out: "Long live the March Front. Long live the people's Hungary."[83]

The March Front aroused a response far beyond what any of the organizers had expected. All the daily newspapers reported on the meeting

with the exception of those of the extreme Right. News of the new movement spread like wildfire throughout the country; the group received
invitations to speak everywhere. Excitement was great, especially in the
countryside, where members of farmers' clubs, reading circles, student
groups, peasants, middle-class citizens, and intellectuals gathered to hear
and discuss the twelve-point program.

Then, during the spring of 1937, the works by the young reformers
began to be published one after another, awakening public opinion to the
deplorable conditions of the peasantry. First came a work by Géza Féja,
Stormy Corner, about the rebellious people of the south Tisza region; one
month later Imre Kovács's *Silent Revolution* appeared; then Illyés *People
of the Puszta,* Ferenc Erdei's *Windblown Sand,* and Zoltán Szabó's study,
Situation at Tard. The huge successes of the publications galvanized public opinion. But the series of publications critical of the social situation
were too much for the authorities. The government press and rightist
papers mounted a campaign against the March Front, with the customary
charges that the movement was infiltrated by communists. In April, the
authorities confiscated Féja's book. Kovács's book sold out and a second
edition was printed, but it was also confiscated.

In reaction to the government measures differences began to appear
within the Front as to the purpose of the movement—whether it should
be first of all an intellectual movement or a political one. The differences
increased in the fall as the government initiated trials against two of the
authors, the first against Féja and the second against Kovács. A ban was
placed on meetings of the March Front and participants were placed
under police surveillance. Sándor Kiss, a student in Szeged, discovered
that students who had attended a March Front organizational meeting at
Makó were watched by the police: ". . . we got the news that we also
were under police surveillance. This news frightened off many who were
interested."[84]

Kovács was charged with "inciting hatred among the lower classes . . .
against the social classes in a more fortunate economic situation, first of
all the landowning class. Also, that he stated false facts which would be
capable of damaging the honor of the Hungarian state and Hungarian
nation and violating its trustworthiness."[85] In his defense Kovács explained that he spoke only of what he had experienced as a child living
on such an estate: "I saw the Hungarian peasantry, but especially the
three million agrarian workers and estate servants and their terrible social
situation. . . . I saw the distorted way of life of the Hungarian peasantry
with the 'one-child syndrome' and the flight to the sects."[86] Kovács asked

the judge to call as witnesses his professors, Count Pál Teleki, former prime minister, and Gyula Szekfű, the highly respected historian, as well as Protestant bishops and parliamentary representatives. The judge refused the request, but Szekfű wrote in the press as a witness, claiming that both books contained ideas that expressed his views as well.[87]

In countering Kovács's defense, the judge explained: "Your charge is not that you carried out village research and wrote a book about it, or the subject of the book, but the charge is about the manner and tone of your writing." Kovács was sentenced to three months in prison. Among those protesting the sentence were parliamentary representative Mátyás Matolcsy, who read out a declaration in the assembly signed by Béla Bartók and Zsigmond Móricz. As a result of the sentence Kovács was expelled from the Technical University, even though he had completed his studies and had only the examination left to complete his degree.

The March Front movement gradually lost momentum. Criticized for being too radical and too critical of Hungarian society, the members were also unsuccessful in gaining the support of the workers and the Social Democrats. Because of their concentration on reforms for the peasantry, they were criticized for not addressing the needs of the urban workers. Members of the liberal opposition parties, themselves divided by questions of power and influence, viewed the dynamic March Front as a new rival for influence among the population. The opposition parties, with much of their support from Budapest and the Jewish population, suspected anti-Semitism in the points of the program targeting the banks, cartels, and monopolies, all of which were in Jewish hands.

By March 1938 the March Front was disintegrating. Disappointed by the obduracy of the regime and the lack of reform, many radicals— including some who had formerly held leftist views—turned to the right for reform.[88] The government crack-down on suspected communists and leftists in the first half of the thirties as well as the measures against the March Front had made reform from the left appear increasingly unattainable. The increasing strength of the radical Right reflected the widespread dissatisfaction of large segments of the population; discontent with the economic situation, disillusionment with the government's failure to carry out long-needed reforms, frustration—especially among young intellectuals—with the ongoing and serious unemployment situation. The failure of Gyula Gömbös to carry out his ninety-five-point program of reform had only contributed to greater disillusionment.

Hungarians were influenced by the general rightist trend pervasive throughout Europe.[89] The capitalist system was seen to be in decline and parliamentary government to be ineffective, while the concept of the corporatist state was gaining popularity. In the wake of the Great Depression democracy was said to be suited only to wealthy or prosperous countries, and even countries with established parliamentary systems struggled to deal with widespread unemployment and budget crises. In France, in the 1920s, suffering from the terrible destruction of the Great War, both the Left and Right shaded off into antidemocratic groups hostile to the parliamentary republic, and agitation of the fascist type began to make headway during the depression.

Mussolini's reforms and progress made by the Italian corporatist state was widely admired in Hungary, and the Salazar clerical-corporatist state, which had brought stability to Portugal, was considered an example to be studied.[90] Fascist parties were gaining in the neighboring countries; the Catholic Hlinka party in Slovakia, the Usztasy in Croatia, the Iron Guard in Romania. The events of the Spanish Civil War, which broke out in 1936, showed the strength of fascism and the weakness of the Western powers, as the government of the Second Spanish Republic struggled against the fascist forces of General Francisco Franco. Fascism came to be regarded as a possible alternative to democratic or parliamentary government—as an actual corrective to troubles whose reality no one could deny.

According to a former student at the University of Szeged, although the majority of students supported the regime, those who took an interest in politics and recognized social ills were more likely to lean to the extreme Right. They had grown up with the view that Trianon was the source of all their problems—that first Mihály Károlyi and then Béla Kún had taken the country on the wrong road and destroyed it. From here it was only a small step to anti-Semitism; the leaders of the Soviet Republic of 1919 were Jewish. Rather than seeing a danger in National Socialism they regarded it as a model; they viewed Hitler's machinations with admiration, the way in which step by step he kicked aside the Treaty of Versailles, and they saw the possibility for the success of Hungarian revisionism in following the German example.[91]

Jews had become an ever-greater target during the depression years, blamed for economic problems and conflicts in society. There was a generally held view that the wealth of the Jewish population was so great, that if it were seized by the state and redistributed it would make possible much needed social reforms. Radicalized youth saw possibilities for the improvement of their own existence only by systematically removing the Jewish middle class and intelligentsia from positions in economics and the free professions that they dominated. Traditionally, this strata of youth had studied law in preparation for the positions they aspired to—government and civil service—but because of the difficulties in securing employment, more were turning to some of the free professions; medicine, engineering, and the liberal arts, which provided a good preparation for teaching. These professions, which had previously been disdained by middle-class Christian youth, had often been the only choice for Jews, who were prevented from access to positions in the government and civil service.

In the late 1930s both the leftist reformers and the rapidly growing radical Right focused on the same problems; domestic tensions caused by extreme class divisions, the unequal distribution of land, the lack of career prospects for university graduates. Both sides realized that the system had to change, but they disagreed completely on the means. The leftist reformers saw the causes of conflict in the class system and the unhealthy division of land, leading to the misery of the landless peasants, dwarf holders, and servants on the large estates; they saw the means of reform in the democratic program of the March Front and land reform. The Right, which was becoming ever more strident, attributed the origin of problems to monopolistic capitalism and the over-representation of Jews in the professions and large industry. They looked to some kind of redistribution of Jewish wealth and the ouster of Jewish professionals from their jobs.[92] Their solution was to eliminate the liberal market economy and bring in a planned economy. It was not only Hitler and Stalin, with their four- and five-year plans, but also Roosevelt with his New Deal who provided their models.[93]

3   The Last Year of European Peace

The last year of European peace, 1938, was a year of turmoil for the Hungarians, ranging from panic over the German *Anschluss* (annexation) of Austria and pride in hosting the International Eucharistic Congress to jubilation with the recovery of part of northern Hungary, the Felvidék. On March 12–13 Hitler's troops marched into Austria, incorporating the country into the German Reich. The rapid takeover, accompanied by cheering Austrian crowds, shocked the Hungarian public. The *Anschluss* brought the territory of the German Reich to the western border of Hungary, completing the encirclement formed by the Little Entente countries, Czechoslovakia, Romania, and Yugoslavia. Many feared the Germans would keep marching right on into Budapest and panic broke out with an announcement that interrupted the Hungarian Radio Program I— German troops were at the Hegyeshalom border. The government ordered a block on news and banned assemblies.[1]

The *Anschluss* gave a tremendous surge to the extreme-right movements, which had been gaining power since the collapse of the reformist March Front. The messianic leader of the Hungarian National Socialist party, known as the Arrow Cross Party, was making great strides in uniting the many fragmented extreme-right parties. The Arrow Cross Party had already declared 1938 to be "our year," the year when their leader, Ferenc Szálasi, would take over power as dictator. The domestic political situation became so tense that the regent found it necessary to calm the public, addressing the nation for the first time by radio in a speech reminiscent of Roosevelt's Fireside Chats. Horthy, who had become something of a father figure, reassured his people that order prevailed, and that Hungary experienced no danger from the newly established Hungarian-German common border, stating that ". . . the union of Austria with Germany means nothing else than the union of an old and good friend of ours, whom the peace treaties had involved in an impossible position, with another old and good friend and companion-in-arms of ours."[2]

The XXXIV International Eucharistic Congress

Despite international tensions the Catholic Church held its International Eucharistic Congress as planned in May 1938. The event had been scheduled to mark the celebration of the nine hundredth anniversary of the death of St. Stephen, the founder of the state and symbol of the former Kingdom of Hungary.[3] Only after years of negotiations had Archbishop Jusztinián Serédi been able to secure the right to organize the congress. He had gained the support of the head of the Permanent Committee of the International Eucharistic Congress, Bishop Heylen of Namur, Belgium, and on November 17, 1936, in Paris the Permanent Committee supported the request unanimously. In Hungary, Catholic newspapers held back the news until after Regent Horthy's visit to Italy, where he was received in a private audience with Pope Pius XI, whose approval raised the congress to a matter of international import. The choice of Budapest for the celebration was not only a matter of pride for Hungarian Catholics but brought the international recognition, which had been denied Hungary for almost twenty years.[4]

The pageantry of the XXXIV International Eucharistic Congress was perhaps the most magnificent celebration of Hungarian Catholicism in the twentieth century, crowned by the participation of Bishop Eugenio Pacelli, the Vatican state secretary, soon to become Pope Pius XII.[5] As he stepped off the train at Budapest's East Railroad Station on May 23, the papal legate was greeted by the regent, dignified in the uniform of an Austro-Hungarian Admiral. Hungary's highest state and ecclesiastical dignitaries looked on as Pacelli and Horthy greeted each other warmly with a prolonged handshake, renewing their acquaintance made on the regent's visit to Italy in November 1936. On that visit, his first official state visit after sixteen years in office, Horthy had been received with a "pomp that far exceeded what would be expected" for a Hungarian head of state.[6] Present on the reception platform were Archbishop Jusztinián Serédi, main organizer of the congress, the newly appointed Prime Minister Béla Imrédy, the presidents of both houses of Parliament, Count Bertalan Szécheny of the upper house and Gyula Kornis of the lower house, Minister of Culture Count Pál Teleki, Minister of Foreign Affairs Kálmán Kánya, and other members of the cabinet, along with other state and church officials.

Horthy and Pacelli proceeded before a military honor guard to the closed auto, which carried them through the rain to the coronation church, where the ecclesiastical representatives awaited Pacelli to take over presidency of the congress. Pacelli's presence and his position as

president of the congress emphasized the support of the Catholic establishment for the regime and Hungary's emergence from its long diplomatic isolation. Despite his own Protestant faith, Horthy had supported
the Catholic Church throughout his reign, and his strong anti-Bolshevism
could not but appeal to the Church in its campaign against "godless communism." The regent's wife, Magdolna Purgly, a devout Catholic, had
been asked to accept the post of patroness of the congress which she
graciously accepted. In the papal message to the regent which Pacelli
delivered that evening, Pope Pius XI commended Horthy and the Hungarian state for organizing the congress and again emphasized that the Hungarian regime enjoyed the full support of the Catholic Church.[7]

Two-thirds of the Hungarian population belonged to the Catholic
Church in Hungary, which wielded considerable influence. Bishops were
ex-officio members of the upper house of Parliament and there were numerous church-affiliated social movements and associations, publishing
houses, extensive press, and trade unions. The churches, including the
Protestant Calvinists and Lutherans, had a near monopoly in education,
with 68.6 percent of elementary schools and 51.9 percent of secondary
schools in 1930. In return they pledged loyal support to Horthy.[8]

The events attended by thousands of Catholics from all over the world
placed Hungary in the international spotlight. This celebration of Christian European culture was perceived in Western Europe as a form of
opposition to Nazi power. The absence of Catholic representatives from
Germany and Austria, prevented from attending by Hitler's government,
highlighted the tension existing between the church and the Nazi regime.

The five days of the congress were full of pageantry, displaying the
magnificence of the Catholic establishment for all the world to see. The
weather had been terrible—cold, rainy, and windy—but on the day of
the opening, Wednesday May 25, the sun came out. At 5 P.M. every
Roman Catholic church bell in Budapest pealed out the opening of the
congress to the city and the world. The prominent guests were hosted at
a dinner given by Horthy and his wife at the castle, and the reception for
1,500 afterward included all of Hungarian officialdom.[9]

The next evening the most spectacular event of the congress took
place, launched by the ceremonial procession from the St. Stephen Basilica to the banks of the Danube. The Papal legate, Pacelli, in full cardinal
vestments, carried the Eucharist from the Basilica to the ship, accompanied by the peal of bells. When the Basilica bells began to ring, the gar-
lands of lights decorating the nine ships flashed on and sparkling lights
illuminated both banks of the Danube which were lined by half a million

people. The emblem of the congress on the Chain Bridge, a burning red chalice on the Elizabeth Bridge, the royal castle, the coronation church, and the parliament, were all brilliantly lighted.

The flotilla of boats displayed the elite of the Horthy regime, both notables and clergy, giving credence to those who labeled it a semifeudal society. The first ship bore a huge illuminated cross, followed by a ship with fifty trumpeters dressed in ancient Hungarian costume to emphasize the thousand years of Hungarian history. The *Prince József* carried the upper clergy in colorful regalia, while forty Dalmatian priests stood at the back of the ship waving burning incense into the air. The *Zsófia* yacht was filled with local and foreign aristocrats as well as political and military elite. The procession circled Margit Island, returned to Eötvös Square, then continued to Miklós Horthy Bridge before returning to the square. At this point, a magnificent firework display burst out from the Gellert hill, and as the finale, a huge fifty-meter cross painted the sky red.[10]

The organizers had left nothing to chance; every detail had been arranged. Pupils in all the Catholic schools and churches had been taught the anthem for the congress. The traditional Easter religious custom, according to which all of the members of the military and gendarmerie took communion together, had been postponed to take place during the congress. When it appeared that school principals were not planning to bring their students to attend, Cardinal Serédi ordered that they perform the usual end of the year Holy Communion at the congress instead. Students were given the school day off to make their confession, and in order to persuade civil servants to take part they were given a holiday on May 27, 29, and 30.

The mass at Heroes' Square on the evening of May 27 demonstrated the power of the Church, as 150,000 men gathered for the religious event. In the square, lighted only by the brilliantly illuminated altar, 150,000 men carrying torches and candles marched by as in a political demonstration. After the mass, in an enactment of a miracle play, Jesuit Father Elemér Csávossy called on all those gathered to protest against godlessness, against atheism. With lighted torches and candles in their hands, the 150,000 men answered him as one: "We protest." In like manner they protested the unjust imprisonment of priests, the communist horror, the robbing of schools by Nazis. As a finale, in answer to the call, "those who are with me against godless actions" they shouted in unison, *"Ott leszünk!* (We will be there!)"[11]

The congress symbolized the inner renewal, which Catholicism had undergone in the difficult years of the truncated state, when people had found an outlet in the spiritual powers of the church. Especially in youth circles the religious and ethical movements gained mass influence. The revival can be seen in the expansion of religious orders that had started at the turn of the century. Numbers in holy orders grew phenomenally; there were more male monks in truncated Hungary than in all of the former Hungarian kingdom and the number of nuns doubled.[12] Women's orders, which had played little role in the nineteenth century, sprang up in surprising numbers, surpassing the number of men's. Women's societies with characteristics of orders such as communal living were also formed, although the sisters wore modern dress and devoted their lives to social work in the community.[13] With the growth of numbers there was also an increase in discipline and activity, new churches were built, new church societies formed, large numbers of church publications were founded. There was hardly any public social area—education, care of the sick, social welfare, and culture—in which one did not find members of orders.

Yet the congress itself totally neglected the festering social problems, which had been brought to the foreground by the March Front and were providing fuel for the rapid growth of extreme-right parties. The featured speakers at the May 28 meeting, devoted to the subject "The Hungarian Village and the Eucharist," were the least likely to understand the village problems: a retired government minister, the mayor of Újpest, and the church official who possessed the greatest church fortune. They believed the main problem of the village was that the villagers were not sufficiently religious. They complained that the villagers seemed to be bored by the mass, only waiting for it to be over! It was necessary to stop their loitering and looking around. In their opinion the primary issue was to intensify the piety of the believers.[14]

The only speaker at the meeting to address the serious social problems of the village and of village youth was a young Jesuit priest, Jenő Kerkai, leader of a dynamic new movement of agrarian youth. Kerkai urged the church to turn its attention to the national and social problems of the village. In a challenge to the traditional attitude of the conservative Catholic clergy, he suggested that the church and its priests should not only instruct the village youth in religion but also undertake to solve their problems.

Kerkai had begun to organize agrarian youth on his return in 1935 from the theological seminary in Innsbruck, Austria, where he had been influenced by the French artisan and agrarian youth organizations, Jeunesse Ouvriere Chretiene (JOC) and Jeunesse Agricole Chretien (JAC). Kerkai believed the position of peasant youth to be unjust; the youngsters lived in cultural isolation and economic backwardness, scattered throughout the countryside in small villages and farms. He was determined to change the situation with the organization Catholic Agrarian Youth, known by its acronym KALOT, which he founded. At the time when the sociological writings of the Village Explorers and Populist writers were being published, youth leaders—both Catholic and Protestant—were intensifying their efforts to reach out to village youth, beginning a movement to educate a new self-confident generation of leaders. KALOT experienced phenomenal growth in the next three years.[15]

One of the KALOT leaders recruited by Kerkai, György Farkas, explained: "We saw that the economic and social structure built on capitalism and the great estates could not, would not, did not even want to solve the problems of the peasantry and workers. . . . We decided on the need to call for a new economic and social system. . . . In all of Europe there was not another country with such a distorted social structure, where at the one pole were millions of peasants, and at the other—medieval feudalism in the twentieth century."[16]

At first the conservative upper clergy of the church regarded the movement as too radical and tried to restrict its growth. The official church with its large landholdings strongly opposed reform, especially the land reform called for by KALOT as well as much of the peasantry and liberal reformers. By siding with the semifeudal power of the landowners they were partially responsible for the social tensions and growth of hostility to the church among the poor. But by1938 the upper clergy had come to the realization that the popular movement could be an aid to the church in its struggle against Godless communism, the leftist worker movement, and class warfare. KALOT was recognized by the Church as an organization, and by 1939 already had 150,000 members.

The Jesuit leaders had learned from modern mass political movements. The organization derived its strength partially from the lack of political representation of the agrarian population, but also from the charisma and methods of Jenő Kerkai and his helpers, who unashamedly copied the methods of the Fascist and Nazi mass movements—marches, flags, demonstrations. Their efforts through weekend leadership training courses had succeeded in preparing 15,000 village youth, both men and women, to march at the Eucharistic Congress.

The gathering of the 15,000 KALOT youth on May 29 clearly demonstrated the strength of the new movement. At 6 A.M., 11,000 village lads and 4,000 village girls began their march into the great Industrial Hall, carrying the movement's flag—a huge cross of sheaves of wheat—at the head of the procession. The speakers' manner of addressing the gathering was reminiscent of political agitators; József Ugrin proclaimed that the agrarian youth represented the future of the Hungarian nation, Father Kerkely urged the young people to become more Christian, more cultured, more active, and self-confident Hungarians—the four goals of the movement! The massive organization of peasant youth, a social class known for its passivity and largely ignored by the urban population, astonished the population of Budapest.[17]

The Effects of the *Anschluss*

The celebratory atmosphere of the congress could not disguise the tension caused by the German threat and the increasing political swing to the right. Just two and a half months earlier the very celebration of the Eucharistic Congress had been put into question. Shortly after the *Anschluss* thousands of foreign pilgrims withdrew their applications to participate, fearing for their safety. The Bishop of Namur, head of the International Eucharistic Congress Board, wrote to Esztergom questioning whether the Hungarians intended to go ahead with plans for the congress; the German government had already made clear that German Catholics would not be allowed to attend. Hitler's condition had been that the Vatican should take the responsibility to assure there would be no anti-German or anti-Nazi incidents. Although the Vatican reiterated the Hungarian Archbishop's pronouncement that the congress was completely nonpolitical, participation by German Catholics was effectively blocked. Added now to the 1,000 Germans who had intended to participate were 7,000 Austrians, who were also forbidden to take part.[18]

The *Anschluss* radically changed Hungary's political situation, its foreign political possibilities, and its domestic relations. Hungary was now surrounded on all sides by threatening powers. Hungary had long been concerned over Austria's fate and the danger of its annexation by Germany. Mussolini had strongly opposed German annexation, and the treaty signed in 1934 between Austria, Hungary, and Italy had been intended to prevent it. But German and Italian relations had improved greatly during the period of the Spanish Civil War and now Mussolini made no protest.[19] Yet the *Anschluss* ended the possibility of an alliance centered on Austria and also devalued Italy's bilateral treaties with Hungary and Yugoslavia. None of the Western powers, which had forbidden annexation in the Treaty of Versailles after World War I tried to prevent Hitler's move.

Alarm in Hungary was increased by the fact that the German government made no declaration recognizing the actual frontiers of Hungary, which it had done in relation to Italy, Yugoslavia, and Switzerland. For years, Germany had shown interest in the half million Hungarian Swabians, an agrarian German population living primarily in the south-central part of the country. In 1934 a young Protestant theology student, Balint Kovács, on a German fellowship in Marburg, remembered his shock at seeing a map on the classroom wall showing western Hungary already occupied by the German Reich.[20] Only after some delay, at the request of Foreign Minister Kálmán Kánya, did the Germans agree that they would not object to publication of a declaration on recognition of Hungary's frontiers.[21]

While the occupation created panic in many circles, it strengthened pro-German elements, especially the forces of the extreme Right. That spring it appeared to everyone, including high church officials and KALOT, that the extreme Right, uniting around the Arrow Cross, was poised to take power to establish a national socialist state. Prime Minister Darányi, who had been appointed to reverse the rightist trend under former Prime Minister Gömbös, now gave free play to the Arrow Cross. His government was the first to congratulate Hitler, and he introduced a press law banning four hundred liberal and left-wing papers. Two months later, on May 12, Horthy asked for Darányi's resignation on the grounds that he had not done enough to break the rightist trend in domestic politics and had not reduced dependence in foreign affairs on Germany.[22]

On May 14 Béla Imrédy, a staunch and pious Catholic with excellent financial connections in London, was named prime minister. He began his ministry by taking strong measures against the extreme Right; his order forbidding state employees to be members of political parties was directed against the many civil servants and military who supported rightist parties. He also ordered the arrest of the leader of the Arrow Cross, Szálasi, to prevent the Arrow Cross from attempting to take power with German support. Imrédy's program, based on the ideals of social justice and popular national unity enjoyed the support of the progressive Catholics, including Kerkai's KALOT movement, which he in turn supported financially.[23]

The massive gains in support made by the Arrow Cross in the months after the *Anschluss* can be seen in the numbers and composition of its members. Although Arrow Cross hysteria subsided when it became apparent that the Nazi advance had stopped at the country's western frontier, its mass influence continued to rise. The number of registered party members grew from about 10,000 in July 1938 to an estimated 200,000 by the elections in 1939. The following came from very mixed social backgrounds, ranging from army officers and civil servants to railroad workers and postmen, and the base was now being broadened. There were potential members from the large unemployed or underemployed bureaucratic middle class, which had increased after the truncation of the territory. To accommodate them rump Hungary had retained the same size civil service as before but with much less money, generating miserable salaries and great discontent.[24]

In 1937–38 the membership base had come from rural districts; in 1938–39 it was shifting to Budapest, the suburbs, and country towns.[25] Contrary to the view that Arrow Cross followers consisted of the dregs of society, recent research shows that at the high point of its popularity in 1938–39 a number of members were highly educated. Among the 466 Budapest party members at the beginning of 1938, ninety-nine had doctorates. In their disillusionment with lack of reform in the 1930s a number of leftist radicals—former Social Democrats and Communists—also joined the party and gained a prominent role in the leadership.[26]

The extreme-right parties, which had been fragmented, were now uniting around the Szálasi party. The police reported that in 1938 the number of meetings of rightist groups far surpassed the number in any other year, although it is important to note the definition of left and right in Hungary at the time. The Left was considered to consist solely of Communists, Social Democrats, and the trade unions; all other groups were considered to be on the right, including parties such as the Agrarian Party, the Independent Smallholders, and Catholic movements like KALOT. The reports written by police officers indicate the increasingly varied nature of the rightist constituency, as well as the growing popularity of the rightist party led by Szálasi.

Permission from the police or gendarmes was required for all organized meetings and an officer was present at each meeting. If the group deviated from the agenda, the officer had the right to dissolve the meeting—the rapping of a pencil often indicated that the meeting was getting off track. According to the police notes, major issues that concerned the public in 1938 were Jewish economic dominance and the need for social reform:

> The February meeting of the party with the same name as the Szálasi party, the Hungarian National Socialist Party, led by Festetics, was attended by about 1,500 people. Márton Buzás, father of nine, demanded healthy land reform and settlement so that every working Hungarian would have land. He considered it wrong that 3,500,000 hold of Hungarian land should be in Jewish hands—Jewish ownership and the burden of the large estates made land reform impossible.
>
> On January 7, at a meeting of the National Front, Kálmán Hubay charged that the Jews in recent years had enriched themselves disproportionately while Christian Hungarians were becoming poorer.
>
> At the January 23 meeting of the United Christian Party, at which the speakers were parliamentary representatives, there were about 1,200 people in attendance. It was said that Christians have to win back what the "foreigners" have taken away from them. Workers work from morning to late night, but can't earn their daily bread, while financial institutions, factories, estates are in foreign hands![27]

A number of the police reports showed that the Arrow Cross was growing in strength among the numerous extreme-right parties, indicating the success of the leader, Ferenc Szálasi, in attracting new members. At a meeting of the rival Hungarian National Socialist party a member stated that the party in Miskolc is falling apart, the members all want to join the Szálasi's party. It was reported at the Budapest center of the Arrow Cross Party that more and more people were joining—not seldom including some of the better social class. "They make large donations of money." Reports came in that the Arrow Cross was organizing in a number of country towns, and that the Szálasi name was soon to be known in the smallest settlement. "They speak of him as someone long awaited by the National Socialist movement."[28]

THE FIRST JEWISH LAW

With the increasing discontent exhibited by the public and the increasing strength of the extreme-right parties, momentum had been building within the government to introduce some measure limiting Jewish strength in economic life. A memorandum, originally submitted by the former Prime Minister Darányi, suggested that a law be formulated to accommodate the aspirations of the Christian middle class at the expense of the Jews, and thus block the increasing popularity of the pro-Nazi Arrow Cross. The government introduced the Jewish law in April 1938 with the intention of pacifying the increasingly strident Right.

The Bill of May 1938 was designed to create "more effective safeguards of balance in economic life" and "conditions to combat unemployment among the intelligentsia" by opening up areas of employment to the Christian middle class; but it was carefully designed so as not to affect the powers of the large Jewish capitalists, who were so important to the Hungarian economy and central to the government plans to expand and modernize the military.[29]

In contrast to the Nazi Nuremberg Laws, the definition of Jew used in the Hungarian Jewish law was based primarily on religion rather than race. Those qualified as Jews who belonged to the Jewish faith, including those who converted after August 1, 1919, or were born after that date if their mother and father had been of the Jewish faith at that date. However, since it included those who had converted to Christianity after 1919, it also relied on the idea of race.

The bill limited to 20 percent the number of persons of Jewish religion in professions in which they were heavily represented—the press, theater, and film industry—by the end of 1939: and within five years in commercial and industrial enterprises employing more than ten persons. The bill also ordered the establishment of a network of professional chambers in most of the liberal professions, similar to the lawyer, doctor, and engineer chambers that had long been in existence. The purpose was to limit the numbers and influence of Jewish lawyers, physicians, engineers, journalists, and actors—professions in which there was a heavy representation of Jewish practitioners. No Jew could be admitted to any local chamber unless the ratio of Jewish members to that particular chamber was below 20 percent. Practicing Jewish professionals at the date of establishment were automatic members of local chambers and were not forced out.[30]

The Jewish law was presented on April 8—four days after the *Anschluss*—and passed on May 29 after a month and a half of violent debate. A protest against the Jewish law, read in parliament by Imre Németh, was signed by fifty-nine Christian Hungarian writers, artists, and public figures—including Béla Bartók, Zoltán Kodály, Zsigmond Móricz—and the liberal opposition and Social Democrats. The protestors emphasized that the law broke with the principle of the equal rights of citizens and pointed out that the law would not solve the real economic and social problems; it would not only humiliate the Jews but it would harm Christian middle-class youth, who would achieve a secure future by taking away rights from others.[31]

In the upper house of Parliament the bill was initially debated in committee, where Imrédy explained that the Jewish presence was too strong and needed to be limited. The church leaders raised objections; Cardinal Serédi objected to a retroactive law, and Bishop Gyula Glattfelder tried to moderate certain points. However, the committee voted for the bill, and after general debate in the upper house, in which there were serious differences, the bill eventually passed. Even Leo Goldberger, a member of Jewish origin, voted for it since he believed it was not too harmful and it would solve the problem and take the Jewish question off the agenda.[32]

The effects of the law at this stage were felt mainly by Jewish salaried professionals, new graduates, and potential migrants. In many areas only members of a chamber were eligible for a position, so acceptance into a chamber became a tool for selection. Not affected by the bill were most independent artisans, merchants, industrialists, and laborers. The bill allowed for an adjustment period of five years. Although relatively moderate for the time, it brought an abrupt departure from the constitutional tradition of the 1867 emancipation, and importantly it broke with the principle established since 1848 of the equality of all citizens.[33]

The first Jewish Law was never implemented in full. Since the only criterion of Jewishness was in reference to religion, it had been relatively easy for churches to agree to it. After it passed there was a proliferation of conversions. Interestingly, the law came into effect just at the time of the first peaceful successful revision—the first Vienna Award—which affected the public to such an extent that they did not feel the full significance or repercussions of the racial law.

A government reform was passed almost at the same time to reorganize the middle schools. The graduation diploma from technical schools was now to be recognized equally with that from the classical *gimnázium*. This reform was intended to enable middle-class children to enter careers in the economy, as well as making possible upward social mobility for the children of lower classes who did not usually attend the elite *gimnázium*. Combined with the Jewish law the two-fold purpose was to reduce the number of Jews in those positions and make it easier for members of the Christian middle class and lower classes to enter them.

THE GYŐR PROGRAM

Shortly before the *Anschluss*, on March 5, 1938, in the industrial city of Győr, Prime Minister Darányi announced a large-scale program to expand and equip the military. Hungarians had long been concerned over possible threats from the Little Entente countries, Czechoslovakia, Romania, and Yugoslavia. Even though truncated Hungary was weak in terms of economic resources and military strength, it was still regarded as a threat by the neighbor countries, not because of its military power but because of the strength of the Hungarian minorities within their borders who retained their Hungarian identity. The intent of the Győr Program was to overcome the gigantic lag in the military's equipment and armaments, which had been restricted by the peace treaty—restrictions that had prevented Hungary from developing manufacturing for military purposes. In the 1930s Hungary had succeeded in purchasing some weapons, but they were later found to be antiquated and substandard.

In comparison with the armies of its neighbors, the Royal Hungarian Army was extremely weak. At the time of the *Anschluss* the whole army consisted of only seven mixed brigades and two cavalry brigades. By the early 1930s Czechoslovakia had twenty-eight divisions as well as an advanced military industry. The Romanians had thirty-two divisions, all equipped with motorized and armored units, while Yugoslavia had twenty-three divisions. The military estimated that if war broke out with the Little Entente countries, they might be able to fight one of the neighbors, perhaps delay two, but certainly not fight all three.

War preparations were accelerating; Germany had introduced compulsory military service in 1935. Already in the mid-1930s the Hungarian high command had realized the increased chance of a European war, one in which Hungary would inevitably be involved, not only because of its geographical location but also its aspirations to territorial revision. The chief of the general staff, Jenő Rátz, pointed out in 1935 that the military was so backward that it was not even prepared to defend the country. In 1937 both the press and military, noting the increased pace of Axis armament, urged rapid and open rearmament, but it had been necessary to await a more favorable economic situation. With a good harvest, an improvement in foreign trade, and some reduction in the national debt in 1936–37, the moment had finally come.[34]

Under the program the ministry authorized the amount of one billion pengős in excess of the appropriation of the state budget to be spent on military and defense aims over a period of five years. This was a significant sum, since in the mid-thirties all of Hungarian industrial capital development was not more than 180 million pengős per year. Six hundred million was designated to strengthen and modernize the army; the rest was allocated for the development of the country's military structure, construction of roads and bridges, development of railways and waterways, and the equipment of the post, telegraph, and telephone network. The program included several kinds of social investment, including expenditure for education in agriculture, works to promote irrigation, and health centers for villages, but no concrete division of funds was fixed in the act. The sum was to be raised partly by taxes and four hundred million by loans.

The goal of the program was to have 107,000 men in peacetime and 250,000 in wartime—3 armies and 7 army corps with 21 divisions, 2 rapid deployment brigades, 2 cavalry brigades, 1 air division, and 3 divisions of border forces, as well as accompanying general headquarters and army corps units. In preparation for a possible attack by one of the neighbors it was necessary to strengthen the border defenses and build up rapid deployment forces and the air force. All of the divisions would be ready to march at the same time, with the exception of the rapid and cavalry brigades, border troops and air force and anti-aircraft artillery. The advantage was the simplicity of mobilizing equally well in peace and war; the disadvantage was that it was not possible for one part of the army to be ready to march earlier.[35]

Although the plan was much less than the military had requested, it pleased the leadership, not only because the government could not be expected to do more in the difficult economic situation, but also since the general staff had not yet worked out their views on the ways to develop the technical and economic plans for the army. They had no idea of exactly what was needed or what it would cost, so it seemed that for the time being the amount was sufficient. Of course, the leadership hoped that the program would be expanded and speeded up, but they were awaiting further developments.[36]

CONTINUED GERMAN AGGRESSION

After the annexation of Austria it was clear that the German pattern of aggression would continue. Publicly the Nazis claimed that the *Anschluss* was simply a realization of German national self-determination, but to Hitler it was a necessary move to improve Germany's strategic position in Central Europe. He needed possession of Austria and Czechoslovakia before launching the conquest of German *Lebensraum* in the East. Hitler's plans for the destruction of Czechoslovakia had been long in the making and included Hungarian involvement. In Berlin at the end of November 1937, he had informed Prime Minister Darányi and Foreign Minister Kánya of his plans. Despite a promise to the Czechs that they would have nothing to fear from Germany, on April 21, 1938, he sent orders to draft plans for invading Czechoslovakia and in May 1938 he approved the plan for military and political action, Operation Grün [Green]. The plan included the role that Hitler expected Hungary and Poland to play—that they demand to reclaim the territories they had lost in the World War I peace treaties. The German propaganda machine concentrated now on the Sudeten Germans in Czechoslovakia, becoming more and more virulent in their accusations against the Czechoslovak government.

From the time of the foundation of the Czechoslovak state, the Czechs had been concerned about the threat to the stability of the republic from the large minority populations. The population of Czechs was estimated at only six and one-half million, while there were three million Germans, almost one million Magyars, as well as Ruthenians, Jews, and other minorities. To balance the minorities they had incorporated the Slovak population, estimated at about two million, to form one Czechoslovak people—the census reports contained no separate category for a Czech or a Slovak nationality, but only that of Czechoslovak. The language of the Republic was officially Czechoslovak, although many Slovaks had difficulty understanding the Czech language.[37]

Now the Czech leaders faced not only increased German pressure and the radicalization of the Sudeten German Party, but also increased activism of the other minorities, including the Slovaks. The Slovak population, overwhelmingly Catholic, resented Czech measures against the Catholic Church, as well as the pressure against the Slovak language in schools and universities. In the early years of the republic, the Czechs had brought in large numbers of Czech administrators because of the lack of qualified Slovak personnel. Despite the rise of a new educated generation, qualified to take the positions, the Czechs had remained.

Popular discontent was increased by economic hardships; the depression hit particularly hard, real income fell by one-third between 1929 and 1932, and overall one-third of Slovakia's inhabitants were without steady income. In 1920 there had been no strong Slovak national consciousness among the general population. By 1938 a new generation of nationalistic Slovak youth, educated in Czech universities, had become radicalized. Unlike the older Slovaks, who were grateful to the Czechs for the republic, the young Slovak intelligentsia took Czechoslovakia for granted and had less tolerance for Prague's failure to deal with the Slovak question. The Slovak People's Party, with its goal of Slovak autonomy, was gradually becoming the most popular among the Slovak electorate.[38]

From the founding of the republic Czechoslovakia had a plethora of political parties and had been ruled by a coalition government. The Czechs had relied on the so-called activist minority parties—those that cooperated with the government—to maintain the coalition majority in Parliament and to resist the demands for greater minority rights. But in 1935, in the last elections to be held in the republic, the new Sudeten German Party led by Konrad Henlein won a stunning victory, receiving two-thirds of all German votes—more votes than any other political party. Two weeks later it was joined by two other German parties, giving it 55 out of 300 deputies in the Chamber of Deputies. After the elections the German parties, which had formerly cooperated with the government, went into opposition.[39]

Influenced by the Sudeten Germans the other minority populations agitated for greater minority rights and equal rights as citizens. Czech inflexibility and unwillingness to compromise not only frustrated the Sudeten Germans, who escalated their demands, but also led to the gradual building up of a unity of purpose with the other minorities, groups that had not previously held common cause. The Germans and Ruthenians demanded autonomy, the Poles and Hungarians demanded equal rights, while the Slovak movements became more radical.

In contrast to the early years, when Hungarian statesmen had dwelt on the political injustices of the Treaty of Trianon, a new, more flexible generation had emerged by the late 1930s. In June 1936 the two Czech Hungarian political parties, led by Andor Jaross and Count János Esterházy, joined to form a common front, the United Hungarian Party. Esterházy, who was thirty-five at the time, represented a younger generation of Hungarians who had come to maturity in Czechoslovakia and were more sympathetic in their attitudes to the Slovaks and their desire for autonomy. He spoke fluent Slovak as well as German and Polish, and gave many of his speeches in Slovak in his attempt to increase understanding between the two peoples.

Yet the younger generation was still staunchly Hungarian. In answer to a promise by Beneš, elected president of the republic in 1935, to grant him a position as minister if his party would become activist, Esterházy countered that just because he was of the younger generation, there was no reason to think he was not just as staunch a Hungarian. "I feel it necessary to make it clear that the Hungarians living here, without generational differences, are Hungarian and will remain Hungarian and will serve Hungarian interests."[40]

In May 1938, with a crisis approaching, the Czech government under German pressure decided to introduce a nationalities statute in Parliament which would have given the Hungarian and Polish minorities the same privileges as were to be given to the Sudeten Germans. Yet, in their concern over the threat to the stability of the republic, the leadership was reluctant to act, fearing that if they gave concessions to any minority the state would self-destruct. In the tense situation the Czechs called for partial mobilization.

At this point, the Sudeten party attempted to form a common front with the minorities, including the Hungarians, although in the past the two had not cooperated. In a meeting with Henlein, the Hungarian parties stated their conditions for cooperation. The Sudeten Germans should stop their propaganda in the Slovak and Ruthenian areas, where it appears they hoped to win the vote of the German population who were pro-Hungarian. Conscious of the dangers of the Nazi ideology, the Hungarian party did not want to ally themselves with the Sudeten party and thus come under German protection.[41]

During the spring and summer of 1938 Hungarian leaders hoped for a diplomatic solution to the revision of their northern borders, and many expected British support for the long-awaited revision of Trianon by peaceful means. Fearing Germany's growing power they were determined to avoid becoming dependent on Hitler's Germany. Since January 1937 the Hungarian government had been involved in negotiations with the countries of the Little Entente, initiated by the ministers of Czechoslovakia, Romania, and Yugoslavia, who were more willing to make concessions with the rise of German power. It was suggested that the Little Entente would acknowledge Hungary's right to rearm in exchange for a nonaggression pact. Yugoslavia, which had the fewest problems with Hungary, went further and proposed a treaty of friendship.

At the beginning of July the Nazi press began to work up hatred against the Czechs, accusing them of reckless suppression of national self-determination. With the increased German pressure, Hungarian Foreign Minister Kálmán Kánya attempted to preserve the country's freedom of maneuver while still continuing negotiations. The Hungarians were in an odd position; although they wanted to get approval for rearmament and to settle the problems of the minorities, they also wanted to avoid a final agreement with Czechoslovakia because of the expected German actions.

In summer a provisional agreement was signed at Bled, stipulating that in return for recognition of Hungary's right to rearm and the settlement of minority problems, Hungary would agree to abandon the use of force in disputes over territorial boundaries, but the agreement would not go into effect until all conditions had been met, and each country was obliged to ratify it separately. The vague wording of the agreement made it open to various interpretations, and in the end it was never ratified.[42]

Horthy and Hitler in Kiel

As a way to honor Horthy as the last commander-in-chief of the Austro-Hungarian fleet, a state meeting between Germany and Hungary had been planned from August 20–26 in the northern German city of Kiel. Horthy was to attend the launch of a heavy cruiser and his wife was to christen the vessel, the *Prinz Eugene*. However, by August the visit had been turned into an opportunity to press Horthy to take military action against Czechoslovakia. Horthy commented: "I was always inclined to be suspicious when my natural and understandable fondness for my former avocation was too blatantly invoked. In this matter of Hitler's invitation, the purpose was clear and it displeased me. And events were soon to prove how well founded my forebodings had been."[43]

The journey had been carefully arranged by the Germans with all the proper protocol. The cautious planners asked Horthy whether the opera he had chosen for the gala performance, *Lohengrin*, might not cause offense to the Hungarians because of the line "O Lord, protect us from the wrath of the Magyars!" But Horthy was actually rather fond of the line: "I could not pretend to myself that I would be sorry to hear of a time when Hungary's might was greater than it was at that moment."[44]

Hitler received the party—which included the regent and his wife, Prime Minister Imrédy and wife, Foreign Minister Kánya, and Minister of Defense Jenő Rátz—at Kiel and presented Madame Horthy with a large bouquet of lilies of the valley, her favorite flower. Lavish entertainment included a huge military parade, a naval review, and the christening of the new cruiser.[45] But despite the celebratory atmosphere the visit ended up causing strained Hungarian-German relations. Not only were the Hungarians unwilling to commit to military action against Czechoslovakia, but the meeting coincided with the publication of the provisional agreements made at Bled. Hitler, furious about the agreement, took it to mean that Hungary had renounced use of force against Czechoslovakia.

Horthy had come to the meeting determined to reject any German offer to join in the attack on Czechoslovakia. Not even Hitler's willingness to allow Hungary to acquire all of Slovakia and Ruthenia could tempt the Hungarians to commit themselves to military action. Conscious of their military weakness the Hungarians realized that an attack might lay them open to an immediate attack from the Czechoslovak ally, Yugoslavia. Also, the Hungarian leaders believed Germany would not win the war if it became a general conflict.

On a cruise to the island of Helgoland on the second day of the visit, the Germans pressed hard to commit the Hungarian government to military action. In one of the most dramatic personal encounters of his career Horthy met alone with Hitler. Since there were no witnesses to the meeting, the events can only be reconstructed from Horthy's accounts and of those close to him, but Horthy's accounts given at various times were unvarying. Hitler opened the conversation by explaining his plan for attacking and dismembering Czechoslovakia, Operation Grün, and asked if Hungary would be willing to attack Slovakia simultaneously. Horthy refused, expressing his regret. He repeated his answer in an interview with the historian C. A. Macartney in 1945: "Ja, sehr gerne, aber wir haben leider keine Armee und ohne Armee kann man keinen Krieg führen." (Yes, with pleasure, but unfortunately we have no army, and without an army one cannot conduct a war.)[46]

At one point during their discussion Horthy warned Hitler, to his extreme annoyance, that it would be best not to undertake the campaign at all, since England would intervene, and because of her superior naval strength would triumph in the end. "You can mobilize in five days," said Horthy, "and put thirty Army Corps here and forty there, while England will take perhaps five months to mobilize, but in the end she will inevitably win." Hitler, unaccustomed to being lectured at, interrupted and shouted: "Unsinn! Schweigen Sie!" (Nonsense, shut up!) Horthy, not about to permit anyone, let alone an ex-corporal, to treat the Hungarian head of state in such an undignified way, walked out.[47]

In the meantime, Foreign Minister Kánya and Prime Minister Imrédy met with Foreign Minister Joachim von Ribbentrop, who expressed bitter anger over the Bled agreement, claiming it could be interpreted by an impartial observer as, in effect, a renunciation of revision. Kánya went to great pains to explain that renunciation of the use of force became operative only after the outstanding problems, namely those of the Hungarian minority, had been settled, but the somewhat vague wording of the agreements led Ribbentrop to understand them as a renunciation of Hungarian revisionist aims. The matter was only exacerbated when Kánya indulged his propensity for sarcasm to drive home his point. When Ribbentrop said that he was unconvinced by this interpretation, Kánya, who disliked the German intensely, said: "Ich erkläre es noch einmal, ganz langsam. . . . Vielleicht hat es sogar der Herr Ribbentrop verstanden." (I'll explain it once more, very slowly. . . . Perhaps now even Herr Ribbentrop has understood it.)[48] Not surprisingly, Ribbentrop was highly insulted. Unfortunately, the dislike that he felt for Kánya he extended to all of Hungary which resulted in far-reaching and damaging effects. Events conspired to intensify the diplomatic misunderstandings. The Czechs, always adept at making use of a propaganda opportunity, sent a delegation to meet the Hungarian party at the train station in Berlin, indicating that the Bled agreement had indeed signaled Hungary's renunciation of revision. The Germans were so annoyed by the Czech demonstration that no official delegation was sent on the Hungarian party's departure from Germany. Hitler privately expressed his disgust over the attitude of the Hungarians, who seemed incapable of steeling themselves for action and preferred to sit around "listening to gypsy music."[49]

The Hungarians returned home fearing that Europe was on the brink of war. Horthy commented to the German minister in Budapest of the peculiar situation in which he found himself. For years he had had no more burning desire than to fulfill Hungary's revisionist aims as soon as possible, but was now compelled because of the pressure of world politics to sound a note of caution.[50]

Hungary was in no way prepared to fight a war in 1938. The Győr program to improve the military had only been announced in March. The system for mobilization was highly questionable, condemned by General Lákatos, who pointed out that the result was only self-deception and led the Axis allies astray. In the plans for mobilization, the Hungarian brigades were to be doubled. This enabled a smaller unit to keep a higher than usual number of officers, noncommissioned officers, and trained soldiers. When mobilization began a twin would be set up, and the extra officers would be available to train the new recruits. The Germans assumed the Hungarian troops were much stronger than they actually were. "To build an army facing its hardest challenge on such a system was badly mistaken! If we take into account the lack of weapons and equipment caused by the weak war industry, . . . then it is clear that in preparation for the coming storm the Hungarian leadership was miscalculating in a dangerous direction."[51]

British Policy Toward Hungary

The policy of British Prime Minister Chamberlain combined warnings to the Germans against the use of force with pressure on the Czechs for far-reaching peaceful revisions of the Treaty of Versailles. Hoping to pacify Hitler, the British and French sent Lord Runciman as an independent delegate to Czechoslovakia to mediate between the Sudeten Germans and the Czech government, expecting the Czechs to make concessions. The leaders of the United Hungarian Party in Czechoslovakia, who believed that any rights gained by the Sudeten minority should also be accorded to the Hungarian minority, had high hopes that Runciman would also deal with their concerns. Count Esterházy succeeded in arranging a meeting between Runciman and the representatives of the Hungarian party. Runciman, who had met with a cool reception from the Czech public, was pleased with the warm Hungarian reception. He explained that his mission only applied to the Sudeten problem and he could not negotiate with the Magyars, but he did assure them that the Hungarians would receive the same rights that were granted to the Sudeten Germans.[52]

By early September Henlein and Hitler had worked out their plan of action. The Sudeten Germans assumed an openly provocative attitude. Rome was now pressing openly for German annexation of the Sudetenland, but the Italians, who wanted to lessen the range of German expansion into Central Europe, were also working to satisfy other minority claims, chiefly those of the Hungarians. The Czechs, seeking to gain time, found themselves isolated, with Paris reacting more and more weakly to appeals from its ally. Thus, on September 12, when Hitler made his aggressive Nuremberg speech, proclaiming his patience exhausted and demanding self-determination for the Sudeten Germans, conditions already existed that made possible the agreement soon to be made at Munich. In his final ultimatum Henlein demanded the annexation of Sudetenland to Germany.

The Czechs ordered a state of emergency and dissolved the Sudeten German party. The Sudeten Germans pressured the leaders of the other minorities to sign a prepared public statement, in which they would agree to make common cause with the Germans and to press their demands together. Monsignor Jozef Tiso, in the name of the Slovaks, rejected the demand, saying that he needed to consult with his party. Esterházy also refused to sign, pointing out that it would be dishonorable since negotiations with the Czech Prime Minister Hodža were still underway. Despite the refusals, the statement that appeared in the next day's paper included the names of those who had not signed. Esterházy appealed to Hungarian party leaders to maintain quiet in the countryside, maintaining that the rights of the Hungarian minority should be realized only by democratic and parliamentary means.[53]

In September Hitler continued to urge Hungary as well as Poland to step up their pressure on the Czech government. Chamberlain decided to seek a solution by meeting with Hitler personally, taking his first plane trip to Berchtesgaden, and surprising Hitler by offering to cede the Sudeten territories rather than only seeking autonomy. Two days later, on September 18, Hitler, who still wanted to destroy the Czechoslovak state with military force, hastily arranged a meeting with Imrédy and Kánya at Berchtesgaden. He urged Hungary to take military action while he was conferring with Chamberlain, allowing him to break off negotiations and intervene in the fighting. Imrédy pleaded lack of readiness to face a force five times the size of Hungary's, and he and Kánya made vague promises of military preparations that fell far short of Hitler's expectations.[54]

Both the Poles with their strong army and the Italian governments criticized the Hungarians for not taking a stronger stand, but Hungary was negotiating from a position of weakness. Mobilization began in secret but the divisions were not on a war footing. The army troops in Budapest did not even have the necessary trains for mobilization. According to plans of the general staff they would only be ready to march at the end of December, and then weakly armed. In attempting to keep Hungarian mobilization secret, call-up papers were sent out individually, greatly slowing down the process. Yet, as the commander of the Budapest First Army Corps commented, everybody could tell they were mobilizing.[55]

In the meantime, all European States were involved in frantic military preparations. On September 18 France, which had begun partial mobilization, accepted the idea of detaching the German minority from Czechoslovakia as long as no force was used. If Prague accepted Great Britain would join in an international guarantee of the new frontiers in the event of unprovoked aggression. Prague finally capitulated, and Chamberlain flew to Germany to meet with Hitler and explain the plan on September 22.

Munich and the Vienna Award

The Munich Agreement of September 29, 1938, signed by the four powers, stipulated that Czechoslovakia hand over the Sudetenland to Germany by the middle of October. The mountainous Sudeten areas to be annexed contained the Czech army's main fortifications, thus making the rest of the country indefensible. Chamberlain returned home to Britain, claiming that he had brought peace in our time, but the appeasement policy of Britain and France had tragic results. The Allies, which had created a new European order through the peace conference in Versailles, had now brought about its destruction.

Hitler had wanted to destroy Czechoslovakia and was furious at having to accept Chamberlain's offer. He blamed the Hungarians for not taking military action; thus it was left to Mussolini to raise the issue of Hungarian and Polish demands for equal treatment with the Sudeten German minority. Hungarian Foreign Minister István Csáky flew to Munich the day of the conference to ask Mussolini to intercede for the Hungarian minority, and Mussolini promised to present the Hungarian demands as coming from himself. His draft for the solution of the Polish and Hungarian minority question was modified in an alternative version by the British and was attached to the Munich Agreement. It stated that the Polish and Hungarian minority questions should be settled within three months by negotiation with the Czechoslovak government. If the problems could not be settled within three months, then the heads of governments of the four powers would meet again.

The heads of the governments of the four powers declare that the problems of the Polish and Hungarian minorities in Czechoslovakia, if not settled within three months by agreement between the respective governments, shall form the subject of another meeting of the heads of the governments of the four powers here present.

Munich, September 29, 1938.

Signed by Adolf Hitler, Neville Chamberlain, Edouard Daladier, Benito Mussolini.[56]

As a consequence of the attachment, the promise of international guarantees of the new boundaries of Czechoslovakia was postponed until the question of the Polish and Hungarian minorities should be settled. The Poles had never forgiven the Czechs for winning their claim to Teschen just when they were in desperate straits with the Soviet's advance on Warsaw in 1920, and now they were not willing to wait. They issued an ultimatum to Czechoslovakia for the immediate surrender of Teschen, threatening dire consequences, and the Czech government agreed: the Poles marched into the area on October 2.[57]

At the time it was widely believed in Hungary that there would be a plebiscite in Slovakia, and the government began preparations for a possible reannexation of the Hungarian inhabited territory. It would be vital to win the vote of all Hungarian speakers in the plebiscite, and Prime Minister Imrédy was well aware of Hungary's backwardness in comparison with Czechoslovia's numerous social welfare reforms, which were far in advance of any central European state.[58] Although the Czechs' radical land reform had favored the Czech legionaries and Slovaks, still many Hungarian agrarian workers received small parcels of land. In general health conditions were better than in Hungary, the remaining middle class were better off than in Hungary, and intellectual unemployment, although not unknown, was no where near the Hungarian level.[59]

In preparation for a takeover of all or parts of southern Slovakia, the government began to evaluate conditions there. Amazingly enough, despite their almost twenty-year-long campaign for revision, the Hungarians had made no plans for the administration of returned territories. It had long been known that the social conditions in those territories differed greatly from those at home, but the details of the social situation of the Hungarian minority were almost completely unknown.[60] At a meeting called by Imrédy on October 6, an expert on social policy, Béla Kovrig, predicted that tremendous amounts of aid would be needed in retaking the Felvidék and proposed a countrywide drive to collect funds. The planned collection, labeled Hungary for the Hungarians, would not only ease the return of the territory, but also show the love of Hungarian society for their fellow Hungarians. In the euphoric days after the Munich Agreement the plan was received with tremendous enthusiasm.

NEGOTIATIONS WITH THE CZECHS AND SLOVAKS

By the time negotiations began between Hungary and Czechoslovakia only ten days after the Munich Agreement the political situation had changed radically. The Slovaks declared their autonomy on October 5, and on October 8 the new leaders took charge of an autonomous Slovakia.[61] Beneš had resigned, and the new prime minister, František Chvalkovský, introduced a pro-German policy in hopes of retaining Germany's guarantees of the new borders. Before the Munich Agreement Hitler had been eager for Hungarian assistance. Now he had no more interest in Hungary. It also appeared that the Czechs, after giving in to Poland, were reluctant to give in to the weakly armed Hungarians, and had been assembling troops on the border.

With the Slovak declaration of autonomy, the Czechs decided that the frontier with Hungary was the Slovaks' concern. When the two delegations met on October 9, the Czechoslovak delegation was led by the new Slovak prime minister, Monsignor Tiso, and consisted almost entirely of

Slovaks, Dr. Ivan Krna being the only representative from Prague. The Hungarians were represented by Foreign Minister Kálmán Kánya and Minister of Education Count Pál Teleki; Ruthenia, now autonomous, was represented only by an observer. Tiso informed the Hungarians: "Today it is the Slovak Government that is here. Now the Slovaks represent Czechoslovakia." It was agreed that officially the language of negotiation would be French, but for practical reasons—a reminder of their common past—discussion would be in Hungarian since almost all of the Slovaks spoke Hungarian.[62]

The Slovaks were in a difficult situation. This was their first official negotiation and they were understandably reluctant to meet Hungarian ethnic demands, wanting to offer only the minimum; the newly formed government would be at a political disadvantage if it started out with territorial concessions. While the Hungarians had come armed with a staff of experts, complete with detailed statistical data and maps of the Hungarian minority in Slovak territory, the members of the Slovak delegation had only a vague idea of the ethnic situation. They claimed that they had not been informed of earlier negotiations in which the Czechs had made certain concessions to the Hungarians. Tiso announced that the promises of the Czech foreign minister did not obligate the Slovaks.[63]

The two sides were far apart in their views. The Hungarian delegation was determined that the agreement made at Munich for the Sudeten Germans based on ethnic borders should be accorded to the Hungarian minority as well, ethnic frontiers on the basis of the 1910 census, and plebiscites in other contested areas. In the spirit of the Munich Agreement all the Hungarian territories should be returned where 50 percent of the population was Hungarian by mother tongue as given in the 1910 census. In preparations for the negotiations Teleki had attempted to draw the most exact ethnic borders possible, based on two decades of study with his staff at the Institute of Political Science, but the negotiating principle of the Slovaks was to give no more than absolutely necessary— they were determined to hold on to the major cities, industry, and the transportation network.[64]

At first the Slovaks offered very little. Their first proposal—offering only autonomy to the Hungarian population within the Czech state— stunned the Hungarian delegates. On October 12, when Tiso made a new offer of the Csallóköz, an island between branches of the Danube populated almost entirely by Hungarians, Teleki indignantly countered that the Hungarian proposal had not been prepared in order to bargain; it was based on the principle of ethnic boundaries.[65] An ethnic line definitely existed, more or less coinciding with the geographic line where the foot-hills of the mountains ended and the plain began. The language border was quite sharp, and in many places agreed with the Czech census of 1930, with the exception of the towns where large numbers of Slovaks had been resettled during the years of Czechoslovak administration. Thus the population of those towns on the ethnic line was mixed, including populations that were bilingual or of mixed origin and could be claimed by either nationality. There were also a large number of Jews who were counted by both regimes in their statistics.

The Slovak and Ruthenian delegations then met separately and ac-knowledged that they would have to accept the ethnic principle to some degree. After much discussion it was decided to work out the so-called maximal offer. At the fifth plenary session meeting at 9 A.M. on October 13, Tiso announced the third offer, an area of 5,405 square kilometers of pieces of territory, almost totally populated by Hungarians. This was only 38.3 percent of the territory and 31.7 percent of the population demanded by Hungary.[66] Teleki countered that they were ridiculous borders which did not follow the ethnic principle; that the Slovak offers were based on economic considerations, while the past twenty years had proved that the only stable frontiers were those based on ethnic considerations. The Hungarian delegation then asked for a recess. Teleki and Kánya returned to Budapest to confer with Imrédy, who, nervous and upset by the pres-sure of public opinion and the radical Right, insisted on breaking off negotiations. Kánya, although not believing that the negotiations would be successful, did not want to break them off, since perhaps the Slovaks would continue to make concessions—but his hands were tied.

When the conference reconvened at 6 P.M., Kánya explained: ". . . we came here to negotiate with the best, most sincere intentions, and in the hope that in a short time we would succeed in reaching an agreement that would establish relations between our nations on a solid basis. Unfor-tunately, our hopes have not been fulfilled. . . . The new borders offered to us this morning differ so widely from our conception, . . . in our convic-tion they are unbridgeable. . . . Therefore, the Hungarian Royal Govern-ment has decided to consider the negotiations ended." The Hungarians would seek negotiations by the four powers. Then, bowing in the direc-tion of Tiso, he hurried out of the room, the Hungarian delegation following.[67]

The Slovaks accepted the breaking off of negotiations with relief; it was in their interest that a new conference decide the debate. If and when they had to give up territory they would do so through pressure from the Allies. They were also influenced by a meeting between Hitler and Ferdinand Duranský and Alexander Mach on October 11 while the negotiations were taking place. The Slovak representatives complained of the Hungarians' excessive demands, and also let it be known that they were ready to subordinate themselves to Germany. The two representatives had returned from their meeting with the impression that the Germans stood behind them, and that in case of a four power decision they would get more favorable results than in negotiations with the Hungarians.[68]

Up to this point the Hungarians had been careful not to offer anything to Hitler. Now, fearing his lack of support and his growing closeness to the new Czech government, they offered major concessions. Hitler had been unwilling to receive any Hungarian minister since September, but on October 14 he received the former Hungarian prime minister, Kálmán Darányi, who had been chosen as the person to ask Hitler's assistance. Hitler was unreceptive at first, lecturing Darányi on Hungary's behavior, but he was somewhat mollified when Darányi offered that Hungary would join the anti–Comintern Pact and was ready to make a ten-year economic agreement. Hitler was against the idea of the four power conference, but after much hesitation agreed that he would attempt to mediate.[69]

On the same day, Foreign Minister Csáky went to Rome to meet with Mussolini and Ciano. Mussolini supported the Hungarian demands with the exception of plebiscites, and was ready to call a four power conference, preferably in a northern Italian city. It became ever more apparent that Italy supported Hungary while Germany, although recognizing the ethnic principle, was inclined to support Czechoslovakia. None of the great powers wanted another four power conference except Italy, which looked forward to playing an international role. Hitler was against the idea since England and France would probably support Czechoslovakia, and then he should support Hungary which he was not inclined to do. The British feared that Hitler would make more demands while the French wanted to avoid any further complications.

In the tense atmosphere negotiations continued. In a compromise move the Czechs made a new proposal on October 22 in which they recognized the Hungarian ethnic borders but without the disputed cities of Pozsony, Nyitra, Kassa, Ungvár and Munkács. The Slovaks gave their consent with great reservations. Budapest accepted the Czech offer but added amendments requesting plebiscites in zones including the important cities. If the Czechs did not accept the amendments then the question of the disputed areas should be submitted to Italian-German arbitration.

To the Hungarians' surprise, since they had believed the question of ethnic borders had been decided, the Czechs now proposed to submit the entire question to arbitration.[70]

The Czechs informed London that the Hungarian demand for plebiscites was unacceptable and asked to know the views of Her Majesty's Government on Axis arbitration. The British responded that, "His Majesty's Government saw no objection to the settlement of the Czech-Hungarian question by means of arbitration by Germany and Italy."[71] The Hungarian ambassador to London, Barcza, noted that the Foreign Office greeted arbitration by Hitler and Mussolini with satisfaction and relief, pleased that the decision could be reached without England's participation.[72] Hitler and Ribbentrop were at first reluctant to carry out arbitration, but Ciano was able to persuade Ribbentrop in Rome on October 28 to agree and to give in on Kassa, Ungvár, and Munkács. Although agreeing to arbitration Hitler instructed Ribbentrop to give in only to the minimum of Hungarian demands.[73]

Just days before the Vienna decision, without the Germans' knowledge, an unofficial Hungarian delegation traveled to Rome in order to agree on the exact border. In the final map showing the northern borders Ciano drew a straight line, making a significant turn away from the language border to the east of Pozsony, thus giving Hungary a fairly large territory with a Slovak population. János Esterházy, who arrived by private plane too late to participate, only learned of the results, which he surely would have criticized. On learning of the Ciano line Teleki was chagrined; he had worked hard to create a true ethnic border.[74]

THE FIRST VIENNA AWARD

The so-called first Vienna Award, declared on November 2 in the Belvedere Palace, returned most of the Hungarian-inhabited areas to Hungary, excluding Pozsony (Bratislava) and the surrounding area (see Map 3). Hungary received 12,103 square kilometers and about 1,050,000 in population of which 751,951 (86.5 percent) were Hungarian. Those Hungarians remaining in Czechoslovakia according to the 1939 Slovak census numbered 66,000. Hungarian army units began to reoccupy the areas awarded, and on November 11 Horthy, astride a white stallion, entered the city of Kassa in a grand procession. He spoke also in Slovak, assuring the Slovak minority of the free use of their language, but the general mood of the Hungarians was one of national jubilation; the population shouted revisionist slogans—Everything back! On to Transylvania.[75]

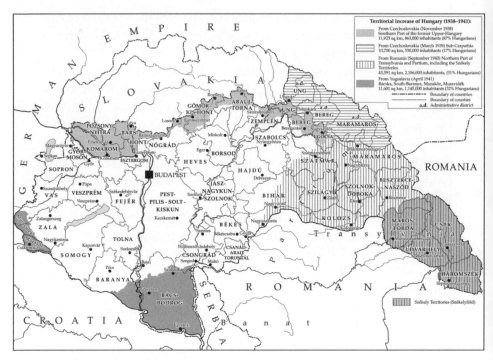

Map 3. Territorial increase of Hungary, 1938–1941.

During the celebrations János Esterházy announced that he had chosen to stay with the 66,000 remaining Hungarians in Slovakia as their representative. "We, Hungarians who remain here, promise that we will shake hands with our Slovak brothers living here and work with them for a better future."[76] With Polish politicians in Warsaw he confided his regret that the Hungarians had failed to make a generous gesture to win Slovak good will, by voluntarily giving up about 1,000 square kilometers, which were inhabited by a Slovak majority. This lack of consideration did not bode well for the future.

The first Vienna Award was only a half solution; the new border brought disappointment on both sides. The Slovaks were furious. On receiving the decision Tiso exclaimed: "We have lost everything." That evening he addressed the Slovak nation by radio, claiming: "Nothing will stop us from notifying the whole world that the Slovak nation has suffered a tragic wrong."[77] The Hungarians also remained unsatisfied. The extreme Right, which had demanded all of Slovakia and Ruthenia, began attacking the government's position, urging that in the future it cooperate fully with the Germans. Supported by the public outcry for further terri-torial revision, Imrédy's government now planned for a military seizure of Ruthenia. The attack, ordered for November 20, was halted only at the last moment by a German-Italian veto—a humiliating blow, especially for Horthy whose personal order as Supreme War Lord had to be revoked.[78]

The Hungarians had failed to realize the change within the Slovak population over the twenty years of Czechoslovakia's existence. In their minds it was only Czech power that had kept the Slovaks from returning happily to Hungary. The Slovaks had developed resentments against the Czechs for denying them the autonomy their leaders had expected, and monopolizing jobs that a newly educated younger Slovak generation craved, but over those years a strong Slovak nationalism had developed. The combination of intense anti-Hungarian Czech propaganda, intended to convince the Slovaks that they had suffered "1,000 years of Hungarian oppression," along with the creation of a new educated Slovak middle class, had created a sense of national identity that barely existed before 1920.[79]

In retrospect it was a mistake that the Hungarians were not more generous to the Slovaks in the first Vienna Award. In 1940, Tiso tried to persuade Hitler to modify the treaty and to give back areas with a Slovak population. Hitler didn't agree at the time but left the question open for after the war. Also in 1940 the minister of the interior, Vojech Tuka, spoke with Esterházy and asked him to intervene in the request to reclaim 2,400 square kilometers with 140,000 in population and possibly the city of Kassa. Later the Slovaks asked for a gesture from Hungary to maintain good relations, since sooner or later the question would come up again. But the Hungarians were unreceptive and for a time the Hungarian gov-ernment even cut off official relations with the Slovaks. 1938 would have been the moment to conduct two-part discussions in the interest of future relations between the two countries.[80]

Imrédy's Dictatorial Turn

At the Eucharistic Congress in May of 1938, Imrédy, recently appointed prime minister, had been hailed as the man to stop the Hungarian Na-tional Socialists. He was considered a moderate, self-confident, ethical statesman, and it was agreed that he was brilliant.[81] When they wanted to flatter him, his friends and acquaintances would comment on his like-ness to Savonarola. The thin, stooped body, the demonic pale face, dark cold eyes, and aquiline nose—all were reminiscent of the Florentine monk burned at the stake. But behind the ascetic exterior lay a desire and longing for power which, according to a colleague, disrupted the clear sightedness and judgment of this otherwise worthy well-educated person of superior intellectual ability.[82] He had no interest in wealth and was incorruptible, but he was possessed of a devouring personal ambition and convinced that he would benefit the world. Impatient of opposition and dictatorial in his claims to leadership he made many enemies.

At the beginning of September, after the visit to Hitler, Imrédy made a surprisingly abrupt and unexplained about-face. As Count Bethlen noted: "Hungarian parliamentary history knows no other about-turn as bedazzling as was the one Béla Imrédy carried out at the zenith of his political career in front of a flabbergasted public."[83] At a provincial political rally in Kaposvár on September 4, Imrédy came out with a sweeping program to transform the social structure of the country. His ambitious plans with himself at the helm alarmed conservative and liberal groups alike. Although his ideas were based on the corporatist system popularized by Pope Pius XI, he even lost the support of the Catholic movement after his Kaposvár speech with its suggestion of a fascist-style dictatorship.

Imrédy's domestic program was truly revolutionary. To win over the poor agrarian population he proposed the creation of a fund for assistance to large families, a more steeply graduated income tax, extensive land reform, a new rural housing program, a final settlement of agricultural indebtedness, and a program of *dopolavoro*, similar to the fascist leisure organization in Italy.[84] The impulse for his dramatic action may well have originated from his visit with Mussolini in July of 1938. In conversation with the Duce, Imrédy had brought up the agitation by parties of the extreme Right. The Duce advised him "to defeat his political adversaries by announcing and applying programs of social reform more concrete than those advanced by his opponents." Mussolini went on to explain the development of the Italian corporatist organizations, the *dopolavoro,* and Italian assistance schemes.[85]

In his program for the reorganization of society on a corporatist model, Imrédy made use of ideas that had gained much popularity throughout Europe in the 1930s. While the capitalist system was widely seen to have failed and Western parliamentary regimes had been unable to solve economic problems, the corporatist system seemed to offer an attractive model for a new means of organizing the state. Corporatist systems had been introduced first in Italy, but also in Austria and Portugal, and the Portuguese model especially had aroused much interest throughout Europe and in Hungary as well. Pope Pius XI had popularized the idea in his *Quadragesimo anno* of May 15, 1931, in which he recommended the corporatist structure as a way of mitigating class differences and the economic disparities under free capitalism. In the corporatist system, parliamentary institutions were replaced by civic assemblies representing industrial, agrarian, and professional groups, which exerted control over their respective areas of social and economic life. The system was an attempt to create a modern version of the medieval concept of a united society in which the various components each play a part in the life of the society, just as various parts of the body serve specific roles in the life of a body.

Imrédy's revolutionary domestic program was partly motivated by the preparations necessary for the takeover of parts of Slovakia. Collection of funds for the program Hungary for the Hungarians began in early November and everyone wanted to contribute. After almost twenty years of propaganda demanding the return of the lost territories, even the poorest and most destitute wanted to join in with whatever they might spare. Especially in the villages, where cash was scarce, contributions were made in kind, placing those who were collecting in an impossible position. They didn't know what to do with the ten kilo of wheat, rye, or maize, and the one or two dozen eggs. The cost of storing them would have been more than they were worth, but it was politically impossible to refuse them.[86] Contributing became a matter of pride, with various organizations joining in. Concerns such as the sugar factories and the large estates gave produce. A large proportion of the Jewish population contributed. Even the Social Democrats, always in opposition to the government, were forced by public opinion to participate.[87]

Immediately following the reannexation, serious problems arose with distribution of food and the lack of trained people to carry out the aid programs. Much of the collection work was done by Catholic organizations, but, as was customary with charitable functions, upper-class women—wives of high county officials, the aristocracy, local landowners—played an important role. Imrédy caused great astonishment by placing his wife at the head of the movement, since it was Horthy's wife who traditionally was asked to head national charitable organizations.[88] Since there was no social welfare training in Hungary the movement was forced to borrow trained social workers, who could only take off a few weeks from their jobs. It became apparent that the organizers had not thought out how distribution of provisions would be carried out, and distribution of food packages went very slowly. The retreating Czechoslovak troops had confiscated almost all edibles, while the local grocers continued to hold back the stores that they had hidden in case the Hungarian troops should continue the Czech practice of requisitioning. The result was that for days—even for weeks—the population starved.

A much greater number of families were without provisions than had been expected. In Komárom, for example, the entering troops had planned to give central assistance to 8 percent of the families, but on the fourth day of the military administration it became clear that the minimum was 15–17 percent. Reports sent by social workers to the central office commented on how much more advanced the Czechoslovak welfare system had been than that in Hungary. Almost every report emphasized the high quality of Czech social welfare services, and that the hopeless poverty found in some places in Hungary was unknown here.[89]

Assistance was given mainly in goods rather than money because of the antiquated attitude of Hungarians to poverty, with the belief that the poor were socially fallen and untrustworthy. This attitude was unfounded in Hungary but even more so among many of this population who had enjoyed quite a high standard of living within Czechoslovakia. The military administration, as well as public opinion, urged that monetary aid should not be given without compensating work, since it would only breed laziness. Despite the urgency the plan to provide work for the poverty stricken was continually delayed; the work offered was similar to that in Hungary—sweeping squares, shoveling snow—but there was never enough work.

The Hungarian administration was suspicious that the minority population had been contaminated by Czech ideas under the eighteen years of Czechoslovak rule, and many treated the Felvidék as an occupied territory. During the years when Hungarian parties in the Czech parliament had concentrated only on protests against the unjust peace treaty, many in the Hungarian minority had turned to the Agrarian Party or the Communist Party, which at the time had defended minority rights and the right to self-determination. Middle-class Hungarians of former Slovakia had been promised positions in the new administration but very few received positions. Some were even removed from elected positions, which under the Czechs had been essentially democratic.[90]

The Budapest government was especially mistrustful of members of youth groups who had become sympathetic to communist ideas. Still it attempted to win them over with a free student mensa, hostels, and help with tuition. The regime felt it important to influence education by changing the textbooks and paying for patriotic Hungarian texts filled with Hungarian literature. In the few Slovak villages the Slovaks were treated badly. Years later a Slovak historian recalled with bitterness the day that Hungarian gendarmes entered his classroom and threw around their textbooks proclaiming, "you can't use these anymore." The Slovak teachers in the classroom, young girls, were using old Slovak texts—of course there were no others.[91]

The military occupation and temporarily organized offices were often motivated by a spirit of revenge against Czechoslovak rule. Names of streets, squares, and so on, were immediately changed back to Hungarian, and signs in two languages on the street or shops were forbidden, exactly as the Czechs had done in the 1920s. In offices it again became obligatory to use the antiquated titles of address used in Hungary. Officials sometimes used the humiliating familiar form to the inhabitants—as in the German *du* or French *tu*—as if they were subordinates.[92]

Despite the help given, which was generous in Hungarian terms, the condition of the population barely improved. The press, which was rarely critical of Hungarian policies, exercised sharp criticism because of the lack of results, and a number of social workers considered resigning. A Gendarme report dated December 21, 1938, describes the situation well: "The enthusiasm of the population is quickly waning. . . . There are many who say, bitterly, that under the twenty years of Czech rule they had never been so cheated as in the days after the Hungarian occupation."[93] In the meantime, the Hungary for the Hungarians movement ran out of money. Lacking money it put the emphasis on propaganda with patriotic celebrations in villages and cities.

Imrédy's Downfall

Imrédy's plans to restructure the domestic political system had run into opposition. His political style and drive for power threatened to alter the traditional methods of political negotiation, which had been based on balance and compromise. In November he attempted to gain permission from Parliament to govern the returned territory by decree, which produced a political crisis. In an unusual coalition, Bethlen, the leader of the opposition conservatives, met with leaders of the Social Democrats, the Independent Smallholders, and members of the government's liberal-conservative wing to move against Imrédy. Imrédy's government lost a vote of no confidence on a point of procedure—an unprecedented event during the interwar period when the government party had always remained in control. Imrédy resigned on November 23, but because of fear of the German reaction, Horthy was persuaded to ask him to form a new cabinet.

The result was a further turn to the right. On November 26, realizing that his government depended on German support, Imrédy authorized the formation of the *Volksbund der Deutschen in Ungarn* as the sole recognized representative body of the German minority. He dismissed Foreign Minister Kálmán Kánya, whom Ribbentrop particularly despised, and named Count István Csáky as his successor. In January, Csáky, subjected to Hitler's rage against Hungary for preventing the destruction of Czechoslovakia, promised to give in to Hitler's demands, including leaving the League of Nations. Imrédy attempted to create a mass movement modeled on the Austrian Patriotic Front, and on January 1, 1939, he introduced his gentlemanly fascist movement, the Movement of Hungarian Life, with which he intended to replace the government party.[94]

The opposition decided that they must force his resignation and in this they used Imrédy's own weapons. He had prepared a second Jewish law, and in its preparation suggested that in contrast to the 1938 law, racial origins rather than religious belief should determine who would be considered Jewish. During the summer, two of his opponents—the liberal politician, Károly Rassay, and Legitimist leader, Count Antal Sigray—gathered information on Imrédy's family. A document was discovered showing that one of his great-grandmothers had been baptized into the Catholic faith with her parents at the age of seven, suggesting that she and her parents had been Jewish. Members of the opposition went to Horthy on January 4 with the memo, asking for Imrédy's removal. Horthy hesitated, but a bomb attack against the Dohány street synagogue on February 3 convinced him.[95]

Horthy had been growing more and more frustrated with the seeming arrogance of his prime minister, who did not consult him on upcoming legislation in the customary fashion. In late 1938 and 1939, evidence suggests that Imrédy had no political discussion with Horthy, and he failed to discuss the new Jewish law with him. When Horthy saw the draft of the proposed second Jewish law, he announced that he could not support it in that form. It was "inhuman and harmed patriotic Jews long resident in the country who were as much Hungarian as he was." He had told Imrédy's wife that he would not allow the Jews to be treated brutally, and that two of his bridge partners, Lipót Aschner and Leó Goldberger had performed real service for the country.[96]

Horthy sent for Imrédy on February 11 and accused him of acting unconstitutionally by tabling two important bills on the Jewish law and land reform without first submitting them to the regent for his preliminary sanction. Horthy may have hoped that Imrédy, realizing he had lost the regent's confidence, would resign, but Imrédy showed no reaction. Then the regent brought out the papers that had been gathered by Imrédy's opponents attesting to his Jewish ancestry, and asked, "Please, what is this?" After reviewing the documents, Imrédy fainted. After he had recovered Horthy told him: "I am not saying this; the papers have been brought to me. If you tell me they are false, I will throw them in the waste-paper basket." Imrédy responded, "I think it is true."[97]

Imrédy announced his intention of resigning to the Council of Ministers, giving the Jewish strain in his ancestry as the reason, but Barczy pleaded that he give some political reason for his step. He consented and stated that the reason, technically, was the regent's loss of confidence in him, but he announced the actual facts in a public speech. Despite his resignation from office Imrédy continued his political activity as leader of the party he had formed. Both he and his gentlemanly fascist party were to remain a significant force throughout the war, pressing for greater cooperation with Germany.

In their enthusiasm over the return of the first of the lost territories in 1938 few Hungarians guessed at the costs they would have to pay. The decision on October 13 to ask for German intervention marked a turning point in Hungarian-German relations. Despite efforts to maintain its independence, Hungary was now beholden to Germany and Italy. Hitler could—and did—threaten to take back the award numerous times. Although the British at the time had agreed to Axis arbitration, Foreign Minister Csáky had failed to get written confirmation. On January 30, 1941, the Foreign Office argued that Great Britain was not bound by the Vienna Award because it had not been reached in accordance with the procedure laid down at Munich.

The breakdown of negotiations with the Slovaks may have been inevitable. The two parties truly had irreconcilable differences. A predominantly Hungarian population did exist in territories that the Slovaks deemed essential to the existence of their state. Although the territory returned to Hungary in the Vienna Award did essentially follow ethnic boundaries, the Slovak sense of injustice with the decision contributed to the tense and often hostile relations between Slovakia and Hungary which have continued to the present day.

4   Clinging to Neutrality

During the two years of the ministry of Count Pál Teleki, from February 1939 to April 1941, the government faced increasing pressure, both external and internal, to join forces with Germany. Hungary was already beholden to Germany and Italy for the return of southern Slovakia. In the winter of 1939, the population was in a frenzy to reclaim all of the lost territories. The extreme Right was gaining in power and Imrédy, despite his resignation, was still a force to be reckoned with, highly respected and supported by his followers in Parliament.

In exacting payment for the Vienna Award the Germans increased their economic demands, making clear their intention to turn Hungary into a raw material and food supply base for the German economy. Hungary and other southeastern European countries were an essential part of Germany's New European Order—the plan to enhance German industrial production with raw materials and agricultural goods for its eastern expansion. The southeastern European countries were to adjust their economies to produce primarily cereals and oil seeds. Bethlen explained to a parliamentary commission: "During the talks we had recently . . . [the Germans] repeatedly warned us: 'Don't keep insisting on a Hungarian industry. You are an agrarian country; be a country of peasants and sell us your agricultural products; we shall supply you with industrial goods.'"[1]

The only possible balance to Germany's ever-increasing aggressiveness was Great Britain, which had become of primary importance to Hungary. To avoid complete dependence on Germany Hungary offered to sell the entire 1939 wheat surplus to Great Britain but Britain refused. The British had considered Hungarian requests for economic assistance, but the British ambassador in Budapest, Sir Geoffrey Knox, reported that there was no sense in helping Hungary for it was bound to fall into German hands. Therefore it would be better to give economic help to those countries where it would be useful. The British Interdepartmental Committee on Economic Assistance to Central and South Eastern Europe,

which was established to examine countries according to their importance to Britain, decided that the situation in Hungary was almost completely hopeless, and it was not advisable to make greater endeavors to
support the country. Germany then took over the promise of the entire
surplus.[2]

After Imrédy's forced resignation, the regent prevailed on Count Pál
Teleki to accept the appointment as prime minister.[3] Disappointed in Imrédy's increasingly pro-German policies, he wanted someone he could
trust to maintain Hungary's independence. The two men held similar
views of the European crisis and Hungary's goals.[4] Horthy, with his naval
background, realized the significance of Britain's sea power, and both he
and Teleki were convinced that the Western democracies would triumph
over Germany in any military conflict.[5]

With Teleki's appointment many in the liberal parties as well as the
old guard of conservatives around Bethlen had high hopes that he would
reverse Imrédy's policies and stand up to German demands. Yet, Teleki
had little room to maneuver. He faced two powerful forces at home, a
pro-German military leadership, eager to ally with Germany in order to
regain more of the lost territories, and an extreme-right movement fueled
mainly by a younger generation demanding radical social change—if
necessary through a dictatorship. Frustrated with Hungary's antiquated
social and economic structure and Parliament's failure to enact reform,
they looked to countries like Portugal, Italy, and Germany as models for
modernization.

Teleki was determined to maintain Hungary's neutrality and independence; in his first speech to Parliament, on February 22, he admonished
the nation to remain true to Hungary's thousand-year-old traditions and
not to pursue foreign examples for needed reforms—in other words those
of Germany and Italy. Yet at the time of his appointment the challenge of
the extreme Right was at its peak. The Vienna Award had been greeted
with euphoric celebrations and mass demonstrations demanding the return of all of the lost territories. Arrow Cross members appeared more
and more often on the streets. The terrorist action, which occurred on
February 2, 1939, when a hand grenade exploded as the worshipers were
leaving the Dohány street synagogue, was of a type unknown in Hungary
over the past twenty years.

In some ways Teleki was well qualified to achieve the balancing act
between resisting German power and maintaining good relations with
the West. Teleki himself believed that his international experience would

enable him to form a sound foreign and domestic policy. An internationally renowned geographer, he had traveled extensively, including trips to the United States, spoke German as well as several other languages fluently, and was regarded as a friend by the Western powers. He represented those Hungarians who valued Hungary's constitutional government and were admirers of the British government and culture. The British knew him not only through his scholarly work but as a familiar figure at international scout activities in his role of Honorary Chief Scout, dressed in his Baden-Powell cap and shorts. Offspring of a historical Transylvanian family, he had lost the major part of the family estates after World War I and lived modestly, but often visited his remaining small estate around his castle at Pribékfalva in Romania. But Teleki was a scholar, not a politician.[6] He was a poor speaker which became painfully obvious during parliamentary debates. Former Prime Minister Bethlen, although he respected his knowledge and vision, believed that Teleki possessed a childlike romanticism and as a politician was too idealistic.[7]

Teleki, the geographer, viewed the Danubian Basin as a natural geographical unit, and considered it inevitable that this area would eventually be united again politically. In his extended view of the area's history he was one of those Hungarian statesmen to realize that the strategic interests of the country might call for moderation of the campaign to revise the Paris peace treaty—or even postponement of Hungary's demands. He realized that Hungary would not be able to keep any returned territories unless it gained the approval, or at least the tacit consent, of the Western powers.

Reactions in the German press were cool when Teleki took office. To dispel German suspicion he emphasized that he would not change the composition of the government or its policies. He retained Imrédy's ministers even though many were still supporters of Imrédy, and only gradually replaced some of these ministers with those who supported his policies. He did, however, take immediate measures against the extreme-rightist parties. His minister of the interior, Ferenc Keresztes-Fischer, referring to the Arrow Cross attack on the Budapest synagogue, banned the Hungarian National Socialist Party led by Szálasi, confiscated the funds of the German National Socialist Workers Party, and arrested the leaders.[8]

Ruthenia and the Final Destruction of Czechoslovakia

Immediately following the Vienna Award, the Hungarians planned to take back Subcarpathian Ruthenia/Carpatho-Ukraine,[9] but at the last minute a German-Italian ultimatum halted the occupation. The ultimatum embarrassed not only the Imrédy government but also the regent, who, as Supreme War Lord, had given the military order. The Carpatho-Ukraine, formerly the northeast corner of the Hungarian kingdom, had been granted to Czechoslovakia in 1920, which had promised autonomy to the region but reneged on its promises. Many in the population, which consisted of Ukrainian poor peasants and forest workers along with a Hungarian and Jewish middle class, resented the failed promise as well as the large and paternalistic Czech bureaucracy.[10]

Ruthenia was of major importance to Hungary because the largely forested territory contained the headwaters of the river Tisza; deforestation was endangering the Great Hungarian Plain, often subject to disastrous flooding. Teleki gathered together geographic documents to explain to the governments of Britain, France, Germany, and Italy that the region was essential to Hungary. But his second unspoken motive for regaining the territory was to secure a common border with Poland which Teleki hoped would be protection against German expansion.[11] With a new crisis developing in Czechoslovakia the Council of Ministers decided to prepare the military to occupy the territory secretly, whether the Germans agreed or not, but once more instead of acting independently Hungary ended up being beholden to Germany.

The results of the Munich Agreement left Hitler profoundly dissatisfied. He had been intent on crushing Czechoslovakia in order to gain a strategic base to continue his plans of eastern conquest. On October 21 several weeks after the intervention of Chamberlain and Mussolini had deprived him of his prize, he ordered the armed forces to prepare the invasion of rump Czechoslovakia. He had concluded that the Western statesmen were unlikely to oppose him, but he was still undecided on his next step. In October he had Ribbentrop meet with Polish Ambassador Lipski, evidently with the idea of making use of Poland as a partner in the eastern conquest.[12] Poland's leaders, although willing to make concessions to Germany, were unwilling to adhere to the Anti–Comintern Pact, seeing in it a form of subservience to Germany. In the following months Berlin authorities tried to obtain Polish acquiescence with alternating offers and threats, but the Warsaw government continued to reject politely Germany's demands.[13]

On March 13, taking the Hungarians by surprise, the Germans informed Hungary that they intended to occupy Bohemia and would raise no objections to Hungary's entry into Ruthenia. In preparation for the takeover Hitler encouraged the Slovaks to declare their independence from Prague, which they did on March 14. The Slovaks, who at most had hoped for autonomy within Czechoslovakia, were not prepared for independence. However, they placed the country under the protection of the German Reich, thus dissolving the Czechoslovak state. Then, on the night of March 14–15, Hitler forced the Czech president and prime minister to turn over the country to him, and in the early hours of March 15 German troops crossed the Czech border. By nine o'clock Prague was firmly in their hands, and on March 16 Hitler proclaimed the establishment of the German protectorate of Bohemia and Moravia, wiping the Czechoslovak state off the map.[14]

Only partly deployed, the Hungarian army marched into Ruthenia on March 15 and the troops reached the Polish frontier on March 17, where they were greeted by Polish officers and soldiers. By March 18 the Hungarians had completed occupation of Ruthenia and achieved the goal of a common border with Poland. Unfortunately, Hungarian government propaganda glorified the Hungarian military actions, creating a false belief that the Hungarian military was strong, since the takeover appeared to be an independent act, rather than with the blessing of Germany. Since the Hungarian occupation was greeted calmly by Western public opinion, it seemed they had avoided Western disapproval. State Secretary Cadogan told Barcza, the Hungarian minister in London, that he was happy that at least Ruthenia had fallen into Hungarian instead of German hands. The establishment of a Polish-Hungarian border was considered a defeat for German diplomacy.[15]

The Italians had also been taken by surprise by Hitler's move. A very disturbed Ciano wrote in his diary of March 15 that German troops had begun occupation of Bohemia during the night:

"The thing is serious, especially since Hitler had assured everyone that he did not want to annex one single Czech. . . . What credence can be given in the future to those declarations and promises, which concern us more directly?"[16]

Ciano noted that Mussolini, on receiving an explanatory message, did not want to release it to the Italian public. He quoted Mussolini, who exclaimed: "The Italians would laugh at me; every time Hitler grabs a country he sends me a message!"[17] After the takeover of Czechoslovakia it was clear that Hitler's declarations were not to be trusted and that he would have no qualms about breaking any treaty he had made. The week after the surprise attack on Czechoslovakia the Germans brought intense pressure on Lithuania, which was forced to return the Memel district to Germany—an opening wedge into the Baltic region. Slovakia had become a German satellite and accepted German garrisons. Poland again responded to the renewed German demands presented on March 21 with a polite refusal. Almost immediately the German press began to make accusations of Polish mistreatment and persecution of Germans in Poland.[18]

The destruction of Czechoslovakia by Nazi aggression aroused the anger of democratic public opinion and led to an about-face in Britain's foreign policy, bringing an end to Britain's appeasement policy. On March 17 Chamberlain stated that the British government could not accept any further expansion of German power in Central and Eastern Europe. British attention turned to Poland, a likely victim of possible German aggression. On March 31 Chamberlain made a public announcement that if there were any action to threaten Polish independence, "His Majesty's Government would feel themselves bound at once to lend the Polish Government all support in their power."[19] Polish Foreign Minister Beck came to London in early April and agreed on an exchange of commitments pending final settlement of precise terms of a treaty.

The unexpected brutal liquidation of Czechoslovakia completed the destruction of the central European system planned and set up in Paris in 1919. Even those who benefited from Hitler's new venture felt apprehension rather than satisfaction. In Budapest Teleki looked to the future with undisguised anxiety.

At this time Teleki made his obligatory diplomatic visits to Italy and Germany, traveling first to Rome as had become the tradition. Mussolini assured Teleki and Foreign Minister Count Czáky of his continued commitment to Hungarian revision. Teleki announced Hungary's withdrawal from the League of Nations, which had been planned for May but was moved to April 11, 1939, as a gift to Mussolini. Teleki had often complained that although the Hungarians had been trying to achieve peaceful revision of its borders for twenty years, the League had not secured protection of the minorities and had made no moves toward treaty revision.[20] In addition, Czáky had gained the impression from London that Chamberlain would not be bothered by the further weakening of the League, which he believed was useless.

During Teleki's visit to Berlin on April 29 the atmosphere was friendlier than expected, especially since Hitler had slighted him by inviting two former Hungarian prime ministers, Darányi and Imrédy, to his fiftieth birthday celebration. Still, Teleki remained taciturn leaving the discussions to Csáky. The Germans had prepared an extensive program; breakfast at Göring's, dinner at Ribbentrop's, wreath laying at Unter den

Linden, a May 1 procession of German youth in the Olympic Stadium. However, as a result of the visit Teleki became convinced that Germany's next goal was Poland. Hitler and Ribbentrop had explained that Germany did not want war, but if forced they would meet force with force against Poland and even against Britain and France. Conscious of Hungary's friendship with Poland, they did not demand Hungarian participation but emphasized that southeastern Europe was a German sphere of interest. After the visit the tone of the German press to the Teleki government changed from hostility to benevolence. Hungary now came under continuous pressure to follow an Axis policy.[21]

The Second Jewish Law

On taking office Teleki had taken measures against the Arrow Cross, but he also felt it necessary to pacify the supporters of the extreme Right. One of his first acts was to bring before Parliament a second Jewish law, prepared under Imrédy in response to complaints that the first law was not stringent enough. Teleki was convinced that passage of the law was necessary and unavoidable, but he believed that with this law the Jewish question, for Hungary at least, would be closed.[22] The law aimed at the limitation of Jewish encroachment in public life and the economy, but it went much further than the first in a radical shift in criteria of those to be considered Jewish which became partly racial and partly religious. Not only those of Jewish faith were considered Jewish, but also those whose parents or two out of four grandparents were born in the Jewish faith. Exceptions included those who had been converted to Christianity before August 1, 1919, those who were wounded in World War I or had received medals, ministers of the Christian faith of Jewish origin, and Olympic champions.[23]

Discrimination was to extend into all aspects of political and civil life. No Jew, apart from the two officially appointed rabbis in the upper house, was eligible for election to Parliament or to any elected post in municipal councils. Jews could no longer obtain Hungarian citizenship. Jews could not be appointed to any public office or to the legal system. Jewish officials in the public sector, down to the lowest position, were to be dismissed or forced into early retirement. Finally, Jewish citizens were deprived of voting rights unless they could prove their ancestors' continuous residence from 1867 on, a clause intended to distinguish between long-time Hungarian residents, who, in general, had assimilated into Hungarian society, and the more recent immigrants.

Through quota restrictions the number of Jewish employees in a firm was to be limited to 20 percent instead of the 6 percent in the first Jewish law, and 12 percent in some free professions. Over a period of two to five years Jewish tradesmen were to be banned from all businesses requiring professional licenses, from pharmacists to taxi drivers. The law was intended to remove Jews from these areas so that they would be replaced by gentiles, an idea that was totally unrealistic considering the number of Jews in the professions and trades. There were 80,507 Jewish shopkeepers and 73,887 independent artisans. In Budapest alone 58.7 percent of the 1,480 nonpublicly owned industrial establishments were owned or managed by Jews. Close to 2,900 of about 8,300 medical doctors in Hungary were Jewish. One fifth of the pharmacists were Jewish and close to one half of the lawyers. Also, the law did not take into account the prejudices of the younger generation against careers in economic life. In December 1942 the National Socialist Party official daily wrote of difficulties in finding Aryan successors for economic life in Hungary: ". . . Youth still does not want even to hear of commercial or industrial pursuits."[24]

Intense debate accompanied the proposal, both within and without Parliament. Debate began on the bill in the lower house on February 24, 1939, but the upper house did not accept the proposal, intending to modify it. According to house rules a joint committee of the two houses had to be formed to negotiate. Members of the upper house proposed various modifications for baptized Jews and those who had conspicuous accomplishments, but in the joint committee negotiations the right-leaning lower house would not accept the changes. This was the first time in the history of the parliament that such a conflict erupted between the two houses on an important political matter.[25]

Despite their reservations, the upper house representatives, hesitating to weaken Teleki's position or to strengthen the extreme Right, finally accepted the proposal by a large majority on April 28. They hoped that by placing restrictions on the Jews the law would take the wind out of the sails of the extreme Right. They also were justifiably hesitant to give the public any more reason to question their right to exist. Imrédy's party program in 1940 included the elimination of the upper house and the establishment of a one-house parliament. The law was still not sufficient to quiet agitation by anti-Semites, who wanted Jews to be placed outside the law. At the same time the harsher laws against the Jews in Slovakia and Romania meant that thousands of Jewish immigrants sought refuge in Hungary.[26]

If the Jewish laws had been carried out as decreed it is estimated that the loss of jobs in Budapest would have been close to 59,000 out of the population of about 185,000 Jews. In the countryside, the damage would have been slightly less. But for a number of reasons the laws were not carried out with the same rigor in every walk of life, or they were circumvented with the awareness of the authorities.[27] Soon after the second Jewish law was passed, the country entered a period of economic growth and the major immediate cause for the legislation, the eight-year economic depression, disappeared. The severe unemployment problem vanished with the war boom, and already in 1939 the availability of labor became the major problem. The overall motive for the law disappeared in less than one year after the laws were passed.

A second reason was that full implementation would have risked severe damage to the economy, which was not in the interests of the regime. The war effort was in its early stages and the Jewish owners and managers were the ones who knew the business and had contacts at home and abroad. They were also on good terms with the Hungarian upper class. In a letter to Teleki of October 1940, Horthy wrote: ". . . when I consider the raising of our standard of living as one of the most important tasks of the Government . . . it is impossible to discard the Jews, who have everything in their control, in one or two years, and to replace them by incompetent, mostly valueless and vociferous elements, because we may flounder."[28]

The actual decline of Jewish industrialists was relatively small. According to the statistics, the ratio of Jews to gentile industrialists fell from 44 percent in 1939 to 34.4 percent in 1941, but even these figures were inaccurate because of the large number of fictitious registration of Jewish establishments as Christian. Through the *Strohman* (straw man) system non-Jews were registered as holders of these establishments, while the original owners continued operations as usual, apparently with full knowledge of the authorities. Even large Jewish agricultural estates were not confiscated, despite the explicit injunctions to prevent Jews from holding agricultural land. Jewish estates of one hundred acres and above remained almost untouched. This tolerant negligence was probably the result of two considerations: the desire not to touch the issue of large estates, and the overall productivity of agriculture, which was in decline from the late 1930s on.[29]

One measure that greatly affected the Jewish population was the introduction of the forced labor service of Jewish males; the harsh treatment in labor companies had severe repercussions.[30] Labor service significantly reduced the number of Jewish men in the economy. The number subjected to forced labor service fluctuated substantially in accordance with needs and policy, but at one point over one half of the men in certain age groups were called up for forced labor. In 1941, the military authorities reported 14,413 Jews in battalions. Two years later the reported number was 106,113. The large numbers of Jewish men shipped away further reduced the need for sweeping changes in the occupational structure of the Jewish population.[31]

The British attitude to the second Jewish law and its execution in Hungary is an interesting commentary on the political cultures of the two nations. Even though the law was on the books there were a number of individuals and groups who refused or delayed in carrying it out. The mayor of Budapest delayed enforcement. Various liberals did not comply with the regulations. Even in the military exceptions were made. The passage of the law made no change in the practice of the upper house, which continued to elect its Jewish members to the various committees as in the past.[32] The British, justifiably, condemned the Hungarian laws, but such a law-abiding people as the British could not understand or believe that there would be laws on the books that would not actually be carried out, or only partially enforced, or actually sabotaged by the government.[33]

A Victory for the Extreme Right

On April 30, after his return from Berlin, Teleki called for new elections to be held according to the new electoral law passed in early 1938. The law, which had been hotly debated for months, provided for election with the secret ballot in the countryside as well as the cities. The elections, held on the traditional Hungarian holiday of Whitsun, May 28–29, were the first with a universal secret ballot since 1920 and resulted in a major victory for parties of the extreme Right—a political earthquake.[34] Although the government party still received an overwhelming majority, 187 mandates of the 260 up for election, an influx of extreme-right representatives completely changed the composition of the house. The extreme-right parties, which favored an unconditional pro-German policy, won forty-nine seats together, becoming the second strongest political force.

Teleki had promised to limit the left wing in the elections but he had failed to recognize the dimension of the rightist danger. He also made a major blunder in refusing to work with the liberal-conservative dissidents, who had left the party in 1938 in their objection to Imrédy's dictatorial ambitions, and none of the Bethlen dissidents were elected. Instead

Teleki, who had been working closely with Imrédy, allowed him to choose from twenty-five to thirty members to stand for the safe seats.[35] This brought another pro-German rightist group into the Parliament, the make-up of which was to continue unchanged throughout the war years.

The victory of the extreme Right was even more surprising—they had little money, their press had been banned, and a number of their leaders had been arrested, although Szálasi in jail was considered a martyr. The legend that the success of the rightist parties was partially due to German financial support appears to be without foundation. Their success can rather be attributed to discontent with a parliament that was seen to be passing useless laws and the impact of the modernizing efforts of Italy, Germany, and the Soviet Union with their planned economies and industrial development. The younger generation, who had little knowledge of the outside world, were impressed with what they knew of Germany.[36]

The election results also revealed the dissatisfaction of the workers and lower middle class in Budapest and the suburbs who in the past had supported the Social Democrats or the liberal parties. Changes in the makeup of the working force, with more young, politically naive workers, weakened the socialist party, and in 1938–39 the Arrow Cross organized successfully among the workers. The radically minded but politically naive young workers who wanted social reform were impressed even more with the promises to bring about effective and rapid solutions to social injustices than by the anti-Semitic slogans. The numbers of Arrow Cross supporters increased not only in Budapest and the suburbs but also in the countryside. Some of the petty bourgeois, who had voted for the liberal bourgeois party up until then, now voted for the radical Right.[37]

Also, the second Jewish law had seriously weakened the liberal opposition, since it deprived Jewish citizens of their voting rights unless they could prove continuous residence of their ancestors from 1867 on. Thus 150,000 citizens were disenfranchised. Many in the liberal opposition chose not to participate in the elections, protesting the limits on civil rights. Despite the secret ballot, which the liberals had demanded for years, the Social Democratic Party received only five mandates—down from fourteen. The Independent Smallholders Party received fourteen mandates, down from tweny-three. Only Rassay's Bourgeois Freedom Party managed to keep its five mandates.[38]

The radical-right representatives, who entered the lower house in large numbers in 1939, were members of a new generation. The number of representatives under the age of forty almost doubled from twenty-six to fifty-four between 1931 and 1939. These extreme-right reformers had received their political education in the radical, often anti-Semitic, university and veterans' movements of 1919–20. Interestingly, as a group they were better educated than earlier representatives. With Germany as their model they criticized the landowners and conservative lawmakers—especially those in the upper house—and demanded radical social and land reform. They supported the Jewish laws, truly believing that the Jews presented a problem.[39]

In the early 1930s a number of the new representatives had been socialist or communist reformers, but the inability of the Left to bring about reform and the government crackdown on Communists had turned them to the right for reform. Former extreme leftists gained prominent roles among the Arrow Cross party's highest leadership. The well-known poet János Kodolányi, in the late 1920s a Communist, had become a rightist by the late 1930s. The sculptor István Péntek, who had called for the permanent communist world revolution in 1933, became the Arrow Cross Party's head ideologist in 1937. István Párkányi, who was thrown out of the Social Democratic Party in 1934 for being too leftist, became an Arrow Cross district leader in Budapest and a party ideologist. (He rejoined the Communist Party in 1945.)[40]

The new political tone became evident on the first day of the new Parliament. At the opening session the Arrow Cross Party representatives appeared in the party uniform, green shirts and Sam Browne belts, instead of the customary urban street dress. The head of the faction, István Magyary-Kossa, greeted the surprised house with an Arrow Cross outstretched arm. Some members of the Hungarian Life Party and sympathizers in Mátyás Matolcsy's National Socialist Party arrived at the session in black Hungarian dress to emphasize the Hungarian and historical dimension of their reform program. In the black and green sea of clothing, the middle class in their light-colored suits stood out as unpatriotic. The new style appeared not only in dress but also in the form and tone of debate. The parliamentary diary noted an unprecedented number of incidents of verbal aggression, representatives shouting out at the speaker during debate, especially against the Social Democrats. From that time on actual opposition to government policies came not from the Left but from the Right.[41]

In 1939 no one could know that this was the high point of the extreme-right movement. With the wartime economic boom they lost much of their popularity, but since no further elections were held during the war they remained in office. In fact, the influence of Parliament in national politics had been declining.[42] The executive power had been strengthened in 1931 and the Hungarian parliament extended the authorization from year to year. A committee of thirty-three handled certain political questions with the agreement of party representatives but without public debate. Thus the new representatives took part in a parliament that had lost much of its influence over the government.[43]

As a result of the 1939 election, Teleki developed his plans to reform the government. He found that the level of political debate, already marked by noisy outbursts and political intrigue, had descended to a new low. "In today's parliamentary system . . . the lower house . . . does not reflect a true picture of the nation, often slips from the serious level; a party political arena which offers circus much more than bread, not so much to the nation but rather to an audience."[44] He planned to create a more modern state structure, incorporating aspects of the corporatist system, in which representatives would rise above the clamor and act in the best interests of the nation. His plans, reflecting the Catholic teaching on society expressed in the *Quadragesimo Anno* Papal encyclical of 1931, combined current ideas on the corporatist system as well as his opposition to any kind of dictatorial system for Hungary.[45]

Ultimately, the growing power of the military became a greater threat to parliamentary government than the political right. The Defense Law, passed in 1938, had opened the way for military direction of the economy. It increased censorship of the press, expanded the jurisdiction of courts martial, and limited the right of assembly, as well as introducing universal military conscription. The armed forces ultimately blocked Teleki's plans to grant autonomy for Ruthenia. Distraught by the undisciplined persecution of Communists, Jews, and Ukrainian nationalists during the period of military rule, he managed to replace the military with a civilian administration. But with the outbreak of war in September 1939, plans for autonomy were halted by the military, which argued that it was dangerous to experiment just when Soviet troops had established themselves on the Ruthenian border—a result of the Russian occupation of eastern Poland in late September of 1939.[46]

The Polish Crisis

The Hungarian government faced a new crisis in the summer of 1939 with the increase in Hitler's anti-Polish propaganda. After the Poles rejected Hitler's proffered alliance and accepted the British offer of a treaty of mutual assistance, the *Führer* decided on the Polish invasion. A long tradition of friendship and sympathy existed between the Hungarians and Poles, and Hungary was determined to follow a policy of neutrality in the Polish-German conflict. Foreign Minister Count István Csáky formulated the policy in a letter written from the Hungarian embassy in Rome on April 27, 1939. Hungary would take no part in any armed action against Poland, and any demand to allow German troops on foot, by vehicle transportation, or railroad to cross for an attack on Poland would be rejected. He added that if they were to allow the Germans to cross through Hungary to attack Poland, "a revolution would break out here."[47] The Hungarian minister to Berlin, Szótay, explained to German Secretary of State Ernst von Weizsäcker that in its thousand-year history Hungary had never been involved in war against Poland.

In late August the Hungarian government learned of the German plan for an attack on Poland. On Mussolini's urging, Teleki had written identical letters to Hitler and Mussolini, declaring that Hungary would follow the Axis policy in case of war, but in a second letter he emphasized: ". . . if no serious change occurs in the given circumstances, Hungary cannot, on moral grounds, be in a position to take armed action against Poland."[48] The letter was received in Berlin with such indignation that on his following visit Csáky was threatened with the possible loss of the Hungarian territories recovered with German assistance. A frightened Csáky, without receiving authorization, asked that Teleki's letters be regarded as not having been written. The Germans continued to exert diplomatic and propaganda pressure on Hungary to join in the attack, which the Hungarians countered with various excuses—including the Hungarian-Polish soccer match in Budapest which had received such enthusiastic press coverage. On the last days of August, Berlin officially notified the Hungarian minister that it considered Hungary's conduct untrustworthy and therefore would hold back the delivery of certain war materials as long as the Hungarians' conduct persisted.[49]

After Poland's rejection of the German threats Hitler decided to seek an alliance with the Soviet Union. The Russians were involved in diplomatic conversations with France and England on a mutual assistance pact, but at the same time had been enticing Germans into the opening of negotiations on a nonaggression pact. The most immediate obstacle to the pact with the French and British was the adamant opposition of the Poles to allowing the forces of the Soviet Union, their traditional enemy, to operate on their soil. While diplomatic conversations continued, Stalin entered into negotiations with the Germans. Ribbentrop set off for Moscow on August 22, authorized to make extensive concessions to the Russians. Finland, Estonia, and part of Latvia, to be partitioned along the Dvina River, were to come into the Russian sphere of interest, and in addition the Russians were to have a free hand to take Bessarabia. Stalin wanted all of Latvia, and Ribbentrop agreed after receiving Hitler's approval. Poland was to be divided along the Narew, Vistula, and San rivers.[50]

The Molotov-Ribbentrop nonaggression pact signed between Germany and the Soviet Union on August 23, 1939, shocked all of Europe. It ended Hungarian hopes for a compromise between the West and Germany against the Soviet Union, and it became evident that the German-Polish conflict would lead to the outbreak of war. However, the agreement did not convince England and France that it was hopeless to support Poland as Hitler had expected. Hitler put off the invasion until September 1, after Mussolini informed him that Italy would not be able to actively assist her ally before 1942 because of the state of Italian armament. Through Barcza in London Teleki sent a message to Foreign Secretary Halifax stating that although Hungary would make no open declaration, it would not cooperate with Germany against Poland and would continue to strive for neutrality.[51]

On September 1, 1939, Hitler attacked Poland and two days later Great Britain and France declared war. Teleki made no declaration of an official policy of neutrality, but he urged the population to support the government's efforts to maintain the country's noncombatant stand. Friendship with the Poles had deep roots among the Hungarian population, and the public supported the Teleki government, as did the opposition liberal political parties, the Social Democrats, the Independent Smallholders, the Legitimists, and the conservative group around Bethlen. Even many of the Right were prepared to support Teleki's stand. The regent, extremely popular at the time, backed him completely. With the attack on Poland and his alliance of friendship with the Soviet Union—the main enemy in the eyes of the public—Hitler had lost the popularity he had enjoyed at the time of the return of southern Slovakia.[52]

Hungary's neutral position surprised London since it indicated that Hungary still remained an independent country. Realizing Hungary's difficult position the British elite's respect for Teleki increased. Berlin, on the other hand, complained about the friendly position to Poland taken by the Hungarian press. Ribbentrop tried to tempt the Hungarian Foreign Minister Csáky at a meeting on September 7, asking whether Hungary did not wish for some "border corrections" with Poland, but Czáky declined the offer explaining that Hungary had no territorial interests that fell outside the territory of historical Hungary. At the time there was no discussion of German troops crossing Hungarian territory.

Thus, Czáky was surprised when at 4 P.M. on September 9, Ribbentrop called him at his home to ask for a small favor. Would Hungary make the Kassa railroad line immediately available to transport German troops to the Polish border. In return it might be possible for Hungary to take over the oil fields in the area of Sambor. Ribbentrop wanted an answer within an hour, but Csáky put him off until the next day at noon, explaining that only the regent could make the decision in such an important question, and at the moment the regent was on a shoot.[53]

Csáky turned to the Italian allies asking for advice from Mussolini and Ciano through Villani, the Hungarian Minister in Rome. He explained that the Hungarians were in no case willing to grant the German request, which they considered the first step in an occupation of Hungary. Ciano agreed that the step was "a prelude to an actual occupation of the country," and after returning from a meeting in Salzburg he told the Duce that the Germans were using the same language to the Hungarians that they had used six months previously to Poland. Mussolini and Ciano advised the Hungarians to turn down the German demand in the most courteous form possible.[54]

That evening Teleki, Foreign Minister Csáky, Minister of Defense Bartha, and Chief of the General Staff Henrik Werth, consulted with the regent on how to formulate the response to the Germans and what steps to take to prevent a possible German invasion. Horthy recommended that if the Germans attempted a forceful crossing, they should blow up all the bridges. He later recalled: "I would sooner have died on the scaffold than have permitted Hungarian territory to be put to such a use."[55] The next day at noon Csáky communicated the memorandum to Ribbentrop: the Hungarian government rejected the German request as incompatible with Hungarian honor, reminding him that on various occasions Budapest had informed the German government that Hungary could not take part in a war against Poland. To agree to the German request would violate Hungarian neutrality and also lead to a declaration of war by Britain, France, and Poland. If the Germans should attempt to invade Hungarian territory without the consent of the government, the royal Hungarian government would be forced to resist.[56]

In the following days, with Poland close to military collapse, the Germans put no pressure on Budapest, but Ciano entered a prophetic note in his diary of September 11: "I believe that this refusal will not be forgotten by the Germans and that at some time or other the Hungarians will have to pay for it."[57] To the Poles the denial of the German request was of huge significance; it meant that the frontier section between Poland and

Hungary remained under Hungarian control, and the open border made it possible for Polish soldiers to flee to Hungary.

The first Polish military units crossed the border on September 10 and in the following days a stream of Poles fled into Hungary. Within two days, on September 12, the Polish minister to Hungary, András Hory, asked the Hungarian government to enable refugees to cross the border more easily.

According to international law the units were disarmed and interned, but the Hungarians faced the question of what to do with the large numbers of Polish civilians, refugees from all walks of life, intellectuals, peasants, women and children, who were greeted warmly by the Hungarian population. The League of Nations convention in 1929 provided for the treatment of military personnel, but there was no corresponding legal provision for civilians. The government determined that Polish citizens who could provide for themselves would be treated like any foreign visitor—free to move about or leave the country at will. Those who needed assistance would be housed in refugee camps and provided for by the state. The Ministry of Defense announced on September 22 that the Polish soldiers were not prisoners of war but were sent to internment camps as interned foreigners simply because of the war conditions.

By October so many refugees had arrived that various nonprofit groups stepped in to help with their care—the Red Cross, the Polish-Hungarian Society, churches, and private individuals. In caring for the civilian refugees an important role was played by the Hungarian-Polish Refugee Committee, a voluntary social service organization established by the Hungarian-Polish Alliances League, and the Hungarian Red Cross. The number of refugees designated as civilian increased rapidly—partly because the Budapest Polish military attaché declared many of the officers to be civilians so that they could move on more quickly. At this point the civilian refugees were placed under the Ministry of Interior and Keresztes-Fischer gave the job to the Ninth Department of Social Services, appointing as head Dr. József Antall, a ministry councilor under Teleki who held the position until the German occupation.[58]

With financial help received from the government for social services, Antall and his workers succeeded in rapidly settling the refugees. In the first weeks, 141 military camps were set up, many in the southwest of the country. The soldiers and lower-ranked officers were placed in camps in factory buildings, schools, and villages, while the staff officers went to special camps in military recreation places, sanatoriums, hotels, and summer holiday places. But the number of camps quickly dwindled to twenty-one since the majority of soldiers went on with the goal of joining the army in France to fight the Nazis.

As time went on care for the refugees became more organized. The refugees received a daily allowance for each member over twelve and a family supplement for younger children. They were housed in various places in the country in vacation spots, villas, with families, and the allowances were handled by the local administration. The exact number of refugees has not been determined but estimates are that about 140,000 arrived in Hungary.[59]

Twenty-seven Polish-language elementary schools were opened for the children, with Polish teachers and textbooks as well as a Polish-language secondary school at Balatonboglar. Father Béla Varga, the parish priest, had a large community center erected in the village which he presented to the Poles for their secondary school.[60] The school became the only independent Polish secondary school in all of Europe during the war, since the Germans closed all those in Poland. Three hundred thirty students studied with Polish teachers and some also went on to the university where they received financial aid. About three hundred Polish graduates received diplomas and were able to return to Poland after the war to help fill the gap of Polish intellectuals, who had been wiped out under German occupation.

The situation of Polish Jewish refugees was to some extent unclear—the numbers estimated vary greatly from between 5,000 to 15,000. Many had left the country by May 1940, but it was also difficult to judge the numbers since many received false papers certifying that they were Christian from the Polish Pastoral Office which the Hungarian authorities accepted. As atrocities against Jews in Poland increased from early 1942, more and more Polish Jews fled to Hungary. Some were smuggled across the border by various groups and about 2,000 fled through Slovakia. A number landed in Jewish religious communities, and many got the false papers. In 1942 Jewish soldiers were put into separate military camps, supposedly at the request of Polish officers, although it appears they were treated well until the Arrow Cross leadership took over.[61]

The Germans considered the acceptance of refugees an unfriendly act and frequently protested against this violation of neutrality. They were especially upset that Polish officers in the internment camps openly agitated for soldiers to join the Polish legion in France, and that the government provided opportunities for Polish soldiers and officers to make their

way to Western Europe. The Hungarian government promised to investigate concrete incidents but the refugees continued to leave until the collapse of France in June 1940. The responsible ministries passed decrees
that would prevent the Polish refugees from reaching Allied territory, but
in practice the authorities closed their eyes. The friendly attitude of the
Hungarian authorities continued under the tacit agreement of Minister
of the Interior Keresztes-Fischer, Prime Minister Teleki, and the regent
himself.[62]

With the French capitulation the situation became more difficult. The
Germans gained much information from Polish soldiers, who had landed
as POWs in France. Although Hungary did not recognize the provisional
Polish government, the legation functioned legally for almost one and a
half years after the war broke out, until the Germans forced Hungary to
close the Polish legation on January 15, 1941.[63]

According to the military plans the Poles had made with the French
and the English, the Polish Army was only expected to hold off the Germans for the two weeks necessary for the Western Allies to launch a
major offensive. The Poles continued fighting for four weeks defending
their country, but the British and French did not arrive. On September
17 the Soviets joined in the German attack, the Red Army invading Poland from the east, and during the second half of September the Soviet
Union occupied eastern Poland; thus Hungary's one hundred fifty kilometer border with Poland became a border with the Soviet Union.[64]

Under German pressure Hungary again established diplomatic relations with the Soviet Union on September 23 and sent József Kristóffy to
Moscow. The government in Moscow tried to reassure Hungary, informing Budapest that it would honor the Hungarian borders and wished to
establish friendly relations, but despite the assurances the anti-Soviet nature of Hungarian foreign policy did not change. When the Soviet-Finn-
ish war broke out in November, volunteer Hungarian troops joined the
Finns and war materials were sent to the Finnish army.[65]

In the following months it became more and more difficult to refuse
German demands. In addition to intensified German economic demands,
Teleki was under pressure at home from both the government right wing
and the military. The right wing around Imrédy, backed by the Arrow
Cross, believed that Hungary should give up its neutral pose and embrace
a pro-German policy. The top military elite, who had fought as allies with
Germany in World War I, were impressed with German support for Hun-
garian revision and saw possibilities for the return of Transyvlania. They

had been imbued with the traditional German orientation of the dual monarchy where German was the language of command; more than half had been born in the lost territories.[66]

Following the Polish invasion and Hungary's neutral stance, the German leaders reacted violently to any minor Hungarian move considered harmful to German interests. With a gradual British economic blockade German foreign policy focused even more on its economic needs. Romania and Yugoslavia became more prominent targets of German diplomacy, Romania for its crude oil and Yugoslavia for ore, and Germany wanted Hungary to repress its industrial development and increase her agricultural production. In preparation for the German-Hungarian economic negotiations of 1939, Ribbentrop suggested that economic ties be based on these conditions; Hungary must also stop production in certain areas in order to increase its capacity to absorb German industrial products.[67]

The actual negotiations in 1939 led to a stalemate. In the interest of a closer integration of the two economic systems, the Germans put forth demands that the Hungarians could not accept, including a revaluation of the Hungarian currency—the pengő to the mark—which Lipót Baranyai, the Governor of the National Bank, resisted vigorously. Teleki also refused to grant the Germans the right to control exploration and exploitation of oil in Ruthenia. With the failure of talks the Germans maintained their veto on fulfilling the armaments contracts that Hungary had placed with Germany. Since Germany had become the only supplier of weapons after the fall of Czechoslovakia, Hungarian military leaders had to be content with the purchase of outdated German weapons and vehicles. The military were upset by the German embargo on war materials, and pressure increased on Teleki from enemies who hoped to remove him from office.[68]

Under pressure from the military the government finally reached an agreement in negotiations in December and January 1940. Baranyai modified his exchange policy and Hungary promised in the future to aid Germany economically with all her resources. In return, Germany promised to fulfill the orders already placed and perhaps take on new orders in the future. Even so, economic cooperation was half-hearted. The Office of Foreign Trade made up various devices for keeping up trade with other countries. Hungary succeeded almost entirely in avoiding any integration of her economic system into that of Germany other than the armaments industry.[69]

THE THREAT OF GERMAN OCCUPATION

In March 1940, with rumors that the "phony war" would soon come to a close, Molotov hinted strongly that the Soviet Union would soon demand the return of Bessarabia, which had been granted to Romania after World War I. At the time Germany considered that it might be necessary to occupy the Romanian oil fields, even though it had made an economic pact with Romania in March 1939. At the end of March, the German general staff asked Budapest for right of passage for German troops to garrison Romanian oil wells, but Teleki feared that close cooperation with the German military might prejudice his determination to maintain Hungarian independence. Yet, opposition to the passage of German troops through Hungary would increase the danger that Germany would decide to occupy Hungary.

Teleki, in a quandary, made a private trip to Mussolini on March 23 to ask for support from his Italian ally, but Mussolini's answer was equivocal. According to historian Macartney, Mussolini had just made up his mind to enter the war.[70] He told Teleki he could not remain neutral forever; at a certain moment he would side with Germany. Disheartened, at luncheon with Ciano, Teleki asked abruptly, "Do you know how to play bridge?" Ciano asked. "Why?" "For the day when we are together in the Dachau Concentration Camp."[71]

A few weeks later, on April 8, Teleki again asked for Mussolini's support, sending his friend Lipót Baranyai to Rome, ostensibly to discuss financial matters but in reality to ask Mussolini and Ciano about their position if the Hungarian government should refuse the German request for transit. Mussolini speculated about the war, predicting that after German bombing Great Britain would collapse, France would be defeated, and the United States would never enter the war. Then in his usual manner he evaded giving a specific answer. When Baranyai asked directly if Hungary should resist a German crossing with military force could they count on Italian support, he answered laconically, "How can you imagine that? I am Hitler's ally and I want to remain so."[72] Teleki was forced to recognize that Italy was no useful balance against German aggression.

With the possibility of German armed action against Romania, the Hungarian military leaders were eager to seize an opportunity to advance their territorial claims for Transylvania. Chief of the General Staff Werth and part of the general staff urged not only military cooperation with Germany but even a political alliance. At the Council of Ministers meeting on April 1, Teleki called attention to the British-French guaranties for

Romania, pointing out that he did not want to sacrifice Hungary's independence over Transylvania. Csáky, in opposition, foresaw an end to the country's independence if Hungary should oppose the German transit request, and he was supported by most of the government members. It was decided that Werth could work out a plan for a common German-Hungarian action, but Teleki strongly opposed it and complained to Horthy that Werth with his German origins did not consider the country's true interests.[73]

Teleki was again under attack from the government right wing around Imrédy, supported by the Arrow Cross. On March 15 Imrédy broke his self-imposed silence, advocating closer ties with Germany, a move possibly calculated as a bid for personal power. Teleki was able to weather the immediate storm—he had the strong backing of Horthy who had given him a signed authorization to be used at will to dissolve Parliament—but his concessions weakened his position for the future. The Germans were making constant and multiple economic demands and demanding complete subservience from the Hungarian press.[74]

PLANS FOR A GOVERNMENT IN EXILE

It has been claimed that Teleki at the time was eager for armed action to reclaim Transylvania, but his actions indicate that he had other priorities. In spring of 1940, he was planning the possible formation of a government in exile, arranging to transfer five million dollars to the Hungarian minister in Washington, János Pelényi, in preparation. The idea had probably originated with Pelényi who first spoke of the possibility to Teleki and Horthy in September 1938, and on April 17, 1939, sent a memorandum to Teleki and Csáky outlining his ideas for the government in exile. When Pelényi met Teleki in August while on vacation in Budapest, the prime minister agreed to the plan and promised that in the necessary circumstances it would be realized. On March 17, 1940, in an official letter he asked Pelenyi to place the money in the name of the Magyar National Bank in a safe, and specified exactly who had access to the funds and under what conditions.[75]

The British Foreign Office, of course, knew of the plan and were encouraging. Assistant Secretary of State Orme Sargent told Barcza that if Germany should force passage through Hungary to Romania and Hungary at least protested against it, this would give Hungary the same status internationally as Denmark. Three days later, on May 17, State Secretary Cadogan repeated the advice, and further suggested that if a Hungarian government—the existing one or another nominated by the regent—

should go abroad, His Majesty's Government would recognize it as the legitimate government of Hungary.[76]

Concerned over the question of the passage of German troops, Teleki wrote Hitler on April 17 asking for German-Italian-Hungarian negotiations on the Balkan problems, but Germany was now preparing to launch its offensive in the West. Since the maintenance of peace in southeast Europe had become more important, the German general staff altered its plans to attack Romania. Finally one month later, on May 14, after the start of the offensive in the West, Hitler replied that Germany did not intend to start military action in the Balkans and therefore it was not timely to discuss the issue. On May 20 Teleki acknowledged Hitler's communication and the next day he wrote to Pelényi in Washington letting him know that the idea of forming a government in exile was to be dropped for the time being. A few months later he instructed Pelényi to repay the five million dollars to the account of the National Bank of Hungary.[77]

Plans for the government in exile were revived in late 1940 with the encouragement of the new British minister in Budapest, Sir Owen O'Malley. Horthy met with his close political advisors, and it was decided that if Germany made unacceptable demands on Hungary, he would appoint a government that would function in exile and then he would abdicate. Bethlen would fly to London to serve as the new prime minister and György Barcza, the Hungarian minister in London, would become the foreign minister. Tibor Eckhardt, head of the Smallholders Party, who had made a lecture tour of the United States earlier in the year, would represent the Hungarian government in exile in Washington.

O'Malley urged Horthy to consider moving to Szeged with loyal troops, from where, if necessary, he could cross the border into Yugoslavia and travel to join Bethlen in London, but Horthy seemed reluctant to leave the country and made no commitment. He also disliked the idea of Bethlen or Eckhardt departing the country before a real emergency arose. Thus when Eckhardt—at the urging of Teleki and Bethlen—left on the mission in early 1941, he did so without instructions or authorization from Horthy. In his report to London, O'Malley expressed himself willing to accompany an exile government to London, and the Foreign Office told Barcza that if Horthy and the members of his cabinet flew to England, His Majesty's Government "would be honored and pleased, and would recognize them as a Government."[78] But plans for the government in exile remained incomplete, since the Hungarians received no answer on their request for explicit assurance that the British would regard the émigré government as the legal government of Hungary no matter what happened in the future.

Reaction to the German Victories in the West

On April 9, 1940, the German army attacked Denmark and Norway, then Belgium, Holland, Luxemburg, and France. On June 22 the French army capitulated unconditionally. The German victories appalled Teleki. Earlier he had formed a research department on economic policy, the sub-rosa assignment of which was to assess the situation of Germany's raw materials and how long they would be able to continue the war given the resources available. At the time it was calculated the materials would last only until the end of 1943. Now with the raw materials available from the Western countries the situation had changed radically. No wonder Teleki was so shocked by the German victories.[79] The rapid German advance encouraged his opponents, emboldening the extreme Right. They renewed their attack against Teleki in early June, and Imrédy asked him to resign. The fall of Paris was celebrated with feasts and receptions.

Hungary was finding it almost impossible to continue straddling the fence. Churchill replaced Chamberlain as prime minister on May 10, and the British ambassador in Budapest had already warned Hungary that her ties to Germany seemed too strong for a country claiming to be neutral. Britain halted shipments of firearms, and with Italy's entry into the war on June 10 and consequent developments in the Mediterranean, shipping routes were blocked, effectively terminating all British trade with Hungary. With the loss of neutral Italy, Hungary was forced into even greater reliance on Germany. The danger of war appeared so imminent that the regent called home his older son, István Horthy, from his honeymoon trip in the Near East, sending a telegram that German troops had occupied Belgium and Holland and that war was coming.[80]

Hitler's stunning victories in the West surprised and shocked the leaders of the Soviet Union as well. In acceding to the Molotov-Ribbentrop Pact of 1939 with an imperialist enemy, Stalin had looked to long-term goals, planning to play off the capitalist powers against each other. He had calculated that after the Polish invasion Britain and France would be drawn into war with Germany and Germany would become involved in a long drawn-out war on the Western front, just as it had in World War I. After the imperialist Western powers had exhausted each other, revolutions would arise and the continent would be open to communist domination.

Now Germany's victories gave it control of much of the continent and assured it of the raw materials it needed, reducing its dependence on the Soviet Union; there was even the possibility of a German-British peace agreement. In June while much of the German army was concentrated in the West, the Soviet Union decided to lay claim to territories lost at the end of World War I, activating the secret clauses of the Molotov-Ribbentrop Pact. They marched into Latvia, Lithuania, and Estonia, and during the summer quietly incorporated them into the Soviet Union as constituent republics. On June 26 Molotov, after receiving German assent, handed over an ultimatum to the Romanians demanding the return of Bessarabia, which had been taken from Russia, but also, as compensation, to turn over the Ukrainian inhabited northern Bukovina.

On receiving the unexpected ultimatum the Romanian government panicked. It could no longer count on support from its former allies; France was defeated and England stood alone against the Germans. With no support from the Germans the government accepted the ultimatum and on June 28 Soviet troops crossed the border. The loss of territory inflicted a stunning blow to the Romanian political and military leadership since it belied their thesis of "Great-Romanian indissoluble unity" which had been hammered into the public for the last twenty years. Shortly before the Soviet ultimatum King Carol had praised the strength of the Romanian army and the Bessarabian fortifications. The Romanians hoped that German protection would prevent further Soviet demands and block Bulgaria and Hungary from following the Soviet precedent and demanding the return of territories taken after World War I.[81] On June 29 to guarantee German protection, the new foreign minister announced that Romania openly expressed its friendship for Germany, and on July 1 it terminated English and French guarantees.[82]

THE QUESTION OF TRANSYLVANIA

The day after the Soviet ultimatum to Romania, the Hungarian Council of Ministers met and agreed that if Romania accepted the Soviet ultimatum, they would demand that Hungary receive equal treatment for satisfaction of its territorial demands. After accepting the Soviet ultimatum, King Carol ordered general mobilization, sending troops to the Hungarian border and new forces into Transylvania. The Romanian press intensified its anti-Hungarian campaign, noting that the Treaty of Trianon had not even satisfied Romanian demands, which laid claim to eastern Hungary up to the Tisza River.

In 1940 Hungarian popular opinion called for nothing less than the return of all of Transylvania to Hungary, while Romanian politicians, backed by intense popular Romanian nationalism, insisted that Romania would give back "not a single furrow" of Greater Romania.[83] Both countries considered Transylvania vital to their national existence. Romanian claims were primarily ethnic, but also based on a historic claim, which they dated back to the Roman province of Dacia. The Romanians claimed that their ancestors were the ancient Daks, who had been conquered by Roman Emperor Trajan and Latinized. When the Romans left in 271, the Daks had retreated to the mountains to avoid the waves of Germanic and Asiatic migrations, but by the eleventh century they had reemerged in the Transylvanian lowlands, where they were conquered by Hungarian intruders. The Romanian theory of origins reduced all other nationalities in Transylvania to historical interlopers in a native Romanian homeland.

Hungarian claims were partially based on history, since Transylvania had been part of the thousand-year-old Kingdom of Hungary, but they disagreed with the Romanians, asserting that Transylvania was uninhabited in the eleventh century, when it had been united with the kingdom. Rulers had brought in Hungarians, Székelys—the ethnic relatives of the Hungarians—and Saxon Germans to protect and develop the area. According to the Hungarians, Romanians had started to enter Transylvania in larger numbers from the south starting in the late twelfth and thirteenth centuries. The newcomers were lowly shepards and had little political or cultural impact on the original Hungarians, Székely and Saxons who made up the historic Three Nations of Transylvania. After World War I when Romania was granted the area known as Transylvania—which also included the eastern part of the Great Hungarian Plain—two million ethnic Hungarians were cut off from Hungary.

In the period after World War I, when Romania acquired the lands that made up Greater Romania, Romanian leaders had been ill prepared to deal with their new multiethnic population. Under pressure from the great powers they had signed the Minorities Protection Treaty, but only after strong opposition. Disregarding the multinational and regional nature of the enlarged country, Romanian politicians aimed to make Romania a Romanian national state following a policy of centralized rule.[84] Their goal was to build a nation of true Romanians, with little regard to the multiethnic nature of the population, which included Romanians, Magyars, Székelys, Germans, Jews, Ukrainians, Gypsies, and Serbs. The Romanians, who made up over half of the population, were overwhelmingly rural, while Hungarians, Germans and Jews formed 88.5 percent of

Transylvania's urban population.[85] Hungarians and German Saxons maintained their national identities throughout the interwar period, and the Hungarian-speaking Székelys formed a solid block in southeast Transylvania. The Székelys were strongly independent with a long tradition of self-government and resisted all Romanian attempts to assimilate them.[86]

In light of the critical situation on the border, Csáky notified Berlin, Rome, and Belgrade that the Hungarian government must initiate protective military measures, since it seemed that a Romanian attack was possible. The Hungarian military had already mobilized part of the second army and the first army was making preparations. After Romania renounced the British guarantee, Teleki believed the danger of British intervention had been eliminated, especially since relations between Britain and Romania had continued to deteriorate.[87] At this time Hitler faced a dilemma. Preoccupied with plans for the invasion of England, for which he sorely needed Romanian oil, he was also concerned about the aggressive manner of the Soviet Union and did not want trouble in the Balkans. Ribbentrop notified Csáky that a Balkan war, which might come about through a Hungarian military move, was diametrically opposed to Germany's current interests, and that Hungary could not count on any kind of assistance from Germany. However, on July 10 he invited Teleki and Csáky to Munich to meet with Hitler. As a consequence the planned Hungarian attack was cancelled, but the situation remained tense.[88]

In a surprising change of policy, Hitler—who up until then had flatly refused to satisfy Hungary and Bulgaria's territorial claims on Romania—suggested a settlement through negotiations. He promised to write to King Carol and ask him to come to an agreement with Hungary. Ribbentrop informed the Romanian king by telegram that Berlin considered territorial revision necessary to assure peace in the Balkans, and that Romania should plan to give up certain territories inhabited by the Bulgarians and Hungarians. The message shocked the king who had believed that Hitler supported his stand. Under German pressure King Carol agreed to take up negotiations, but pleaded for German assistance to support the idea of systematic population exchange rather than the granting of territories.[89]

At the end of July, Hitler's position underwent a further change as he considered the possibility of an attack against the Soviet Union. In addition to his concern over the Soviet expansionist moves during the summer, he was aware that in July Stalin had contacted the British government, suggesting the possibility of an alliance in which the Soviet Union would change sides. On July 31, 1940, Hitler mapped out plans with his military leaders for the attack he was considering against the Soviet Union.[90] He realized that the price to be paid for the use of railroad lines in Hungary might be the satisfaction, at least in part, of Hungarian revisionist demands.[91]

In early August, under German pressure, the Bucharest leadership was forced to take the first steps toward negotiations with Hungary and Bulgaria on territorial revision, but pleading with the Germans that they needed time to prepare Romanian public opinion, the Romanians aimed to delay negotiations as long as possible. They stood firm on their position that population exchange must be the basis of negotiations, and only afterward might there be discussion of possible territorial exchange.[92] In discussions among themselves the Romanians considered different plans for the resettlement of the Transylvanian-Hungarians. The greatest difficulty was presented by the Székely population because of its geographic position as a solid block of Hungarians in the southeast of Transylvania, far from other Hungarian settlements.

Negotiations took place at Turnu Severin and lasted from August 16 through August 24; during this period the positions of the two delegations remained essentially the same. The Romanian delegation refused to propose any territorial changes and was only willing to negotiate on the basis of population exchange. The Hungarian plan asked for two-thirds of Transylvania but would leave the richer economic region to Romania. It has been suggested that Hitler knew well that the negotiations would be fruitless. When negotiations failed, as they were bound to, he would step in to arbitrate, and so would hold both governments in his hands.[93]

Leaders of both delegations were native Transylvanians. Valeriu Pop, the leader of the Romanian delegation, stated Romania was only willing to negotiate if the starting point was based on the principle of population exchange, asserting that even the Székely problem could be solved by exchange of peoples. The Hungarian leader, András Hory, judging that future negotiations were futile, telegrammed Csáky asking for permission to break off discussions. Czáky, probably under Axis pressure, replied not to break off negotiations yet. As a last resort Hory suggested that the Hungarian delegation would return to Budapest to discuss difficulties, but before he left he asked Pop privately if there was any hope that the Székelyföld would have any contact with Hungary. Pop responded that the Székely territory was an integral part of Romanian land and they would never negotiate about giving it over. If Hungary wanted the Székelys they could get them through population exchange.

In his report to a special sitting of the Council of Ministers on August 22, Hory explained that the only benefit he could see from the negotiations was that they had made clear Romania's firm intention of keeping the pure Hungarian territory. The ministers were struck by the Romanian admission that they had only given back territory to the Soviet Union because of the danger of a Russian military attack. Bartha, minister of defense, broke in: ". . . that means that for our part if we start military action Romania will talk differently." The next day Chief of the General Staff Werth announced the start of military operations against Romania. Troops were to be ready to start the operation at dawn on August 28.

On the final day of negotiations, August 24, the two sides were no closer to agreement. Hory again stated the Budapest position—that the starting point had to be the new border and then it would be possible to discuss any necessary population exchange. Hungary would never agree to the Székely population being resettled from the Székelyföld. The Romanian delegation still clung to the formula of population exchange as the only possibility of negotiation. The Romanian government was seemingly convinced that Hitler supported them in this stand.[94]

In the meantime, Bulgaria had gained back Southern Dobruja under an agreement concluded on August 21 and formalized by a treaty on September 7. On the last day of negotiations, the Hungarian government took steps to prepare for a military attack against Romania, canceling the leave that had been given for soldiers to bring in the harvest and mobilizing about 400,000 troops. The Romanians already had 450,000 troops in Transylvania with new troops expected, and border incidents broke out between Hungarian and Romanian troops.[95]

With alarming news arriving in Berlin about the tense situation on the Soviet-Romanian border where the Soviets had massed their troops, Hitler decided that the Axis must intervene to prevent a Hungarian-Romanian armed conflict. The Soviets had assured the Hungarians that they supported their just claims for revision, and Hitler feared that they would use military conflict as an opportunity to move in and take over the Ploesti oil fields. German and Italian diplomacy went into action on August 26. Ribbentrop and Ciano recalled their ministers from Budapest and Bucharest for advice, in the meantime instructing the Hungarian and Romanian governments to take no action that would increase the seriousness of the situation.[96]

On August 27 a small council called by Hitler made the decision on the border question. There are no written records of the meeting but evidently there were two recommendations made to Ribbentrop on the territory to be given to Hungary by W. Fabricius, the German minister in Bucharest, and German economic deputy, Karl Clodius. Ribbentrop added the city of Kolozsvár to the recommendation made by Fabricius, and Clodius warned that the Székelyföld must be included. Both suggestions were presented to Hitler. On the way to Berchtesgaden, Fabricius warned Ribbentrop that if the two suggestions were combined, the result would be unacceptable to Romania. His fears were soon realized: Hitler combined the two plans, giving to Hungary a territory larger than either one of the suggestions—43,000 square kilometers. Thus the new Hungarian-Romanian border was decided by Hitler, and presented on August 30 with only minor changes.[97]

THE SECOND VIENNA AWARD

When the foreign ministers of Hungary and Romania, Csáky and Manoilescu, arrived in Vienna on August 29, they expected to conduct further negotiations in the presence of the Axis foreign ministers. The Romanians were convinced that Hitler supported their stand on population exchange and that the Axis decision would be favorable to Romania. Ciano commented: "It is a difficult problem to solve; in fact, impossible to solve with any absolute justice. We shall try to be as fair as we can."[98]

The Axis first took steps to persuade both sides to agree to accept the arbitration decision unconditionally before they knew the terms. Ribbentrop and Ciano met with Foreign Minister Csáky, with Teleki as an observer. In a threatening tone Ribbentrop complained about the Hungarian stand in the Polish war; that they were not thankful enough to Germany. Teleki hesitated to give unconditional acceptance to the arbitration decision, fearing Hungary would not receive the Székelyföld, but finally after conferring with Budapest Csáky agreed. In the meeting with the Romanians the Germans rejected the solution of population exchange, and Ciano explained that it would be too difficult, that one could not move people around like that. They mentioned the Russian threat, but assured the Romanians that Germany would guarantee Romania's borders. Manoilescu left the meeting in great distress and the decision to accept arbitration was reached only after long midnight discussions of the Council of Ministers.[99]

At the Belvedere on the afternoon of August 30, the Axis delayed the presentation of the map showing the division of Transylvania. Ribbentrop first read out the conditions for the division, made both in German and Italian, to establish the final border between Romania and Hungary. Within fourteen days the Romanian authorities were to leave the ceded territory and the Hungarian occupation was to take place peacefully. The exact demarcation was to be made later by a joint Hungarian-Romanian committee. Romanians in the Hungarian section were ensured of Hungarian citizenship, but if they should choose to retain Romanian citizenship they should leave within one year. Equal treatment was to be given both sides.

Only after this reading was a map handed over to each delegation (see Map 3). In accordance with the decision approximately 43,000 square kilometers of Northern Transylvania was returned to Hungary, including the cities of Nagyvárad and Kolozsvár, and also the Székelyföld.[100] The population of 2.5 million included more than one million Romanians, while approximately 400,000 Hungarians remained in Romanian territory. The second Vienna Award, called by the Romanians the *Viennese Dictat*, shocked both parties. When Manoilescu looked at the map and saw the new borders, he fainted. In less than three months Romania had lost a third of its population and territory. For the Hungarians the shock was the Axis powers guarantee of Romania's borders, thus freezing Hungarian claims to the rest of Transylvania.[101]

The new border was just as artificial as that of the borders specified in the Treaty of Trianon.[102] Béla Bethlen, who became governor of two of the returned counties, described the division as a Solomon decision, which divided families and destroyed livelihoods: "Just to mention those closest to me; my elderly mother, two brothers, my older sister, and one of my children, with their families, remained in southern Transylvania, cut off from me."[103] On August 30, the day of his daughter's wedding, as the family sat down to dinner he turned on the radio to hear the twelve o'clock news. "Just then they were giving the results of the Vienna decision, listing district by district the new borders. That's when we learned that we were cut off from our child. We would return to Bethlen in Hungary, while right after dinner our daughter and her new husband drove to Mezőpagocsa in southern Transylvania, a pistol shot away but now on the other side."[104]

The Hungarian population was jubilant. The newsreels showed Horthy's celebratory entrance into Kolozsvár and the radio played a popular song, "Dearest Transylvania, we are here. We live and die for you . . ."[105] Vilmos Nagy, head of the newly established First Army, rejoiced to visit his birthplace after twenty-two years, especially since his troops had been prepared for a possible Romanian conflict. Instead they marched into Kolozsvár, where they were greeted with tremendous enthusiasm by the

Transylvanian population. When a Greek Orthodox Romanian priest protested that the Romanians had lost their home, Nagy replied that, although he understood his pain, the speech was out of place when the Hungarians were celebrating their freedom from "Romanian bondage."[106]

The Romanian reaction to the decision was so violent that it fatally weakened the position of the bumbling, corrupt Romanian king. Blamed for the loss of northern Transylvania, King Carol's government collapsed on September 6, and in a volte-face he called on General Antonescu, whom he had had arrested on July 7, 1940, to form a new government. Known for his personal integrity, Antonescu enjoyed widespread public support—especially because of his past opposition to the king. After forcing the king to abdicate, Antonescu was appointed president of the Council of Ministers by the new king, the nineteen-year-old Michael. The new regime under General Antonescu openly declared it would not acquiesce in the loss of northern Transylvania and the Székely lands. Anti-Hungarian demonstrations increased and the press clamored for northern Transylvania to be taken back from Hungary.

While Hungary celebrated, Teleki was on the brink of despair. He had not wanted an award with Hitler's help; his explicit policy was that Hungary would not ask Germany for arbitration in the Transylvanian question. Chief of the General Staff Werth had interfered, telling the German Air Force attaché in Budapest that Hungary did want arbitration, a position that Foreign Minister Csáky then had to deny.[107] The results of the decision threw Teleki into depression. He refused to come out to greet the crowds on the celebratory train ride back to Budapest or to sign the proclamation, which announced the terms of the award; he realized that the forced solution would only increase hostile relations with Romania. Still convinced that in the end Germany could not triumph over the Allies he believed that the territorial gain—won through a decree rather than consultation—could only be temporary. In contrast to the first Vienna Award the correctness of the second decision was questionable according to international law. The United States and Great Britain both took it to be a forced *dictat* against the Romanians and questioned its validity.[108]

THE COST OF THE SECOND VIENNA AWARD

Over the next months Hungary paid the price for regaining northern Transylvania. A few hours after the announcement of the second Vienna Award, Czáky signed the *Volksbund* protocol, approving the Volksbund as the only legal organization for the German minority in Transylvania and Hungary. For some time the Germans had demanded that the *Volks-deutschen* be recognized as a German ethnic group, which Teleki had opposed. The German-speaking population, known in Hungary as Swabians, lived in communities mainly in western Hungary and had never formed a uniform historical community.[109] Primarily peasants, they had been relatively apolitical until the 1930s, but German propaganda and Hitler's successes succeeded in making many conscious of their German background. The number of the Hungarian-German minority in Hungary had grown significantly after the Vienna Awards, and the idea of belonging to a vast German ethnic community was gaining ground. It was seen most clearly among the youth, many who wanted to leave the Hungarian paramilitary youth organization, the *levente*, to join the *Deutsche Jugend*, which was modeled on the *Hitler Jugend*.

Teleki was at first unwilling to sign the measure but eventually gave in to German pressure. The Volksbund could now openly proclaim to be a National Socialist ethnic association. According to the protocol anyone in the German-speaking population who chose to consider himself a member of the *Volksbund der Deutschen in Ungarn* was to enjoy special rights, essentially creating a state within a state. Teleki's amendments, however, made the agreement obscure enough to allow different interpretations, and it was never sanctioned by an act of Parliament.[110]

On October 10 Hungary signed another substantial economic agreement with Germany, setting higher quotas for Hungarian deliveries of grains as well as lowering the pengő's value in relation to the mark. It also committed Hungary to pay for its imports with exports. Since the Germans delayed their own shipments while pressuring Hungary not to fall behind with theirs, this was translated into a credit arrangement highly advantageous to Germany.

In October the government also permitted German training troops to pass through Hungarian territory by rail to the Romanian oil fields. The decision was explained away by the fact that the Romanians themselves asked for help in updating the training of their army.[111] Even though the Romanians had terminated the English guarantees, the decision brought a protest from Britain. Perhaps most important, on November 20 Hungary joined the Tripartite Pact of September 2, in which Germany, Italy, and Japan agreed that any two would come to the defense of the third if attacked. Slovakia and Romania also joined, since supposedly it would secure them a voice in the territorial reorganization of Europe, but effectively it meant the end to Teleki's policy of neutrality.

Conflict Between Werth and Teleki

Differences had been building up between Prime Minister Teleki and Chief of the General Staff Werth. Teleki was concerned about the increasing political influence of the military leadership and their interference in the economy. Werth, the highest-ranking officer next to the regent, had tremendous powers; he needed to consult only with the minister of defense and the regent himself. Werth believed it imperative to build up the military more rapidly and to improve relations with Germany in order to ensure delivery of promised military equipment, since there was constant fear of a Romanian attack.[112] The Romanian army was much better equipped than that of Hungary, and German delivery of promised military equipment was continually delayed. The government of General Antonescu, who would establish his dictatorship on January 27, 1941, enjoyed the closest possible relations with Nazi Germany; Hitler had taken a liking to Antonescu when he visited Berlin in November 1940 and treated him with a trust and cordiality very different from his attitude toward any of the Hungarians. Hitler assured him he intended to revise the Transylvanian award in favor of Romania.[113]

Accompanied by a list of conflicts between the military leadership and the civilian government, Teleki submitted his letter of resignation to Horthy in September 1940. In effect, Teleki explained, two governments existed within Hungary, one legal, the other the military, "the influence of which is growing in almost every branch of administration, and which the legal government is unable to supervise."[114] The armed forces did not answer to the cabinet in matters of finance. Their staff in the ministry of industry refused to answer to the appropriate minister and contracted foreign trade and domestic labor agreements without authorization. The military leadership made arrangements with Berlin without the knowledge of the government, countering Teleki's aim to reduce commitments to Germany and maintain ties with England. These arrangements included agreements on exports and imports, of which the responsible ministers of foreign affairs, trade, and industry had no knowledge. Later, in foreign trade discussions, it was of course impossible to withdraw these promises.[115]

After his resignation, Teleki proposed to continue as government commissioner of the regained Transylvanian territories, to deal with the problems of transportation and communication that had plagued Hungary for months after the second Vienna Award. When the Romanians evacuated northern Transylvania they had taken the vast majority of railcars in violation of the Vienna agreements. But even worse, the rail line connecting

Hungary with the Székelyföld in easternmost Transylvania passed through territory that had been left in Romanian hands. Badly needed food and other supplies had to be trucked over poor roads. The Romanians denied oil from Ploesti, and Hungarian workers were no longer allowed to commute to Brassó and the surrounding area.[116]

Teleki, who believed in governing the non-Hungarian peoples with tolerance and respect for their cultures, also feared the brutality of military administration to the non-Hungarian nationalities, as had been experienced in the reannexed territories in Slovakia and Ruthenia. He had intended to give Ruthenia autonomy as a model of his plan for the future Hungary to again become a multinational state, but the military forced him to set aside his plan. Now he attempted to ensure that the remaining Romanian population would be treated fairly, but as the military moved into Transylvania and established administrative control they murdered dozens of Romanians and Jews in the villages of Szilágyipp, Ördökút, and elsewhere.[117]

On September 29, 1940, the regent summoned Teleki, Werth, and Minister of Defense Bartha to review Teleki's accusations. In the past, Horthy had been sympathetic to the military, but in his desire to have Teleki remain he made several concessions; he ended the military's practice of presenting extremely general and unalterable budgetary estimates and he terminated the military's jurisdiction over Transylvania on November 26. He also made Teleki government commissioner in Transylvania and awarded him the highest decoration, the Grand Cross of the St. Stephen Order.[118]

In order to incorporate northern Transylvania quickly into the Hungarian system of public administration, it was decided that, until elections could be held, representatives to Parliament would be appointed, chosen by the prime minister and approved by both houses. The original idea had been to appoint deputies who had served in an elected body, but all such bodies had been eliminated under the royal dictatorship of King Carol. Therefore Teleki selected a number of representatives who had earlier been members of the Hungarian party, most of whom could speak Romanian and had served in some civic or religious office.[119] He also appointed young intellectuals whom he felt represented new ideas of the younger generation, such as György Váró from the Székelyföld who was not yet thirty years old at the time of his appointment.[120]

Of the planned sixty-three representatives in the lower house, twelve were to have been Transylvanian Romanians and three Saxons, but the plan to appoint Romanians ran into conflict with the terms of the second

Vienna Award, according to which all such measures were to be reciprocal. Since the new military dictatorship in Romania eliminated all parliamentary bodies there were no Hungarian minority political representatives; therefore no Romanian representatives could be appointed.[121]

The new representatives formed the Transylvanian Party, which attempted to defend the special interests of Transylvania. In setting out the party program the president of the party, Béla Teleki, emphasized the need to concentrate on production in agriculture and organization of the small farmers, the need for technical training, and the great need for industrialization, especially in the Székelyföld in order to exploit its natural resources. In education great efforts were made to see that every Hungarian child attend a Hungarian school. In Romanian-speaking schools Hungarian was introduced as part of the curriculum, and where Romanian teachers had left, they were replaced with Hungarians who spoke Romanian. The former Kolozsvar University, which had been transplanted to Szeged, was returned, with departments of law and state, medicine, philosophy, language and history, mathematics and natural science as well as economics added. Teleki appointed eighty-three new university professors, most of them young and almost unknown, since it had been impossible for them to find academic positions in truncated Hungary. These new professors included his protégées and his own son Géza Teleki.[122]

As part of his program of reconstruction Teleki sent out a number of young social workers to the returned Transylvanian counties. Viola Tomori, who had been born in Transylvania but fled after the war, was sent to the Székelyföld, where economic development had been neglected under the Romanians. "My work in Udvarhelyszék, which was 98 percent Hungarian, was to initiate the county social service organization so that it could function independently after one year."[123]

She and two assistants sought out the crafts people of the old cottage industries, and with their help set up cottage industry courses for the youth, securing materials and orders for them: "We procured enamel for the people in Korond to make tiles, special thread for the bone lace-making of Szentkirály, yarn to weave the homespun cloth in various villages, seed grain for farmers, and good milk-producing cows for families with many children. For small self-employed craftsmen and house builders we secured long term, interest free loans."[124]

In reviving the cottage industries, they added useful features. Straw-plaiting could be used to manufacture modern women's handbags, and wide-brimmed straw hats which could also be sold in the city. A small folkart shop, opened to sell the handicraft goods directly, also provided a place for people to drop by and chat. With the attractive furnishings, books to read, and items for sale, they were able to make close contact with the people.

The need to reverse the economic and cultural backwardness that had ensued under the twenty years of Romanian rule was clear, but the interests of the Hungarians in Transylvania and of those in Hungary diverged. With the reclaimed territories the Hungarian government aimed to achieve a major reduction in unemployment at home, while many who had left after the Romanian takeover wanted to return to Transylvania. On the other hand, the Transylvanians expected positions for their own people in the various offices and public services, which until then had been held mainly by Romanians. In order to change over the administration from Romanian back to Hungarian, the government sent in a large number of officials versed in all the details of Hungarian administration. The situation was further complicated by the fact that more Romanian officials remained than the Hungarian government held desirable. To remove them police made use of terror and brutality, then announced they had decided to leave voluntarily. For similar reasons Hungarian officials from southern Transylvania came across to northern Transylvania.[125]

Hitler's Strategic Dilemma

Hitler's about-face during the summer with the surprisingly favorable terms to Hungary in the second Vienna Award may be attributed to his growing concern over the Soviet Union and the strategic dilemma he faced. After the armistice with France he had expected that the British would be ready to make peace. While waiting he took a vacation, toured the World War I trenches where he had fought, visited sights of Paris, and wandered through his favorite landscapes in southern Germany. Then he waited for a week in his Black Forest retreat for word that Churchill had finally recognized the reality of defeat. He intended his speech to the Reichstag on July 19, 1940, to expose the hopelessness of the British position: "In this hour, I feel it to be my duty before my own conscience to appeal once more to reason and common sense in Great Britain as much as elsewhere. I consider myself in a position to make this appeal since I am not the vanquished begging favors, but the victor speaking in the name of reason. I see no reason why this war must go on."[126]

With Britain's refusal to admit defeat he faced a difficult decision—whether to concentrate on Britain or the Soviets. The bombing raids had not brought Britain to the peace table, but he had not given up hope that eventually he would be able to persuade Britain to cooperate. On the other hand, from the beginning of his political career he had desired to defeat Russia and Bolshevism. Russia's acquisitions of territories, which had moved her boundary westward, infringed directly on German interests. Since the fall of Poland in September 1939, the Soviets had added about 741,000 square kilometers (about 286,000 square miles) and 20 million people. Soviet occupation and integration of the Baltic states— Latvia, Lithuania and Estonia—threatened Finland, which was effectively a German protectorate, and extended the Soviet area of control in the Baltic. An annexation of Romania's Danubian provinces would have threatened Bulgaria, a country with traditional affinities to Russia, and improved the Soviet's chances of seizing the Mediterranean entrance to the Black Sea. Although he did not believe that Russia planned to attack, the boundary changes enlarged her opportunities for further strategic expansion while narrowing those of Germany.[127]

The terms of the second Vienna Award had further strained German-Soviet relations. Germany's guarantee of Romania's new borders was aimed not only at Hungary but also at the Soviet Union. The Soviet's expansionist moves in the summer of 1940 persuaded Hitler he could not put off his planned attack on the Soviet Union. At the end of July, Hitler reversed his decision to demobilize 35 divisions, deciding to increase the army to 180 divisions and to accelerate transfer of forces to the east, so that by the spring of 1941 Germany would have 120 divisions close to the Soviet border. The Germans assumed that the war against the Soviet Union would be over quickly in summer and early fall 1941, and thus they made no preparations for winter fighting, a move which they were to sorely regret. Hitler had information on the great military purge of 1938, which had decimated and demoralized the Soviet military, and the Germans assumed that the Soviet system would rapidly collapse.[128]

Molotov was invited to Berlin on November 12, 1940, to discuss current problems in German-Soviet relations as well as the possibility of joining the Tripartite Pact, and he arrived anticipating a new general agreement with Germany. In a preliminary meeting Ribbentrop explained the German side of a bargain, directing Russia's expansion away from southeastern Europe to lands of the British Empire in the east. In return, the Soviet Union should join the Tripartite Pact. Molotov agreed in principle to joining the pact but wanted the details made clear, especially since the pact included Japan, Russia's old enemy in Asia. He showed no interest in the offer of despoiling the British Empire.

Molotov quickly clarified the Soviet Union's determination to hold Germany to all the terms of the Molotov-Ribbentrop Pact, and to pursue its own interests as a great power. The Soviet Union wanted to annex Finland, which had been assigned to its sphere of influence by the pact, to guarantee Bulgaria's frontiers, and to improve its rights of passage between the Black Sea and the Mediterranean by way of the Turkish straits. Molotov believed that the differences could be worked out, but the Germans refused to honor the prior policy on Finland; Soviet annexation of Finland would block the further advance of Germany in southeast Europe. Molotov's visit only strengthened Hitler's conviction that there was no way to deal with the Soviet Union other than war. When Molotov's draft of the treaty arrived in Berlin on November 26 with a revised protocol to join the Tripartite Pact, Hitler instructed Ribbentrop not to reply.[129]

The End to Hungary's Policy of Independence

Hoping to create a counterweight to German pressure, Hungary signed a treaty of eternal friendship with Yugoslavia in December 1940. With Germany dominating lands to the west and north and a hostile Romania to the east, neutral Yugoslavia seemed to offer the only opportunity to keep an avenue open to the West. By resigning Hungary's claims to Croatia it was hoped that an understanding might be reached on the return of other former Hungarian territories. In communications with England and neutral countries Hungarian leaders emphasized the Yugoslav treaty of eternal friendship as opening a window toward the West. Those opposed to German power greeted it enthusiastically, seeing it as an independent political step. It was unfortunate that the Hungarians agreed to accept the wording *eternal friendship*, which they had rejected at first.[130]

Despite the treaty, increased German pressure made it ever harder to maintain an independent foreign policy. By joining the Tripartite Pact Teleki had compromised Hungary in the eyes of the British, who were also extremely concerned about Hungary allowing passage of German troops to Romania. Anthony Eden, now head of the foreign ministry, explained that he understood Hungary's difficult geopolitical situation but complained that German troops continued crossing through Hungary to Romania, that Hungary had joined the Tripartite Pact, and that the Hungarian press had adopted a pro-German tone.[131] Although Britain had verbally accepted the first Vienna Award as in agreement with international law, they now informed Barcza that His Majesty's Government did not recognize the award since it had not been granted by all four powers.

In January Barcza was also informed that His Majesty's Government did not recognize Hungary's possession of Ruthenia, even though at the time in March 1939 they had rejoiced that it had come under Hungarian and not German control.[132]

From the time of Mussolini's failed attack on Greece on October 28, 1940, Germany had exerted unrelenting pressure on Yugoslavia to accede to the Tripartite Pact. As a result of the attack, the British occupied Crete and received permission to establish troops in southern Greece within bombing range of the Ploesti oil fields. Hitler now felt himself bound to mount an invasion of Greece and needed to secure his rear with Yugoslavia. The Yugoslavs resisted with great courage, despite an unusually favorable offer from Hitler, who was prepared to guarantee Yugoslavia's territorial integrity. Yugoslavia would not be required to furnish military assistance or even to allow its territory to be used for stations or transporting alien troops. Germany continued its pressure, pointing out that if Yugoslavia refused it would no longer be allowed to remain politically neutral but would be considered an enemy country.[133]

During the period of prolonged discussions between Yugoslav and Hungarian representatives, the news that the Germans were ready to guarantee Yugoslavia's territorial integrity created unease in Budapest, since a clause in the Treaty of Eternal Friendship left open the possibility of the peaceful agreement over Hungary's lost territories. The newly appointed foreign minister, László Bárdossy, strongly criticized the recognition of the Yugoslav borders, emphasizing that Hungary had never given up its territorial claims, of which the Yugoslav government was well aware. In the now familiar German practice of making conflicting promises, the Germans assured Bárdossy that Germany recognized Hungary's revisionist claims and nothing in the Yugoslav assurances would interfere, that Hungary's rightful territorial claims were in good hands.[134]

Eventually, on March 17, in a mixed vote of the Crown Council session headed by the Anglophile Prince Regent Paul, Yugoslavia agreed to join the pact and the signatures were entered at Vienna on March 25. But the Serbian population perceived the signing of the treaty as a betrayal of their national interest, tradition, and honor, going against the grain of Serbia's history. On the night of March 26–27, a group of Serb officers led by General Borivoje Mirković carried out a bloodless military coup, denouncing the treaty, forcing Prince Paul to resign as regent, and installing the young King Peter as monarch. Although the coup was bound to provoke the Germans, the Serb patriots, egged on by the Americans and the British, ignored the danger.[135]

In Belgrade the street crowds were ecstatic, shouting: "Bolje rat nego Pakt" (Better war than the pact); "bolje grob nego rob" (better the grave than a slave); "nema rata bez Srba" (no war without Serbs). But Croats in Zagreb and Slovens in Ljubljana were resentful that the Serbs had unilaterally committed the country to the almost certain war. Hitler was enraged. The new premier, General Dušan Simović, desperately tried to stave off German retribution, announcing that the postcoup government accepted all international obligations of its predecessors—that the causes of coup were exclusively internal, but all efforts to appease Hitler were futile.

With the arrival of news of the Belgrade coup on March 27, 1941, Hitler sent Döme Sztójay, Hungarian minister in Berlin, on a special plane to personally deliver his urgent message to Horthy. Teleki hastily returned from his family home in Pribékfalu in Hungarian northern Transylvania, arriving several hours after Sztójay. He and Foreign Minister Bárdossy hurried to the regent, where an excited Sztójay reported with enthusiasm his unexpected reception by Hitler. Hitler informed him that he was preparing for armed action against Yugoslavia, and it would be appropriate if Hungary too were to take certain military measures, making it clear that Hungary would naturally regain its former territories, including the Bácska, Bánát, and perhaps even Croatia.[136]

Horthy, who had become obsessed with the slogan Justice for Hungary, reacted with unrestrained enthusiasm, immediately composing a letter offering Hitler unconditional participation in the planned invasion. Aghast, Teleki protested that Hungary could not stab in the back people to whom they had sworn eternal friendship. With Bardossy's help, after a discussion lasting late into the night, they persuaded Horthy to sleep on his decision.

Teleki realized it would be extremely difficult not to accept the German proposal. The situation offered an unparalleled opportunity for revision which otherwise might have to wait for years. The territories included the rich food reserves of the Bácska, the mineral oil fields of Muraköz, and the Bánát, densely populated by Swabians. Formerly pro-Hungarian, the Swabian population had become intensely nationalistic and had formulated plans to create a German autonomous region, the Prince Eugen Gau, including the former Hungarian territories of Yugoslavia. If Hungary refused the Germans might make this territory autonomous or offer it to Romania. Yet the proposal completely upset Teleki's plans to regain southern Transylvania and to consolidate the newly re-claimed territories. Even more importantly, Hungary would be breaking the recently signed treaty of eternal friendship with Yugoslavia.

German troops would have to cross through Hungary to carry out Hitler's plans. If the Hungarian government refused, the troops would cross anyway. Teleki was most concerned about the British attitude, since he had hoped all along to win their understanding for Hungary's unten-able position. At the time that Hungary had allowed German training troops to pass through their territory to Romania, Britain had announced they would break diplomatic relations if Hungary allowed its territory to be used as a military base to launch attacks on Britain's allies.

In their response to Hitler, Teleki and Bárdossy managed to include a formulation to evade certain possibly dangerous obligations. Hungary would support Germany *in accordance with its power,* but it needed to take into account the Soviet and Romanian danger. Teleki believed that the letter was ambiguous enough to enable Hungary to avoid action, but the Germans, encouraged by Sztójay who delivered the message, took the letter to indicate Hungary's willingness to participate in the attack. Their interpretation was enforced by the clause that the German High Com-mand should get in touch with the Hungarian military command which also signified to Hitler that Hungary was ready to participate. He had already sent Colonel Kinzel from the German general staff to carry on preliminary negotiations with Werth, who demanded the mobilization of five army corps and two motorized and two cavalry brigades.[137]

During the following days, Teleki tried for a solution that would per-mit armed occupation of the proffered territories without breaking off relations with Great Britain and going to war. He persuaded the Council of Ministers to agree to conditions stipulating that the Hungarian army should join in action only after Yugoslavia had already disintegrated and Croatia had declared independence, which would create a power vacuum in the ex-Hungarian territories. Mobilization should be limited, large enough only to protect the Hungarian minority in Yugoslavia. Hungarian troops should not be deployed outside of the former Hungarian territories and should not become subordinated to the Germans. In an effort to prevent breaking of relations with Britain he wrote a long secret letter to Barcza in London with instructions on how to present the Hungarian cause to the British.[138]

In the meantime, disregarding Teleki's stipulations, Chief of the Gen-eral Staff Werth and Colonel Dezső László, chief of the operational staff, were negotiating with General Friedrich Paulus for large scale mobilization. Werth believed the German army invincible and that Hungary needed to give evidence of its unshakeable friendship. They ignored the warning that such large-scale mobilization would have alarming consequences at the time of important agricultural work in springtime with the danger of floods harming the harvest. In contradiction to the conditions set by the Council of Ministers, they agreed on Hungarian military operations in Croatia, which had once been part of Hungarian territory, but also, if needed in Serbian territories, thus undermining Teleki's efforts to keep Hungarian troops within the borders of the former Hungarian territory.

Horthy, influenced by one of his moderate advisors, Count Maurice Esterházy, had become less sure of the wisdom of Hungary's participation. At the meeting of the Supreme Council of Defense on April 1, Werth submitted the agreements, which had already been made with the German and Hungarian general staffs, and asked for authority to mobilize, but Teleki and Bárdossy were able to persuade the regent to make some compromises. Horthy's role as commander in chief was to be strongly underlined—only Horthy could order mobilization, and the Hungarian army was not to enter Croatian or Serbian territories. Teleki, the last to speak, expressed anxiety about the delicate nature of the dangerous undertaking but agreed that they should go ahead.[139]

Teleki had been under intense stress for months, realizing that he had ever decreasing ability to maneuver. It is probable that at the end of March, he received information that his wife, who had been ill for some time, had only a few months to live. His mother, his confidant in political as well as family matters, was also suffering from deteriorating health. He had long been subject to depression and during the last months struggled with insomnia. On April 2 Teleki appeared to behave normally. He showed up in parliament and chatted with the members. He visited his wife in the Park Sanatorium and participated in pre-Easter religious exercises for scout officers in the chapel of the Basilica. In a letter to a personal friend, Gábor Apor, Hungarian minister to the Vatican City, which remained unfinished, he wrote, "This Yugo affair has put us into a most dreadful situation. . . ." About his efforts to put limits on mobilization, he explained: "But my position is incredibly difficult, because the regent, the army, half of the government, and the majority of Parliament in this case are against me."[140]

At some point he called on Bárdossy where he found a telegram from Barcza awaiting him with the information that if the Hungarians allowed the Germans to use the country's territory as a military base the British would break off diplomatic relations. If they joined in a German attack the British would possibly declare war. Barcza explained that Hungarian reasons and motives "will hardly be understood here, and if either of the mentioned exigencies arise the whole Anglo-American world will charge us with breach of treaty and possibly with attacking our new friends from the rear." Bárdossy tried to calm Teleki, but he was distraught. "I have done all I could! I cannot do any more!"[141]

That night from his office and residence at the Sándor Palace, Teleki called Elemér Újpétery, the Foreign Service secretary on duty in the Foreign Ministry on Dísz square, and asked him to bring over the copy of Barcza's message. Újpétery, who had known Teleki—his favorite professor—since student days, found Teleki perfectly calm, and told him to call if he needed anything more.[142] On Teleki's return to his office he probably had received several more pieces of information, including the news that German troops had already started to press forward through Hungary. In the early morning hours of April 3, 1941, Teleki committed suicide.

In a suicide note to the regent, he wrote: "Your Serene Highness: we have become breakers of our word—out of cowardice—in defiance of the Treaty of Eternal Friendship based on the Mohács speech. . . . We have placed ourselves at the side of scoundrels. . . . We shall be robbers of corpses! the most abominable nation. I did not keep you back. I am guilty. April 3, 1941. Pál Teleki."[143]

In his last conversation with Teleki around Christmas 1940, Barcza had asked: "What will happen with us, Bóli?" Teleki answered: "I'd like to know myself. We have to go with the Germans, nothing else is possible, but only to a certain point. And that point is taking part in the war. On no account will we do that, ... But it's unbelievably difficult, maybe impossible to oppose it. Revision, and I'd only say this to you, is the greatest danger that threatens, but I cannot do anything against it, because I would be finished. The public has gone crazy. They want everything back! No matter how, and no matter at what price. . . . I'll struggle as long as I can hold out, . . . I'll defend our honor, I won't give up the nation and the country, but if I cannot succeed I will shoot myself in the head."[144]

Teleki's death was not made public until the afternoon of April 4; no one could believe that Teleki, known to be a devout Catholic, had committed suicide. In his report to the German foreign minister, Erdmannsdorff explained Teleki's death on his personal crisis at the breaking of the Treaty of Eternal Friendship with Yugoslavia. On learning the news the regent ordered mobilization stopped, but in a typical pattern he later relented and agreed to the mobilization of two army corps.

The decision to join the war on Yugoslavia ended any hope for an émigré government. Horthy told O'Malley, when he came to see him soon after Teleki's death was announced, that the decision on Yugoslavia had been made. Horthy considered it his sacred duty to restore the frontiers of Hungary. He also complained that Hungary could expect no help from Great Britain; he had received no invitation from London for the émigré government. O'Malley tried to persuade him that Hungary should not take advantage of Yugoslavia, but Horthy declared that his mind was made up.[145]

The Invasion of Yugoslavia

As foreign minister, Bárdossy had worked closely with Teleki on negotiations with the Germans over the Yugoslav crisis. Now named prime minister he remained true to the Teleki formula, only to enter the Hungarian populated territories after Yugoslavia fell apart. In his meeting with the government party, the members voted that the Yugoslav treaty remained in effect. Only if the Yugoslav state broke up would Hungary take back its former territories.

On April 6, 1941, Germany, Italy, and Bulgaria all declared war on Yugoslavia. Hitler, furious at the Belgrade coup, took devastating revenge on those who had dared to cross him. Within hours of the coup he had directed the Wehrmacht, Germany's unified defense force, to smash Yugoslavia, ignoring all pleas for consultation. He was not even deterred by Stalin's last-minute Treaty of Friendship and Nonaggression with Yugoslavia on April 5. The Germans conducted a massive four-day attack on Belgrade, turning the center into smoking ruins, and the German army poured across the Yugoslav borders from different directions. Bulgarian troops crossed the Yugoslav-Macedonia border on the April 9 and Italy occupied Dalmatia and Ljubljana.

Hungary still remained passive. Withstanding intense German pressure Bárdossy told Erdmannsdorff that Hungary would take action only if the Yugoslav state disintegrated and Croatia declared independence. On April 10 retired General Kvaternik proclaimed Croatia's separation from the Yugoslav kingdom and the formation of an independent Croatian state, which provided the proof for the disintegration of Yugoslavia, that Hungary had anticipated. Soon afterward Radio Budapest broadcast Horthy's order to the military to take back the Hungarian populated Délvidek up to the former border of the kingdom. Late that evening at a meeting of the council of ministers, a long, carefully worded proclamation was drawn up, signed by Horthy and Bárdossy, stating that Hungary must protect the Hungarian population broken off from Hungary in 1918 and secure their safety. Bárdossy hoped that the wording of the proclamation would win the understanding of the Allies.

Early on the morning of April 11, the Hungarian army marched into the pre-Trianon southern provinces, with the exception of the Bánát, which had been occupied by Germany. The Yugoslav army had already withdrawn. The territories included the Bácska, the triangle of territory between the Danube and the Drava rivers, the Muraköz and the Muravidék, in all another 11,417 square kilometers of territory.[146] There were about 370,000 Hungarians among the population of over one million, while large numbers of non-Magyars left the newly annexed territories.

The military annexation precluded the possibility of any further talk of peaceful territorial expansion. On April 7 O'Malley notified the Hungarian government that Britain had broken off diplomatic relations. British First Secretary Eden told the departing Barcza that at the future peace conference Britain would not forget that Hungary had violated its pact with Yugoslavia. But since this was the only immediate reaction it strengthened the conviction among much of the Hungarian population that a close alliance with Germany would lead to the regaining of former Hungarian territories. Yet since none of the states from which Hungary had regained territory accepted the territorial gains, the Germans gained even more leverage to play off one country against another and increase their influence.[147]

5

Hungary Enters the War

Less than three months after Teleki's suicide, Hungary entered into a state of war with the Soviet Union. With the declaration of a state of war by the new prime minister, László Bárdossy, Hungary took the fateful step, deviating from the policy of neutrality under Teleki and the early Bárdossy ministry. At the time everyone expected that it would be another short war with Germany emerging victorious. Hungarian Chief of the General Staff Heinrich Werth predicted a six-week blitzkrieg. A year earlier the Germans had swept through western Europe, conquering one country after another, and Hitler expected to be in Moscow in the fall of 1941. Participation seemed a small price to pay for Germany's favor.

In the meantime, Hungary was experiencing a wartime economic boom.[1] The public enjoyed the first period of prosperity in decades, with increases in employment, development of heavy industry, better conditions for the agrarian population, and the beginnings of social reforms. Hungary was an island of plenty in the middle of Europe; the country did not participate in the war until June 1941 and then with only a small force. The official press lauded the Hungarian military and its supposed victories in regaining the territories in southern Slovakia, Ruthenia, and northern Yugoslavia.

Each week the newsreels, playing dramatic music in the background, depicted Hungary regaining its lost territories: First came the map of the thousand-year-old kingdom outlined in white, and superimposed on it the map of truncated Hungary. Then, piece by piece, a white line delineates each of the recovered territories, first northern Hungary, then Ruthenia, then Transylvania, and then northern Yugoslavia. With the war boom the film industry prospered—the weekly cinema became a favorite source of entertainment for young people, workers seeking inexpensive entertainment, soldiers on a day off, shop assistants, minor clerks, servants. The Horthy regime had never been so popular. With the return of part of the territories and the startling German victories, it is not surprising that much of the population believed that the German alliance continued to be favorable for Hungary. Yet problems with the expansion of industry, the efforts to provide equipment for the troops, mobilization, and the increasing German demands signaled problems to come.

The Kassa Incident

By spring 1941 Hungarian leaders knew of Hitler's plans for the attack on the Soviet Union, codenamed Barbarossa, but the Hungarian political leadership had no intention of joining Hitler's campaign. Hungary had no claims against the Soviet Union and nothing to gain from entering the war. Bárdossy, carefully following Teleki's program of armed neutrality, resisted pressure from military officers who were eager to join Germany in the war.

Hitler himself did not consider Hungarian participation necessary. He planned to drive through the Soviet frontier positions with three army panzer spearheads, then quickly encircle and crush the Red Army, thus avoiding the fate of Napoleon. He did count on Finnish and Romanian cooperation since both countries were strategically located for attacks against parts of the USSR. Unlike Hungary, which had no territorial demands against the Soviets, they had each recently lost territory to the Soviet Union. Contrary to the situation with the invasion of Yugoslavia, the Germans did not need to use Hungarian territory. A few of Hitler's senior commanders and staff officers had their doubts about the invasion, worrying about being engulfed in the vast spaces of the Russian interior, and individual generals believed it better to conquer Britain first and avoid the danger of a war on two fronts. Still the war with Russia appeared inevitable and collectively they kept their doubts to themselves.[2]

Hitler was astoundingly optimistic about the success of his invasion. The poor showing of the Red Army in the Winter War against tiny Finland had encouraged him to write off the Soviets' ability to resist a German invasion. He believed that Stalin's drastic purge of the higher officers of the Soviet military had fatally weakened the Russian army.[3] Because of faulty industrial intelligence he knew nothing of the progress made by the Soviet military industry in the development of new and advanced armored vehicles, especially the new tank, T-34, which proved to be the best tank in any army. He was also ignorant of the Soviet's new industrial cities being built east of the Urals. He remarked to his general staff: "In terms of weapons, the Russian soldier is as inferior to us as the French. He has a few modern field batteries, everything else is old, reconditioned material . . . the bulk of the Russian tank forces is poorly armored. The

Russian human material is inferior. The armies are leaderless."[4] He assumed that the German forces would defeat the Soviet army as quickly as they had defeated the French in May. It would be only a matter of weeks until they reached Moscow.

However, Gerd von Rundstedt, commander of Army Group South, did consider Hungarian support desirable. He indicated the need to strengthen his right wing with support from Hungarian territory, but Hitler rejected his concerns, referring to the reluctance of the Hungarian political leadership to join in previous attacks against Czechoslovakia and Poland. In June Hungary received indications that the Germans would welcome Hungarian voluntary participation in the war, but that Hitler did not want to request participation, fearing that in return Hungary would make further territorial demands.

The initial German attack on the Soviet Union, beginning on June 22, was extremely successful. The advance of the Panzer spearheads was so rapid that the German infantry had difficulty catching up. Taken completely by surprise the Soviets were unprepared; in light of Russia's newly gained territories in the west, Stalin had advanced his line of defense close to the frontier, and the fortifications were far from complete. The German Panzer spearheads broke through the Stalin line easily, leaving the Soviet troops open to attack by the advancing infantry who were able to encircle and destroy them at leisure. The armored divisions launched forward at eighty kilometers a day, while the plodding infantry labored across the steppe at thirty-two kilometers a day or less, with fifty pounds of equipment on their shoulders.[5]

Confirming the doubts of Rundstedt, the progress of Army Group South was slower than that of the other two army groups; the Seventeenth Army pushed forward only ten to twelve kilometers on the first day. On June 25, 1941, the chief of staff of Army South repeated his request for the intervention of troops from Hungary. He pointed out that this would be a significant unburdening of the Seventeenth Army's south wing and help the attack of the Eleventh Army. The answer came from the Oberkommando des Heeres (OKH), Nazi Germany's High Command of the Army—"the question of Hungarian participation is still open."[6] Halder noted in his diary of June 25: "Hungary's collaboration would be desirable. Hungary, however, wants to be asked officially. The Führer will not do that, for political reasons."[7]

All this changed on June 26 at a few minutes after one o'clock in the afternoon when three unidentified planes dropped bombs on the Hungarian city of Kassa. The bombs struck the post and telegraph office, a settlement and several homes, leaving several dead and a larger number wounded. One bomb failed to explode and was found to be of Russian manufacture. The planes then disappeared toward the southeast, the direction from which they had come. The local military authorities concluded that Soviet planes were responsible, but to this day the question of responsibility has not been solved. Many Hungarians believed that the Germans had used the bombing as a trick to bring Hungary into the war, but absolutely no German documents have turned up to support this thesis. The Russians denied responsibility.[8]

When the news reached Budapest, the minister of defense, Károly Bartha, and Chief of the General Staff Henrik Werth rushed to tell the regent what had happened. Horthy's immediate reaction was indignation—the country had been attacked! His sense of honor required that he act. On the spot he ordered that appropriate retaliatory measures be initiated, but it is not clear if he was thinking of a declaration of war or only reprisals. Horthy, who was apolitical, was always prone to making quick impulsive decisions, which he could be talked out of later by calmer minds. His respected advisors, Moricz Esterházy or István Bethlen, had been able to talk the regent out of hasty actions in other situations, but both Bartha and Werth were eager for war.[9]

By the time Bárdossy heard of the incident and reached the regent, Horthy had already given the order for retaliatory measures. A career diplomat, Bárdossy had never had close relations with Horthy, and he did not attempt to counter the impulsive decision. He believed that Horthy wanted immediate action—and that this action would be war. He explained that he must first go to the Council of Ministers since only they could make a declaration of a state of war. Horthy seems to have believed that after council deliberation Bárdossy would return to him with the decision for his approval, but Bárdossy believed he had been ordered to put a decision on war into effect. Therefore there was no need to consult the regent further. Later Horthy charged that Bárdossy had presented him with a *fait accompli.*[10]

One hour and twenty minutes after bombs fell on Kassa, Bárdossy summoned an emergency session of the Council of Ministers, which met so hurriedly that several members were missing. Dezső Laky, minister of public supply, arrived only at the end, and Ferenc Zsindely, secretary of state, was absent, while Antal Ullein-Reviczky, head of the foreign ministry's press division, was attending a lunch party and sent a deputy in his stead. In that short time Bárdossy had made up his mind to a complete reversal of his whole policy. At the council meeting he announced that the Soviets had bombed Kassa, and in his view Hungary should declare that as a consequence she regarded herself as in a state of war.

Opinions were divided. Minister of Defense Bartha condemned the Soviet attack as an uncalled-for provocation and made vigorous pleas to carry out reprisals. The moderate minister of the interior, Ferenc Keresztes-Fischer, thought it was too early to declare a state of war, reasoning that the bombing was not that serious an action. He believed the army was not strong enough, and that it was against the country's interests to start a war against a great power. Bálint Hóman, the pro-German minister of culture, and Reményi-Schneller, minister of finance, both supported the prime minister, claiming that Hungary should not be the only one left out of the action. Italy and Romania had joined in the war the day of the German attack and Slovakia had also joined.[11]

Bárdossy summed up the opinion of the council, that all were in favor of reprisals, and all, except Keresztes-Fischer, were in favor of stating that Hungary regarded herself as being in a state of war with Russia, but participation in military action should be as limited as possible. Evidently no vote was taken. The ministers did not seem to have realized that Bárdossy's summing-up was equivalent to agreement to a binding resolution. According to the official record of the meeting signed by Bárdossy, the ministers' decision to declare the existence of a state of war between Hungary and the USSR was unanimous, although at Bárdossy's trial in 1945, it was charged that he had falsified the evidence—that four ministers had voted against the decision.[12]

Without consulting the regent, Bárdossy immediately drafted and issued a communiqué describing the attack on Kassa as an act of unprovoked aggression by the USSR and ended by stating that in consequence "Hungary considered herself from this moment on as at war with the U.S.S.R." Later, on the advice of Ullein-Reviczky, he modified the wording to state: "In consequence of the repeated attacks made by Soviet aircraft, contrary to international law, against Hungarian territory, Hungary considers a state of war to have come into being between herself and the USSR."[13] That day he did not inform the regent of his communiqué.

The question remains why Bárdossy made the fatal step so precipitously. The Kassa incident was no *casus belli*; Molotov strongly denied Moscow's involvement.[14] There was no overt German pressure. Bárdossy said the step was inevitable but in later years historians have blamed him directly for Hungary's entry into war. Since the fall of State Socialism in 1989, many World War II officers and political figures charged with war crimes have been rehabilitated, but there is still no discussion of clearing Bárdossy's name.

Bárdossy had been appointed prime minister hastily, immediately following Teleki's suicide. Although acknowledged to be brilliant, he was often impatient. He could be charming and had been an excellent representative for Hungary in England, and successful in Bucharest in improving Hungarian Romanian relations, but he was a novice in domestic politics, not familiar with parliamentary rules and conduct. A proud and sensitive man, he was prone to make quick decisions and to make them on his own. Not patient with those around him who were less bright, he was not good at consulting others nor taking advice. To add to his impatience he had serious stomach problems. It seems that at this point he had come to the decisions on what he believed to be the correct course.[15]

The next day, June 27, Bárdossy appeared before Parliament. The standing chairman, Jenő Szinyei Merse, announced with outrage that there had been an air attack by the Soviet Air Force the day before, but there was no mention that the identity of the attackers could be questioned. He then introduced Prime Minister Bárdossy to acclamation by the House ("Hear! Hear!"). Bárdossy repeated the news of the Soviet attack. "Thus the Hungarian Royal Government decided that as a result of the attack a state of war exists between Hungary and the Soviet Union."[16] The parliamentary record states that his news was greeted by long and lively cheering and clapping from all sides. From the extreme Right came the shouts: "Out with the Social Democrats." Bárdossy continued, stating that the Hungarian army would take the necessary measures. There was no further parliamentary discussion, the house continued with a long drawn-out debate on the need to further restrict the activities of the Jews.[17] According to a later report there were at most forty representatives present. The one or two Smallholders and Social Democrat representatives immediately left the chamber and the loud clapping came from the ten to fifteen Arrow Cross representatives. The leader of one opposition party, Rassay, asked as he left the chamber, "Are you happy about this?" The government party representatives were surprised and clapped politely.[18] Bárdossy did not even appear in the upper house which received the same notification read out by the president. His failure to consult the upper house, which was taken as an insult, greatly reduced his esteem in that body.

The declaration of war was not unpopular—none of those in the opposition, neither the liberal parties nor the Social Democrats challenged the declaration. The prominent opposition leader, Bajcsy Zsilinsky, even sent a message to Bárdossy praising him for defending the country's interests, and the military were especially jubilant. Hungarians had been permeated with anti-Bolshevism ever since the catastrophic Soviet Republic of 1919, and the officers, indoctrinated with an anti-Bolshevik attitude, were infatuated with Germany and its technical advances and rapid victories. A number of the younger officers saw in Hitler's social reforms a new society. Three military commissions, which had gone to Germany in 1940–41,were unanimous in their opinion that no power on the continent could defeat the Wehrmacht. In light of Germany's rapid victories everyone thought that it would be a short war. There was no thought that Hungary's participation might entangle the country in hostilities with the West.

But the simple peasant or worker felt no enthusiasm at the prospect of fighting Russians, who meant nothing to him. Closer association with Germany was still unpopular among many Hungarians. The regent preserved a curious reticence about the war. It was many days before any Hungarian paper suggested that Horthy had ordered the campaign and he signed no order to the troops. In a speech given on June 29 to unveil a monument to the World War I fallen, he did not include a single reference to the new war.

Wartime Boom

The Győr program of March 5, 1938, had opened a new chapter in economic life, injecting one billion pengő into the system and creating a demand for labor. With the plans to use 60 percent for military purposes and the rest for infrastructure, the development of transportation and telecommunications, the way was opened to develop heavy industry, which received huge state orders for weaponry, aircraft, and tanks. In one year Hungarian industry as a whole experienced a higher degree of growth than in the whole of the previous two decades.

Despite fears of inflation the government program created a quick rise in employment and a real increase in the turnover of goods. The amount for direct armament had been raised with the increased possibility of war in 1939, and the Győr program was speeded up, to be carried out in two years rather than five. 1939 became one of the best years ever for the Hungarian economy, with the best harvest during the entire interwar period and the disappearance of marketing problems. For the first time since the end of World War I, Hungarians experiences rapid industrial expansion, full employment, and an increase in consumer spending.

The economic boom was not solely due to the impact of the rearmament program. With the territorial gains, which almost doubled the area of the country, the Hungarian population increased by 5.4 million to 14 million.[19] The return of the lost territories increased the work force and domestic market and supplied new food-growing regions and raw materials previously in scarce supply, including iron and other ores and a rich supply of timber. The recruits who swelled the army automatically raised demand; the soldiers had to be fed, and those who came from the poor peasantry consumed many more calories and animal protein than they had during peacetime. The former unemployed who flooded the workplaces created demand both for agricultural and industrial goods. Although wages in actual value stagnated this did not lead to a lessening of consumption since there were more people employed per family.

With the rise in employment and the new demands on agriculture Hungary's greatest social problem of the 1930s, the unemployment and underemployment of the agrarian population, was coming to an end. The early war years began a shift of the agrarian work force into industry which brought a significant change in the composition of the working class. As a result of the war boom over half of the working class was employed in mining, steel, and metallurgical industries, machinery production, and the chemical industry.[20] The wartime boom also affected small-scale industries and a part of the unemployed went to work for small businesses. An influx of poor workers from the returned territories migrated toward jobs in Budapest factories, and in the years from 1938 to 1943 the labor supply increased 100 percent, from 288,512 to 542,688. At first the rise in the labor force was largely due to hiring the former unemployed but soon the available unemployed were not enough to meet the demand.[21]

A combination of factors also helped to solve the serious interwar problem of unemployed young intellectuals. A number of those young people now found positions in the returned territories in the civil service, in education, and in social services. They were nicknamed parachutists and resented by those Hungarians who, after the long period of subservience to Czech or Romanian rule, had expected that they would receive these positions. The Jewish laws also provided new positions for the Christian middle class in the management of firms as well as in the theater, press, and other cultural institutions.

Since the improvement in living conditions coincided with the return of territories, it seemed to prove that the regime had been right in attributing all social and economic ills to Trianon. The country benefited from the increased trade with Germany and new agreements for agricultural goods. The wide-scale discontent, which had resulted in the rise of extreme-right parties in 1939, largely dissipated. After close to two decades in power the regent had become a father figure, a fixed point in a changing landscape, now enjoying his greatest national popularity. Horthy was a cosmopolitan figure, treated as an equal by foreign dignitaries; he appeared often in the newsreels and in public, showing off his happy family as well as his giant tattoo, acquired during his naval tours.[22] The people also loved his wife, Magda, for her gentle manner and active work in national charities. The price of these benefits was increased dependence on Germany, but the harmful effects were not experienced until later in the war.

PROBLEMS WITH INDUSTRIAL DEVELOPMENT

On receiving the first orders placed through the Győr Program, industrialists discovered that they needed to enlarge the capacity of their plants, modernize their technology, and above all increase the number of skilled workers. A continuing problem throughout the war was the small number of skilled workers, partially because of the low level of education and general lack of mechanical knowledge. Few men knew how to drive a car. Even the large state-owned MÁVAG ammunition factory had to double its capacity in order to produce the planned five hundred artillery pieces in three years.

At first the Ministry of Defense tried to save money by not setting a final price for its orders and attempting to avoid giving any initial payment, hoping to whittle down the price during production. Since the factories had to make major investments to order material, new machinery, and increase their capacity, this caused major difficulties and foot-dragging. The industrialist Ferenc Chorin protested that the burdens of military orders were endangering the industry. As a result, the Ministry of Finance made capital available for loans to firms, but even this did not solve the problems. Many plants asked for the extension of deadlines since the necessary materials were not reaching them in time because of delivery and coordination problems.[23]

The general staff had counted heavily on German support, planning to buy licenses for tanks and other equipment from the Germans so they could produce these on their own. They were sorely disappointed when, in consultations in 1937, the Germans let their Hungarian partners know there was absolutely no hope of purchasing licenses for important weapons. They were unwilling to sell licenses for manufacture and only reluctantly agreed to sell certain weapons—namely those weapons produced for export which were of lesser quality.[24] This was a blow to Hungarian hopes for modernization, which depended heavily on the availability of German imports.

At the time the Germans were following their policy of discouraging or even preventing industrial development in the southeast European countries. Hungary should supply raw materials in return for those goods that Germany chose to export. The head of the Foreign Ministry's department for economic policies, Alfréd Nickl, commented that the "Germans want to send us those goods that we really do not need, . . . and take from us those goods that we would need. . . ."[25] The Germans let it be known that industrial development in Hungary and other southeastern European countries "was incompatible with the agricultural character of these countries." They would have to adjust their economies "to the demands of the continental economy."[26]

Industrialists also worried that after increasing production capacity to meet the sudden need they would be left with superfluous capacity. Soon after the return of northern Hungary in the first Vienna Award, the Weiss-Manfréd factory sent a worried letter to the Ministry of Industry: "Over the past weeks the Ministry of Defense has wished to accelerate the production of war materials to such an extraordinary extent, that the manufacture of the quantities in question at the required pace needed the considerable extension of the workshops and facilities. After the termination of the present war preparations, probably in the near future, these costly investments would become redundant."[27]

Prime Minister Teleki also feared unemployment and unused industrial capacity after the target for war production had been met. But in fact overall production increased during 1939. By summer, the volume of manufactured goods was 22 percent greater than a year before, and the employed number reached 769,000—a new high.

The first half of 1940 again brought an increase of about 10 percent in production, although there was a downturn in the economy in the second half of 1940. A bad harvest decreased purchasing power in agriculture, which led to some food shortages and curtailed the amount of goods for export. Italy's entry into the war meant that certain supplies of raw materials were cut off, which harmed light industries in particular. Shortages of cotton, wool, and leather produced serious reduction in the output of these industries. Still, the achievement of the past years—with the vast increase in demand for labor, an end to mass unemployment, and a rise of income as a result of the increased labor force and improved wages, as well as a sharp increase in investment—all contributed to a much stronger economy than ever before.[28]

Yet working conditions in wartime heavy industry were less than ideal. The changeover of industry to wartime production was complicated by conflicts between military and civilian authorities. In 1938 war production was completely disorganized—there was no chain of command and it was not clear who had what powers and responsibilities. Officials from the Ministry of Defense could intervene directly in a factory, even giving orders that disturbed productivity. The plan to mobilize industry for wartime production soon spun unforeseen problems. Factories declared necessary for war production were to be placed under military supervision, and the military commanders assigned to the factories were intended to be experts in the industries to which they were assigned, but retired officers with little or no knowledge of industry had been called in temporarily as a forced solution. It soon became apparent that the great majority were completely incapable of fulfilling their responsibilities.[29]

The commanders were granted extensive powers. They were to supervise the workers, oversee their social situation, pay attention to workers' mood, and watch for spying, sabotage, and propaganda. In factories with more than two hundred workers the military commander could pressure workers through fines or even put them before a military court. No strikes were to be allowed, and if a strike should occur participants could be sentenced for ten to fifteen years or, depending on conditions, even for life. Reprisals like those at the National Worsted Mill were common. Some of the workers charged with absenteeism were sentenced to three and four weeks' imprisonment, augmented with one day of fasting weekly.[30]

Conflicts also developed between orders for mobilization and the need to exempt skilled workers in war industries. Those workers who were considered absolutely necessary to carry out the wartime tasks—such as engineers, technical experts, and skilled laborers—were to be exempted from military service. The most necessary industries were placed in an A category, and at the time for mobilization on August 15, directors were to give a list of exempted names to the district military command which would forward it for approval to the Ministry of Defense. Those industries considered less essential, the B category industries, were to submit the list of exemptions to the responsible minister—but only six days after mobilization. The increase of military orders brought more factories into war production that had not been included in the original categories. As a result some of the protected workers were called up in the mobilization of September 1938, but then it became necessary to demobilize them. This was not a simple matter since the troops had already been taken to the border for arms practice, and each worker had to be demobilized individually.[31]

Some officers would have liked to fully militarize the factories but the idea was foreign to political leaders and to industrialists who considered it too dictatorial.[32] Finally, in March 1939 a new defense law was passed which opened the way for the military direction of the economy. The law spelled out conditions stipulating that even during peacetime factories should work out detailed plans for war production and should stockpile various materials. With the German attack on Poland signaling the outbreak of war, the government went over to a war economy, and the law of September 1, 1939, proclaiming a state of emergency powers, came into force.

HUNGARIAN WORKERS IN GERMANY

With the introduction of a war economy and increased demand for labor, the government looked less favorably on German demands for workers, especially because of German working conditions. The labor shortage in Germany led to an increased demand for Hungarian labor, and in 1941 a joint government agreement determined that 6,000 Hungarian workers would be sent. At the time the Hungarian government was happy to make the agreement, since their extra manpower would be occupied and would be trained in various branches of machine production and the aircraft industry in German factories. In the beginning a fair number of workers signed up, taken in by the promises of German propaganda, but the German work conditions quickly made them lose their illusions and regret their decision.

Often living conditions were poor, with workers housed in wet, flea ridden, poorly furnished places. There were problems with German food, very different from what the Hungarians were accustomed to. In their weekly allowance of foodstuffs, the workers received potatoes, milk, bread, porridge, rye flour, wheat flower, lard, and salt, but Hungarians missed the staples in their traditional diet—fat-bacon, paprika, wine. For that reason, in 1939 the government arranged that Hungarian workers could buy per head and per month duty-free fat-bacon, *tarhonya* [barley pasta], and wine. In 1940, red paprika was added.[33] One worker complained: "We can't say anything good about the food, ... We ate potatoes all the time, every day dinner was potatoes. Only on Sunday when everyone cooked for himself I made a little meat soup. Luckily, after a while we were able to get discounted bacon and paprika from Hungary. We got seven deciliter of milk a day, milk made up our breakfast and supper. We got four and a half kilo of bread a week, but always one and a half kilos were missing. . . ."[34]

The minister of industry, Jószef Varga, asked for 4,000 pengő from the Council of Ministers in December 1941 to send Christmas packages to the workers in Germany, to try to lighten their conditions, which were much worse than expected. He also suggested that officials be sent to visit the workers and listen to their complaints. The flight of some workers and those put into punishment institutions showed the seriousness of the situation. In 1941, at a time when the state of German provisions was worsening, two representatives from the Ministry of Agriculture reported on the quality of workers' provisions: "In comparison to the past, the provisioning of our workers is weak. The German employers . . . cannot provision the workers as in the past. For example the majority of the employers give margarine instead of lard, or in the best case they give the workers butter, with which the Hungarian worker does not know how to cook. Often they don't get legumes and they seldom can eat meat."[35]

Hungarian workers also had difficulty keeping up with the pace expected of German workers. "The unaccustomed work tempo is very hard on the weak, poorly fed workers. The employers complain a great deal about the Hungarian workers' lack of productivity." Hungarian workers who went to work were often ill or not prepared; some had tuberculosis, some of the women were pregnant. Some of the older men who could not do the work were sent home. The women were paid less but often put to even harder work, and were at the mercy of foremen.[36] Under such conditions it was not surprising that in May 1942 the Germans complained that according to the agreement there was a lack of 1,500 workers. For the Hungarians the work there had lost all its appeal, while the new demand for workers in Hungary made it more difficult to export labor. It was decided that it would be desirable to bring the workers home as soon as possible for vacation, and to use the skilled workers to man the Hungarian airplane factories.[37]

THE AGRARIAN POPULATION

The wartime boom of the early war years was especially favorable to the agrarian population. During the depression years there had been no market for their produce, and many small landowners had been unable to pay their debts and faced the auctioning off of their land, while agrarian workers on the large estates worked fewer days, and day workers' salaries were cut in half. But now there was new reason to work hard and strive for something better. The peasants were able to produce surpluses, knowing that they would be bought and paid for. The government began requisitions in 1940 and 1941 but when government prices were set too low, independent peasants increased their own consumption or sold their goods on the flourishing black market. With a market for their produce and higher overall employment, people in the villages had more expendable income and a healthier diet. Electricity was introduced in some villages, cheap radios and bicycles were available, as well as manufactured small engines that could be used for various purposes. Now that they had a little spare time and money, there was some hope to get ahead if you made an effort.

Beginning in 1939 the Hungarian government faced the problem of securing adequate food supplies. The harvest of 1938 had been excellent, but from 1939 on the agricultural surplus of the depression years suddenly changed to scarcity. Toward the end of 1940 there were already shortages of food, mainly as a result of hoarding, but then serious floods during the cold rainy autumn and renewed floods in February made a bad harvest a certainty. It was now necessary to feed an enlarged army, provide food to the recovered territories, and deal with the increased domestic consumption as a result of the economic boom.

In addition, demands of the German government for agricultural goods kept increasing. By 1939, because of their dwindling reserves, the Hungarians were less interested in exporting to Germany, and one of most delicate issues of Hungarian-German economic relations became the size and composition of Hungarian agricultural exports versus industrial growth. The Germans pressured Hungary to reduce her industry and increase her agricultural production, but Germany was recalcitrant in supplying Hungary with the industrial goods it needed, particularly military supplies. Spare parts ordered from Germany which were indispensable for the production of Hungarian vehicles and weapons became more and more difficult to procure.[38]

At first the government attempted to use forceful methods to collect surplus agricultural products, but their methods were often counter-productive. Before the harvest of 1940 an order stipulated that the remainder of wheat and corn from the previous year be offered for central collection, but since there was no registration of yields, the government had no way to force producers to sell their excess. In addition, the government was dealing with two very different modes of production and interests. The landed estates were capitalistic enterprises producing for the domestic and international market, but the market played a secondary role for the small peasants, who farmed mainly to provide subsistence for their families. The prices, set through central price regulation, were considered much too low, well below the black market prices, which angered both large landowners and peasant farmers. Low prices encouraged large farms to leave land fallow and smaller producers to consume more, as well as to hoard. There was a danger of a real drop in production.

The large enterprises formed a strong agrarian lobby, which was represented in Parliament and controlled local governments as well. The lobby, which considered the prices "offensively low," demanded a price rise of over 40 percent, and warned the government to give serious consideration to their proposals. Landowners cut back the sowing area of winter crops by 30 percent and announced that they would refuse to obey mandated deliveries unless the fixed prices covered costs of production and left far larger reserves for estate consumption than before.[39]

Various government measures, including the calling-in of troops in the spring of 1941, were not only costly but also resulted in unfavorable yields and turned both large and small producers against the government. In addition the government confounded the situation through contradictory measures, actually rewarding peasants who had not fulfilled the compulsory delivery by offering to pay more if they were willing to sell their reserves to the state. In response to army intervention, large estates threatened to cut back production, while the smaller ones began to withdraw from trade, dynamically increasing their livestock to tide over the bad times. With the continuation of restrictions producers reduced the sowing area of those crops most liable to delivery, cutting back exactly those goods that were needed.

The solution finally was found in November 1942 with the plan proposed by Béla Jurcsek, new head of the National Office for Public Supply. The Jurcsek plan changed the procedure of imposing compulsory levies, reversing the sequence and encouraging production. Rather than turning over excess crops after the harvest, a fixed quota of crops was to be handed in irrespective of harvest yields. The requirements from each producer were prescribed in advance and broken down by individual estates, and the quota determined in the spring on the basis of the size of the arable area which forced the peasants to produce instead of leaving the fields fallow. After that the producer could dispose of the remaining crops as he pleased. The Jurcsek plan, far more successful than earlier measures, halted the decline of agricultural production and increased the sown area for cereals.

Although wages of agricultural employees generally remained behind those in the industry, wages were paid partially in crops, so that consumption of food products was not reduced. Rather it grew because of increased employment and as a result of the draft.[40] The government had learned from World War I that it had to pay families something if their young men were taken as soldiers. The effects of mobilization were not too onerous until total mobilization under the German occupation in the spring of 1944.

social reforms

The period of prosperity and relaxation of social tensions made possible the introduction of several social reforms. In September 1939 the government introduced a proposal for an allowance for the widows of workers, and in December a law was introduced to modify the public health law by adding a number of health protection measures, including raising the number of beds in hospitals and compulsory medical treatment. In 1940 a ministerial order was issued that united all healthcare agencies under a National Health Protection Association.

The most far-reaching reform was that for social housing, ONCSA, the National Foundation for the Protection of the People and the Family. The project aimed to support large agricultural families with four or more children by providing them with family homes and a vegetable garden. The foundation was to provide 402,308 families whose existence was endangered with housing, social welfare co-operatives and possible resettlement to land where economic conditions were better. The plan was intended to bring about more social equality and to promote an increase of population.

ONCSA was only to be the beginning of a larger social welfare program. The greatest allotment was for the building of houses, help with kitchen-gardens, live stock, home industry, materials, and organization of production and sales. It also included some charitable aid—free milk and sugar, food for children's day care, and summer children's homes. ONCSA grew to become a huge organization, active in almost every village, where social workers taught the women cooking and health protection. The work was supported by the populist writers, and young engineers and architects were involved. With the help of interest-free loans some 12,000 one- and two-room flats were built.[41]

A debate on land reform began in the house on October 10, 1939. A redistribution of land had long been on the list of reforms demanded by the agrarian population, but the question of land reform was fraught with difficulties—some of political consideration, but also questions of practicality and economic benefit. Horthy had once commented that there was not enough land in Hungary for all of the peasants who demanded a piece of it. Large landowners, and especially the Roman Catholic Church, were natural opponents of land redistribution. Also the example of land reform in other countries showed that the results were not necessarily as beneficial as had been expected. The plan was criticized both by liberals and conservatives, and because of disagreements the law was not announced until April 1940. From the details it is clear that the reform would have been the most acceptable change of land ownership in the Horthy era, but with the outbreak of war nothing came of the land reform.[42]

EDUCATION FOR THE PEASANTRY

With the improved economic situation attention turned to improving the education of the peasantry. In 1941 a School Reform Bill introduced eight years of required elementary school education to extend the former required six years. But providing education for peasant youth was not as simple as the passage of a bill. It was extremely difficult to reach village youth, who lived in scattered villages and settlements and often had little contact with the outside world. Although elementary schools existed in most villages, many peasant children attended school only irregularly and dropped out early because their labor was required at home.

In the 1930s leaders of a Protestant YMCA, in an education program for village youth, found that many of the youth, ages sixteen to twenty-one, had forgotten how to write and had little opportunity to read. With intensive effort the program grew and by the late 1930s more than 75 percent of the Calvinist and Lutheran congregations had YMCA groups, which met once a week during fall and winter when farm work was at a minimum. The meetings concentrated on Bible reading and discussion, games, songs, and prayer, with the aim of developing skills and increasing the self-confidence of the members, encouraging them to take pride in their identity as Calvinists, Hungarians, and peasants.[43]

The program led to a movement of continuing education for young peasant adults through so-called folk high schools, which aimed to revive the declining village communities and create a new peasant leadership. During the winter agricultural break the peasant youth attended short sessions, which concentrated on broadening their horizons and giving them the tools to continue their self-education. Students heard lectures on history and literature and were encouraged to participate in discussions of current social and economic problems The residential aspect of the school, with teachers and students living together, became an essential element of the effort to break down class barriers and increase the villagers' self-confidence and self-respect—for a short time agrarian youth were removed from the narrow world-view of their villages. The unofficial nature of the schools freed them from the established curriculum, and populist writings, often forbidden works advocating radical solutions to the nation's problems, provided a springboard for discussion. Although the character of the schools varied widely, most advocated a new type of self-governing citizen leadership; common to all was the demand for land reform and the establishment of independent cooperatives.

Small farmers had been reluctant to send bright youngsters for schooling beyond the six years of elementary school, partly because they needed their labor, but also because of the fear that their child would join the educated elite and never return to the village. With increased prosperity more parents could be persuaded to release the young men for a short period in winter. Sándor Jakab, twenty years old at the time, was invited to attend a folk high school session in January 1939. His parents let him attend, probably because it was the winter quiet season, and he was given twenty pengő from the Reformed Church District for train fare. A year later when he was invited to attend the Veszprém school, his parents were reluctant; they needed his work—but the crux was, "if you take Sanyi away, we won't see him again."[44]

László Kovács, the son of a poor peasant who attended a folk high school session in Sarospatak in 1941, explained the effect on the village youth: "We wage-laborer youth from the village felt that a whole new world opened up to us. . . . Afterwards I took part in the village community work. We felt that we were learning things that would help us to shake up the life of the village that had gotten bogged down."[45]

At a YMCA conference on Lake Balaton, the sociologist Ferenc Erdei noted a new spirit among peasant youth. They appeared before him as the village youth he knew, "sunburned, slow moving people, a little timid, unsure . . . but when they spoke out my blood sang. They are no longer meek village peasants. Revolutionary, impatient, they don't want to be peasants anymore but men."[46]

Catholic folk high schools began somewhat later, after overcoming great resistance from the conservative Catholic hierarchy, but the movement expanded rapidly, drawing on the large Catholic population and church resources. It was difficult for the three million Hungarians who were part of the agrarian proletariat to get any further training, and for the 1.8 million small farmers, there were only fourteen agricultural schools and ninety-three three-month winter agricultural practical sessions. Initiated by KALOT leaders, the folk high schools concentrated on practical matters but also tended to be more radical in their demands for land reform. The first Catholic folk high school, established in 1940 in the former Jesuit monastery at Érd, was a permanent one offering three types of courses: one concentrating on folk culture, a leadership course, and a course in practical farming. In 1941 five more schools opened. In the following years the Catholic folk high schools multiplied rapidly.

Leaders of the Catholic and Protestant folk high schools met informally to exchange ideas and experiences. This cooperation was unusual at a time when tensions were high between the official Catholic and Protestant churches. KALOT leader Father Kerkai suggested that they form a commission of folk high schools, and in May 1941 a National Folk High School Commission was established, with representatives from both Protestant and Catholic folk high schools—the first major cooperative venture between Protestant and Catholic churches of the period. The efforts of these young intellectuals to transform young villagers into leaders was amazingly successful, with approximately 10,000 peasant youth having participated in the folk high schools by 1944. It was often the graduates of the folk high schools who presided over the land reform initiated by the democratically elected government in 1945. Brought to an abrupt halt by the Communist regime after 1948, the movement and its leaders emerged again briefly in October 1956.

THE JEWISH LAWS

The Jewish laws of 1938 and 1939 contradicted the nineteenth-century liberal policies, which had encouraged widespread assimilation by extending civil and religious equality to Jews. Ironically, the attempts to carry out the laws demonstrated the extent to which Jews had been thoroughly assimilated into Hungarian society. Assimilation was reflected in the number of mixed Christian-Jewish marriages, the cooperation of Jews and gentiles to circumvent the restrictions in business, and the difficulties faced by the military in simply attempting to certify non-Jewish background, not to mention the fact that the owners of the huge industrial complexes producing war materials were assimilated Jews. The new laws in effect turned Jews into second-class citizens, although in typical Hungarian fashion the laws were not always observed and various ways were found to circumvent their intent. Many Hungarian Jews suffered materially and psychologically and some Jews left the country, but in general the Jews considered themselves Hungarian and had faith that Horthy would protect them from the fate of Jews elsewhere in Europe. Hungary was seen as a place of refuge for the Jews of Europe and Jewish immigration into Hungary from Slovakia, Poland, and elsewhere continued until the German occupation in 1944.

The general effect of implementation of the laws was regressive, widening the economic differences within the Jewish community and increasing inequality both in income and wealth. Income from property was not jeopardized, intensifying regressive tendencies, and the industrial magnates, directors of major financial institutions, big commercial establishments, were very little affected. Even self-employed, well-established members of liberal professions, senior physicians, attorneys, engineers, and so on, remained members of their respective professional chambers and pursued their professions without major disturbances. The family of Lilly Vigyazo, whose father was a respected surgeon, lived their lives undisturbed until the Germans came. Patients of her father brought them foodstuffs so that they lacked nothing. "One man from the countryside brought milk products and eggs. My mother, who was a wonderful cook, made the best *kalács*. Before the German occupation a butcher brought us meat, including very scarce tenderloin, only for guests."[47]

The main blow fell on the middle and lower classes. The principal victims were small retailers, peddlers, artisans working in a workshop with a couple of workers, and salaried professional employees and lower clerks, particularly in the public sector, who had made a decent though modest living and were the most liable to lose their livelihood through the withdrawal of licenses or by dismissal. The law requiring professional chambers to be set up where they did not yet exist—and making membership obligatory—also restricted possibilities for young Jews in the professions. Lilly Vigyazo was refused admission at the university medical school. The head of the Dean's Office of the medical department said she could not be admitted, but that it was for her own good, since the medical chamber would not accept any new Jewish doctors. Instead she studied chemistry in the Philosophy Faculty at the Pazmany Péter University.[48]

A parody of the situation appeared in an article by a writer under the pen name of Tempefői commenting on a recent film about Bánk Bán, the Hungarian hero. The play of Bánk Bán had been written by a famous Hungarian playwright, József Katona:

"Hello, Mr Rajonghy? It's Vezér. I've just become terribly upset. This 'guy,' this 'Katona' who wrote that thing, Bank Ban—is he a member of the chamber?"

"Oh, for heaven's sake, József Katona died just 110 years ago!"

"Oh thank heavens, a stone just fell from my heart. But . . . how can I say this: if he were alive, could he be a member of the chamber?"[49]

Interestingly, a group that was relatively unaffected was the class of manual workers, but there were not many Jews among them.[50]

A group that suffered greatly from the laws was the liberal political opposition, many of whom lost their voting rights and frequently their jobs. Journalists were among those that suffered almost total deprivation of the right to pursue their profession. Simon Kemény, a founder and editor of the publication, *Az Est*, lost his job through the second Jewish law, when the proportion of Jewish-origin journalists was reduced from 20 percent to 6 percent. In his diary, which he began on January 1, 1942, he records how empty his days are since he lost his job: "Freezing, bitter cold winter—coldest in years. Don't have money to play cards—which would help pass the time. Go with my wife to her shop, then to a café. Sleep off and on. Listen to the radio."[51]

A number of papers were refused permission to publish, and a new guard took over in many newspapers and editorial staffs. It was no longer possible to publish many Hungarian and foreign authors. The laws led to a wave of emigration of artists, intellectuals, musicians, actors, film writers, and journalists whose jobs had been taken away. Rusztem Vámbéry, the editor of *Századunk*, was not admitted to the newly established Press Chamber, and soon immigrated to the United States.[52]

The radio profession was especially hard hit. The director of the Radio and Hungarian Telegram Office, Miklós Kozma, complained of the dangerous decline in the cultural level of the radio programs. The new head of the Radio Office, Antal Náray, appointed by Horthy after Kozma's death in early 1942, was often called a rescuer of Jews and Jewish hireling because he prevented the Jewish employees at the radio from being called up for labor service and also performed works of Jewish authors. The German embassy in Budapest, as well as Ribbentrop, often objected to the radio station' activities.[53]

One piece of music that could no longer be played was "Hungary, you are lovely, you are beautiful." In a bizarre way the Jewish laws showed how successful assimilation had been. Jews had become part of Hungarian society. The Hungarian culture of which the regime was so proud was only complete with what had been added to it by the Jews, including the slightly cynical shade to Hungarian humor: After 1938, in the cabarets a kind of gallows humor was poked at the Jewish laws and the Nazis: "Out with your documents!" "Let's learn English."[54]

Although the Jewish laws were never carried out to the extent that had been intended, the laws still had dramatic effects on the Hungarians—not only economic but also psychological, cutting deep into the fabric of society. The law forced the whole population of the country to consider their family heritage, as thousands of men and women researched letters, archives, and church records. Alice Somlai Pók remembered: "In 1939 with the Jewish laws, everyone had to prove that they had no Jewish origins—anyone who had a job. My mother had come from Eger and had to go back to get papers, the records of birth certificate of all four grandparents."[55] People had migrated into Hungary over hundreds of years, and after Trianon large numbers of the population had come from regions now in Romania, Yugoslavia, Austria, and Czechoslovakia, and were far removed from their family records. The population who had declared themselves enthusiastic Hungarians, now, to their dismay, realized that among their ancestors were German, Czech, Slovak, Romanian, Serb, Croat, and Italians. They asked themselves, "In what way am I Hungarian?"—a spirit contrary to that of St. Stephen's reign, which aimed to receive people of many nations held together by the language.[56]

The radical shift in the criteria of the second law from religion to race had a powerful impact. The respected professor and Piarist priest, Sándor Sík, wrote in his diary at Christmas 1938 that the new Jewish law was the greatest blow in his life:

. . . according to the suggested law I am a Jew. In a few weeks I will be fifty years old: up until now, never, even in my dreams, did it occur to me that such a thing could be, that my Hungarian-ness could be placed in doubt. I was ten years old when I was told that my parents—at some time before I was born—had been Jewish; but since then it never occurred to me for a minute that one could draw such a conclusion from that fact. My life is an open book, I have said, and one can find it in my more than a dozen books too: in them everyone can read my Hungarian-ness as clear as the day.[57]

CIRCUMVENTING THE JEWISH LAWS

At the time of the passage of the Jewish laws many Jews joined earlier converts by converting to Christianity.[58] The family of Gábor Támas could be considered the prototype of the assimilated Jewish family. They were nonobservant Jews and did not celebrate Jewish holidays but held all the Christian celebrations—St. Nicholas on December 6, Christmas with a Christmas tree—although he remembered that his mother did fast at Yom Kippur. His father, who was director in a large knitware factory, did very well and the family was financially very comfortable. Gábor's father looked Jewish, although his mother didn't. Everyone knew his father was Jewish; he had a large hooked nose and big ears. The firm where his father worked was Swabian and his father was "their Jew." The owners of the firm, Christian and rightists, had good connections with the government, and also with the Germans who wooed the Hungarian-German Swabians and tried to get them to join the *Volksbund.* Since the factory also manufactured heavy sweaters in khaki and other clothing for the military, it was considered to be in military production.[59]

In the summer of 1938, the family was baptized in the Calvinist church in Pestszenterzsébet, a town near Budapest. A friend of his father's who was Calvinist knew the priest and arranged for the baptism. They all received original birth certificates saying they had been born Calvinist. Gábor attended a Lutheran school and in the first years paid the tuition designated for a Calvinist student; only later was he required to pay the tuition for Jewish students. Although he knew something about the first and second Jewish laws passed by the government, they didn't affect him much except for the anti-Jewish measures in the scouts. He became a Wolf Cub in 1938 and looked forward to going to a scout jamboree like the International Scout Jamboree that had been held at Gödöllö in 1933, a tremendously exciting event with scouts attending from all over the world. Two years later he was told that Jews could not be scouts.[60]

The most effective way found to circumvent the Jewish laws regarding ownership of businesses was the *Strohman* system, which functioned to hide the Jewish ownership of firms. The informal development of this system revealed the ways in which Jews had assimilated and become an integral part of society. Under the *Strohman* system, non-Jews were often registered as holders of firms while the original owners continued operations as usual. József Litván, a manager of an international holding company, explained that companies, banks, and other businesses that were to a great extent in Jewish hands, solved the problem posed by the laws by taking advantage of their Aryan relatives and friends. In this way they were able to keep good technical management and maintain continuity of ownership. This was not only important to the firms, but to the country's credit worthiness, particularly in foreign trade which, of course, did not disappear in German-occupied Europe.

In some concerns the old and new leadership worked in symbiosis. The owner of the firm—the Magyar Kender-, Len- és Jutaipari Vállalat (Hungarian Hemp, Flax, and Jute Company)—was Jewish, but his daughter married a Swabian manufacturer from the Bácska, Dr. János Ertl. The son-in-law carried out the director-general's functions and also the proprietary rights while his father-in-law continued to run the firm. In another example, Emil Just, the director-general of the Linum-Pannónia concern, which was the property of the Magyar Általános Hitelbank, remained in his position but divided his responsibilities with his friend, Dr. Sándor Hardy. It was relatively simple to make tolerable compromises, often with consensus, in the cases when the ownership was in domestic hands and the owners were present within the country, because no expropriation law was passed until March 19, 1944. The principle of honoring personal property remained valid until that point.[61]

THE IMPACT OF THE JEWISH LAWS ON THE MILITARY

The Jewish laws caused major problems for the military, both practical and psychological. Those generals and officers who had begun their military career before the World War I were opposed to bringing the Jewish question into the military at all. The principle followed by the monarchy had been apolitical, and the military by its nature was not organized on the basis of class, religion, or race. The spirit of comradeship was felt especially strongly by the officers who had fought together with their Jewish comrades during the Great War. Among the retired officers were a number of well-known individuals, who held an honored place within the army and society, such as Baron Samu Hazai, a former minister of defense, and General Sióagárdi Márton Zöld, who was with Horthy in Szeged in 1919. But many of the younger generation who received their training after 1920 had been affected by anti-Semitic propaganda and believed in a radical solution to the Jewish question.[62]

The army, undergoing expansion in preparation for war, was struggling with a serious lack of officers, and carrying out the law's provisions meant that many generals and officers would have to be removed. It was necessary to evaluate who among the army leaders would be considered Jewish. Data had to be collected on more than 10,000 officers, including reserve and retired officers, and those officers considered Jewish according to the law, or whose wives were considered Jewish, had to be retired, including generals in high commands. Officers who received only a *not Jewish* or *not to be considered Jewish* label faced numerous restrictions. Many members of the officers corps with only the *not to be considered*

Jewish label did not want to accept the restrictions and asked for retirement or to be placed on inactive duty. Among these a number joined the Resistance Movement in 1944.[63]

A number of prominent military personnel, including Lt. Gen. Ferenc Szombathelyi, later the chief of general staff, were not able to authenticate their pure Christian origin or that of their wives.[64] The list prepared in 1940 of about seventy such generals and colonels included such prominent military personnel as Lt. Gen. Emil Barabás, head of the Ministry of Defense I Group, Lt. Gen. László Horváth, commander of the Pécs IV Army Corps, Lt. Gen. István Náday, group head of the military operations of the Chief of the general staff, General Ödön Domaniczky, commander of the Twentieth Infantry Brigade, later commander of the Third Army Corps, General Guysztáv Hennyey, commander of the Fifth Infantry brigade, later commander of the Second Army Corps, and foreign minister of the Lakatos government.[65]

There was also the difficult question of Jewish conscripts and their use of weapons, since the army counted on 3,000 Jewish recruits each year. Until the laws were passed Jews had served under arms, although not in certain protected divisions such as the air force, intelligence, or border protection. In 1939 the regulation and directive was passed according to which those considered Jewish could not be officers, noncommissioned officers, or junior officers. However, they could serve in armed units, except the protected ones, and those Jews not able to bear arms would be put in labor units. This regulation remained in effect until April 1941.[66]

At the time the labor service system was introduced under the Teleki administration, it was not exclusively anti-Jewish or even discriminatory in character. The law, signed by Prime Minister Teleki on May 12, 1939, was originally intended for all "unreliables," including the minorities—Romanians, Serbs, and Slovaks—and also "opposition Hungarians" or Communists. It was to apply to all Hungarian citizens twenty-one years of age and older classified as unsuitable for military service. Recruiting agencies would determine which recruits were fit for armed or labor service, and those selected for labor service were to serve for a period not exceeding three months at a time. The system went into effect on July 1, 1939, and was not very different from the system in the army as a whole. The labor servicemen had to report to their particular recruitment centers, and after the usual checkup and classification they were assigned to camps under the jurisdiction of the eight army corps commands existing at the time. The recruits received the same pay, discipline, and board as other draftees, and the same family assistance and welfare benefits for the disabled.[67]

The status of Jews in both the military and labor service system remained fundamentally the same until April 1941. In summer and fall 1940, labor service companies were used in various projects of interest to the military—clearing forests, especially along the Romanian border, road construction, and so on. The working conditions were still quite tolerable, which was surprising at a time of widespread anti-Semitism. During the general rearmament and mobilization program in the summer of 1940 the special labor service companies were also brought up to war strength. However, the Law of 1942, XIV decreed that all Jewish military duty was to be carried out in labor service, thus closing the Jewish question in the military.[68]

The example of a talented young lawyer, Béla Reitzer, illustrates the uncertainty of life for Jewish conscripts. Although Reitzer had been made a permanent member of the Chamber of Commerce and Trade in Budapest and had converted to Catholicism in 1936, he was still considered Jewish under the second Jewish law. From then on, his life began to be uncertain. Called up for service in a labor company in August 1940, the five months spent there deeply shattered and humiliated him. Around Christmas he was demobilized and immediately got married. He and his wife had no material problems, official work and social life gave content to their daily lives, but this calm was broken when he was called up again in 1941 with the occupation of the territory in the former Yugoslavia. When he was demobilized two or three months later, his friend, Ferenc Erdei, wanted to save him with false papers, but—for whatever reason—he didn't accept this solution. In the summer of 1942 he was again mobilized and sent to the Ukraine, where he died at the end of 1942 or beginning of 1943. Later research found only that he had died in a labor company hospital around Sepetovka. The Germans set fire to the wooden barracks, which held the patients who were not able to walk.[69]

Hungary's Early Participation in the War

With the declaration of the existence of a state of war on June 27, 1941, the military leadership began to prepare the Carpathian Group, the force to be sent against the Soviet Union. The force was under the command of Lt. Gen. Ferenc Szombathelyi, who was later to become Horthy's chief of general staff. Despite the efforts of the Győr Program the army was still woefully lacking in weapons and equipment, so weapons and equipment were taken from all the various army units in order to equip the force. The Carpathian Group consisted of 90,000 troops, which included the recently formed elite First Mountain brigade, the Eighth Border Patrol brigade, and the First Cavalry brigade, as well as the Rapid Corps, the most modern, best-equipped, and only rapid division of the army, with two motorized brigades. The name Rapid Corps was somewhat of a misnomer since the corps was only mechanized in comparison to other Hungarian units.

The Rapid Corps, under the command of Maj. Gen. Béla Miklós, was much less well equipped than the comparable German or Soviet units. It depended for mobility on the motorized riflemen, the cavalry, and bicycle brigades. The armored vehicles were small light tanks, almost exclusively the Italian-made Ansaldo two-person vehicles, which were already obsolete. It had been necessary to requisition a large part of the horses and vehicles from civilian life, which naturally caused problems. On the battlefield a number of the vehicles became useless. According to a report from August 1941, the route of the Rapid Corps was littered with broken-down, dilapidated vehicles of the most unusual types. One observer pointed out that it had been a shame to bring them to the battlefield in the first place, since more of them were under repair than in use, aside from the eyesore that they presented, the requisitioned vehicles bore the most fantastic logos, advertising products such as Elida cream or Zwack liquor.[70]

Although most of the officers corps, especially the general staff, were overjoyed at going to war, Szombathelyi was reserved from the beginning. According to a staff captain's memoirs, before embarking on the military operations Szombathelyi predicted catastrophe: "What will come of this, good Lord! What will come of this? Did we really need this; to jump into this stupidity?" At the time his words shocked everyone.[71]

The mobilized units of the Carpathian Group were ready to roll out on June 30, and since the Soviet troops were retreating before the Germans they met no resistance at first. The motorized riflemen battalions reached the Dniester July 6, while the major part of the Carpathian Group arrived on July 8. The next day the nature of the original force was radically altered in response to a request by Hitler to Horthy that the Rapid Corps be placed under the command of Army Group South, and to continue the advance with the Seventeenth German Army. The Carpathian Group command remained in the occupied territory at the border. The First Mountain Brigade and the Eigth Border Guard Brigade became the first Hungarian occupation forces in the Ukraine.

Throughout July and August it became clear that there was no possibility of a six-week blitzkrieg. Despite their huge losses Soviet resistance did not diminish. In his estimation of the Soviet troops Hitler had been badly mistaken. Russian soldiers had always proved themselves to be brave, hardy, and patriotic fighters, and the quality of the Russian artillery material had always been excellent, the infantrymen tenacious in defense and aggressive in attack. Since the Soviet Union was not covered by the Hague or Geneva conventions, Soviet soldiers were not protected from mistreatment. Word had spread of the slaughter of numerous POWs and the horrendous mistreatment of the rest, and as a result the Red Army soldiers were more afraid of being taken prisoner than of dying on the battlefield.[72]

The Rapid Corps under the command of Army Group South took part in German operations to encircle, cut off, and destroy the large Soviet forces gathering west of the Dniester. After the German Seventeenth Army broke through the Stalin line and most had crossed the Bug River, the Rapid Corps was given the task to break through south to southeast of the Bug and surround and destroy the opposition. The second motorized brigade met a completely unexpected Soviet attack on July 27 as the battalion was trying to extricate itself from the sodden road. The unit was in danger of being surrounded when the Eleventh Tank and Second Reconnaissance battalions and the First Mounted Tank battalion succeded in restoring the position, but only after the unit suffered heavy losses.[73]

By early August the Hungarian troops were completely exhausted, their technical equipment in terrible shape. On August 3 Maj. Gen. Béla Miklós reported: "Need eight to ten days rest and to repair equipment. The bicycle brigade members' hearts and lungs are ruined. The advance has gone on for thirty-two days without rest."[74] A high-ranking military medical committee had arrived to inspect the Hungarian Bicycle Brigade, and one member of the brigade wrote: "They found that about two-thirds had enlargement of the heart—probably from the strain of the long, unbelievably difficult bicycle trip, since we had to keep step with the German infantry who were transported in modern land rovers."[75]

Major General Miklós explained that the bicycles and motorized equipment were in need of repair, and pleaded for time to await the replacements, which were coming by train. But the liaison officer, Lt. Col. Sándor Makray, denied the request. The Hungarian brigades became involved in more and more difficult battles, their losses grew, their equipment was destroyed or rendered useless. By the end of August it became apparent that the only way to save the divisions from annihilation was to withdraw them from battle.[76]

CHANGE IN MILITARY COMMAND

The early rapid German advances had pleased Horthy, but as the summer went on he became concerned. The Red Army had not collapsed after six weeks, Churchill had offered Britain's full support to Stalin's war effort with an agreement of mutual aid, and his meeting with Roosevelt on August 14 and the issuance of the Atlantic Charter suggested that the Anglo-Saxon powers were forming a powerful coalition against Germany. News of the German treatment of the occupied peoples appalled Horthy.[77] He began to look at the anti-Soviet campaign realistically and seemed to regret that he had allowed his country to be swept into this war.

On August 26 he received a long letter from Prime Minister Bárdossy, complaining bitterly that his chief of general staff, Henrik Werth, was once again attempting to insinuate himself into political and diplomatic affairs. Werth criticized the government and its conduct in domestic and foreign affairs, as if such affairs belonged to his own sphere of authority. He had submitted a memorandum to the cabinet in which he criticized Hungary's minimal participation in the war and stated that only through total mobilization could Hungary realize its cherished national goals to regain its borders and to deport non-Magyars and Jews. Furious with the brazen fashion in which Werth interfered in his and the regent's prerogatives, Bárdossy announced that in the intolerable situation the regent must choose between him and the chief of general staff.[78]

Bárdossy's complaints echoed those that Teleki had made a year earlier, but at the time Horthy had been hesitant to force Werth's resignation. Werth's early predictions of German military victories had been on target, but his latest prediction that the war against the Soviet Union would be over in six weeks was dismally mistaken. Horthy decided that Werth would have to go, but who could replace him? Horthy had lost contact with the higher officers who might have come into question for the position of chief of staff. At seventy-three, he no longer was as engaged in military life as he used to be, and he had become more and more isolated from the members of his officers corps. The members of the general staff, leaders of the Ministry of War, and high officers of the troops were relatively unknown to him. He met military leaders mainly at the various military ceremonies and celebrations since he did not invite the higher officers to his home as he did his political advisors and friends.

He knew of their military abilities, political attitudes, and human qualities only through the subjective opinions of Bartha and Werth.[79]

A chance meeting in Kassa in August between István Horthy, the regent's older son, and Lt. Gen. Ferenc Szombathelyi, commander of the Carpathian Group, was to determine his choice. An apolitical officer of German background, Szombathelyi was much better educated and his theoretical knowledge was far beyond that of most Hungarian officers. His skepticism about a rapid German victory differentiated him from most of his fellow officers. Over dinner he explained that the Germans were in serious trouble in the Soviet Union. István, highly impressed with Szombathelyi's analysis, asked him to put his conclusions about the strategic situation in Russia in a memorandum to the regent.[80]

Szombathelyi suggested that there was no possibility of a blitzkrieg for the German army in the vast Russian steppe: "At the beginning of September 1941 I handed the regent a memorandum, the essence of which was that the Russian war would not be a 'Blitzkrieg' but a long drawn out, bloody struggle, the results of which were completely uncertain. Our troops, if possible, should be withdrawn before we plunge further into the war."[81] He argued that since a complete German victory was unlikely, Hungary would do best to conserve its power in order to be able to deal with smaller wars against its neighbors which were likely to come at the end of the larger war. Horthy greatly admired his son, an engineer serving as director of the Hungarian railways at the time. István, who had spent a year in the United States studying the auto industry, was pro-Western and shared his father's antipathy for the Nazis and the Hungarian Arrow Cross. After receiving the memorandum Horthy resolved not only to reject Werth's call for total mobilization and formation of a new Hungarian army but to actually reduce Hungary's participation in the war. In late August he dismissed Werth, appointed Szombathelyi over the heads of his seniors to replace him, and in November promoted him to the rank of three-star general.

Szombathelyi's education, stature, and intellectual abilities made him exceptional among his fellow officers. After completing his cadet and officer's training with the Hungarian army, he attended the elite Viennese War Academy and was made staff captain at the age of twenty-eight, serving during World War I as a staff officer.[82] Tough, but at the same time a sensitive soldier, he loved literature and in his lectures often referred to French culture as well as to the great military strategies used throughout history. He was an excellent horseman, liked fine food and wine, had eyes for pretty women, and was an amusing companion in society. A friend commented that he was good looking, with finely chiseled features, friendly, smiling, and relaxed when he met someone he liked. Above all he was a Magyar patriot, his highest goal to serve his country faithfully. Like his Hungarian and German comrades he held the professional career of a military officer to be above other occupations and was convinced that an officer must be apolitical.[83]

Szombathelyi had been against the idea of Hungary participating in the war, and he worked steadily to keep Hungary's participation to a minimum, even going beyond Horthy's views. Pál Lieszkovszky, who had been Szombathelyi's adjutant from 1941 in Kassa and accompanied him when he became head of the general staff, explained: "Szombathelyi was an extremely closed person, a strict soldier. Already in Kassa it was his habit to take a long walk in the evening before going to bed. I was obliged to accompany him. During his walk he would go through the day's happenings aloud. At such a time he released the tensions. Of course, I learned a lot through this."[84]

In early September, Horthy took his new chief of staff on his visit to Hitler's new headquarters in the small Ukrainian town of Vinitsa. As all higher Hungarian officers before him, Szombathelyi had received his military training in the Austro-Hungarian common army and spoke perfect German. Hitler, who knew of Szombathelyi through his command of the Carpathian Group, gave him an unexpectedly warm greeting. Szombathelyi conducted the negotiations, requesting the withdrawal of the Hungarian combat units from Russia as the only way to save the valuable Rapid Corps from complete destruction. He reasoned that the Rapid Corps was no longer useful because of its debilitated condition and destroyed equipment. Although Ribbentrop and the German military were against it for propaganda reasons, Szombathelyi eventually succeeded in reaching an agreement to bring the Rapid Corps home. Germany was making steady progress on the eastern front and the Hungarian forces, even the Rapid Corps, had not satisfied German expectations as participants in modern warfare. In return the military had to agree to send two more infantry brigades in addition to the four already there as occupation troops to the Ukraine. The troops were to be brought home gradually, in steps.[85]

Szombathelyi faced a difficult situation in dealing with his own general staff who were convinced that Hungary's fate and future depended on Germany: "Since the high ranking officers and generals were completely pro-German, I was under their supervision to a certain extent. . . . I knew that changing the attitude of the leaders had to be done step by step, and I often felt that I had come too late to change the poisoned attitude."[86] At the cadet school in Pécs, attending his thirty-fifth reunion, he met with Gyula Kádár, a young officer, and over a private breakfast Szombathelyi told Kádár, "You know, we don't have an army; but a badly equipped poor peasantry." He felt as if he was only a shadow commander, not able to make the changes he wanted, but he wanted men he could depend on. Less than a year later he appointed Kádár to serve in the office of the chief of general staff.[87]

He attempted to bring order within the general staff by ending the constant gossip and the insulting criticism of the nation's leaders. One of his first moves was to stop the practice of officers making promises to their German colleagues with no attempts to clear them with the government. An immediate opportunity occurred on his return from Hitler's headquarters, when he received a request from the German command to send two more occupation brigades, asking for an immediate response. The German leadership were surprised to find that the accustomed "good old direct route" to the chief of the general staff no longer functioned. Szombathelyi informed Halder that the request must be initiated with the government through political channels. The Germans assumed that this was only the result of a temporary misunderstanding, never presuming that the new chief of the general staff and the government were in complete agreement. When further misunderstandings became apparent, Bárdossy informed Sztójay, the Hungarian minister to Berlin, that from now on the government of the Third Reich must turn to the Hungarian government with any kind of request.[88]

RETURN OF THE RAPID CORPS

Starting in October with the beginning of the *rasputiza,* the mud season, the daily rains made the Russian roads impassable. A part of the Rapid Corps cavalry brigade was taken home by train on October 10. The rest of the army corps began the return home on November 24. Sándor Jakab, a member of the bicycle brigade, described the situation in October: "Merciless mud—everything sank in it, including our food provisions. One day was a beautiful warm fall day—the next the temperature sank to minus 18–20 Celsius. Our uniforms were thin, hands and feet were frozen, our vehicles couldn't even start. My toes froze, needed medical attention. . . . Then a miracle happened, our longing for home was answered. They brought home the so-called Rapid Corps and us with it. They put us on a train at Berdicsev—crossing Slovakia through Kassa we arrived in Munkács. For Christmas and the New Year we were sent home on leave."[89]

During the four months of the campaign the Rapid Corps had pushed 2,000 kilometers deep into the southern territory of the Soviet Union—the troops had not been prepared for traveling such a distance. In the fighting, the corps had lost 3,730 men—fallen, wounded, or taken as prisoners of war. Another 830 returned home seriously ill, a number of them psychologically scarred. Equipment lost included 1,200 motor-driven vehicles, 30 planes, 28 pieces of artillery, all the Italian-made tanks, 80 percent of the Hungarian light Toldi tanks, and 90 percent of the Csaba armed personnel carriers.[90]

The public had heard only of the spectacular German victories, the Hungarian radio broadcast only favorable news; losses and defeats were never mentioned. Since the Rapid Corps had involved a fairly small number of troops, the impact of losses was felt only by a few. For this reason the following event—an incident in the apartment house of Simon Kemény—was particularly shocking.

The husband of the concierge had returned from the Russian front on January 3. His wife found him a changed man, beaten down and sad, but she thought he was only tired. One night she woke to find him in the kitchen among some broken dishes and asked what he was doing: "He looked at me in great surprise. 'Don't you hear the terrible shelling and gunfire? Look, how many dead, wounded, suffering, there are. Look at my hands all covered with blood, because I killed, murdered!'"[91] Realizing something was really wrong, she went out to telephone for the ambulance. When she came back the poor guy was in the courtyard, kneeling in the snow and shouting up toward the sky: "Dear Jesus, forgive me. I didn't want to kill, massacre people. They took me there, put a gun in my hands, gave me orders. What should I do, poor wretched man. I couldn't do anything else, I had to obey. I committed a terrible great sin, dear Jesus, forgive me."[92]

Everybody from the apartment house had come out to see what was going on. The man kept on shouting, accusing himself, asking for forgiveness. Some of the tenants cried when they heard him. Then the ambulance arrived. They had seen lots of things but this appalled them. One of them took off his cap, kneeled next to him, and began to pray with him, sobbing. Later they took him to a military hospital. The next day the head doctor told Kemény: "Unfortunately we see this fairly frequently. Nowadays every fifth soldier comes back from the war in this condition."

His wife said: "My God, what could these soldiers have seen at the front that broke their spirit like this?"[93]

Declarations of War on the Allies

In late autumn 1941 all seemed calm on the Hungarian domestic scene. It appeared that Hungary's entrance into the war had brought no serious repercussions, other than Britain's recognition of the Czechoslovak government in exile. The Carpathian Group was on its way home and German and Hungarian military commanders were still confident of victory. Then, on December 7, came the news of the Japanese attack on Pearl Harbor. On the day of the attack the Hungarian public received the news that Britain had declared war on Hungary as well as on other German "satellite states" that were taking part in the war against the Soviet Union.

The Soviet Union had been pressuring its allies to make this declaration. At the end of November, Herbert C. Pell, the United States minister in Budapest and intermediary with the British, delivered a British ultimatum that if Hungary had not ceased all military operations and withdrawn all active participants from hostilities against the Soviet Union by midnight of December 5, His Majesty's Government would "have no alternative but to declare the existence of a state of war between the two countries." Bárdossy told Mr. Pell he was extremely surprised at the communication, arguing that Hungarian troops had already been pulled back, and that it was physically impossible to accede to the British ultimatum. He continued, rather arrogantly, that Hungary could not have her policy made dependent on the decisions of the British government.

When Pell asked whether the Hungarian government did not have something to convey to the British government, for he was at their service, Bárdossy answered in the negative. Pell made every effort to prevent the declaration of war, attempting to bring the British government to change its mind and sending messages to President Roosevelt, but Bárdossy adopted an air of "aggrieved innocence." On the evening of December 6, 1941, Pell informed the Hungarian government that the state of war would become effective at midnight, with expressions of his deepest regret.[94]

Four days after Pearl Harbor, Germany declared war on the United States, making it known that it expected Hungary to follow suite in the spirit of the Tripartite Pact. In an effort to avoid a declaration of war, a special session of the Council of Ministers adopted a formula proposed by Bárdossy. This formula would involve breaking off diplomatic relations but not necessarily a declaration of war; instead, in support of her responsibilities under the Tripartite Pact, Hungary would declare her solidarity with the Axis powers. They hoped that the declaration would satisfy the Axis powers but agreed that the wider interpretation, which would be a declaration of war, could be used if necessary. The regent agreed. The next day the Germans and Italians made it clear that severing diplomatic relations was not sufficient. It was the duty of those powers adhering to the Tripartite Pact to declare a state of war.

Believing that the step was inescapable, Bárdossy, acting on his own, wired the Hungarian legations in Rome and Berlin that if the Axis powers considered the declaration of a state of war to be indispensable, then the declaration of solidarity could be thus interpreted. He had told Pell the day before that the formula did not mean war. Now he informed Pell that the formula of the previous day had after all meant that a state of war now existed between Hungary and the United States.[95] Pell made a last effort: "I suppose you are doing this under heavy pressure from Germany, and that the declaration reflects no hostility on the part of the Hungarian people towards the people of the U.S.A.?" But Bárdossy, refusing the proffered alibi, answered indignantly: "Hungary is a sovereign and independent State. . . . Her Government and her people are entirely at one."[96]

Bárdossy made no special announcements of the declaration of a state of war to the Council of Ministers, simply reporting it in their regular meeting. He included the announcement of a state of war with the United States in his routine report to the foreign affairs committee of the upper house on the December 15. The committee, appalled by the announcement, gave Bárdossy a frosty reception, and the person soon to replace Bárdossy, Miklós Kállay, suggested that they should continue unofficially to maintain relations with the Anglo-Saxon powers. The upper house attitude toward Bárdossy had changed radically after he failed to ask their opinion in the war against the Soviet Union. Now the hope for a continuation of the policy of neutrality was completely destroyed.

Evidently Bárdossy had realized that he would be unable to get the consent of Parliament or of the regent to a formal declaration of war. Horthy told American First Secretary Travers during his farewell visit that the so-called declaration of war was not legal, not approved by parliament and not signed by him. Under pressure from the Axis powers, Bárdossy had taken it upon himself to declare war. The former United States minister to Hungary, John Flournoy Montgomery, opined that whether Bárdossy was a patriot or a scoundrel was a matter of opinion.[97] President Roosevelt believed that the declarations of war from the small countries were forced by Hitler and decided to ignore them. He did not send a message to Congress that Rumania, Hungary, and Bulgaria had declared war on the United States until June 2, 1942, but added that the three governments had acted not on their own initiative but as "instruments of Hitler."[98] On the same day, Congress declared that a state of war existed between the United States and those countries. The state of war with Britain and the United States changed the whole complexion of the war. For the first time Hungarian public opinion began to consider seriously the possibility of the defeat of the Axis powers and of Hungary. Just as enthusiasm for the war dissolved, Hungary received a demand from Hitler to join in with full force for his final campaign to defeat the Soviet Union. After taking command of the German army in mid-December, Hitler had determined to wind up the war in the East before the Western Allies would be able to develop their full war potential. Again he underestimated his enemy.

6   Disaster at the Don

In October 1941 Hitler was jubilant; he believed the war was over! He had planned on wiping Moscow from the face of the earth and replacing it with an artificial lake. In a routine speech at the Berlin Sportpalast on October 4 he announced the "greatest battle in the history of the world; that the Soviet enemy had been beaten and would never rise again."[1] He still believed that the Soviet Union was a rotten structure that would collapse as the suppressed citizens turned against the Russian tyrant. But by the end of November the situation had changed. The Germans were almost at Moscow but the army was expiring on its feet, the soldiers almost incapable of movement. The German army had suffered serious losses; death, wounds and sickness had reduced its strength by half a million. The losses had convinced Hitler that he would need to rely more on his minor allies, primarily Romania and Hungary. For the first time he asked directly for Hungarian participation.

German military leaders had seriously underestimated the Soviets, not counting on the stubborn Soviet resistance. Their weapons were not effective against the new Russian tanks, the T-34 and the KV, nor were they prepared to fight in the bitter Russian winter, which had started early, when temperatures started to fall below minus 20 degrees Celsius. Although the advancing German troops were approaching Moscow, the 650-kilometer march at 45 to 50 kilometers per day had been excruciating and morale was low; medical reports showed that twenty-year-old youth looked like old men. General Alfred Jodl, the OKW operations officer, had refused to allow the public collection of winter clothing fearing it might cast doubt on assurances that Russia would collapse before winter. Soldiers stuffed newspaper inside their uniforms to repel the cold, while their iron-nailed soles accelerated the onset of frostbite—100,000 cases of frostbite were recorded, 2,000 required amputations. The Russians were used to and equipped for the cold; every Russian, military or civilian, had a pair of felt boots, which best protected feet against frostbite.[2]

Refusing suggestions to postpone the final stage of the drive on Moscow and dig in for the winter, Hitler was determined to carry on. The German commanders urged a general withdrawal that would enable regrouping for the spring offensive, but Hitler flatly refused. Realizing that a withdrawal would cost time and might lead to a general disintegration of the battle line, he had no sympathy for the ill-clad and over-committed frontline troops. A desperate attempt was made to reach Moscow and beat the winter, but on November 25 Guderian's Panzer Group Two ordered a halt. The Russians, under Marshal S. K. Timoshenko, recaptured Rostov-on-Don a week after it had been taken, Rundstedt's tanks were forced back 80 kilometers behind Rostov where they dug in for the winter, and Army Group North halted outside Leningrad.

At first there had been panic in Moscow. On October 13, with the German army approaching, Stalin ordered the evacuation of the bulk of the Communist Party, the Supreme High Command (*Stavka*), and civil government offices to be evacuated to the east. Factories and offices were closed down and desperate people swamped the trains. There were riots and looting, but then Stalin made the historic decision to stay in the capital, halting the evacuation and setting the NKVD to shoot looters and restore order—a state of siege was declared on October 19. A flood of people from all walks of life volunteered to join the army, intelligentsia, factory workers, and a substantial number of women who served in a variety of roles. Against the advice of his generals Stalin celebrated the anniversary of the Bolshevik Revolution with a military parade in Red Square, making a tremendous impact on Russian morale.[3] The Red Army had also been reinforced by Siberian divisions, which Stalin had been holding in reserve, fearing a Japanese attack. The Russian counteroffensive began on December 7 and by Christmas Day 1941 they had retaken almost all the territory won by the Germans in the last stages of the drive on Moscow.

Hitler went into a rage, accusing the high command for the failure to take Moscow. He dismissed Guderian, accepted Rundstedt's resignation, and relieved Brauchitsch as commander-in-chief of the army. In an ominous decision he announced that he would take the command into his own hands. In words that must have filled the hearts of his senior commanders with dread, he asserted that being in charge of the army was no more than "a little matter of operational command that anyone can do."[4]

Request for Hungarian Troops

Up to this point the German Reich Foreign Office had clung to the pretense that Germany did not request military support from its Hungarian ally. But now that the outlook had changed, Hitler asked Regent Horthy for Hungarian participation in a letter dated December 29. He explained the German army's temporary setbacks due to the bad weather, not mentioning of course that the Russians had faced the same conditions. "My candid wish, Your Excellency, is that Hungarian units may participate in the decisive fight once again in the coming year."[5] He then announced that he was sending personally his Foreign Minister Ribbentrop and Field Marshal Wilhelm Keitel to Budapest. As Chief of the General Staff Szombathelyi wryly commented: "If up until now their attitude to us had been that if we wanted to take part in the war at any cost then let us take part, now at the end of 1941 they suddenly turned the voluntary participation into an obligation."[6] It was no secret that the guests would request Hungary's participation in the German army's spring operations—the question was to what extent.

Ribbentrop's visit, which had been planned previously as a courtesy call, began in traditional fashion with a hunting party hosted by Horthy, but in the negotiations that started on January 8 he placed heavy military and economic demands. Announcing to the regent and Prime Minister Bárdossy that Bolshevism must be defeated in the coming year, he referred to the losses the Wehrmacht had already suffered—which he surprisingly interpreted to be "for Hungary"—and emphasized that the Hungarian government should express its gratitude and take part in the final victory. In transmitting Hitler's demands he mentioned that Romania had placed greater Hungarian participation as the condition for its full participation. Using the already well-known German method of promises and threats, he noted that if Hungary's response was not satisfactory, the Führer would be very angry which would affect Hungarian territorial claims.[7]

Hungarian leaders realized that in the face of the extreme German demands they would have to give in to some extent, but they wanted to commit the fewest troops possible. Bárdossy referred to the army's weakness in weaponry and equipment, the difficulties of the wartime economy, and the always-present danger of a Romanian attack, which was a real concern—German dispatches noted the continuing tension between the two countries and the constant border incidents. Hungary had massed troops along the new border and Romanian threats appeared daily in the newspapers. In a long letter to Hitler, Horthy wrote that as a loyal ally Hungary would take part in the coming battles, but that one had to take under consideration the strained relations between Hungary and Romania. After intense bargaining, Bárdossy agreed that although Hungary could not fully commit the army into the eastern war, it would take part with much greater strength than previously, and Ribbentrop left satisfied; he had received a positive answer, as well as the promise of increased oil and grain deliveries.[8]

The public's reactions to Ribbentrop's visit were hardly enthusiastic. In his diary Simon Kemény wrote:

January 9: After 5 P.M. I went out on corner of Eötvös and Andrássy street—saw long line of cars standing in huge snowfall. Every ten steps a policeman in full dress. . . . People were unable to move. Thus they had artificially created a large crowd—as if they had come in honor of Ribbentrop. People were patient, but didn't talk, didn't make comments. Cafes were closed—couldn't go in or out. Gates were closed. Lots of detectives in civil moved around. . . . A few minutes after the last car in the procession went by one could cross the street. The crowd broke up, becoming impatient, annoyed and loud. Relieved, the people hurried on their various paths to make up for the delay. The atmosphere was as if they had become liberated from some great danger.[9]

Count Galeazzo Ciano, the Italian minister of foreign affairs, visiting Budapest five days later, noted Hungarian exasperation with the Germans: "You can't remain long with any Magyar before he speaks ill of Germany. All of them are like this from the regent to the last beggar on the street. Admiral Horthy said 'The Germans are a brave people, and I admire them for this, but they are also an unbearable, tactless, and boorish people.' Kanya was even more cutting. Bethlen weighed his words, but in talking about German interference he was so violent, even though restrained, that I can't describe it."[10] Ciano, who may have enjoyed the Hungarian reactions, did not find it necessary to recount his impressions to the Germans.

On January 20, the arrival of Keitel, who was now Hitler's right-hand man, signified the importance Hitler placed on the military negotiations. Keitel's demands were much higher than expected; he seemed to want participation of the whole armed forces. Szombathelyi and Bartha saw no way to meet the German demands. Not only was the army weak and lacking in equipment and training, the Hungarian army was not psychologically prepared to be involved in such a far-off action. Even many officers found it difficult to understand how the battle against the Soviet Union was essential to Hungary's defense—yet they realized if they refused German demands there might be serious consequences. Ribbentrop's threats revived the fear that Hitler might reconsider the Vienna

Awards, but even more serious, the Hungarians feared German occupation. As Szombathelyi later explained: "We might have lost our independent Hungarian army, lost our independent state, . . ."[11]

Keitel demanded a minimum of twelve infantry brigades, but after hard bargaining, including shouting and table pounding, a compromise was reached. At a dinner at the Gellért Hotel on January 22, Szombathelyi agreed that the army would send nine infantry brigades, an improvised brigade-sized armored division, and a token air-force formation—207,000 troops in all, making up one-third of Hungary's military strength. The army would be under German command. Keitel, knowing the Hungarian army's deficiencies in antitank and heavy weapons, gave an oral commitment that the Germans would supplement them with weapons and equipment at the front. He wrote later that he could not avoid acceding to Hungarian requests for German weaponry, since without modern equipment the Hungarian troops would have been worth little against the well-equipped Russians. All this was drawn on the back of the hotel menu, no written agreement was signed.[12]

The promised nine infantry brigades were to be light divisions— much smaller than German divisions—in order not be such a burden on the military and the country. This solution was misleading, especially to the Germans who expected more from the Hungarians than they were able to give. The Germans had no knowledge of Hungarian military organization or the value of a light division. Although the real strength of a Hungarian division equaled that of a reinforced brigade, the Germans assigned full-value combat duties to such divisions.

The military leadership, believing in the continued success of the German blitzkrieg, expected a short campaign and a rapid return of the improvised Second Army in the same way that the Carpathian Group had returned after four months. The Soviet Union was in a position of acute weakness in the spring of 1942. Three million of its soldiers had been captured, 3.1 million killed—the tank and air forces were depleted. Russian bread rations were halved since the Germans occupied the grain-producing lands of the Ukraine and one-third of the rail network was behind German lines. In Hungary the favorable German propaganda had continued as usual, noting the rapid German advance on Moscow and the successes of army groups North, Center, and South. Not only was the general public completely ignorant of any German problems, but many in the officer corps as well. No doubt much of the Hungarian political and military leadership shared Hitler's belief that his spring campaign would lead to the final defeat of Bolshevism. At the time few would have gambled on a Soviet victory.[13]

Since the Second Army's role was only to back up the attacking German army there was no thought that the troops would be involved in active fighting. In the original discussion the Hungarian soldiers were to be used for maintenance of security and public order in occupied territories; half of the troops sent were noncombat personnel. The reluctance of the military leadership in agreeing to send the Second Army was not so much for fear of possible losses but because of the fear of the Romanians. At the time they were satisfied that the country had gotten off by giving a relatively smaller force than originally demanded, and they failed to clarify the details of how the army was to be used or for how long—the exact locations, duration, and the tasks awaiting them. No provision was made for reinforcements in the case of losses or for the relief over time of the rank and file. The failure of the leadership to determine these questions and to gain a guarantee of German equipment was to cost them dearly.

THE ÚJVIDÉK MASSACRE

During the period of negotiations with the Germans a dreadful event occurred in the Voivodina—the territory Hungary had reclaimed after the dissolution of Yugoslavia—which was to have dire repercussions. Between January 21 and 23, 1942, the Hungarian military and gendarmerie slaughtered about 3,000 inhabitants in the city of Novi Sad, known in Hungarian as Újvidék—under the pretense of putting down partisan attacks once and for all.

Before the German invasion, Yugoslav-Hungarian relations had been relatively good, leading to the Pact of Eternal Friendship signed only months before. For Hungarians the Voivodina—made up of three natural subdivisions, the Baranya, the Bácska, and Bánát—had never carried the emotional significance of the Felvidék (northern Hungary) or Transylvania.[14] The great flat area was an extension of the Great Hungarian Plain, a fertile black-earth belt. It was purely agricultural with no industry except that directly related to agriculture. The population of Serbs, Hungarians, Germans, Romanians, Gypsies, and Jews was inextricably mixed, with Magyars most numerous in the north and Serbs in the south. The inhabitants of the Serb regions had a strong sense of their history, national feeling, and culture. Their Orthodox church had been protected under various governments, and they had long-established, wealthy cultural centers such as that around Novi Sad. In negotiations for the treaty signed in December 1941, the Yugoslavs had indicated some readiness to resolve Hungarian claims to certain Magyar-inhabited areas at some indefinite time, although no agreement was included in the treaty since any concessions would have brought territorial claims from both Romania and Bulgaria.

Hitler's decision to destroy Yugoslavia put pressure on Hungary to allow German troops transit and to join in the occupation. Passage of German troops could hardly have been refused, and the offer to reclaim the Baranya, Bácska, and Bánát was too tempting to resist, especially for the extreme Right and those who clamored for "everything back," but in occupying much of the former territory—the Germans held on to the rich Bánát where they had once planned an independent state—the Hungarians not only reneged on the Pact of Eternal Friendship, but the occupying forces carried out harsh measures against the local populations.

Following the start of the war with the Soviet Union, partisan movement flared up in the German-occupied Serb territory. Incidents in the Hungarian-occupied territory increased in the fall of 1941 with attacks by partisans on Hungarian troops and gendarme patrols, which escalated in December.[15] In January 1942 Serb partisans from German-occupied Serbia and the Bánát, infiltrating the so-called Sajkas area, attacked a number of gendarme patrols killing some gendarmes. Although it was fairly obvious that some in the local population were helping the partisans, the perpetrators were nearly always Serbs who had infiltrated across river frontiers and returned to their bases. Hungarian authorities took severe measures against any of the partisans caught but without stopping the incidents.[16]

With the situation getting out of hand, a local gendarmerie commander requested military aid through his superior, who called upon Keresztes-Fischer, minister of the interior responsible for the gendarmerie. Keresztes-Fischer received authorization to employ the military from the Council of Ministers, and Chief of the General Staff Szombathelyi entrusted the mission to the senior military officer in the neighborhood, General Feketehalmi-Czeydner, commander of the Szeged Corps. Szombathelyi, who knew Czeydner as a fellow officer, did not know that he was a fanatic National Socialist with sadistic tendencies. Czeydner had decided to repress the disorder with an iron hand, perhaps hoping to win favor with the Germans.[17]

On January 12, after initial reprisals against those accused of supporting the partisans, including women and children, Czeydner applied for authority to extend the purge to the whole area, including the local center of Novi Sad, claiming that the partisans had pulled back into the city. The Council of Ministers authorized the necessary defensive measures but stipulated that no superfluous or exaggerated measures should be taken.

On January 20, a new detachment of troops and body of gendarmerie entered Novi Sad, throwing a cordon around the town and cutting off telegraphic and telephonic communications. Placards were posted informing the inhabitants that no one was allowed to go into the streets except to buy food. Czeydner called the local authorities together and announced that for three days the military would take charge and clean things up. On the next day the raid began, with about 6,000 to 7,000 persons considered suspicious taken to a central headquarters to have their papers examined. Most were let go but about forty to fifty were taken to the banks of the Danube and shot.

A survivor of the massacre, Eva Volcevic, described how a soldier came to her house and ordered her and her mother onto the back of a truck which was crowded with dozens of others, mostly Jews like her. "That day all soldiers on the streets were drunk," she said. "The truck was driving us around for a long time, making circles. We finally stopped at the former theater building. We went in and took seats as if we had been waiting for the play to begin."[18] After having their identities checked the people were separated into two lines—one line allowed to return home but the rest taken to the Danube where they were shot. On January 22 not only suspected partisans but a large number of people, including a number of wealthier citizens, many of them Jews, were taken into custody as hostages. There was little resistance but soon thereafter there was some random shooting in the vicinity, and in reprisal Czeydner ordered a wholesale execution of the hostages. With horrifying brutality victims were taken to the banks of the Danube and shot in batches, stripped, and looted of their valuables. Weeks later naked bodies, some mutilated, were found when the ice melted.[19]

With all communications cut no one had been able to notify authorities in Hungary, but on January 23 the Lord Lieutenant of the city succeeded in slipping out through the cordon and walked to where he could telephone Budapest. He brought back an order that shooting was to stop instantly, and Feketehalmi-Czeydner ordered that military measures cease by 9 P.M. More than two thousand Serbs, several hundred Jews, but also Hungarians, Germans, Slovaks, and Russians were murdered, including many women, children, and older persons. The mother-in-law of the Lord Lieutenant was among the victims.[20]

The effect of the incident was devastating. The bloodbath became known worldwide, damaging Hungary's reputation more than any other wartime event. The story came out bit by bit as bodies floated down the Danube and Tisza to Belgrade and was published in the world press. Attempts to deny the magnitude of the massacre by the Hungarian press brought violent attacks on the Hungarian government. Within Hungary the news filtered in, brought by refugees from Novi Sad. On January 28 Kálmán Shvoy wrote in his diary: "Had lunch at the Modern, Tóni Klein, Pista [Shvoy], Boross. Tóni Klein related terrible things over Újvidék, the military slaughtered, pillaged, executed 3,500, robbed large sums of money. Monstrous. No one will admit responsibility! What have we come to? Worse than the Balkans."[21]

On January 29, Endre Bajcsy-Zsilinszky in the Foreign Affairs Committee of Parliament demanded an investigation of the Novi Sad massacre. Bárdossy, who knew little about the matter, said he would make inquiries. Czeydner of course denied everything and the highest military officers, including Szombathelyi, believed him, unable to imagine that any officer would betray the code of honor through deception. Later Szombathelyi remarked to a friend that he and Czeydner were general staff comrades and had been teachers together at the War Academy: "How could he lie to me? Who can I believe if not him?"[22]

In his memoirs written in 1945, Szombathelyi explained:

Most Hungarians and almost all of the extreme right and the Officers Corps viewed the events at Újvidék . . . as a National Heroic act. . . . Public opinion was completely under the influence of rightist propaganda and formed their opinions. I myself did not believe that the Újvidék events were so terrible. For a long time I did not believe it. And if I never fell into that error that the events were heroic, for a long time I was convinced that the troops had taken harsh but justified reprisals in Újvidék to put an end to the atrocities of the Serbs, who had carried out numerous actions against Hungarian public safety and security forces, as well as train bombings.

I completely believed the reports of the responsible commanders, Colonel General Ferenc Feketehalmy-Czeydner and Lieutenant General József Grassy, who I knew as upstanding trustworthy soldiers. In word and writing they denied that any uncalled for bloodletting had occurred. To the extent that any excess had occurred it was provoked by the conduct of the Serbian population. I never was able to receive a report on the numbers or make-up of the victims, but they denied that there were women or children among the victims. I believed that I faced the exaggerations of the civil administration. On the basis of this belief, as well as the international situation, but above all German relations, and the Serb massacres against each other, the German and Croat situation . . . I did not consider the time favorable to uncover such a mess, which would disturb the country's peace. I was too young a Chief of Staff to go into such a fight alone. . . . On the government's request I put aside the matter.[23]

Horthy, also unwilling to let civilians interfere, sent a minor official to investigate, and he and Czeydner put together a short report with statistics of persons executed as partisans. Bárdossy was suspicious and thought of resigning, but it was a critical period, with discussion of the election of a vice regent. Horthy had been seriously ill in November and his doctors feared his death. The responsible officers were only brought to trial in December 1943.[24]

After the Novi Sad massacre, relations between Hungary and Serbia have never been the same. Known in Serbian history books as the *Racija,* it has also featured prominently in Hungary in books and films and is still one of the most-discussed atrocities of the Nazi era. As late as 2006 an elderly man in Hungary, Sandor Kepiro, aged ninety-two, was identified as a junior police officer who had taken part in the raids and his guilt was being debated.[25]

MOBILIZATION OF THE SECOND ARMY

The Hungarian military had been prepared to fight only to protect its borders against one of its neighbors. The Second Army was totally unprepared to cope with the requirements of fighting a mobile war against modern heavy artillery and armored troops, the army woefully lacking in equipment and experience. Although the Ministry of Defense ordered that the troops should get the best quality of everything and the Second Army got about half of all the weaponry in the country, it was still poorly equipped, especially in comparison to the German and Russian armies. There was a shortage of vehicles but the shortage of antitank weapons was the most devastating. The Germans had promised one hundred antitank guns but the Hungarians received about a dozen, which were useful only if they came with tractors, for horse-drawn guns became immobile once in battle; the Hungarian army itself had mainly horse-drawn vehicles. The equipment they did receive from the Germans—guns, tanks, radios—was not only second hand and run down but unfamiliar. The troops did not know what to do with the weapons they suddenly received. Lacking training and experience with modern weapons, many soldiers were not even familiar with motorized vehicles; few knew how to drive.

There was also the problem of lack of education; many recruits had six years or less of elementary education.[26]

In an attempt to burden each part of the country equally and not to weaken Hungary's defenses at home, mobilization of the Second Army differed from the existing military practice. Minister of Defense Bartha and Chief of the General Staff Szombathelyi were concerned to maintain homeland defense and at all costs to prevent a repetition of the disaster at the end of World War I when Czech and Romanian troops invaded the country. They made the suggestion that the troops should be raised from all parts of the country, not only from the territory of the already mobilized three army corps. Thus the mobilization would have little effect on the best-trained age groups. Horthy agreed to the suggestions, adding only that the Sixth and Ninth Corps defending the Romanian border should not be touched by the mobilization.

This form of mobilization—a major departure from the usual method—had lasting consequences. In the traditional system, men were called up together with others from their region. They knew each other, served together, went through training and maneuvers together, building up a sense of comradeship. They felt the closest relationship with those in their section of ten, then with the company, and felt some loyalty to the division or regiment. In contrast, in the mobilization of the Second Army, for example, the mobilized armored division was an improvised force drawn from different parts of the country. Although an armored division required a year of training and relied on cooperation, these men had not trained together and therefore had trouble in battle with incorrect signals and poor communication.[27]

The commander of the Second Army supply division, General Staff Major József Tóth-Halmay, commented on the manner of mobilization: "Unfortunately, this conception, fine in principle, turned out not to be fine in practice. The ordinary man only saw that, while he was here in Russia for almost a year, bearing the full burden of the war, those who remained in the village were able to conduct their daily work in peace and quiet, in fact, with the departure of the recruits their earning possibilities kept improving, while those called up were continually worrying about their families' subsistence. It was impossible to explain this situation in any logical way to the masses."[28]

Collection of the troops for the Second Army began in February. The call-up of enlisted men was not to exceed 20 percent in order to take only a small number of the younger men most valuable in the eyes of the army. To make up the numbers it was necessary to call on the reserves, with the remaining number to be supplemented from those between thirty and forty-five years old. Non-Hungarian nationalities were to make up 20 percent, and Jews and members of leftist organizations not more than 10 percent.[29] Of the non-Hungarians, many were Romanians and Ruthenians from the reannexed territories who served primarily in service and provisioning. It had been intended to include many Swabians, but this did not happen, perhaps because the government had just given permission for 20,000 Hungarians of German origin to be recruited into the Waffen-SS.[30]

György Váró, one of those mobilized from the thirty- to forty-five-year group, was called up just a few weeks after his wedding on May 20, 1942, in a seemingly politically motivated decision. As a member of Parliament with parliamentary immunity his mobilization was illegal. "As I later heard, they said that we young representatives had not been called up, but had volunteered ourselves to go to the front. This was not true. . . . As far as I know it was arranged by the Transylvanian party leadership."[31] Váró believed his call-up was in retaliation for his protest against Hungarian landowners regaining forestland, which had been taken away in the Romanian land reform. Imre Mikó, another prominent young Transylvanian representative who did not protest was not called up. Ivan Boldizsár was called up for the second time in June 1942, leaving behind his wife and two-week-old son, Gábor. He commented bitterly about those recruited with him: "All men in group over 30. Horthy wanted to keep young ones at home. I was youngest—30th birthday at front. . . . Everyone going to the front is sure he will die."[32]

Before leaving for the front the troops received six weeks of training—often extended by a few more weeks because of problems with transportation—but it still was not enough time to develop the cohesion and spirit of cooperation needed. Increased war maneuvers were conducted with sharp shooting and artillery fire so that the troops would not arrive completely unprepared, but lack of ammunition hindered preparation for battle, while the Easter and Whitsuntide holidays interrupted training. In a meeting of the Supreme Defense Council in October 1942 Szombathelyi explained that troop training had been primarily theoretical because of the lack of weapons, but also because Hungary had no training ground large enough for the troops to train together. Officers later realized that not enough emphasis had been placed on protection—the building up of a system of covered trenches—which was to prove disastrous at the front. The young recruits, who had never seen a tank before, suffered from tank panic; they had no practical experience of aircraft bombing and did not know how to hide.[33]

General Gusztáv Jány was chosen to be in command of the tragically fated Second Army. Jány had been passed over for the position as chief of the general staff in favor of Szombathelyi, who was lower in rank, and because of the slight he asked to be retired, but Horthy would not hear of it. He valued Jány's long experience and personal and military bearing, and also that he was completely removed from anything political. Jány only learned of the details of the summer campaign and the role to be played by the Second Army when he met with Hitler on May 16; Operation Blau [Blue] was to destroy the Soviet forces facing Army Group South, take Stalingrad and the oil fields in the Caucasus. The Hungarian command was to operate in the Lower Volga territory along with the Romanians and Italians. Jány was dissatisfied with the limited training of the troops, but on complaining to the Hungarian military leadership he was told that there would be time to perfect their training at the front where the Germans would provide them with modern antitank guns. Yet, once more the German promises remained unrealized and there was no time at the front for further training.[34]

The military leadership tried to prepare the officers for the conditions they could expect; Szombathelyi personally held lectures on the Red Army and gave detailed explanations on the experiences and battles faced by the Rapid Force the year before, but the Hungarian army was top-heavy with generals who had served in the Austro-Hungarian army and were too old for World War II. It was unavoidable that many officers landed at the front who had spent years in administrative positions and had been more interested in social than professional duties; during the interwar period dashing officers in fancy uniforms were an attraction at balls. The military also reflected class divisions in society. Hungarian officers had many servants in contrast to the Germans—a Hungarian officer would not sit at the same table as his driver. The weakest point of the army was the regiment and battalion commanders, who had had only occasional contact with troops and could not keep up with modernization, especially technical developments. Their experience had prepared them for a war similar to the Great War, and they were often shocked to realize the realities of fighting a highly mobile war; a number were completely incapable of enduring the battleground conditions and in a few months returned home sick. The Jewish laws had also depleted the ranks of officers at the time when the army was struggling with a serious lack of officers.[35]

The Need for a Vice Regent

The recruiting of the Second Army and its departure to the front received less public attention than one might have expected, since the country was distracted by a momentous political event—the debate over the election of a successor to the regent. Now seventy-four, Horthy had been taken seriously ill in November 1941 and the weight of his office was bearing heavily on him. He urged Prime Minister Bárdossy to settle the matter of his succession, asking that Parliament choose a vice regent who would automatically succeed to the regency in the event of his resignation. The Act of 1937 was no longer effective. The act provided that both houses of parliament would choose one of three individuals named by Horthy to be his successor, but of the three nominees one was dead and the other two were almost as old as Horthy. Horthy feared that if he became incapacitated or died suddenly the Far Right would take advantage and install its own candidate as regent. His concern appeared justified, as the far-right Archduke Albrecht, a Habsburg member of the upper house of Parliament and extremely ambitious, had advanced his own campaign to succeed the regent.[36]

Horthy's older son, István Horthy, had been recommended as his successor, an attractive idea in that it offered political continuity and stability. Horthy and his son were very close and Horthy would be able to cooperate with him unconditionally. At thirty-seven István's credentials were excellent: a man of high integrity and an Anglophile, he would be a bulwark against the Far Right and growing German pressure. István Horthy was a mechanical engineer and had traveled widely, including eighteen months working at the Ford Dearborn factory in Detroit, where, rejecting every privilege that he would have received as the son of the Hungarian head of state, he had gone through every step as a worker until he reached the position of engineer. Henry Ford personally followed the experimental work of the young engineer and invited him to his home a number of times.

On his return to Hungary he became chief engineer at MÁVAG:Vas-, Acél, és Gépgyárak, [the Royal Hungarian State Iron, Steel and Machine Works], and after seven years in that position he was named head of MÁV, the Hungarian State Railways. He was an enthusiastic pilot, the owner of a one-motor sports plane, in which he and his wife, Countess Ilona Gyulai Edelsheim—with whom he had a small son—had spent their honeymoon visiting Egypt and the Near East.[37] István had also volunteered for military duty, training as an air force officer, taking part in annual air force military maneuvers, and volunteering with the First

Army fighter plane regiment on the return of northern Hungary, when he served for four months as a pilot. On the return of Ruthenia he again volunteered for military maneuvers, becoming a flight commander and was named air force second lieutenant. along with his class in 1939.

The question of concern for many was not so much that István had no political experience, but whether his election would be a significant step toward establishing a dynasty. Those still hoping for a return of the Habsburg monarch, the legitimists and higher clergy, feared the move as a possible obstacle. István Horthy was a Protestant like his father, and the head of the Hungarian Catholic Church, Prince Primate Jusztinián Serédy, did not favor the proposal. Serédy had always viewed the regent first as a Protestant and then as head of state. The Reformed (Calvinist) Church naturally supported the candidacy. The proposal created a major domestic upheaval with criticism from all sides—the government party suspected that István had dynastic ambitions, and some did not like his Anglophile leanings; the extreme Right opposed it mainly because he was an Anglophile, as well as having many Jewish friends; the middle-class opposition wanted to prevent the continuation of the present conservative regime. István himself turned down the suggestion point-blank when it was first formulated at the home of a member of the upper house, Béla Somogyi. He was perfectly happy with his present life and devoted to his engineering career.[38]

The public knew little of István Horthy other than rumors that he liked the good life and loved to party—His wife Ilona explained: "Those who saw him [when invited for dinner or when dancing at some club] believed that he never worked, and those who knew him from the work place believed he was a serious person who worked without pause."[39] The government attempted to promote István but without much success, the press describing him as a modern man, characterized by a sense of industry and duty, with a sensitivity to social problems—all of which was true, but did not increase his popularity in conservative circles or with the public. The gossip on the grapevine, which emphasized his western orientation and decided anti-German feelings, was much more successful. There was hardly anyone in the country who had not heard how, in the presence of German diplomats at the Arizona nightclub, István had played the British Anthem (or in another version Tipperary) with the band.

The Far Right under Imrédy supported Habsburg Archduke Albrecht, but despite his rightist views he got no support from Germany—in fact Hitler refused to receive him. The Arrow Cross party initiated a campaign of defamation, with fliers flooding cities, castigating István as a "thoroughly debased drunkard and an immoral, degenerate womanizer, an Anglophile traitor, and a dandy with Jewish morals, wallowing delirious in the delights of depravity."⁴⁰ The fliers did not improve Albrecht's cause with Hitler, but they did increase Horthy's antipathy to Szálasi and his party. They rallied the Smallholders and Social Democrats who otherwise would probably have opposed István's vice-regency. Even Imrédy denounced the Arrow Cross campaign. István Horthy was elected vice regent on February 19 at a joint sitting of Parliament with 280 members of the lower house and 203 members of the upper house present, two-thirds giving their written endorsement. In the course of debate on the bill, the conservative and liberal opposition, while expressing their reservations, had been willing to compromise, partly because the proposal to make István vice regent did not include the most controversial clause, the right of succession, but also because of the ever-more-aggressive measures of the extreme Right. Albrecht and other Habsburgs, Imrédy and his party and most of the Arrow Cross representatives were demonstratively absent, and István was elected by acclamation. The papers of the liberals and the opposition expressed their high esteem of István. *Népszava* and *Esti Kurir* emphasized that he had worked alongside the working class and was sensitive to their needs, also that he was a fine soldier. In the military, no one showed enthusiasm except for Szombathelyi; most were indifferent.⁴¹

The German press was cool. German leaders considered István an Anglophile and a friend of the Jews who could be considered an opponent of National Socialism, but with their increasing economic and military needs they had not wanted to officially move against the election. The Italian press was more favorable, reporting that István was a modern man to his fingertips, while the Allies were uninterested. Goebbels in his diary of February 20, 1942, wrote: "Horthy's older son has been elected Vice Regent in the Hungarian Parliament by acclamation. This is a matter of major political rigging. But we are refraining from taking any position on it. . . . The older son of Horthy is a pronounced Jew-lover, an Anglophile to the bones, a man without any profound education and without broad political understanding; in short, a person with whom, if he were Regent of Hungary, we would have some difficulties to work out."⁴²

Horthy's wife described István's reaction on the evening following the election after they returned from a family supper and the customary bridge game with the regent and his wife. István stood in the middle of the room, gazing in front of him with an infinitely sad expression. "What a responsibility and how black the future seemed. I knew what it meant to him, that he would no longer be able to follow his calling, his engineering work."[43]

Prime Minister Bárdossy Out, Miklós Kállay In

As the Second Army was being mobilized Horthy resolved to remove Prime Minister Bárdossy, whom he blamed for the state of war with the Soviet Union and the United States—and that Hungary was now in the process of sending a large army to fight in the vast steppes of Russia. Bárdossy had lost the confidence of the upper house leadership when he did not even consult them on the question of taking Hungary into the war against the Soviet Union. His decision, under German pressure, to declare Hungary at war with the United States in December 1941 had stunned leading Hungarian circles, who believed it important to keep doors open to the West. It was also under his administration that the Novi Sad massacre had taken place.

Horthy decided that in the current crisis what was needed was a "real Hungarian"—a man who would be able to stand up to the Germans, neutralize the noisy right-wing extremists, and protect the country's interests in wartime. To Horthy there was only one man, who seemed to fit this description—Miklós Kállay. The British historian C. A. Macartney, who was personally acquainted with the leading figures of the time, described Miklós Kállay as "a Kállay of Szabolcs County; and that itself, to any Hungarian, was a characterization. Szabolcs County, on the left bank of the middle Tiza, had always been one of the most Hungarian parts of all Hungary."[44] The county was ethnically pure Magyar, except for a very considerable Jewish population which had established itself in the towns in the nineteenth century. "If Szabolcs might be called the quintessence of Hungary, and the Kállays of Szabolcs, Miklós Kállay was the quintessence of the Kállays."[45]

In early January Horthy had already been considering Kállay to replace Bárdossy. Kállay noted, "Horthy had even dropped certain hints of his intention to appoint me when we met in January, at a shooting party given for Ribbentrop."[46] Kállay obviously annoyed Ribbentrop by suggesting to him that it was a mistake for Germany to draw small nations like Romania and Hungary into an offensive war, asserting that in general "a small nation's radius of activity could never extend beyond its historic frontiers. . . ." Horthy praised him afterward saying, "that was the way to talk to the Germans; great changes were imminent, and I should prepare myself for them."[47] Shortly after March 4 Horthy summoned Kállay to the Royal Castle and explained that he had been completely disappointed in Bárdossy, whom he had appointed after Teleki's suicide because he was a career diplomat. His task was to steer the country out of the Yugoslav crisis as smoothly as possible, but instead Bárdossy confronted him with one *fait accompli* after another, and was now trying to force loyal people out of the cabinet such as Minister of the Interior Keresztes-Fischer. In asking Kállay to become prime minister, the regent affirmed his complete confidence in him, whose views he knew and approved. As prime minister he would have a completely free hand and could proceed as he wished. As regent he would not interfere in the selection of the cabinet except to retain his control over military affairs, and the appointment would be for the long term. If ever there was a problem with Parliament, he would dissolve it and Kállay could call for new elections. The unusual conditions offered demonstrated the regent's eagerness to persuade Kállay to take on the post; not since Bethlen had a prime minister been promised so much freedom of action.[48]

At first Kállay respectfully declined; he pointed out that the majority in the government party did not trust him and that the Germans would be hostile. As he later mentioned to a friend, the only foreign policy that he would pursue would be that of Teleki, but if "Teleki had found no way except suicide of remaining true to his principles" at a time when the country had not yet gone to war, "how could one follow this policy now, with Bárdossy's four wars on one's back?"

The regent persisted, calling Kállay daily, and finally he relented. When Kállay appeared in the regent's office to announce his decision, Horthy embraced him warmly with tears in his eyes and thanked him for undertaking this grave responsibility. As Kállay was leaving he met István Horthy, who when he heard the news exclaimed, "Now everything is all right; everything will be all right."[49]

Kállay's appointment surprised the nation's public but in general it was welcomed. It had been possible only because he had been inactive in politics since 1935, thus no one knew his views. Although an expert in agricultural matters, Kállay's political experience had been limited to the administration of his county and as minister of agriculture in the Gömbös government. People suspected that he was part of the conservative group, but being an unknown made him acceptable to the extreme Right and to Berlin. His political views were moderately conservative, hostile to all extremist movements, protective of the interests of the great landowners and respectful of Hungary's constitutional traditions. As a member of the upper house he had voted against a third anti-Jewish law, a signal to the extreme Right that on the Jewish question he shared the relatively tolerant views of his friend, Keresztes-Fischer.[50] In his diary of March 21, 1942, Goebbels notes: "In a report from Hungary we learn that Kállay in reality is everything other than friendly to the Germans. He comes from the Anglophile Clique and only pretends today to be friendly to the Axis. . . . This whole magyar Clique is so offensively egoistic that one can spare oneself paying them any attention. They fit into the Axis circle like a fist in the eye."[51]

Horthy and Kállay shared certain fundamental principles and assumptions. In the spring of 1942 neither believed that the Germans would be defeated—the Germans were at the height of their power, with control over Poland, Holland, Belgium, France, Denmark, Norway, Yugoslavia, and Greece and alliances with Hungary, Romania, Bulgaria, Slovakia, Croatia, and to an extent Finland. They had a foothold in North Africa and were advancing ever further into the Soviet Union. The two men calculated that there might be a stalemate in the war and a compromise peace. In domestic affairs they intended to resist the pressure of the radical Right—Horthy emphasized that the Arrow Cross and local Nazis should be considered enemies of the nation and outside the law—and they were also prepared to make certain concessions to moderate and left-wing forces.[52]

Although Kállay was determined to oppose new German demands and preserve the little elbow room that the country still had, he realized that he would have to make gestures friendly to Germany and if necessary anti-Semitic declarations. Imrédy's rightist group and the Arrow Cross contingent were daily growing more daring. Although their strength was estimated at only 5 to 6 percent of popular support, they were provocative and dangerous, and both German and right-wing propaganda influenced much of the population. He was prepared to promote his policies by a series of back-and-forth steps, which must be cautious enough to avoid provoking a German occupation and also to allow Hungary to coexist with Germany if a negotiated peace should leave the Reich dominant in Eastern Europe. This pragmatic policy became known as Kállay's "seesaw policy" or—after a Hungarian dance—the "Kállay two-step."

Still very much a political novice when he took office, Kalláy had few people whom he could ask for advice and had to maneuver with great care during the first months. From his memoirs it is clear that he could not express his policies openly, especially in the rightist dominated lower house. The only person with whom he could speak frankly was the minister of the interior, Ferenc Keresztes-Fischer, who shared many of his thoughts and plans; for a long time he did not even share his plans in detail with the regent in order to protect him.[53]

After discussing the need to introduce some kind of anti-Jewish measure with Keresztes-Fischer, he decided on the expropriation of large Jewish estates with compensation as being the least damaging to the Jewish population. Kállay was convinced that with the demands for land reform sooner or later the whole question of the large estates would have to be addressed, and he was able to convince prominent Jewish individuals that the law was in their interests. He hoped to keep new Jewish measures to the economic sphere, measures that would not hurt the majority of Jews and could always be revised after the war.[54] The law was accepted by Parliament with little discussion and announced on September 6, 1942. Further anti-Jewish measures included Law VIII revoking the law of 1895, which had made the Jewish religion equal with other recognized religions. Also Jewish schools would no longer receive any state or local government support. The upper house accepted these without any major opposition.

The following apocryphal story suggests his attitude: "One Sunday the local Jews sought out Kállay on his estate in Kállósemjén, and anxiously asked him if it was true that he intended to pass new radical rules against the Jews. Kállay answered: 'Did I ever ask for money from you?' 'Yes, Excellency, you did.' 'Did I promise that I would pay it back promptly?' 'Yes, you promised.' 'Na, and did I pay you back?' 'No, you surely did not give it back.' 'Then what do you fear from me and my promises?'"[55]

Kállay followed his see-saw policy, attempting to pacify the Germans but without becoming more committed to the war. His speeches were filled with pro-Axis, anti-Russian, and anti-Semitic utterances, and in his first months in office he followed the policies of his predecessor, including keeping Bárdossy's cabinet to reassure the Germans. He had barely taken office when the police arrested the leaders of the emerging independence movement, and soon after that about four hundred leftists, mainly Social Democrats, were conscripted and sent to the front in labor companies. From April the police started carrying out raids on communist cadres, leaders, and other leftists. In the uncertain situation with regard to the war, he made some very careful moves to make contact with the Western world, but did not go beyond that.[56]

The Independence Movement
Despite the wartime prosperity and passivity of much of the population, resistance to the war had already begun with the attack on the Soviet

Union. The various middle-class liberal groups, the Social Democrats, some pro-British political figures, as well as the tiny Communist Party saw as their first duty to make propaganda against the war. The most influential slogan was the demand for an independent, democratic Hungary. Although it was not possible to express anti-German attitudes openly, people found ways to make their feelings known. The frequent literary and artistic evenings presented opportunities to express views, and in the press journalists found means to evade censorship, counting on their readers to read between the lines.[57]

The day before the outbreak of the war in June 1941, an article appeared in the recently founded anti-German daily, the *Magyar Nemzet*, entitled "Insane or Emperor: Sleepless, misogynist; mortal enemy of democracy; cultural dictator; Eagle's Nest in the Alps." The subject of the account, written by a civil servant under the pseudonym János Lénárd, was the mad King Louis II of Bavaria, but it was hardly surprising that the readers of the daily recognized not Louis but Hitler in the description. The timely portrait and parable-like account caused an uproar.[58] According to gossip the German minister in Budapest, Otto Erdmannsdorff, even complained to the foreign minister that the article could be easily misunderstood.

Hungary had a long-standing tradition of using memorials and the anniversaries of national martyrs for political demonstrations. The laying of wreaths on the graves of national heroes was—and still is—a favored way of demonstrating political views. On the October 6, 1941, less than four months after the declaration of war, an antiwar demonstration took place at the eternal flame memorial to Count Lajos Batthyány, the martyred political leader of the 1848 revolution for independence who had been executed on October 6, 1849 by a military firing squad along with thirteen generals.[59] On November 1 a larger group of demonstrators gathered for a wreath-laying ceremony at the grave of Lajos Kossuth, the leader and hero of the 1848 revolution.

The Christmas 1941 issue of *Népszava*, the newspaper of the Social Democrats, celebrated Hungarian independence and antifascism with articles written by Social Democrats, Communists, Village Explorers, and two prominent figures, Endre Bajcsy-Zsilinszky, a nationalist and prominent leader of the Independent Smallholders party, and the respected Catholic historian Gyula Szekfű. Szekfű's participation as a representative of the middle-class intelligentsia was especially notable. He had become a patron of the Village Explorers, some of whom had been his pupils. The issue, named the "Independence Front" issue, caused a great sensation, not so much for the content of the articles but for the mixed composition of the contributors. It surprised pro-Fascist Hungarian society and won approval from those opposed to the Right, as well as of the BBC.[60]

Early in 1942, as the Second Army was being mobilized, two movements began which were to gain significance as the war proceeded, one by a leftist opposition and the other by conservatives. In February, the Hungarian Historical Memorial Committee came into being—including Social Democrats, Smallholders, the Peasant party, as well as Communists. Their goal was the cultivation of Hungary's historical traditions, especially the upcoming centenary of the 1848 revolution. Although the respected Szekfű became president, members of the board included known critics of the government, including the Village Explorer, Imre Kovács. The committee, with the approval of the minister of the interior, Ferenc Kereztes-Fischer, organized a demonstration with antiwar slogans on March 15, the greatest national holiday, at the statue to Petőfi, the poet and martyr of the 1848 revolution.[61]

In January 1942 a more conservative group gathered around István Bethlen in informal friendly gatherings to discuss how to break away from the German alliance. Bethlen had been reviled by the opposition parties during his ten-year administration in the 1920s as hindering reform, but now had become the grand old man of Hungarian diplomacy. A member of the upper house of Parliament, he was instrumental in bringing together the dissimilar opposition parties, conservative and liberal politicians, in an Independence Front. The diverse group included several legitimists, Count György Apponyi and Count Antal Sigray;[62] Ferenc Chorin, a member of the circle close to Horthy, owner of a huge industrial complex who had close links to other wealthy Jewish families; and the former diplomat, Rudolf Andorka, who had resigned as minister to Madrid because of his opposition to the pro-Nazi policies. The group also included several leaders of the liberal opposition parties: Károly Rassay, editor of the *Esti Kurier* and founder of the Independent National Democratic party, Árpád Szakasits, Social Democratic leader and editor of the *Nép Szava*; and Zóltan Tildy, a Protestant minister and leader in the Independent Smallholders Party. The general consensus was that until the policies of the government changed there was little that they could do.[63]

The March 15 demonstration by the Historical Memorial Committee ended unfortunately. Although the planned participation of Social Democrats, who were held suspect for their slogans of class warfare, was called off, and the attendance of masses of workers was also called off at the request of the police, it was unfortunately too late. Several thousand participants gathered at the statue to Sándor Petőfi and then marched on through the center of the city to the statue of Kossuth, shouting slogans against the war and the Germans. Police broke up the demonstration and arrested about ninety participants. A deputation of Social Democrats, aided by Szekfű, was able to get most of them released, and on the promise of future good behavior Kállay agreed not to take any further action against the Independence Front, but in the next weeks the Communists initiated several activities on their own, circulating leaflets and carrying out minor deeds of sabotage.

At this time the administration began to carry out the series of anti-leftist raids, which lasted for several months and resulted in the arrest of a number of Communists and other leftists, including Communist Party leaders Zoltán Schönherz and Ferenc Rózsa. Rózsa died from torture and Schönherz was executed. A number of Social Democrat union organizers and party leaders were sent to the front in labor companies. Others were saved by the intervention of moderate members of the Independence Front.[64] Through the investigations information came to light that was an embarrassment to the noncommunist members of the Independence Front. The discovery of the so-called Davidson letters, delivered by the English wife of the Hungarian Consul-General in Istanbul to Szakasits and Imre Kovács, suggested that the two men might be involved in activities detrimental to the existing regime. The letters contained the message that the United States and Britain hoped for a strong popular opposition that would eventually be able to take over government. The affair led to Szakasits' resignation as secretary of the Social Democratic Party and Kovács doing a turn in prison.[65]

As a result of the arrests and revelations of undue communist influence, the committee was dissolved, deciding to wait for a more favorable situation. The Social Democrats were seriously affected since the leading role of the Communists in the Independence Front Movement had become clear. During the spring and summer both the Social Democrats and the Smallholders remained passive.[66]

Hungarian Troops to the Front

Movement of the Hungarian troops by train to the eastern front began in April. Slow at first, it did not reach its full compliment until July 7. When the Second Army reached the Don at Voronezh the troops arrived exhausted. The very success of the German attack meant that they had had to advance much farther than expected. There had been difficulties with transportation, and most had spent eight days sitting on a train. It often happened that because of lack of fuel the troops were immobile. Along the way Soviet partisans had damaged the railroad line, and even if the tracks were not blown up there was the possibility of mines, making it perilous to get off the train and walk. Troops detrained from whatever station they ended up at, and from there they had to march 1,000 to 1,200 kilometers under the summer sun.[67]

After the first phase of Hitler's Operation Blau, Hitler ordered that all available forces be concentrated on the southern sector. He intended to destroy the enemy before the Don and to secure the Caucasus oil fields and high-mountain passes. The goal was to cut off the Soviet Union from the wealthiest part of their country, including its oil supplies. Hitler was also obsessed with the fear of losing the Ploesti oil fields in Romania. Despite the losses during the winter campaigns, Hitler was convinced that the German force would be sufficient to finish the Soviets. The Germans had been able to raise thirteen new divisions in January, with another nine created soon afterward, but they still had to count on the assistance of troops raised from the minor allies to back up the German attack. The contributions of the minor allies included six Italian, ten Hungarian, and five under-strength Romanian divisions, but the minor allies were less well trained than the Germans, generally had fewer weapons, and less reliable equipment. Only one Italian division was considered the equivalent of an average German formation.[68]

The Soviets were ill prepared. Until the fall of Voronezh the *Stavka*, misled by German deception operations, had continued to regard Moscow as the primary target. On May 8 General Erich von Manstein began his attack into the Kerch peninsula of the Crimea and by May 19 his eleventh army had taken the peninsula. He then redirected his forces to Sevastopol where he methodically reduced the fortress between June 7 and 4 July.[69] By July 9 the northernmost German armies on the southern front had reached the Don opposite Voronezh. The Soviet forces crumbled. On June 28, designated as D Day, the attack began as scheduled, as four German armies—the Sixth Army, Fourth Panzer Army, First Panzer Army, and Seventeenth Army—faced and defeated four Russian armies. The way was open before them to cross the southern steppe—the treeless, roadless, sea of grass. A German survivor recalled: "It was easily the most desolate and mournful region of the East that came before my eyes. A barren, naked, lifeless steppe, without a bush, without a tree, for miles without a village."[70]

In July as the Hungarian troops were arriving at the Don the odds were heavily in Germany's favor. Stalin's spring offensive to retake Kharkov, a vital German rail junction, had failed, and the attempt to drive the Germans out of the Crimea had also failed at great cost. The Soviet forces were in disarray. Rostov fell, abandoned by panicking soldiers. On July 28 Stalin issued Order No. 227, *Ni Shagu Nazad!*—not a step backward. The order mandated that any commander or political officer who retreated would be assigned to a punishment battalion; penal battalions, much worse than the Hungarian labor companies, were given the most dangerous work, sent ahead through minefields. Yet, despite the use of force the war had become more than just a defense of communism—it had become a patriotic struggle.[71]

In July 1942 the young officer, György Váró, described the destruction he had seen traveling from Pest to his assignment at the Don. On reaching Kiev he described the ruins of this huge city:

On the main street on each side the walls were blown up, burned out houses, reaching to the sky although the more elegant part of the city was comparatively intact. From Staryy-Oskol to Semidesjacko we were directed to a railroad coach complex. On the way I was surprised by how many discarded tractors one could see next to the shot up deserted tanks. . . . It was a bitter experience to see the neglected and suffering wounded, who were waiting in the courtyard of a camp hospital for their wounds to be bound and cared for. . . . As the commander of the railroad post, luckily I only had to see to the delivery of feed for the horses, and thus only heard the gunfire on the Don from far away.[72]

Since the fast-moving German units had already destroyed the nucleus of Soviet resistance the Hungarians at first did not meet serious Russian opposition. Still the officers were shocked by the vastness of Soviet terrain in which their soldiers nearly disappeared. With consternation they remarked that they lacked experience to know what to do with the mass of equipment they received.

Despite the training they had received in war maneuvers before leaving for the front, a number of higher officers felt unsure and not up to the task. In January 1942 Major General Jenő Major assessed their situation: "Our Hungarian Army still does not know itself well enough to believe blindly in its own strength, but this self-confidence is necessary in war or peace."[73]

By the end of July Hitler was so confident that he agreed to a change of plan—dividing his forces in half—which turned out to be disastrous.

General Ewald von Kleist was to take the First Panzer Army with Army Group A to the Caucasus, while General Maximilian von Weichs's Army Group B moved eastward across the Don to take the city of Stalingrad. In order to take the city of Voronezh, Field Marshal Fedor von Bock diverted the Fourth Panzer Army to attack the city, leaving Paulus' Sixth Army alone without tank cover to cross over from the Don to the Volga at Stalingrad. As Hitler had feared, Bock's tanks were drawn into the battle of Voronezh, and although Hitler intervened personally ten days later on July 13, ordering the tanks to continue as planned and replacing Bock with Weichs as commander of Army Group South, the damage had been done.[74]

The Russians had also become wilier. The German advance had failed to take in the massive prisoner hauls of the previous year. Stalin and Timoshenko had learned from their mistakes, and on July 6 the *Stavka* issued an order to the Soviet forces to conduct a strategic retreat, allowing the troops to slip away out of danger. In the days between July 8–15, while the Germans were experiencing a fuel crisis, many Russian soldiers were able to escape. During the first three weeks of fighting Army Group A only took 54,000 prisoners.[75]

On July 23 Hitler ordered the continuation of Operation Blau, code-named Brunswick. Kleist's Seventeenth Army and First Panzer Army were to follow the Russians across the great bend of the Don, destroy them and then go on to Rostov; List's Sixth Army and Fourth Panzer Army were to push on to Stalingrad. Kleist's Army advanced rapidly at first, but then slowed when it reached the foothills of the Caucasus at the end of August. Its lines of communication covered 480 kilometers, leaving it open to Russian attack from the steppe.

The Germans continued their rapid drive forward. Army Group B moved across the Don River toward Stalingrad, becoming increasingly engaged in what was to have been a minor battle. The Red Army was pushed back toward Stalingrad day by day. On August 23 German units reached the outskirts of the city, while bombing destroyed most of it. Paulus, supported now by the Fourth Panzer Army, expected to seize the city and cut off the Volga route in a matter of days.

BRIDGEHEAD BATTLES

The Hungarian troops, exhausted from the long march and initial battles, took over the defense of the Don riverbank from the German rapid corps. Along with the other allied armies they were to fill in the gap as Army Group South began to extricate its forces for the drive to the Caucasus and the Volga. The Hungarians were placed in defense of the 200-kilometer-wide sector between Voronezh and Pavlovszk on the Don, but the Second Army had only eighteen infantry regiments to occupy the two hundred kilometer long line. With their reserves there was no possibility that they could defend the whole territory. The fighting troops numbered about 80,000 to 90,000; more than half of the army's members were technical, supply, railroad and sanitation workers. They also lacked the necessary equipment; there was a shortage of heavy armaments and antitank weapons and the supply of ammunition was intermittent. The first unit to reach the Don, the Third Army Corps, which took part in the June 28 attack with Army Group Weichs, lost 20 percent of its troops in four days of heavy fighting.

Under German pressure the Red Army had abandoned the west bank of the Don opposite the Hungarians, but it had retained three fortified bridgeheads in the areas of Uriv, Korotoyak, and Storozevoje. The bridgeheads were built on the bends of the river so it was not possible to go around them but they had to be attacked head on, and the Soviets were able to get reinforcements easily.[76] The assignment for the Hungarian Second Army was to take back these fortified positions. The width of the Don varies, in places not more than sixty meters, in others up to three hundred meters. The banks on both sides are swampy, with vegetation of sedge and shrubs as tall as a man. Because of the boggy swampy terrain on the banks, the main resistance line with light machine gun nests for defense had to be set up two to six kilometers from the river, with only weakly defended watch points directly on the bank. This meant that both sides could hide relatively unnoticed.[77]

From the end of July to the middle of September the Hungarian Second Army made three major attempts to drive the Russians from the bridgeheads. The first action from July 18–20 appeared at first to be a success, but because of the nature of the riverbank the Soviets were able to bring in reinforcements that could not be seen. To retaliate would have taken many more troops than Jány had. The only possibility was to build up the line of defense with observers. In the meantime, all the German troops had withdrawn and Jány had no reserves and lacked ammunition. The Soviets soon realized the weakness of the Hungarian army and started a forceful attack to occupy the west bank of the river. After the more mobile German armies , had disappeared, the Second Army could not defend the long front. The Hungarian line actually offered a target to the Soviet attackers; the 200-kilometer-long front could only be patrolled, and the German artillery units promised to them had not yet reached the Don.[78]

The soldiers were completely exhausted. The Germans did not supply them with sufficient food or equipment—even water was lacking and those at the front seldom had warm meals. The commander of the Third Army Corps reported: "I do not consider the moral resistance of the (7th) division such that they can stand against the ever increasing pressure from the enemy. . . . As I recommended before, the relief of the division is desirable."[79] The commander of the Twelfth Light Division opposed a command for the units to attack and stated on August 6 that it was mistaken to order the unrealistic attack—the infantry and bicycle battalions—exhausted from the six-week march and without battle experience, were not trained for the unfavorable terrain, and without air protection the order was irresponsible.[80]

Váró, commander of the railroad post, reported:

I had the opportunity to speak with many soldiers and officers of the Second Hungarian Army, and a united opinion emerged from their words, that the whole Hungarian army was a sacrifice, abandoned by the Germans. They complained about the lack of weapons, the lack of firepower, in contrast to the Russian artillery. They spoke of a bridge across the Don, which lay just below the water level—thus could not be seen or bombed—but that the Russians could cross it easily and keep in touch with their positions on the right bank of the Don. . . . They spoke of certain officers who robbed carpets from the churches. The regular officers said that they were certainly protected by the army command.[81]

In August, with the second phase of the battle for the bridgeheads, the Hungarians asked for and finally received German support. Since the German troops were mobile they could attack the Russians in a frontal attack. They broke up the Soviet formations which the Hungarians with their horse-drawn artillery were unable to do, especially in the marshy terrain. Even if they received antitank weapons they could not put them into place. Chief of the General Staff Szombathelyi turned to the German military leadership several times to request that the Second Army's front be shortened or to strengthen them with reserves. All through the summer and fall the Hungarians were promised that the line would be shortened—that German or Italian troops would cover part of it, but nothing happened.

From April 23 to October 1, 1943, the Second Army suffered grave losses. There were about 1,000 officers and 29,000 men among the fallen, wounded, or disappeared. Lost were 15 percent of the commissariat, 20.5 percent of combat troops, 20 percent of the officers corps, and most commissioned officers and candidates. Losses of 89 percent hit the infantry, which they replaced with the noncombat personnel. The material losses were huge and could only be replaced with German equipment, but the Germans gave little—forty-six antitank guns and two light howitzers. They tried to replace needed weapons from confiscated supplies.[82]

In general, the Germans were not particularly critical of the Hungarian effort. The tank commander, German General Langermann-Erlencamp, wrote on September 14: "The Hungarian troops did everything that they were able in order to destroy the opposition and to retake the lost territory." Some of the Hungarian commanders explained that the troops were completely unprepared for a war against Bolshevism. The real reason for their courage was the desire to survive. Gyula Kovács, staff colonel, in a report from August 17, 1942 explained: "The army and probably the homeland itself did not see clearly the meaning of the war and their participation in it . . . they do not hate bolshevism or their opposition, the Russians."[83]

DEATH OF VICE REGENT ISTVÁN HORTHY

In reports of war news from the Second Army and the unfolding battle at the Uriv bridgehead, it had been suggested that the press should emphasize the activities of the air force and the performance of the vice regent, István Horthy. Shortly after his election the vice regent had asked to be sent to the Russian front where he joined a fighter air force squadron, the Szolnok flying unit, as a lieutenant in the Hungarian air force. On August 5, in a radio program, "The Front Speaks," several members of the fighter battalion gave a war correspondent their impression of István. They emphasized his leadership abilities, bravery, and his warm friendly manner, and that he did not take advantage of any privileges. Horthy himself said a few words about the significant events on the front, then briefly repeated his earlier appeal to adventurous youth to take pilot training and report to the air force.[84]

The press reports strengthened the impression that István Horthy was being prepared to be crowned. News spread on the front and at home that he would fly home on August 20, the celebration of St. Stephen's Day,[85] and with an enthusiastic crowd be taken to the castle to be crowned at the people's will. Nothing was farther from the truth. When his squadron commander suggested to Horthy that he fly home to celebrate his name's day on the twentieth he refused, insisting that he would not leave until he had completed his service tour.[86]

Instead, on the traditional celebration of St. Stephen's Day, as the seventy-four-year-old regent made his way along cobbled streets acknowledging the cheers of the crowds, Prime Minister Kállay was given the message, "István Horthy has had a flying accident. He has been killed." Kállay waited until after the mass celebrated in the Coronation Church when Horthy returned to the Royal Castle to break the unbearable news. Horthy fainted in Kállay's arms, recovered, and then fainted again.[87]

The question was not so much why the plane crashed; the Heja, of Italian design, was notoriously fragile. Rather it was why the second in command of the nation was at the front at all. The decision to send István to the front had been initiated by Szombathelyi, with the idea that he would gain military experience, build contacts with the officers' corps, and gain loyalty and prestige for his later duties. István was more interested in gaining information on the conditions of the troops, but also to divert criticism since he had been accused of cowardice. From the front he wanted to report on the lack of equipment and weapons, the troops situation, and to criticize the behavior of the German ally, who, he believed, exploited the Hungarians but also treated them as subordinates.

The regent agreed to Istvan's request although Prime Minister Kállay tried to dissuade him, believing that István was needed at home. Opposition leaders and legitimists also thought that the decision was unwise. Many pointed out that if István Horthy wanted to go to the front he could join the army command. Several government party members and opposition representatives—among them Imrédy and Andor Jaross—served at the front during the summer, but most were placed in the army staff under relatively safe conditions although they received great publicity at home.[88]

István's friend, Antal Náray, had tried to talk him out of going to the front, and two months later urged the regent to order him home, which he did on August 11. On the basis of the resolution passed by the Hungarian cabinet, István was recalled from active duty to assume his political responsibilities as deputy regent. But it took nine days for the order to arrive. Horthy died in action on August 20 at 5 A.M. when his plane crashed near Aleksejevo-Lozovskoje. The hopes that had been attached to him died with him.[89]

Few details were released about the crash, leading to all sorts of rumors. Some said that István had been celebrating his name's day the evening before and had been drunk. Others suspected German complicity, especially because a few weeks later Horthy's son-in-law also died in a crash, but it seems the deputy regent's crash was simply a fault of the airplane itself. It was a terrible loss for Horthy and his wife who went into a long period of mourning, but it was also a loss for the immediate future. István had been sending information to the regent through his wife and Gyula Tost, his aide-de-camp, in which he held the general staff responsible for the overly German-oriented policy and urged that the minister of defense, Bartha, be removed, that Hungarian participation at the front be reduced, and that no more troops be sent.

Shortly before his death in a visit with his wife, he told her that being at the front had convinced him even more strongly that the Germans were losing the war, and he could see that neither at the front nor at home would he be able to do anything to improve the situation. Therefore he had decided on his return to go either to England or the United States to see if he could do anything there for his country.[90] Hungary's fate might have been ameliorated if he had been able to carry out his plan. The younger Horthy son, Miklós Horthy Jr., who had been serving in Brazil as minister, returned home and later played an important role in preparations for the attempt to withdraw from the war, but he was never considered for the deputy-regent position.

The Conditions of the Second Army

In early September at the time of the third unsuccessful attack on the bridgehead of Uriv, Chief of the General Staff Szombathelyi visited the Second Army. The son of one of his close friends, István Csicsery-Rónay, reported fondly how the general had ordered that he—a lowly artillery ensign—be present in the review with other officers. The commander, József Grassy, probably could not understand why Szombathelyi would spend so much time talking to a lowly officer. Szombathelyi had brought him a package from home and saw that the camera men included him in the film they were making for the newsreel that would be played a week later in the *Pesti híradó* so that his parents could catch a glimpse of him.[91]

But the picture that met Szombathelyi was grim. At first hand he could evaluate the serious losses and could see that the level of equipment and training was not of the quality that the German command expected. But the army had not received the up-to-date weapons that the German leadership had promised, and there were serious problems with the German provisioning. Soldiers were united in the opinion that the provisions were unsatisfactory and insufficient, a problem caused partly by the limited Soviet railroad lines which did not have the capacity for delivery and were plagued by partisan activity. The Hungarians also had trouble with the German food—especially the *ersatz* (substitute) supplies. Hungarian cooks didn't know what to do with the puddings; the men had a hard time getting to like the cheese squeezed out of tubes, the anchovy paste they called snail meat, the artificial honey and weak tea.[92] From the fall of 1942 the army received Hungarian supplements in the form of bacon, paprika, and palinka. The horses were in a worse situation. Because of lack of fodder they had to be placed about 100 kilometer behind the front line and only a few remained at the front, which meant that most of the artillery was immobile.[93]

Yet Szombathelyi had no solutions to offer. He warned the commanders that the army would have to remain at the front throughout the winter and that they could not count on another round of weapons or other supplies from home. On his way home he visited the German headquarters at Vinnyican, appealing to the Germans to deliver the much-needed supplies and the promised weapons, but to no avail. On his return on October 5 Szombathelyi delivered his assessment of the situation of the Second Army to the Supreme Military Council. He ruled out a German victory and informed the council members that the war would go on for years, and they would have to count on the fact that the Second Army, already worn down, struggling with the lack of weapons, would have to remain at the front in 1943. In his opinion the Wehrmacht was trying to win time, and the war would drag on until Germany reached an acceptable peace. Recalling the events after World War I he emphasized the importance of keeping a military force at home to protect the country. Thus the council decided that they would not replace the Hungarian losses at the front but continue to develop the forces remaining at home.[94]

In September 1942 no one could have imagined the fast-moving collapse of the German armies and rapid advance of the Russians. The military high command still did not expect that the Second Army would engage in significant fighting, and they kept counting on German promises for supplies, simply believing that the Second Army needed to hold out on the Don while the Germans and Russians fought out the war. It was possible to imagine a retreat—but never the whole scale success of the Russian counteroffensive. The German collapse was quite different from anything in their experience.

Soon after Szombathelyi's visit to the front, Horthy appointed a new minister of defense to replace General Károly Bartha, who had been criticized for his pro-German policies. Horthy had begun to receive reports on the plight of Jews in the labor companies at the front. The military law under Bárdossy of April 1941 under which all Jews were ordered to serve in labor units in place of armed service, had applied only to those Jews who were conscripted. Now it was applied to all Jewish men between the ages of 18 and 48, including those who had been honored for their roles in World War I. Horthy received reports of cruel and sadistic treatment and acted favorably on a number of petitions for the recall of individuals, mostly from physicians and scholars.

The reports prompted him to dismiss Bartha and appoint General Vilmos Nagy, a former military attaché in London, who had a reputation for integrity and humanitarianism. On September 20, 1942, Horthy instructed Nagy, who had been brought out of retirement, to restore discipline and end the political activity that had become fashionable among the officers. But Nagy was to find that task impossible—the extremist right-wing and pro-German tendencies were too firmly embedded in the officer corps. He did achieve some success in ending the most blatant abuses in forced labor units, although officers at lower levels often sabotaged his orders.[95]

One of the most serious problems facing the new minister of defense was the provisioning and relief of the Second Army. Horthy had recently received firsthand witnesses on the situation at the Don from György Váró and several of his fellow officers, just returned from the Soviet front, who had been called to a session of the regent's cabinet. The regent was primarily interested in what they might know from close range about the death of his son, the deputy regent. Váró explained: "Of course, all we knew was what we had heard from the soldiers, who had mentioned the possibility of German sabotage."

The young officers recounted their experiences, the essence of which was that the whole army felt itself outcast. "It was their feeling that they had been abandoned as a sacrifice. The artillery of the Hungarian units was weak, the German allies were arrogant in their treatment of them and did not give them the requested and necessary air and tank support, they awaited their relief in vain, even though the time was long past. They heard from other soldiers, especially the Germans, that they were entitled to be given leave. From letters they received they knew that their lucky acquaintances, who had not been mobilized to the Second Army, were living happily at home. It was incomprehensible to them why exactly they had been condemned to this fate. They looked with longing at the members of the labor companies, since they worked behind the front and were not exposed to the Russian artillery."[96]

Nagy announced his intention to review the Second Army in connection with the obligatory visit to German headquarters. Before his departure he consulted with Prime Minister Kállay, who explained that relations with the Germans had greatly deteriorated. The latest battlefield events had shaken the Germans' belief in the legendary heroism of the Hungarian soldier. More importantly, according to German opinion, the Hungarian leadership had not proven equal to the task. Another point of dispute was the Jewish question, which the Hungarians had still not solved to Hitler's satisfaction. Ominously for the Hungarians, German relations with Romania had developed more favorably. Antonescu explained to his people that Romania was fighting on the German side to gain favor so that the second Vienna decision could be reviewed and Romania's borders would then reach westward into Hungary to the Tisza![97]

In his meeting with Nagy Hitler acknowledged that he had underestimated the military strength of the Red Army, since the Russians had only used the old type tanks in the war against Finland. But he continued with his expectations for success. According to Hitler the capture of Stalingrad was only a question of a short period of time; the Russians would not be able to withstand German artillery power. He did not expect the Russians to attack the line held by the Second Army.

After his meeting with Hitler, Nagy flew to the Second Army headquarters, located at a factory site at Aleksejevka, where he was met by the army commander, Gusztáv Jány. Although a well-qualified senior officer, Jány had gained his practical experience in the trenches in the Great War, and was described by Géza Lakatos, who had served under him, as a blood-and-guts officer, a forceful person, extremely brave, with an attractive manner and looks, but not without fault. He could be difficult to deal with because of his inflexibility, and he sometimes lost his temper, flying into a rage.[98] Jány was still offended that he had been passed over by the Szombathelyi appointment even though he had been next in line to be chief of the general staff.

Jány reported on the limitations of the army in defending the 200-kilometer stretch, pointing out that it was much too wide for the division's fighting ability. In comparison, the Fourth Italian division of the Eighth Army on their south flank had the task of defending about 180 kilometers, but covered only 30 kilometers. The Hungarian army had only 5,000 to 6,000 rifles, and neither the number of armored units at their disposal nor their equipment were adequate; antitank weapons were lacking; there was not enough artillery and larger caliber mortars; the reserves and supplies of food were not adequate, and there was not enough fodder for the horses. The German army corps, which was to be their reserve, was not under Jány's command; it could only be activated with the direct permission of Hitler. Jány explained that the Don was not a real barrier—not suited for defense. At the moment the Russians did not show any intention to attack, but with the next attack they would break through the army's front. Nagy promised that he would do everything within his power to solve the complaints.[99]

Jány, who had asked to be relieved on several occasions, may have realized the approaching catastrophe months beforehand. He was in an impossible position and got no help from home in delineating the extent to which he should remain loyal to the Germans. This became a problem when a few days before the Soviet offensive he had to decide whether to carry out German commands or try to save the army. Sacrifice of the army for the Germans was pointless but as an obedient officer he would not refuse a command.[100]

Nagy was especially concerned with the problems of the Jewish labor companies. In addition to the new law, which meant that Jews were called into labor service no matter what their age or social position, the Jews had been mobilized in a manner contrary to the usual mobilization practice by which men were called up by age group; they had been mobilized by the so-called SAS (an urgent call-up ordering individuals to report within forty-eight hours). This form of mobilization led to various kinds of abuse. Conditions were made worse by regulations that specified that Romanians, Serbs, and Jews were to get no favors and that they should not be relieved from service at the front.

Nagy issued orders forbidding that labor service men be treated as prisoners, that their provisions be adequate, and that the sick and those unable to work be immediately demobilized. He inspected the hospital and was distressed by conditions, especially for Jewish workers lying on straw pallets or just on straw. The next day he spoke with the commanders of the Fourth and Seventh Army Corps, Lieutenant Generals Csatay and Gyimessy, and again emphasized humane treatment of Jews. In checking on the troops he spoke to men in a worker company but he saw that it didn't please the commanders.[101]

Before returning home Nagy flew to the headquarters of the German commander, Weichs, in Bjelgorod, hoping that if he described the Second Army deficiencies he would be able to secure supplies and replacements. The town was so full of Germans that there were no lodgings available, so that he was put up in a railroad salon car, which had once been used by French President Poincaré. Weichs promised to help but explained that the Germans were having a hard time even supplying their own soldiers. The Soviets had begun to surround Stalingrad and would soon begin a counteroffensive. On his return, speaking to the regent, the Council of Ministers and the two houses of Parliament, Nagy criticized Hitler and the German military leadership for not delivering the promised weapons and emphasized that there was no way that the Second Army in its present state could hold the line against the approaching Soviet attack.[102]

News of state of the Second Army placed the leadership in a dilemma. The officers' corps, under the influence of the continuous flood of propaganda praising the Axis and repeating the news of the approaching common victory, was not prepared for the unfortunate turn of the war. Since it was forbidden to make any mention of losses or defeats, the actual situation had been kept hidden from them as well as the public. At the end of 1942 the greater part of the officers' corps believed the repeated broadcasts that promised the final victory and stood staunchly behind the German alliance, while the military leadership cautiously described the seriousness of the situation only to the highest corps of generals.

STALINGRAD

The Germans had become mired down in Stalingrad. On August 23 General Friedrich Paulus had expected to seize the city and cut the Volga route in a matter of days, but Stalin was determined to hold the city at all costs and the war raged around Stalingrad for the next four months. The siege was a departure from the mobile warfare at which the Germans excelled. The Soviets had time to mount a careful counteroffensive, and the Germans failed to sufficiently protect the flanks of the Sixth Army which were held by the allied armies: the northern flank by the Romanian Third Army, the northwest along the Don front by the Italian Eighth Army, and farther to the northwest the Hungarian Second Army. It was common knowledge that these allied armies had only inferior gear and the front they occupied extended for several thousand kilometers. But the Germans, who were short of troops, could not place significant reserves behind the allied armies and were unable to supply them with the weapons and equipment they lacked, especially antitank weapons to cope with Soviet tanks.

In Stalingrad there was bitter house-to-house fighting in mid-September. The Russian defense, led by General Vasili Chuikov, had retreated underground to tunnels and bunkers. By October the fighting had been going on for eighty days and eighty nights, and from October 18 the front was essentially stabilized in utter exhaustion. Hitler, who had the tendency to obsess with details and lose perspective, had forgotten why he wanted to take Stalingrad in the first place. The city was strategically important—but not that important.[103]

In the meantime, Stalin had brought in Marshal G. K. Zhukov, the savior of Leningrad and Moscow. Zhukov and A. M. Vasilevsky planned a dramatic advance—the wide encirclement of German forces on the lower Volga and the destruction of Paulus' Sixth Army—but the preparations took time. The defenders of Stalingrad were not informed of the plan because of the fear that their defense might falter. On November 11 Paulus made his final effort and the Fourth Panzer Army succeeded in reaching the Volga in the south, but this was to be their last success. On November 19 the counterattack began.[104]

THE SECOND ARMY IN FALL 1942

After the battle at Uriv in the fall of 1942, the Second Army was left with the 200-kilometer section to defend, but since it was unsure if the Germans would keep them there, they made only partial preparations for winter. They underestimated the size of fortification work to be done and began to build the trenches late. Their clothing was 25 to 20 percent worn out, footwear was 40 percent worn out, and the Wehrmacht failed to hand over the delivered food. At home people took up collections of warm clothing for the soldiers and on the initiative of various social organizations women and girls knit pullovers and woolen wristlets for the men.[105]

The replacement of the army's losses and gradual relief of those at the front became ever more urgent in the fall months. In his report to the Supreme Military Council of October 5, Szombathelyi explained that it was impossible to relieve whole formations; therefore, after replacements were made, they would start a slow exchange, but only for the combat troops who would be used to train others through their experience. The country had a minimal amount of weapons remaining and the general staff was concerned by the increasing number of incidents at the Transylvanian border and the ever-greater possibility of conflict with Romania.

On October 17, 980 officers and 33,400 troops were mobilized, and from September to December a number of worker companies were sent to the front, each with 250 men, to build fortifications. The replacements received only four weeks training and arrived almost completely without weapons—thirty rifles for a company. When they arrived at Belgorod or Korovino they were obliged to march on snow-covered roads for forty to sixty kilometers to the training camp, suffering losses on the way from partisan attacks. They had been trained by German officers but only in machine guns and automatic machine guns since other equipment was lacking.[106] Those sent to the front were not given special winter clothing but were, in principle, to ask for it from the troops returning home, an attempt to save money which led to catastrophe.[107]

At home there was still peacetime prosperity. No one knew how bad conditions were at the front. Iván Boldizsar, a young officer, who had taken an early Christmas leave from the front, was called in by his former editor, György Ottlik of the *Pester Lloyd*, a highly regarded German-language newspaper.[108] At first Ottlik did not want to believe the condition of the army—how poorly equipped they were—until Boldizsar gave him details comparing the Hungarian equipment to the German. He told him how the soldiers were freezing, that they had not distributed winter clothing, saying that they had to be kept in reserve for the next winter at the Volga! The next day, the editor, who was a member of the upper house, took him to a member of the Ministry of Defense to tell the story.[109]

In his memoir Boldizsar wrote how his leave-taking to go back to the army was worse than when he had first left, especially since his wife had thought he was coming home for good. He remembered thinking how could one face the front after seeing the peaceful conditions in Budapest, and he burned with anger: "Damn it—here you are eating, drinking, and dancing, amusing yourselves, watching soccer matches, going to the movies, and at the same time we are put out in the cold to freeze, or to perish in some other way." In the railroad coach he met others who had also been on leave, and they said to each other that it was wonderful at home, but it would have been better not to come. "They have written us off. These words we repeated again and again. They have written us off!"[110]

Defeat at the Don

The destruction of the Second Army at the Don over half a century ago is considered one of Hungary's great national tragedies, but it is only recently that the full chronicle of the war has been made known to the public.[111] Péter Szabó dedicated his work, *Don Kanyar* (The Don Bend), published in 2001, to the memory of the soldiers and labor company workers lying in unmarked graves in Russia. Reporting on the war was one of the last tabus to be lifted. Since the army had fought against the

Soviet Union historians avoided the subject, and after the turn of the year 1946/1947, survivors did not dare to talk about the Don. According to party historians, the Horthy regime had made up the Second Army from the poorest elements of society and political opponents—leftists, Jews, minorities—who were sent to the Don to die. For a long time the only story the public knew was that the unwilling army was sent out at German urging as cannon fodder and conducted itself poorly.[112]

The massive Soviet counterattack, beginning in November 1942, sealed the fate of the Second Army. The Soviets made their dramatic counterstrike on November 19 when the counteroffensive moved against the two Romanian armies holding the northern and southern flanks of the German Sixth Army and overran them. As Soviet units closed the ring around the Sixth Army, Field Marshal Erich von Manstein, head of the New Army Group Don, had to give up the effort to relieve Stalingrad and to evacuate German forces from the Caucasus. The battle of Stalingrad claimed enormous casualties—by the end of the year the Red Army had closely encircled the Germans in a defeat so serious that it proved decisive for the outcome of the war. Even the Soviets were surprised that their plan had worked.

Chief of the General Staff Szombathelyi realized that Germany's situation at Stalingrad was hopeless, but military circles remained convinced of the final victory of the Third Reich and could not comprehend that the Germans were losing—or recognize the weakness of their own army. At Christmas time Hitler telegrammed the regent describing the German troops' temporary setbacks. He warned that the Hungarian troops would experience a powerful attack, but he emphasized that it was essential for the whole eastern front that the Hungarian forces hold—even if the opposition should break through the defense line. He urged the regent to prevent the Hungarian soldiers from even thinking of retreating.[113]

Horthy replied that he would order tough resistance, but he complained that the Hungarian troops were not adequately equipped and lacked the means for prolonged resistance: "Please let us have some assistance in this regard." Hungary had been assigned too long a sector of the front and the troops were backed up by too few reserves. The Hungarians were still short of large caliber antitank weapons to cope with heavily armored Soviet tanks. On December 27, General Szombathelyi sent a telegram to Jány implementing Hitler's request. The order to Jány, issued in the name of the supreme commander, read that our positions must be held at any cost. "No one is allowed to retreat; there is no backward, only forward." On the same day Hitler ordered "all possible measures" to support the Hungarian army but the German military authorities were slow. The command, which has been much criticized, turned out to be mistake both for Szombathelyi and for Horthy.[114]

On January 12, 1943, the Soviets launched their attack against the Hungarian-held segment of the front at Voronezh. The Russian attack came as a surprise even though it should have been expected. The Soviets had an overwhelmingly superior force—three times as many soldiers and ten times as much artillery. The Don, thickly frozen, was no obstacle to the Soviet troops. The Hungarian troops were spread out in a thin line and were short of equipment. The Soviets broke through the Hungarian defense line at Uriv on January 12, and again at Scsucsje two days later. At first the army put up a tenacious resistance, but since it did not receive German support and the Soviet attack intensified, the units were separated. The German Army Group B failed to provide the necessary support.[115]

On January 15 the army headquarters' operational division could see that they would be unable to regain their original front since they lacked the resources for a successful defense. Jány asked permission to retreat but was told by Weichs that only Hitler could make that decision. By January 16 Jány realized that if they did not withdraw the divisions south of Uriv the army would be unnecessarily destroyed. In the afternoon, under pressure from his general staff officers, he again asked permission to move back to where the Seventh Corps was still holding, asking for notification at 8 P.M. At 7 P.M. the officers of the general staff gathered in Jány's room—he had the usual smile on his face although his nerves were shot. A little before eight the phone rang. His officers heard Jány's answer: "I understand, yes, to the last man, shell, hold at the Don." At the suggestion of one of his officers he then called Szombathelyi, then Horthy. Both were sorry, but said it was necessary to carry out the German command.[116]

Jány was caught between absolute obedience and the protection of his troops; his tragedy was that he chose the first. When a Soviet tank army broke through the German Twenty-fourth Panzer Corps line on January 14, endangering the Hungarian army from behind, it would have been reason enough for a responsible commander to avoid encirclement and retreat against orders. It seems that he simply fell apart under the responsibility, although his bravery was unquestioned; he remained with his troops, experiencing firsthand their conditions and sharing their fate. That day, he wrote: "I have to emphasize that the troops are doing everything of which they are capable." In his choice he differentiated himself from the mass of the Hungarian generals, but also from the German. Of the 352 Hungarian generals, fewer than ten fell at the front, and of the 1,400 generals of the Wehrmacht and the Luftwaffe, the German Air Force, only 500 were among the disappeared, either fallen or through suicide.[117] His actions and the measures taken after January 15 were characterized by his despair and hesitation, although it is questionable whether there was any brave and determined individual among the Hungarian Royal Army's general staff in the critical days of January 15–16 who could have resolved to take any independent step.[118]

Finally, on January 17 at dawn, with Army Group B's tacit knowledge, Jány gave the command for the Seventh Army Corps to retreat. His belated order meant that the troops came under attack a number of times and were only able to fight through with great difficulty. One part of the retreat was covered by the Italian Alpine Army Corps who had started their retreat on January 16 without informing the Germans or their Hungarian neighbors.

With the Soviet attack and the rapid collapse of the Hungarian units Jány issued an extraordinary command: "The Second Army has lost its honor, because with the exception of a few—true to their oath and duties—they have not carried out what everyone could have expected of them." He explained that the disgrace consisted not in losing the battle, but in the cowardly flight of the panic-stricken troops, bringing on the contempt of the German allies and the fatherland. The order continued, "No one will be allowed to return home, not for illness, for wounds, for frostbite, . . . everyone will recover here or perish."[119] This humiliating command was that of a distraught, broken man. It was a slap in the face for the troops under his command and had immeasurable consequences. The command reached the Germans, and even the Romanians translated it in southern Transylvania.

On the January 24, when the Germans decided to withdraw the Second Army from the front, there was not one word of praise; in fact it appeared that they were blaming the catastrophe on the Hungarians. Jány's command gave them every reason to disparage the Hungarian soldiers and make more demands of them. The disorganized retreat of the remains of the Second Army and the terrible losses and suffering were partially the result of German conduct. The soldiers and labor companies went through terrible suffering, the retreating stream on foot in the sea of snow. Some officers used brutal measures to stop the troops from fleeing, ordering them shot in the head if retreating, but discipline lost its effect. Some soldiers responded in defiance, demanding to be shot in the head rather than freeze slowly to death.[120]

The Wehrmacht's retreat was no more organized than that of the Hungarian army, but it took place on better roads and with the use of more motor vehicles. Jány soon came to himself out of his severe depression and later withdrew his command. On February 8, in a report to the chief of general staff he wrote that it was his impression that the Germans were using the Hungarians—even if without weapons—to secure their own units. His impression was born out by the fate of the Third Army Corps.

When the Soviets attacked, the Third Army Corps, under the command of Marcel Stomm, was cut off from the Second Army and placed directly under the German Lieutenant General Siebert, who commanded the German Seventh Army Corps.[121] Siebert, who was reputed to have gained his command through the influence of his Nazi brother, kept delaying the order for his corps to retreat and would not allow the Hungarians to join the retreating German units or to use the roads reserved for the German troops. "The attitude of Siebert and his chief of staff toward us was noticeably reticent and uncommunicative. From this we drew the conclusion that Siebert and the chiefs of staff were trying to cover up their own mistakes with the German Supreme Military Leadership through finding fault with the Hungarian III Corps."[122]

In the morning of February 2, 1943, Stomm received the notice from Siebert that his troops could break out from the encirclement by going west, an area that even the Germans had been unable to take. The Germans, who disdained the Hungarians, seemed to be sacrificing Stomm's troops to protect themselves. In light of this clearly impossible command Stomm chose to take a unique course that has been debated ever since. He announced that his unit was not able to carry out the German commands, and he believed the only way to save his troops was to let them break up into small groups and try to reach safety. In an unprecedented action he dissolved his corps and told everyone to take command of his own future since there was no food and no ammunition, leaving it to the men to decide whether to surrender or try to break through the Russian encirclement in small bands.[123]

Stomm was correct in assessing the situation as impossible, but as a result of his command his troops fell apart completely. Acting on his humanitarian principles he was not thinking of the simple soldiers who were being left on their own. His staff tried to talk him into remaining with the unit but he was a desperate man, sick and dispirited, and incapable of action. Part of the troops were eventually saved but after incredible horrors. Some higher officers of the army corps decided to stay with the troops and try to break out, but they were only allowed to use the road parallel to the main road used by the Germans. Stomm and his small staff tried to escape to the West. Two of his officers, Jenő Sárkány and Zoltán Buzinkay, committed suicide, and two days later, with frozen legs, Stomm was taken prisoner of war by the Russians.[124]

Taken to a command post, Stomm was cared for by white-coated doctors and nurses. On February 6, as he and his companions were being moved, they saw the dismal scene of the retreating Second Army—hundreds of frozen dead on the side of the road. To Stomm this was proof "that what the German leadership had asked of us was inhuman." His experiences strengthened his belief that the Second Army had suffered as many losses from the inflexibility of the German leadership as from the enemy.[125]

Iván Boldizsar described the retreat of his unit in the minus 38 degrees Celsius cold. The officers had all fled, the last one, an ensign, on January 16. He saw them taking their belongings in personal cars. As the highest-ranking member of the unit, Sergeant Boldizsar took over and decided to open up the warehouse where goods were stored. It was full of fur outerwear—fur hats with earflaps, long fur coats, fur boots, and also canned goods. His unit had only one truck, but later found a broken-down German truck and fixed it so all could ride. It was their luck that they didn't have to walk. Otherwise they would have joined all those who froze to death on the way.[126]

One of those in the Second Army who escaped was Kálmán Dreisziger. He retreated from the front lines, walking long distances alone or with small groups usually at night, often in minus 40 degrees Celsius temperatures. As a soldier allied with the Germans he risked being captured or killed by the Red Army or by Russian partisans operating behind German lines. As an unauthorized fugitive from his unit, he risked being arrested by Hungarian or German military police and being shot as a deserter.[127]

Lieutenant. László Szabó was one of those few officers, who were able to bring their troops home safe. He had been in command of an antiaircraft artillery unit defending the railroad station at Korotoyak. Early in 1943 Soviet warplanes began to attack the command in the early morning and late evening. With their four automatic guns the unit shot down eight Russian planes, but when the main attack came they lost their guns and fled—traveling southwest from Korotoyak toward Kharkov. At the end of the war Szabó and his family were taken prisoner by the English to the Ruhr garrison, where they received news from a relative that everything at home was fine. Although the English told them they could stay and they had a chance to go to America, they decided to go home. Because Szabó had fought against the Russians and been a prisoner in the West he was considered an enemy of the state; the family was left with nothing. A friend let them stay in his summer home. Unable to find any employment Szabó was finally able to work during the harvest as a thresher.[128]

Within one week the powerful Soviet forces had almost completely annihilated the Second Army. About 50,000 Hungarian soldiers were killed or froze to death in the course of the fighting and retreat. Seventy thousand were taken prisoner or disappeared. Of the 50,000 unarmed labor company members, only 6,000 to 7,000 returned home. The army lost 80 percent of its equipment, including almost all of the artillery and tank material.

Most of the remnants of the army returned home in early May. The commander of the Second Army, Jány, with a small group of officers, was received with a pro-forma celebratory welcome May 1 at the Budapest Eastern Railway station, but Jány was then retired and removed from public life. Returning soldiers were kept sequestered for a time as the government attempted to cover up the extent of the losses, but throughout the country it was easy to access "Kossuth Radio," the Hungarian broadcast from Moscow, as well as the Hungarian-language broadcast from England, about the disaster on the eastern front.

The defeat had a sobering effect on the Hungarian people. The bulk of the population had no sympathy for the war; it was not clear what Hungarian participation had to do with the national interest; neither the simple soldier nor his family, nor the industrial workers, were particularly interested in the crusade against Bolshevism. Long before the Don catastrophe the war had undermined morale. It produced no new marching songs, myths, or acts of heroism. Bitterness was especially strong toward the German high command, which had used the Hungarian soldiers, along with other minor allies, to sacrifice themselves as cannon fodder in order to cover the German retreat. Hitler and others criticized the Hungarian army, but Jány himself noted that the Germans seemed to have given the Hungarian forces the task of protecting the German units with the live bodies of Hungarian soldiers.[129]

7   Efforts to Exit the War

Despite the catastrophic loss of the Second Army, 1943 became a year of cautious optimism for Hungarians. For the first time it seemed that there might be another choice between the German alliance or the much-dreaded Soviet Union and Bolshevism. It even seemed possible that the war might end by giving the Anglo-Saxons a predominant voice in the peace settlement. The North Africa landing of the Anglo-American forces in November 1942, and the defeat of the Germans at Stalingrad in February 1943, made it clear that the war had reached a turning point. German losses had a dynamic effect on the country. As the student leader Sándor Kiss put it: "Hitler lost battles on the eastern front one after another . . . only those who were blind, obsessed or stupid believed in the increasing use of the 'miracle weapon' in propaganda. The soldiers returning from the front were unanimous in reporting that the Germans would not be able to win the war."[1]

The Allied landing in North Africa was the first successful Allied operation. The rapid occupation renewed faith that the Allies were capable of decisive action and strengthened those politicians and members of the general staff who from the beginning had doubts about German victory. It showed that the Allies were capable of surprise and that they could take on a large-scale military operation, one that could change the strategic situation in Europe. The fact that the Vichy French in Algeria had been willing to join the Allies—and that the Allies had been pragmatic enough to accept—made many think that negotiations with official Hungary might somehow be acceptable to the Allies.[2]

In Hungary one of the most important results of the North Africa landing was that the pro-British element came again to the forefront as a serious factor to be considered. The Independence Front, which had remained dormant after the dissolution of the Historical Memorial Committee in the spring, had been newly formed just a few days before the Allied landing and became more active in the changed situation. With the urging of the Independence Front and the conservative opposition group around Bethlen, the government of Prime Minister Kállay increased its efforts to make contact with the British and Americans.

At the same time, fear of German occupation affected every action of the government. The fear of occupation was especially paralyzing because the overwhelming desire of the Hungarian public was to maintain the status quo. As the diplomat Aladár Szegedy-Maszák remarked, "During the war we held that maintaining the status quo was of absolute importance," even though "we counted on unavoidable and necessary change . . ."[3] The majority of the population had not yet experienced the reality of war. Despite the German alliance and Hungary's involvement in the war, the government and institutions remained intact, the parliamentary system continued, there was active participation by the opposition democratic parties. In spite of censorship the press remained fairly colorful during the war and living conditions were much better than in the neighboring countries or in Europe in general.

Rezső Peéry, a journalist from the Felvidék, who had criticized the Hungarian government in the 1930s as being "hopelessly anachronistic, lacking democracy, and allowing deplorable cultural and social conditions," wrote:

"Who could have guessed that in World War II—in comparison to radical fascist Slovakia—conservative and reactionary Hungary would appear to be the last liberal European reservation among the East European countries—where during the World War II years there was a legal opposition, an existing social democratic party, and press freedom was not abolished, . . . until the German occupation in 1944."[4]

Fallout from the Don Disaster

The debacle of the Second Army at the Don and the defeat of the Germans at Stalingrad placed a different complexion on the war. From that time on, the arrival of the Red Army in the Carpathian Mountains became an obvious possibility. The destruction of the Second Army, one of the worst disasters in modern Hungarian history, affected every part of the Hungarian community. Although the government tried to hush up the losses, the loss of men and equipment meant that the army could not be used for the country's own defense, and government leaders and public opinion were forced to recognize that they had underestimated the fearful strength and fighting ability of the Red Army. Chief of the General Staff Szombathelyi, returning from a visit with Hitler on February 12, 1943, explained that the Hungarians must prepare themselves for a dark future:

"We have to reckon that during the spring the Anglo-Saxon powers will attempt a landing in the Balkans. . . . Hitler, is of the opinion that such a landing is very probable . . ."[5]

REVIVAL OF THE CONSERVATIVE OPPOSITION

With the Allied landing in North Africa both the conservative and liberal opposition went into action. The Independence Front, reorganized by Endre Bajcsy-Zsilinsky, again brought together the representatives of the parties that had made up the Historical Memorial Committee, although the participants presented an extreme divergence of views. The parties ranged from Social Democrats to Legitimists, and even Mgr. Vilmos Apor, the bishop of Győr attended. The Legitimists believed the question of the restoration of the Habsburg Monarchy was not a matter of party politics but could be supported by the whole country. To that end, they were willing to cooperate with political groups quite opposite in their views. It was the Social Democrats that posed the real difficulty for cooperation among the various groups. Both Catholic and Protestant churches rejected cooperation with the Marxist-influenced party. The nonsocialist parties insisted that in order for cooperation the Social Democrats must abandon their principles of class warfare and the dictatorship of the proletariat.[6]

The always-cautious Prince Primate Jusztinián Séredi took a stand in his New Year's speech, telling the government that it must change its policies, follow national interests, and break with former friends; that Hungary could not tie its fate to a foreign country. Catholic bishops in their Christmas and New Year's proclamations took up the struggle against National Socialism and called for support of Jews who had lost their jobs because of the Jewish laws. Cardinal Séredi's article, published in the Catholic daily in March, brought strong criticism from the German ministry, but the government responded that it could not interfere with publications of church leaders.

The conservative opposition group around Bethlen, spurred to action, met several times in the days after the landing in North Africa. In an effort to influence the government's policies Bethlen and a few of his supporters, with the approval of Prime Minister Kállay, prepared a memorandum for Horthy, who, in mourning for his son, was ill and out of touch. The memorandum was delivered to the regent late in January 1943 by a committee of Bethlen, the Prince-Primate, and Géza Töreki, head of the Supreme Court. It included three points on what should be done:

> Request the withdrawal as soon as possible of Hungarian fighting forces from the front.

Reinforce the army at home in expectation of a power vacuum after the war.
Urgently reestablish constitutional rights and respect for law, including punishment of the military responsible for the atrocities at Novi Sad/Újvidék,
as well as implementation of Jewish laws in the spirit of humanity and
Christianity.

The first news of the tragedy of the Second Army arrived a few days
after the three men had met Horthy.[7]

With growing collaboration among the conservative and liberal
groups, leaders of the Independent Smallholders Party, Legitimist aristocrats, liberal-conservative bourgeoisie, liberal democrats, and Bethlen's
loyal followers relegated old party disagreements to the background. On
February 27, 1943, to hold the disparate groups together, Bethlen formed
the Hungarian National Social Circle, which met informally at dinners
and in private. This exclusive elite group of about two hundred members
was able to exert influence on Horthy and Kállay and thus on government
policy.

To the government and the Anglophile circles it was clear that Hungary should make contact with the Allied powers and attempt a gradual
withdrawal from the German alliance. The majority blamed the defeat of
the Second Army on the Germans, and believed that the remains of the
army should be brought home at once. The extreme Right on the other
hand blamed the government for not ordering full mobilization and sending the whole armed forces into the battle.

This political polarization erupted in a stormy session of the Foreign
Affairs Committee of the lower house on February 19, 1943. Kállay explained that the fighting in the East would probably shift to the Balkans
and that an Anglo-American landing could be expected, but he emphasized that Hungarian participation in the war was limited to the struggle
against the Soviet Union and had nothing to do with the other conflicts.
Imrédy, speaking for the Right, accused the government for not arming
the Second Army sufficiently and for not committing Hungary to total
war and complete allegiance to Germany. He disputed Kállay's statement
that Russia was their only enemy, pointing out that the Czech and Yugoslav émigré governments in London were busy preparing the further dismemberment of Hungary, and therefore the government must realize the
need to fight England as well. Representatives of the leftist opposition,
Tildy and Rassay, condemned Hungary's entrance into war in the first
place. Kállay ended debate, explaining that since the Second Army had
lost all its weaponry it was necessary to build up a new army. Then it

would be possible to decide in what way and where it would be used in the war.[8]

Taking advantage of the shock produced by the loss of the army, Bethlen at the February 19 session of the Foreign Affairs Committee of the upper house gave the same arguments he had given Horthy in the January memorandum. He declared that the Germans had clearly lost the war, and that the government must do everything to see that the war should not end with Hungary on the side of Germany. He demanded that those who took the country into war be called to account, and the remnants of the Don army be withdrawn immediately.[9]

Yet efforts to allow the remains of the Second Army to return home were unsuccessful. When Szombathelyi traveled to the German general staff Headquarters in February to get permission for their return, the Germans instead demanded that the remains of the army should be pulled together into an army corps to carry out occupation duties, and demanded another six divisions as a Hungarian occupation force in addition to the existing ones. The government backed by Horthy refused the demand, emphasizing that the Second Army was utterly destroyed. The German High Command then proposed an alternative; Hungary should send two to three divisions as occupation forces to Serbia in case of an Allied landing. Quite probably the intention was not so much for military purposes as to increase Serbian hostility against the Hungarians as well as compromising the Kállay government in the eyes of the West.[10] Szombathely agreed, welcoming the possibility of having Hungarian troops in the Balkans in preparation for a possible Allied landing, but also fearing that denying German demands would further strain relations.[11]

The Council of Ministers at meetings on March 10 and March 30 strongly rejected sending a force to the Balkans; it would damage their cause with the Allies with whom they were trying to negotiate and would mean giving in further to the Germans. The excuse given was that the Hungarians lacked the arms, but the Germans countered that they were prepared to equip three divisions now and two more later. Kállay and Keresztes-Fischer threatened to resign if the troops were sent, and on March 30 the Supreme Defense Council decided that the whole Second Army should be brought home, except for the two light divisions which were to be left in the Ukraine for occupation duties only. No troops were to be sent to the Balkans, although the government did consent to setting up two light divisions from the remnants of the Second Army for occupation duties.[12]

Despite the defeat of the Second Army and the lack of sympathy for the war, the great majority of the population paid little heed to international events or even to the military situation; they went about their business occupied with their own daily cares and troubles. Gyula Gueth, a Protestant military pastor, described the atmosphere at the officers' military resort and hospital on historic Lake Balaton after the army's defeat.

In spite of the presence at the hospital of remnants of the Don army suffering from the terrible catastrophe, Gueth explained: "there was an effervescent life among the well-to-do at the holiday resort. . . . [T]he prosperous vacationing people lived and amused themselves as if everything was in the best of order, even though the events at the front after the Don breakthrough to every forward-thinking person meant clearly that the future looked hopelessly black."[13]

The conditions of the population were still relatively good. Annual wages for workers had more than doubled between 1938 and 1943, partly because of the extension of working time, but also because of the grave shortage of laborers, especially of skilled workers, in nearly all the major war factories. Since small businesses continued to operate—unlike in Germany where they had been closed down—in Hungary it was not possible to recruit the needed workers from the small businesses. The shortage increased during the summer months when some workers went home to help harvest their crops. Although there had been an actual decline in real wages, the constant labor shortage enabled several members of a family to work, keeping family incomes stable. Food rationing limited consumption to some extent, but in 1943 people were still living well.[14]

The introduction of the Jurcsek system had halted the decline in agricultural production and the small peasantry were more prosperous. Favorable natural conditions between 1943–44 increased the drive for production. Sown area for cereals increased, and producers turned in 157 percent of the bread-grain obligation, 111 percent of meat and lard, and 75 percent of freely chosen crops, although as was expected, performance of smaller holdings were not as successful as larger estates.[15] Landless agrarian laborers and farm hands who lived on fixed wages were less well off, but since most owned their own cottages and gardens, they were able to supplement their slender resources with their own produce, contradicting the assertion during the communist period that requisitioning seriously reduced the food consumption of the agrarian population.

There were other signs of prosperity, including statistics showing that on the large farms and among the wealthier peasantry the stock of tractors increased, as well as machine stock in general. In the villages the consumption of manufactured goods also increased: bicycles, radios—battery-powered, since most villages were not electrified—and other consumer goods were consumed in greater quantities among the wider circles of the peasantry.[16]

SECRET ATTEMPTS TO CONTACT THE ALLIES

The Don catastrophe and German defeats stirred Kállay to action. In contrast to his hesitant steps to contact the Allies in 1942, he now took every opportunity to make contacts to determine what steps were needed for Hungary to leave the war.[17] In the following months, in concert with his secret advisors, Kállay carried out a one-man policy behind the back of Parliament. This was a paradoxical situation in which the extreme Right used Parliament for their propaganda while the prime minister had to go through secret channels, a situation which the Allies would have been completely unable to understand.[18]

The process was not easy. Hungary had no government in exile, no official access to the Allied powers. Attempted contacts had to be made through the neutral countries and neither Great Britain nor the United States were particularly receptive. The government attempted contacts in Lisbon, Bern, Madrid, Stockholm, as well as the United States, as opportunities arose; all steps, of course, had to be made with the utmost secrecy. The historian Fenyo points out that it is impossible to give a well-organized account of the negotiations since they were not well organized "but fumbling, bumbling, intermittent, and at times absurd efforts on the part of elements of the Hungarian government to find some miraculous way out of its well-nigh hopeless predicament."[19]

The difficulties entailed in making overtures to the Allies without arousing German or Hungarian rightist suspicions were almost insurmountable. Barcza explained: "The Germans had such a well-organized, wide-spread spy system then that they knew everything—through their own spies and through Hungarian spies. The Minister of Finance, Reményi-Schneller, delivered the minutes of every Council of Ministers meeting to the German Embassy on that same day. They knew whom Kállay met with, even what they spoke about."[20] It was later learned that Péter Hain, who had been responsible for the regent's security for a decade and accompanied him on every foreign trip, was in German pay and gave exact details to the Germans about Horthy and Kállay's negotiations with the Allies.[21] The possibility of a German occupation of Hungary was always present.

Kállay's task was made more difficult by the noisy propaganda of the extreme Right in the lower house of Parliament. Thus the upper house became increasingly important as a moderating body, and the upper house committees—especially the Committee on Foreign Affairs—became increasingly active in carrying out the work of government. After 1942 their meetings, which had been open and well attended, were kept secret and no records were kept of their closed sessions in which the most important matters were discussed.[22] Most of the key personalities in the conservative branch of the Independence Front were members, and members of Jewish origin served on the most important committees.

Through both private individuals and diplomatic efforts it was made known to English and American diplomats that Hungary was ready to enter into negotiations, although it considered it impossible to negotiate with the Soviet Union. Messages had been received from the United States that representatives in Switzerland would meet with someone independent of the government for discussions. István Bethlen was the person considered most suitable to lead the negotiations, but he hesitated, concerned at the lack of guarantees without which successful Hungarian policy in exile could not be conducted. Also he was almost seventy years old and experiencing the first signs of physical and mental decline.[23]

Instead, the choice fell on György Barcza, former Hungarian minister to London, who had built up a multitude of diplomatic contacts over his long career. When contacted by Bethlen in the fall of 1942 Barcza agreed to accept the mission, but only on the condition that he can go as a private person with free hands. He would loyally keep Kállay informed, but his mission was to save the country, not the government. The patriotic opposition, who were concerned that nothing was being done to make contact with the Allies, considered Barcza to be the best candidate, and in February 1943 before he left, Barcza met with all the main opposition leaders, including the regent's younger son, Miklós Horthy Jr.

Although Kállay approved the terms, weeks went by before he and Barcza met in secret for dinner at the home of a mutual friend. Barcza later criticized Kállay who kept delaying, fearing that if the Germans realized the plans to break away they would immediately occupy the country, get rid of the Jews, and imprison the political leaders. Typically for Hungary during this period, which was full of gossip as well as informers, Barcza's secret plan was first revealed to ten or twelve people, who in turn told another twenty to thirty friends, who then told another forty to sixty. Finally, even his barber asked him when he would be leaving on his mission. He did not actually depart until March 22.[24]

Barcza's mission began in Rome, where he had been minister to the Vatican and had close connections with Pope Pius XII and D'Arcy Osborne, the English ambassador to the Vatican. His timing was lucky since Osborne was leaving for a visit to England three days later and promised that he would do everything in London to ensure that the Foreign Office in Switzerland would contact him. Barcza recalled that the Pope had received him warmly: ". . . after the usual ceremony, three genuflections, etc., he hugged me. Noticed immediately how much he had aged since I had last seen him—thinner, face more pale, looked tired, eyes and mouth had melancholy lines."[25]

In their long political discussion the Pope spoke of the terrible, inhuman treatment by the Germans of innocent people, especially the Jews. He said that if it were possible he would happily sacrifice himself if he could save people from their terrible suffering, but he was powerless—and only through prayer could he turn to God to end as soon as possible such suffering. Barcza answered that the Church and its head were the world's greatest and strongest spiritual power, and in his view the power was not being used enough against the war and suffering. If the Pope would speak out—use his spiritual power to speak out against Hitler's breaking of international law, perhaps it would not achieve the end of the war, but it would be a great service to humanity and to the Church as well.[26]

Pius XII answered that many times he had sent peace messages, instructions to Papal nuncios to protest to the governments about the German authorities' measures against the Church, but unfortunately in vain. He was afraid if he took stronger measures—such as excommunication—it would poison the situation even more. The Germans would persecute the Church more, make the fate of the thirty million German Catholics worse, which he would like to avoid, since he had seen how the Germans treated the Polish Catholics. Barcza pointed out that it was a question of Catholics in the whole world who were awaiting a public position from the Church and the Pope. Again the Pope spoke of his extremely difficult position—that his only powers were spiritual weapons—which were weak to break Hitler's and the Germans' brutality. He had often thought of moving the seat of the Church elsewhere, but it was a really sensitive question—flight could be taken as a sign of weakness. The Pope told Barcza: "I'm powerless. . . . Believe me it is the most terrible feeling to see the suffering of so many people and to know that I can do nothing to prevent it."[27]

Barcza was surprised at his own audacity in speaking so openly and forcefully with the Pope, but the Pope realized that his words expressed his true fear and did not hold it against him.[28]

After Rome, Barcza found it good to breath the fresh air of neutral Switzerland. Even though material life in Hungary, especially in the villages, was still plentiful and good, the atmosphere was poisoned by Nazi ideology and their Hungarian imitators; here papers carried news from all over the world. He was contacted by a Mr. Van den Heuven, press attaché for the Bern British Embassy, who turned out to be the leader of the British Intelligence Service in Switzerland. The head of the American OSS, Allen Dulles, was also based in Bern along with Royall Tyler, an American who had many friends in Hungary from his years there as a representative of the League of Nations.

Barcza explained that he came as a private citizen but he represented the Hungarian patriotic opposition, which aimed to free the country from German pressure, but because of their isolation from the Allies resistance had to be secret and passive. Van den Heuven countered that the future judgment of Hungary would depend on whether they were able to break with the Germans—and to what extent they could interfere with German war activities. It was the British stance that opposition groups should use sabotage against the Germans—or rise up against them—which Barcza knew in Hungary's situation would be pure suicide. The British urged them to withdraw their troops from the Soviet Union, which the government was eager to do, but unfortunately all means of transport were in German hands. Barcza answered that for the time being they could do nothing, everyone was afraid of the Germans.[29]

A number of Hungarians placed their hopes in Archduke Otto von Habsburg, who had received a warm reception from President Roosevelt when he arrived in the United States as a refugee. Roosevelt was fairly well informed on Central European affairs and was interested in Otto's ideas for a new order in Central Europe, a Central European Federation, an idea which was being considered by the committee set up by Roosevelt to consider United States postwar foreign policy. Both the British and Americans generally acknowledged that the dissolution of the Austro-Hungarian Monarchy had been unfortunate. Kállay and the Legitimist leader Sigray sent a joint message to be given to the Archduke, asking him to establish contact between the Hungarian government and the government of the United States to prepare the way for Hungary to leave the Germans and join the Allies at the appropriate moment. Otto received the message in March and passed it on to the president. Unfortunately for

Hungary, their hopes were dimmed by the strong position of the Czech émigré government, headed by the intensely anti-Habsburg and anti–Hungarian President Benes, who used the large funds at his disposal for anti-Hungarian propaganda.

The most important site for Hungary's contacts with the Allies turned out to be the neutral country of Turkey, with which Hungary was on good terms. Antal Ullein-Reviczky, head of the foreign ministry press division, had a personal connection through the father of his English wife, who worked with the British consulate in Istanbul. He and his wife spent summer holidays in the villa on the Bosphorus, and in the summer of 1942 he was able to make contact with the British. He succeeded in reaching an agreement with the British representative at the Cairo general headquarters through which the Hungarian government would send a representative to Turkey. András Frey, foreign policy editor of the *Magyar Nemzet,* was chosen and arrived for his mission to Turkey on February 1, 1943.[30]

Frey had been authorized to make a declaration to an Allied diplomat in Constantinople that Hungary did not intend to oppose Anglo-American or Polish troops if they reached the Hungarian frontier; that in principle Hungary was prepared to take positive action against the Germans and, if possible, to work out in advance a practical plan for cooperation between the armies concerned.[31] He had no success in contacting the Americans but was set up by the British with a Hungarian of dubious reputation, György Pálóczi-Horváth, a contact that was particularly disappointing since Pálóczi was with the secret service, Special Operations Executive (SOE), and not the Foreign Office. Pálóczi responded to Frey that he was not empowered to discuss political matters or Hungary's future; the Hungarian government should send out two high-ranking officers to negotiate. Kállay, who was upset that the British had chosen an agent known to be hostile to the Hungarian regime, and nervous that there had been information leaks, was concerned that it would not be possible to find two senior officers with whom the secret would be safe. Their very presence in Istanbul would reveal their mission.[32]

Despite the rigid stance of the SOE, the British attitude toward Hungary was softening. In February Foreign Minister Eden mentioned Hungary's success in maintaining its constitutional government and relative political independence and formulated conditions on which the British government would be ready to negotiate with the Hungarians. These included the provision that Hungary would send no more troops to the

Soviet front, and that in the case of a European invasion from the southeast, Hungary would offer no opposition but would open its borders to British, American, and if necessary Polish troops. Eden's conditions were sent on to the American and Russian allies, but both of the responses were negative.

The State Department sent an answer on May 4, 1943, pointing out that neither the present Hungarian government nor the opposition was in a position to offer anything positive to the Allies. Rather, such a hurried step would lead to liquidation of exactly those persons who could give the greatest aid. Molotov's answer was much harsher—the Hungarian troops were still on Soviet soil carrying out violence for which the Hungarian people must be held responsible. The Allies should not negotiate with the Hungarian government but hold to the doctrine of unconditional surrender. In addition to returning all of the territories taken, Hungary must pay reparations and carry out punishment of war criminals.[33]

Molotov's insistence on holding to the doctrine of unconditional surrender referred to Roosevelt's pronouncement immediately following the Casablanca Conference in January 1943, at which he declared a doctrine of unconditional surrender for the Axis powers. The policy, supported by Churchill, was designed to stiffen the morale of the Russians who were locked in the epic battle for Stalingrad. It demonstrated that both the British and Americans intended to permanently eliminate the threat of Germany, and assured the Soviets that the United States and Britain would fight to the end. It also crushed any hope Hitler may have had for peace negotiations. From the time that the United States had formally entered the war Roosevelt had turned American participation into a crusade, and often emphasized the need to declare complete victory without compromises. The British as well were determined that Germany must be utterly destroyed. They had refused Hitler's offer of peace at the close of the German-Polish war and again when they rejected his generous peace offers after Dunkirk.[34]

The impact of this pronouncement on the prolongation of the war and on the promotion of communist aims in Europe has been much debated. The declaration probably stiffened German resistance and prolonged bloodshed. By the summer of 1942 the desire in Germany for a compromise peace was not confined to the German opposition against Hitler. Even Heinrich Himmler was willing to envisage a compromise peace on the basis of Germany's territorial position on September 1, 1939. In reaction to the doctrine the Germans fought on with the courage of despair, and it impacted Italy's stance as well. Mussolini told Hungarian Prime Minister Kállay on his visit in early April 1943: "We cannot even think of a separate peace. Firstly, because honor would not allow it. Secondly, because Italy would achieve nothing by it. . . . In any event, the Allies' insistence on 'unconditional surrender' excludes the possibility of such a step."[35] Unfortunately, the declaration was made as a blanket ultimatum and did not exclude the satellite states, an oversight, since by the time it was issued, most of the satellites, beginning with Finland and Hungary, were sending various peace feelers to London and Washington.[36]

The British did not react strongly against Molotov's stand, but in a memo sent by Eden to Lord Halifax, British Ambassador in Washington, he instructed him that British diplomats should not enter into contact with any Hungarian diplomat who was an official representative of the government in Budapest without authorization. At the moment it was necessary to strengthen Hungarian opposition against German pressure, and reduce willingness to cooperate with the Axis. Furthermore, it was necessary to inform Hungary that they were expected to give back the Allied rights, referring to the territory taken from Czechoslovakia and Yugoslavia.[37]

In April, instead of sending the two senior officers requested, Kállay sent László Veress, a talented young foreign service official who already had experience with the British in Lisbon. Veress was to attempt to organize contacts on a political plane and eliminate the need for Pálóczi-Horváth, but his mission was only partly successful. After Eden's suggestion had been rejected the British would not negotiate with a representative of the Hungarian government. Veress on his own initiative stated that his message came from a resistance group within the government—a group that included the prime minister, minister of the interior, and the foreign minister—which was resolved to dissociate Hungary from Germany as soon as the approach of the Allies made this possible. Hungary would undertake not to resist the Allies and would assist them actively by all available means. In return, Hungary asked that operations on Hungarian soil should not be conducted by non-Western Allied troops (except Poles) and that Hungary should not be occupied exclusively by Soviet troops.[38]

Veress was received in a friendly way, agents acknowledged that contact was now on an official level, and they would be happy to accept the offer of free information. Since they were aware of Hungarian intentions no further political conversations were necessary; the next step was to send down two officers, but if Hungary was unable to do that there was no point in continuing conversations. They also continued to insist that information go through the Hungarian György Pálóczi-Horváth much to the dismay of Kállay and others who mistrusted Pálóczi-Horváth and suspected him of communist sympathies—which were later to prove correct.[39]

Of several private initiatives to Istanbul during the spring months, surprisingly the most significant was that of Professor Albert Szent-Györgyi, an internationally known Nobel Prize winner. Szent-Györgyi made contact with the British in early February 1943, presenting himself as representative of a popular front which could overthrow the government and bring about democratic reform. He claimed that with the exception of the Arrow Cross, every party and social group would accept him as prime minister. If he came to power he would clean out the general staff and German sympathizers; he was also willing to carry out sabotage in the interests of the Allies. In his opinion Hungary could only free itself from the existing regime of the army, priests, and feudal landowner class with Allied intervention. The British overestimated Szent-Györgyi's role and influence, but they did take him seriously; his dilettante action contributed to the British finally being willing to enter into contact with Hungary. Unfortunately, while in Istanbul, Szent-Györgyi was contacted by persons purporting to be American agents who were in fact agents of the Gestapo; thus his whole story reached Hitler within a few days, who was—not surprisingly—furious.[40]

At first the Kállay government peace feelers did not bring the hoped-for results. The British were cautious, the Americans more so, and the Soviets stuck to the formula of unconditional surrender. Barcza's semiofficial diplomatic mission to Rome and then to Switzerland had no immediate results. But the private trip of Szent-Györgyi to Turkey—although it had no measurable effect—did make the British begin to think that the Hungarians might be taken seriously.

ALLIED PLANS FOR POSTWAR EUROPE

From the early years of the war both the Americans and the British had been discussing plans for postwar Eastern Europe. In the United States the Advisory Committee on Post-War Foreign Policy, established within the State Department in early January 1940, was particularly concerned with the need for closer economic and political cooperation within the Danube region against penetration from the two powerful neighbors, Germany and Russia, as well as to ensure economic viability.[41] The committee was inclined to accept a plan for two east European federations—a

Balkan union and a northern union. A possible third sub-unit would be a Danubian federation. By the summer of 1943, probably in consideration of the animosity existing among the countries involved, the Advisory Committee decided that instead of a federation there should be a loosely organized union of independent and sovereign states, cooperating for limited objectives. The committee assumed that cooperation would ease tensions, but they also realized the need to adjust political frontiers on the basis of ethnic dividing lines wherever possible, as well as the exchange of populations living near border areas.[42]

In the case of Hungary they recommended revising every one of the borders decided by Trianon in Hungary's favor with the exception of the Austro-Hungarian border. They believed that a straightforward adhesion to the ethnic principle on the northern border would end the Slovak-Hungarian antagonisms once and for all, and if border modification was accompanied with the exchange of population they would also be able to ameliorate Yugoslav-Hungarian relations. Only in Transylvania with its mixed population did the modification of borders and population exchange appear to be insufficient. The committee preferred the idea by which most of Transylvania should belong to Romania with a small border revision in favor of Hungary, but that the Székely region should receive wide-ranging autonomy. The next most favored plan was the notion of an independent state of Transylvania as a member of a proposed mid-European union.

The committee, also concerned in helping democratic regimes come to power, leaned toward support of a Hungarian government which would include Social Democrats, Independent Smallholders, liberals and some of the so-called populist writers. They did not consider it desirable that Horthy or Bethlen should play a leading role. Unfortunately for Hungary not a single one of their proposals was carried out.[43]

The British committee as well as leading British politicians also favored the federative principle, while Winston Churchill conceived of a confederation of an all European United Nations. In 1942, negotiations with the Czech and Polish émigré politicians based in London resulted in the outlines of an east-central (Polish and Czech) confederation and a southeast European (Yugoslav-Greek) confederation. When Churchill visited Washington in 1943 he added that he would also like to see a Danube Federation with Vienna as the capital in addition to the outlined northern and southern confederations. To a certain extent this would fill the vacuum left by the dissolution of the Austro-Hungarian Monarchy.[44]

The border suggestions worked out by the British Committee greatly resembled the American and were relatively favorable to Hungary. In the case of the Slovak-Hungarian border they went further than the American, essentially following the line of the first Vienna Award. To the south, they were uncertain and did not delineate exact borders. They considered the situation of Transylvania, with its mixed population, to be the most complicated problem of the whole region. Among the various possibilities, the most hopeful one would make Transylvania a member of the confederation as an independent political unit, along with Romania and Hungary, or possibly make it a completely independent buffer state.

The British also supported the democratization of the Hungarian government, and among the progressive forces they considered the Social Democrats, favored by the Labour Party, especially important. At the same time, in contrast with the Americans, they would not have shut out the conservative liberals from the new governing group. Earlier they had been prepared to greet István Bethlen at the head of an émigré Hungarian government, and they planned that he would assume a leading role.[45]

The Czech émigré government based in London exerted considerable political influence and was especially hostile to any border changes that would benefit Hungary; it insisted on a return to the 1938 borders, as did the Yugoslavs. On August 5, 1942, Eden reversed earlier British policy when he announced to the lower house that Britain officially negated the Munich Agreement and did not recognize any later changes of territory, including the areas taken by Hungary which had initially been approved by the British—the Felvidék and Ruthenia. Churchill, although he sympathized with the Hungarians, said that Britain could not recognize the second Vienna Award that divided Transylvania between the Romanians and Hungarians since it was the result of a *dictat*.

The Soviet point of view countered the American and British plans, reflecting their expansionist strategies. They considered every viable confederation that would possibly come under Anglo-Saxon influence as directed against them, and thus rejected any such plan. In June 1943, Molotov officially informed the Western Allies of this point of view, and at the Teheran meeting in November 1943 Stalin strengthened Molotov's communication. Answering Churchill, who again recommended the establishment of an Austrian, Hungarian, and possibly Bavarian peaceful and nonaggressive confederation, Stalin announced that after partitioning Germany the stupidest thing would be to establish a new combination, Danube or whatever. With the decision at Teheran to make the

Allied landing in Normandy rather than through the Balkans, debate between the Allies over the question became essentially mute, leaving the area to the Soviets.[46]

In regards to Hungary Stalin planned a return to the Trianon borders, not only because of Hungary's participation in the war against the Soviet Union, but also to be able to compensate Romania by granting it Transylvania in return for Bessarabia, which the Soviets had taken back in 1940 and intended to keep.[47] The Soviet Committee to Prepare the Peace also considered the possibility of an independent Transylvanian state. Cynically they supposed that an independent Transylvania could act as the root of conflict between the two neighbors and the Soviets could play the mediating role between the two. Up until 1944 Stalin considered it possible that Horthy would play a role in the transition period between the war and postwar era, but after the unsuccessful ceasefire attempt by Horthy in October 1944 this possibility disappeared.[48]

Worsening Relations with Germany

While attempts were being made to contact the Allies, relations between Hungary and Germany continued to deteriorate. After Voronezh there were mutual recriminations; the Hungarians blamed the Germans for neglecting the Hungarian troops before the battle and then purposely sacrificing them for the safe retreat of the German troops, while Hitler blamed the Hungarians for the loss, telling Szombathelyi during his visit in February 1943 that the Germans would have been better off if the Hungarian troops had never joined them. Szombathelyi answered that he was of the same opinion and always had been.[49]

In addition, increasing German economic demands created a constant source of friction. German losses in 1942 had led to a change in German policy—rather than discouraging Hungarian industry they now counted on its factories to supply the German army. Hungarian factories received an increasing number of military orders, and more and more work was done on commission, supervised by the *Deutsche Industrie Kommission für Ungarn*, which eventually became the instrument by which the Germans controlled the Hungarian industry. One aspect of the system was joint aircraft manufacturing; the Messerschmitt plan expanded aircraft manufacturing in Hungary by increasing the existing capacity, and a large new facility was founded, the Danube Aircraft Factory (Dunai Repülőgépgyár). The Germans also encouraged the development of the processing capacity in aluminum and aluminum factories, and bauxite deliveries increased.[50]

A sharp conflict arose in the fall of 1942 over the annual renewal of the German-Hungarian commercial agreement. The German representative, Karl Clodius, had negotiated an agreement in July for an increase in Hungarian deliveries of oil, bauxite, and processed food products in return for more coal and manufactured goods from Germany. But in September a new negotiator, Walther Funk, dismayed the Hungarian negotiators by proposing much more extensive economic cooperation, as well as an extension of credit to 2,000 million reichsmarks, which, he assured the Hungarians, Germany would easily pay off after she had won the war.

The proposal would have integrated Hungary more fully into the German war economy, making it an obvious target for Allied bombers. Certain bombed-out German factories or those likely to be bombed in the future were to be transferred to Hungary, where—supposedly—they would work to serve the needs of both countries; the danger was that if Hungary rejected the proposal Germany might reduce supplies for the rearmament program. The Hungarian government did reject the request for the transfer of factories, and in the end also rejected the full credit request, although only after a disagreement between Reményi-Schneller, the finance minister, and Baranyai, president of the National Bank, which led to Baranyai's resignation.[51]

While increasing its demands, Germany paid for a diminishing proportion of deliveries and commission work, which a member of the German delegation to the 1942 commercial talks acknowledged officially: "The bulk of the Hungarian consignment . . . should in fact be regarded as a contribution to the common war effort. . . . The ways of settling the sums recorded is a question that will arise and be dealt with after the end of the war."[52] The task of paying the suppliers fell to the Hungarian government, which had to finance some of the deliveries to Germany as well as its own military expenditure. In the spring of 1943, the president of the National Bank told a parliamentary committee, "We are, in fact, lending the German treasury 60 percent more than we have lent to the Hungarian treasury."[53] Between 1942 and 1944 German indebtedness to Hungary more than doubled to over one million reichsmarks, so that about half of the banknote issue was serving to cover their debt.[54]

Another ongoing source of conflict was the German demand to recruit minority German-Hungarian citizens into the Waffen-SS. In continual need of new manpower the Germans pressured the Hungarian government to allow SS recruiting among the Volksdeutsche, whose numbers had increased after the second Vienna Award. The first SS recruiting in

January 1941 was carried out illegally since the Teleki government was firmly opposed to it. Himmler aimed to get five hundred youth on the pretext of participating in sports training and work, but succeeded only in recruiting one hundred. When the volunteers arrived at a training camp in Brünn, to the great surprise of the Germans many rejected the SS uniform and refused the oath to Adolf Hitler. Clearly, many didn't know what they were becoming involved in. One volunteer who got home on a visit in September 1942 told that he had gone to Germany with the others in August 1941 for three weeks training, but instead he was forced to join the SS, and taken to Finland to serve on the Karelia front.[55]

The first legal SS volunteers were recruited at the time that Ribbentrop demanded troops for the Russian front in February 1942. The Hungarian government reluctantly agreed, but set conditions that only Volksdeutsche volunteers could be recruited, that they would lose their Hungarian citizenship, and that they must receive their parents' agreement. Many parents had protested earlier against the illegal recruiting into the Waffen-SS, asking why the government had not prevented it. The number agreed on was 20,000, and recruitment was to be organized by the Hungarian Volksbund and carried out quickly without any publicity.[56]

After the first enthusiastic sign-up, many were sorry they had joined and began to realize what they had committed themselves for. Some parents remembered the year before when their sons were lured into going to Germany for the sports course and ended up in the German army at the front. For this reason most of the parents of the youth under twenty did not give their permission. In some places young men, fearing the call-up, resigned from the Volksbund. The recruiting continued until April 3, and according to German data they collected 25,709 men within 52 days.[57]

Himmler wanted to raise the number of recruits to 30,000 but the Volksbund could only promise 4,000 since most of those in the age group had already enlisted in the Hungarian army. On Kállay's visit to Germany in June 1942 he was relieved that the Germans did not demand any further Hungarian forces for the eastern front but wanted more German-speaking volunteers for the SS. He agreed to raise the allowance to 30,000, reasoning that if they could get more German-Hungarians perhaps they would not ask for more Hungarian troops, but there were not that many Volksdeutsche available.

Some SS volunteers who had returned to Hungary at the end of 1942 because of health problems told how the Volksbund leadership had forced them to take service in the SS. The German soldiers had been told that the SS from Hungary were only penniless unmarried German-speakers. When they got to Munich and the German soldiers realized that among them were married and propertied individuals, they asked them if they were crazy? They only wanted volunteers and unmarried people who were with them in the fight heart and soul. Those demobilized from the SS were treated by the Hungarian authorities and the public as homeless noncitizens, which contributed to the fact that fewer Hungarian Volksdeutsche responded to the next recruitment action.[58]

In early 1943 the Waffen-SS leadership aimed to raise the number of Volksdeutsche recruits from 30,000 to 50,000, but this would only become possible if German speakers were to be allowed to fulfill their Hungarian military duty in the SS. The radical leader of the Hungarian Volksbund, Ferenc Basch, suggested that the Germans demand the Hungarian government allow them to recruit those Volksdeutsche who were serving in the Hungarian army. At first the request was rejected but a second recruitment treaty was signed with the Kállay government on May 22, 1943, concerning individuals of German origin in the Hungarian army who were released to serve with the SS.[59] This added another 20,000 Volksdeutsche to the SS, half of them from the Bácska.[60]

THE JEWISH QUESTION

Tensions continued to increase over the dissatisfaction of the German leadership with the failure of the Hungarian government to carry out actions against the Jews. While Jews were being deported from all over Europe, the Hungarian Jews and the hundred thousand who had fled from persecution and deportation in the neighboring countries were being protected.[61] At Kállay's introductory visit in June 1942 Hitler had urged him to act to bring about the Final Solution to the "Jewish problem." Five months later, the Germans decided the time had come to pressure Hungary to participate in the Final Solution. On October 17, 1942, the German government demanded that Jews be completely shut out of economic and cultural life, that they wear the yellow star, that deportations begin, and that 300,000 Jews be sent to the Ukraine. Ribbentrop gave Sztójay detailed suggestions, first as friendly advice and then as an official demand. Sztójay reported from Berlin that there would be fatal consequences if Budapest did not respond appropriately.[62]

Horthy, who favored a relatively tolerant policy toward the Jews, was not prepared to act on the anti-Jewish measures the Germans were demanding. The note came just at the time Horthy had taken action to improve the treatment of Jewish men in the labor companies at the front, replacing General Károly Bartha as minister of defense with General Vilmos Nagy. Horthy had also objected to a proposal by pro-German Minister of Finance Lajos Reményi-Schneller to expropriate Jewish wealth by a capital levy. Although he believed that the Galician Jews would have to be excluded from the life of the country, all those Jews who had served Hungary in science, industry, and finance were to be regarded as patriots.

On April 15, 1943, Ambassador Jagow sent a telegram demanding that the two members of Jewish origin, Ferenc Chorin and Aurél Egry, be removed from the Committee for Foreign Affairs of the upper house of Parliament, but Horthy said that he would not tolerate mistreatment of the Jews who had served as his advisors or as members of the upper house. At this time five members of Jewish origin served in the Financial Committee: Ferenc Chorin, Aurél Egry, Baron Móricz Kornfeld, Jenő Vida, and Baron György Ullman. A German survey of 1940 showed that five families of Jewish extraction had controlling influence over Hungarian industry: the Manfréd Weiss, Fülöp Weiss, Jenő Vida, Pál Biró and Ferenc Chorin families.[63]

Kállay and Horthy, knowing they had the support of the conservatives and liberals as well as the Socialists, rejected the German demands. The Hungarian government answer, delivered through Sztójay on December 14, flatly rejected the request to force Jews to wear a distinguishing mark or to make preparations for deportation. On the matter of sending 300,000 Jews to the Ukraine, Kállay raised a variety of objections—that it would disrupt the economy, cause inflation, and hamper delivery of war material to Germany. He would not allow Jews to be deported until he had a better idea of the fate of the Jews in the East, and whether they would be provided with the means of livelihood. Besides Jews could be usefully employed on work projects in Hungary. In any case, the Jewish question was an internal affair, and Hungary would not tolerate any interference from outsiders.[64]

At Christmas time Sztójay arrived with a dramatic appeal to give in to the Germans on the Jewish question or Hungary's fate would be sealed. He threatened Kállay that the German reaction to a negative response would mean the end of German cooperation; if Kállay remained stubborn the Germans would force his resignation. But Kállay, who believed that acceptance would mean the end to Hungarian independence, discussed his decision only with Keresztes-Fischer and informed the regent, who agreed with his decision, to reject the German demands.[65]

In addition to conflicts over the Jewish question, the Germans—through their extensive spy network—knew of the missions to contact the Allies. On March 29 Ribbentrop sent the German minister in Budapest, von Jagow, to Kállay to inquire about the negotiations in Turkey. Kállay insisted that the purpose was to bring Turkey closer to the Axis powers, and that he had broken off the negotiations when he realized the German government did not view the matter favorably. Again, on April 9, von Jagow approached Kállay to ask about the purpose of Barcza's trip to Rome; he received the impression that the query discomfited Kállay.[66]

A further irritation came when the Hungarians informed the Germans that a Hungarian squadron being trained in night flying in southern France should on no account be used in active fighting, since it was only intended to be used against the Soviet Union. Jagow wired the foreign ministry that this official communication indicated that the Hungarians intended only to take part in the war against the Soviet Union. Since he had heard that the Führer planned to meet with Horthy in person, he considered it extremely important that the Führer clarify Hungary's willingness to take part in the war against the Western Allies, in case they should open a second front in the Balkans.[67]

MEETING AT KLESSHEIM, AUGUST 16, 1943

On April 11, 1943, the regent received an invitation to meet with Hitler at Klessheim Castle near Salzburg in accord with Hitler's habit of meeting the leaders of his allies on a rotating basis once or twice a year. But in contrast to their previous meetings, in which Hitler had been somewhat deferential to Horthy, this audience on April 16 was carried out in a sharp unfriendly tone. According to Goebbels who was not present, the meeting on the first day took place in a very heated atmosphere. The Führer minced no words and above all pointed out to Horthy how wrong his policies were, both in general and especially in regards to the conduct of the war and the question of the Jews.[68] In his memoirs Horthy blamed Hitler's hysterical behavior on the visit just before he arrived by Mussolini and Romanian Marshal Antonescu, who had told Hitler bluntly that he should sue for peace.[69]

Hitler indulged in an hour-long monologue on the Russian danger and the vital role Germany was playing against the Bolsheviks during which Horthy was obliged to sit and listen. Then, without giving Horthy an opportunity to comment, he launched into recriminations against the Hungarian government; the Hungarian armed forces had fought badly during the previous winter offensive and the performance of the soldiers was very bad; the poor morale of the Hungarian soldiers was due to Jewish influence and propaganda. He claimed that the German government had concrete evidence that Kállay was making preparations to defect to the enemy, and said he had lost all confidence in Kállay. Ribbentrop showed Horthy diplomatic telegrams that had been intercepted and decoded, dwelling at length on the trip of Albert Szent-Györgyi to Istanbul and referred to the Hungarian activities in Switzerland.[70]

The death of his son had taken a visible toll on Horthy. He was thinner and had lost some of his vivacity and robustness. His tendency in conversations to ramble and lose his concentration, which had been present even in 1920, became more pronounced. He no longer read newspapers on a daily basis and began to lose track of developments in Europe and the wider world. Less attentive to the stream of memorandums and reports that came to him, only seldom did he have the interest or energy to write down his thoughts in letters or memos.[71]

Now Horthy, who was accustomed to dominating the conversation himself, was forced to listen silently to the long hostile monologue. Not surprisingly, according to the German protocol, he sometimes seemed disoriented and often lost track of the trend of the conversation. It was remarkable that he remained calm and retained his dignity. In briefing him beforehand, Kállay had told him to argue that he was not prepared to deal with political matters. Rather than arguing with Hitler over the conduct of the Hungarian army, he merely pointed out that "the best troops cannot put up a good show against an enemy superior in number and arms; that the Germans had promised us armoured vehicles and guns but had not supplied them; and that the heavy losses of our troops were the best testimony to the strength of their morale."[72] Hungary had had a very late start in rearming and was fighting in Russia even though Hungary had no territorial claims. He would leave the performance of the Hungarian army for future historians to judge, observing only that the army had lost 146,000 regular soldiers, 36,000 labor servicemen, and all its equipment, and had surely not disgraced itself.[73]

Since Horthy had never been known for being discreet or diplomatic, and his occasional lapses of memory sometimes led to confusion and misunderstandings, Kállay had purposely not kept him informed of the attempted negotiations with the Allies, fearing that he might blurt out something. At various times throughout the sessions, Horthy vigorously defended his prime minister. He insisted that the accusations against Kállay were 100 percent false and that he was completely trustworthy. They were good friends, conversed on a regular basis, and that no one was thinking of coquetting with the enemy. When Hitler told him that Kállay should be dismissed in the interests of Hungarian-German friendship, Horthy countered that he saw no reason to dismiss his prime minister. The next day, Hitler continued to harp on Kállay, but when he tried to convince Horthy to appoint a new prime minister, Horthy responded: "You know, I'm very hard of hearing. It seems I only understood half of what you were saying yesterday."[74]

Occasionally his abrupt changes of topic may have been maneuvers to avoid answering the German charges. In one digression from the main theme he proposed an idea he had to solve the main weakness of submarines—the fact that they could not see very far. From his experience during the Great War he remembered that a sailor had been sent up on a one-man kite to survey the terrain. Why not have all the submarines send up such one-man kites at a predetermined time. Hitler then proceeded to explain the technology of radar.[75]

Some of the most significant exchanges between Horthy and Hitler concerned Hungary's lenient treatment of the Jews. According to Hitler, the Jews were responsible for the communist revolution and the two world wars, they destroyed the economy, and, it seemed clear to him that it was their influence and propaganda that was responsible for the poor morale among the Hungarian soldiers. Horthy agreed that the large number of Jews in Hungary created problems, but he pointed out that since Magyars regarded money-making as vulgar, they were partly responsible that the Jews played such a vital role in the Hungarian economy—there was simply no easy way to replace them. As for the presence of Jews in the upper house of Parliament which Ribbentrop had complained about, he could do nothing about that without violating the constitution. He asserted that he had done everything he could against the Jews within the limits of decency, but he could hardly murder them or do away with them in some other way. Ribbentrop replied that the Jews had to be either destroyed or brought into concentration camps, there was no other alternative. Horthy's next remark must have startled Hitler and Ribbentrop. According to historian Sakmyster, Horthy declared that he was ashamed to have to confess that he had sent 36,000 Jews in labor battalions to the Front, and that most of them had been killed in the Russian advance.[76]

The Germans were clearly dissatisfied with the meeting. Horthy remained stubborn in his defense of Kállay although he promised an honorable investigation of the German charges. His humanitarian arguments for the Jews indicated that he had no intention of changing Hungarian policy. Just before his departure he refused to approve the wording of an official communiqué prepared for the press which was the same as that issued after the recent visit of Marshal Antonescu. The communiqué called for the continuation of the struggle against Bolshevism and the Anglo-American Allies but Horthy wanted no direct reference to the Western Allies. On learning that the communiqué had been issued without his approval he denied having given his consent and Hungary issued its own communiqué in Budapest without any reference to the Allies.[77]

A long letter of May 7, signed by Horthy but apparently written by Kállay and government officials, rebutted Hitler's accusations at great length. In regard to German charges of suspicious government contacts in neutral countries, a detailed report was presented on each. For example, the report stated that the journalist András Frey was not on a governmental mission but that the possibility existed that as a private person his views were not the same as those of the government and that his activities would be observed. The rebuke that Hungary was not taking a great enough part in the war was deemed inexplicable since an ever-greater part of Hungarian industrial output was at the service of the German Reich. On the matter of Hungarian pilots in France, since Hungary "is not on a war-standing with France" it would be against international law for Hungarian air units to take part in military actions on French soil.[78]

Despite German displeasure with Horthy he was still treated with courtesy. On Horthy's seventy-fifth birthday in June, Hitler informed him that he was sending him a yacht. Horthy responded with effusive letters of thanks but privately scoffed at Hitler's gauche ways: "What the hell can I do with a yacht? Cross over to Pest? . . . If he were a gentleman, he would send me a riding horse or a team of horses. . . ."[79] Horthy had increasing doubts about Germany's ability to win the war and was prepared to conceal Kállay's overtures to the Allies. But despite his hatred of the Nazis his insistence that he would never betray his ally was completely sincere. It was a matter of principle that an honorable person would never betray an ally.[80]

Edmund von Veesenmayer, an SS officer sent by Ribbentrop to evaluate the situation in Hungary, explained that the toppling of the current regime could only be accomplished with, and not against, the regent. The report contained devastating criticism of the men directing Hungarian policy officially or behind the scenes—Kállay, Bethlen, Ullein, Chorin, and Goldberger—who allegedly kept Hungary's contribution to the war effort at only a fraction of what it could be. The regent's standing with the general public was so high that he himself must not be attacked, but the clique around him needed to be eliminated. Veesenmayer opined that Szálasi's movement had degenerated and become totally unimportant, while politicians of the right-wing opposition were intelligent but too intellectual to become leaders of a serious opposition. Only two men were to be seriously considered—Imrédy and Bárdossy—but both were anathema to the regent.[81]

Hitler and Ribbentrop decided that as long as the military situation in the Balkans remained stable, and Hungary continued to supply Germany with industrial and agricultural goods, they would not undermine Horthy's position. On the other hand, intense pressure was to be put on Kállay in an effort to topple the government. German officials in Budapest were instructed to ostracize him and to encourage the Hungarian radical right-wing parties to attack the government even more vehemently. The right-wing parties urged Horthy to appoint a pro-German government and get rid of Kállay, Keresztes-Fischer, and Nagy, but Horthy ignored their demands.

DISAPPOINTING MEETING WITH MUSSOLINI

At the beginning of April, Kállay finally made his official trip to Rome which had been delayed the year before. It had become customary for each new prime minister to make his first foreign visit to Italy, but when Kállay planned to visit, Mussolini announced that he must first visit Hitler, an indication of the change that had taken place in the balance of power between the two allies. The visit proved inconclusive. Kállay found Mussolini much changed from 1938; he looked ill, with his head bald, his skin yellowish-white; the loss of Tripoli to the Allies had affected him deeply.[82] He confided in Kállay that his true reason for entering the war was his desire to make Italy a great power; it was for Italy the moment of destiny. If she missed the opportunity, Italy would remain a beggar among the great powers of the world.[83]

Kállay suggested an alignment of Italy, Hungary, and Finland within the Axis alliance as a means to take independent steps, but Mussolini urged him to be careful. He would try to help Hungary but it was impossible even to think of a separate peace. This was not just a matter of honor but a direct result of the Allied Casablanca formula of unconditional surrender. A separate peace on the basis of unconditional surrender would only turn Italy into a battlefield. The one thing Kállay achieved was that Mussolini promised not to apply discrimination against the Jews of Hungarian nationality living in Italy.[84]

Kállay had drawn up a memorandum for the Pope with the help of Cardinal Serédi, appealing to His Holiness to use his influence to save Hungary and other countries in a similar plight from both Nazism and Communism. Now he proposed the idea of a peace initiative by the Pope, who assured him of his sympathy and understanding; he would offer to mediate between belligerent parties if the Italian government asked him to do so, but Mussolini refused to discuss the matter. The Duce said everything must depend on his anticipated interview with Hitler. Kállay returned with the conclusion that one could no longer count on Italy.[85]

Political debates in Parliament grew increasingly acrimonious, as Imrédy and the rightists attempted to bring down the government. At one point the government survived by a margin of only nine votes. Imrédy's party planned several challenges to the government through interpellations, the practice of putting questions to a minister on a point of government policy which were traditionally posed on Wednesday. One challenge was the campaign to get rid of Vilmos Nagy, the minister of defense, who had been working to improve the treatment of Jews in the labor companies. Kállay met with Imrédy and appealed to his patriotism, explaining that the interpellations could lead to the fall of the government, but Imrédy was not willing to compromise. In order to block the troublemakers, Kállay took the highly unusual step of requesting that the regent suspend the parliamentary session, to which Horthy agreed on May 4, the day before the scheduled interpellations.

On the afternoon of May 4 Kállay called together the Council of Ministers in an extraordinary session and explained his plans. The next day, at the beginning of the parliamentary session, Kállay gave the president of the house the regent's letter, which announced that according to the 1933 Twenty-third Law Parliament would be prorogued to an undetermined date. Unless fifty representatives called the body together, they would not meet again until the budget debate in the fall. In the interval, according to the above law, the so-called Forty-two Committee—a committee of forty-two members of Parliament empowered to create decrees, would govern. There was a noisy outburst from the Right, but the leftist opposition, sensing what was at stake, agreed. In London, Kállay's strategy was misunderstood, and Radio London spoke of a fascist dictatorship.[86]

Summer of Hope

In July, the Allies landed in Sicily and on the morning of July 27, Hungary learned that Mussolini had fallen. The effect of the news was electrifying—all of Hungary jumped to the conclusion that within a few days

Italy would join forces with the Allies. The triumphant Allies would take Italy quickly and march up to the Hungarian border. It was taken for granted that Germany had already lost the war. Instead of making plans on how Hungary could get out of the war, efforts were devoted to making plans for the future.[87]

Both government and society believed that they had escaped the worst of the war. In the name of the Independent Smallholders Party Bacsky-Zsilinszky and Tildy urged immediate action—withdrawal from the war, resumption of neutrality, recall of troops from the Russian front, and repeal of the Jewish laws. Various groups of the democratic opposition planned and published their postwar programs.[88] All reckoned with the approaching arrival of the British army and Hungary's democratic trans-formation.[89] No one considered the possibility of negotiating with the Soviets. The end of the war seemed so close that at the August 24 meeting at Balatonszársó, the distinguished writer, László Németh, spoke of the war as if it was already over: "The Hungarians have lived through this war to the end in much better condition than the first world war. War losses have been smaller, [there is] greater prosperity . . ."[90]

In early August the reformers took their first step toward bridging rivalries and ideological disputes. In a major breakthrough the Indepen-dent Smallholders Party made an alliance with the Social Democrats, the first time that the Social Democrats had been willing to join with a party in the liberal opposition. The two parties in the alliance urged the admin-istration to change sides even if it meant fighting the Germans, and in-vited other opposition parties to join them. They got little response, other than the support of the former Communists who had formed the Peace Party after the Comintern dissolved itself and their party in May. The Social Democrats were still associated in the political mind with interna-tional Marxism.[91]

In his efforts to gather together the pro Anglo-Saxon groups, Bethlen hoped to shut out the radical leftists. From among the members of the Hungarian Social Circle he founded a group called the Democratic Citi-zens Alliance, but their stance against radical leftists contributed to pre-venting an agreement and made the Independent Smallholders hold more firmly to their alliance with the Social Democrats, even those who had been lukewarm before. The Independent Smallholders were caught between their desire to keep the alliance with the Social Democrats but also to join Bethlen. Bethlen set the date of decision as March 20, 1944, as it turned out one day after the Germans occupied the country.

CONFERENCE AT BALATON SZÁRSZÓ, AUGUST 23–29

In this spirit of optimism, a meeting of reformers was held to debate the question of Hungary's future; the very fact that the government permitted the meetings indicated the mood of the time. The conference of approximately six hundred participants brought together varied social groups, several of them did not usually cooperate. Almost all the populist writers were there as well as representatives of peasant parties, including Béla Kovács of the Peasant Alliance.[92] Minister of the Interior Ferenc Keresztes-Fischer, a strong anti-German and supporter of the Peasant Alliance, was also in attendance as were journalists of major papers and publishers. The conference was hosted by the anti-German Calvinist Soli Deo Gloria youth society, who had long been sympathetic to the populist movement but who were neither leftist nor revolutionary. Other youth groups included the Catholic youth group KALOT, the Student Unity movement, and the pro-Communist Győrffy College students, as well as a few worker groups. The aim of the meeting was to clarify the reformers' goals for the future of Hungary's economic and social life.

At the conference, held at the Soli Deo Gloria Balaton summer camp, a vacation atmosphere prevailed. Speeches and intense discussion mixed with summer relaxation, campfire singing and story telling. In spite of the political situation, with the government forced to prorogue Parliament, people met and spoke freely—something that would not be possible in the future. The major speakers came from among the populist writers who had built up a national following through their works, which had changed society's view of peasant life. Their loosely joined movement had remained relatively apolitical, with the exception of a few writers, who had started the National Peasant Party, which represented the landless and dwarf-holding peasants.

Differences emerged during the conference that revealed conflicting views of the possibilities awaiting Hungary at the end of the war. The first speaker, Ferenc Erdei, a leftist writer who had been instrumental in founding the National Peasant Party, startled his audience by taking an open political stand, declaring himself pro historical materialism and examining the development of modern Hungarian society through Marxist principles. He explained that Hungary had only two possible choices—if not fascism, then socialism—clearly meaning the Soviet model, which shocked many of the participants. Imre Kovács, who with his friend Erdei had organized the National Peasant party, was startled by Erdei's open political stance. A minority—including some of the students of peasant origin and young workers—supported Erdei's view, but the majority felt such a choice was not possible.[93]

Countering Erdei's Marxist stance was the well-known writer László Németh, who reflected the hopes that Hungary would emerge unscathed from the war. He declared that Hungary had been treated as a colonial country, both from within and without, with a leadership foreign to it. Between fascism and communism he offered the possibility of a third way through which Hungary would retain its independence. He took New Guinea as his example. "Let's say that one faction in New Guinea want New Guinea to belong to the English. The other says that New Guinea will only prosper with the Dutch. And then someone stands up and asks: Isn't it possible for New Guinea to belong to the Papuans?"[94] Emphasizing that European society had not developed in the way that Marx predicted, that instead of a few capitalists and a massive proletariat there were more and more landed peasants, free artisans, merchants, and public employees, he rejected both a British-type capitalism and Soviet-style socialism in favor of the third way.

István Bibó, considered one of the foremost political analysts of recent Central European history, commented later that the conference would have provided the ideal opportunity to initiate an anti-German, anti-Fascist People's Front movement. Bibó felt that Erdei made a mistake by placing Marxism at the center of the debate. By shocking the whole gathering he halted the possibility that a movement could be initiated which would have formed a united opposition. Then Németh responded with the third-way alternative. Bibó found that the two lectures proposing the two alternatives confused the mainly Protestant listeners and left them without direction. Others tried to moderate, but in the end the first two lectures determined further debate. From this point on the conference began to divide into two groups. In spite of the spirit of community and general anti-Fascist stance, there had been a definite split between the leftist and the more moderate groups, and the Szárszó conference ended with no follow up.[95] This meeting of representatives of the intellectual community was to be the last public debate of the populist ideas, which had been so influential during the 1930s.[96]

In August 1943, a reform movement of progressive Catholic leaders that was to play an important role at the end of the war gained momentum. At a secret meeting in Győr the leaders agreed on the urgent need to prepare for a democratic transformation of authoritarian semifeudal Hungary. Count József Pálffy, the leading figure, became president, but since he was comprised by his position in Parliament throughout the war, the journalist and editor of *Magyar Nemzet*, thirty-seven-year-old István Barankovics, became the leader as secretary-general. The progressive Catholic movement was strengthened by KALOT with its half million members, and EMSZO, the association of Catholic Urban Workers with 15,000 members. Together the two groups created the Catholic Social People's Movement, based on Jacques Maritain's ideas of integral humanism, a Christian view of man and the world. The people's movement drew up concrete proposals for transforming Hungarian society and restructuring the economy through radical land reform, rapid industrialization, and the expansion of education.[97]

Although those in the opposition were united behind the Kállay administration's efforts to shorten the war, they differed greatly in their ideas for postwar Hungary. One prevalent point of view, including Bethlen and his group, was to keep the existing system in order to maintain law and order and prevent a repetition of the chaos and social turmoil after World War I. Others thought that Kállay should reduce the huge deliveries of foodstuffs and war materials to the Germans, reduce military participation, and prepare the citizens as well as the military for a switch of sides, despite the risk of German occupation. The Social Democrat, Szakasits wanted an active turn against the Germans, but other leading Social Democrats, including their leader, Peyer, supported the Kállay-Bethlen view.

NEW ATTEMPTS TO CONTACT THE ALLIES

Negotiations between László Veress and the British in Istanbul started up again in summer. With the Allied landing in Sicily and Mussolini's downfall on July 25, the Italian capitulation seemed imminent, suggesting that an agreement was urgent. It could not be foreseen that with Mussolini's capture by the Germans and the foundation of his puppet republic the war in Italy would drag on.[98] Veress's earlier mission to Istanbul in the spring had been inconclusive not only because of the British call for Hungarian military officers to conduct negotiations. The Kállay government had been reluctant, partly because of the danger of discovery by the Germans but also because Paloczi-Horvath—as well as Royall Tyler in Bern—had spoken of sabotage, recommending the blowing up of bridges and derailing of trains. As Szegedy-Maszák remembered, all in the Foreign Office were appalled at the proposal of sabotage, especially that there was no concern expressed that such actions would bring about a German occupation of Hungary.[99] Still the Kállay government decided it would be unfortunate to allow the contact to end. The British had declared August

20 as the deadline to continue negotiations, and it was decided to make one last attempt and to send Veress as special envoy to Istanbul with authorization to discover what conditions the British would set to make it possible to carry out serious negotiations.

Veress, who was strongly pro-British, was convinced that only by accepting the formula of unconditional surrender would it be possible for the Hungarians to establish contact on the diplomatic level. In Istanbul, at the beginning of August, with the new Hungarian consul-general, Dezső Újváry, Veress formulated a communication according to which the Hungarian government offered to accept unconditional surrender if the Allies would make it possible. The message, confirmed and sent by Újváry on August 16, informed the British ambassador in Ankara, Sir Hugh Knatchbull-Hugessen, that Veress—who represented the group within the Hungarian government made up of the prime minister, the minister of the interior, chief of staff, and foreign ministry political department—wished to announce to the Allies that Hungary would accept unconditional surrender and would do everything to make it happen as soon as possible. The note stated that the Hungarian army was ready to defend Hungarian borders against the Germans and assured the Allies' use of airports and other military facilities to facilitate the Allies' occupation.[100]

The British Embassy in Ankara took Veress seriously and a high-ranking deputy of the ambassador's staff, John Cecil Sterndale-Bennett, met with Veress and Újváry on August 20 and recognized Veress' authorization. To his question whether the group would be able to carry out the capitulation, Veress answered that it was a technical question that could only be answered by a military expert who the Hungarian government would send to Istanbul.[101]

With an armistice agreement about to be signed by Italy, Veress' offer aroused great interest in London. Eden immediately informed the Americans and Soviets of the Hungarian initiative and included his four-point response: First, the British government would like to see a more valid authorization. Second, His Majesty's Government will expect the Hungarian government to make a public announcement of their acceptance of unconditional surrender and to take the necessary steps at the earliest possible moment. Third, if the Hungarian government should find that the time was not yet ripe for a public announcement, it should prove its good intentions by ceasing all cooperation with the Germans. Fourth, if the Hungarian government agreed with point three, the British government was ready to discuss ways and means with a Hungarian military person.[102]

Feverish activity followed. On September 6 the proposed text was sent to Moscow, Washington, and Quebec City, where Churchill and Roosevelt were in conference. The response from Molotov and Churchill indicated a fundamental divergence of views. In his reply of September 7 Molotov recommended leaving out the third and fourth points; the Soviets wanted only to recognize the Hungarian willingness to surrender. Churchill sent an urgent reply also dated September 7 that Hungarian defection from Germany would be a tremendous advantage, but only if it took place at the appropriate moment: ". . . it would be most improvident of us to squander the Hungarian volte-face and merely produce a premature outbreak followed by a German Gauleiter or super-Quisling installed by force. . . . We should not be impatient in this matter."[103]

Eden, concerned over the divergence in views, immediately wrote the prime minister that the Soviet opinion should be considered, and the next day Churchill accepted the original text, but with a single essential modification; that the words *at a suitable moment* be added to the second point. The definitive text now read: "His Majesty's Government will expect the Hungarian Government to make at a suitable moment a public announcement of their acceptance of unconditional surrender." Eden then wired Molotov that the British government believed it to be right to keep all four points. The decision was thus passed and instructions were sent to Istanbul for the text to be conveyed to Veress.[104]

In the middle of the night of September 9, 1943, under extraordinary secrecy the British ambassador, Sir Hugh Knatchbull-Hugessen, met Veress on a yacht in the Sea of Marmora. After showing Veress his own authorization in the shape of a telegram from Mr. Eden, he informed him in the name of the United Nations that His Majesty's Government had "taken note" of Hungary's communication and read out the following "preliminary conditions," which Veress took down from his dictation.[105] According to the conditions, the Hungarian capitulation was to be kept secret and made public by the Allies and the Hungarian government simultaneously, but in no case before the Allies reached the frontiers of Hungary. Hungary was to progressively reduce military and economic cooperation with Germany and withdraw its troops from Russia. It was to resist any attempt made by Germany to occupy Hungary and to prepare the persons and material for the cease-fire. An Allied military mission would parachute into Hungary in an advisory capacity.[106] The change of sides would only take place when the Anglo-Saxon powers reached Hungary's borders. Until then it was to be kept secret, and the Hungarians were not to provoke German occupation.[107]

Veress reached Budapest on September 14 with a memorized account of the document and two wireless transmitters. The members of the government, several who only now learned of the negotiations, were somewhat shocked. The foreign minister, Jenő Ghyczy, feared that Veress had overstepped his authority and committed them to more than they could deliver. Kállay reacted against the acceptance of unconditional surrender since it would be an infringement of the national sovereignty. Keresztes-Fischer strongly urged acceptance. According to Szegedy-Maszák the main point of view was that if Hungary's initiative had finally gotten beyond the sabotage and spying bureaucracy to a kind of political agreement, "we would harm our own work and trustworthiness if we pulled back."[108] Eventually Kállay consented that if the Allies would accept a compromise—that there would be no admission of unconditional surrender—the Hungarians would carry out any conditions imposed.

Although some doubted that the Hungarian government would be able to carry out the conditions, the government agreed to accept. Dezső Újváry, representing the Hungarian government, gave the verbal agreement on September 9 or 10. Andor Wodianer, consul in Lisbon, speaking with British Ambassador Sir Ronald Campbell, supported Újváry's word. When the formalities were finally agreed on, Wodianer formally presented Kállay's compromise. Campbell, acting for the Allies, said he could not accept, but Wodianer suggested that the point could be left in abeyance since the surrender would not take place until the Allies reached Hungary's frontiers; thus the disagreement was shelved, and it was agreed that the Hungarian government could consider the agreement to be in effect. Kállay wrote that the Hungarian offer amounted in essence to unconditional surrender and was received as such by the British.[109]

Yet the British and the Hungarians had differences in their interpretation and expectations of the agreement. Kállay regarded the agreement as a political gesture. He trusted that the Allies would honor the fact that Hungary had kept its constitutional parliamentary structure, was the first country to agree to go through diplomatic channels voluntarily to break with the Germans, and that it would be "struck off the list of enemies" and given British protection. The Allies sought only to derive military advantage. The British point of view was that Hungary needed to carry out such acts that would hasten their victory over Germany, and demanded action—including sabotage—on a serious scale, which would have brought immediate occupation.[110]

All through autumn it was assumed that the Western armies would soon reach the Drave or Danube, and the Hungarians had reasonable grounds for believing the Allied armies would eventually reach Hungary. Veress had brought two radio transmitters on his return to Budapest and started to work in the foreign ministry political department. He sent information to the British—official and precise data on the military situation, movement of German troops toward the Balkans, and acceptance of the mission of British parachutists to Hungary according to the Istanbul agreement. Kállay was in touch with the British through a secret radio transmitter that was kept in Horthy's residence in the castle, but since the Allies never reached the Hungarian borders the agreement never came into play.[111]

SZOMBATHELYI AND THE OSS

Also in late summer of 1943, with the expectation that Allied troops would soon take Italy, the Kállay government entered into new negotiations, this time with representatives of the American Office of Strategic Services (OSS). It has been known that the Hungarians made contact with OSS-Istanbul in late 1943, but the negotiations had been considered of minor importance since they appeared to have been inconclusive. The full significance of the negotiations has only been revealed through recently declassified files of the OSS, which show that there was much greater Hungarian involvement than heretofore realized; in fact, a final agreement had been reached between OSS-Istanbul and the Hungarian government at the end of February 1944. According to the plan the agreement would only be made public after American troops landed at an airport close to Budapest.

Director of Military Intelligence Colonel Gyula Kádár recalled that in September 1943 he received a written request from the Hungarian military attaché in Bulgaria, Ottó Hatz, to attend the international fair in Smyrna (Izmir), where he might meet various people from whom he could learn something; Kádár gave his permission.[112] At the fair Hatz made friends with American officers who organized a get-together a few days later for him to meet with the responsible American agents of the OSS in Istanbul. Hatz presented his credentials to the OSS officers and explained his interest in negotiating a change of sides to the Allies. In contrast to the long drawn-out efforts to work with the British, the OSS agents and Hatz came to a quick understanding. They drew up an agreement by which the Hungarians would begin to provide intelligence information.[113]

On October 8, 1943, Hatz flew to Budapest where he appeared in Kádár's office and after some pleasantries explained that he had made friends with American officers at the fair; then he showed Kádár the radio receiver-transmitter, which the Americans had given him. He and the Americans had come to an agreement that if the Hungarian government or the Hungarian chief of staff should be ready to take up negotiations, a message should be sent through the official Hungarian radio service. Three days in succession in the 8 P.M. evening news an announcement should be made including the two words *Izmir Fair*. The American radio, in turn, would respond three days in succession at a determined time with a certain wording.[114]

Since the matter went beyond his sphere of authority, Kádár took Hatz to Szombathelyi, who expressed his delight with the possibility of establishing contact with the Americans. Szombathelyi arranged to speak with the prime minister and the regent and received authorization to continue with the negotiations but that the radio transmitter was not to be used. Further arrangements were to be handled by permanent Assistant Director of Foreign Affairs Andor Szentmiklóssy, one of the most important figures in the anti-German group. Kádár himself composed the text for the radio message and personally gave it to the director, Antal Náray, and the message was duly sent.

The announcement, repeated every ten minutes, first in German, then English, finally French, read: "According to the Turkish press report the Smyrna fare resulted in a complete Hungarian success." The English text added: "We hope that in the future Hungarian-Turkish commercial contacts will continue to strengthen."[115] To give proof of their good intentions, the Hungarians regularly sent intelligence information to the OSS-Istanbul local office. Hatz, transferred from Sofia to Ankara, negotiated with the Americans a number of times. Each time, either personally or through the diplomatic post, he reported to Kádár, who then informed Szombathelyi and Szentmiklóssy. Hatz's first discussions did not contain concrete recommendations; the Americans emphasized that they were only willing to negotiate if the Hungarians did so with complete sincerity.[116]

Neither Kádár in his extensive memoir published in 1978 nor Szombathelyi in his account of his activities written in American prison in June 1945 mention delivering intelligence information to the OSS.[117] At his trial in Budapest in 1946, Szombathelyi did acknowledge his role in taking up contact with the Americans but he denied that he took part in spying against Germany.[118] Yet the OSS dossier indicates that the Hungarians delivered a large amount of information, including details about the Hungarian divisions on the Russian front, on the war materials produced for the Germans, on German units transiting Hungary into Yugoslavia and Russia, and of especial importance to the Germans, data on Hungarian crude oil production, refining, and volume of petroleum exports of fuel to Germany. The head of the OSS in Washington, William Donovan, in a report to the Joint Chiefs of Staff, dated November 20, 1943, wrote that the committee of the Hungarian chief of staff had given its first proposal to OSS-Istanbul "to give detailed military intelligence concerning the German Army and German operations."[119]

From the beginning of his tenure, Chief of Staff Szombathelyi had attempted to minimize the Hungarian alliance with Germany. His contributions indicate his intention to assist American troops to land in Hungary. A package with materials signed by Szombathelyi on December 28, 1943, which arrived at OSS-Istanbul February 23, 1944, included a seven-hundred-word analysis of the European war and of the strength of the German divisions as well as of their allies, commenting that the German forces were exhausted. Attached to Szombathelyi's report he had included four detailed hand-drawn desktop-size maps, clearly designed to make possible an American landing on the Hungarian sites designated, with special attention devoted to new and newly improved roads, one which led to a new airfield near Budapest. Another map linked the city of Kecskemét to the central military airport of Hungary and to the city of Szeged, close to the prewar Yugoslav border. It appears that such a landing was definitely planned. Former OSS Lt. Col. Abram Gilmore Flues stated in 2002 that the OSS team he commanded was to land in the latter part of 1944 just south of Buda.[120]

Despite the initial agreement, attempts to make a more formal pact foundered in the next months, as OSS officers became more impatient in their demands, and the Hungarians realized that the Americans were primarily interested in gaining intelligence information and rejected any political guarantees. On December 18 Hatz was presented with a new draft, which ruled out a formal political instrument and proposed an agreement to merely define the extent of a collaboration between military executives. The Americans pointed out that simply by agreeing to collaborate the Hungarians would prove their moral disassociation from the Axis, and promised to give the Allied committee dealing with Hungary at the postwar peace conference all of the relevant information. The new draft of American demands was submitted to Szombathelyi and to Kállay in late December 1943 with a deadline of January 7 to return concrete and binding offers.[121]

At this time the Hungarian military attaché in Berlin, Sándor Homlok, arrived to announce that Ribbentrop had gotten word that Hungary was involved in separate peace negotiations in Turkey. The news aroused consternation since rumors were already circulating that the Germans were planning an occupation. It was decided that Kádár and Hatz, who was called to Budapest, would arrange a meeting with Admiral Wilhelm Canaris, the head of the German *Abwehr*, with whom Hatz was on good terms. Hatz would explain that as military attaché he had met some American officers and the possibility existed to make friends. Would Canaris give his permission to deepen the contact, perhaps the Americans would provide useful information. According to Kádár, at the meeting on January 9 in Munich, Canaris listened silently to Hatz' presentation—then replied that in no way could he give his permission. The suggestion was naive—the Americans were much too crafty to give any significant information, and they would come under suspicion of spying, which carried with it unforeseeable consequences. It was at this point that Hatz told Kádár that he had mentioned his meeting with the Americans to his friend Otto Wagner, the head of the Abwehr (Defense) station in Sofia.[122]

Admiral Canaris' activities against the Nazi regime revealed at the Nuremberg Trials, as well as Kádár's failure to mention Hungary's involvement in spying for the OSS, would suggest that this was not a full account of the Canaris meeting. It is extremely unlikely that the Hungarians would have gone ahead in negotiations with the Americans if the head of the German Abwehr had prohibited further contact. It is known that Canaris, who had connections with both the British and United States secret services, had met secretly with William Donovan, head of OSS, in Spain in the summer of 1943 to propose a peace plan.[123] It later turned out that Otto Wagner was working with Canaris in this anti-Nazi conspiracy.[124]

At any rate the OSS files show that negotiations were not broken off, although the Hungarians did not meet the January 7 deadline. In contacting the Americans the Kállay government had hoped to receive some political guarantees and also ensure that the country would not be occupied by the Soviet Union. Kállay's representatives had also been negotiating with Alan Dulles in Switzerland.[125] By this time the initial enthusiasm attached to the American contact had waned. In February, the Hungarians sought a guarantee that if they accepted the American proposal, Russia (and Britain) would respect Hungary's status as a virtual ally and adjust their attitudes and action accordingly; the Americans responded that no assurance could be given as long as Hungary remained an enemy of the United Nations.

Finally, on February 14, the Hungarian government called the disagreement so serious that they would be unable to advance without direct conversations with an American well-acquainted with Hungary's situation which the OSS interpreted as a rejection and definite break-off of negotiations. Despite the reservations, on February 22 Hatz delivered Kállay's reluctant approval in principle of the American proposal. Perhaps he still hoped that the OSS would fulfill its promise of landing an American contingent on Hungarian soil. The Hungarians agreed to furnish the intelligence material the Americans had requested, which included precise diagrams of landing fields and signals. A few weeks later the Germans occupied Hungary.[126]

Although the OSS plans called for the arrival of an OSS team at an airport near Budapest in the latter part of 1944, after which a United States–Hungarian alliance was to become public, the question arises whether there ever was such a plan—or whether it was all a deception on the part of the Americans to mislead the Germans and distract their attention from the planned North Atlantic invasion. Operation Bodyguard, created to deceive the Germans—and their allies—into believing in a Balkan landing, seemingly convinced Hitler, the Hungarians, and perhaps even those among the Allies who were planning for such a landing.[127]

ATTEMPTS TO IMPROVE RELATIONS WITH NEIGHBORS

A major concern in the attempt to leave the war was that of the territories won back between 1938 and 1941 since no one in Hungary was willing to lose them. A problem in the negotiations with the British had been the Hungarian government's attempts to gain a commitment to help them retain some of the reclaimed lands, as well as to avoid a Soviet occupation; negotiations with the OSS-Istanbul almost foundered for the same reasons. In its efforts to improve relations with its neighbors, Kállay's government attempted to open negotiations with the surrounding governments despite the intense anti-Hungarian propaganda, but each neighbor demanded return of the annexed territories. Relations with Romania were constantly worsening.[128] The deputy premier, Michael Antonescu, was willing to enter discussions but not the fanatically pro-German dictator, Marshal Ion Antonescu. At a general meeting of the Liga Culturale, he announced that after fighting ended in the East the Romanian soldiers would have to turn their arms against the chief enemy. The meeting passed a resolution that the Romanian frontier must extend to the Tisza, deep inside truncated Hungary.

In an effort to explain and justify the governance of the returned territories at the future peace conference, the Hungarian government began a large-scale review, with detailed questionnaires to be filled out by all ministries in the Felvidék, the Carpathian/Ukraine, and northern Transylvania, outlining the problems they met, the solutions carried out, the monies spent, and the treatment of minorities.[129]

At the request of both the Hungarians and Romanians, a special commission was appointed by the German and Italian governments to investigate the conditions in north and south Transylvania. The special commission, the *Sonderbeauftragtenkommission,* carried out parallel studies of conditions in southern and northern Transylvania with exemplary thoroughness, examining in detail conditions relating to requirements for military service, borders, the economic situation, cultural situation, movement of refugees, and so on. The conclusion reached in their *Denkschrift* dated Berlin, March 1943, was that neither the Romanian nor the Hungarian governments had fulfilled their responsibilities from the Vienna Award, which they had signed. The conclusion also mentioned that the recommendations made by the governments of the German Reich and of Italy to the Romanian and Hungarian governments to establish peace in Transylvania had remained essentially unfulfilled. Both sides were guilty of serious discrimination against the population of the other ethnic group through their official and military personnel.[130] There is no question that each side carried out harsh and unjust measures against the other minority population.

A foreign office official confessed: "I am not proud of Hungarian minority policies in northern Transylvania. I never approved of the reciprocity measures which punished people for things about which they could do nothing. . . . Both Teleki and Kállay had good intentions but were unable to carry through their policies. In southern Transylvania the situation was probably worse, more death sentences, internments, longer prison terms, forced labor. But that did not justify what happened in northern Transylvania."[131]

OFFICERS ON TRIAL

After taking office Prime Minister Kállay had begun to investigate the Újvidék massacres. In response to an interpellation in Parliament by a Serbian member, Milán Popovics, on July 15, 1942, Kállay affirmed that he was looking into the matter. He was also anxious to cultivate friendly relations with the Serbian leaders, Nedić and Mihailović, and sent a message through a Serb officer to Mihailović, expressing his sincere regret for the Újvidék atrocities and promising that the culprits would be punished. At his request Szombathelyi assigned a military court judge-advocate to make an extensive report detailing the events, according to Kállay the most heinous crime in Hungary's military history.[132]

It was a unique event for a country to put its own officers on trial during wartime. The formal inquiry initiated by the Ministry of the Interior began in fall of 1943. Although the gendarme officers were tried in regular court on the order of the Ministry, at Szombathelyi's request the high-ranking officers who led the raid were tried before the court of the chief of the general staff. Szombathelyi had been bitterly disappointed by his formerly honored comrades and officers. He had come to realize from police reports and individual reports, that those responsible had not only misled him but had carried out a heinous crime, which for the Hungarians was a national tragedy. "When this painful reality hit, I finally took action and energetically. I could almost say that I made the whole matter mine. I took it on my shoulders—therefore I placed it before the Court of the General Staff. In order to do this I raised the charge to treason, although my prosecuting attorney did not consider that correct. I did not want to pass off this horrible matter to others. To place on anyone else's shoulders, although the minister of interior warned me that this did not come under the authority of the Chief of Staff—it was not a matter of treason but of public murder and robbery. I feared that in other hands the verdict would be drawn out and might get lost"[133]

The special military court began the trial on December 13 against those officers immediately responsible, above all Lieutenant General Feketehalmy-Czeydner, Lt. Col. László Deák, Maj. Gen. József Grassy, and Gendarme Captain Márton Zöldy. According to the Hungarian military code a senior officer accused of a crime could be left on parole unless the charge was so severe as to tempt him to flee. Thus the high-ranking officers were not taken into custody but remained free while defending themselves. The sentences were announced in December and January. Along with minor offenders who received punishment, eight officers were sentenced to long terms of imprisonment. Of the four main officers charged, Lieutenant General Feketehalmy-Czeydner was sentenced to fifteen years, Major General Grassy to fourteen, Lieutenant Colonel Deák to thirteen, and Captain Zöldi to eleven.[134]

On January 18, 1944, all Hungary was startled by the news that the four main officers had broken their parole and fled across the Austrian frontier. Never before in the annals of the Hungarian military had such a disgraceful incident occurred. It had been held unthinkable that an officer should fail to appear duly before the court unless committing suicide, the proper course for the guilty. Flight was something unheard of, and the public was enraged. The officers, smuggled into Germany with the assistance of Archduke Albrecht, were welcomed in Germany and received high positions in the Waffen-SS. It was not possible for Kállay to ask for their extradition since Hungary did not have a reciprocal agreement with Germany, but also because he feared the Germans would demand extradition of the thousands of Polish, French, British, and Jewish refugees.[135]

The affair strengthened the old suspicion that the Germans had been involved in the events leading up to the massacre in 1942. Szombathelyi, distraught at the escape, believed that the nation's honor was at stake; the flight of the officers proved that the whole Újvidék matter was a German affair.[136] The thesis is supported by exchanges between Werkmeister, the Budapest chargé d'affaires, and the German foreign ministry. Werkmeister reported in a telegram on January 17, 1944:

. . . a few days ago when I met the chief of the general staff in company, I mentioned the news circulating in the city about his conduct in acting against those responsible for the Újvidék matter. The chief of the general staff became very serious and expressed that the Újvidék events were a national misfortune. He was ashamed to acknowledge that terrible things had happened there. . . . In such a case it was impossible that the military commanders under whom such heinous deeds were carried out should get away with it. They must count on serious punishment.[137]

The OKW, the Supreme Command of the Armed Forces, answered to ignore the matter, but Werkmeister reported in a second telegram that the chief of the general staff this morning continued the official discussion. He received a telegram from the foreign advisor to the Budapest ministry, Hilger, telling him that if someone brings up the fact that the Hungarian officers crossed the border say that you know nothing about it.[138]

The Road to Occupation

For a time Kállay and his supporters thought that by contacting the Western Allies they had achieved their aims; they would only have to wait for the end of the war, which seemed to be very close. They believed that they would be able to avoid negotiating with the Soviet Union and by making some reforms be able to establish a government after the war. Antipathy to Bolshevism was almost universal, intensified by the deeds of the Soviet Union under Stalin: the famine in the Ukraine, the show trials, the purge of the military.[139] But the spirit of optimism began to dim with the slow progress of the Allies in Italy and the steady advance of the Russians. Coalition armies with their mixed command advanced slowly and the front remained static from October 1943 until May 1944. The government plan based on surrendering to the Allies at the border became ever less plausible; yet the government held fast to its resolve to avoid negotiations with the Russians.

While Kállay had counted on the Allies to enable him to collaborate with them, the British were more interested in sending secret service members to organize underground activities and sabotage, a form of resistance that made no sense to the Hungarians. Former Ambassador Barcza criticized Radio London, which kept urging Hungary to open opposition. Only someone who had no idea of their situation could think that Hungary could openly take up weapons against the Germans—surrounded and infiltrated as they were.[140]

At the end of November at the Teheran Conference, Roosevelt and Churchill had given in to Stalin's demands, allowing Russia hegemony over Central and Eastern Europe. The British then urged Kállay to seek contact with the Soviets before their army reached Hungary's borders. The Americans also urged an immediate bailout and urgent negotiations with the Soviet Union. Yet Horthy's intense anti-Bolshevism and the pro-German stance of the military made it next to impossible for Kállay to act on their suggestions. Responding to a question posed by Barcza in February 1944, Kállay answered that if they had to choose between a Germany on the defensive or an expansive Russia, they had no choice other than to stick with the Germans; Hungarian politicians had long considered Russia the greater danger.

The Hungarians did not have exact information on the diplomatic agreements at Teheran, but the Beneš trip to Moscow and the ensuing Czech-Soviet alliance, as well as a Soviet mission to Tito and Allied assistance to Tito's partisans, made the general terms of the agreement clear. A report came from Ullein-Reviczky, now in Stockholm, that he had learned from Japanese colleagues that 1944 would start the British offensive in the West and that there would be no serious attack in the Balkans.[141]

At the time of the Italian armistice in the fall of 1943, Hitler had decided that to prepare against another betrayal it would be necessary to plan for a possible occupation first of Hungary and then of Romania. The OKW completed a plan for a Hungarian invasion, code-named Margarethe I, on September 30. The plan included the use of Romanian and Slovak troops, although at the time Hitler had no actual intention of occupying Hungary, having decided that as long as things remained calm he would leave the regent in charge.

The situation changed early in 1944 with the spectacular victories of the Red Army and rapid Soviet advances in the Ukraine. As Soviet armies drew nearer to the Carpathians the importance of the lines of communication across Hungary increased enormously. Besides, if the Russians reached the Carpathians there would be direct contact with the Hungarians who might use the opportunity to defect. In light of Hungary's strategic position it was clear that Hitler could not leave Hungary in the hands of a government whose loyalties were suspect, while the Hungarian economy had become of even more crucial importance to Germany. With the retreat of German troops and the advance of the Red Army, Hungary was almost the only significant foreign territory under German control. Hitler was especially anxious to hold out in western Hungary, the source of Hungarian oil.[142]

The Germans also lacked trust in the Hungarian military. Their view was colored by the fact that the military had been unable to push through the measure for Hungarian troops to join the Wehrmacht in the occupation of the Balkans—exactly as Szombathelyi had feared.[143] Hitler had also been angered by the attempts of the Hungarian military to secure the return of the Hungarian units remaining on the eastern front. During his visit to Hitler's headquarters in January 1944, Szombathelyi again requested the return of the Hungarian occupation units, explaining to Wilhelm Keitel that Hungary intended to defend the border on the Carpathians with Hungarian troops alone. Keitel found the idea ludicrous, partly because he found it inconceivable that the German lines should have to withdraw so far west; Hitler as well considered there was no possibility that the Russians would push forward to the Carpathians. When Horthy repeated the request in a letter to Hitler on February 12, 1944, Hitler was furious and did not answer Horthy or Szombathelyi.[144]

OPERATION MARGARETHE

It is difficult to determine when Hitler made his decision to order the execution of Operation Margarethe. The plans for the occupation had been changed several times depending on the political and military situation. His decision may have been precipitated by Horthy's letter requesting the return of the Hungarian troops, as well as a report from the

German espionage service that Horthy and his son were attempting to make contact with the Allies. The timing of the invasion may well have been influenced by the Allies' deceptive strategy to hide their plans for the Normandy invasion, Operation Overlord. At Teheran, Roosevelt, Stalin, and Churchill had agreed on the strategy code-named Operation Bodyguard to deceive the Germans about the planned Normandy landing, leading them to expect an invasion of Norway, an invasion at Calais, or a landing in the Balkans. The operation to suggest the imminent invasion of the Balkans, Operation Zeppelin, was intended to take advantage of Hitler's obsession over the vulnerability of his southern flank and tie down German troops in preparing for the attack. The deception probably misled Hitler, whose fears would have been confirmed when he received the report at the end of February that Hungary was expecting an American mission.[145]

The deception was also intended to fool the Hungarians. Since the Allied invasion in Normandy required that German troops be removed from the Western theater of war, it would be an advantage if Germany's allies should attempt to change sides, bringing on a German occupation. In Hungary's case these policies were somewhat contradictory since a German invasion was likely to destroy the democratic elements the Allies needed for democratic reconstruction, as well as the last intact Jewish community in Europe.[146]

For Hitler the question became not whether to occupy Hungary, but if there were enough German troops available, or whether he should allow Romanian, Slovak, and Croat troops to take part—and then to allow the neighboring countries to take over parts of the country. He even considered the idea that Hungary should disappear from the map. Romania and Slovakia would be rewarded by cancellation of the two Vienna Awards; Croatia would get the Muraköz. By March 7, when the Red Army was only about a one hundred sixty kilometers from the Hungarian borders, Hitler could delay no longer.[147]

The German secret service in Hungary got wind of Hitler's plans to use troops from the hostile neighboring countries. Dr. Wilhelm Höttl recalled: "When Hitler found out that Horthy, in spite of every warning, was continuing negotiations with the English, he decided in his choleric manner: 'Occupation! And with the cooperation of Romanian and Slovak troops! I already arranged it with Antonescu!' Probably with Tisó as well."[148] According to this plan the Hungarian army would have been disarmed, divided up, and put into work brigades. At the most Hungarian battalions would have been mixed in with German units. "This is how the original order went out. And you have to know that an order from the Führer could not be reversed. There was no precedent."[149]

In what he termed perhaps the greatest success in his secret service career, Höttl explained: "Knowing Hungarian conditions, I saw that if they carried out this order there would be big trouble. If we carried out an open military action against Hungary, at least several garrisons would oppose us."[150]

Höttl wrote a memorandum recommending a political solution with military force, but without Romanian and Slovak troops. Most important, the solution needed to be carried out to give the appearance that everything happened with Horthy's knowledge and consent! This would result in a Hungary friendly to Germany with Horthy still at his post and the army and police collaborating. Hungary's economic resources would be at the full disposal of the Reich. Romania would be free to send her troops to the front.

Getting the memo to Hitler was the most difficult part, since both Himmler and Ribbentrop were in favor of Hitler's drastic occupation plan, Margarethe II. Schellenberg, chief of the SS secret service, sent the memo to a minister assigned to Hitler's staff, who then gave it to the Führer's aide-de-camp, telling him to put it on Hitler's night table. It was Hitler's custom before he went to bed to read the most recent messages. Höttl was certain that Hitler had read his memo. "Clearly he read my memorandum too, because the next morning he arranged that they invite Horthy for negotiations."[151]

Hitler agreed to make a last attempt with Horthy, but it was clear that the occupation would take place. The concession was only that it would be restricted and the country would not be dismembered immediately— everything would depend on Horthy. The restricted occupation was to be carried out while Horthy was with Hitler so he would be confronted with a *fait accompli*. If he could put a good face on it, order the Hungarians to accept it, pretend to the outer world that it had his consent and would guarantee Hungary's full cooperation, then Hitler would also pretend it had all been a transaction between friends. He would even let the occupying troops leave the country when the situation stabilized. If not, total occupation, using satellite troops, would be put into effect. The orders for Operation Margarethe I were issued March 12, signed by Hitler.[152]

In early March 1944, unrealistic optimism prevailed in Hungary. Despite the spectacular Soviet victories with their armies within one hundred sixty kilometers of the Hungarian border, there was no move for a general Hungarian mobilization. Only two divisions were given definite orders to mobilize. The Second Armored Division was warned, but left at peace strength. The remaining troops in the country were given no orders at all. Horthy still hoped to persuade the Germans to let Hungary defend the Carpathians, thus motivating the Russians to go around through the flat Polish plain.

It was carnival season. Life in Hungary went on as if there was no cloud in the sky. The former minister to London, Barczy, writes that never "was the season so filled with dinners, déjeuners, teas and cocktail parties."[153] Streets were still crowded, shops with ridiculously expensive luxury goods still found buyers. "Jews occupied the best tables in the restaurants and the best seats in the theatres."[154] Moderate politicians, the Independent Smallholders, and even the Social Democrats, addressed the largest audiences of their lives and made promises of a democratic world around the corner. Much of the public was under the illusion that the most difficult parts of war were behind them. Although German troops had been moving up to the Hungarian borders since early March, no one believed in the danger of German occupation.[155]

Along with plans for the traditional celebration of March 15, the Hungarian national holiday of independence, a special celebration of the fiftieth anniversary of the death of Kossuth, the great Hungarian patriot, was to be held on March 20. Expectations were high for the speech Kállay was to give in Parliament. People thought he might proclaim a Hungarian surrender and perhaps the arrival of Allied air-borne divisions.

A three-member American mission, code named Mission Sparrow, actually landed March 15 close to the Yugoslav border near a village named Podturen. The landing had to take place during the full moon from March 10–15, and a storm had delayed their takeoff from Bari, Italy. Their long-planned mission originated in OSS headquarters with Allen W. Dulles in Bern. The idea was to help the Hungarians break with Hitler's Germany and join the Allies. They chose a village close to the Yugoslav border for the landing so if captured, the men could say they had landed in Hungary by mistake. After burying their parachutes and supplies they met a Hungarian, a former waiter in France, who introduced them to the villagers. In celebration, the women brought quantities of food to the village hall— eggs, ham, butter, rolls, dumplings. They toasted with slivovitz. To the Americans it was like an operetta. Where was the war?[156]

After some questioning by the Hungarian military, they were taken to Budapest where they expected to be received immediately by Kállay. They had no way of knowing that at the moment Horthy and Szombathelyi were meeting with Hitler.

MEETING AT KLESSHEIM, MARCH 18, 1944

On March 15 Admiral Horthy and his wife attended the gala premiere of the opera "Petőfi," arranged by students at the university, along with government officials, diplomats, and other dignitaries. It was the first time that the regent's wife, Magda, had appeared in public since the death of her son István. During the intermission a member of the German legation interrupted them, saying that Minister von Jagow requested an urgent audience to deliver a personal letter from Hitler. The letter turned out to be a belated response to Horthy's request in February for the immediate withdrawal of Hungarian forces from the eastern front. Now Hitler was prepared to discuss the matter personally and asked that Horthy kindly meet him at Klessheim Castle before March 20. Hitler asked him to bring Chief of Staff Szombathelyi and Foreign Minister Csatay, but not the prime minister, Miklós Kállay, nor the minister of the interior Keresztes-Fischer whom he also distrusted.

On the morning of March 16 Horthy met with Kállay, Foreign Minister Ghyczy, Csatay, and Szombathelyi to discuss his response. Kállay urged him not to go, arguing that his absence from the country could lead to disorder and arbitrary actions by Germany and her Hungarian sympathizers: "I warned Horthy it would be extremely dangerous to leave Hungary before it was clear what the Germans meant to do with the troops they had lined up on our frontiers." No important decisions could be made in his absence, and the country as well as the army "would remain without the supreme leadership at the mercy of the arbitrary will of the Germans."[157] Kállay of course knew of the landing of Mission Sparrow and its ramifications.

Horthy seemed to accept these arguments and to agree that Chief of the General Staff Szombathelyi be sent instead, but Szombathelyi—although willing to take on the assignment if necessary—argued that if Hitler was finally willing to discuss the withdrawal of Hungarian troops, only the regent himself would be able to achieve the desired result. In the past Hitler had only been willing to give in to Horthy. For twenty-five years the regent "had shouldered every burden for the nation's sake," and could not now refuse to undertake this difficult task. Szombathelyi did not consider a German occupation likely—as he told his adjutant, Pál Lieszkovszky, "for Hitler it would be madness: such an aggressive move would make it impossible for Hungarian and German soldiers to continue to fight together as allies."[158] Horthy could not resist this call to his patriotism.[159]

Horthy and his party—Csatay, Szombathelyi, and Ghyczy—left Budapest secretly on the evening of March 17, arriving at Klessheim Castle the morning of March 18. Greeted by Hitler, Ribbentrop, and Keitel, they found the atmosphere frigid. Hitler asked Horthy for a private conversation, and since Horthy who spoke fluent German objected to the presence of Hitler's interpreter the two were strictly alone, thus there was no exact record made of their discussion.[160] The Führer said that in light of the terrible catastrophe of the Italian surrender he had to prevent Hungarian betrayal. He knew that Hungary planned to double-cross Germany and he would not allow it. He had to defend himself and therefore would take necessary measures. Horthy was furious at the charge of betrayal. In its thousand-year history Hungary had never betrayed an ally, and if it should be in the national interest to ask for a ceasefire, he considered it a matter of honor to first tell the Germans.

At the end of the hour-and-a-half meeting , Hitler announced that he had already decided on a military occupation of Hungary. Horthy now became really furious. As he told the historian C. A. Macartney later, "If I had had my revolver with me, I would have shot the scoundrel; all my life I'll regret that I didn't do it."[161] He jumped up and ran out of the room. According to witnesses, Horthy, with a face red with fury, ran toward his rooms. Hitler came after him at the door, also furious. He tried to talk Horthy into coming back, but Horthy shook him off and shut himself in his room. Hitler turned around and went back to his own room, calling Ribbentrop to him. Not long afterward he asked that the regent join him for lunch. Members of Horthy's entourage assembled to hear the regent's account of the meeting but he was so agitated he was unable to give a lucid account. When the invitation to lunch was delivered Horthy replied he would attend only if the talks were to continue. The lunch took place in icy silence.

In their second conversation, the regent took the offensive, telling Hitler he should reconsider, that the Hungarians were the only people still friendly to Germany. The Germans had behaved so badly that even the Hottentots and Laplanders hated them. Hitler rehashed the accusations made at the earlier meeting at Klessheim and handed Horthy a protocol, which listed the objectives of the German occupation. It called for the appointment of a new Hungarian government with Imrédy as prime minister and General Jenő Rátz as minister of defense, as well as a German minister plenipotentiary to be sent in with the occupation army. The regent was to issue a proclamation instructing the Hungarian people and army to receive the Wehrmacht in a friendly way.[162]

Horthy indignantly refused to sign the proposed protocol, declaring that never in his life had he told a lie and he would not do so now. In desperation Horthy told Hitler that if he refrained from attacking Hungary he would give his solemn promise that Hungary would not defect to the enemy, and if the promise were broken he would commit suicide. Hitler replied, "But what good would that do me?"[163] On this bizarre note the conversation ended in deadlock. Horthy changed into travel clothes and announced his intention of departing immediately. To delay him Ribbentrop staged a fake air raid with a smoke screen over the castle.

Szombathelyi, convinced that any resistance would have disastrous consequences, seems to have persuaded Horthy to make one final effort with Hitler. Both Hitler and Ribbentrop had hinted that some compromise was possible—if Horthy agreed he could return to Budapest and appoint a new government acceptable to Germany. Once the guarantees were achieved Hitler told Szombathelyi that he would withdraw his troops from Hungary. This promise may have begun to tip the balance. Around 8 P.M. Ribbentrop appeared to tell Horthy that Hitler was prepared for further discussion. Making an effort to appear conciliatory Hitler implored Horthy to remain at his post and promised "that the German troops shall be withdrawn as soon as a new Hungarian government that has my confidence has been formed."[164] There is controversy over just what Horthy agreed to at Klessheim, but there definitely was some kind of agreement.[165]

Horthy would not resign; he would dismiss Kállay and appoint a government that had the Germans' trust. But Hitler had promised that he would withdraw the troops as soon as Horthy named an acceptable government, and Horthy later affirmed that this was the most important point on which he made his decision. It seems that the regent did not continue to request that the Hungarian troops be brought home but would send the whole Hungarian army to the Russian front, and of course the massive deliveries of foodstuffs and war material to Germany would continue. At their departure, Hitler accompanied the Hungarian party to their train to send them off.[166]

Evidently, Horthy's assurances were enough to convince Hitler that the occupation could be accomplished without major complications. He ordered certain changes in Operation Margarethe, calling off plans for a military seizure of the castle. The number of units to be used to occupy the country was somewhat reduced, and Hungarian troops were to be confined to their barracks but their weapons were not to be confiscated.

As he left Klessheim Castle, Horthy had little idea of the seriousness of the situation. He could hardly have imagined that the German occupation would put an end to what has been called the most remarkable accomplishment of the so-called Horthy era—the preservation of a degree of political freedom and pluralism in face of repeated attempts by the radical Right to introduce one-party dictatorship.[167] Until the German occupation Hungary was one of the three islands of cultural and intellectual freedom in Europe, along with Sweden and Switzerland. Book publishing flourished, with a great and increasing interest shown in foreign literature, especially English. Even a few Jewish authors were published at a time when elsewhere in Europe Jewish books were being burned.[168] Although civil and political rights had been eroded, Hungary had remained one of the few countries on the Continent and the only one in Eastern Europe that permitted the functioning of a multiparty system and some freedom of assembly and the press.[169]

The regent's train left Klessheim around 9:30 P.M. and arrived in Vienna at 1 A.M. There it was held up until at least four in the morning, the moment when German troops began their advance into Hungary. When Horthy awoke on March 19 he was surprised to find himself still several hours from Budapest. By the time his train crossed the Hungarian border, German troops were near the capital, and when he reached the railroad station in Budapest he was greeted by a German honor guard. The troops marched into Hungary unopposed.[170]

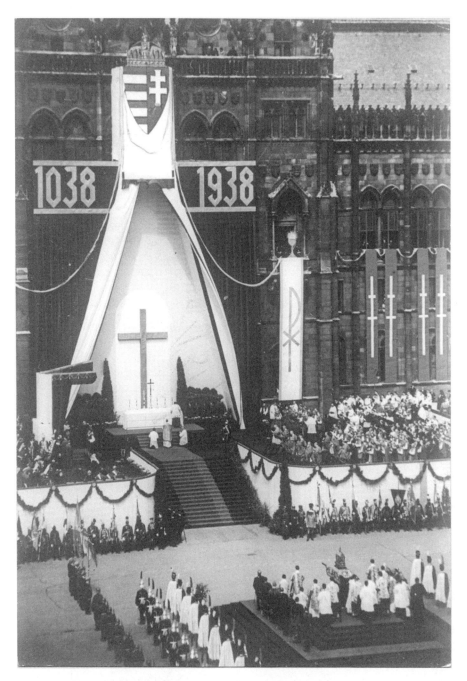

Opening of World Eucharistic Congress before Parliament, 1938.

Above: Regent Horthy and wife with Hitler at Berlin Opera House, 25 August 1938.

Below: "Long Live Greater Hungary": Marching into Losonc after first Vienna Award, 10 November 1938.

Soldier to the front—
leave-taking, 22 July 1941.

Northern Transylvanian village after second Vienna Award, 1941.

Above: Entering a Soviet village, summer 1942.

Below: Vice-Regent Horthy and the Regent, 1942.

Above: Vice-Regent preparing for flight before fatal crash, 20 August 1942.

Below: Jews being taken to train station, 18 June 1944.

Hungarian family fleeing from Transylvania before Soviets, 2 October 1944.

Prime minister Ferenc Nagy and Mátyás Rákosi, general secretary of the Communist
Party, 4 April 1947.

8 German Occupation

German troops occupied Hungary on Sunday morning, March 19, 1944, virtually without resistance. The occupation took the inhabitants of Budapest completely by surprise. It was a beautiful early spring day, and the cafés, beer gardens, and terraces of Budapest were crowded. The occupation troops entered Hungary ceremonially as if on parade, with bands playing—they were the cream of the German army, the elite, good looking and well educated. As they drove through the streets of Budapest, their disciplined, motorized convoy provided an impressive display to those on the streets and café terraces, who may not have understood the true meaning of the occupation. A young Budapest woman and her friends, leaving the pastry shop after their usual Sunday outing, were not surprised to see them; Babi explained that they were used to seeing German military around.[1] By midday, German officers were sitting in the finest restaurants and cafés enjoying their Sunday dinner. Yet there was no cheering in Budapest as there had been in Vienna. The population looked on passively as the Germans entered.

Sándor Kiss, a student leader, recalled: "I happened to go up to the castle on that . . . Sunday morning. . . . I hiked up from the streetcar stop on the Széll Kálmán square. When I reached the gate, I was surprised to see two soldiers standing on either side, their weapons at the ready—the cannons on either side of the gate. So this was it. I got cold shivers up my spine. . . . I knew that there was big trouble, and it suddenly hit me: the Germans."[2]

Hungary—Enemy Country

Very few knew of the circumstances surrounding Admiral Horthy's visit to Klessheim. Because the Germans delayed his return, sidetracking his train and keeping his company incommunicado, Prime Minister Kállay received no instructions. He had been waiting for news from the regent since March 17 and had gone to bed at midnight after taking a strong dose of sleeping medicine. "I was hardly in my bed when my direct phone with the ministry of the interior rang. Keresztes-Fischer . . . told me only to get dressed and that he would be with me very quickly because serious events were under way. A few minutes later he arrived to tell me that the frontier guards had reported that the Germans had crossed the border in trains, tanks, and armored cars, the various units evidently heading towards Budapest."[3]

Reports from the army then began to come in. "According to the general staff the following forces had been concentrated against us: on the western frontier, five German divisions; in the north and around Kassa, one German and one Slovak division; along the southeaster frontier, ten Rumanian divisions; in the Belgrade area, four to five German divisions; westward of this, important Croatian forces had been disposed against us. The only forces that we had ready for action were those in the Carpathians."[4]

Kállay called in the three army commanders who were in Budapest—István Náday, Károly Beregffy, and János Vörös. At that moment two telegrams arrived, one addressed by Foreign Minister Ghyczy to his deputy, Szentmiklóssy, which ran: "Please Let My Wife Know That I Am Well."[5] According to the agreed code, this meant military occupation to be expected, but the Germans had purposely delayed transmission of the telegram. The second telegram from Chief of Staff Szombathelyi to his deputy chief of staff, General Jósef Bajnóczy, stated that nothing should be done until the regent returned, and that German troops were to be received as friends. The German military attaché, General Greiffenberg, then arrived with a long telegram from Keitel saying that the German troops were going to occupy Budapest in accordance with an agreement reached between the Führer and the regent. The regent and the new German minister plenipotentiary would arrive the next morning. The Germans would act in a restrained manner but would relentlessly crush any resistance, and if Hungary resisted, the armies of the neighboring countries which were standing in readiness on the borders would march on Budapest.

Kállay faced the dilemma whether to act independently or wait for the regent. When he asked the army commanders if they were prepared to accept his instruction to order resistance in the absence of the regent, all three immediately replied that resistance against the Germans was absolutely impossible. Kállay pointed out that the issue was not one of relative strength but of showing that the Hungarians were prepared to defend their independence. Both Beregffy and Vörös refused, adding that they would forbid their subordinates to carry out orders to resist in the absence of the regent. Náday was willing but believed resistance would be dangerous if the army was not united. It was finally agreed that if the Germans attacked any Hungarian military unit they were to be resisted. Army commanders were to issue orders that officers and other ranks be concentrated in barracks, the gates to be bolted, ammunition to be distributed, and guns made ready for action; then to await the regent's orders.[6]

During the next three hours, Kállay ordered the burning of the secret archives of the ministries of foreign affairs, the interior, defense, and other more important offices, including his own. Kállay's son, Cristopher, sat at the telephone all night calling individuals to warn them of the imminent danger, beginning with the members of the left-wing parties, prominent Anglophiles, and Jewish representatives. The commanders of the refugee camps were warned and given orders that the internees were free to leave if they wished and were to be given a month's wages in advance.[7]

When German troops began appearing the military was in a quandary—the Germans were their allies, yet German troops were invading Hungary—a sovereign nation. Their dilemma was partially solved by the telegram from Chief of the General Staff Szombathelyi, instructing them to receive the German troops in a friendly manner. Thus armed resistance took place only in a few pockets that had not received the command.

At the Ludovika Military Academy the cadets had been looking forward to a Sunday cross-country race, then perhaps Sunday afternoon leave. Instead, in the early morning hours they received the news that the Germans had occupied Hungary. One of the cadets, Tibor Petrusz, summed up their reaction: "I have to say honestly we didn't know how we should react, what we should feel. The Germans were our military comrades, we were allies. But this, that they should occupy Hungary, offended our national pride. At the Ludovika we got the order to 'hold together' (együtt-tartást), but we didn't understand what that command meant. That we should stand against the Germans?—or perhaps that we were to carry out something with the Germans? They handed out ammunition, so that if there actually should be a skirmish with the Germans, they could bring in the Ludovika classes trained to carry out policing actions."[8]

General Jenő Major, commander of the First Armored Army Corps, awaited information on how they should conduct themselves. In his memoirs he recalled:

Only around noon a directive came from Budapest through the Ist army corps command that German troops were marching into our country. We were instructed not to resist but to protest against being disarmed. Troops were to remain in their barracks, but still no explanation. . . .

German troops moved into all our barracks—set up guards. In some places they didn't allow them to leave the barracks—in other words held them prisoner. In others had complete freedom. Our officers in many places greeted and entertained the German officers in friendship. Over white tablecloths and wine the sad truth came out—Hitler had really given the command to occupy Hungary during the time that the country's regent and chief of staff were his guests. Over wine the German officers explained that the written command began: *Ungarn Feindesland.* [Hungary—enemy country] They themselves were the most surprised when they got the command to occupy a friendly allied country and were ashamed to carry it out.[9]

The occupation did not take place smoothly everywhere. At several border locations there was firing on German troops and several airports also fired on the occupiers. At Bicske railroad workers tried to oppose them. But in German military documents of the time, there is hardly a word about Hungarian opposition. In his diary from March 19, 1944, commanding general of the occupying forces, Field Marshall Baron Maximilian von Weichs, who had been transferred from Belgrade to carry out the occupation, noted: "Morning: the occupation is going according to plan. Only one place where Hungarian troop disarmament took place. And only because my command did not arrive in time. But we took care of it. In Budapest everything quiet. Nowhere any opposition. . . . Evening: we achieved all of our goals. Parts of the army received us ceremonially. In other places some resistance—but by mistake. . . . In Budapest there is quiet."[10]

Next day, after meeting with Hitler's new minister and Reich Plenipotentiary, Edmund Veesenmayer, and discussing the Hungarian domestic situation, he wrote: "The situation is quiet. The Hungarian troops accept us loyally. The population is in general neutral."[11] Veesenmayer later said that in Hungary he felt completely safe, one year in Hungary was less dangerous than one day in Yugoslavia The regent's train approached at a snail's pace, finally arriving at the Kelenfóld station at 11 A.M. When Kállay arrived at the station he found a large German honor guard drawn up and German staff officers led by Field Marshall Weichs. When the regent's special train opened its doors, "at every door an armed SS soldier appeared instead of the usual Hungarian bodyguard."[12] Kállay reported that the regent was deathly pale, "and he looked worn out but still master of himself."[13] The regent presented Veesenmayer, the new German minister to Budapest; following him was Döme Sztójay, the Hungarian minister in Berlin, with whom Kállay avoided shaking hands.

At the crown council, ordered by the regent for one o'clock, Horthy told of his conversations at Klessheim, including Hitler's threat to invite Romanian, Croatian, and Slovak troops to join in the attack. He asked the cabinet to continue in office until new decisions were made, but both Kállay and Keresztes-Fischer argued that all such actions were legally null and void since they were taken under foreign duress. Kállay offered his resignation and would not sign the notes of the sitting or the resignation document. He recommended that either Keresztes-Fischer or an administrative government take over the cabinet, but from the beginning it was clear that a government acceptable for the Germans had to be found. In the midst of the meeting Keresztes-Fischer gave the alarming report that the Gestapo had already arrested forty-five prominent Hungarians—including some members of Parliament. Severe measures against the Jews were apparently being planned; not a single Jew was being permitted to leave Budapest. Ilona Horthy, István Horthy's widow, who had been in Szolnok for an unveiling of a statue to the regent's son, was only able to pass through the roadblocks and return to the city in the company of a German officer.[14]

Throughout the afternoon Horthy agonized over critical decisions, struggling with conflicting advice. A Jewish delegation, headed by Ferenc Chorin and Móric Kornfeld, implored him not to abdicate but to appease the Germans by appointing a new government. Otherwise the Jews would face certain extermination.[15] In the evening, Kállay, who had been shocked by the reports of brutal Gestapo actions, tried to persuade him to resign. According to Kállay, it "was the only way we could refute the story which the Germans were spreading that he had consented to the military occupation."[16] Horthy answered: "The captain cannot leave his sinking ship; he must remain on the bridge to the last. Whom will it serve if Imrédy sits here? Who will defend the army? Who will save a million Magyar lads from being dragged away to the Russian shambles? Who will defend the honorable men and women in this country who have trusted me blindly? Who will defend the Jews or our refugees if I leave my post?"[17] Kállay then suggested that he follow the example of King Christian X of Denmark—retire to Kenderes, withdraw from all state business, and adopt a completely passive attitude, but Horthy insisted he could not abandon his people in the time of extreme emergency.

István Bethlen, Horthy's trusted advisor, had made his way to the Royal Castle through an underground passage and was waiting for the regent on his return. He advised him not to appoint a prime minister or to form a government. Forced to leave March 22, since Magda Horthy feared the consequences if he was discovered, Bethlen again warned Horthy: "If there is no government the Germans have no one with which to negotiate. Public opinion at home and abroad will see that there has been an end to legitimate government."[18] He gave Horthy two lists of names—those trusted anti-Nazis and those who might be traitors or too weak to hold up against the Germans. Early on the morning of March 19, the Gestapo began to arrest all of the possible opposition leaders according to a carefully prepared list. Those arrested were the elite of traditional political, economic, and diplomatic life, leaders of the opposition parties, known anglophiles, industrial leaders and bankers. Among those arrested were thirteen members of the lower house of Parliament and nine of the upper house members. Parliament met on the March 22 as scheduled but only to be adjourned indefinitely. Only one deputy, József Közi-Horváth of the Christian Party, protested the violation of the Hungarian constitution and arrest of members of the house by a foreign power, but he was stopped by the speaker of the house and shouted down by other members.[19]

One civilian put up armed resistance, Endre Bajcsy-Zsilinsky, the vehement leader of the opposition for Hungarian independence. When the SS rang the doorbell his unsuspecting wife said he was sleeping, to call again at 11 A.M. While they continued to ring the doorbell, Bajcsy-Zsilinsky called the captain of police, asking for protection as a free Hungarian parliamentary representative, but the police had been occupied themselves. Meanwhile the Germans kept knocking on the apartment door. Then there was quiet. The SS, who had not expected any resistance, sent for help. When they returned they succeeded in shooting out the lock, pushing their way into the hallway. Bajcsy-Zsilinsky's widow recalled the dramatic encounter:

Holding his pistol ready to shoot, my husband stood in front of the bedroom door. One of the armed SS. . . . shouted, "Hinaus! Hinaus!" . . . That's when Endre took his first shot. The SS answered with a machine gun round. Again Endre shot and the Germans returned it with another round. Pieces of the glass from the glass door, the window, the mirror flew around the flat. They also hit the radio. . . . In the middle of the shooting I heard Endre say: 'A shot in the stomach . . . one in the shoulder . . .' I thought he wanted to tell me of the targets he had hit, but it turned out that he spoke of his own wounds. . . . After he had shot the last bullet from his pistol. Endre then threw the pistol through the door into the living room, at which the SS rushed into the room, tied his hands behind him and took him away bleeding from several wounds.[20]

The arrest of Károly Rassay, leader of the Budapest liberal opposition, was typical of the morning arrests. At 6 A.M. Chorin telephoned him, warning that the Germans were detraining at the Kelenföld station near Budapest. Then came the news that Bajcsy-Zsiliszky had been arrested. Soon afterward two German soldiers arrived at his home accompanied by a young Hungarian, probably an Arrow Cross member. With only his overcoat and glasses he was taken to a cell already filled with about five prisoners, where a file for him had been prepared with the number 18, a number he had noticed on his villa some weeks before.[21]

Some prominent individuals managed to escape. Kállay and his family escaped to the castle and the Turkish minister, Sevket Fuat Kececi, offered Kállay refuge, while his family remained in the castle.[22] Chorin and István Bethlen fled to the countryside. Bethlen, disguised as a colonel of the Hussars, found refuge in Transylvania at the headquarters of General Veress. Social Democrat leaders, Szakasits and Mme Kéthly, and Smallholders Tildy and Varga had been at political meetings outside of Budapest and were warned not to return. Peyer gave himself up when the Germans threatened his family but Szakasits managed to remain free. The German police took over the Royal Hotel where they kept prisoners in the basement. By April 28, 8,240 individuals were being held. Those arrested included the Allied prisoners of war: 812 French, 5,450 Polish, 39 English, 11 American, 16 Belgian, 12 Dutch, 180 Soviet, as well as members of the Royal Italian Legation.[23]

On Sunday, Budapest Radio made no announcement and many people were not aware that the occupation had taken place. That evening the radio began to broadcast news solely of German origin in contrast to the usual practice of news based on the British radio. The head of the *Magyar Távirati Iroda és Rádió* [Hungarian telegraphic news agency and radio], Antal Náray, bewailed the fact that on Monday, April 20, Ferenc Schaub, who had been empowered to control the radio, dictated the news, "using a tone against the Jews which was unworthy of the Radio's serious and objective tone before March 19."[24]

For three days the Hungarian press made no mention of the German occupation. Papers published news of the war and the home news as if nothing had happened, although only news from German sources appeared. The only indication of the German occupation was the announcement in all morning papers on March 20 that the minister for internal affairs had prohibited all theater and cinema performances as well as dancing and public meetings. Morning papers on the March 21 carried the item that the Kossuth anniversary celebrations, to have been held the morning of March 20, had not taken place because of the ban on public meetings. At the time that Kállay was scheduled to deliver his long awaited speech to the Hungarian population the radio played a philology lecture.

In London, émigrés who followed events in Hungary closely got their first indication of the occupation by the change in tone of the radio broadcasts. Actual news of the occupation arrived on Monday afternoon in a message from the Bucharest correspondent of the *Agence Anatolique* and broadcast by Ankara radio. The same day news was received from all neutral capitals that telephone and telegraph communications with Hungary had been cut. Since Germany dominated all the surrounding countries it was impossible to get news of the occupation. Hungary was now completely sealed off from the outside world.[25]

Formation of the Sztójay Government

Horthy soon discovered how difficult it was to navigate without the aid of his advisors and fellow officers. He had to rely increasingly on his dwindling entourage at the castle and close family members—his wife, Magda, his daughter-in-law, Ilona, and his son, Nicky. Veesenmayer, although relatively moderate and pragmatic, was a formidable opponent. He had been given three days by Hitler for the formation of the new government, but if the negotiations were not successful a total occupation would be put into force. Thus Veesenmayer put all his efforts into persuading Horthy to cooperate, believing that his subordinates would then obey orders. The prevailing atmosphere was tense, the Gestapo was rounding up victims and all public events were canceled. Negotiations moved slowly and threatened to break down.

Horthy rejected out of hand the idea of naming Imrédy prime minister; he favored a caretaker government, but Veesenmayer demanded Horthy appoint a government from the radical right-wing parties, excluding the Arrow Cross. An ultimatum arrived that if the new government was not formed by 6 P.M., the Germans under Field Marshall von Weichs would occupy the castle and take over complete power.[26] Weichs, who had received instructions to prepare to occupy the Palace and disarm the army, expressed his reservations about such a base policy "A step like this on our part would immediately line up against us the various circles of the Hungarian opposition . . . The government just established would resign, along with the regent. A general Hungarian uprising would take place. Instead of gaining new troops for the eastern front with the Hungarians, we would have to withdraw troops from there in order to keep order."[27] The Red Army had advanced 265 kilometers between March and April on the southern front and inflicted irreparable damage on Army Groups A, South, and Center.[28] Weichs concluded that the radical measure would achieve exactly the opposite of the object of the occupation.

Horthy finally prevailed upon Sztójay, a professional soldier and longtime Hungarian minister in Berlin, to take the position of prime minister. Although Horthy did not like Sztójay, he believed that as a professional soldier he would be honorable and loyal. He had participated in the regent's Crown Council meeting, but he was a sick man, a diabetic, and felt himself unfit mentally and physically.[29] Horthy finally convinced him, promising that if they succeeded in winning the Germans' trust, they would erect a statue to him in one of the most beautiful places in Budapest.

On March 22 at 3:45 A.M., an agreement was reached, with a final slate including rightist ministers from the government party and several followers of Imrédy. It was a compromise solution but Reményi-Schneller, Szász, and Jurcsek were specialists in their respective fields, and Horthy had succeeded in keeping General Csatay as minister of defense.[30] Since one half of the ministers had already held office and a number were members of the traditional government party, the new government had credibility. But of most importance was that Horthy had appointed it as a legal government, which satisfied the German desire to have a constitutional government still under the regent. On March 23 at 6 P.M., shortly before the ultimatum would have expired, the Sztójay ministry took the oath in the auditorium of the Royal Castle.

The change of government was announced as if nothing untoward had happened; the population learned about it only after the new government had been sworn in. The official notice read: "In order to assist Hungary in the common war . . . against the common enemy, and in particular in effectively combating Bolshevism . . . German troops have arrived in Hungary as the result of a mutual agreement. . . . The two allied Governments have agreed that the measures which have been taken will contribute towards Hungary's throwing into the scale every resource calculated to help on the final victory of the common cause, in the spirit of the old friendship and comradeship in arms between the Hungarian and German peoples."[31]

While much of the population greeted the German presence passively, there were many who welcomed the Germans as friends and allies against the much-feared Russians, whom the all-pervasive propaganda depicted as brutes and rapists. Judit Stúr, the daughter of an upper–middle-class family in Köszeg, made friends with a German soldier with her family's blessing. Her father, a mid-level government official, was right-wing and anti-Semitic, believing the Jews were too intelligent and had too much power for their numbers. He would not allow the family to shop in Jewish stores, but—rather typically of the attitude of many so-called anti-Semites—her mother went to a Jewish hairdresser because she was good, while Judit's best friend in school was a Jewish girl.[32]

Horthy removed himself from day-to-day affairs, living in relative isolation, although his name was given to all measures taken by the new government. His way of protesting was to remain secluded in the castle, asserting that he was a prisoner of the Germans. Through his self-imposed isolation he wished to disassociate himself as much as possible from decisions by the Sztójay government, but this also served German interests. Ribbentrop had instructed that the Hungarian political role be reduced to the barest minimum.[33]

With his earlier contacts broken, surrounded by a foreign army, it appeared that the regent had decided he could do nothing more for the time being than try to collect some trustworthy people around him, settle down and bide his time. The government leaders and heads of the political parties were in prison or concentration camps and most of the officers with whom he had worked up to then were either under arrest or scattered, with the exception of his minister of defense, Csatay. At the same time the officers who had been sentenced for their roles in the Újvidék massacre and had escaped to Germany returned and were reinstated and promoted. His suspicion of General János Vörös, whom he had been forced to appoint as chief of the general staff, replacing Szombathelyi, proved correct since Vörös began to press to reactivate pro-German officers who had been retired.[34]

Horthy's decision to remain as regent has been one of the most intensely debated questions among Hungarians ever since. Would Hungary have been better off if Horthy had resigned—or if he had removed himself from all government affairs as had the king of Denmark? The country would have received more brutal treatment from the Germans but perhaps have gained more at the peace settlement. In an audience with Szálasi, whom he received reluctantly, Horthy told him that he would have nothing to do with the government—his sole concern was to keep the army in his own hands. In Horthy's view, Hungary needed to have a powerful army at the end of the war in order to avoid a similar fate that had befallen Hungary after World War I. He later said that Hitler's promise at Klessheim that he would withdraw German troops as soon as a Hungarian government was formed that enjoyed his confidence was the most important factor in his decision to maintain a semblance of legal continuity and to remain as regent. Unfortunately, because he retained his position as regent, the Allied powers regarded Hungary as a Nazi vassal state and not as an occupied country.[35]

In the days after March 19, the German occupiers and the Gestapo basically transformed the domestic situation, replacing officials loyal to Horthy with those loyal to the Germans. Veesenmayer, who had visited Hungary in the spring and fall of 1943 as a private person, had decided then that it was necessary to reorganize the Hungarian government. His impression was that most of the political leaders were ready to collaborate and cooperate with the Germans; it was only necessary to replace the highest leadership, the so-called "castle clique" which he proceeded to do.[36]

In one of his frequent telegrams to Ribbentrop, Veesenmayer informed him on April 28 that he had succeeded in exchanging nineteen of the Lord Lieutenants who ruled the government of the counties. In all out of forty-one Lord Lieutenants twenty-nine were removed. He replaced many high government and administrative officials, including the mayor of Budapest and two-thirds of the mayors of other cities, men who would probably have been loyal to Horthy.[37] The opposition parties were banned, including the Social Democrats, as well as their newspapers, trade unions, and worker associations. The press and radio were tightly controlled, and it was forbidden to listen to foreign newscasts.

Until this point German-Hungarian relations could have been referred to as "equal" but now they clearly became hierarchical. Though the Hungarian army kept its formal independence, and restrictions imposed in March were lifted, subordination of its operations became final. Even Hungarian troops not destined for operational tasks were now used in the front lines. The Germans replaced military leaders whom they disliked and some were even arrested. István Náday and Ferenc Szombathelyi were relieved of their duties, while Major General István Újszászy, Staff Colonel Gyula Kádár and Staff Major Károly Kern were arrested by the Gestapo.[38]

Soon after the German occupation the full horrors of war descended on the Hungarian population. There had been no Allied bombing raids against Hungarian targets in the time of the Kállay government but now they became a regular event. Allied bombing began April 2 with a daylight attack by American aircraft and on April 3 a nighttime attack by the British. Both attacks involved several hundred airplanes, inflicting extensive damage, and from then on blanket bombing hit the factories on Csepel, the airplane factory, the oil fields and railroad centers, but also population centers. For the first time the population had to black out windows, cease using car headlights, make use of the air raid shelters and shelters in the cellars of large apartment blocks. The start of the bombing had a powerful effect on public opinion—the sirens and radio alerts heightened the atmosphere of fear and destroyed the German legend of invincibility. Rather than rallying the population in support of the fighting, as it had in Great Britain, the bombing increased the desire to get out of the war.[39]

The new Hungarian government proceeded to carry out the measures urged on them by the Germans. Despite the fact that the occupying force was small—many troops had been withdrawn soon after the occupation—members of the military and government agreed to German demands even when aware that they could not be fulfilled. Mobilization was speeded up. The Germans began the reorganization of the Hungarian economy with the aim of subordinating war and weapons production and the delivery of raw materials completely to their interests. And the solution to the Jewish question in Hungary—so long demanded by the Germans—was immediately begun under the supervision of Adolf Eichmann, the *Schutzstaffe* [SS] commander in charge of deportations.

Mobilization of the Hungarian Troops

Hungary had never fully mobilized, intending to keep the best forces intact for the fighting which they expected to come after the war, as had happened after World War I, but now mobilization was intensified. The Germans, short of men ever since Stalingrad and especially after the battle of the Kursk salient in the summer of 1943, were desperate for men by the spring of 1944. At the military conference on March 29 it was determined that all forces in Hungary that were already on a war footing were to be sent immediately to the Carpathian front, while those forces at peace or only at cadre strength were to be brought up to war strength and sent to the front as soon as possible. Reserves of military age were to be called up and trained.

With the advance of the Soviet troops the Germans demanded more Hungarian troops and more and more reserves were called up. The First

Hungarian Army, which had been mobilized for the first time in January 1944, grew to more than 300,000 men. The First Cavalry division, the elite unit of the army, was mobilized against Horthy's opposition and sent to the front in June, together with four divisions.[40] The Germans were also pressuring the Hungarian authorities to recruit students from the universities and schools of higher education, young men who in most cases had not felt the effects of the war up to this time. Students had seldom been required to serve during the war years, and many students enrolled in order to escape the draft, especially in departments of law and economics in which one was not required to attend classes but only examinations.[41]

Under German pressure military circles increased their efforts to get rid of or greatly limit the student exemption from the draft. The decree of May 11 from the Ministry of Defense, eliminating the student exemption for all except medical, engineering, and veterinary students, aroused general protest from the university departments, which tried by any means, including the use of their personal connections, to protect their students from the draft. Representatives met with the Ministry of Defense asking that the law be softened and offering to provide shortened training to allow the students to receive their diplomas within the time stipulated by the order. Lajos Csatay, minister of defense, accepted the university's requests and liberalized the order; exemption would be extended to those students who took part in shortened courses of study and would be finished by October 1, 1945, or for medical students by November 1, or for those who had one more year, by October 1, 1946.

Interestingly, the plan to mobilize many of the university students in July 1944 was never carried out. No university students were called up in the Horthy army, or if they were, they could ask for an exemption.[42] Those in authority tried to save the university youth as insurance for the country's future intellectual life. Among them was Miklós Mester, state secretary in the Ministry of Religion and Education, who was instrumental in preventing the mobilization of the students. Greatly upset when members of the military operations department explained that they planned a decree to require all university students to do military service, he went to Gyula Ambrózy, the head of the cabinet office, who immediately took his side.

Mester later explained that they had recommended that the students not be placed under the Ministry of Defense, but if the Ministry was going to designate work groups to fortify the Carpathians and Székely-föld, the students could be sent there for summer work. He emphasized that in formulating the decree to order students to perform required labor service, they had given it a strict tone, in order to cover our evasion from the German group.[43] Of course, the students knew nothing of these arguments to determine their fate. They only knew that they were being ordered to serve in labor camps during the summer, an experience that radicalized a number of them, and some would later join the resistance.

Reorganization of the Hungarian Economy

A major goal of the occupation was to gain total exploitation of Hungary's economic resources.

German economic experts arrived along with the occupation troops to prepare for the economic changeover, intending to exploit every economic aspect of the country—to take over war and weapon production, and send unlimited quantities of raw materials and food products to Germany. The Germans, their own sources of materials depleted, had placed great hopes on the still unexploited capacity of Hungarian industry and its material resources, especially bauxite, manganese, mineral oil, and antimony production.[44] Minister of Foreign Affairs Clodius had given special instructions for the "quick and relentless exploitation of the economic resources of the country . . . no Hungarian contribution of any significance must be neglected simply because of a lack of means of payment."[45]

Hungary was also to bear the burden of financing the German occupation. Veesenmayer and the pro-German minister of finance, Reményi-Schneller, reached an agreement on June 2, 1944, by which the Hungarian government would pay 200 million pengő monthly for the occupation troops, this in addition to the huge debt already piled up by the Germans through the method of exchange through the clearing system. Between 1942 and 1944, German debts more than doubled to over one million reichsmarks. That the Hungarian economy did not collapse can be explained by the extensive confiscation of Jewish wealth.[46]

Prime Minister Sztójay agreed with Veesenmayer on the complete reorganization of the Hungarian economy. The Hungarian army would be supplied with weapons by the Germans, and the freed-up capacity of war production would be used for commonly planned production—in other words for German war aims, all this to be carried out within the shortest period. From now on the Hungarian army would be armed with German equipment and ammunition in order that the remaining Hungarian capacity could be used more economically. The Sztójay government and the military leadership had little choice but to agree to all the German conditions, even though they must have known that it would be impossible for the Germans to carry out the promised deliveries. The Hungarian military representatives knew from past experience that the Germans never carried through on their promises of equipment and supplies. In the ever more difficult battlefield and homeland situation it appeared impossible that the Germans could make the deliveries which earlier, in more favorable situations, they had not been willing or capable of delivering.[47]

Despite the efforts of the German commissioners they soon faced complete failure. Conditions in war production were already deteriorating. Worker discipline had been on the decline before the occupation, since workers had problems with living conditions, many had been called up for military service, and many had been lost on the battlefield. The military had increasingly tightened control over factories involved in war production, tying the workers to the factories, infringing on their rights, and imposing increasingly harsh measures, with punishments including imprisonment. One person recalled that his father, a carpenter, was one of those workers sentenced to a labor company. Since his father was not political and would not have made any political statement, it was likely that he had complained about something—for example, the pay.[48]

Under the occupation, new military mobilization and the deportation of the Jewish population reduced the numbers of available workers, especially Hungary's small number of skilled workers. The systematic bombing that began in April led to widespread damage in communications, transportation and industrial production. The result of the bombing damage, the increasing difficulty of providing the machines and materials necessary, as well as the increasing lack of man power and skilled workers, made the conversion of production more difficult and industrial output rapidly declined. The Germans were hoping to replace some of their tanks lost at the terrible battle of the Kursk salient in July 1943, but under these circumstances, production of armored vehicles stopped completely. More and more the German and Hungarian troops were limited to the repair of broken-down motor vehicles.

The German presence in the factories increased resistance against them. Although there was no open opposition they found themselves faced with an insurmountable passive resistance—obtuseness, slowness and malingering, problems with organization of work and provision of materials, breakdowns of machinery, a flood of complaints and increasing restlessness from the workers. In the end Germany had neither the strength nor the time to turn Hungarian industrial capacity over to its service; thus Hungarian industry contributed a minimum to the German war effort.[49]

Measures Against the Jewish Population

Although Jews were not the reason for the German occupation, they became a primary concern once the decision to launch Operation Margarethe had been made. The preparations for the occupation included plans for the deportation and eradication of the Hungarian Jews. Adolf Eichmann. arrived shortly after the occupying troops at the head of the Eichmann Kommando, consisting of not more than 200 to 300 people. He had received the command from Himmler, the leader of the SS, to "sweep out the Jews from the country in the direction from east to west, and deport every Jew to Auschwitz as quickly as possible. To start in the eastern counties which the Russians are approaching, and to take care that no event similar to the Warsaw ghetto uprising takes place."[50]

The Germans' task was facilitated by the fact that they had destroyed the traditional Hungarian political leadership; the anti-German groups of the Hungarian economic, diplomatic, and military elite had been removed from positions of influence. The conservative-liberals, leftist liberals, and social democrats who had protested against the Jewish laws had either been taken into German prison or concentration camps or had gone into hiding. Veesenmayer's replacement of the Lord Lieutenants and other county officials lessened the chance of any possible protest against the deportations from the provinces. Jewish leaders hoped that with the worsening military situation and scarcity of transportation, the Germans would not be able to remove the 825,000 Jews in the few remaining months of the war, but they did not reckon on the breakneck speed with which the deportations were carried out.

Relying on the model developed through deportation of the Jews elsewhere in Europe, the Germans accomplished their goal in an amazingly short time with the full cooperation of the Hungarian authorities. The fact that Horthy remained in office, giving the new government the appearance of legitimacy, increased the assurance that commands would be followed. The SS followed the pattern used in other countries; first isolation laws and the confiscation of Jewish wealth, then the gathering of Jews into ghettos, afterward deportation, then annihilation. Veesenmayer wrote to Berlin that the Hungarian government took the job seriously— and carried it out in a praiseworthy fashion. In the space of a few weeks after the occupation, Jews were confined to ghettos, internment camps and "yellow-star houses." Then, in only fifty-six days starting with May 16, all 437,402 people from the countryside were deported to Auschwitz-Birkenau, except for some 15,000 who were taken to Strasshof, Austria.[51]

ESTABLISHMENT OF THE JEWISH COUNCIL

On the day following the occupation the Gestapo demanded the establishment of a so-called Jewish Council with the goal of providing the means by which they would round up the Jews. The majority of the Budapest Jewish community lived on the Pest side of Budapest.[52] On the morning of May 20, leading members of the Jewish community were commanded to report to the main office of the Pest Israelite congregation. Hastily gathering the evening of May 19, the leaders, who were all good law-abiding citizens, called the Hungarian government's Ministry of Culture to ask what their attitude to the Germans should be. After repeated calls and evasive answers they were told the next morning only that they should follow all of the Germans' orders.

At the Pest Israelite headquarters at 12 Sik Street, they were greeted by SS officers, the Gestapo's infamous Jewish Division, accompanied by machine-gun carrying soldiers. The officers of the Eichmann Kommando issued the order to establish the Central Council of Hungarian Jews. The leaders of the congregation were to prepare reports on the structure, organizations, property, and associations of the Jewish religious community.[53] The SS informed them that the Gestapo alone was to be responsible for Jewish affairs; anyone who did not follow their orders would be executed. Reassuringly they added that if the Jewish population complied with their orders they would come to no harm. Although there would be certain restrictions, individuals and property would be safe and there would be no deportations. They emphasized that Jewish religious ceremonies should continue as usual. The council was to represent the Jewish community and receive and carry out all orders given them by the SS. As president they chose the seventy-year-old Samu Stern, a culturally assimilated Hungarian and long-time president of the Pest Israelite Religious Community, who had made a brilliant career in economic life.[54] Eichmann met with the Jewish representatives on March 31 and repeated the assurances that Jews as such were not going to be harmed.[55]

It was vitally important for the Germans that the Jewish communities throughout the country accept the Central Jewish Council as legitimate leader of the Jewish community, thus ensuring compliance with Nazi demands. On March 24 the chairmen of Jewish congregation districts throughout the country were invited to Budapest to attend a meeting to organize a national committee. The leaders, who had traveled on permits issued by the German authorities, resolved to establish a unified national organization under the leadership of the Jewish Council and adopted a foundation document in the first days of April. The founding of a national organization gave the impression of a longer-term operation; yet there is no document to prove that any council other than the Jewish Council actually functioned. Existing data mentions only the above-noted meeting of March 28. Even the Central Council did not hold regular sessions. Many of the meetings were held in the office of the chairman and often in the presence of others than the chief officials.[56]

On April 6, the Jewish Council sent a circular letter to the provincial religious leaders in Hungary informing them of the establishment and powers of the council, and that by order of higher authorities Hungarian Jews were to be organized all over the country under the direction of the Jewish Council. The circular called on the provincial religious communities to organize and lead local Jewish councils. From documents recovered it appears that in some places local organizations were set up by the Jewish Council itself. In others, leaders representing the interests of the Jewish population were appointed by local administrative authorities, while in some places local Jewish councils were never organized.[57]

On the same day as the circular was issued the readers of the *Magyar Zsidók Lapja* were informed that the Jewish Council had been established. The paper, heavily censored by the Germans, continued to call on the Jewish population to remain calm, be disciplined, and execute orders unconditionally. In the early weeks the Hungarian authorities effectively ignored the existence of the Jewish Council, which remained entirely under German command. It was not until April 19 that Minister of the Interior Jaross submitted a proposal that would establish a self-governing organization of Hungarian Jews—the already existing council—to be supervised by the Ministry of the Interior.[58]

PROCLAMATION OF ANTI-JEWISH DECREES

The first decrees to isolate the Jewish population were published at the end of March. Jews were instructed to wear the six-cornered star which was to be made to specific directions: ten by ten centimeters in size, of silk or velvet, in canary yellow, a color that was easy to see. The Jews were removed from their jobs and workshops, and their businesses were to be turned over to Christians. Jews were forbidden to travel, except on urgent business when they might get a special permit on payment of a fee. They were not allowed to use cars, taxis, trains, ships, or other vehicles except trams or omnibuses in towns. Jews also were not to use public baths, restaurants, or places of amusement. Radios, telephones, and cars, if they had them, were confiscated.[59] Támas Gábor had just received a bicycle for his sixteenth birthday, and now he had to give it up. Up to this time, anti-Semitism had not affected him, but now students in his Lutheran secondary school began to taunt him.[60]

Jewish assets, estimated to make up 20 to 25 percent of the nation's wealth, were impounded. Ironically, this measure affecting the Jews was to be used by the communists a few years later to nationalize the wealth of all Hungarians. One result was that the Weiss-Manfréd Works, essential to the nation's war production, was sold to the Germans. Competition had begun among the German political groups over the plundering of the country, with the Weiss-Manfréd complex a sought-after prize. The Hungarian government had agreed to a proposal that some factories be turned over to a Göring Works subsidiary, but through a startling move the SS was able to take over the works. The SS representative Kurt Becher carried out secret negotiations with Ferenc Chorin, the head of the Weiss-Manfréd family, after securing his release from an internment camp and threatening him, as well as his two brothers-in-law, Baron Móric Kornfeld and Baron Jenő Weiss, with a return to the camps if he did not sign. He succeeded in getting Chorin to sign an agreement essentially giving over the whole fortune into the hands of Himmler's SS in exchange for allowing the extended family to escape to Portugal with much of their portable wealth.[61]

Chorin, a member of Horthy's close circle, felt obliged to write a letter to the regent explaining the decision, although there was little to prevent German agents from taking over the Weiss-Manfréd complex without consulting the owners. Chorin commented that the regent had surely learned that he had been arrested, during which time, "unfortunately and surely under pressure, under the serene highness's aegis the Jewish question was regulated, and a whole series of illegal decrees were put through. These decrees blocked, but actually expropriated Jewish wealth and created a terrible precedent, the consequences of which we can already foretell."[62] Chorin took pains to emphasize that the family had not betrayed the country's interests, but—as he believed—he had ensured that the factory would remain in Hungarian hands. He concluded: "In saying farewell to your serene highness . . . I especially thank you for the kind disposition which accompanied my activities in service to Hungarian industry throughout twenty years. And to me personally for which I am and will always be sincerely thankful."[63] The loss of the Weiss-Manfréd Works was such a dramatic blow to the independence of the country that even the rightist Imrédy protested against it. The SS action alarmed Hungarian leading circles, and led Horthy a few days after the agreement was signed on May 22, 1944, to agree to name Imrédy minister of economics, although he had rejected the idea up to then. The hope was that because of his German connections Imrédy would be better able to protect Hungarian capital.

ESTABLISHMENT OF GHETTOS

The ghettoization of the Jews outside of Budapest began in mid-April in the larger towns and cities according to an order of the Hungarian Ministry of Interior. In the provinces, the Jewish population was to be collected in designated camps; in the cities and larger towns in designated Jewish houses or ghettos. According to these regulations, ghettos were to be established in all towns and cities with populations of more than 10,000. However decisions about which streets were to be used were left to local officials. In practice, county officials decided which towns and cities would have ghettos and to which of these ghettos smaller towns and villages would send their Jews. In Vas county, for example, it was in early May that the deputy prefect decided that seven ghettos were to be established in the county, one of them in the town of Körmend. The Jews from the town and surrounding villages were ordered to move into the planned ghetto area by May 12, and the chief administrative officer ordered the local Jewish council to erect a fence around the ghetto by May 20.[64]

In accord with Himmler's instructions, Eichmann divided Hungary into six geographical zones, starting in the east. The areas in northeastern Hungary were considered particularly critical; military commanders of the operational zones insisted that the Jews constituted an element of military insecurity and must be cleared out of those areas completely. The process took place by gendarme districts, beginning April 16 in Ruthenia and northeast Hungary, followed by northern Transylvania. Afterward, the process was to continue from east to west—Miskolc, Debrecen, Szeged, Pécs, Szombathely, Székesfehérvár, and finally Budapest. It appears that local Jews in the Bácska had already been rounded up and put in camps.[65]

The rounding up of Jews in northeastern Hungary was accompanied by extreme brutality. Usually they would be collected from the village by early dawn, taken to the local synagogue, and a few days later moved to a nearby city, to lumber yards, brick factories, tobacco sheds, or empty factory yards, often under the open sky with inhuman conditions. The Jews were often beaten, humiliated, and robbed of their valuables. The possessions left at home were either distributed by the army or simply carted off by the local population. In a letter smuggled out from a brick-yard at Kassa/Kosice, one Jew wrote: "We lie in the dust, have neither straw mattresses nor covers, and will freeze to death. . . . We are so ne-glected, that we do not look human any more."[66]

The brutality accompanying the collections and inhumanity of the conditions under which they were confined—when they first became known—brought forth protests from the Jewish Council and from official leaders and prominent individuals among all the Christian churches. The two officers placed in charge of the campaign, State Secretary László Endre in the Ministry of the Interior with special responsibility for Jewish affairs, and State Secretary László Baky, reported to Horthy that for rea-sons of national security the Jews were to be removed from possible com-bat zones since they were all procommunist. The two had been former officers under Horthy at Szeged and Horthy tended to trust them.[67]

In the meantime in early April, in a separate move, the German gov-ernment requested a Jewish labor contingent of 100,000 men from the Hungarian government. Since Horthy had agreed to supply the Reich with Jewish labor at his meeting with Hitler at Klessheim, the Hungarian authorities saw no problem in granting the request. Sztójay promised 50,000 Jews by the end of April and another 50,000 in May. Hungarian military authorities informed Veesenmayer that 5,000 men could be made available immediately and another 5,000 every three to four days until the quota was fulfilled; on April 14 he reported to his superiors that both the government and the regent had approved dispatch of more than 100,000 Jews to carry out forced labor in the *Reich*. According to Macart-ney the agreement to send the Jewish laborers, as well as the frightful conditions in the camps where Jews had been collected, provided Eich-mann with the excuse to offer to transport the entire Jewish population to Auschwitz and other camps.[68]

Already on April 20, Baky received a report that the conditions in the large camps in northeastern Hungary were intolerable. The inmates could not be fed or housed and there was a danger of epidemics. Eichmann suggested that he would see that these Jews were transported to Ausch-witz and other camps, although he insisted on receiving a request from the Hungarian government, a request that was submitted by Baky. On April 25, Veesenmayer cabled Berlin and Eichmann that beginning in mid-May it would be possible to transport 3,000 Jews daily from north-eastern Hungary, and if transport allowed, from other ghettos as well to the final destination, Auschwitz.[69]

The process began on May 15, when the original inmates of the Kassa camp were entrained, and ended on July 9. Veesenmayer's notes, which appear to be the most accurate, report that from May 14 to June 7, 289,357 Jews were deported from Ruthenia and northern Transylvania. The next stop was in northern Hungary, where from June 14–16, another 50,805 were taken. From June 25–28, 41,400 were taken from southeast Hungary. Veesenmayer's notes sent from the western parts of Hungary were abbreviated. The total number of deported was 437,402. Since the number of trains the Germans could provide was limited, the usual compliment per wagon, forty soldiers per wagon, was increased to seventy persons. Thus the operation could be completed in sixty days. The deportations themselves were carried out with sickening brutality—during summer heat, gross overcrowding, hardly any food or water, doors padlocked, and windows boarded.[70]

In his testimony at the Nuremberg Trials, Veesenmayer said that if the Hungarians had refused to meet German demands the deportations would not have taken place, since the Germans did not have a sufficient force available, but his statement was only partially true. Although some were enthusiastic in carrying out the deportations, like Baky and Endre, Hungary was under German occupation; the German shadow government was everywhere and supervised the measures against the Jews. Yet there seems no doubt that Horthy consented to the deportation of at least the Jews from the northeast and probably of all Jews outside Budapest, and that the majority of the population supported measures to remove the Jews. Even the churches hardly moved against the decrees.[71]

WHY DID JEWS NOT TRY TO RESIST?
The question has often been asked, why did the Jewish population not resist? Why were there relatively few attempts to escape? Jewish leaders in Hungary must have known that Jews had been or were being deported from countries occupied by Germany. Yet they were prepared to cooperate with the Germans. In fact the rounding up of Jews for deportation was carried out not by the German SS or even by the Hungarian gendarmerie but in much of the country by the local administration, with the cooperation of Jewish representatives who executed the orders they received.[72]

In recriminations against the Jewish Council after the war, the question was often asked why the members had accepted membership in the council—the charge being that they had done so to protect themselves, their own families and relatives, and to gain extra privileges. Samu Stern explained that with his connections it would have been quite possible for him to escape to the United States or elsewhere. However, he "considered that to be cowardly, unmanly, irresponsible conduct, a selfish flight and desertion." He believed that perhaps with his long experience of leadership he would be able to help. He also hoped that he might be able to win over the regent, whom he had known for twenty years, in the interest of saving the Jews. He added that the other assigned members of the council, who had also served the Jewish community for a long time, must have felt the same way.[73]

The Jewish leaders have been criticized for not informing the Jewish population earlier about what was transpiring in the neighboring countries and for advising them to keep calm after the occupation. Randolph L. Braham claims that by not informing the Jewish masses before the German occupation Jewish leaders gave them a false sense of security. By telling the masses to remain calm after the occupation and to obey and execute orders, Braham holds the Jewish leadership, along with the Nazis and their Hungarian accomplices, responsible for the murder of over half a million Hungarian Jews. Yet, Judit Molnár points out that before the occupation there was plenty of information available to the population from various sources, including Jewish forced laborers home on leave; the numerous Jewish refugees from Austria, Poland, and Slovakia; as well as radio broadcasts from neutral and antifascist countries. After the occupation it was a question of how the council could have informed the Jewish population. The *Magyar Zsidók Lapja* was under tight military censorship, as were all forms of publication.[74]

Yehuda Bauer comments that those who addressed the question of whether the Jews knew what was in store from them sometimes seem to have "mistaken information for knowledge or understanding." Even when members of Zionist youth movements tried to warn local Jewish councils that they were going to be "deported to their deaths" they were not listened to. "Until the very last, Hungarian Jews chose to believe they were being transported to labor camps within Hungary."[75]

Those who heard of the horrors from the radio or from refugees simply could not—or refused to—believe the inconceivable. One survivor who had been deported from the city of Pécs wrote decades later, "I was unable to comprehend reality, it seemed too unreal to me." Later he added. "What curse was it that inflicted complete blindness upon us?"[76] During the 1961 Eichmann trial in Jerusalem one survivor commented: "If I had known what Auschwitz was, then no power on Earth would have forced me onto that train. But there was no power on Earth that would have made me believe that such a place as Auschwitz existed."[77]

As late as spring 1944, when they were locked up in ghettos and collecting camps, Jews still did not believe the young Zionists who traveled illegally to provinces trying to encourage people to escape. In many cases the identification papers they had smuggled into a particular ghetto were not used. Those who did not believe the warnings—a majority of the Jews—could not see the logic of breaking up a family in the hour of need. Some warned the youth not to spread panic and create confusion at a time when the reputable leadership of the entire Jewish community was announcing in the official press that no harm would come to anyone if they would only maintain law and order. They could not imagine that the Jewish press was being censored, with the contents at times dictated by Gestapo.[78]

In his history of the Jewish population of Csorna, a town in western Hungary, Endre Berecz comments on the lack of attempts at rescue among the Hungarian Jewish population. People simply could not imagine that in Hungary the things they had heard of could happen. As an exception he mentions one successful rescue, when the Weiner couple managed to escape from the Csorna ghetto with the help of Kálmán Dreisziger, the man whose near-miraculous escape at the time of the disaster at the Don is mentioned in Chapter 6. Records indicate that it was common practice for local non-Jewish inhabitants to request Jewish labor from the ghettos. In the town of Körmend, groups of Jewish men, women, and children were mobilized from the ghetto into makeshift labor units largely to satisfy local requests for labor. Children were taken out to carry out minor tasks such as rag collection, and women were often called on to do gardening or farm work.[79]

In Csorna as well the inhabitants were sometimes called on to perform labor for non-Jews. The Dreiszigers declared that they needed the help of Sandor and Kati Weiner for an evening. Kati Weiner was working in the fields for someone else, and Kálmán fetched her by bicycle, a trip of six kilometers, and brought her back to Csorna. There a truck came for the couple to take them to Budapest under cover of darkness. Afterward Dreisziger was severely criticized by the Jewish leaders for helping the Weiners escape.[80]

It was primarily women and children who were called on for local labor, since Jewish men between the ages of eighteen and forty-eight were being mobilized for service in labor companies. In a decree issued at the end of April 1944, Jewish labor battalion members on active service were explicitly exempted from the ghetto, illustrating a degree of conflict between the Hungarian army and the German security police. The army had ordered mass conscription despite the claim by the security police that according to the Ministry of Defense agreement Jews could not be called up in areas where the Jewish population was being rounded up. Those who were with the army's labor battalions escaped deportation to Auschwitz and thus had a greater chance of survival.[81]

The Jewish Council agonized over whether to refuse to carry out the Germans' command to notify those who were to report to detention barracks. They faced a moral dilemma, with no acceptable alternative. They knew they would be condemned for helping with the internment but decided that it was better that the people receive some notification, giving them the opportunity to flee, hide, or procure a medical excuse. At least they would have time to prepare belongings to take with them. "Thus we felt we had to accept, even if we would be criticized. The text we sent out stated that we sent the notice on the order of higher command, and that they should take their things with them. In this way everyone would know what it was about. They could choose whether to hide or report. There were many who got a doctor's certificate which they sent instead of reporting themselves, or went to a hospital—perhaps for a long-considered operation—and thus saved themselves. Or simply hid with false papers. But there were many more, sadly, who reported."[82]

REACTION OF THE CHRISTIAN CHURCHES

The German occupation had taken the leaders of the Christian churches as much by surprise as it had the ordinary citizen, and they were just as much at a loss as to what course of action to follow. At first the leaders of the Protestant churches decided on a policy of passive resistance, to avoid all contact with the puppet government and the occupiers, but this proved completely unrealistic because of the tremendous number of requests for assistance which forced them to intervene with the government and administration.[83]

The Jewish Council appealed to church leaders but they were slow to respond. In the first weeks the main efforts of the leaders—Prince Primate Cardinal Jusztinian Serédi for the Catholic Church, Bishop Ravasz, head of the Calvinist Synod and Convent, and Béla Kapi of the Lutherans—were to have their own converts exempted from the new regulations, for example, wearing the Star of David, and they met with some success. On April 3 Bishop Ravasz submitted his first protest in writing to the Sztójay administration, requesting that converts be spared from wearing the yellow star, and on April 6 the Lutheran and Calvinist Convent joined in the request.

On April 5 Prime Minister Sztójay informed Cardinal Serédi that priests, nuns, and lay church official converts would be exempted from the anti-Jewish measures. Converted Protestant civil functionaries, presbyters (elders in the Presbyterian church) and their families were also exempted. But when the Prince Primate visited Sztójay on April 13 and 23, handing over a written memorandum stating the position of the Church against government violation of human rights and protesting the cruel treatment in the internments of Jews in the northeastern provinces, Sztójay told him that the Church should concentrate its energies on the struggle against communism instead.[84]

Despite censorship news of atrocities began to reach the capital, but the prime minister and other ministers feigned ignorance or denied everything. On April 12, Bishop Ravasz rose from his sickbed to warn Horthy, who summoned Andor Jaross, minister of the interior and Nazi sympathizer, and told him to conduct an investigation. Jaross sent State Secretary Endre on an inspection tour with Eichmann. The ghetto Endre visited had atrocious conditions—not enough water or food, and the Jews were often beaten, humiliated, and robbed of their valuables. But the report Endre brought back was filled with outlandish lies—that the provincial ghettoes were like sanatoria—healthy life in open air. Horthy was able to convince himself the alleged atrocities were only the "usual gossip of cowardly Jewish sensation-mongers."[85]

Ravasz, who had never before intervened in such a direct way in government affairs, was so alarmed that he requested a second audience with the regent. At their meeting on April 28, he implored the regent to ensure that his name not be associated with atrocities against the Jews. Horthy, irritated by clerical meddling, explained that he had responded to the first reports by making a commotion and ordering an investigation, but he was now convinced that any scandalous treatment had ended. Those Jews who could not be in the military were pressed into labor service, and they would work as did several hundred thousand Hungarian workers in Germany. Their families would accompany them. Ravasz was shocked at how Horthy was being misled by his ministers and generals.[86]

From the end of March to early April desperate appeals came to Cardinal Serédi from those calling for the Church to raise its voice against the persecutions. Bishop Ravasz proposed a plan for a united action by all the Christian churches, which would be more effective than single actions, but the cautious Cardinal Serédi rejected the plan for a joint proclamation. As the persecutions continued some members of the Catholics Bishops' Council became impatient, urging the Prince Primate to take stronger steps and publicly protest. They judged that further discussions with the government were futile and demanded that Cardinal Serédi publicly and openly denounce the government. The retired Count János Mikes, former Bishop of Szombathely, made a concrete proposal for a joint pastoral letter, and on April 12, 1944, Vilmos Apor, bishop of Győr, wrote to Serédi that it was necessary to take action, but the cardinal did not believe it expedient. According to Serédi's reasoning, such open condemnation—which the censorship then in effect would prevent from reaching the public—would also not alleviate the fate of the persecuted. He felt it would do nothing to help the persecuted Jews but would enrage Hitler and merely worsen their situation. This was the same consideration that prevented Pope Pius XII from publicly denouncing Hitler.[87] Serédi feared incurring the wrath of the Germans, and also counted on the knowledge that some in the government did not agree with the bestial measures.[88]

Serédi's reluctance can be partially explained by the anti-Semitism of the population. Anti-Church propaganda raised the perception that the Hungarian churches offered sanctuary to Jews, which angered many on the radical right. State Secretary László complained in a public speech that the pastors of all kinds and ranks of the Christian confessions were in first place in the saving of Jews. Even after the deportations ceased, the director of Catholic Action reported to Serédi that the mass baptism of Jews had resulted in waves of anti-priest and anti-Catholic agitation in Budapest.[89]

In a pastoral letter of May 17 to the bishops, Cardinal Serédi summarized the measures taken by the church on behalf of the converts and admitted the results achieved were meager, but explained the reason for keeping negotiations secret and not publicly opposing the grievous regulations. "We did not wish to furnish anybody with a pretext for launching, parallel to our official negotiations, attacks upon our Catholic brethren—not yet affected by the regulations—and upon the rights and institutions of our Church, which might have resulted in the curtailing of its rights or the withdrawal of the concessions granted. We had neither abandoned nor betrayed the true cause or our Catholic brethren, but under the prevailing circumstances we could achieve no more."[90]

After the order for mass deportations on May 15, 1944, officials in the Vatican, speaking through the nunciate in Budapest, Angelo Rotta, began urging the Prince Primate to take a more vigorous stand. The day after the deportations began on May 18, the Bishop of Transylvania, Áron Márton, in a sermon in Kolozsvar stated bluntly that the church rejected differentiating between one human being and another. On May 27, Bishop Vilmos Apor, after witnessing the brutal cruelty with which the deportation of captives of the ghetto of Győr was carried out, appealed again to the Cardinal's conscience. He deplored his resolution not to publicize the violations of human rights and pleaded with the cardinal that as head of the Hungarian Catholic Church he issue a pastoral letter on the religious and moral implications of the situation, or give the bishops a free hand to inform and guide their parishioners.

HORTHY'S REACTION TO THE DEPORTATIONS

Meanwhile in late May, Regent Horthy began to become aware of the reality of the atrocities taking place. He received a detailed memorandum from Ernő Pető, a longtime friend of the family, and other members of the Jewish Council, which gave a graphic account of the brutal deportations and warned that unless countermeasures were taken the entire Jewish community would be destroyed. Through the compelling personal stories and graphic detail—of Jews crammed into railroad cars with only one bucket of water to drink, the deportation of the sick, the aged, even of war heroes—Horthy was finally convinced that there was inhuman treatment, but he still did not grasp the purpose of the deportations. He was slow to move, fearing confrontation with the Germans. The Final Solution was beyond his imagination, as well as that of many others. At this time the true fate of European Jewry was not universally known. Although Jewish leaders passed warnings on to the Allies, the Department of State and the British Foreign Office, for various reasons suppressed this information.[91]

At some point, realizing that he was not actually a prisoner of the Germans, Horthy began to regain some of his old self-confidence and attempted to take action to stop the excessive brutality and inhuman treatment of the Jews. He wrote a letter to Sztójay in early June, saying that recently things had been brought to his attention of which he had not been aware, especially over brutal and inhuman treatment of Jews and measures taken interfering with the essential contributions of the

Jewish population. He considered it necessary to carry out immediately measures to prevent the excesses of brutality and to provide exemptions to baptized Jews and those of special merit, especially engineers, leaders in the economy, and particularly doctors, whose services were needed in wartime. In order to stop any continuation of uncalled-for merciless and inhuman measures, direction of Jewish matters should be taken out of the hands of State Secretary László Endre, and State Secretary László Baky should be removed from his position. He asked Sztójay to see that his ministers take action on his memorandum without delay. Angry that Hitler had not answered his letter in which he reminded him of his promise to end the occupation after a satisfactory Hungarian government had been formed, he asked Sztójay to deliver a second letter on his trip to Berlin June 6.[92]

In the last week of June an unprecedented international campaign was launched on behalf of the Hungarian Jews after a copy of the Auschwitz Protocols was smuggled into Switzerland. The Protocols contained the report by two prisoners, Rudolf Vrba and Alfred Wetzler, who had escaped from Auschwitz on April 7, 1944, and made contact with the Jewish Council in Slovakia fourteen days later when they wrote down their report. Their report for the first time gave a precise description of the geography of the camp and an account of the mass murders in the gas chambers in Auschwitz. They also reported on preparations being made in Auschwitz for the impending reception of the Hungarian Jews which had started as early as January 15, 1944. Slovak Jewish leaders sent the report to the Jewish Council in Hungary, as well as to other key people in Hungary including church leaders, although—for reasons still debated—they did not release the information to the Jewish community at large.[93]

It has been debated exactly when the Auschwitz Protocols reached Hungary and when they were passed on to key leaders. It appears that the German language document reached the Jewish Council in early June. In a letter to Tsvi Erez, dated March 30, 1974, from Fülöp Freudiger, a member of the Jewish Council, Freudiger writes that the Protocols were brought on the eighth or tenth of June by courier from the Hungarian mission in Bratislava. Yet they were not passed on to either Horthy's circle or to other diplomats until the second half of June. The reason for the delay is unclear except that Freudiger was having the nearly forty-page text translated by his assistants. Then, on June 19, the protocols were sent out of Hungary. Freudiger personally handed the protocols to the head of the Magyar Quartermasters Corps, and the general was shocked by the descriptions of the atrocities.[94] Sándor Török, the Christian member of the Jewish Council, mentioned in regard to the documents: "I visited various leading people with our documentary material, such as the highly important secret reports we had about the Auschwitz camp; most had the opinion that they were not true, merely 'Jewish exaggerations.'"[95]

According to Vrba, none of the 437,000 Hungarian Jews deported to Auschwitz between May 15 and July 9 were ever given the information from the protocols. Failure of the official Jewish representatives in Hungary to inform the Jewish population contributed to Eichmann's stunning success in so rapidly organizing the deportation of the majority of the Hungarian Jews. "It is my contention that this tragedy could have been greatly impeded if our warning had been effectively and swiftly communicated to the intended victims."[96]

When the news about Auschwitz was published in Switzerland, although in an abridged form, it led to an extensive newspaper campaign, which eventually caused an international chain reaction. It triggered a major grass roots protest in Switzerland with glaring headlines protesting against Europe's barbarism and its dark age in the twentieth century. Publication of the report also triggered Sunday sermons in Swiss churches expressing deep concern over the fate of Jews. In addition there were various street protests.

Perhaps to counter the effect the Germans prepared a German propaganda film, which was shown in various Western countries. The film demonstrated the brutal conduct of the Hungarian gendarmes, showing them beating women with their gunstocks, hounding children with blackjacks, packing people like cattle into the railroad cars—with nary a German in sight. Only after crossing the Hungarian border did the humane Germans appear, arriving with Red Cross nurses, bringing fresh water, food, and aid to the suffering. Through his son, Nicky, Horthy received a report of the film from the Swiss Hungarian Ministry, and even more damning, an article in a Swiss paper mocking the Hungarians who claimed to be "the chivalrous nation" yet were involved in such shameful acts that would remain a dark stain on the nation's honor forever. Horthy, who had always been fiercely proud of Hungary's reputation for honor and chivalry, was appalled.[97]

Then, on June 23, the Jewish Council through Nicky sent a memo to the regent warning that the Germans intended to deport the Jews of Budapest in the near future and imploring him to halt the deportations. Near the end of June he received a long memorandum from Bethlen condemning the "inhuman and stupid persecution of the Jews with which the present government stain the Hungarian name."[98] He urged the regent to get rid of the present cabinet, appoint a new government of nonpolitical experts, and sue for armistice. On June 25 a personal letter arrived from Pope Pius XII, asking Horthy for his personal intervention, although not mentioning the Jews by name. He received a message from President Roosevelt, with remonstrances in a threatening tone, and a personal cable from the King of Sweden, requesting him in the "name of humanity" to take all steps to rescue all who can yet be saved. As an additional blow Horthy discovered that in the meetings on June 21 and June 23 his cabinet had failed to carry out his directives to Sztójay. Through the letters, messages, and the cabinet's failure to follow his orders, he was stirred to action.[99]

On June 26, Horthy summoned a meeting of the Crown Council—the first such meeting to be held since the early days of the German occupation. He spoke of the deportations and that he had received messages from all the Protestant bishops, from the Pope, from the Swedish king and also Roosevelt, making him responsible for the fate of the Jews in Budapest. Eden, the British prime minister had spoken in Parliament. Horthy denounced the two state secretaries in charge of the anti-Jewish campaign, László Baky and László Endre, as sadistic scoundrels, demanded their resignation again, and insisted that the Hungarian administration and gendarmes take no part in the deportations. If the Germans wanted it at all costs, they should do it themselves.[100]

Despite his directive to stop the deportation of the Jews of Budapest, freight trains crammed with Jews continued to depart from Szeged, Sopron, and other cities in southern and western Hungary in the last days of June and early July. As a concession, Baky and Endre were temporarily relieved of their duties, but this was only for the sake of appearances, and the date for the beginning of deportations from Budapest was postponed from June 30. Horthy was allowed to exempt a small number of favored Jews from the anti-Jewish laws. Veesnemayer believed these concessions would satisfy Horthy.[101]

Following the Pope's letter to Horthy, the Papal nunciate in Budapest, Angelo Rotta, again urged Cardinal Serédi to act, recommending he take action publicly to protest the deportations in a pastoral letter from the pulpit. At the same time, on June 15, Bishop Ravasz, head of the Reformed Convent, again attempted to initiate an action by all the Christian churches, suggesting in a letter to Serédi that they meet personally and formulate a common standpoint. But the cardinal, who had been reluctant to take any public action, continued to reject a public denunciation of the deportations in unity with the Protestant churches. The Protestant leaders decided to go ahead on their own and act in unison. A memorandum, formulated by Bishop Ravasz and signed by nine Bishops, was handed over to Prime Minister Sztojay on June 23; the protest received no answer.[102]

In late June, under pressure from his own bishops as well as the Papal Nuncio, the cardinal began to draft a pastoral letter to the faithful to be read in parishes throughout Hungary, although his assistant, Archbishop Gyula Czapik of Eger, reminded him of the popular reaction that any statement on behalf of the Hungarian Jews would arouse. The church had been virtually accused of treason by the radical right, even for insisting on certain minimal exemptions for its converts. Czapik suggested that the text give "as little unnecessary pretext as possible to the expected anti-Church attacks . . ."[103] The letter also reflected the Primate's ambiguity. Serédi declared that the Church deplored the new anti-Jewish measures as an affront to divine law, but still made accusations that some Hungarian Jews were guilty of a harmful influence in the economic, social, and moral life of the nation, and there was no doubt that the Jewish question must be regulated by law.[104]

The pastoral letter, dated June 29, was brought to the attention of István Antal, minister of justice, religious affairs and education, who promptly stopped its distribution, although some archdioceses did receive the letter and it was reportedly read out in some churches. Prime Minister Sztójay, accompanied by Antal and Imrédy, met with the cardinal, who was by this time seriously ill, and warned him of an Arrow Cross coup if the legitimacy of the government should be undermined. The government promised to investigate the atrocities, punish those involved, and stop the deportations. After negotiations, an agreement was finally reached by which the pastoral letter would be retracted if the Hungarian government would not permit further deportations.

The Hungarian-American historian, István Deák remarked: "The tragedy is that the Prince Primate kept discreetly protesting the atrocities in the ghettoes at a time when hundreds of thousands were already on their way to the gas chambers. One cannot help feeling that timely protestations in public . . . would have slowed down the deportation process. They would not have stopped Eichmann but they would have thrown confusion in the ranks of the allegedly Christian gendarmes and civil servants without whose assistance the deportations were impossible. The Prince Primate's pastoral letter of June 29 came far too late."[105]

A pastoral letter of protest by Bishop Ravasz in the name of the Reformed Church was sent out on the last Sunday of June to be read July 9. There was no mention of Jewish individual or collective guilt or of the necessity of solving the Jewish question. On the suggestion of other bishops, the letter mentioned that the Jews had not been guilty—as had been charged—for the start of Allied bombing. But under similar circumstances this letter was also not read. On July 16 leaders from both churches told their congregations that they had taken steps on behalf of the Jews—especially the converted.[106] By this time the deportations had been halted through actions by Horthy. The prime minister declared that the deportations had been stopped at the request of the church.[107]

The question of when Horthy knew of the actual fate awaiting the Jewish deportees is still debated.[108] After the occupation Horthy spoke of himself as a prisoner of the Germans, and removed himself from the actions taken by the government. By having the cabinet pass decrees rather than laws Horthy did not need to countersign the decrees, thus—to his thinking—absolving himself from responsibility. In his letter to Sztójay he acknowledged that he was out of touch with recent measures taken. Various dates have been given for the time when Sándor Török, a well-known writer and member of the Jewish Council, delivered a copy of the Auschwitz Protocols to the regent's daughter-in-law, Ilona, who then took it to Horthy's wife, Magda. Mme. Horthy then showed the report to Horthy which convinced him the reports were not mere exaggeration.[109]

Ilona Horthy, in her memoirs published in 2000, tells of receiving the Auschwitz Protocols from Török on July 3 and taking them to Horthy. Commenting on the dispute about "when Horthy knew," she points out, "I am the only one with a record of when the Hungarian translation of the Protocols were brought to Horthy,"[110] since she had recorded the date in her diary, while other accounts relied on memory. She recorded that on July 3, after she had completed her nursing duties, Török came up to her apartment in the castle and gave her the Auschwitz Protocols, which she read in his presence, and—confessing that she was utterly shocked—took them down to her mother-in-law, Magda Horthy, since Horthy was busy in his study. Ilona recalled: "I gave the protocol to her without saying anything, I only asked that she read it immediately. In tears, Magda-mama read it to the end, and promised that she would give it to Miklóspapa when he came out of his study. . . . I wasn't there when my father-in-law read them. But Magda said afterwards how deeply he was affected—that such horrible things couldn't be true. He said then that the deportations must be stopped."[111] Three days later, on July 6, the Hungarian government stopped the Jewish deportations. Prime Minister Sztójay informed the Germans, who accepted the decision only because their military situation was so perilous.[112]

If Horthy had attempted to intervene earlier, it is quite possible that he would have been removed or silenced, but by the end of June the general military situation for the Germans was desperate. The Normandy landings of the Western Allies had begun on June 6 and by the end of the month it was obvious that they could not be thrown back into the sea, despite the reinforcements Hitler sent to the new front, troops he could hardly afford to send. Much worse was the situation on the eastern front. On June 22, the Soviets had started Operation Bagration in which 166 Soviet divisions launched an all-out attack on the 3,200-kilometer front. The Soviets had not only numerical superiority—166 divisions versus some 30-odd German ones—but had superiority in heavy armor, artillery, even air power. Within ten days they inflicted enormous losses on the Germans. One historian calls the Red Army's success in destroying the German Army Group Center the "most spectacular single military success of the war."[113] For the Germans it was a catastrophe greater than that of Stalingrad or Kursk. The three German armies lost more than 196,000 men—over 130,000 were killed and 66,000 were taken as prisoners of war.

LÁSZLÓ BAKY'S COUP ATTEMPT

In early July the regent learned of a plan by László Baky to carry out the rapid liquidation of the Jews of Budapest through a government coup, using the gendarme brigades which had served in his anti-Jewish operations. By early July several thousand gendarmes armed with bayonets were patrolling the streets of the capital in groups of two and three, breaking with the very strict division maintained between the police who served in the cities, and the gendarmerie, which was in charge of the countryside. Gendarmes were not supposed to be in the city except when they were off duty, and certainly not when armed.[114] An attempt by Baky to assassinate Horthy's friend, István Bárczy, state secretary and keeper of the minutes, on June 29 galvanized the regent to action.

Acting quickly, with uncharacteristic boldness and discretion, Horthy bypassed his Chief of Staff Vörös, and authorized Lt. Gen. Károly Lázár, the commander of his personal bodyguard, to assume military command in Budapest and take measures to prevent both the coup d'état and deportation of the Jews.[115] Concerned that there was not an armed force on hand, Lázár happened to meet his friend, Colonel Ferenc Koszorus, on the banks of the Danube on July 2. Through a trick of fate the Germans did not know of Koszorus' First Armored Division, which was stationed north of Budapest. When the remnants of the First Armored Division returned from the Don in March 1943, they were not divided up among other units but dispersed to prevent the Germans from sending the army to the front. Since they were not placed within the order of battle the Germans did not know of their existence. On hearing of Baky's plan and the danger involved since the regent lacked an armed force, Koszorus asked Lázár: ". . . to tell the regent that if I received the command I would get rid of the gendarme units with force!"[116]

On July 5 around 11 P.M. Koszorus received the order from the regent to remove the gendarmerie from the capital—that Baky was planning the putsch for July 6. Koszorus had determined that the Germans had only three police battalions in the capital, motorized with excellent weapons, but Koszorus commanded a larger force: "On July 6 at 7 A.M. I sent an officers' patrol to László Baky. . . . I ordered that within twenty-four hours the gendarme units should evacuate Budapest, otherwise I would carry out the evacuation by force."[117]

Although a crisis atmosphere prevailed in the capital on July 7 and 8, with rumors of an imminent entry of German military units, by late July 7 the gamble was succeeding. Vörös had warned Horthy that the Germans would never stand for a unilateral action to stop the deportations, but General Faraghó, the gendarmerie commander, was unwilling to disobey a direct command from the regent, and Sztójay felt compelled to carry out Horthy's orders. The Germans, caught off guard, were not prepared to risk a direct confrontation. On July 7 at 9 A.M., Baky informed Koszorus that the gendarmes would evacuate within 24 hours. The gendarmes began an orderly withdrawal and Baky and Endre were relieved of their duties. According to an account by Endre, there were 170,000 Jews registered in Budapest and at least another 130,000 hiding with false papers, who were saved for the time being.[118]

Veesenmayer, who was often successful in persuading or threatening the regent, was convinced that he could resume the deportations later, but Eichmann was more alarmed: "In all my long practice this is the first time such a thing has happened to me; this won't do at all. It is contrary to all agreements."[119] It was the first time that a leader had succeeded in halting deportations of Jews through the threat of military force. Eichmann moved quickly to test the regent; with the cooperation of Andor Jaross he organized a rapid action to deport a group of 1,500 Jews held in a camp on the outskirts of Budapest, but Horthy, alerted by the Jewish Council, dispatched troops in time to intercept the train and return the transport safely back to camp. By subterfuge Eichmann succeeded in a second maneuver. While holding the members of the Jewish Council incommunicado in an all-day conference, Eichmann kidnapped the 1,500 Jews with an SS detachment and spirited them out of the country.[120]

There is ongoing debate about the numbers of Jews who were deported from Hungary, the number killed at Auschwitz, and the total number of survivors. István Deák comments: "Let me note here that statistical data on such things as the number of Second Army soldiers and forced laborers, . . . or the number of Hungarian Jews gassed at Auschwitz, or the total number of wartime Jewish dead, are not much better than guesses. There exists no reliable information on these subjects."[121] According to Tamás Stark, who has extensively analyzed statistics concerning Hungarian Jews, what is generally agreed is that 437,000 Jews were deported from Hungary in the summer of 1944; most of them were sent to Auschwitz. Those who were not fit for work were killed. In the fall of 1944, another estimated fifty thousand Jews were force-marched to the Austro-Hungarian border for fortification work, and many didn't survive the experience. The greater part of Jews in Budapest survived and tens of thousand Jews in labor battalions also survived the persecution.[122]

HORTHY REGAINS THE INITIATIVE

After his success in preventing the putsch and deportations, Horthy began to realize that he did have some room to maneuver and considered the appointment of a new government. In times past he had considered the possibility of appointing a government of military officers loyal to him, and once he had told Barcza in conversation that if ever he could not find a suitable prime minister he would just name a military government.[123] Yet still hesitant, he delayed his decision a number of times.

At the end of May, Horthy had told General Lakatos that he planned to name him prime minister sometime soon.[124] Now, incensed at how the treatment of the Jews had endangered the Hungarian reputation, he called Lakatos to his residence on July 7, telling him that he intended to force the Sztójay government to resign and appoint an apolitical government. Lakatos asked for twenty-four hours to consider the situation, and in a meeting with Bethlen, who was often smuggled into the castle to advise the regent, Lakatos referred to his complete lack of experience in domestic politics. Bethlen, who had recommended him to the regent, said that was exactly why he was suitable. Lakatos, hesitant whether the Germans would tolerate the change of government, conferred with Vörös, who emphasized that the Germans were still strong enough to resist. It was decided to wait.[125]

About two weeks later, Horthy again attempted to replace the Sztójay government, calling Lakatos to Budapest and demanding the resignation of Sztójay, but he was foiled by Veesenmayer and his own military officers. He felt it necessary to inform Veesenmayer, who said he must first notify Hitler. Veesenmayer immediately telephoned Ribbentrop and the next day, July 17, he called on Horthy to deliver Ribbentrop's message from Hitler. Hitler had reacted with extreme displeasure to the intention to replace Sztójay, which he regarded as nothing less than treason, and warned that any departure from the ways decided at Klessheim might jeopardize the very existence of the Hungarian nation. In his telegram to Ribbentrop, Veesenmayer wrote: "After the conclusion of this conversation Horthy was completely finished, his whole body trembled, and he was an old broken man."[126]

But evidently Horthy quickly pulled himself together. On July 17 he called in his generals, Csatay and Vörös, and without mentioning the conversation with Veesenmayer, asked, "what would happen if we were to undertake armed resistance against the Germans here?"[127] Vörös answered that it would mean the end of Hungary's national existence; thus the decision to replace the Sztójay government was again postponed. Afterward Vörös briefed his officers staff at headquarters, and they unanimously agreed that Hungary must avoid fighting against the Germans, and restore smooth relations with them at the earliest opportunity, a reaction that was to resonate during the armistice attempt on October 15.[128]

The effects of Horthy's new stance soon began to be felt. In summer the situation of the Jews was alleviated in many ways. Through negotiations opened up by the Red Cross with various neutral countries a few thousand Jews, mainly children, were allowed to leave for Palestine, Sweden, or Switzerland, and hundreds of Jews bought their way out through complex financial negotiations with Himmler's men in Germany.[129] On July 18 Horthy made an offer through the International Red Cross to the United States and Britain to permit the emigration of Jewish children under ten with visas to other countries and of all Jews who had Palestine certificates. The overture put pressure on the United States and Britain, and within ten days the War Refugee Board in the United States assured that it would find havens for all the Jews released, but not wanting to act alone, informed the British that it would wait until August 7 for them to join in accepting the offer. The British stalled, alarmed at the pressure Horthy's proposal would place on their Palestine policy but unwilling to be the ones to reject the offer. It wasn't until August 17 that the two governments publicly issued a statement accepting the responsibility for finding havens for all the Jews allowed out, but they had delayed too long. While they were negotiating the Nazis who controlled the borders made it clear that they would bar any Jewish emigration.[130]

During the summer the Allied air raids were remorseless, devastating cities and disrupting communications. The stream of refugees fleeing before the Red Army began to swell, and public security was deteriorating rapidly. In Budapest itself the police were authorized to use firearms against anyone who refused to halt when challenged. Growing discontent among the workers became evident with the increase of resistance in the war industries, the reduced output of the harvest, and workers more openly agitating against the system. At the end of summer, bathing in the unusual heat, the majority of the Hungarian population waited in helpless passivity, expecting the country soon to become a battleground.[131]

Romania Turns on Its Allies

A major change in the war situation came on August 23. With the rapid approach of Soviet troops King Michael of Romania staged a well-planned palace revolution, arresting Ion Antonescu and replacing his government with one of national unity. Hitler, in his fury, responded by bombing Bucharest on August 24, giving the king reason to declare war against Germany which he had promised the Soviets. By September 2 the Germans had lost control of the Ploesti oil fields and Bucharest. The Soviets at first treated the Romanian army as a conquered foe, but then demanded their participation in continuing the advance against the Germans. Since the Soviets agreed in return to help them recover the northern part of Transylvania, the Romanians agreed enthusiastically, but had no enthusiasm for continuing to fight alongside the Soviets after Transylvania had been occupied.[132]

The Romanian desertion was a monumental blow for Hungary. Politically it gave Romania a huge advantage in the constant competition for the favor of the Allies, while it was devastating strategically. Unless they were stopped, the Soviet forces could sweep through the gap torn in the defense and penetrate the South Carpathian passes and easily overrun the country.

Following the Romanian bailout and the invasion of Transylvania by the Romanian army, many believed that now was the time to get out of the war. Lakatos received the long-awaited telegram from Horthy the day after the Romanian defection and arrived in Budapest on August 25. Together with István Bethlen they examined the new situation. Bethlen was of the opinion—which the regent accepted—that now was not the moment to bail out of the war but to prepare for it. They should make use of German weakness and prepare for their next moves. The role to be assigned to the new government was to prepare to leave the war. Thus they were playing a dangerous game under the German occupation— pursuing the war but in secret plotting to leave.

The Germans had suffered staggering losses over the summer. On the eastern front they had lost 215,000 dead and 627,000 missing against the Red Army. Including the wounded the total reached almost two million, as many casualties as the army had suffered from the beginning of the war through the battle of Stalingrad in February 1943. For the first time in the war the territory of the German Reich itself lay under threat. The political implications were even worse. At the end of August a national uprising broke out in Slovakia against the fascist Tiso regime. Bulgaria, never a true German ally, asked Russia for a truce on September 5. Marshal Carl Gustav Mannerheim, national leader of Finland, broke relations with the Germans on September 2 and signed a treaty with the Soviets on September 19. Although Finland was peripheral to Hitler's strategy, Hungary was central to the defense of the Reich, next in the firing line after Romania and Bulgaria.[133]

The cabinet chosen by Horthy and Lakatos was to be apolitical—half military and half professional—and the designated ministers assembled on September 28. The new prime minister was introduced to Veesenmayer in the obligatory audience, but Lakatos persuaded the regent to allow him to conduct the discussion, remembering how in July Veesenmayer had wiped out the regent with his threats. Veesenmayer, surprised at the naming of a new government, made all sorts of demands to include extreme rightist representatives in the government, especially his own trusted ministers, László Endre as minister of work, and Jurcsek, his most trustworthy spy, as minister of agriculture. But the German position had become much weaker and he was inclined to compromise. He left saying that he would deliver the German answer the next day.

After waiting in vain for the promised German response, on September 29 Lakatos and Horthy decided to act. They sent a message to the German minister that in the existing situation the regent considered that he had regained complete independence. Under the pressure of the situation they decided to keep two sitting ministers which Veesenmayer had insisted on, Jurcsek and Reményi-Schneller, an unfortunate decision, since both continued to deliver information to the Germans.[134] The new government, which took the oath that day at 10 A.M., was received throughout the county with great acclaim. In public and to the Germans they made as if to continue the war, but despite the urgency indicated by Romania's change of sides, the negotiations for a cease-fire dragged on, giving the Germans time to prepare.

Obstacles in the Armistice Proceedings

On September 6 Lakatos informed Horthy that the Soviets had broken through Hungarian defenses and were marching through Transylvania. The regent, deeply concerned, ordered a meeting of the Crown Council for the next day at 6 P.M. to discuss the initiation of armistice proceedings. He began the meeting expressing his hope that a peaceful agreement with the Russians would lead to milder treatment when they occupied the country, now a forgone conclusion. In the debate that followed the pro-Nazis, Jurcsek and Reményi-Schneller, naturally opposed a cease-fire, but the other members, the anti-Nazis, were also fearful. They had vivid memories of what had happened after World War I when the armistice and disarming of the soldiers led to catastrophe. Violent antipathy toward the Russians dated back to the Revolution of 1848 and the Bolshevik regime of Béla Kun, and German and Hungarian anti-Bolshevik propaganda was intense during the war. The publication *Magyar Futar*, directed at a wide public audience, depicted the Russians with fangs, blood streaming down their cheeks, vicious creatures raping women.[135]

Defense Minister Csatay offered a compromise; an ultimatum should be sent to the Germans that day that they should send five armored divisions within twenty-four hours or Hungary would be forced to ask for an armistice since it would be unable to defend itself without such assistance.[136] The members accepted this appalling idea as a clever suggestion. The Germans, greatly surprised, of course promised to send the requested units.[137] Lakatos realized only much later that the decision would inevitably lead to the worst possible consequences: "With this we delayed the step for an armistice. At the same time we drew the Germans' attention to our preparations. This decided our fate. Militarily we did not get serious assistance, while more and more German troops were brought in to the capital and surroundings . . . they armed the Arrow Cross and prepared them so that with the first possible instance, power would be given to Szálasi and comrades. At the time I did not see this clearly. . . . Now of course I know, that in that moment the scales were tipped."[138]

On August 25 several young Transylvanian Hungarians, who were much more in touch with the reality of events on the ground, asked Béla Teleki, president of the Transylvanian party in Parliament, to go to Budapest to request an audience with Horthy and tell him how urgent it was to make an armistice agreement before the fighting came to Transylvania and Hungary. But in their meeting Horthy explained to Teleki that there were still huge German forces in the country and there was danger of civil war; he did not see that the time had come for a change of sides. On September 6 several Transylvanians met with Nicky, who spoke out heatedly against the members of the government: "They live in illusions! There is no truth that the Anglo-Saxons are carrying out any kind of negotiations. We have to make an armistice with the Soviets; we are fighting with them!"[139]

On September 10, Horthy called together a privy council with a larger number of his trusted councilors, both political and military, to announce that it was time to get out of the war. Lakatos, Hennyey, and Csatay represented the government as well as Vörös. Others of his trusted advisors included Count Móric Esterházy, Count Gyula Károlyi, Kálmán Kánya, Baron Zigmond Perényi, head of the upper house of Parliament, as well as Bethlen, and the retired generals Vilmos Röder, Hugó Sónyi, and István Náday. Representatives of the Transylvanian party, Béla Teleki and Baron Dániel Bánffy, who had met with Horthy that morning also took part. Horthy opened the meeting with a short account of the general military situation and the conclusion that Germany had lost the war. Lakatos announced that the divisions demanded from the Germans had not arrived.[140]

After Lakatos spoke on the political situation and Vörös on the advance of the Soviet troops, Bethlen, who had been smuggled into the castle, asked to speak. Supporting the regent he demanded immediate action—there was no point in further bloodletting, Hungary must get out of the war or it would be wiped off the map. But the others, especially the military officers, were uneasy, not only because of their fear of the Russians, but because most of them, including Horthy, believed in the old code of honor—that Hungary could only leave its allies in the traditional way. Yet clearly in a situation of total war and the demand for unconditional surrender this was not possible.[141]

At the end of five hours of debate a broad consensus was reached to seek an armistice following the Finnish example, but in order not to be considered traitors to let the Germans know. Lakatos, who earlier had been concerned that as a military man he had no experience in domestic politics, was determined to stick to constitutional principles. He asked to be allowed to bring the matter to the cabinet since the ministers were responsible to the public, this even though the Parliament was no longer representative of the nation.[142]

The cabinet meeting on September 11 was disastrous. The cabinet unanimously rejected the decision to call for an armistice and threatened to resign should the regent disregard its recommendation and sue for an armistice. One member after another spoke against taking on the responsibility for the cease-fire. The minutes of the meeting reported the wavering ministers' comments: "I understand the regent, but that is difficult to take on . . .", "If the regent orders it, I would accept the responsibility, but . . .", "The Germans would take dreadful revenge," "It's still early to ask for a cease-fire!"[143] Horthy was appalled by Lakatos's report of the meeting. With great disappointment he asked about the ministers he thought he could count on, "Rakovszky too? Vladár too? And even Csatay?"[144]

Without the support of the government, the regent was forced to turn to a narrow group of personal advisors. That evening in the regent's study a small group gathered—the regent and his wife, his son Nicky, daughter-in-law Ilona, Lt. Gen. Szilard Bakay, commander of the First Army and officer in charge of Budapest security, Lt. Gen. Károly Lázár, commander of the body guard, Lt. Col. Gyula Tost, aide-de-camp, Gyula Ambrözy, head of the cabinet bureau, and Antal Vattay, head of the military bureau. The regent gave the results of the Council of Ministers meeting and recalled what a difficult struggle it had been to finally name this government. Now the whole government had left him in the lurch. There was no time to go through the naming of a new cabinet. He remained alone, and he had decided to carry on; he would take personal responsibility for contacting the enemy, sending an emissary to Italy—and if necessary to Russia. It was a formidable task. It had to be kept secret from the Germans but also from his own prime minister, foreign minister, and chief of staff. Horthy at this point was seventy-six years old. Considering that he often had difficulty in making decisions, was easily influenced, and often blurted out sensitive information, he did amazingly well. With the help of his wife, son, daughter-in-law, and a handful of aides, he managed to carry it off. In late September the Allies were informed that Hungary was prepared to sue for peace.[145]

At the time it seems that the regent had no clear concept of what kind of armistice would be feasible or acceptable. He made one more last-ditch effort to contact the Western Allies, still hoping that they would take part in an occupation of Hungary. He chose retired General István Náday as his emissary to fly to the Allies main war base in Italy; Colonel Charles T. Howie, a British officer nominally a prisoner of war in Hungary but working with the underground, was to accompany him. They finally found a trustworthy pilot, János Majoros, who put aside and gradually fueled an old Heinkel and conveyed it to an obscure airfield near Budapest. On the evening of September 20, Howie and Náday were given a final briefing at the castle by Horthy although Náday's orders were only verbal because of fear of Gestapo inspection. They flew to Foggia on the night of September 22 in the "rickety old Heinkel" and crash landed, but since Náday had only oral authorization he was received with suspicion by Field Marshal Henry Maitland Wilson, the Allied commander-in-chief in the Italian theater.[146]

On the same night, the Red Army crossed the Hungarian frontier and had already reached the Hungarian plain. There could no longer be a question of an agreement with the West without Moscow. It seems that only then did Horthy realize that Hungary must turn to the Soviet Union for an armistice. The decision was an extremely difficult one. For years Horthy had insisted that it was Russia that presented the greatest threat to Hungary and the Western world. "It was a cancer to be excised, a poison to be removed from the system, a vile Mafia run by the scum of society."[147]

EN ROUTE TO MOSCOW

After much delay a three-member delegation with the regent's authorization was to start off for Moscow by way of Slovakia on September 28. In a fairly bizarre story, Count Ladomér Zichy, a Hungarian citizen living in Slovakia, prepared the trip of the armistice delegation. Zichy's estate in Divény (which the Slovaks call Divin) had remained in Slovakia after the first Vienna Award. "Since a part of my estate was in Hungary I had passes and in general could move freely between Slovakia and Hungary. I was in a good position with the Slovak border guards, customs, and population too."[148] As a result of the uprising in Slovakia, anti-Nazi partisan forces controlled considerable portions of the country in September 1944.

Zichy knew from his brother-in-law, Dániel Bánffy, a representative of the Transylvanian party, that the decision had finally come for Hungary to get in touch with the Soviets. After conferring with Bánffy as well as the head of the Transylvanian delegation, Béla Teleki, in Budapest, Zichy agreed to go back to Slovakia and try to make contacts, leaving on September 11. After a series of adventures Zichy ended up as a guest at dinner where he met the commander of a large Soviet partisan unit and his political representative, Lieutenant Colonel Makarov. They discussed conditions of the armistice and talked about how the Hungarian delegation would get to Moscow. The partisans vouched that they would take them by plane.[149]

On September 18 Zichy returned to Budapest and through the regent's son arranged to meet the regent and his advisors the next day at 6 P.M. He explained the results of his negotiations with Makarov—that if a serious authorized delegation would come he would be able to get them by plane to Moscow. According to Makarov, Hungary would get very advantageous terms for an armistice. All of the assembled group were against the idea except for Bánffy, young Horthy, and Zichy himself. Then there was an interruption by Chief of the General Staff Vörös, who urgently needed to speak to the regent. Horthy went out and came back with the news that a message had come, signed by some Russian colonel called Makarov, who offered armistice negotiations with Hungary. From then on only the technical questions remained.[150]

Earlier, an informal mission had gone to Moscow to try to make contact. Nicky had recommended Baron Ede Aczél, a maverick left-wing aristocrat from Transylvania, to travel to Moscow with two communist companions, Jozsef Dudás and Imre Faust. They returned from Moscow on September 24 also with a favorable reply—that the Soviets would welcome an authoritative Hungarian negotiator.[151] The messages from Makarov offered very advantageous terms for a speedy armistice, and that the Allied powers would refrain from interfering in Hungarian domestic affairs. Hungarian independence would be guaranteed, the Hungarian army and police forces would not be disarmed, and the Transylvanian question would be settled definitively by the peace treaty.[152]

It took days for the membership of the delegation to be determined. It was finally decided that the head of the mission would be General

Gábor Faragho, head of the gendarmerie, who had been military attaché in Moscow and spoke fluent Russian. Despite his role in the deportations he had been loyal to the regent during the July coup attempt. Also, the Germans would not suspect him. The other members were Count Géza Teleki, son of the former prime minister and a university professor, and Domokos Szent-Iványi, who was appointed envoy extraordinary and minister plenipotentiary. The mission set off much encouraged by the letter from Makarov.

It was necessary to proceed with utmost secrecy. The official delegation started off at 2 P.M. in separate cars. It was not apparent that they were planning to travel anywhere. The three men traveled separately through German occupied Hungary, then on foot across the river, and into Slovakia. Several days later they were taken to an airport where a plane sent by Stalin awaited them.[153]

Julia Zichy, a Red Cross nurse with a military hospital at the front, recalled meeting the delegation, although she only realized their identity later. She was told that some patients were coming in who were to be put into isolation. Since there were no isolation facilities a room was found away from the surgical unit. The seven or eight elderly men who arrived by ambulance got off jauntily. "We put them up and they were no problem." The next morning one came and asked for hot water for shaving. She explained that they were not prepared for that sort of thing—but she would hunt and finally came up with some warm water for him. They ate there, spent a few days, and then got back into their ambulances.[154]

The delegates carried with them the letter that Horthy had written to Stalin in English. He addressed himself to the field marshal: "in the name and for the sake of the Hungarian people in their extreme danger . . ." In his letter Horthy referred to misleading information which had led him to declare war on the Soviet Union in June 1941. "For the sake of justice, I would like to inform you that we have never ever wanted to take but a single inch from anybody that was not ours by right." Horthy begged Stalin "to spare this unfortunate country which has its own historic merits and the people of which has so many affinities with the Russian people."[155]

Communications between the delegation and the castle were carried out in secrecy through a shortwave receiver-transmitter unit. Since the transmitter located in the castle belonged to the Ministry of the Interior, there was concern about security, but the telegraph operators assigned to it agreed to allow the secret contact with Moscow without the knowledge of the ministry. Only two copies of the special cipher key had been pre-pared—one for the delegation and the other for the little group of ama-teurs in the castle, Horthy's aide-de-camp, Lt. Col. Gyula Tost, his son Nicky, and his daughter-in-law, Ilona. Ilona recalled that "Every time the secret radio transmission began to work, German airplanes appeared above the castle—they surely wanted to decipher the code."[156] The inexpe-rience of the team undoubtedly contributed to problems with the commu-nications. Messages came through garbled and had to be repeated, and instructions to various negotiators were not always clear.

During the first ten days of October, the delegation conducted negotia-tions for preliminary conditions for the Hungarian armistice but the negotiations went slowly. The whole process was fraught with misunder-standings and miscommunication. The Soviets and Horthy had quite dif-ferent ideas on what constituted the preliminary armistice. The Soviets thought the agreement was to be purely military, and that Hungary would begin cooperating immediately. Horthy believed the armistice would be truly preliminary and only finalized with the signing of the actual armistice. From the arrival of the negotiating team on October 1 it was clear that the Soviets wanted a rapid agreement and were mainly interested in achieving military cooperation. The team was received by the deputy chief of staff of the Soviet army, Colonel-General Kuznetsov, who started discussion from the principle of unconditional surrender and wanted to discuss the Hungarian army's desertion and entry into war against Germany. Since Faragho's task was to negotiate a preliminary armistice agreement with favorable conditions, he asked to meet a pleni-potentiary of higher rank to whom he might present Horthy's letter to Stalin.

Discussions resumed on October 5 with Chief of Staff Army General Antonov as Stalin's representative. Antonov emphasized the matter of military co-operation, for if the defection of the Hungarian army were successful, Soviet forces could pass quickly through Hungarian territory without the country becoming a theater of war. He was disappointed to find that Horthy's letter did not contain a detailed description of the methods of desertion. That same night Kuznetsov called on Faragho in his quarters to tell him that without authorization to sign the armistice the Soviet government saw no reason to negotiate.[157]

Not satisfied with the delegations' powers the Soviets demanded that a higher representative be sent. The small group in the castle had diffi-culty with the decoding of the message, which arrived asking urgently for a written statement of the delegations' full authority to sign a cease-fire and other agreements. Finding the telegram difficult to decipher, they requested that the Soviets resend the first two telegrams. The Soviets were impatient, believing the Hungarians were not negotiating in good faith.[158]

Molotov received the delegation on the night of October 8 and presented them with the terms of the preliminary armistice in the name of the three main Allies. On October 6 Molotov had informed the British and U.S. ambassadors in Moscow of the proposed terms, which were approved by both the British and the Americans. If the terms were accepted, the Allies would be ready to discuss in Moscow the terms of the definitive armistice, but they must have a plenipotentiary with necessary written authorization. Szent-Ivány brought up the favorable terms offered in the Makarov letter, but Molotov explained the Allies' position that the principle of unconditional surrender was the only solution and told Faragho to inform Horthy that the Soviet government considered the Makarov letter to be void. His message that the Soviet government negated the Makarov promises shocked Horthy's advisors who had counted on the favorable terms.[159]

The telegram with the preliminary terms was sent on October 9, and after meeting with Lakatos and others the next day, Horthy decided to accept the terms. The delegation was informed on October 11 at 12:30 A.M., and Faragho immediately called on Molotov. He sent a telegram two hours later: "At 4 A.M. today we informed Foreign Minister of the content of the telegram on Hungary's acceptance of preliminary armistice terms. The atmosphere became warm and friendly. British Prime Minister and Foreign Secretary are here, their presence secures solemnity and prompt action on our case. . . . They demand repetition of authorization to sign with simultaneous recapitulation of the state preliminary terms. Please grasp the importance of the situation and take the necessary measures to enable us to fulfill our obligations."[160]

That afternoon Molotov conferred with Foreign Secretary Eden, British Ambassador Clark Kerr, and the U.S. Ambassador Averell Harriman, showing them the Horthy telegram with acceptance of the preliminary terms. Eden and the U.S. ambassador agreed with the Soviet suggestions. At 10:30 P.M., Horthy sent a telegram repeating the authorization to sign and announced that Major József Nemes would leave on October 12 with written authorization. But before the telegram reached Moscow, Molotov summoned the delegation to tell them it was needless to wait. Thus at 7:57 P.M. on October 11, Molotov and Faragho signed the preliminary armistice agreement. The Soviets said they would stop the advance of their troops for one or two days. At half past nine in the evening Faragho sent a telegram that the armistice agreement had been signed and that he would be told which Hungarian commanders should go over to which Russian commanders through the front line.[161]

In essence, the terms reached stated that Hungary would cease hostilities against the Soviet Union; within ten days Hungary should pull out its military forces and administration from the territory that had been taken after 1937. In order to supervise the agreement the Allied Supervisory Committee would come into the country. The Hungarian government was to break all contacts with the Germans and immediately declare war against Germany, after which the Soviet government would offer help to carry out the change of sides.

Through German spies Veesenmayer learned that in the first days of October a delegation led by Gábor Faragho was seeking an armistice in Moscow. Thus, while the delegation was negotiating in Moscow, the Germans took steps for the take-over of power in conjunction with the Arrow Cross, despite their earlier reluctance to deal with Szálasi whom they had discounted, doubting his ability as well as his *hungarista* ideology. The decision to give power to Szálasi and his party was determined mainly because he and his followers were the only ones prepared to hold out to the end and accept the seemingly hopeless struggle.[162]

Szálasi and Veesenmayer met on October 11 and made an agreement for the take-over and the preliminary make-up of the government. Emil Kovarcz, a former general staff officer who had earlier fled the country to escape imprisonment, was named commander of the Arrow Cross forces; he immediately began to organize the movement, putting his people into key positions in the radio, centers of public utilities and communication, and the police and gendarmes.[163] Otto Skorzeny and his detachment arrived in Budapest September 20, 1944.

REVIVAL OF THE OPPOSITION

The shock of the occupation and arrest of prominent members had left the opposition Hungarian Front in disarray. Any opposition had become extremely difficult under German domination, especially since the leaders had been arrested by the Gestapo or forced into hiding. Gradually, the group began to rally as it seemed safe to move about more freely; the grapevine began to operate and parties that had once formed the Independence Front began to come together to formulate a common strategy against the German occupation. The group, with its extremely varied political and class interests, had very different views of the future; they were united only by their anti-German and anti–Arrow Cross stance. At the time, the only possibility for an opposition movement seemed to lie in persuading Horthy to stand at the head of the resistance.

In the middle of May, at a meeting at the villa of Marquis György Pallavicini, representatives of the Independent Smallholders, Legitimists, Social Democrats, and the Peace Party agreed on a manifesto calling on the Hungarian people to defeat the German conquerors and establish a free democratic Hungary. The Independent Smallholders were able to build up regular contacts with their imprisoned party leader, Bajczy-Zsilinsky, and Zoltán Tildy in hiding. The Communist Party, now the Peace party, despite its small numbers still had a working organization and reestablished contact with Szakasits and Tildy. They managed to print and distributed some leaflets. The Social Democrat representatives, Szakasits and Kádár, aimed to bring the unions into the plans. In the name of the Hungarian Front a leaflet was issued in early June, signed by the Peace party, Independent Smallholders, and Social Democrats, calling on the workers, peasants, and intelligentsia to resist.[164]

The establishment of many small resistance groups showed a growing opposition to the German occupation among the population. One called the Hungarian Patriots Freedom Alliance published leaflets and illegal newspapers. An opposition group gathered around Albert Szent-Györgyi, joined by the followers of János Vázsonyi, prepared to carry out armed resistance. In Budapest on the premises of the Taurus firm, they began to gather weapons and train their members, most who had never held a gun in their hands. University students also founded the National Resistance Student Movement.[165]

The strength of opposition grew with the increased Allied bombing and the advance of the Soviet armies during the summer and began to affect more influential circles, especially with the success of the Allied landing in Normandy. There was no question of active resistance from below—although worker morale was low there was no sabotage in the factories—but meetings and contacts multiplied. There were regular contacts between the Independent Smallholders, the Social Democrats, and representatives of the Peace party, as well as with representatives of some circles in both the Roman Catholic and Protestant churches. Legitimist spokesman G. Pallavicini again agreed to cooperate with the Left. Contact with the castle was reestablished through the regent's son, Nicky, and his assistants. At the time, all but the Communists still hoped to made contact with the Western Allies.[166]

After the Romanian change of sides and appointment of the Lakatos government, the Hungarian Front set up an Executive Committee as an action committee, with Árpád Szakasits, the oldest member, as president.[167] In early October members of the Front in contact with Horthy Jr. managed to get a memorandum taken to the regent's office listing their goals. The main points were the need to leave the war, to turn the fight against the Germans, and to set up a coalition government. They stressed that these measures would require careful political and military preparations. The Peace party, again named the Communist Party, insisted on armed action and organized its own military commission. However, Horthy rejected a suggestion made by László Rajk to Horthy Jr. that armed workers be used, saying that he didn't want a bloodbath with Germans shooting the population. On October 10, the Communists and Social Democrats agreed to organize a united front, and when the Hungarian Front had received no response from Horthy they sent a second memorandum in which they made no conditions for taking part in the fight against the German occupiers.[168]

Horthy finally announced that he would meet with representatives of the Hungarian Front, Zoltán Tildy and Árpád Szakasits on the evening of October 11, although he refused to meet with a Communist representative. It was planned that Mihály Hőgye, an acquaintance, would drive Tildy to a rental building directly across from the Foreign Ministry on Disz Square, where they would meet Szakasits. After a short discussion the two would go on to the castle. The day was full of excitement: who would take part in the discussion at Disz Square, with what password would they get past the fully armed guard at the castle, how should one dress for a meeting with Horthy? Szakasits wanted to dress in a dinner jacket—to which Tildy replied: "Tell him then that I won't go anywhere."[169]

On October 11, the day the preliminary armistice was signed in Moscow, Hőgye drove Szakasits and Tildy from their secret hiding places to the castle. The meeting lasted an hour and a quarter. On their return the two men recounted their experiences to Hőgye, who was waiting in the car. While the regent had been recounting, loquaciously, of his love for the Hungarian people, Tildy began to feel uncomfortable, fearing that no important question would be discussed, and finally interrupted the regent. Supposedly they got him to agree that after the war Tildy would form a coalition government and carry out land reform.[170]

Afterward the participants wrote their own accounts of the meeting. In his memoirs, Horthy wrote that the meeting had come to nothing; Tildy wrote that the regent said he had come to a final decision and in a few days would make the deciding step. Szakasits wrote in more detail, saying that in the name of the Hungarian Front they expressed the need to leave the war urgently, set up a coalition government between the Front and the army, and to arm the workers of Budapest's factories and protect the bridges and railroads. According to Szakasits, Horthy agreed to weapons for the workers and to the coalition government. He did not speak of an approaching cease-fire and the conditions but said that the decisive step would be around October 18. On this basis the Hungarian Front prepared their actions.[171]

Later Szakasits told a party congress that a plan had been made by which workers would announce a general strike on October 17 and start huge peace protests in and around Budapest. This would bring out police detachments and then they would use trusted troops who would join the workers and possibly give them arms. Horthy's decision to start the action early—on a Sunday—precluded any possibility of worker participation.

After the signing in Moscow, Horthy asked the Soviet military leadership to halt the attack by the Red Army troops in order to allow enough troops from the front to come to Budapest or the surrounding area, but the transfer of Hungarian units to Budapest was slow and drawn out. The reinforcements ordered by the regent did not arrive, partly because of betrayal, a bombing attack, and the blowing up of a railroad bridge. Chief of Staff János Vörös, who was not trusted by the regent or his close advisors, was not fully informed of the plan and did not know exactly how it was to be carried out, even though he alone had the right to give a command to the Royal Hungarian Army troops.[172]

Horthy instructed his trusted commanders, Béla Miklós and Lajos Dálnoki-Veress, commanders of the First and Second armies respectively, to establish contact with the Soviet army the moment they would receive his orders and then to stop fighting, but they did not share the information with their subalterns and failed to make preparations. The commander of the First Army Corps, Lt. Gen. Szilárd Bakay, who was to play an important role in the bailout, was kidnaped by the Germans on October 8.[173]

The date of the planned announcement of a provisional armistice with the Soviets was set for October 20, although Horthy had not informed the Soviet government of this date. On the morning of October 14, the regent decided that he would wait no longer but would announce the armistice the next day, making the decision without consulting anyone outside his immediate group. It is not known what determined his decision, but it was probably influenced by the increasingly worsening war situation, especially since reinforcements from the Tenth Division became impossible after the railroad bridge at Csap was blown up. Horthy was also receiving reports of the German reinforcement of their troops around Budapest and Arrow Cross preparations for a takeover, as well as Faragho's insistence from Moscow that he must begin military measures.[174]

On October 14, Horthy informed the abbreviated Council of Ministers of the necessity to agree to an armistice. Without knowing that the preconditions had already been determined, they proceeded to work out the conditions. Both Lakatos and Vörös warned that the necessary preparations had not been made and that the attitude of the officers' corps was unclear. Lakatos, who thought the wording of the proclamation to be too harsh, made one change which proved to be crucial; he deleted the sentence "from this day Hungary considers herself to be at war with Germany."[175]

October 15—Szálasi Takeover

On the morning of October 15, during the operation Panzerfaust, a German contingent commanded by SS Maj. Otto Skorzeny, kidnapped the regent's son, Nicky, who had been active for months in an organization nicknamed the Bail-Out Bureau, establishing contact with anti-Nazi and left-wing elements. He was lured from the castle to meet with supposed partisans of Tito. Skorzeny's target had originally been the regent, but the German High Command decided that Horthy's obedience could be gained by holding the son hostage. Horthy had ordered his son not to leave the castle, but he had given him permission to negotiate with the Tito representatives, believing the meeting would take place in the castle. At the time that Nicky entered the building to meet the Tito agents the building was already surrounded by Skorzeny's detachment. When two of Skorzeny's men entered the building, Horthy's escort opened fire. After a few minutes of shooting, Horthy Jr. was captured and badly beaten, then rolled inside a carpet, and driven off to the airport to be taken first to Vienna and then to Mauthausen.[176]

Horthy had called for a meeting of the Crown Council at 11 A.M. Shortly before the meeting, as the Hungarian cabinet and Horthy's aides assembled in the castle, his daughter-in-law told him of Nicky's kidnapping. The regent was shocked but pulled himself together and the Crown Council started only half an hour late.[177] Horthy railed against the Germans who had kidnapped his son, and then announced that he had decided to ask for an armistice but without informing the cabinet of the secret negotiations. As prearranged, Lakatos offered the resignation of the cabinet on the grounds that he had promised the leaders of Parliament to consult them before concluding an armistice. Horthy accepted the resignation but refused to consult Parliament, citing his right as Supreme War Lord. He said he would reappoint those who would support him, and to his astonishment and that of Lakatos, all the ministers agreed, including the pro-Germans, Jurcsek and Reményi-Schneller, and the Crown Council unanimously accepted the plan.[178]

The meeting was adjourned because of the arrival of Veesenmayer for a meeting that had been scheduled the day before. With Lakatos and Hennyey in attendance Horthy attacked Veesenmayer, recounting the German anti-Hungarian actions, the kidnapping of his son, that Germany had plundered Hungary and failed to keep a single promise, and announced that he would ask for an armistice. According to his promise to Hitler he was giving notice that Hungary was about to withdraw from the war. Veesenmayer went pale and begged Horthy at least to receive Ambassador Rahn, who had come to Budapest to consult with him. He left shortly before 1 P.M.

The reading of the proclamation was delayed because of the caution of those Horthy had entrusted to carry out the carefully timed procedure. As planned, Ilona Horthy had been listening to the Veesenmayer meeting in the next room, and the minute it was over went to inform Ambrózy to give the word. The old lawyer asked whether they shouldn't ask the regent if he wanted to change the wording after his talk with Veesenmayer. "I couldn't believe my ears. Why this stalling?"[179] Then she saw Endré Hlatky, who was supposed to be waiting at the Radio Central. She agreed to wait with Ambrózy but said that Hlatky should leave immediately and await the decisions at the radio station. They entered Horthy's office after Veesenmayer left, and Tost asked if the proclamation had been announced, but Lakatos answered that they must wait until Ambassador Rahn arrived. The regent heard this with the greatest astonishment, saying that he didn't understand—why had the proclamation not gone out. See that it happens immediately. Ambrozy, who was at the door, hurried to the telephone.[180] The proclamation was read over the state radio at 1 P.M. at the time people were enjoying their Sunday dinner, but it only stated that Hungary was "about to conclude a military armistice with our former enemies and to cease all hostilities against them," leaving out the clause that Lakatos had deleted—that "from this day Hungary considers herself to be at war with Germany." As the Supreme Commander of the Army Horthy called on soldiers to carry out faithfully and unconditionally his commands given through the commanders he had appointed, and on every Hungarian to follow him on this path "of saving the Hungarian nation."[181]

Rather than the electrifying impact that had been expected, the reaction was subdued and apprehensive. How would the Germans respond? How would the Soviets act? A good deal of confusion existed about the state of affairs, not only among officers in the field but also at general staff headquarters in Budapest. The Hungarian Front was caught totally unaware. Frantic efforts were made in the afternoon to patch together a plan of action, but the workers had not yet been provided with weapons and a general strike on a Sunday was not likely to have much effect. Around 1:30 P.M. there was a second reading.[182]

The troops had not gotten the needed orientation and remained immobile. At the most, some units prepared for an attack from all sides. In Budapest in the afternoon the units were put into a waiting position, while the commander of the First Army Corps, Lt. Gen. Béla Aggteleky, was taken prisoner by his own officers led by Iván Hindy. In the same way his subalterns captured Lt. Col. Kálmán Hardy, the commander of the river forces. Officers of the staff who were for holding out as German allies to the very end, Staff Col. Lajos Nádás and Staff Lt. Col. György Porzezinsky did everything in their power to make sure the bailout would fail.[183]

In a fateful step, Vörös sabotaged the whole enterprise. He and his aides had agreed earlier not to allow hostilities between German and Hungarian troops. Shortly before 3 P.M. he authorized a message to all field commanders that stated that the proclamation meant only that armistice negotiations would be embarked on. In the meantime, the war would go on and the troops were to defend themselves—in effect continuing the fight against the Red Army. His order was broadcast on the radio later that afternoon.[184]

Vörös's message may have been decisive for those officers, who otherwise would have sided with the regent if they had realized his true intentions. But the majority of officers were appalled on hearing Horthy's radio proclamation, which they regarded as treason against the Germans. They were not prepared to stab their former ally in the back. The coded message did go out to the two commanders in the field. The commander of the First Army, General Béla Miklós, went over to the Soviets with a few aides but without his troops, who fell under the command of officers still loyal to the Germans. The commander of the Second Army, General Lajos Dálnoki-Veress, was preparing to line up his units to do the same but was arrested by German officers. A few Hungarian units went over to the Soviets or retreated but there was not much disruption.[185]

One eyewitness describes a seemingly quiet Sunday morning, although something in the air was oppressive. The newspaper was full of calming news from the front while the radio played the usual boring program.

We knew that the . . . German troops were pulling back from the Duna-Tisza and the Red Army was moving with its relentless force from Szeged in the direction of Budapest. Then the radio announcement at 13:27 with Horthy's speech—which really is vague, doesn't say a great deal, although seems to signal withdrawal. In his command to the army, he says that it is decided they will ask for a ceasefire—not that they have done it already. That they should all follow his command. But not really clear what the command is. Later heard an unfamiliar voice—János Vörös—the chief of staff—reading out a command to continue resistance, Hungarian troops to keep on fighting! Then, at first Hungarian marches—but then German marches: Erika, Lili Marleen, Prinz Eugen March— and brutal German voices.[186]

Most of the afternoon Horthy was unaware of the plan miscarrying. He reconvened the meeting of the Crown Council at 2:30 P.M. and told of the negotiations with Veesenmayer and his instructions to his army commanders, but he still did not reveal that an armistice had already been signed. The ministers, most of whom were unpleasantly surprised by the regent's proclamation, were uneasy with the absence of detailed plans for dealing with German countermeasures.

Horthy began to realize that things had gone wrong in the late afternoon when the radio station seized by German forces began to broadcast a "war command to the armed nation" by Szálasi, and the order by Vörös for the troops to continue to fight. By late evening it seemed that only the castle with its three-hundred-man force remained securely under the regent's command. Lakatos and Hennyey, who tried to reach a compromise with Veesenmayer, only now learned of the preliminary armistice.

Lakatos suspected the cabinet would never accept such severe terms. Horthy—weary and dejected—apparently agreed that the terms were unacceptable.[187] Meanwhile German troops occupied Budapest and the most important public buildings, the Hungarian radio offices and the barracks. Not long after, the radio broadcast Szálasi's battle command—and requested that General Károly Beregfy report to Budapest.

Lakatos, Vattay, and Ambrózy dreamed up a plan that the regent would abdicate allowing the Germans to appoint the government they wanted, and Horthy and family to be taken under protection. But Lakatos insisted Horthy be consulted. Vattay woke him up after midnight and Horthy, irritated, perhaps disoriented, angrily rejected the proposal. Vattay, fearing the danger to the lives of Horthy and his family decided to take the initiative and on his own reported to Lakatos that the regent approved their proposed settlement in its entirety. Around 4 A.M., General Lázár, realizing an attack on the castle was imminent, awakened the regent and persuaded him to send his wife, Ilona, and grandson to the papal nuncio's. Unaware of Lakatos's negotiations, Horthy decided if the Germans attacked he would order resistance. Around 5 A.M., he and Vattay were sitting on the steps of the castle loading their pistols. Suddenly Lázár appeared, saying that Lakatos had phoned and had directed that military conflict was to be avoided at all costs.[188]

Several minutes later, Lakatos arrived with Veesenmayer in a German military car at the main entrance. Lakatos reported that a tentative agreement had been reached with the Germans and urged Horthy to call off resistance and accept. Veesenmayer said the attack would begin in twelve minutes and Horthy gave in. Veesenmayer suggested taking the regent to the nearby Hatvany Palace—Horthy went meekly. The whole event proceeded with such formality and politeness that Hungarian officers observing from a distance didn't realize they were witnessing the arrest of the regent and his entourage.

In his memoirs Horthy explains that only in 1947 did he realize why both he and Veesenmayer were so perplexed with the situation. Veesenmayer had learned from Lakatos that the regent had accepted the plan proposed by Lakatos, Vattay, and Ambrózy during the night, and the Germans thought the regent had completely capitulated. Horthy explained:

Shortly before 6 A.M. Dr. Veesenmayer appeared and asked me to go to the Hatvany Palace, "to spare me the pain of seeing the occupation of the Royal Palace." That, I thought, was a definite, if courteous, form of arrest. On our arrival at the

Hatvany Palace, the headquarters of the SS, Dr. Veesenmayer said "Here Your Highness is under the Führer's protection." My reply to that was that I had sought no one's protection and did not consider that I needed it in my own country. Dr. Veesenmayer stared at me in amazement. My words were as incomprehensible to him as his behavior was to me.[189]

In the early hours of October 16, a short fight broke out in the castle between the German assailants and the bodyguard who had not been notified of the agreement. The fight left several dead. This was the end of the attempted bailout.

Szálasi appeared before Horthy twice, at noontime and at 7 P.M., but Horthy refused to appoint him prime minister. The Germans, intent on preserving the face of constitutional procedure, threatened Horthy that they could only guarantee his safety and that of his family if he were to appoint Szálasi and abdicate. Finally, to protect his son from the brutal measures threatened, Horthy gave in, but only after receiving Veesenmayer's word of honor that his son would join him on his train the next day in Austria. On October 17 he and his family were taken under guard to the western train station, Horthy in hunting attire since his clothing had been stolen by German soldiers.[190] His son, of course, did not join him, although he later learned that Veesenmayer had made repeated attempts to keep his word to obtain his son's return, even approaching Ribbentrop, Baron Dörnberg, and others in the Foreign Ministry and Himmler himself.[191]

Thus began the catastrophic reign of Szálasi and the Arrow Cross.

9   From Arrow Cross Rule to Soviet Occupation

The failure of Horthy's attempted armistice with the Soviets and the ensuing Szálasi putsch was a catastrophe for Hungary, prolonging the war for five agonizing months. Instead of an armistice the country was subjected to the "most destructive fighting ever to take place on Hungarian soil."[1] On October 16 the Arrow Cross government began its efforts to establish Szálasi's vision of the Hungarista state, while Arrow Cross hoodlums initiated a reign of terror against the Jewish inhabitants of Budapest. Yet the Szálasi administration governed only Budapest and western Hungary. The Soviets had already taken over much of the eastern half of the country, initiating the exodus of primarily middle-class officials, professionals, and property owners who tried to escape from the Bolshevik Red Terror. In the western half of the country the former opposition leaders began to organize a Hungarian resistance, but the resistance was in its infancy, its leaders naive and inexperienced, counting on support from the Red Army, although it is doubtful whether the Soviets ever had any intention of providing support. During the bitter siege of Budapest, which was to last from Christmas 1944 until February 12, 1945, the city was destroyed, as the whole country turned into a battlefield between German and Soviet forces.

The Arrow Cross Putsch

A few hours after the failed armistice on October 15 an announcement was made that Ferenc Szálasi had been appointed the new prime minister, entrusted with the temporary direction of state affairs. The announcement gave the appearance of legality to the change of government, although it was not until the next day that Horthy finally gave his assent to the appointment.[2] The German and the Arrow Cross leadership had prepared for resistance, issuing numerous orders, including a curfew and a ban on assembly, but the measures were not needed; the population greeted the change passively. Shops and factories remained closed in Budapest on October 16 but trams and buses ran as usual, and on the morning of the October 17 factories had resumed production and shops were open. There were only a few absentees among the ministerial staff, amazing the Arrow Cross leadership who had expected resistance.[3]

Following a meeting of the Council of Regency on October 27, which discussed whether Horthy's abdication was authentic, the ceremony for Szálasi's swearing in was prepared. On November 3, Szálasi took the oath as leader of the nation at the Royal Castle before the Holy Crown, swearing to uphold Hungary's laws and ancient customs. He became simultaneously prime minister and head of state, essentially assuming the role of a dictator. Although Parliament was not dissolved, actual power was in the hands of the Arrow Cross. Only 55 members out of the 370 members of the lower house appeared when Parliament convened on November 2, but most public officials complied with the required oath to Szálasi as national leader, and Cardinal Serédi advised all Catholic school teachers to comply, probably to keep the schools intact.[4] Many military officers, like the long-time officer, Jenő Major, who was named commander of the Second Army on October 16, did not question taking the oath to Szálasi as new commander of the army. Major had always been loyal to legal authority and never got involved in daily politics.[5]

Szálasi, believing that Hungary's only hope lay in full cooperation with the Germans, placed the country's material resources completely at the disposal of German military interests. The amount to be paid to the Germans was raised from the monthly 200 million pengő to 300 million. Szálasi hoped to raise fourteen new army divisions based on the idea of national service for all. The government ordered general mobilization, threatening the population with the coming Soviet atrocities, and issued a flood of orders calling up all different categories of the population, but the result was so chaotic that the orders had to be rescinded. There were no arms—not even uniforms—for the supposed new recruits.

Szálasi planned to reorganize the country on the basis of his confused ideology of national unity. The Hungarista state, to be known as Hungarian United Ancient Lands, was to encompass the Danubian basin, including all the Magyar-populated territories, as well as areas inhabited by non-Magyar nationalities, Slovaks, Ruthens, Croats, and so on. The Magyars would have the dominant position, but other nationalities would enjoy administrative and cultural autonomy; Szálasi had no doubt that all peoples would be happy under Magyar supremacy.[6]

The constitution of the Hungarista state had been prepared long before, with numerous projects worked out in minute detail. Work began for a complete restructuring of the life of the nation, to build a new social-political system for the independent Hungarista state. The plan of national reconstruction included the reorganization of the economy and society on a corporatist basis, similar to Mussolini's corporative system. The corporatist model, in which the economy was collectively managed by employers, workers and state officials at the national level, had gained many supporters in Europe during the 1930s and early 1940s.[7]

Replacement of personnel in the military leadership and higher positions in the state apparatus began immediately. All of the institutions, organizations and schools were placed under the so-called Home Army Command by the end of the month, and ministers and leading functionaries began to occupy themselves with the "work plan for the building of the country." In grandiloquent terms the leader of the cultural office, Kálmán Hubay, explained that the new state would establish the intellectual face of the Hungarista Empire, meaning to establish Hungary as the leading nation of southeastern Europe in the greater European community.[8]

Yet, except for a few hastily issued decrees, none of the projects could be realized, since the advancing Soviet troops occupied ever-increasing portions of the country. The Germans allowed Szálasi and his regime to function unhampered, as the takeover gave the illusion of a continuation of the Horthy regime. Even the Arrow Cross terror was useful to them since it took care of police functions.[9] But there was no clear division of power under the Szálasi regime. The Germans, concerned with fighting the Soviets, controlled the military; the Arrow Cross was trying to establish its authority, and inevitably at times the two came into conflict. In addition to the German military and police, there were three other armed groups: a relatively large number of mostly disciplined armed Arrow Cross troops, a mob numbering in the thousands wearing the Arrow Cross armband and carrying guns, and the conventional police and military forces who often obeyed the Arrow Cross leadership reluctantly or even resisted some of their orders.[10]

Arrow Cross members immediately began terrorist actions against alleged leftists and Jews. In a new round of political arrests thousands were taken, including the biochemist and Nobel Prize winner, Albert Szent-Györgyi, and the resistance group around him, as well as former Prime Minister Kállay and his son. All were transported to German concentration camps. The state security system, the Hungarian Gestapo, and the military security service were reorganized. Party members, supervising the activities of the state, had power to decide who should live and who should die, instilling fear into the hearts of the population.

The Arrow Cross mob, which carried out most of the atrocities, was made up of those attracted to the party by the possibility of spoils, the uniform, guns, and the Arrow Cross armband. By October 15, 1944 many of the intelligentsia who had joined the Arrow Cross in 1938 at the high point of the movement had left the party. Of the forty-nine representatives elected to Parliament in 1939, only two took part in the Arrow Cross takeover.[11] One Arrow Cross man explained to the young Jewish woman he was escorting to the collection area, that he was a barber by profession but had joined the Arrow Cross since the supreme leader had promised him a higher position.[12]

MEASURES AGAINST THE JEWS

The Ministry of the Interior under Gábor Vajna, which began to function soon after the Arrow Cross putsch, worked out a plan to divide the Jews into five categories: Jews under foreign protection, baptized Jews, members of the clergy of the Jewish race, Jews possessing certificates of distinction, and all of the rest of the Jews in Budapest. The first four categories were to enjoy total or partial exemption, which was important since there was a flood of new protective passes issued, either real or forged, with the number rising from 15,000 to 33,000 within a few weeks.[13] Of those in the last category of about 125,000, the able-bodied men aged sixteen to sixty were requisitioned for military forced labor service, and women sixteen to forty were called up to wash and mend soldiers' clothing.[14] Most of the men were set to work digging trenches around Budapest. Ironically, the Hungarian military in many cases saved Jewish men from deportation by calling them up for labor service.[15] The protected, but not exempted Jews, about 33,000, were moved into smaller international ghettos, where they were sometimes butchered by Germans or Arrow Cross members. Hundreds were dragged down to the banks of the Danube, tied together and shot.

Szálasi, who considered himself a good Christian, seriously believed in the theory of a worldwide Jewish conspiracy. His Hungarista ideology differentiated between anti-Semitism and "asemitism"—the removal of Jews—which was to be achieved not through extermination but through resettlement; now under the pressure of manpower shortages, he first wanted them to work for the good of Hungary. The Germans, who wanted construction of a huge wall of fortifications along the Austro-Hungarian border, had already sent demands for 50,000 able-bodied men to be taken to the German Reich. Szálasi replied that only a Jewish work force was available, and he could send only the limited number of 25,000.

The transfer of the first work force began on November 2 at Hegyeshalom. Because of the lack of transportation the unfortunate workers had to set out for the border on foot. Along with the deplorable conditions they were treated with horrendous brutality and a number of them perished on the way.[16]

Szálasi could not ignore the deteriorating military situation, and Veesenmayer finally persuaded him to send a total of 50,000 Jews to the Reich, the males to work on the wall and the females to work in war production factories. According to Eichmann, who was once more in Budapest, 27,000 started for the German-Hungarian border on November 13. On the same day Veesenmayer mentioned that they could count on another 40,000 able-bodied Jews, of which two to four thousand would start out every day. Eventually, the Arrow Cross, Hungarian gendarmes, soldiers, and police deported thousands of Jews, marching them to the border—the old and the sick, as well as young children, of whom great numbers died along the roads.[17]

In late November Szálasi seemingly had a change of heart; after first announcing that the women workers could leave only with transportation, he ordered the forced marches to be stopped entirely. He was greatly concerned that his government receive international recognition, thus his decision was affected by the protests from neutral countries and the Papal Nuncio, but also possibly because of protests by the Germans themselves. Even Himmler sent a critical comment and SS Lt. Col. Kurt Becher commented that the forced marches were pure murder.[18]

The German leadership itself was divided. In his quest for a separate peace, the Reich SS leader Himmler had ordered the extermination camps to be shut down in November, probably without Hitler's knowledge, and afterward the Germans were only interested in receiving able-bodied Jews from Hungary. Eichmann, on the other hand, strove for the total elimination of the Budapest Jews, and was supported by Foreign Minister Ribbentrop. After learning that Szálasi had stopped the massive deportations he sent a first-class telegram to Veesenmayer, urging him to explain to Szálasi that a speedy elimination of the Jews was essential for the defense of the capital.[19]

On November 21 Veesenmayer had to report that it would be impossible to reach the 50,000 Szálasi had promised, and at the end of November Eichmann regretfully announced that only 38,000 could be taken although another 20,000 trench diggers were needed. The last train of deportees took off in the first days of December with an estimated 3,000 to

3,600 Jews, and on December 11 the last march on foot started from the Budapest detention barracks with 1,200 prisoners.[20]

By early November it appears that Szálasi and his administration had decided on the manner in which they would resolve the Jewish question. On November 3 an order confiscated all Jewish property for the benefit of the state, with the exception of a fortnight's supply of food, fuel, a few articles of personal use, and a nominal supply of cash. Plans were made to establish the Budapest central ghetto. The plans were handed over to a representative of the Jewish Council on November 18. The proposed area had housed up to then about 7,000 people and contained 162 star-marked buildings, only 18 of which were inhabited solely by Jews. The Christians living there were to move out, given a list of buildings to which they could move, or told they could take over any evacuated Jewish apartment. It was calculated this would make up 4,725 rooms for about 63,000 Jews—thirteen to fourteen people per room. On December 2 all non able-bodied Jews were ordered to move to the ghetto, with the exception of those with safe-conduct passes. Approximately 70,000 Jews were forced to move; the number of those with safe-conduct passes and those who were in hiding is impossible to establish.[21]

Conditions in the crowded ghetto were catastrophic. The most serious problems were caring for the sick and food to feed the inhabitants. The Jewish Council did its best to provide food supplies and safety, but their resources were extremely limited. They could count on some help from the diplomatic corps, the International Red Cross, and Budapest representatives of the Red Cross in Budapest. Members of the Arrow Cross prevented the delivery even of what was provided by the officials of the capital. The number of deaths was increased by the terror attacks of the Arrow Cross bands, who attacked hospitals, homes, and the streets and dragged the Jews to the banks of the Danube and shot them. After the Soviets had pushed the frontline closer to Budapest, SS General Winkelmann put up a guard of SS soldiers to protect the ghetto. The Germans feared that the continuing atrocities could provoke an uprising and endanger the protection of the city.[22]

There were numerous individuals who worked to rescue the Jews personally or through institutions. Many Christian families, priests, and ministers offered their own homes, provisions, and even lent their own baptismal certificates. In their efforts they often put their own security at risk. Ferenc Dira, a small boy at the time living in Óbuda, a poor section and factory center on the outskirts of Budapest, told how they tried to help. "[W]e took bread to the ghetto . . . the yellow star house on Mókus street next to the Goldberger factory. We had to look around carefully not to be observed—we did it as good Catholics."[23]

The Arrow Cross had set up their headquarters on Bécsi Street 71 and moved out the inhabitants. For two months, starting on October 15, the Arrow Cross terrorized the country. Dira, who was walking on the street with his mother, recalled seeing one group of Jews who were being taken away. "An old woman who had been shopping pulled a piece of bread out of her basket and gave it to a Jewish woman who immediately hid it. The Arrow Cross saw it—shot the woman dead, not the Jewish woman but the Christian who was trying to help."[24] His mother quickly took him by the hand and pulled him away.

A young woman, Alice Somlai, and her mother were one of the Christian families who had to move from their building when it was declared a Yellow Star house, but they were lucky to be able to trade with a wealthy Jewish family who had an elegant apartment on Andrássy Street. Alice recounted a traumatic experience she had while taking help to the ghetto:

Someone in our building had an acquaintance in the ghetto. Wanted some food taken to them. We lived not too far away at the beginning of Andrássy street. The people lived at Klausal Square, which was in the ghetto. One could visit between 12 and 2. At the time people didn't have identity papers but I had a passport since I had been in Italy in 1937, so I could show my papers and go in. I was also blonde and blue-eyed which helped. The ghetto was surrounded by police, but I showed my passport. What I saw was horrifying. In a three room apartment one room with people lying side by side on straw. A long line in front of the bathroom. As I started to leave, a policeman stopped me—asked where I thought I was going. I showed my passport but he said that Alice was a man's name, even though my photo was on the passport. He said it was not mine and didn't want to let me out. I started to cry. As luck would have it an acquaintance was passing by and recognized me. He bawled out the policeman and got me let free.[25]

She could have been kept there, her passport thrown away, and sent to her death.

Besides the numerous personal stories, the best-documented rescue efforts are those of the embassies remaining in Budapest. Neutral countries protested and those embassies still functioning organized rescue operations, mainly by giving out safe-conduct passes, The Swedish Embassy under Ambassador Carl Ivan Danielsson had been the first to issue letters of safe conduct after the German occupation, and the Vatican diplomat,

Monsignor Angelo Rotta, eventually issued more than 15,000 safe-conduct certificates and baptismal certificates, offering the protection of Vatican neutrality; he personally protected numerous safe houses throughout Budapest.[26] Carl Lutz, a Swiss diplomat, issued protective passports from the Swiss embassy. The Portuguese diplomat, Carlos Barnquinho, supplied protection papers. Friedrich Born, chief delegate of the International Red Cross issued 1,300 identity cards. The El Salvador Embassy distributed 800 special certificates of citizenship. The Nicaraguan Embassy distributed 500.

The Italian businessman, Giorgio Perlasca, became an unusual volunteer as a Spanish diplomat. After escaping from German internment, he had taken refuge in the Spanish Embassy where he posed as a Spanish diplomat and joined in life-saving missions with Spanish Chargé d'Affaires Angel Sanz-Briz. But when Sanz-Briz left for Spain on November 29, Perlasca announced that he had been left as chargé d'affaires designate, and as such he was able to save occupants of the Spanish-protected houses.[27]

The well-known Swedish humanitarian, Raoul Wallenberg, together with fellow Swedish diplomat Per Anger, used their diplomatic status by issuing protective passports, which identified the bearers as Swedish subjects awaiting repatriation. Although not legally valid these documents looked official and were generally accepted by German and Hungarian authorities, who sometimes were also bribed. The Swedish legation also succeeded in negotiating with the Germans that the bearers of the protective passes would be treated as Swedish citizens and be exempt from having to wear the yellow Star of David on their chests. With American money Wallenberg rented thirty-two buildings in Budapest and declared them to be extraterritorial, protected by diplomatic immunity. He put up signs such as "The Swedish Library" and "The Swedish Research Institute" on their doors and hung oversized Swedish flags on the front of the buildings to bolster the deception. The buildings eventually housed almost 10,000 people, one of whom was Tom Lantos, who became a member of the U.S. House of Representatives and served until his death on February 13, 2008.

One of Wallenberg's drivers, Sandor Ardai, recounted how Wallenberg intercepted a trainload of Jews about to leave for Auschwitz:

. . . he climbed up on the roof of the train and began handing in protective passes through the doors which were not yet sealed. Wallenberg ignored German orders to get down and the Arrow Cross shots and shouts and calmly continued handing out passports to the hands that were reaching out for them. After Wallenberg had handed over the last of the passports he ordered all those with a pass to leave the train and walk to the caravan of cars parked nearby, all marked in Swedish colors. He saved dozens off that train, and the Germans and Arrow Cross were so dumbfounded they let him get away with it.[28]

The protective passes were not necessarily respected by the Arrow Cross. Lilly Vigyazo told of being taken together with a group of Jews to a brick factory in Obuda, marched through the pouring rain:

We all marched along Andrassy street, crossed the Chain Bridge, going toward Obuda. We arrived at a brick factory which I recognized from an earlier time when I had been there on a chemistry trip. (It was part of studies into chemical technology to visit factories and study the manufacturing processes.) . . . I was saved by two things—my copy of the citizenship paper and my sense not to trust the men in charge. When I left the house my father had given me the original copy of the San Salvador citizenship paper. He had only one original and three copies—he hesitated a bit—and gave me the original. We had to cue in the court-yard. We were told if anyone had documents which would save them, to line up. People lined up, but I didn't trust them. After, they collected the documents they tore them up and threw them in the mud.

Next day, again, we had to go out in the courtyard. A man was ushered in, and a white table and white chair were set up. It must have been Wallenberg. He was elegantly dressed, with a fishbone material overcoat. He was not too tall with a somewhat stern face. Again, those with papers were told to cue. When I came to the table he looked carefully at my document. Said I could leave. I was escorted by two Arrow Cross to an open deck lorry. Taken to a place near the Keleti—had been some kind of school for deaf or blind children. It was being used for foreign subjects who were interned, American and English, mainly women.[29]

Churches and church organizations were one of the greatest resources to provide aid, especially the religious orders. The Benedictine monastery at Pannonhalma used its protection under the International Red Cross to offer refuge to the persecuted, while other religious orders without monastery buildings were also active.

The actions of some ten thousand nuns in schools, hospitals and social organizations have gone largely unrecognized, often known of only through personal remembrances. They rescued innumerable children, young girls and women by taking them into the convents and giving them monastic clothing. Among those that are known one of the bravest was Margit Slachta, the head of the Sisters of Social Service, who carried out rescue actions in the convent which was right across the street from the Arrow Cross quarters.[30] Among the sisters was Sára Salkaházi, who was shot by Arrow Cross thugs at the Danube along with the Jews she had hidden. Vilma Bernovits, a teacher of religion in a home for working girls, was reported for hiding Jews and securing baptismal certificates for them and was executed on December 27. Her main offense was that she had acted as godmother to twenty-four converts between July 11 and October 11.[31]

Church archives show the records of baptismal certificates given out and other life-saving actions. Baron Vilmos Apor, bishop of Győr, not only protested publicly but gave refuge to hundreds in his own home and personally went into the Győr ghetto to save lives. The Protestant churches and civil leadership made numerous protests and demanded action in a common front. But ministers and priests gave out baptismal certificates according to their own moral codes, some holding to the procedures which prevented the necessary haste; others who believed that providing help was their first Christian responsibility. For example, between July 1 and 19, 1944, 114 adults were baptized in the Budapest Rókus parish; on November 11, at the time of Arrow Cross rule, eighty baptisms are recorded on one day.[32]

Under a Red Cross section of the Protestant Good Shepherd Children's Action, Gábor Sztehlo, a Hungarian Lutheran pastor, organized an extremely successful rescue of Jewish children by setting up temporary children's homes. At his request homes were opened to the children in relatively small groups in various points of the city, especially on the Buda side of Budapest. Through his activities he saved approximately 1,600 children and 400 adults. He had first concentrated on saving converted Jews but he later saved those baptized or not, believing that he had to help wherever people were in danger.[33] A number of the children that he saved are still alive today, among them Gabor Vermes, professor emeritus of Rutgers University, who at the age of eleven was hidden in a children's home under the pretext that he and the other children were Christian refugees. The children prayed that the German officers, who came to hear them sing Bavarian songs would not learn their true identity. Vermes explained: "If the Germans suspected that you were Jewish, they would pull your pants down to see if you were circumcised."[34]

Near the end of the siege of Budapest some Arrow Cross men protected Jewish families in the hopes of gaining protection for themselves after the war. The family of Gabor Tamás was helped by an Arrow Cross member who worked with one of his father's business friends:

We lived in the cellar used for an air-raid shelter in the non-Jewish house. Heavy shooting started—after Horthy was removed. We had a warning that the Arrow Cross were going from cellar to cellar looking for Jews. A high-ranking Arrow Cross person who worked with a business friend of my father told us to get ready to move. The friend knew where we were. Uncle Gyula, the Arrow Cross guy, came for us—it was a cold morning. We went to Nádor Street—near the stock exchange. There was a big cellar—air raid cellar. Two rooms plus a small transit area. Lots of people in the big room. In the small one were my family, my father's friend, wife and child, and Uncle Gyulai. All stayed there. When the Arrow Cross came in, Uncle Gyula told them to go to Hell. (He came and went during that time.) He probably hoped to get protection when the war was over. After the war, when trials were held, he asked my father to testify that he had saved Jews. My father did testify even though he was criticized by other Jews.[35]

Yet despite efforts to help, it was the Soviet occupation in the end that saved the remaining Jews.

Hungary Becomes a Battleground

After Romania's withdrawal from the war Hungary became the primary theater of operations on the eastern front (see Map 4). The Red Army made a rapid advance across eastern Poland in the summer of 1944, but their advance stalled when they reached the Vistula in the second half of August. Although they captured the fortified suburb of Praga on the east bank of the river, they did not attack the main part of Warsaw on the west bank, even though the Warsaw Uprising had begun on August 1. Stalin had expected Warsaw to fall by early August but the Red Army, weakened by its long advance, met unexpected German resistance. The Soviets have been accused of standing idly on the banks of the Vistula while the Polish resistance fighters were being decimated, and the explanation for their conduct is still debated.[36] The Red Army made no progress further west in Poland until January 1945. Since the front in Poland remained firm at the Vistula, both sides were determined to resolve the stalemate in the central part of Eastern Europe.

While stalled at the Vistula, the Red Army achieved an unexpected triumph in its offensive against Romania by trapping large Axis forces in the space of a week. When the twenty-year-old King Michael overturned the government of Marshal Antonescu on August 23, the Royal Romanian

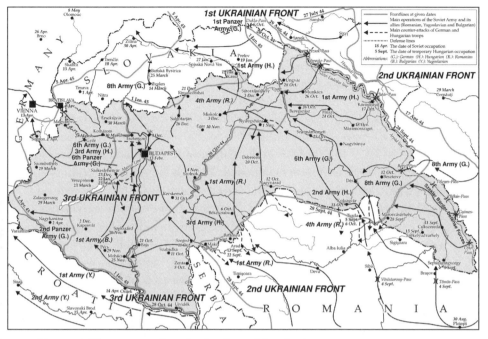

Map 4. Military operations in the Carpathian Basin, 1944–1945.

Army and Air Force turned against the Germans, supporting the Red
Army in its campaign against their old enemy, Hungary. The Red Army
entered Bucharest on the August 31 and within one week Soviet troops
overran most of country and entered the Carpathian Basin through the
passes of the Transylvanian Alps.

The Red Army reached Hungary much more quickly than planned
because of Romania's defection; the Soviets now hoped to repeat their
success and march through Hungary to the Austro-Bohemian border. But
to Hitler, holding the country was a high priority, and he had forbidden
the Hungarian capital to be declared a free city or abandoned. After the
loss of the Romanian oil fields he attached great importance to the oil
fields southwest of Lake Balaton at Nagykanizsa, and Budapest in its strategic position straddling the Danube commanded the main entry route to
Austria and Bohemia. It was also the main railway hub of the region and
the largest Danubian port. The campaign in Hungary turned out to be
much longer and more drawn out than the Soviets had expected.[37]

In early October the Second Ukrainian Front reached the border in
the south of the Alföld, the Great Hungarian Plain, which offered a wide,

flat expanse for their rapid progress. On October 6, acting together with the Third Ukrainian Front, under the command of Marshal Rodion Malinovskii, the Soviets began their general offensive, aiming to encircle Hungarian and German troops. Malinovskii's army took Szeged on the eleventh and Szabadka on the twelfth. His right wing drove up the left bank of the river almost as far as Debrecen, where the Germans had also concentrated their forces to prevent the encirclement of Axis forces in the northeastern regions of Hungary.

The arrival of the Hungarian delegation in Moscow and the Hungarian request for an armistice heightened Soviet hopes to advance quickly to Budapest and cross through the country. Therefore the Soviets pressured the Hungarian delegation to come to a rapid military agreement, but the delegation had expected diplomatic negotiations over a preliminary armistice and had no authority to conclude a military agreement. During the days immediately before October 15 the Soviets waited for Horthy to take action and for Hungarian troops to change sides. Stalin had instructed the troops to suspend active hostilities on the fronts of all three Hungarian armies while waiting for the armistice to be announced, but the failure of Horthy's armistice and the German-engineered Arrow Cross putsch ended that plan.

The political events taking place in Moscow and Budapest actually had little effect in the Alföld. In early October the Axis forces determined to hold the eastern Hungarian front at the Hungarian city of Debrecen in order to allow their forces to withdraw behind the Tisza. A violent tank battle for Debrecen took place from October 10 to 14 with terrible losses on both sides. Although the Red Army had captured the city by October 19, the battle was a marked Soviet defeat. The Germans lost 133 tanks, but the Soviets lost 500, more than 70 percent of their strength. They had lost their mobile forces necessary for the quick offensive toward Budapest.[38]

By October 24 Stalin had lost patience with the unsuccessful efforts to have Hungarian troops change sides. When General Béla Miklós, commander of the First Army, met up with the Soviets on October 17, he came without his troops because he feared they would not disobey Vörös's order to continue fighting. He and his adjutant, Kéri, were welcomed by the Soviets, and he sent letters to all his senior commanders that they should join the Russians who would arm them and set up a Hungarian Army of Liberation, but with no appreciable results. After ten days the Russians dropped the idea, and Stalin ordered that the Hungarian military be treated as enemies in the same way as the Germans.

The Soviet command determined to occupy Budapest and continue on to Vienna. More armies than ever before began to move onto Hungarian territory. By the end of October all of Transylvania, Ruthenia, Tiszantul, and half of the Alföld were in Soviet hands and the Red Army was only one hundred kilometers from Budapest.[39] Stalin wanted Soviet troops to push forward as rapidly as possible; he was already thinking in terms of territorial partition with the Allies and wanted to ensure his supremacy in Central Europe. On his visit to Moscow in October, at the time of the Hungarian armistice negotiations, Churchill had made Stalin nervous by mentioning the plan for Anglo-American troops to march through Ljubljana to the Carpathian basin a number of times. Underestimating the considerable German and Hungarian forces facing the Soviet troops, Stalin ordered Marshal Malinovskii on October 28 to take Budapest immediately; he ignored the reservations of General Antonov, chief of the Red Army's general staff, about deceptive reports on the forces around Budapest.

In their telephone conversation Stalin refused Marshall Malinovskii's request for five days to prepare: "The supreme command can't give you five days. . . . You must start the attack on Budapest without delay." Malinovskii countered: "If you give me five days I will take Budapest in another five days. If we start the offensive right now, the Forty-Sixth Army . . . will inevitably be bogged down. . . ." But Stalin would not relent: "There's no point in being so stubborn. You obviously don't understand the political necessity of an immediate strike against Budapest."[40] He ordered Malinovskii to begin the offensive against Budapest on the next day.

Following Stalin's orders, the Soviet army pushed forward in the direction of Budapest at the end of October, but they were sorely missing the tanks and armored vehicles lost in the battle at Debrecen, while the German and Hungarian armies still possessed some reserves. The Germans had been sending in a steady flow of reinforcements which they could afford to do only because the front in Poland was inactive. In September the number of divisions from the German Army Group South (*Heeresgruppe Süd*) had already reached eleven with four armored divisions. As Malinovskii had predicted, the Soviet advance got bogged down on the approaches to Budapest.

Meanwhile Soviet and Yugoslav units had gained a critical foothold west of the Danube by crossing the Drave, but the line remained stationary on the hills south of Pécs. Then, on November 29, Marshal Tolbukhin, commander of the Second Ukrainian Front, who had been bringing up troops from the Balkans, attacked in force with spectacular results. On a single day his troops entered the cities close to the Yugoslav border— Pécs, Mohács, and Bátaszék—as well as 330 inhabited localities. The troops established a bridgehead across the Danube that was forty kilometers deep and one hundred fifty kilometers wide, and then moved forward. By December 7 their line extended from Barcs on the Drave north to the southwest tip of Lake Balaton and from the northeastern extremity of the lake along a line just south of the Buda-Székesfehérvár road and railway to the Danube at Ercsi.[41]

The Germans did not actually consider the Soviet advance a defeat. They had not been driven beyond the line that they had established as the one where they proposed to make their stand. They had extricated practically all their troops from the dangerous positions of mid-October and inflicted more casualties than they suffered. Now they informed the Hungarians that they would hold the line until the following spring when the lost ground would be recovered.

But the retreat brought about a huge change in public opinion. The population was no longer convinced that German domination was better than Russian domination, especially if German domination meant exile. As yet Budapest had suffered little damage except for the Margit Bridge, which was destroyed on November 4. On the surface the peaceful routine of daily life continued, but with the influx of refugees and general confusion conditions had become exceedingly difficult. Jews were being marched to the border or to ghettos; columns of refugees marched through on their trek to the west. Official rations were cut drastically and often not available. Peasants were not willing to sell supplies in the market except in exchange for clothes or cigarettes. The fuel situation was even worse—unheated rooms, the supply of power for factories and trams in danger. The feeling was growing that resistance would only prolong the agony before inevitable defeat. For the Jews the approaching Soviet troops promised salvation, but for the rest of the population there was only a sense of foreboding.

The Soviet and Romanian conquest of northern Transylvania had started a massive flight of Hungarian refugees westward, which continued as Soviet troops advanced through eastern Hungary. In the city of Hajdúnánás near Debrecen part of the population of about 20,000 did not even wait for the Red Army to approach; the flood of refugees began on October 9 as the front approached the border of the county. The Hungarian authorities had ordered a compulsory evacuation, and the leading officials, as well as the civil servants, and a majority of the professionals—

doctors, teachers, and priests—left the city. The exodus to the west continued the following days; official propaganda about the Bolshevik Red Terror was reinforced by tales about Soviet soldiers' atrocities told by refugees from the already occupied Transylvanian territory.[42]

Margít Makláry from Hajdúnánás explained: "Nánas had not felt much of the war up until now—only once was there a heavy bombing which happened by mistake. . . . We hardly felt we were at war."[43] Her father, a reserve first lieutenant, had been able to remain in Hajdúnánás because of his title of *vitéz*.[44] But on October 7 her father came home saying they should begin to pack; they were to be resettled to Kapuvár in western Hungary on October 9.

Makláry, whose family was one of the few that returned to Hajdúnánás after the front had passed, continued: "Everything was organized. . . . They took the recruiting officers and their whole families. And not only we landed there, but the middle class who fled from the Russians. I don't know what happened to the mayor, where he landed, but the main clerk came with his family, our friends, the reformed minister, higher ranked police officers."[45]

Hitler had declared that under no circumstances could Budapest be given up. On December 4 he finally granted an audience to Szálasi, but he rejected Szálasi's plea that Budapest be declared a free city, saying that the German leadership should prepare for the defense of the city. As time went on the defense of Budapest had become a political issue. The Germans had transferred so many reinforcements that it was vitally important to produce results. By January the number of divisions operating in the country had reached twenty-two, with seven armored divisions, and by early March, thirty-one with ten armored divisions.[46]

On December 1 the Szálasi regime moved the headquarters of the government ministries and most of the state administration away from the capital to cities in the extreme west of Hungary—Szombathely, Sopron, and Kőszeg—setting up the provisional seat of government and Parliament in Sopron. Since Budapest was the administrative, industrial, and cultural center of Hungary, the regime lost much of its ability to govern. Partly on orders and partly voluntarily a number of public officials and public employees as well as their families moved to the western part of the country.[47] The government extended the compulsory evacuation to Arrow Cross members and their families, university teachers, and scientists, while some of those considered necessary to the population were officially forbidden to leave, including workers, doctors, and surviving Jews. The clergy were ordered not to leave by their superiors. The

Arrow Cross leadership also planned to move out all medical facilities. When asked what would happen to the Budapest population, the answer was: "There will be no more Hungarians in Budapest. The place for Hungarians and Hungarian soldiers is in the West." Although few peasants or workers left, the refugees placed a heavy burden on the communities in the west of the country.[48]

The Arrow Cross leadership planned to resettle all the universities to Germany, complete with their professors and students, but when the plan was proposed on November 30 the professorial faculties offered fierce resistance. One of the professors exclaimed: "If I have to perish, then I'll perish here, I won't take one step."[49] The government's answer was to mobilize the students by radio. Two trains transported students to Germany in December 1944, and a second transport of two trains in January 1945 went to Szombathely, but the universities succeeded in preventing the transport of books and many of the students. The scientific equipment of the universities was removed to Halle and Breslau along with a handful of teachers and students of the Technical University. One fourth-year student, Béla Zamory remembered being taken first to Breslau but then as the Red Army came closer moved to Dresden where he and his fellow students attended the local university.[50]

The government, despite having been removed from the capital to western Hungary, continued to make plans for the future. Parliament, with only about 10 percent of its membership, enacted bills including the approval of a provisional budget, and authorized itself to fill the vacancies in its own body. But in reality the government had lost control of the conduct of affairs. The territory still nominally under its control had disintegrated into small units similar to the situation in eastern Hungary. Where the military did not govern directly, it did so through the commissioner of the Operational Zone, but owing to the breakdown of communication the commissioner had to delegate most of his powers to local authorities.[51]

The government of the German Reich had come to an official agreement with the Szálasi government on November 14 for materials to be removed to Germany—including factory equipment, machinery, raw materials, agricultural products, hospital equipment, and art treasures—but the Germans also confiscated anything they wanted and could carry. In their retreat from the Great Hungarian Plain they stripped the big estates, taking agricultural materials, including live animals, machinery, and industrial raw materials. As they moved westward the German High Command ordered a policy of systematic industrial dismantling and removal in order to deny its use to the Red Army. The German and Hungarian forces destroyed much of the transportation infrastructure, blowing up railways, bridges, and roads, ripping up railroad tracks, and taking most of the rolling stock to Germany. Many merchant ships were sunk while the rest were taken to Germany along with autos and motor transport vehicles. About five hundred major factories were wholly or partially dismantled and much immovable property was destroyed by Nazi demolition experts.[52]

Yet worker resistance prevented the removal of much of the factory equipment. In Diósgyőr, Ózd, the Budapest Danuvia, the Mosonmagyaró-vári Vadásztöltény factory, and others, the workers blocked the taking of machinery or destroyed it.[53] In Salgótarján, assistant stationmaster József Hasznos was able to slow down the dismantling of the factories and even stop it completely for days since he was in charge of providing the empty railroad cars. This contributed to the fact that the machinery remained in Hungary so that production could start up again.[54]

József Hasznos recalled the effect of the German military order on his family in November 1944:

The front was coming close. The German military were in command. My father, also József Hasznos, aged twenty-nine, was deputy stationmaster of the Hungarian Royal State railway in Salgótarján, Nograd country. Mother was three years younger. Éva was born in 1942, and I was born in 1943. The Germans ordered us to empty out the station, pack up everything, and leave. We were to take all the equipment, telegraph equipment, etc. so the Russians would not be able to use the railroad station. . . . My father had planned carefully—he had slaughtered a pig, gathered sacks of potatoes, etc. to eat or to trade. We packed up all our stuff in a railroad car, leaving the furniture.

We started out headed for Hungarian territory—probably Galánta—but suddenly found ourselves on the Czech border at Tarno. We turned around and got back to Vienna. Father tried to return home—but he saw that the front had reached Győr, so he came back. The train was still there. We landed in Passau—had to get out—needed the car for soldier transport. Were taken by truck to Vilshofen, then Gelbersdorf, then Hofkirchen, a little village, where we were put up on the second floor of a peasant house. The German widow, Frau Schneider, was not happy—blamed the Hungarians for losing the war because they didn't want to fight. But with the food father had brought she became more pleasant.[55]

From Opposition to Resistance

Since the country had retained its sovereignty until the German occupation, it was only after Horthy's removal that leaders of the Hungarian

Front began to organize a true resistance movement. Until then the opposition had counted on Horthy to carry out a break with the Germans, and much of the military—violently opposed to the Russians—remained loyal to Horthy and the Germans. Now, after the Arrow Cross putsch, opposition leaders who had escaped arrest and were living in illegality began to regroup. They contacted each other in great secrecy to escape the attention of the Arrow Cross police state. New impetus to the embryonic movement came with the release of Endre Bajcsy-Zsilinszky, the main opposition leader, and Zoltán Tildy Jr., leader of the Independent Smallholders, along with several others. Horthy officials, honoring Horthy's promise to the leftist leaders, had bargained with the Germans to secure their release, which occurred on October 15, ironically the day of Horthy's failed bailout.[56]

Bajczy-Zsilinszky, under an assumed name, took refuge in the countryside, moving from one hiding place to another while meeting with friends and leaders of the Hungarian Front. Imre Kovács and Miklós Makay, head of the Nitrochemical Industrial firm, traveled to Bajczy-Zsilinszky's place of refuge to convince him to come to Budapest to head the resistance, and after hearing their plans, Bajczy accepted. Although the exact dates and participants are unclear, the Hungarian Front was recreated soon after his arrival. In their memoirs former participants mention numerous meetings, but since it was impossible to speak of the noncommunist resistance for so many years, their memories are not clear.[57]

The loosely linked members of the Hungarian Front had been united primarily by opposition to the Germans; the group was too heterogeneous to set up a policy or lead resistance. Thus it was decided to set up a united group to organize the antifascist struggle. On November 9, in order to avoid attracting notice, representatives of the various parties met at Szabadság square in front of the Nitrochemical Industrial firm, waiting for an all-clear sign from Imre Kovács to enter the office.[58] The men decided to establish an executive committee, the Liberation Committee of the Hungarian National Uprising (MNFFB), to lead the resistance movement, with Bajczy-Zsilinszky as president and Smallholders representative János Csorba as vice president.[59] The committee declared itself the legal representative of the people, versus the illegally established Arrow Cross regime, with the intention to carry out the actions planned by the regent on October 15.[60]

The resistance leaders began to organize feverishly. A number of groups of the former Hungarian Front joined the Liberation Committee—

the Independent Smallholders, Social Democrats, Legitimists, and the National Peasant's Party. The resistance leaders also took up contact with the communist resistance movement and its military committee. They were joined as well by the Hungarian Student Independence Front, a group made up of eight formerly separate and often competing student groups. Most students had been apolitical, but some had been radicalized by their experience in the summer labor camps. Their movement grew after the Arrow Cross closed all schools and boarding places and suspended all teaching, freeing up about 8,000 male university students in Budapest for total mobilization. Many of the students simply returned home but some chose to join the resistance.

The Liberation Committee realized that it was imperative to have a military arm of the resistance. After the Arrow Cross putsch some officers who had remained true to their oath to Horthy and the nation began to question to whom they owed their loyalty. Although Hungarians in general did not regard the Germans as enemies, the Arrow Cross was feared and hated. Among Hungarian army officers only 3 to 5 percent favored the Arrow Cross, according to German reports, and a number of officers, including German sympathizers, began to doubt their new role of defending the Arrow Cross regime. Many no longer felt bound by the oath they were required to take to Szálasi as national leader, especially since the Szálasi National Unity Government subordinated itself completely to the German Reich.

Bajcsy-Zsilinszky enlisted an old friend, Lt. Gen. János Kiss, to take over military direction of the movement.[61] Kiss, who had been retired since 1939, was brought from Kőszeg in western Hungary, and Staff Captain Jenő Nagy, who had been imprisoned for two years for disparaging the Nazis, became his adjutant. They were assisted by a number of young anti-German staff officers—Vilmos Tartsay, a staff captain, retired at his request in 1941 because of his anti-Nazi sentiments, worked as a liaison officer; technical officer József Kővágó, a captain and mechanical engineer, became adjutant to János Kiss; and Lt. Gen. Pál Almásy, who had been working at the Military Engineering Institute, also joined them.[62]

The organizers made contact with a number of military units that appeared ready to join the uprising, and also with small groups of professional, reserve, or retired officers who had begun to organize. While some promised to mobilize soldiers, others agreed to secure materials—weapons, ammunition, technical equipment—receiving support from the Military Technical Institute. In the meantime more and more higher officers were told of the plans. But the general opinion was that only if the

Soviet troops were close enough to offer assistance would it be possible to carry out open resistance against the Germans.

At a meeting on November 10 Kiss explained the plans and the state of military organization, and discussion began on the exact timing of the uprising. The military general staff planned for three main actions: to blow up the Germans retreat route, prevent the explosions planned by the Germans, especially the bridges of the capital, public works and factories, and to make contact with the Red Army as soon as possible and ensure its support. Vivid in the minds of all was the disaster of the Warsaw Uprising in August–September when the Red Army remained on the eastern side of the Vistula while the Germans decimated the resistance. Kiss referred to the Polish example to explain the necessity of gaining Soviet support and that action could take place only in mid-December, since the Red Army troops, although close, needed to rest. Several members urged that the uprising take place sooner, fearing that actions by the communist partisans would raise German suspicions and increase the danger of discovery.[63]

Previously no party had been willing to deal with the Communists, but now Bajczy-Zsilinszky met with the young Communist leader, László Rajk, in an unprecedented meeting. Rajk, just released from prison, was the dynamic secretary of the Hungarian Communist Party, which had been illegal for decades and vilified as representative of the detested Bolshevism. Shortly before the putsch Horthy's son had arranged a meeting between Major General Ujszászy and Rajk to discuss possible cooperation. Rajk and Imre Kovács then had worked out a memorandum for the regent with recommendations on how to prepare for the armistice.[64]

Bajczy-Zsilinszky met Rajk in the nitrochemical headquarters with the military leaders Kiss and Jenő Nagy also present. From the start Rajk stressed the importance of conspiracy, in which the Communists were well versed but which he knew was foreign to a Hungarian gentleman or especially to a military officer. He urged them to follow rules of security, to move to other apartments, break their earlier contacts, live with false papers, change their outer appearance, but his words gained little attention.[65] One of the grave weaknesses of the novice resistance was the leadership's naïveté and failure to take the necessary precautions.

At a November 14 meeting the Communist and military leaders came to a compromise. The leaders agreed to organize armed action and at the opportune moment to start a national uprising to save Budapest and its population from siege, counting on the help of the Red Army. The Communists would continue partisan activities and the officers the preparation of the uprising—all with the expected support of the Red Army. Kiss and Rajk came to an agreement on the participation of workers. Bajczy-Zsilinszky emphasized the importance of gaining the recognition of the Soviet Union and of bringing their actions into step with the command of the Second Ukrainian Front. But establishing contact with the Soviets turned out to be the most difficult obstacle of all.

In order to make contact with the Soviets and gain their cooperation it was decided to compose two letters, one to be sent to Marshal Malinovskii at the front and the other to be sent to Moscow in the name of the Liberation Committee. The letter intended for Malinovskii informed him that preparation for a political and military conspiracy was underway and that the Liberation Committee was sending a delegation to Moscow. The letter also asked for the Marshal's assistance and explained the historical background to the formation of the committee, justifying its legality as representative of the Hungarian nation. The composition of the delegation to Moscow was determined, with the letter translated into French and Russian. According to the plan the delegation and documents, with the help of a pilot from the Székesfehérvár airport, should be taken across the front.

A member of the military resistance movement, Major Simonffy-Tóth, the Sixth Army's chief of operations, was chosen to provide assistance. Although Simonffy-Tóth had no access to a plane, he had a connection with Air Force First Lt. József Török, a member of the resistance.[66] Together they contacted a mechanic in the repair workshop at the Székesfehérvár airport, Sándor Böröczky, who had the means to ready a plane for take-off. The day before the flight, November 12, Zoltán Tildy explained to Simonffy-Toth the political role of the Hungarian Front, and told him to convince the Soviet government to recognize the Front as the representative of the will of the Hungarian nation, and to entrust the Front with establishing a new government after the liberation of Budapest.

On November 13 at 4 A.M. Simonffy-Tóth and his wife, accompanied by Tibor Vörös, the son of General János Vörös, drove to the Székesfehérvár airport with Jószef Török where Sándor Böröczky awaited them with an unmarked Focke-Wulf 58 type plane. Török was to fly to the emergency airport at Gamásza-puszta near Siófok. There he would again meet Simonffy-Tóth, who would await the car bringing the political delegation. The plan required exact timing, but there was much confusion. At

9 A.M. Török landed at the Gamásza-puszta airport and Simonffy-Tóth's car met him as planned , but the car bringing the politicians was late. They had been held up by German troops approaching them on the road. The pilot was impatient. Germans were camping next to the road. As the politicians were approaching the airport they saw the plane taking off in front of them.

Simonffy-Tóth attempted to carry out the mission by himself. After landing at the Szeged airport which had been occupied by the Soviets, he went on to Malinovskii's headquarters and delivered the Hungarian Front message that he had memorized, as well as the twelve maps of Budapest he had prepared with exact drawings of the positions of fortifications and defense. From there he flew to Bucharest and Moscow carrying the memorandum, but the Soviets prevaricated and the mission turned out to have been in vain.[67]

The weakest link in the activities of the resistance was maintaining security. The Communist members, Rajk and Pálffy, continually warned the leaders they were playing with fire, and asked them in their interests and the interest of others to keep strictly to the rules of security set by the committee. The leaders did take certain precautions, using false names, holding their meetings in different spots, not sleeping at home, but too many people knew about the matter. No password was used at the meetings, and they made the serious mistake of allowing members to bring others with them without question. Sometimes there were as many as twenty to twenty-five in attendance. They had no idea of the rules of conspiracy and hiding was far from their mentality.[68]

On one occasion the military leader, Jenő Nagy, held a discussion at a central Budapest café, where the group was easily seen from the street. On another occasion the group was meeting at a café, obviously one they frequented often, since they were known by the waiters. During the meeting their waiter came to the table to announce: "the conspiring gentlemen are called to the telephone."[69] With such carelessness it was not surprising that the Arrow Cross investigative organ learned about the matter and smuggled their people inThere were various warnings ahead of time that there were spies among them and that they were being watched. Gábor Vajna, Arrow Cross minister of the interior, testified at the trial of Szálasi after the war that already at the beginning of November, he knew a military conspiracy was underway. Vajna explained that Láday, state secretary in charge of the gendarmerie and police, and Norbert Orendy came to him one evening informing him of a planned putsch attempt. He explained, "the men were arrested because they were disturbing public order behind the backs of the German and Hungarian forces."[70]

On November 22, 1944, as the resistance members of the military general staff gathered at the home of Vilmos Tartsay, Arrow Cross members raided the meeting. During the evening the Arrow Cross also caught Bajczy-Zsilinsky and János Kiss. Imre Kovács owed his life to a late arrival: "I had not yet reached Andrássy Street, and already I heard shots in the direction of the Opera. I hurried my steps, and did not want to believe my eyes; the area around the Opera looked like a battlefield. Field gendarmes and party militia were firing like mad from entryways, behind trees, and billboards, at a car, which was returning fire. Already the bodies of four gendarmes were on the road, covered by soldiers' coats."[71]

More than thirty people were arrested. Subsequently the majority of those in the organization, several hundred, were rounded up. The Arrow Cross showed no sympathy. Lt. Gen. János Kiss, Col. Jenő Nagy, and retired Capt. Vilmos Tartsay were sentenced to death by a special court of the Hungarian army and executed at the military prison in Margit Boulevard on December 8. Others received ten to fifteen years in prison.[72] Bajczy-Zsilinsky because of his parliamentary immunity was separated and later sentenced to death by an Arrow Cross military court and hanged on December 24, 1944.[73]

THE HUNGARIAN STUDENT INDEPENDENCE FRONT

With the arrests the most organized group of the military resistance movement ceased to exist. The Student Front continued for a short time and smaller resistance movements, including the Görgey Battalion, continued to function during the siege of Budapest. On the advice of the Hungarian Front leaders the students had organized themselves by cells. They attempted to join workers, peasants, and intellectual youth in a broader organization, the Hungarian Youth Independence Front, but the student groups were disorganized and fragmented. As more students sought to avoid going to the front which meant almost certain death, a number joined two armed groups, the Görgey Battalion, under Air Force Captain Zoltán Mikó, and the Táncsics Mihály Battalion under József Várhelyi, a medical student, with members recruited mainly from the National Guard at Budapest universities. They issued hundreds of false identity papers and carried out several armed attacks on the Germans and the Arrow Cross.[74]

According to student leader Zoltán Nyeste:

Our goal after October 15 was mainly to enlighten the people of Budapest of the need to leave the war. We wrote leaflets, the leaders handed out illegal papers, which they distributed in the streets. Not, of course, openly—it would have been too dangerous. Everyone found his own method. I went into telephone booths and hid the leaflets which I had smuggled in the lining of my overcoat among the pages of the telephone book.[75]

Perhaps most notable of our activities were false papers. Many people needed them for one reason or another. There were many civil and ecclesiastical offices, hospitals, barracks, with brave people who were willing to stamp the documents. The trouble was that as the situation got more and more difficult it was harder to find documents that would satisfy them; we even got papers from the Arrow Cross. I always had with me an Arrow Cross armband hidden in the lining of my overcoat. We had confiscated the pass from a real Arrow Cross member, telling him that there was some irregularity—he should report next day to the party office to clear up the matter. The Arrow Cross guy was scared to death—he protested that everything was in order.[76]

Contrary to later claims by the Communist Party, the communist youth disappeared from the resistance movement several weeks after the Szálasi putsch and did not take part in the Student Front actions. It became known later that the underground party had given the command that the main task of every Communist was to save himself for the period after the liberation.[77]

The first members of the student resistance movement were caught a few weeks after the collapse of the military resistance on December 12. On their way to a planned meeting at the Széchenyi Society, two of the leaders, Tibor Zimányi and Pál Jónás, were warned after seeing too many people, most of them in boots. They went separately to warn the other members but were caught by gendarmes. The political police arrested twelve members between December 12 and 16, and afterward a large number of the students in the resistance were arrested.[78] Jónás, explaining the details of their capture, confessed that they looked like terrorists. When he was caught on Calvin Square he was carrying explosives, which he was to hand over to a comrade.[79]

The twelve leaders were taken to the infamous Margit boulevard military prison where they were tortured day and night. Sándor Kiss recalled: ". . . as a result of the beating on our feet sometimes a two centimeter thick layer of blood was congealed, but the worst was the bright light.

The torture reached such a level that many looked on execution as liberation. . . . after the liberation, we figured that of two hundred prisoners thirty of us lived through the month-long calvary. It's one of life's miracles that the twelve of us survived."[80]

The main reason that the students were captured was their inexperience and lack of understanding of conspiracy; the only reason they had been able to move freely for so long was that the Arrow Cross members were also inexperienced and the Germans were not familiar with Budapest.[81]

The Görgey Battalian, the most organized unit of the student resistance, continued to function under the ingenious Staff Captain Zoltán Mikó. In fall Mikó had been made head of the Supreme Command's defense section, entrusted with organizing subversion and espionage units against the Soviets. He was also placed in charge of the Prónay commandos, and his new position gave him the opportunity to carry out resistance activities. He formed the Görgey Battalion, which was supposedly preparing to carry out partisan activities against the Soviets, but in reality was a resistance group of university students whom he was training and arming to take part in the Budapest uprising. Officially the battalion was part of the Prónay commandos, taking part in exercises while at the same time carrying out acts of sabotage and attacking members of the Arrow Cross. Mikó was also in regular contact with Wallenberg; he procured legitimate identity papers for people in hiding, and through Wallenberg sent food from the battalion's supplies to Jewish protected houses.[82]

On November 21 the existence of the Görgey Battalion was endangered when one of its members, a Jewish deserter from the labor service, was recognized. Afterward a further ten labor service deserters in the battalion were found and executed on December 4. Acting quickly Mikó arranged to transfer the battalion out of danger to the Börzsöny Hills north of the Danube, under the pretext that the soldiers needed training. Mikó had planned on the possibility that the armed resistance fighters he had recruited—some eight hundred—would change sides and join the Soviets. During the siege he made plans to defect and open the front line to the Soviets in Zugló and on Rózsadomb Hill, but in seeking help from a former comrade he was denounced and the plan came to the attention of the Arrow Cross members.[83]

Mikó was able to evade capture but landed in a Soviet prison of war along with his military assistant, Vilmos Bondor. Marshal Tolbuchin interrogated him in his headquarters in Kunszentmiklós, and even though the Russians found his story puzzling they liked it; how could a fascist military unit carry out resistance? Since he had voluntarily cooperated with the Soviets he was treated extremely well, but later the Russians sentenced him to death for espionage and he was executed in Odessa on August 15, 1945.[84] It is suspected that his contacts with Wallenberg led to his execution. Mikó knew of the documents concerning the Katyn massacres that Wallenberg kept in a safe, and Stalin had ordered that anyone who knew of the massacre should be dealt with. Mikó told his friend Bondor that after the Wallenberg safe was found his treatment by the Soviets changed radically. Just before he was executed he advised Bondor never to mention Katyn.[85]

Although the resistance movement had little effect on the military conduct of the war, its very existence was significant. The student movements, despite being small and disunited, were important for their political effect on the younger generation. The revolutionary spirit that they implanted in the intellectual youth contributed to the strength of student movements between 1945 and 1948. After the war European regimes in general made use of resistance movements to legitimize their postwar governments, and in Hungary the provisional government was eager to recognize resistance members; those who had participated could receive a certificate if they submitted their data to a committee. The Communists wanted to record any antifascist activity and a number of studies on the resistance were published, but soon the studies were distorted by Soviet-style history, according to which only the Communist partisans had been resistance fighters. In 1945 a number of the resistance members had been suspicious of the Communists and refrained from sending in their data to the committee; a year later their suspicions were justified when the certificates were revoked and the noncommunist recipients were later hounded. One of the student leaders, Zoltán Nyeste, has asserted that the greatest sin of the Communist leadership, Rákosi and his gang "was not the cruelty, the oppression, the prisons, etc., but in erasing history. Lying about the past, washing out their father's memories, they robbed a whole generation."[86]

THE SOVIETS AND THE PROVISIONAL GOVERNMENT

With the rapid advance of the Red Army, the Soviets were beginning to address the question of how they would deal with an occupied Hungary. In discussions in Moscow with the Hungarian communist émigrés from mid-September through early October, it was decided that there was no necessity to establish a proletarian dictatorship immediately. At the time the Soviets' immediate goal was to enlist Hungary in the final battle against the Germans. The advice for a moderate approach was also inspired by the need to deceive the Western Allies of the ultimate goal, since the speeded-up bolshevization of Poland had aroused their suspicions. It is also possible that the Soviets at this time were uncertain as to their own aims in Hungary. Stalin, who opined that there was no need to frighten anyone, was enough of a tactician not to increase tension through pressing too far in Hungary. For the Hungarian Communists the main task was not to take over power but to decide what tactics to use not to arouse suspicion.[87]

By this time the Soviets had occupied roughly two-thirds of Hungarian territory. In the occupied settlements in eastern Hungary, isolated from the central government and from each other, local municipal councils gradually came into being to deal with immediate problems, cleaning up the war damage, organizing public provisions; a large part of their role was to maintain contact with the Soviet units. Simply keeping up with the ever-increasing demands of the Red Army—along with the atrocities—was not a simple task. The councils were made of up local representatives, mainly from the former parties in the legal opposition, as well as the Communist Party, whose members during the long years of illegality had developed self-assurance and a strong esprit de corps. Despite the party's very small membership—in December 1944 the total membership in Hungary was about 4,000—the party had begun to dominate the scene.[88]

Following the advancing Red Army, Zoltán Vas, one of the Hungarian Moscow émigrés, had been sent in order to scout out the situation. In mid-October 1944 he reached the major Alföld city of Szeged and made contact with local Communists and Social Democrats. Then in the first days of November, Molotov sent four Muscovite Hungarian Communists—Ernő Gerő, Mihály Farkas, Imre Nagy, and József Révai—to Hungary to formally revive the Hungarian Communist Party and assess the political climate. Stalin had decided that the head of the party, the later ruler of Hungary, Mátyás Rákosi, should not accompany them at this time.[89] On November 7 the Muscovites established a temporary center of the Hungarian Communist Party in Szeged. Here they met with some members of the former Hungarian Front parties; these men then became the kernel of the future provisional government, which was to be based on a coalition among parties of the Hungarian Front.[90]

During this time in Moscow the Horthy delegation, considering itself the legitimate representative of the Hungarian state, requested permission from the Soviets to form an antifascist government, which would cooperate with the Allies. In mid-November Molotov received them and agreed to the formation of a new democratic government, even accepting some of their suggestions for delegates. With Molotov's consent, along with General Béla Miklós and General Vörös who had joined them, they began to plan for a provisional government. Miklós, with some competition from Vörös who claimed that Horthy had named him his successor, became their candidate for prime minister. When Simonffy-Tóth arrived in Moscow on November 18 with the memorandum from the Liberation Committee, which also claimed to be the true representative of the Hungarian state, it was decided that the leaders of the Liberation Front should be empowered as ministers.[91] (It was not known for some time that the leaders of the Liberation Front had been caught and imprisoned on November 22.)

Meanwhile in early December in Szeged, under the leadership of Ernő Gerő and the other Hungarian émigrés, a coalition of representatives of the former opposition parties was established and given the title of the Hungarian National Independence Front. It was made up of those representatives from the former opposition parties who happened to be in the liberated area—the Independent Smallholders, the National Peasant Party, the Citizens Democratic Party, the Social Democratic Party, as well as the Hungarian Communist Party and the free trade unions.

On November 30 the Hungarian Communist Party published its program, The Program of Hungary's Democratic Revival and Reconstruction, in Debrecen. The Independent Front Coalition quickly accepted the Communists' program as its own. The program emphasized the need to rebuild the country, to bring about radical land reform, and promised social and socialist reform, regulation of large capital, the recognition of the right to strike, the continuing fight against the Germans, peace with the neighbors, cooperation with the Western powers, and friendly relations with the Soviet Union. Gerő and Nagy, as leaders of the Hungarian Communist Party, were summoned back to Moscow in order to discuss the founding of the provisional government.[92]

In Moscow, Gerő and Nagy joined Rákosi in meetings with Molotov to work out details of the coalition government. Stalin endorsed their proposal to form a provisional government, commenting that a new source of political legitimacy for Hungary needed to be devised after Horthy had allowed himself to be deported by the Nazis. He recommended that a new national council be formed with representatives of local governments and if possible of trade unions, but the Communist Party should take no direct part in it. Between the first and fifth of December plans were developed that were to include elections for a provisional national assembly in the liberated territories. There was to be a preparatory commission, assisted by the local councils, which would conduct elections in the liberated territories for the provisional national assembly. Those chosen would then elect the provisional government.[93]

The lists drawn up by the Horthy armistice delegation were ignored, the delegation members being informed that they should participate or face the consequences of a more left-wing regime. The composition of the government was predetermined: the Soviets recommended Generals Miklós, Vörös, and Faragho as prime minister, defense minister, and minister of food supply. The émigrés proposed Imre Nagy for minister of agriculture and József Gábor for minister of commerce and transportation. Another six portfolios were to be given to members of the National Committee in Szeged.[94] By this time the Liberation Committee members had been arrested and were in custody.

The Gerő group had assumed that the seat of the new regime would be in Szeged, but Moscow decided in favor of Debrecen for the opening of the provisional government. Debrecen had symbolic value as the site of the Hungarian proclamation of independence during the 1848 revolution, in contrast to Szeged, which had been the base for formation of the National Army under Horthy in 1919. After the discussions were completed the assembled group—which included the Horthy delegates, the communist émigré leaders, G. M. Pushkin, later to become Soviet ambassador to Hungary, and General Susajkov as liaison with Field Marshal Malinovskii—left from the Kiev Station for the slow journey to Debrecen. They arrived on December 12.[95]

Discussions were held with the city's leaders and on December 13 the preparatory commission of the National Assembly was established. It was decided which villages and towns in the territory already under Red Army control should send representatives to the Provisional National Assembly, and from December 15 to 20 representatives were chosen in the occupied territories. The official nomination of the delegates was generally staged by the local councils known as national committees, which held public meetings in celebration and elected representatives by acclamation. The Communist Sándor Nógrádi arrived in Debrecen and discovered that he had been elected in his absence by the city of Miskolc, where no one knew him personally. Some local notables were recruited by the Communists, aided by the Soviet security police, resorting when necessary to threats of deportation.[96] According to some historians the choice of delegates was not overly influenced by the Soviets, but Ferenc Nagy,

Independent Smallholders party leader and prime minister of the elected Hungarian government in 1945, asserts that the number of representatives were determined arbitrarily, giving the advantage to towns with large numbers of left-wing workers and landless peasants.[97]

The two hundred thirty members of the National Assembly were said to represent all democratic associations and parties, although, as was to be expected, the left was dominant. The official list showed seventy-one Communists, fifty-five Independent Smallholders, thirty-eight Social Democrats, sixteen National Peasants, twelve from the Citizens Democratic Party, nineteen representatives of trade unions and nineteen unaffiliated. The three leftist parties, the Hungarian Communist Party, the Social Democrats, and the National Peasant Party along with the trade unions held an absolute majority. Among the ministers, on the other hand, there were still three generals and Count Géza Teleki from the former regime.[98]

On December 21 the Provisional National Assembly gathered in the oratorium chapel of the Reformed College, the site of the declaration of Hungarian independence in 1849. As had been arranged in Moscow, on the next day the assembly elected Miklós as prime minister. The rest of his proposed ministers were sworn in as the ministers of the provisional government.[99] Miklós read out a declaration of policy: to seek an armistice with the U.S.S.R.; to carry out a drastic program of internal reform, including the introduction of universal, equal, direct and secret suffrage, to enact comprehensive land reform, and to punish traitors and war criminals. Private property was to be guaranteed. With no debate on the problems facing the nation or on the goals of the new government, the Provisional National Assembly then adjourned.

Although the Western Allies had not been informed or consulted, the Soviets announced the formation of the Hungarian Provisional National Assembly and government on December 23. Sir Alvary Frederick Gascoigne, the British diplomat in Debrecen at the time, commented to his friend Orme Sargent that the Soviets manipulated the members of the Provisional National Assembly behind the scenes like puppets.[100]

The members of the provisional government remained isolated in Debrecen, out of contact with Budapest and the rest of the country where fighting continued throughout the winter. The temporary government lacked funds and resources, and thus was at the mercy of the Soviets. Under close Soviet supervision they were prevented from communicating directly with representatives of the Western Allies.[101] No Hungarian in the liberated districts possessed a usable auto, except for the Communists.

At first members of the government were allowed to reside at the Golden Bull, Debrecen's best hotel, run by the Red Army, where they participated in some of the lavish feasts put on by the Soviet general staff. But they were soon told to leave to make space for the Russians. According to Ferenc Nagy, this was a major blow, especially since it was tremendously difficult to find food for themselves and their families. Instead, members of the cabinet gave up trying to run the country and turned to party organization. Local administration everywhere was in chaos. Most of the officials had fled to the west and a large proportion of reliable civil employees had been transferred forcibly by the Germans. There was no telephone, no telegraph, mail trains ran only on lines that the Red Army ordered rebuilt for their own military replacements. The former police force was disbanded, labeled a tool of the former reactionary government, and the new force became notorious as an undisciplined horde, more interested in looting than in maintaining order.[102]

The Siege of Budapest

The siege of Budapest, one of the longest and bloodiest sieges of a city during World War II, lasted from the arrival of the Red Army on Christmas Eve 1944 until the final surrender on February 13, 1945 (see Map 5). In contrast, Berlin fell in two weeks, Vienna in six days, Paris and other European capitals—with the exception of Warsaw—never became battlegrounds. The intensity of fighting in Budapest can only be compared to that of Leningrad, Stalingrad, and Warsaw.[103] On December 24 the Red Army reached the outer suburbs of Buda, arriving so unexpectedly that people were still out Christmas shopping. When the siege started on Christmas Eve, Lilly Vigyazo reported from the Jewish hospital near the ghetto that the explosions broke all the windows.[104]

The Soviets had surprised the Germans and Hungarians by crossing the Danube and coming up from the west toward Buda, the part of Budapest on the western bank of the Danube, where defenses were extremely weak. Exploiting the complete lack of German reinforcements behind the front, the Soviets broke through the front at Lake Velence on December 22, attacking from the southwest. The commander of the German Army Group South, Colonel-General Hans Friessner, had asked for permission to strengthen the Buda side by withdrawing the Eighth SS Cavalry division from the Pest bridgehead, but his request was denied; Hitler had ordered that they were not to give up one inch of Budapest.[105]

By December 26 Soviet troops had encircled the city after seizing the main road linking Budapest to Vienna. As a result of the Soviet link-up,

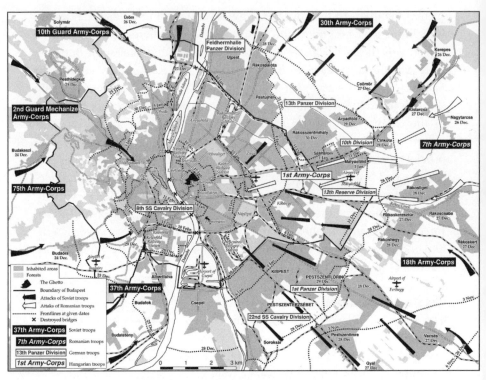

Map 5. Siege of Budapest, December 24, 1944–February 13, 1945.

nearly 33,000 German and 37,000 Hungarian soldiers as well as over 800,000 civilians became trapped within the city. Karl Pfeffer-Wildenbruch, the commanding general of the Ninth SS Mountain Corps, seeing the situation as hopeless, decided to evacuate Budapest on December 27 and attempt a breakout toward the west. Preparations had already been started, but on December 28 Hitler forbade the attempt; he was determined to hold Budapest. Already on December 24 he had ordered troops transferred from Army Group Center in the Warsaw area—the Fourth SS Panzer Corps (*Panzerkorps*) as well as the Ninety-Sixth and 711th Infantry divisions, all together 200 tanks and 60,000 soldiers—to Transdanubia. His decision was to have dire consequences for the Wehrmacht when the Soviet Vistula-Oder offensive began in Poland. After removing the Fourth SS Panzer Corps no reserves remained, and two weeks later, on January 12, 1945, the Soviet attack swept away the front below the Visztula; the Soviets were only stopped at the Oder.[106]

On December 29 Malinovskii, who wanted to avoid a long costly siege, sent two emissaries to negotiate the city's capitulation, offering generous terms. The ultimatum was to be delivered by two Soviet captains, Miklós Steinmetz in Pest and Ilya Afanasevich Ostapenko in Buda. Steinmetz and his driver died before they reached the Germans, although it is unclear whether their jeep hit a mine or whether they were assassinated. Ostapenko and his group handed the ultimatum to a senior officer who contacted Pfeffer-Wildenbruch, but in his response, which came within an hour, he refused the offer of capitulation. On his return Ostapenko fell, but his deputy, First Lieutenant Orlov, lived to recount the events. Since the emissaries did not return, their fate was widely disputed, the Soviets charging the Germans with shooting them deliberately, but historian Kristian Úngváry, who has studied the matter intensively, concludes that the deaths were probably caused by chance and carelessness, and that neither Ostapenko nor Steinmetz were deliberately killed by Germans.[107]

In any event, Pfeffer-Wildenbruch could not have disobeyed Hitler's orders. The Soviet commanders considered the failure of the emissaries to return a refusal of negotiations and ordered the start of the siege. The Soviet offensive started in the eastern suburbs advancing through Pest; they made good use of the large central avenues to speed up their progress. The German and Hungarian defenders, overwhelmed, tried to trade space for time in order to slow down the Soviet advance. With the encirclement, urban warfare in Budapest increased in intensity. The surrounded German and Hungarian army formations and Arrow Cross members carried on the fight from street to street. The inhabitants dug tank-trap trenches around the city, even taking school-age children into the hopeless fight against the Soviet T 34 tanks.[108]

Supplies became a decisive factor after the loss of the Ferihegy airport on December 27. Until January 9, 1945, German troops were able to use some of the main avenues as well as the park next to the Castle as landing zones for planes and gliders, although they were under constant artillery fire from the Soviets. Before the Danube froze some supplies could be passed on barges under the cover of darkness and fog. Nevertheless food shortages were more and more common and soldiers had to rely on finding their own sources of food, some even resorting to eating their own horses; in the extremely cold winter bodies, including those of dead horses, were preserved. The extreme temperatures affected civilians and troops alike.

The Soviet troops soon found themselves in a similar situation to that of the Germans in Stalingrad, but their troops were able to take advantage of the urban terrain by relying heavily on snipers and sappers to advance. Fights broke out even in the sewers, as both Axis and Soviet troops used them for troop movement. In mid-January the Soviets took Csepel Island along with its military factories, which were still producing cheap anti-tank weapons called *Panzerfausts* and shells, even under Soviet fire. Meanwhile in Pest the situation deteriorated with the garrison facing the risk of being cut in half by the advancing Soviet troops. The Russians had brought up dense concentrations of guns and howitzers to reduce German positions block by block. Its garrison began to surrender en masse on January 15 when trapped with their backs to the Danube.

The inhabitants lived through the siege in the cellars, emerging only rarely to forage for water or food. The cellars of large apartment blocks sheltered hundreds of thousands day and night for weeks on end. The shelters had been designed only for short air raids and not for the large crowds who lived there during the siege; most were furnished with a few benches, some fire-fighting equipment and a first-aid cabinet. At first the families who moved into the shelters were those with small children, who would have trouble getting to the cellar from the third or fourth floor when air raids began. Then, in shifts, more and more families moved in. The breath of so many people condensed on the walls and the ceilings, which were constantly dripping.[109]

Organized food supplies ceased almost completely soon after Christmas. Since the population had not been prepared for a long siege people began to starve within a few days. To add to the distress of the inhabitants, the winter of 1945 was an extremely cold one; many survived only because of the 30,000 or more horses brought into the city by the Hungarian and German cavalry and artillery units. The animals starved since there was no fodder. The greatest conflicts among the occupants were those over cooking, water carrying, and washing. Normally between fifteen to twenty families had to share a cooker for cooking and heating water. Some groups organized communal cooking, which was more economical and did not create the sense of inequality. In other places there were more conflicts. People eating in secret sometimes gave themselves away by the sound of chewing in the night.[110]

Drinking water rapidly became a major problem. Only a few buildings had wells of their own and drinking water had to be brought from far away, which was life-threatening since soldiers from both sides would open fire on any civilians who ventured out of doors. Many were killed by hand grenades or phosphorus thrown through cellar windows. By the end of December water for the Pest side could be gotten only from wells near Parliament and Margit Island. The population of Buda got water from medicinal springs near Gellért Hill, but in some places, for example the Castle District, the shortage became catastrophic. People often attempted to alleviate the water shortage by melting snow. Following the breakdown of water supplies, the lavatories also stopped working, and by January, because of excrement lying around everywhere, there was a risk of epidemics in the shelters. Conditions in the sick bays were the worst—there were thousands of civilian and military wounded lying in the cellars of Parliament, the Museum of Military History, and the Castle District.[111]

END OF THE SIEGE IN PEST

On January 17 at 7:25 P.M. Hitler finally gave permission to Pfeffer-Wildenbruch to evacuate all the remaining troops from Pest to Buda, allowing them to shorten their lines and take advantage of Buda's hilly nature. Now the sole objective of the Germans and Hungarians was to cross the two bridges still standing—the Erzsébet and the Chain Bridge—to reach Buda, although many Hungarian soldiers stayed behind. The two bridges spanning the Danube were clogged with traffic, evacuating troops and civilians. On January 18, 1945, at 7 A.M. German troops blew up the bridges despite protests from Hungarian officers about the pointless destruction; there were still some evacuees, soldiers and civilians, on the bridges at the time. After the bridges were destroyed it took the Soviet troops two more days to mop up the last of the German and Hungarian opposition in Pest. The Soviets then took over Pest in the liberation.[112]

When the Soviet liberation arrived on January 18, one Jewish family who had been living in a shelter on Nádor Street decided to attempt to go back to their home.

We had sleds for our belongings. It was freezing cold—and a very long walk. The house was close to Aréna Street, now called Dozsa György Street. Some people were living there—but they left. There was a plank going from my room across to the other side—over the bombed area. . . . Some neighbor's apartment was in better condition. I remember we cooked hamburgers from horsemeat. My mother bathed me from head to toe because I was so filthy. We had spent six to seven weeks in the shelter—early December to mid-January—without washing.[113]

One young man had been hiding since late October in the cellar of a building owned by the Unitarian Church. The night the Red Army occupied Pest, the concierge who had been caring for the mixed group of deserters from Transylvania, politicians and Jews, feared they would be shot by the Soviets, and he only let them out the next day.

When I got out I was blinded—sun, snow, dead Russian, dead horse. Father came for me. Our house had been bombed—it was five stories, but we lived on the first floor and our flat was okay. It was amazing how houses held up. All had cellars. Sometimes one would see a building with the whole front gone but inside furniture, even paintings, were still in place. . . . The Germans were still in Buda; their mortars fired high and would come over the buildings. One day walking with my mother on Hold Street I grabbed her and pulled her down on the sidewalk. I was suddenly struck by the irony—this very upper middle class lady lying on the street.[114]

OPERATION KONRAD

On January 1, under the code name Operation Konrad, the Germans had begun their attempt to relieve the encircled garrison of Budapest. Since they had transferred more reinforcements to Hungary than anywhere else, it was vitally important to produce positive results. Hitler was determined to hold the city at all costs, although all others agreed that Budapest must be given up as soon as possible. Almost every day a request came to Hitler asking him to allow a breakout, but he was obstinate in his refusal, forbidding the German commander, Waffen-SS General Karl Pfeffer-Wildenbruch, to abandon Budapest; he was not even willing to give up Pest.[115]

The Germans debated whether to attack from the south or from the north over the hilly terrain, which would be difficult for tanks. It was decided to attack from the north in hopes that the Soviets had not yet built up strong defenses. Tolbuchin and Malinovskii, however, had anticipated the attack and had placed troops and antitank guns to prevent the German rescue attempt. On January 6 the Soviets stopped the advance, although suffering heavy losses. The next day, the Germans launched a new attack from Esztergom with two hundred tons of supplies, which they hoped to deliver to the capital. As rescue attempts proceeded, it was clear that the intentions of the German commanders deviated from Hitler's commands. They saw no possibility of recapturing the city but instead hoped to rescue the defenders by opening a passageway through which their comrades could escape.

The last phase of Operation Konrad was launched on January 17 as the German Fourth SS Panzer Corps attacked from the south of Budapest in an attempt to encircle ten Soviet divisions. At first the attack was successful; only the lack of an infantry prevented the Germans from breaking through the Soviet encirclement.[116] The attempt ultimately failed, despite the fact that the Germans had employed all their military might available to force an end to the stalemate. A senior Soviet political officer reported at the end of January: "The town of Budapest, especially its central area, is heavily damaged, hardly one building has been preserved intact. The western part of the town, Buda, where fighting is still going on, has literally been transformed into a ruin, the bridges across the Danube have been blown up."[117]

THE FINAL SIEGE OF BUDA

When the troops withdrew from the flat terrain of Pest to the hills of Buda, the defenders were able to place artillery and fortifications above the attackers, greatly slowing the Soviet advance. The main citadel, Gellért Hill, was defended by elite Waffen-SS troops, who successfully repelled several Soviet assaults. Nearby, Soviet and German forces were fighting for the city cemetery, a fight that lasted several days. Fighting on Margit Island, in the middle of the Danube, was particularly merciless. By this time the Danube was almost completely frozen over, and the defenders' strength was rapidly declining with losses that could not be replaced.

On January 26, after Pfeffer-Wildenbrook received news of the failure of the third relief attempt of Operation Konrad, he called a war council.[118] His officers submitted a breakout proposal but he rejected it, saying that they must await the Führer's orders. The Papal Nuncio, Angelo Rotta, representing the Budapest diplomatic corps, visited him in his bunker on February 3 and asked him to urge the German supreme command to end the suffering and prevent the ultimate destruction of the civilian population. Pfeffer-Wildenbrook, who must have realized that the end was only days away, informed the Wehrmacht headquarters of the nuncio's intervention. He asked if there were still plans for the relief of Budapest, undoubtedly hoping to receive permission for a breakout, but the reply was that the Führer's orders remained unchanged—Budapest was to be held to the bitter end. He made the request again on February 5 but was refused.[119]

On February 10, 1945, after a violent assault, Soviet marines established a bridgehead on the Castle Hill, almost cutting the remaining garrison in half. The glider flights bringing in supplies had ended a few days earlier and the parachute drops had also been discontinued. The remaining German divisions, concentrated in less than two square kilometers, were in a state of total battle weariness, suffering from malnutrition and disease. Their supply of ammunition was unsteady and the rations consisted of beans and horsemeat. The state of the Hungarian troops was even more appalling—of the 14,000 combat-ready soldiers of the Tenth Infantry Division in early November, at best only 2,500 remained by January. The German commander had little regard for the Hungarian troops and did not even take them into consideration in the final stages of the siege.

The morale of the Hungarian troops suffered and most Hungarian soldiers attempted to extricate themselves as soon as possible from the seemingly futile resistance. They deserted, defected to the Soviets, or simply lingered behind the front lines. Most of those who defected to the Soviets did so mainly because it seemed pointless to continue the struggle. In January for the first time Hungarian units had been allowed to fight alongside the Soviets, but only because the exhausted Red Army needed reinforcements. Previously, on Stalin's orders, even units that surrendered as a whole had been sent to prison camps, but as the siege progressed defectors were often given the choice between prison camp in Siberia and fighting with the Soviets against their fellow-countrymen.[120]

Pfeffer-Wildenbruch had followed Hitler's orders until the very last moment. Only at the eleventh hour when it was evident that the city would soon fall did he decide to attempt a breakout to lead the remnants of his troops out of Budapest. Throughout the war no German army had chosen to lay down its arms before the Soviets if a breakout operation was a viable alternative; commanding officers could not face the odium of surrender, but also everyone feared Siberia and the Soviets. In Budapest it was known that Soviets did not spare the lives of SS personnel, who constituted half of the German forces in the city. In contrast to his customary neglect of General Iván Hindy, the Hungarian commander of the city, Pfeffer-Wildenbruch included Hindy in this last desperate breakout attempt. He did not radio his intention to German Army Group South until the last possible moment on February 11 at 5:50 P.M. Immediately following the announcement the radio equipment was demolished, making the launching of the operation irreversible.[121]

The Budapest breakout attempt has gone down in history as one of most desperate operations of World War II; it was not by chance that Budapest is often referred to as a second Stalingrad in German memoirs. On February 11 there were 43,900 German and Hungarian troops serving in Budapest. By February 15 22,350 had been taken prisoner, including Pfeffer-Wildenbruch and Hindy, and some 17,000 had been killed. Only somewhat more than 700 of the 43,900 men reached German lines, mainly because of Reserve First Lt. László Szilasy's knowledge of the local terrain. Some German soldiers remained in hiding in the woods until spring.[122]

Several thousand soldiers, mostly Hungarians, remained in the Castle District, either because they never received the break-out order or because they thought the attempt pointless. Some two thousand seriously wounded men were left behind in the military hospital in the tunnel beneath the Castle Hill. The head physician had fled with his staff and only one staff physician, Hübner, turned back when he saw the breakout attempt had failed. The Soviets decided to leave the hospital and one of those selected to help with the wounded, Medical Sergeant Aladár Konkoly Thege, recalled the horrors he experienced as he entered the tunnel: "The air is thick and stifling. Pus, blood, gangrene, excrement, sweat, urine, tobacco smoke and the smell of gun powder mingle in a dense stench, which fills the passage. It is unbearable, nauseating. The light of the torch picks images out of the gloom. On both sides of the passages the wounded are lying in long rows, some on plank beds or in bunks, many on the bare concrete. . . . They are lying there almost motionless, feverish, weakened and helpless."[123]

On February 13, 1945, the remaining defenders surrendered. German and Hungarian military losses were high, whole divisions had been destroyed. Budapest lay in ruins, with more than 80 percent of its buildings destroyed or damaged, and historical buildings such as the Hungarian parliament and the castle lay in ruins. All five bridges spanning the Danube had been destroyed.

Hitler mounted a last offensive in Hungary, Operation Spring Awakening, attempting to push the Red Army back to the Danube and retake Budapest. With the new force, the Sixth SS Panzer Army, the Germans advanced from between Lake Balaton and Lake Velence toward the Danube south of Budapest, but the Soviets resisted bitterly and effectively. The supplies of fuel were limited and the panzers bogged down in the mud. After ten days of heavy fighting much of the Sixth SS Panzer Army was shattered, and by March 15 the operation had ended in failure. Tolbukhin and Malinovskii's forces broke out across western Hungary and by March 30 reached the Hungarian–German/Austrian border. The German front now collapsed. According to historian Evan Mawdsley it was a "most foolhardy deployment of German elite forces" since Soviet forces on the Oder were only sixty-five kilometers from Berlin.[124]

By the end of March Szálasi and the whole leadership had left western Hungary for Austria where the Germans ignored Szálasi. They disarmed the Hungarian troops; volunteers were given German uniforms and were placed in German units, others were treated as POWs or placed in forced labor units. At the end of April Szálasi and his general staff landed in American prison in Salzburg and later were brought home as war criminals.[125]

Soviet Occupation

On February 12 Budapest was still, the streets deserted. The population emerged from the cellars to find fires burning, heaps of bodies lining the streets, the capital city reduced to rubble. The population of Budapest had been reduced in one year from an all-time high 1,380,000 in March 1944 to 832,000 by March 1945. During the siege and the first quarter of 1945, 23,624 Budapest inhabitants died, 12,588 homes were completely destroyed and another 18,775 became uninhabitable, out of forty-five major hospital buildings only four remained undamaged. Of 40,000 Budapest buildings less than 26 percent escaped serious damage. In the first weeks after the siege there were no electric lights in streets and homes.[126]

On February 13 Malinovskii granted his troops three days of free looting to celebrate their victory, including forcing women to act as prostitutes. Coming out of hiding a student greeted his friends in the college shouting, "Hurrah, we've been liberated" but was greeted by dark looks. During the night several women students had been raped and ten to fifteen students had been taken away.[127] Still, for some the Soviet occupation was a true liberation. György Kontra, a young medical student, had spent the siege in a cellar with the noted musician Zoltán Kodály and Nobel Prize winner Albert Szent-Györgyi. The Russians knew their reputations and searched them out after the siege, brought them food, and treated them well. For Kontra who had been living in hiding, it meant that he could go out on the street again and see his family.[128]

The Soviets, justifiably, regarded Hungary as an enemy state. After Horthy's failed armistice the fighting had continued for four long bitter months. The Red Army soldier had little reason to feel sympathy for the Hungarian population, and since few Hungarians could speak Russian they could not communicate. Looting was ubiquitous, accepted, and even encouraged. Soldiers were allowed to send home parcels weighing up to ten kilograms, an added incentive to loot since there was nothing else to send. The soldiers had been told that all Hungarians were bourgeois, which included anybody who possessed a watch, a bed, or a stove. With conditions in the Soviet Union so much worse, most Hungarians must have looked to them as bourgeois, yet, despite rational explanations for the wholesale orgy of rape, looting, and violence by the Soviet soldiers, their conduct brought about a radical change in the minds of much of the population about the liberation.[129]

The Soviets were not the only ones looting; Hungarians were looting too. As in other war-torn societies Hungarian society was in the throws of a deep moral crisis. The normal human order, the way of thinking, had been destroyed by war and occupation. The destruction, plundering, and mass killings had reduced respect for law and private property and weakened morality. Stories were legion of citizens looting Jewish homes and shops, of people failing to return goods entrusted to them by Jewish neighbors. One woman told of an acquaintance, a textile merchant who lived in Buda. He had entrusted his many possessions to a neighbor. Zsuzsa saw with her own eyes that the Hungarian woman piled a wagon full of the family's possessions and took it away; then told the family that the Russians had taken their belongings. "Ethics were destroyed. The whole society had become morally twisted."[130]

Count Mihály Károlyi, prime minister of the Hungarian Republic in 1918, expressed his bitter disappointment when he returned to Budapest for a visit. He told Gascoigne, a British diplomat, he was suffering from "great sorrow, disillusion and disgust; sorrow because of the ruins of a once beautiful capital, disillusion because of the weakness which was obviously being displayed by those in power toward the Communists, disgust because of the wholesale immorality and graft which permeated all strata of the population, both official and otherwise."[131]

In addition to the looting committed by the common Soviet soldiers, looting was carried out systematically by special units of the Red Army to collect valuables for the Soviet Union. According to the Swiss Embassy, shortly after the end of the siege a small but meticulous group of officers plundered the strongboxes—especially American and British—in every bank, and took away all the cash. Officers specially trained in art history systematically robbed public collections, and works of art were stolen from famous Jewish collectors. Looting in the capital became more systematic as the occupation progressed. The equipment of hotels on Margit Island was stolen, as were many sculptures in public places.[132]

The writer, Sándor Márai, who was living in a small village on the Danube during the fighting, observed that the soldiers of the Red Army were always looting. Many of the Soviet infantry and artillery who passed through the village stopped at his house for the night. In his memoirs he recalled that mostly "they helped themselves to something—a pillow, a pillowcase or comforter, a piece of cutlery—but also clothing—shoes, anything they could get their hands on." He saw them strip the villa next door in broad daylight. "They loaded the furniture and furnishings on trucks; they even removed the parquet flooring and tore the insulated tubes for electrical wiring out of the walls; they left untouched only the books on the shelves."[133]

As did many Hungarians, Márai, who lived for months in close intimacy night and day with the Russians, came to the conclusion that he simply was unable to understand them. "They were childlike, sometimes wild, sometimes edgy and melancholy, always unpredictable." He found "there is 'something different' about the Russians that someone raised in the West cannot understand."[134]

Rape was so common that few women were spared. The youngest victims were less than ten years old; the oldest over ninety. In Budapest alone it was estimated that 50,000 had been raped by Romanian and Red Army soldiers. The population was utterly defenseless; drunken soldiers raped mothers in front of their children and husbands. Women were often mass raped by ten to fifteen soldiers—and infected with venereal diseases as well. In general, records were not kept; under the occupation it was not possible to report rapes or make complaints to the authorities, and for a long time the women victims and the civil population remained silent about the Soviet atrocities. Doctors in the hospitals did keep records when women came for help, and because of the crisis the strict rules against abortions were relaxed; 20 percent of women who were raped became pregnant.[135] The head doctor of a major hospital in Budapest announced that in the present unusually serious situation, those who turned to the specialist to interrupt pregnancy should be allowed.[136]

In asking for an abortion, in a signed statement the twenty-six-year old L. M. described the circumstances of being raped:

On June 18 of this year in Lébény county I was going home from the seamstress around 10 P.M., when two Russians wrestled me down and both of them raped me. Exactly one month later, July 16, at 8 in the evening I was going home from Moson on the railroad tracks by bicycle. A Russian wanted to take away my bicycle, but when I began sobbing, asking him to leave the bicycle, he raped me. . . . since my pregnancy was against my will and I did not want to carry it, I requested at the hospital to free me from my pregnancy. . . .[137]

The deeds of the Soviet soldiers were especially painful for the local Communists. On February 19, soon after he had returned to Budapest, Mátyás Rákosi, who had been elected secretary general of the Hungarian Communist Party, appealed to Soviet authorities asking the Comintern leader, Georgii Dimitrov, to intervene against the mass rape of women, since the acts of the Red Army were blamed on the party as well.[138] He did not receive much satisfaction. Milovan Djilas once complained to Stalin about the conduct of the Red Army soldiers; Stalin was surprised that Djilas couldn't understand that the soldiers needed to have a little fun.[139]

A major concern for the population was simply finding enough to eat. Rations, especially in the cities, were at starvation level. In the peace agreement signed on January 20 the Hungarian government had taken full responsibility for feeding the occupation force of 1.5 million, although the Soviet soldiers had already confiscated most of the available food stocks. People bartered anything they owned, paintings, jewelry, for food, or tried to find some way to go to the countryside to find provisions. Zoltán Vas, a Muscovite Hungarian émigré, appointed government commissioner for public supplies with extraordinary powers, confiscated the remaining food, ordered the evacuation of children, emergency kitchens, and introduced food coupons on February 25, allotting 500 calories a day. At the end of March the allotment was raised to 1,000 calories per day. By spring communal kitchens were feeding about 50,000.[140]

SOVIET-DOMINATED ALLIED CONTROL COMMISSION

According to the armistice signed by delegates of the provisional government in Moscow on January 20, 1945, Hungary was to withdraw to its 1937 borders, send troops to fight against Germany, and to liquidate all pro-German and fascist organizations. It was to pay 300 million dollars in reparations within six years: 200 million to the Soviet Union, 70 million to Yugoslavia, and 30 million to Czechoslovakia, an amount that even the Western Allies found excessive.[141] All German and Austrian property was to be given to the Soviets. Even more important to the Soviets, Hungary was to accept supervision by an Allied Control Commission. The establishment of the Allied Control Commission marked a new period in the Soviet occupation. The precedent for establishing such commissions in defeated countries, a system that had not existed previously, was introduced by the Western Allies with the Italian armistice in 1943 in order to prevent the expansion of Soviet influence in the area, a move which the Soviets deeply resented.[142] In establishing the Allied Control Commission in Hungary, in which the Western Allies had only observer status, the Soviets could claim simply to be following the Allied example.

The Allied Control Commission, set up by the Soviets, was to insure that the Hungarians lived up to the terms of the armistice, and was to be headed by the representative of the Soviet armed forces, Soviet Marshal Klimenti Voroshilov. In its function of regulating and controlling the fulfillment of the armistice terms it assumed broad powers. The commission—which also had the authority to ban parties, arrest individuals, and exercise censorship—immediately began to organize Hungary's economic resources. Thus it became the instrument and legal justification for Soviet direct political intervention, as well as intervention in all other aspects of Hungarian life.[143]

The statutes of the commission expressly limited influence from the Western Allies. The chairman or vice-chairman needed only to inform British and American representatives of policy directives and take note of their observations. The Western Allies had the right to put forward proposals of their governments regarding fulfillment of the armistice agreement, but their access to the Hungarian government or ability to travel within the country had to go through the commission. If they wanted to make journeys to the provinces they were to apply to the vice-chairman, and in order to communicate with organs of the Hungarian government they were to go through the chairman or other commission official.[144]

At the Potsdam conference the Allies did attempt to gain greater influence in the Hungarian Allied Control Commission. They proposed that the chiefs of the British and American missions be appointed vice-chairmen of the commission and be free to travel in and out of Hungary and to communicate with the Hungarian government, but Voroshilov rejected the proposal.[145] Concerned with problems elsewhere, the British and Americans adopted a hands-off policy toward Hungary as well as the other countries considered within the Soviet sphere. In the spring of 1945 Douglas F. Howard, Foreign Office head of the Central European department, acknowledged that he did not see how the British could prevent the Russians from taking whatever actions they wanted in Romania, Bulgaria, and Hungary; it would be better just to recognize the situation as soon as possible.[146]

GOODS AND RESOURCES AS REPARATIONS

The armistice agreement gave the Soviets the right to take over and exploit Hungarian industry, but war damage to the industrial sector had left the country paralyzed. Despite the situation, the Soviets expected the reparation deliveries to begin immediately. On February 9, while the siege of Buda was still continuing, a demand came from Voroshilov to Prime Minister Miklós of the provisional government that within five days Hungary should submit a concrete proposal concerning reparation deliveries. A long period of negotiations followed, with an agreement only finalized on June 15, 1945.[147]

Yet, from November 1944 the Soviets had taken over any factory still capable of functioning to produce for the Soviet war effort, and factories were forced to produce at breakneck speed under difficult working conditions while workers were often not paid. Arbitrary street arrests by Soviet patrols and deportation of large numbers of skilled workers to the Soviet Union increased problems with the labor supply. The Soviets also removed industrial installations, requisitioned vast quantities of agricultural goods, and drove away tens of thousands of cattle, horses, and other livestock. According to the armistice agreement they claimed all German- or Italian-owned assets. While negotiations continued the Soviet army removed entire factories or parts of them and reassembled them in the Soviet Union, including the Weiss Manfred works in Csepel, the core of Hungary's industrial center, on the grounds that they were German property. Up until the requisition agreement was signed in June 1945 no credit was given to the Hungarian government for these reparation deliveries made to the Soviets.[148]

To reconstruct and begin deliveries at the same time was nearly impossible. Almost 90 percent of Hungarian heavy industrial production was tied down by reparations orders. Since the rate of exchange was based on the 1938 dollar, Hungary had to deliver goods worth almost four dollars at the current rate of exchange to obtain credit for one dollar of reparation. Deliveries to the Soviet Union placed such a heavy burden on industry that factories could not produce for domestic consumption. Peasants had no incentive to sell their produce since there was nothing for them to buy. In order to begin production the government was forced to issue loans to companies, which was only possible through printing money, and inflation began immediately after the end of the fighting.

The economic situation was made worse by the accumulated foreign and domestic debt; by September 1945 Hungary had a foreign debt of 890 million pengő plus $578 million. Hungarian debts to Germany of 30 million dollars, as well as the nearly 300 million dollars Germany owed Hungary were now owed to the Soviet Union. The Hungarian National Bank ceased to issue bank notes since the gold reserves had been removed from the country; in its place the Red Army issued large amounts of military money, also denominated in pengős. Despite minimal production, demand for food and other necessities was rising adding to rapid inflation. The obligation of paying for the upkeep of the Soviet Army was enormous, adding to inflationary pressure.[149]

FORCED LABOR AS REPARATIONS

In Soviet thinking forced labor was tied to reparations. At the Yalta and Potsdam conferences Stalin stated that the soldiers who had landed in prison from enemy countries should work on Soviet territory as partial reparations for its terrible human and material losses. In 1943 a committee of the Foreign People's Commissariat worked out a plan that the destroyed territory should be rebuilt through reparations, and in June of 1943 V. M. Molotov wrote to the British ambassador to Moscow that the entire Hungarian nation must be held responsible because Hungary provided armed support to Germany.[150]

In order to explain the long delay in the conquest of Budapest, Malinovskii had claimed to the Soviet Supreme Command that the Soviet troops had taken 110,000 prisoners during the siege—an enormously exaggerated figure. In order to deliver the 110,000 prisoners, Malinovskii ordered that some 50,000 men be rounded up. First it was anyone in a uniform—policemen, postmen, firefighters—and those with German names. Then indiscriminately anyone was picked off the streets. There was no precedent in Hungarian history for such actions after a war, that a military enemy deported civilians from the country, and the population was completely unprepared for the massive deportations by the Soviets. Even though the population had heard through German and Hungarian propaganda of the atrocities carried out by the Red Army, the forced removals that occurred after the occupation were completely unexpected.[151]

All together the Red Army abducted an estimated 600,000 to 700,000 people as prisoners of war to the Soviet Union—a large number of them civilians. There was hardly a family that was not affected directly or indirectly. The deportations were presented as the normal treatment of prisoners, although a majority were not actually prisoners of war and at least one third of the POWs had never been soldiers.[152] The collection continued months after the fighting had ceased.

It seems there was no systematic method for collecting the deportees. The deportations started as soon as the Soviets entered Hungarian territory in fall of 1944, beginning with the Soviet occupation of the northeastern Hungarian regions. Men in Maros-Torda county in age groups liable for recruitment were ordered to report to the local Soviet command or to the Romanian gendarmes to get their identity documents. The unsuspecting men who reported were not allowed to go home but were sent to a further locality with the promise of receiving the identity papers; upon their arrival they were marched into collection camps. It took days before the men realized that they had landed in prisoner-of-war camps.[153]

A commonly used method was to round up civilians under the pretense of asking young, able-bodied men and women to participate in short cleanup operations, called *malenkij robot* or little work. Unsuspecting civilians were rounded up off the streets or told to assemble in schools, movie theaters, or public buildings, to perform a few days of communal work. They were not permitted to return home but were force-marched twenty to thirty kilometers or more to reception centers. From there they were loaded into cattle cars holding between forty to sixty people to a wagon and taken to one of the Soviet forced labor camps in the Trans-Ural region.[154]

At one point in Budapest groups numbering a few hundred were lined up in fours, surrounded by Soviet bayonets, and marched toward Gödöllö. The people couldn't imagine what was happening. Then they learned that the Soviets had restored the railroad lines from Gödöllö. The men were packed into the railroad cars and only then did people realize that they were being deported to the Soviet Union.[155] Zoltán Kugyelka was taken from his butcher shop in Budapest with three friends on January 28, 1945, and marched to Gödöllö. They were kept there for two months before being transported by train to Jas, Romania, and then to Novkrematoszk, arriving the day after Easter. Kugyelka was one of the lucky ones who returned home. He worked in an iron-casting foundry where he suffered from bitter cold in a building with no roof and was fed only potatoes, beets, and rye. After the peace treaty was signed in May 1947 he was allowed to go home.[156]

Thousands of young women were among the deportees and many perished. In most settlements they took able-bodied girls and women along with young boys and men. To fill the quotas Soviet soldiers arrested anyone who fit the age categories, including pregnant women. The women received no special treatment but were forced to leave without food or proper clothing to face the extreme weather conditions of Siberian winters.[157]

Soviet soldiers had been told to keep their hands off the church and clergy; the Communists had concluded that violent attacks on the church during the 1919 revolution had alienated much of the population. Prof.

Béla Gyíres and his wife, who had taken refuge during the siege at the Pannonhalma Monastery, were returning to Budapest in April 1945 with some of the Benedictine priests. People called to them from the windows to take cover; the Russians were picking people up off the streets. They had no time to hide, but the Benedictine priests were with them. When the soldiers asked why they were not in robes, they said they had run out of vestments and the excuse was accepted.[158]

Often family members had no idea what had happened to their loved ones and no way of getting any information. In one case as prisoners were on a train, some tried to escape at a stop and the Soviets shot them. To replace them they saw a man with a thirteen- or fourteen-year-old child on a horse-drawn wagon waiting for the train to go by. The Russians took them despite the father's protests not to take the child. The horses were left standing there. The mother would never know what had happened.[159]

The father of Etelka Schwerthner, a retired officer living in Sopron, had taken no part in the war. When the Red Army occupied the city they ordered all officers or former officers to report; friends advised her father not to go, but—accustomed to obeying orders—he reported. He never returned home. The family's last glimpse of him was being loaded with other prisoners into the cattle cars. For years they had no idea of what had happened to him until an Austrian came to tell them that he had lain next to Etelka's father in a hospital in Odessa at Christmastime 1945. Her father was very ill and had died there.[160]

It is not possible to give an exact number of those POWs who returned from the Soviet prison camp world. The statistics suggest that 330,000 to 400,000 survived the Soviet prisons. Most of those who returned were sick, never able to work again. In 1948 after the Soviet and Hungarian Treaty of Friendship and Cooperation, the Hungarian communist government declared the issue closed—that those that remained were war criminals. Mass repatriation began in the autumn of 1957 but the reigning communist regime warned the returning POWs to keep quiet, threatening them with retaliation from the moment they reached the Hungarian border. Local and state governments rejected requests for financial assistance. From the 1960s the majority of those who submitted letters requesting pardon to the Soviet Union Highest Court were accepted; thus the sentences were without basis. Despite this, in Hungary they were treated as second-class citizens.[161]

In 1985 when Tamás Stark began his study of the Hungarian Soviet POWs, it was an especially sensitive area of research; even the mention of these deportations had been off limits for Hungarian historians. This was not surprising in a Hungary still under communist rule and Soviet military occupation. What is surprising is that the subject has not lost much of its sensitivity. Although large amounts of research material are available, very little has been published on the subject. With the collapse of socialism in Hungary, former Soviet POWs published dozens of memoirs, often on their own initiative, and during the early 1990s the opening of Soviet archives revealed that the Soviet bureaucracy had recorded information on the prisoners who arrived in the camps in great detail. In 2005 a mixed committee of Russians and Hungarians published *Magyar hadifolglyok a Szovjetunióban* (Hungarian POWs in the Soviet Union) a volume of documents in Russian. Even though so much material is available, very few Hungarian historians have dealt with the subject, and in general syntheses of twentieth-century Hungarian history it is often only mentioned briefly.[162]

The nature of Soviet intentions in the immediate postwar period have been debated. Exactly what were Stalin's plans for the East European countries, and at what point did he decide to make Hungary and the other East European countries satellites. From the actions of the Soviet Red Army and the Soviet-dominated Allied Control Commission, it seems clear that in the immediate postwar period the Soviets had only one aim—to squeeze out of Hungary everything possible in industrial goods, agricultural goods, and even human resources. The Hungarians were to be punished for joining the Germans and participating in the war and to be despoiled of as many of their resources as possible to contribute to the rebuilding of the Soviet Union.

10

Those making plans for Hungary's future in the fall of 1944 could hardly have foreseen a collapse so complete as that which Hungary suffered in 1945. Hungary—in proportion to its population—suffered one of the greatest military losses of life in the war—about one million people from a total population of less than ten million. According to historian Gyula Juhász, the combined effect of the German occupation, Arrow Cross rule, six months of frontline battles, and the Soviet occupation, not only dissolved the former Hungarian power structure, but brought about decisive changes in the traditional social structure.[1] No one had plans for a way out of such a cataclysm.

Approximately half a million people had fled to the West. The loss of members of the state and local bureaucracy was devastating, making it much more difficult to restart the administration, especially since the exodus included much of the experienced upper–middle class, as well as thousands of ordinary working people. From the point of view of economic reconstruction, most costly was the loss of large numbers of technicians, engineers, plant managers and owners. Although most of the refugees undoubtedly intended to return to Hungary after the war, a large number never returned.

Their decision on whether to return was affected by several factors. People's Courts, set up already in 1945 to eliminate war criminals, considered anyone who had left the country for the West to be guilty of collaborating with the Germans and the Szálasi government; of those who did return, many were detained. A radical Land Reform Act, implemented by Soviet edict even before the fighting stopped, appropriated not only the estates of the landowning aristocracy and the landed gentry, but also of the more prosperous nongentry farmers, eliminating their means of subsistence. These losses created a radical transformation of the social landscape.

Yet, despite the collapse of the former political and social order there was hope that the demise of the old regime would open the way for the building of a new democratic Hungary. The last German units had been driven out of the country by April 4, 1945, and on April 11 the Provisional National Government moved from Debrecen to Budapest. The parties represented in the provisional government began to make their plans for Hungary's future.

Land Reform

One of the few issues on which all political parties agreed was the need for agrarian reform. In the days following the Soviet occupation, leaders of every party feverishly worked on their plans for land distribution to eliminate the former system of large estates, but there were serious issues to consider. Conditions of farming and land ownership in Hungary varied widely, and it was clear that there was not enough land in the country to satisfy all claimants. Furthermore, a dilemma existed between how the land could be divided to satisfy peasant demands and at the same time maintain agricultural production. Other issues included how much land should be taken from each landowner, whether one should differentiate between the so-called gentry landowners and peasant owners, and which strata of peasants should have access to the land. Landless and agrarian workers were the most needy, but they had worked for others and did not have experience in independent farming. Conversely, the self-reliant smallholding peasantry had farming experience and would be able to modernize to form a new class of citizen peasantry.[2]

It had always been assumed that land reform would require careful planning. In the 1930s the Independent Smallholders Party had worked out a program to answer the crucial issues, which combined land distribution to the independent smallholding peasantry with a system of cooperatives to provide leadership and organization for the landless and agrarian workers. The more radical National Peasant Party, founded only in 1939, aimed to distribute land to the poor and landless peasantry, but also advanced the idea of cooperative farming. Unexpectedly, instead of debate and negotiations, the revolutionary program for agrarian reform was decided in Moscow, and the communist-designed program was rushed through in great haste, even while fighting continued in western Hungary.

The issuing of the revolutionary Land Reform Act of March 17, 1945 was the first direct Soviet intervention in Hungarian domestic affairs. On March 7 the Soviet State Defense Committee instructed Marshal Voroshilov, head of the Allied Control Commission, to have land reform carried out immediately. Molotov hoped that rapid execution of land division would encourage the Hungarian peasant soldiers still fighting with the Germans to desert, and would also rally the poor peasantry around the

Communist Party. Voroshilov summoned leaders of the approved political parties to a conference in Debrecen on March 13, 1945, to discuss agrarian reform. Participants believed that this would be a serious discussion in which they would be able to present their own programs and debate various possibilities.[3]

Leaders were summoned precipitously. Imre Kovács, one of the founders of the National Peasant Party, was roused from bed by a Russian colonel who stormed into the room and ordered him to come with him. He and several others known as experts on the land question made the 250-kilometer trip to Debrecen that night in an open jeep, wrapped in blankets.[4] Smallholders party leader Ferenc Nagy was working on his program for land reform when a car stopped at his home and a Russian colonel told him to pack his things; he had orders to bring him to Debrecen that night. When Nagy arrived in Debrecen the next morning discussions had already begun. Moscow émigré Imre Nagy, minister of agriculture, who had been working out a program for land reform in Moscow since September 1944, read out the plan.[5]

The proposed measure affected eight million acres—35 percent of the country's arable land. Owners of estates larger than 1,500 acres were to be fully dispossessed, including the estates of the Catholic and Protestant churches. Estates of extreme rightists and war criminals were also confiscated. Smaller gentry landowners were allowed to keep a maximum of 150 acres, while peasant landowners were allowed to keep 300 acres. The decree provided for compensation to landowners with holdings of 142 to 1,420 acres—which was never paid out—and landowners with holdings larger than 1,420 acres were not promised any compensation. Forty percent of the land thus obtained became state and collective property. The rest was re-allocated among 642,000 families, creating a new landowning class.[6]

Ferenc Nagy made several proposals to modify the plan, suggesting that since it was difficult to differentiate between the so-called gentry landowners and peasant owners, all landholders should be allowed to retain 150 acres, and that landholders with children should retain correspondingly more, but the conference voted down his proposals. He reportedly turned to his fellow Smallholders party leader, Zoltán Tildy, asking: "What's going on here? Why is it impossible to get a single reasonable proposal accepted?" Tildy explained that when Marshal Voroshilov had assembled them the day before he had already settled the extent and timing of the agrarian reform.[7]

Imre Kovács also proposed modifications, rejecting the Communist Party leadership's recommendation and putting forth the modified program of the March Front. He explained: "This was seemingly more radical . . . but I wanted the land reform carried out in two periods: first the estates over 500 hold . . . and after the new owners had gotten equipment and were used to producing on their own . . . then two or three years later would come confiscation of land over 50 hold."[8] He also suggested that the teaching orders and Protestant kollegium be left 1,000 hold each to continue their teaching. Kovács noted: "They were part of Hungarian history, and Hungarian democracy shouldn't go on without them. Not one of my suggestions was accepted. The wording of the decree was already printed and posters prepared with the date of March 15, 1945."[9] Despite objections, the measure was passed as a government decree on March 17, a little over a month after the surrender of Budapest.

Rushed through so quickly the land reform was calculated to win the support of the poor and landless peasantry for the Communist Party—and large numbers of peasants did join the party—partly because they feared that otherwise they would not get their land. Under communist supervision it was peasant claimants to land rather than agricultural specialists who set up the land-requisition committees, which determined what lands were to be distributed, sometimes with the aid of the Soviet army. Ferenc Nagy had advocated that the committees should include agronomists but his proposal was voted down. The distribution was entrusted exclusively to the claimants.

In the beginning there was a great deal of confusion and lawlessness in the process. The most radical acts occurred in the early months after the Soviet occupation. In eastern Hungary, the poorest and most radical part of the country, demand was the greatest but the least land was available to be distributed. At times peasants took more property than the land reform plan called for, but there was no one to stop them. A few months later the process became more orderly, and complaints began to come in over land that had been seized contrary to the provisions of the decree.[10]

The Smallholders had been rightly concerned about the economic soundness of the plan. Despite the radical nature of the reform the land confiscated from the large estates was not sufficient to satisfy the demands of those without land. About half of the landless—several hundred thousand agrarian workers, estate servants, and dwarf holders—did not receive land. Also many poor peasants were still held as prisoners of war at the time of distribution. Many who were included in the distribution received property too small to support a family. The average size of a plot was seven acres, while farms generally considered viable and competitive in Europe at the time were between fifty to one hundred acres. The small strips of land most peasants cultivated were often unable to produce per unit of land even as much as the antiquated system of large feudal estates.[11]

A major problem was that the distribution of land had not been accompanied by agrarian reform. There was no credit available for the new peasant owners, and the drastic loss of draft animals, machinery, and implements during the war added to economic disarray. The simple redistribution of land could not alleviate the dreadful poverty of those living in the country. Reports from Communist Party village agitators in 1946 revealed startling backwardness and poverty—in most villages there was no electricity.[12] The disappearance of the large estates also meant that agrarian laborers no longer had job opportunities, leading to an increase in rural unemployment, a problem compounded by urban relatives without food and work who came back to the villages. The earlier public works programs such as road building were suspended for lack of funds. The radical reform also eliminated the middle class farmers who had been the backbone of the countryside.

The land reform was but the prelude to the radical redistribution of property during the following three years. The reform not only eliminated the traditional large estates, but also their family members, lowering the social position of about one-quarter million formerly privileged social groups in one historic moment. The former elite groups, the aristocracy and gentry, had lost their means of subsistence; thus these groups were destroyed as distinct classes.[13]

Still, despite its defects the land reform was hailed for destroying the antiquated semifeudal pre-1945 social and economic structure and opening the way for the peaceful development of social and political democracy in an independent Hungary. The centuries-old dream of the Hungarian peasant had come true. It was thought at the time that the land reform would open the way to end the status of the peasantry as an under class and raise them into the body politic. But since the new agricultural system based on small farms functioned only for a short time, there is no way to know whether it could have overcome the age-old backwardness of Hungarian agriculture.[14]

Movement Against Reactionaries

As in other defeated countries radical social and political ideas found sympathy in Hungary. To gain legitimacy, governments of liberated Europe had to deal with the legacy of discredited wartime regimes, often by punishing those accused of fascist collaboration. In France, where rightist parties had been discredited by the Vichy regime, the Left, which had emerged with enhanced strength and prestige, pressed for the systematic purge of collaborators. In Italy, the Communist Party became the country's second leading party, proclaiming its role in the resistance and capitalizing on the fact that much of the country's social elite had cooperated with fascism.[15] In Hungary as well, many were eager to place blame for the country's involvement in the disastrous war, and were receptive to attacks on the old political and social elites.

The Communists had immediately begun their efforts to gain control over all the enforcement arms of the state—the political police, the police and the army. As the Red Army occupied the eastern part of the country, national committees were set up in the towns and villages, which then chose the delegates to the Provisional National Assembly. Ferenc Erdei of the National Peasant Party, a Communist in all but name, received the position of minister of the interior. In discussing the reorganization of the police on January 12, the cabinet approved Erdei's suggestion to establish two separate police departments, criminal and political, to carry out the two major tasks of the police, that of maintaining public order and of defending the democratic system. A reorganized and enlarged police force took over the tasks of the gendarmerie, which was disbanded. The task of pursuing fascists and reactionaries, which had been performed by the Soviet NKVD[16] agents who had arrived with the Red Army, was assumed by the newly formed Hungarian political police, the *Államvédelmi Osztály* or AVO. The Soviets made sure that the political police should become the exclusive preserve of the Communists. The organization of both police departments took place under the auspices of Erdei's Communist-dominated Ministry of the Interior.[17]

The activities of the AVO were above the law and beyond the jurisdiction of all but the Communist Party leadership and the Soviet authorities. Gábor Péter, selected to organize the AVO in January 1945, was close to Rákosi and possessed considerable autonomy. The headquarters were set up at the infamous Andrássy Boulevard 60, the ex-headquarters of the Nazis. The AVO became an important weapon for the Communists in their struggle for power as an instrument for repression and terror.[18]

ESTABLISHMENT OF PEOPLE'S COURTS

One of the first acts of the provisional government was to establish a new judicial institution to take reprisals on war criminals. Blame was to be placed directly on the so-called fascist and reactionary Horthy regime. Encouraged by the Soviets, they were also encouraged by the Allies, who in November 1943 had indicated their determination to punish those responsible for war crimes. In the armistice agreement signed with the Soviets, the Hungarians obligated themselves to liquidate all pro-German and fascist organizations, and among other things to cleanse the government and the civil service from those not committed to democracy.[19]

A few days after the signing of the armistice the provisional government published a regulation to begin the process of holding people accountable for wartime activity. The regulation stated explicitly that crimes could be punished even if *ex post facto*, despite protests that people should not be punished for acts not considered criminal at the time. Since these matters were not legal but above all political, it was decided that it would be necessary to establish a new court system.

The traditional Hungarian court system, with its long legal tradition and adherence to the rule of law was rejected, since its members had served under the former regime. According to its proponents, the new system would supposedly include those who had fought against the fascist alliance and was to represent the new democratic people's Hungary. The courts, to be made up by the parties in the national independence front, were intended to establish the legitimacy of the new government.

In all, there were twenty-four courts, the decisions of which were made by five lay people, nominated by parties of the national front and trade unions and then selected by the heads of counties. The use of lay people was intended to create the appearance that it was the "people" who were holding war criminals responsible. They functioned as a jury under the guidance of trained jurists, and the prosecutor was always a professional jurist. The Left was usually dominant in the People's Courts because of the representatives of the Communist-infiltrated trade unions. Appeals were addressed to the National Council for the People's Courts, members of which were also named by the political parties, but were made up of professional jurists and had no trade union representatives. The National Council often reduced sentences, arousing the hostility of the Communist and Socialist parties, who blamed them for taking the side of fascists.[20]

War criminals were to include all those who had played leading roles in the past reactionary and fascist regime, as well as the Arrow Cross leaders; in other words all who had served in the government, military, or civil service were to be held responsible. The category of war criminals was also to include all those who had fled, as well as the many who had been ordered or forced to move, to Austria or Germany. A proponent of the People's Courts writing in 1946, asserted that the judgments were all based on the illegitimacy of the Horthy regime; the war criminals were to be held guilty of all the ills suffered by the people from 1919 and especially the war. He claimed, "The people have never had control of their own fate in recent history. Since 1919 the old regime rulers exclusively ruled. Now it had become possible for the Hungarian people to place responsibility and punish those who brought on the Hungarian catastrophe."[21]

As the courts were being set up, teams within the Ministry of Justice were assembling a list of people to be charged with war crimes, including everyone who could be held responsible for the country entering the war, as well as Arrow Cross parliamentary deputies, and those military men who had prevented Horthy's armistice attempt. The list also included actors, writers, judges and civilians who had collaborated with the Arrow Cross. The process at the outset was haphazard; in the first postwar months only relatively unknown people were tried—journalists, soldiers who had killed Jews in workers' battalions. Important people could only be brought to trial after the end of the hostilities when the Allies were able and willing to return captives to Hungary. Political leaders were concerned that a large number of judges and prosecutors were Jewish and wanted to avoid the impression of a Jewish desire for revenge.[22]

FORMER LEADERSHIP ON TRIAL

Hungary had presented the Allies with a list of people to be repatriated and the first group was delivered on October 3, 1945. The first major trial, beginning on October 29, was that of former Prime Minister László Bárdossy. It had originally been planned that Szálasi would be the first to be tried, but at the last moment Rákosi made the change, perhaps because it had been Bárdossy who had made the declaration of a state of war with the Soviet Union. Because of the sudden change the prosecution was not fully prepared. Imre Kovács tried to dissuade Rákosi from beginning the procedures with the Bárdossy trial, suggesting instead to begin with Szálasi, who would be less likely to enlist sympathy, but Rákosi was adamant.[23] Bárdossy was charged primarily for entering the war against the Soviet Union, but also for the declaration of war against the United States and the operations against Yugoslavia.

Through condemning Bárdossy the trial was intended to teach the population about the crimes of the entire Hungarian political system of the interwar years. Bárdossy was presented as an evil person who had committed monstrous and unprecedented crimes. But Bárdossy, who maintained his dignified presence throughout the six-day trial, aroused much sympathy among the observers. In an intelligent defense he took responsibility for his actions but did not consider himself guilty of war crimes. He was sentenced to death by hanging on November 13, 1945, which the National Council of Judges commuted to the more honorable death by firing squad. Up to the present day he has not been rehabilitated, unlike many of those who were sentenced by the People's Courts.[24]

With other major figures it was often easier to judge their guilt and condemn them. Ferenc Szálasi at his trial appeared completely out of touch with reality, continuing to describe himself as leader of the nation. He was hanged March 12, 1946. Béla Imrédy, who had worked closely with the Germans, was sentenced to death on February 28, 1946. Lajos Reményi-Schneller, who had passed information to the Germans as a member of Horthy's cabinet and later served in Szálasi's government, was sentenced to death by firing squad.

Former Chief of Staff Ferenc Szombathelyi was also brought before the People's Court, although Szombathelyi's name had not been on any of the several extradition requests from Hungarian officials. No one in the government or press mentioned his name as a possible war criminal, and his arrival on the plane with war criminals surprised politicians and the press. Szombathelyi's anti-Nazi views were well known in Hungary, and he had been arrested by the Germans after the occupation. It is not known why he was suddenly arrested by the American military. In the trial Szombathelyi acknowledged his known role in taking up contact with the Americans but denied that he took part in spying against Germany. In his final speech before the court he described his appearance in his general's dress uniform—the gold braid cape lined with magenta, the various medals and crosses—"but the greatest cross was the one on my shoulders. How could I lead this little country out of this senseless War?"[25]

The judges of the People's Court were unanimous in their desire to save Szombathelyi, and they sentenced him to ten years in prison, but at the same time the Yugoslav Military Mission in Budapest was making demands for his extradition in connection with the Újvidék affair. In the end the National Council intervened and decided to prevent his extradition by sentencing him to life imprisonment. He was already in the process of serving his sentence, about to be delivered to the Hartai penitentiary where he was to have a position as clerk, when István Riesz, minister of justice, illegally handed him over to the Yugoslavs; he was put on trial in Újvidék and sentenced to death.

By January 31, 1946, the People's Courts had begun procedures against 29,917 individuals, issued indictments to 20,778 persons and sentences to 10,163. Between 1945 and 1950 all together about 60,000 were brought before the courts and of these 27,000 were convicted; more than 10,000 were put in prison and 189 executed, 167 received life sentences and 2,300 were sentenced to forced labor.[26] Among the rich supply of documents from the trials, a number show how suspicions were often based on mistaken bases, and that the judgments passed did not stand the test of time.[27] Former Prime Ministers Kállay and Lakatos were not charged, since they had carried out anti-German policies, and Horthy was spared for having saved the Budapest Jews.

There were no Hungarians tried at the Nuremberg trials. Horthy participated as a witness but he had been absolved by Stalin. On the visit of the Hungarian delegation to Moscow in April of 1946, Stalin had asked "and how is Regent Horthy?" He then told them, "I ask you, do not condemn Horthy. . . . First, Horthy is an old man; secondly, one should not be permitted to forget that he made the offer for an armistice in the fall of 1944."[28]

Reconstruction

Despite the terrible destruction that had occurred and the depredations of the Soviet Army, by spring of 1945 there were signs of revived hope. It was believed that once the peace treaty was signed the Soviet occupation forces would leave and Hungary would be free to develop independently. The country indeed rebounded quickly as people began to clear away the rubble and attack the most pressing reconstruction tasks. Essential services improved, as health care, education, and transportation services were gradually re-launched. In the first months after the siege there were no electric lights in streets and homes but by May 1945 there was almost a normal supply. The waterworks and burst pipes were repaired by August. With the temporary erection of an auxiliary suspension bridge on the pillars of the demolished St. Margit Bridge, supplies of gas were carried from Buda to the Pest side and suburbs. Private enterprise was strongly encouraged and land reform had created a whole new class of peasant small landowners.[29]

The new circumstances created a spirit of optimism and renewed hope that it would be possible to bring about democracy and enact the ideas of reform which had been broached before the war. Balint Kovács, a Protestant minister, commented that in 1945 life was "sparkling like champagne."[30] According to youth leader Sándor Kiss, all through the war their hopes had been placed in the democratic principles presented in the Atlantic Charter. Originally formulated by Roosevelt and Churchill in August 1941 and approved, among others, by the Soviet Union in September, the charter presented a vision for a post–World War II world in which the victors would not seek territorial gains and all peoples would have a right to self-determination. In the spring of 1945 it appeared that the Soviet Army, which had urged reorganization of democratic parties and the revival of political life along with the destruction of fascists, intended to abide by the Atlantic Charter.[31]

Perceptions of the immediate postwar period differed. In the spring of 1945 the Hungarian anthropologist, Linda Dégh, saw signs that might promise a new start in the bright red flags, hastily put-up posters on damaged buildings , and civilian militia members sporting red armbands on shabby winter coats, and even in the slogans praising the Red Army and Stalin: "Hail to the Heroes, the Glorious Soviet Army and its Great Leader, Comrade Stalin, Death and Eternal Damnation to the Enemy of the People, the Fascist Villains."[32] The first celebration of May Day in 1945 set the pattern of ritualized patriotic festivities, floats and pageants making political statements, happily cheering marchers carrying banners and portraits of champions of the party.[33] But Sir Alvary Frederick Gascoigne, British diplomat in Hungary, commenting on the May 1 parade, noted that people had to line up on the streets—if not they were called nazis. The mob marched with red flags and communist slogans—but looked broken and tired.[34]

Leaders of Hungarian youth groups were among the first to mobilize their members. By the end of February the Hungarian Scout Movement had been reactivated. Despite the danger of being picked up and deported by the Red Army, scouts were active in rebuilding. They tore down collapsed shelters in search of survivors, removed rubble, served at the railway stations giving food to the men and women POWs about to be shipped to the Soviet Union, went to the countryside to help in harvesting crops.[35] In Debrecen in late December Jenő Kerkai, founder of KALOT, received permission from leaders of the Hungarian Front as well as the communist leadership to restart the youth organization, and Catholic youth leaders began hiking through the villages to organize peasant youth.[36]

Soon after the liberation of Budapest, leaders of the youth resistance decided to form a movement designed to unite all Hungarian youth in a democratic association, and Sándor Kiss was chosen secretary general. But in April when the association, the Alliance of Hungarian Democratic Youth (MADISZ), was formally established, a communist leadership gained influence with the intention of organizing it on the Soviet model, and Kiss handed in his resignation. National Peasant Party member Zoltán Szabó became the new secretary general with Communist Party member József Kiss as vice-secretary general.

After the provisional government moved to the capital, Independent Smallholders leaders Zoltán Tildy and Ferenc Nagy returned to Budapest and began to reorganize the Independent Smallholders Party. The affiliated Peasant Alliance, an apolitical body created to unite the peasantry, was recreated in May with the goal of fashioning a united Hungarian peasantry. Using the folk high school model with a curriculum geared to develop peasant confidence and self-respect, they aimed to educate a local leadership that would defend peasant interests in a way similar to the worker trade union movement. The National Peasant Alliance held seventeen three-month folk high school sessions in 1946 and thirty-eight six-to-eight-week programs. In 1947 the number of sessions increased to thirty and sixty respectively.

PLANNING FOR ELECTIONS

According to the declaration at Yalta general elections were necessary, but elections were also needed in order to confirm the legality of the radical changes made only with the approval of the provisional government and legislative assembly.[37] The Western powers had not yet acknowledged the provisional government and declined to do so until the Soviets agreed to hold free elections. In the meantime, the Communist Party had strengthened its organization. At their first national conference in Budapest from 20–21 May, the Hungarian Communist Party enlarged the Central Committee to twenty-five members and created an eleven-member politburo and a five-member secretariat. The five members—General Secretary Rákosi, Mihály Farkas, János Kádár, J. Révai, and László Rajk; all Moscow émigrés except Rajk—directed the party; the four without Rajk held leadership in their hands.[38]

Based on the perceived successes of the May Day rallies, the Communists were convinced that if elections were held, they would be victorious. They accordingly raised the issue of national elections, and by the end of August the cabinet began to discuss election timing. The Communists had eliminated the more moderate members of the provisional government; Gábor Faragho, Public Supply; Ágoston Valentiny, Justice; and István Vasáry, Finance, had been pressured into resigning on July 21. The Communists and Social Democrats now formed the majority in the cabinet and established the timing for the elections. The communist leaders calculated that their electoral chances were best in the Budapest area; they were convinced that the working class districts of the capital would give a sweeping victory to the united Communist-Socialist ticket. It was decided to hold the election in two rounds, Budapest municipal elections on October 7 and national elections on November 4, leaving little time for the political parties to campaign.[39]

For the time being Stalin had decided to maintain a semblance of parliamentary democracy, but the Soviets were still confident in the victory of the Communist Party. Membership in the party had grown exponentially, and by the time elections were held in November 1945 membership had reached a half million. The disintegration of the state and the dissolution of society favored revolutionary change, and the communist program of social radicalism found support, particularly in eastern Hungary. In their program the Communists concentrated on the most pressing tasks of reconstruction combined with reform; they refrained from attacks on the Catholic Church in the villages and posed as a patriotic organization ready to defend national interests and private property. There was no hint of their long-term goal; socialism was not mentioned— they spoke only of democracy.[40]

Many workers joined the party out of conviction, and a number of small peasants joined after the land reform. Some idealistic intellectuals believed in the party's promises while civil servants joined sometimes out of fear, others out of opportunism. Two dramatically different groups signed up in large numbers, Jews and former Arrow Cross members. Jews turned to the party out of gratitude for the liberation and the sense that communism could protect them from popular anti-Semitism. Former low-ranking Arrow Cross members joined to cover up their past activities, but also perhaps because of the appeal of radical change. The party encouraged them to join; since all of the Moscow leaders except Imre Nagy were Jewish, they welcomed the former nationalists. Also all the leaders except

Rákosi had spent the interwar years in the Soviet Union and had little understanding of the situation in Hungary.[41]

The elections by secret ballot were relatively fair and free from interference. Although the Western Allies had a hands-off policy toward Hungary, the Soviets were still not sure how much pressure they could apply to Hungary because of the percentage deal between Churchill and Stalin, when the division of influence agreed on for Hungary had been fifty-fifty. As a result they intervened less in the Hungarian elections than those in other East European countries. Sixty percent of the population had the vote, in contrast to one-third under the Horthy regime and one-sixth under the Habsburgs. Those banned from voting included the leaders of the dissolved rightist parties, volunteers in the SS, and all those interned or being prosecuted by the People's Courts. Of course the hundreds of thousands deported to the Soviet Union were not available to vote.[42]

Of the ten parties that applied to participate, the seven granted permission by the Allied Control Commission were the Hungarian Communist Party, the Independent Smallholders, the Social Democratic Party, the National Peasant Party, the Civic Democratic Party, the Hungarian Radical Party, and the Democratic Popular Party. Other than the former opposition parties, none of the former legal parties in the government of the Horthy regime were represented. Interestingly, the positions of the various parties were not significantly different. All parties spoke of the importance of private property and privately owned means of production. The four largest parties called for a socialized health care system and revision of the pension system. The Communist Party had the most detailed campaign platform and was the best run; they had the most access to print media which was in scarce supply, and the means of transport by the Soviet occupation forces.[43]

In the first round, the municipal elections in Budapest on October 7, the Smallholders won a surprise victory, gaining a resounding 50.54 percent of the vote. The Social Democrats and the Communist Party had run on a common ticket, the United Workers' Front, and won only 42.75 percent. The Communists had been convinced of victory since forty percent of the eligible voters belonged to one or the other party, and they were shocked by the results. They had not reckoned with the workers' suspicion of the Communists as well as their patriotism. Offended by the behavior of the Soviet soldiers, workers were also aware that the Moscow clique had taken over leadership of the party and that the party was full of corrupt elements, including former Arrow Cross opportunists. The

Social Democratic alliance with the Communists also aroused their suspicions, especially since the traditional Social Democratic leadership, including the former respected leader, Károly Peyer, had been pushed aside.[44] The Communists had also failed to note that many of the men were still in prisoner-of-war camps or recruited for *"malenki robot "* thus women made up a large number of the voters.[45]

The Communist Party blamed the loss on the economic crisis, the right-wing of the Social Democrats, the anti-Soviet attitude of the middle class, and the influence of the Catholic Church. The Social Democrats blamed their loss on the United Front and decided to run independently in the national elections. Upset with the results, on October 18 Voroshilov suggested that in the nationwide elections all the parties run together on one common list to avoid a similarly disappointing outcome, but the Smallholders and the Social Democrats insisted on running independently. Furthermore, the Western Allies mentioned that the single list would not meet the Yalta specifications, so the Soviets were forced to compromise. Still they insisted that regardless of the outcome the new government should be a coalition government. The Communists still expected a great victory in the national elections based on the tremendous success of the party in recruiting new members and the effect of the land reform. The Muscovite, József Révai, predicted a victory by 70 percent. In contrast, the actual result was a bitter disappointment.

The national elections of November 4, 1945 have been celebrated as being the first free elections ever held in Hungary. The November elections proved that the population was still profoundly anti-Soviet and skeptical of the Communist Party's ultimate goals. The Smallholders won the contest in all of the sixteen districts, collecting 57 percent of the vote, an absolute majority. Although it had formerly been the party of the democratic peasant opposition, in the new situation, and in the absence of the former traditional parties, the Smallholders attracted the votes of urban and nonpeasant voters alike who were frightened of a communist takeover. The elections were not only a defeat for the Communists but also to a certain extent for the Social Democrats. The Social Democratic Party, now closely aligned with the Communist Party, received only slightly more than 17 percent, while the Communist Party received slightly less than 17 percent. The radical left-wing National Peasant Party, led by the crypto-communist Erdei, received only 7 percent, and the rest of the votes went to the Civic Democratic Party and the new Hungarian Radical Party.[46]

Hoping to avoid confrontation, the Smallholders yielded to Voroshilov's demands that they form a coalition government. The party itself was a coalition, including conservatives who had joined for lack of another party, as well as crypto-communists like Gyula Ortutay. Uncertain whether they would be able to take on the burden of so many difficult tasks, the party leaders decided to ask for half of the portfolios. Of eighteen cabinet posts, nine went to the Smallholders, four to the Communists, four to the Social Democrats, and one to the Peasant Party. The Communists were determined to have the Ministry of the Interior with its immense power and responsibility for administration and public security, including the police. At first the Smallholders had claimed it for the popular leader, Béla Kovács, and the Communists had agreed, but on the day before the official appointment Rákosi again demanded the Ministry of the Interior, stating that otherwise the Communist Party would not share in the government. If this happened the Social Democrats and National Peasant Party would also leave the coalition. Rákosi argued that the Communist Party had to lead the fight against reactionaries. In every country in southeastern Europe the ministry of interior was in the hands of the Communist Party, and Ferenc Nagy believed that Rákosi had his instructions from the Soviets.[47] British diplomat Gascoigne expressed the fear that the Smallholders would give in too much to communist demands, and his fear was warranted.[48]

Debate on the form of government for the postwar Hungarian state began in early December when the idea of forming a republic was introduced. Some thought it not appropriate to change the form of government while the country was under foreign occupation, but on February 1, 1946, the National Assembly passed Law I of 1946 proclaiming Hungary a republic. Interestingly, in the postwar period the monarchy was also abolished in Yugoslavia and in Italy.[49] Zoltán Tildy, a Calvinist minister, was elected president, and Ferenc Nagy, a Calvinist peasant farmer, was named prime minister, an amazing development in the history of Hungary.[50]

The unique situation in which a peasant farmer had become prime minister was pointed up at a dinner in the United States for the Hungarian delegation, hosted by Undersecretary Dean Acheson. Nagy recalled an exchange with Justice Felix Frankfurter—who remarked to him in his jovial manner "that he had come to the conclusion that the Hungarian people chose me [Nagy] for their premier because I had an answer for every question." "No, sir," Nagy responded in an equally jovial fashion. "The Hungarians, as proof of their sincere democratic feelings, wanted a man for the premiership whose cultural training did not go beyond reading and writing, who had never been abroad, and who spoke not a single foreign language. As they could not find these qualifications in anyone but me, I became the premier."[51]

COALITION GOVERNMENT

After the results of the elections it became clear that the Communist Party would not be able to come to power through traditional parliamentary means. From this time on the Communists began to take political life increasingly into their own hands, with the Allied Control Commission providing the instrument through which they were able to control the situation. In the coalition government the Smallholders were constantly outmaneuvered by the Communists, who had the support of the Social Democrat and National Peasant party ministers, Szakasits and Erdei, and used the slogans of class warfare and social revolution. The Smallholders leadership continued to compromise, hoping that they could hold out until the peace treaty was signed and the Red Army would leave the country.[52]

The Communists considered control of the organs of power of the utmost importance, and Rákosi made clear that no matter what the opposition did the police would remain "democratic" meaning under Communist control. Even before the elections the police had been basically in communist hands: 64 percent of the officers belonged to parties of the left-wing blocs and 31 percent were Communists. Afterward, despite its poor electoral results, the party was able to sustain its initial advantage over the police forces through its hold on the ministry of the interior.[53] A transformation of the military was more problematic at this early stage because of the anticommunist orientation of the armed forces.[54] However, the Hungarian Frontier Guards, which was the only combat-ready force in the country at this time, was doubled in size to 10,000. Under the command of Gen. Maj. György Pálffy, who also headed the Ministry of Defense Military Political department, it was converted into a communist armed force and became a strong military organization used as a primary instrument of communist terror.[55]

The difficulties presented by a coalition government soon became evident. Every issue had to be thrashed out in inter-party conferences by the four political parties. As the Communists were often violently opposed to the Smallholders leadership's plans, the result was that little could be

agreed on. The Communists soon realized that they could force concessions from their opponents, and they exploited their position ruthlessly.
Using the slogan of the struggle against so-called reactionaries, they organized mass demonstrations, an easy task considering the collective misery
in the winter months of 1945–1946, the desperate lack of food supplies
and run-away inflation, leading to hunger revolts and waves of strikes. At
the beginning of 1946 the average daily provisions for an adult citizen in
Budapest barely reached 480 calories; the population was also responsible
for maintaining provisions for the one and one half million Soviet soldiers in Hungary.[56] Their goal was not to break up the coalition by attacking the entire Smallholders Party, but to break up the unity of the party
by attacking the more conservative or outspoken members—an approach
referred to as "salami tactics." The Smallholders hesitated to take a tough
line against them, especially after the Communists had engineered the
formation of a Left-Wing Bloc, which was formally consolidated in March
of 1946.[57]

On March 6 the Left-Wing Bloc, made up of the Communist Party,
the Social Democrats, the Trade Union Council, and the National Peasant
Party, made a joint declaration that they were unwilling to cooperate
with the "reactionary right wing" of the Smallholders Party and demanded a supervised purge of the civil service. Two days later at a general assembly at Heroes Square, the Left-Wing Bloc demanded the
removal of representatives in the Smallholders Party whom they characterized as reactionaries, claiming that they hindered the work of the
coalition. The Smallholders leadership gave in to the threat, and suggested that the twenty-two members targeted be advised to leave the
party and thus enable the coalition government to continue to function
peacefully.[58] These representatives were not reactionary, but they had
worked to bring attention to illegal acts of the Communists and had
warned of the growing danger of dictatorship. The members were expelled on March 11, which meant that the party lost its majority in
parliament, although the expelled members did not lose their mandates
and continued to vote with the Smallholders on important matters.

This was the first use of Rakosi's clever salami tactics, the stage-by-
stage removal of those from the political scene who resisted the communist takeover. Many question why Tildy and Nagy gave in to Rákosi's
maneuvers. The Smallholders leaders feared the breakup of the coalition
which could lead to the government being paralyzed by strikes, but one
main reason for the compromises was Soviet pressure. The new Soviet

ambassador, G. M. Pushkin, criticized the Smallholders Party's deputies, calling them reactionary and anti-Soviet.Every time a Smallholder member of parliament criticized something, the Soviets countered with a demand, for immediate payment of reparations, for immediate payment of the food loan to the capital, and so on. Any protest was termed to be "reactionary."[59]

One of the first problems facing the coalition government was the run-away inflation and the necessity to cut expenditures. Because of inflation there was almost no national income; conditions became so extreme that the normal banking system and in particular the lending of money came to a halt. The problem had started during the war with the printing of money and now, with the demands of reparations, reconstruction could be accomplished only by printing more and more. The mint printed floods of paper notes but could barely keep industry moving. Reparations payments lagged. Inflation spiraled—at the black market the dollar was worth 1,320 pengő in July 1945 and 290,000 at the end of the year. At its height the daily inflation rate was 158,486 percent and the value of the dollar at the end of July 1946, 4,600,000 quadrillion, the greatest hyperinflation in history up to that time. This imposed further hardship on an already stressed population.[60]

The bureaucracy, already much too large during the interwar period, had greatly increased during the war; according to one source Hungary ranked fourth in the world in state employment after Germany, England, and Sweden. It was determined that it would be necessary to cut the number of civil servants, and the coalition government agreed to have so-called B-lists drawn up, lists of people who would be dismissed. It was of course to be expected that the reduction in bureaucracy would concentrate on those who were suspected of having actively supported the old regime.

Prime Minister Nagy suggested a commission of three men be established to determine the dismissals, one to be appointed by the prime minister, one by the minister of finance, and the third by the minister of each particular department affected. The Communists violently opposed the plan, demanding the involvement of the trade unions which they controlled. They insisted that instead of the finance minister, a trade-union representative should be a member of the commission, establishing a leftist majority in every ministry held by the workers' parties. The debate went on for weeks during which the Communists ordered worker demonstrations. Finally, on May 6, 1946 through use of a ruse, Rákosi won a decision favoring the Communist-led trade unions; the Communists now had the opportunity to advocate dismissal of individuals they described as reactionaries. According to the decrees issued, those to be examined by the screening committee included civil servants, writers, artists, and scholars.[61] With the introduction of the B-lists over 60,000 individuals were removed from their posts between May and October of 1946, the majority for political reasons; the Communists and to some extent the Socialists placed their people in vacated posts.[62]

Letters to save individuals from the B-list, written by the political scientist, István Bibó, indicate the nature of some of the charges. In one example a procedure was started against the pastor of a church in Debrecen, Pastor Uray, for rabble-rousing during the war, based on a sermon in which he described a Soviet Russian poster as being against God and religion, while in fact, the sermon, with no reference to the war, was against godlessness. In defending the pastor, Bibó explained that Uray had spoken strongly against Hitlerism, and attested to his honesty, purity, and Protestant pietism. Uray was freed. In another case, a certain József Hegedüs was being charged because he moved to the West during the time of the Szálasi government. Bibó attested that Hegedüs was against fascism and nazism and an honorable Hungarian. His removal to the West was not because of his political views but in his official role as a public servant.[63] Despite the isolated victories, however, the vast majority of those on the B-lists were indeed dismissed.

EXPULSION OF THE GERMAN MINORITY

At the Potsdam meeting of the three great powers in mid-summer 1945 one item addressed was the expulsion of German populations from Poland, Czechoslovakia, and Hungary, and in the statement released August 2, 1945, the powers recognized that "the transfer to Germany of German populations, or elements thereof, . . . will have to be undertaken" but stated that any transfers that take place should be effected in an orderly and humane manner. A week later, General Lieutenant Swiridow, leader of the Allied Control Commission, informed Béla Dálnoki-Miklós, president of the provisional national government, that Moscow demanded from the Hungarian government the expulsion of 400,000 to 450,000 Germans. Miklós informed the coalition partners on August 10 and called for a special session of the Council of Ministers for August 13, since Swiridow demanded the submission of the outline of a plan within three or four days.[64]

At the cabinet meeting Communist Party and National Peasant Party members also insisted on the expulsion of all Germans. Ferenc Nagy pointed out that there were not enough Germans in the whole country to fill the number demanded, adding that those who were guilty of crimes should be expelled, but that he was against collective responsibility. It was only later learned that the Potsdam decision had not required that Hungary expel the Germans but only gave them the authority to do so.[65]

In late 1944 there had been no comprehensive plans for the expulsion of the Hungarian-German population; Hungarians felt no particular animosity toward the German minority. In December 1944 the provisional government called for the punishment of war criminals and traitors, but without treating the question of minorities. In fact the Soviet deportation of tens of thousands of Swabians at the end of 1944 was greeted with widespread protests.[66] The attitude of the Hungarians changed with the hastily executed land reform and influx of refugees from the neighboring countries. Forced to leave their land and possessions, the refugees needed new homes, and the properties of the German minority became more attractive. The decree which gave authorities the right to confiscate the property of all traitors suggested the acceptance of a policy of collective guilt, since members of the Volksbund had been judged equally with fascist leaders and war criminals.[67]

Regardless, the Potsdam agreement, stating that the transfer of Germans should be carried out in an orderly humane manner, was interpreted by the National Peasant and Communist parties as legal permission to carry out deportations. After receiving the Soviet demand, amid heated debate, the Council of Ministers agreed to expel 303,000 individuals, including 60,000 children and 37,000 people over sixty, despite the protests of foreign minister János Gyöngyösi, who warned that the use of collective punishment would set a precedent for the treatment of Hungarians in neighboring lands. The number of Swabians deported remained much below government expectations: about 120,000 were deported in 1946 and another 50,000 in 1947–48.[68]

But as Gyöngyösi had warned, the expulsion of the Germans became intertwined with Czechoslovakia's determination to rid the state of the entire Hungarian minority. The Czechoslovak government had already begun to carry out plans to expel the Hungarian minority in the spring of 1945, having decided that the Czech prewar policy of minority protection was counterproductive, and the minorities a source of unrest and instability. The multiethnic state was to become solely Czech and Slovak, the goal to be reached by the expulsion of most of the minorities and successive assimilation of the rest.[69]

CIVIL SOCIETY

The victory of the Independent Smallholders Party was greeted with enthusiasm and relief by much of the population. The democratic beginnings represented a distinct break with the conservative, nationalist authoritarianism of the interwar period, and there were hopeful signs throughout the country, with genuine achievements in reconstruction and peasant production. People were optimistic, many believing in a brighter future. The rich associational life that had flourished in prewar Hungary, the youth groups, caritative societies, religious associations, Protestant and Catholic folk schools, showed signs of being revived with promising democratic initiatives.[70]

In competition with the Communist-influenced MADISZ, the Independent Smallholders Party formed its own youth group, the Independent Youth Alliance, FISZ. KALOT at first had sought contacts with MADISZ, but after MADISZ accused it of being reactionary and fascist, and demanded that it be dissolved, KALOT increased active cooperation with FISZ, coming to an agreement to democratize economic and political life. The National Peasant Party also formed its own youth group. On March 3, 1946 the independent youth groups, including the Protestant YMCA and Scouts set up the democratic youth organization, the National Hungarian Youth Council, MIOT to unite worker, peasant and student youth.

Invigorated by the elections, the Peasant Alliance developed a program for a network of folk high schools, as well as one that would lead to high school graduation equivalence.[71] The more radical National Peasant Party at first opposed the revival of folk high schools, believing in the need for a quick build-up of an eight-grade general school and possibilities for the peasantry to continue with their education. They held that the folk high schools, earlier sponsored by church organizations, would block the development of peasant self-confidence. But it quickly became apparent that conditions were missing for the development and expansion of a general educational system, and thus, under the name of peasant universities, they set up a few folk high schools in Debrecen and Pécs.[72]

The National Council for Public Education, created in April 1945 and chaired by Albert Szent-Györgyi, initiated the transition to an eight-year required elementary school system that had originally been proposed in 1940. The Elementary Education Act of July 1946 was intended to make the educational structure more democratic, with all students to be educated equally. The plan was accompanied by a review of textbooks, which resulted in the elimination or modification of the majority of texts, most changes being made in literature and history texts. From a political point of view teaching was to be neutral; students were to choose for themselves their own world views and political orientations. In reality, of course, this was impossible to realize. The new textbooks of 1947–48 eliminated all conservative or nationalistic material which was replaced by leftist political writings. In literature the works of beloved national poets and writers were reduced and religious writings almost disappeared. Latin was eliminated and was to be replaced by a living language, but the teachers' lack of knowledge often meant that no language was taught at all. A separate Russian Institute was established in order to initiate the teaching of Russian. Yet because of the lack of teachers and school buildings it took years to try to establish the new system, with over-crowded classrooms and ill qualified teachers.[73]

A major initiative aiming to bring about a rapid change in the elite was the founding of the National Association of Folk Colleges, NÉKOSZ, intended to educate talented peasant, worker, and urban youth for leadership positions. About one hundred twenty People's Colleges were established throughout the country between 1946 and 1948, patterned after the Györffy kollégium, the first college established for peasant youth. The colleges combined community living with special instruction, similar to the Oxford and Cambridge system of colleges. NÉKOSZ, which became immensely popular, was an elite organization, with the aim of creating a new generation, the future leadership.[74]

Students attended regular schools, but in addition they had special studies in politics, Marxism, and literature in the colleges, and even read the populist writers. The majority attended middle schools, but many still needed to complete elementary education, while some attended schools of higher education (estimates range between 400 and 1,000). Information at the time gave the students' origins as about 30 percent poor peasants and 20 percent small or middle peasants. By the beginning of 1948 peasant, worker, and urban students from all over the country lived, studied, and engaged in politics in the colleges. Estimates of the numbers of students range from between 2,500 to 6,067.[75]

At the time that the democratic youth organization MIOT was established in March 1946, its position seemed to be secure, but in June the leftist parties decided to weaken the position of the Smallholders and clerical powers, beginning a press campaign against FISZ, KALOT, and other religious-based youth groups. On July 4, 1946, the minister of the interior, László Rajk, who had replaced Imre Nagy, dissolved the so-called reactionary association KALOT, with its some hundred thousand members, and also the Hungarian Scout Alliance, a decision that aroused such a strong reaction by several members in Parliament that the government backed down, although it continued to limit the scout organization.[76] In the following two weeks Rajk dissolved a further 1,500 civil societies and church youth groups. The orders signed by Rajk were intended to eliminate all autonomous organizations of civil society. He continued to compile ever-newer lists of right-wing elements, and often through carefully orchestrated public meetings denounced accused individuals and forced them to resign.[77]

The long tradition of church-sponsored education was an immediate target of the new regime. As early as spring 1946, shortly after the elections, Catholic clergy were accused of participating in a reactionary fascist conspiracy. In response, in a pastoral letter issued in May 1946, Cardinal Mindszenty and other Catholic bishops linked the right of the Church to operate schools with that of parents to control the education of their children. Strongly supported by the population, the Catholics won a respite and the immediate crisis passed; the government did not move to take over the Catholic schools in 1946.

At the same time, the reform of public education met with strong resistance, with intense debate over the revision of textbooks. There was violent protest against the elimination of required religious education, which was to be made optional in spring of 1947. Growing communist influence and the elimination of religious education led the minister of religion and education, Dezsö Keresztury, to resign on March 14, to be replaced by Gyula Ortutay, nominally a member of the Smallholders Party, but actually a secret Communist. Ortutay supported the plan, but the plan ran into such public protest that the government was forced to drop it for the time being.

Preparations for the Paris Peace Conference

Since April 1945 foreign affairs experts had been holding deliberations to prepare for the Paris peace conference, but the difficulties presented by dealing with the coalition government soon became evident. The new foreign minister, János Gyöngyösi, appointed a foreign affairs professional, István Kertesz,[78] to organize and supervise the new division of the ministry to prepare the Hungarian case, but the work was to take place under the most difficult political and technical circumstances. The Foreign Ministry building and most of its contents had been destroyed during the siege, but even more disruptive—in every important division of the ministry was a Communist who reported to the party, and the Soviet authorities were consulted about all issues of importance.[79]

Kertesz's first question to the foreign minister was to clarify the peace aims of the government—but he never received an explicit answer. Gyöngyösi only explained that political difficulties in the coalition regime hindered an agreement. So Kertesz and the team of officials and scholars that he had put together concentrated on gathering materials and data and preparing a variety of alternative proposals.

Hungarians were eagerly awaiting the treaty because of the widespread understanding that Soviet troops would leave the country once a peace treaty was signed. There were also hopes that minor territorial adjustments could be made in favor of the minority ethnic Hungarians living on the border with Hungary in Slovakia, and also with ethnic Hungarian populations in Romania. This pursuit of territorial revision on ethnic grounds was an intensely patriotic cause with virtually unanimous public support and was endorsed by all the noncommunist parties. But the Communist Party, constrained by Stalin's preferential treatment of Czechoslovakia and Romania, refrained from taking a position. When public outrage at official persecution of the Magyar minority in Slovakia finally compelled the Communists to attempt to intercede, representatives of the Slovak party reminded them that Stalin supported the Czechoslovak stand.[80]

As previously noted, the Czechoslovak government charged the entire Hungarian minority with collective guilt for the war, and Beneš demanded that all Slovak-Hungarians be resettled to Hungary. In negotiations the Hungarian government pointed out that the majority of the Hungarians in question were an agrarian population who had lived on these same lands for centuries. When the Hungarian government refused the Czechoslovak proposal for massive minority resettlement, the Czechs continued their alternative plan to resettle and re-Slovakize the Magyars, forcing them across the border or removing them from their homes and transferring them to the formerly German-populated Sudetenland. Finally, impelled to negotiate in an attempt to protect the minority, the Hungarian government signed an accord on February 27, 1946, agreeing to a voluntary people's exchange.[81] It was difficult to find enough Slovak-Hungarians interested in resettling to Slovakia, but eventually 60,000 Slovaks were recruited, primarily agrarian workers and youth, in exchange for 90,000 Slovak Hungarians.[82]

The suggested proposals prepared for the peace conference were completed in February 1946 and essentially reiterated the Hungarian belief in the injustice of the Trianon dictate and asked for modification along ethnic lines in Transylvania and Slovakia. In March the Communist Party politburo debated the proposals but reached no conclusions, and recommended that a delegation led by Prime Minister Nagy visit Moscow.

The Hungarian peace delegation, led by Prime Minister Nagy, set out on the visit to Moscow, the first of several visits to the Allied capitals to make personal contacts before the meeting of the peace conference. The delegation brought proposals for modest readjustments of the Trianon borders and requested autonomy for the Székely area in Transylvania as well. They hoped to improve the relationship with the Soviet Union and the nine-day trip, from April 9 to 18, was somewhat successful. The delegation was received with elaborate hospitality and Stalin devoted several hours to discussions with members of the delegation. The burden of reparations was eased somewhat—the period of fulfillment being lengthened from six to eight years. Regarding the Czech demand for the resettlement of the entire Hungarian minority, Stalin said he believed in population exchange but would support the delegates' desire for equal citizenship rights for the Hungarian minority. On the Hungarian request for a minimum amount of land to be returned from Transylvania, 4,000 square kilometers, Stalin pointed out that if Romania fulfilled its obligations according to the armistice agreement, it would be granted Transylvania or the larger part of it, a clause which, he said, gave them the opportunity to raise the question at the peace conference.[83]

The delegation thought they had done good work in Moscow, naively believing that friendship between the two countries would be sincere. They soon realized how mistaken they had been when on May 7 they received a message that the Foreign Ministers' Conference in Paris had reached a decision on Transylvania and would recommend that Romania receive all of the Transylvanian territory. Later the Americans told Nagy that they had favored some adjustment in favor of Hungary but Molotov was adamantly opposed.[84]

The next trip was to the Western capitals. Nagy, aware of the danger of alienating Moscow, hoped to assuage the Soviets by persuading Rákosi to join the delegation. Ironically, Rákosi was the only member of the delegation who spoke English and was often the spokesman. In their visit to the United States in June their first meeting was with Undersecretary Dean Acheson, where the discussion concentrated on two main topics, the final negotiations for the peace treaty and the return of Hungarian national wealth, $30,000,000 of gold bullion. The delegates were impressed by the friendliness and cheerfulness among lawmakers at the luncheon by the House Foreign Affairs committee. Secretary of State Byrnes, who met personally with Nagy and according to Nagy treated him like an old friend, told how the question of Transylvania had slipped entirely into Soviet hands and the decision of May 7 was entirely at their insistence. Before the delegation left Washington, Acheson handed Nagy a note with the response that the United States would unconditionally return the gold bullion, as well as other treasures, including the fleet—if it were to be owned by Hungary. The surplus credit of $10 million, which had been granted a short time earlier, was to be raised to $15 million.[85]

During the trip Rákosi's pro-Moscow and anti-U.S. attitude was demonstrated by his harsh and partisan criticism of everything the delegation did and saw, combined with his unrelenting praise of conditions in the Soviet Union. Upon visiting the Tennessee Valley Authority, a major New Deal project, he compared it unfavorably to the power plants of the Soviet Union. He expressed similar opinions when shown some well-furnished prefabricated houses, commenting: "Once the bedbugs get into these houses, they'll never get them out again." In answer to another delegate who said, but "there don't seem to be any bedbugs in America," he snapped: "Don't you know that bedbugs originated in America, and were exported from here to Europe and Russia?" Still, at a dinner in New York he commented, "I better enjoy something as long as I am here. The way I see the international situation, they will never ask us to come to America again."[86]

Upon their return, Rákosi reported to Stalin that aside from the promise to return Hungarian gold and some other Hungarian properties the trip had brought no political benefits. The Americans had demonstrated that they were not in a position to give concrete help in preventing Soviet domination, while the British had shown even less inclination to support any Hungarian aims.[87]

After the reception in the United States the trip to London was disappointing. Secretary Philip Noel-Baker listened to the delegation's peace aims but gave little encouragement, saying he could hardly conceive of a reintroduction of the Transylvanian issue. In regard to the Hungarians in Slovakia, he said courteously but pointedly, "Don't you find it slightly unusual that you desire support for a defeated nation at the expense of a victorious one?" Nagy pointed out that it was debatable if Slovakia could be regarded as a victorious nation, since "during its short independence, [it] pursued the war against the Allies much harder than Hungary."[88] But he emphasized that Hungary was only seeking human rights and liberties for the Hungarian population living on Czechoslovak soil. Prime Minister Clement Attlee gave them a lecture on democracy, stating that no country is truly democratic unless its government has an active opposition in parliament—a dig at Hungary where all political parties were in the governing coalition.[89]

In May 1946 István Kertesz arrived in Paris ahead of the Hungarian peace delegation, which he was to lead, full of hope that he would be able to make contact with the Allied committees preparing for the peace conference and present some of the proposals of his committee. But he soon became aware of the stark realities of peacemaking in 1946. His request for a hearing in connection with two main questions—the persecution of the Hungarian minority in Czechoslovakia, and the council's decision to reestablish the Trianon boundary between Hungary and Romania—was turned down. The council would examine only the draft peace treaties prepared by the deputy foreign ministers, indicating that the work on their carefully prepared proposals had been in vain. The peace settlement was to depend on the respective power, national interests and ideologies of the major victorious powers.[90]

There was little similarity between the Paris peace conference of 1946 and the peace conference of 1919. Peace treaties were not concluded with the major enemy states, Germany and Japan. The conclusion of peace treaties was restricted to the five less important ex-enemy states: Italy, Bulgaria, Romania, Finland, and Hungary. The major Western states signed a peace treaty with Japan only in 1951 and Western and Communist countries later concluded patchwork agreements with the two Germanys. In no way was this a comprehensive peace settlement.

Discussion of the Hungarian peace treaty at the Paris peace conference lasted from the end of August 1946 until the beginning of October; yet none of the Hungarian requests were granted. The treaty was finally signed on February 10, 1947, along with the Romanian, Italian, Bulgarian, and Finnish treaties. Contrary to the period early in the war, when the Western powers had been in favor of giving back some of the territory lost with the Treaty of Trianon, views had changed. With Czechoslovakia, after sacrificing the Sudetenland to Hitler at Munich in 1938, the Western powers were in no position to insist on anything, not even the ethnic principle. But the final obstacles were presented by the Soviet Union for whom Romania was strategically more important than Hungary; the Soviets, who intended to keep Bessarabia, favored Romania keeping all of Transylvania to compensate for the loss. The Western powers supported minimal Hungarian territorial claims against Romania but without conviction, and consequently the Soviet position prevailed.[91]

In essence the treaty re-established the Trianon borders, but with Czechoslovakia granted an additional three Hungarian villages, which it demanded for the enlargement of the Bratislava bridgehead on the right bank of the Danube. The Western Allies refused Beneš's insistence on collective punishment and the forced resettlement of 20,000 ethnic Hungarians from Czechoslovakia to Hungary, but paid little attention to the misfortunes of the remaining Hungarian minority.[92] Even though the Hungarian minority had not been pro-Nazi—in fact had been alienated by the nationalist policies of the Slovak fascist regime—the Allies equated them with the German minority in the Sudetenland. The Hungarian request for an international commission to supervise treatment of the Hungarian-populated part of Slovakia was refused; after the war the United Nations did not re-establish international guaranties for minorities, leaving the question of minority rights to individual countries.[93] The outcome of the peace conference caused much bitterness, but unlike the hysteria after the signing of the Treaty of Trianon in 1920, was accepted by the exhausted and disillusioned Hungarians with a general sentiment of resignation.[94]

The greatest disappointment of all, however, came with the realization that Soviet troops were to remain in Hungary. It had been fully expected that the Soviet troops would leave the country upon the signing of the peace treaty, and the treaty in fact stipulated that within ninety days of the ratification of the treaty all Allied armed forces were to leave the country which they had occupied. Yet the Soviets slipped in an additional clause that effectively annulled this promise. The clause gave the Soviet Union the right to maintain such armed forces in Hungary and Romania as were needed to secure communications with its occupation forces in the Soviet occupied zone of Austria; no numbers were attached to the number of forces the Soviets would be entitled to maintain. Troop withdrawal was tied to the conclusion of a peace treaty with Austria, thus postponing it indefinitely and granting the Soviet Union the legal right to maintain the occupation of Hungary and Romania for an unspecified period of time.[95] Soviet troops finally left Hungary nearly forty-five years later, on June 16, 1990.

Destruction of the Democratic Coalition

The final blows to the democratic coalition came in 1947. The result of the peace treaty greatly enhanced the position of the Communists, who immediately launched the next phase of their campaign to liquidate their political opponents. On February 19, only nine days after the treaty was signed, in a fabricated conspiracy charge centering on the popular Smallholders party leader, Béla Kovács, Rákosi eliminated a number of politicians. Although the National Assembly refused to waive Kovács's parliamentary immunity, the Soviet military authorities intervened and arrested and deported him on February 25, 1947. Imre Kovács, who on that evening had been waiting to take a walk with Béla, recorded this eyewitness account: "In front of his house stood a covered truck, around it NKVD people who closed off the road; the courtyard and hallway were full of them. They dragged Béla Kovács from his first story flat, knocked him down the steps, and forced him into the waiting truck, in exactly the same way the Germans had done. . . ."[96]

In May 1947, Prime Minister Ferenc Nagy left with his wife for a rest cure in Switzerland. Rákosi, who was the deputy prime minister, chaired an extraordinary meeting of the government on May 28, presenting "damning testimony" against Nagy which supposedly involved him in the conspiracy. At first the cabinet decided to ask him to return and defend himself; then the government called on him to resign and remain abroad. Nagy realized from the fate of his friend Kovács that if he returned there was no chance that he would be treated justly, but he refused to resign until his five-year-old son was handed over to him safely. Finally, on June 1 Nagy handed in his resignation in exchange for his son at the Swiss-Austrian border; he never returned to Hungary.[97]

While the elections held in August 1947 were still relatively free, the elimination of Prime Minister Nagy sounded the death knell of the democratic government. The Communists decided to hold the elections on August 31 but gave little notice, and a number of groups were denied the suffrage. The elections again led to a coalition government, but in spite of some election rigging, the Communists still gained no more than 22 percent of the vote. Still, with the Social Democrats' 17 percent, the Peasant Party, and the remnants of the greatly weakened Smallholders Party, the coalition received roughly 60 percent of the vote. Newly formed opposition parties won 40 percent and remained for a short time in parliament.

In 1947–48 the Cold War broke out in earnest, fueled by the growth of mutual suspicion between the Soviets and the West. After the death of Roosevelt, whom Stalin had considered an ally, his successor Truman openly expressed his lack of confidence in Stalin. The dramatic deterioration in international relations was matched with the reimposition of harsh controls on Soviet society by the fall of 1946. Stalin and his fellow leaders, concerned about the exposure to the more advanced capitalist West by millions of Soviets, either as soldiers, prisoners of war or laborers, feared for the stability of the regime. It appeared clear to Stalin that if he restrained the Communist parties in France and Italy the West would allow him control in Eastern Europe. By mid-1947 the Soviet leaders no longer cared about Western reactions to their actions in Eastern Europe. Disappointed by the failing performance and uncertain loyalty of Western European Communist parties—they had lost hope for the future of communism in Western Europe in the immediate future.[98]

For the Hungarians, 1948 marked the turning point. The Communists won perhaps their most important victory over their most formidable rival, the Catholic Church, with the nationalization of the schools in June 1948. The Communists perceived the religious schools as an insurmountable block against the re-education of society, and with good reason; a public opinion survey showed that in 1948 more than 90 percent of the population considered themselves believers, 95 percent of them lived in rural areas, and half of the public attended church regularly. Significantly, these percentages were larger than those under the conservative regime before the war.[99] Protestant and Jewish leaders, considering that the nationalization of schools was inevitable, had given in while the Catholics resisted. Those who did not acquiesce were either removed or sentenced in Hungarian "show trials." Among prominent church leaders who were removed, Bishop László Ravasz resigned in April 1948, Lutheran Bishop Lajos Ordass received a two-year prison sentence in October 1948, and Father Kerkai was sentenced to six years in prison in a show trial, with an added four and a half years in a later trial.[100]

About half of the 6,500-odd nationalized schools had been in Catholic hands, and the 18,000 teachers became state employees. In an indication of the attitude of the population, the Communists were forced to continue religious education until the following year. About 5,000 teachers followed the order by Cardinal Mindzenty not to take positions in the nationalized schools, thus increasing the serious lack of teachers already affected by the huge losses during the war and those taken as POWs to the Soviet Union. With the loss of well-trained experienced teachers the level of teaching declined precipitously; the loss was felt especially in the famous historic secondary schools and teachers' education colleges. The renowned elite institution, the Eötvös Collegium, was dissolved a year later, and at about the same time the Hungarian Academy of Sciences, which had been denounced already in October 1946 as a stronghold of reaction, lost its autonomy. A few months later several thousand volumes of supposedly fascist, anti-Soviet and chauvinist literature were removed and destroyed by the AVO.[101]

The measure for nationalization of the schools was passed against the wishes of a majority of the population and aroused far stronger popular opposition than had any other measure; land reform, the nationalization of factories, even the collectivization of land that was soon to take place.[102] The willingness of the Communists to pursue such an unpopular policy by force showed both their newly gained confidence and desire to effect profound change in Hungary.

In 1948 further nationalization took place in industry, commerce, and stronger measures in agriculture. The early nationalization measures had not been particularly controversial; with the desperate need for energy after the war the coal mines were nationalized in June 1946, followed by the four largest heavy industry complexes. By 1946, however, the issue of nationalization had become highly politicized, and strong controversy arose over the attempt to nationalize the banks. Formal nationalization took place only in September 1947, after Hungary had been prevented from participating in the Marshall Plan, and after former Prime Minister Ferenc Nagy had been forced out. A huge change in property relationships came in the spring of 1948 with nationalization of factories employing more than one hundred workers. In this case even the appearance of legality was absent; the law governing the takeover was presented to Parliament at the end of April, a month after the actual takeover on March 25, 1948. With that act the percentage of workers under the state reached 90 percent among miners and heavy industry and 75 percent in light industry.[103]

The Radical Transformation of Society

By 1948 the radical transformation of Hungarian society was well underway, but in a form very different from the restructuring of society envisioned by the March Front movement in the late 1930s, with its demands for democracy, freedom of speech, press, and assembly, universal suffrage, and land reform. It also was not the transformation hoped for by the freely elected government of 1945 for the formation of a democratic multiparty system and an independent peasantry based on land ownership. During the years from 1945 to 1947 there had been some optimism that democratic pluralistic change would occur. Following the total defeat in World War II all had realized that the prewar system would not continue. But few imagined the nature of the regime that would follow.

The process leading to the transformation of society, which began with the German deportations and continued with the Soviet occupation, had dissolved the former Hungarian power structure and the structure of the state. The flight to the West by state and public administration along with many ordinary citizens, the People's Court trials, the B-lists, and the land reform brought about fundamental changes in the traditional social structure, eliminating not only former privileged social groups, but also a large number of the middle class.

The new government attempted to institute a democratic multiparty system, but from the beginning the Communist Party had established its power base, and the experiment ended in 1947 with Nagy's departure and resignation. Nationalization, step by step, eliminated the remainder of private enterprises, and with it the remainder of the property-owning middle and lower middle classes. In the end even the peasantry, who had initially benefited from the land reform, lost out as their gains and holdings were replaced by collective farms. Within the framework of the ever narrower, more dogmatic interpretation of people's democracy, it was ever less possible to fit in an image of an independent peasantry.[104]

In fact, the reversal of land reform dealt a major blow to those who had hailed the reform as the end to Hungary's semifeudal system and beginning of a new democratic society. The reversal occurred more quickly than originally planned because of a radicalization of the Communist Party's program. The party had initially been willing to consider a long, gradual transition from independent to cooperative farming, but this relatively liberal approach suffered because of the break between Stalin and Tito, and the censuring of the Yugoslav party for its indulgent attitude to the peasant issue. In response to these developments, party leader Mátyás Rákosi urged the speeding-up of the collectivization process. In August 1948 he announced a basic transformation of agricultural production, the cooperative program.[105] Those remaining liberals who had believed that the centuries-old dream of the Hungarian peasant might be realized under this new regime were sadly disabused.

The hopes for a new elite leadership from the People's Colleges ended as well with the closing of the NÉKOSZ schools, which were charged with being too autonomous. One of the most popular initiatives of the people's democracy, intended to educate talented peasant, worker, and urban youth to take over leadership positions in the new society, NÉKOSZ was dissolved July 10, 1949, to the vast surprise and disappointment of the students.[106] As part of the new terror, the folk high schools were discontinued, and the new generation of peasant leaders who had emerged were often denounced as *kulaks* or forced off the land. Indeed the peasantry were not to be raised into the body politic but were destined instead to hold the role of a rural proletariat, serving the cause of massive industrialization.

By early fall of 1948, with the disappearance of the last vestiges of pluralism, Hungary as well as the rest of Eastern Europe was firmly established in a Soviet-style system. As the coalition moved to a dictatorial state socialist system, a number of opposition leaders fled the country, and others were forced to leave to escape arrest. Imre Kovács, former National Peasant Party leader, left the country; the conservative Social Democrats party leader, Károly Peyer, fled to avoid arrest, as did Zoltán Pfeiffer, former opposition leader of the Independent Smallholders. By December 1948 when Mindszenty was arrested, Hungarians lived under a totalitarian system.[107] By the next elections, May 1949, the People's Front was credited to have received 95.6 percent of the vote—a far cry from the percentage they had received during the relatively free elections of 1945.

Notes

Introduction

1. M. Kiss Sándor, ed., *Magyarország 1944: Fejezetek az ellenállás történeté-ből* [Hungary 1944: Chapters from the history of the resistance] (Budapest: Nemzeti Tankönyvkiadó, 1994), 316.

1. The Legacy of World War I

1. In ethnically mixed areas in which much of the population is bilingual, ethnic identity is often subjective. In the census of 1919 in Czechoslovakia, individuals asked about their nationality often gave answers such as "Slovak as well as Hungarian," or "Hungarian Slovak," or even "Catholic."

2. The one exception was the plebiscite held in a small area of the Burgenland between Austria and Hungary.

3. The party itself was a weak group with no mass organization and only twenty members in Parliament.

4. Peter Pastor, *Hungary Between Wilson and Lenin: The Hungarian Revolution of 1918–1919 and the Big Three* (New York: Columbia University Press, 1976), 33–36; Tibor Hajdu, *Károlyi Mihály: Politikai életrajz* [Mihály Károlyi: Political biography] (Budapest: Kossuth könyvkiadó, 1978), 265.

5. Tibor Hajdu, "The Hungarian Revolution—Conjunctures, Conjectures, Generalizations," Hungarian Revolution of 1918–1919, International Colloquium, Graz, June 5–9, 1989, 12.

6. Leaders of the two Protestant churches were prepared to give in to land reform, and the Catholic church even thought of giving up most of its lands in order to keep the remainder, as well as its schools (Zsinati Archivesr, 23 f.6 box/II.3).

7. Hajdu, *Károlyi Mihály*, 280–282.

8. Pastor, *Between Wilson and Lenin*, 62.

9. Margaret Macmillan, *Paris 1919: Six Months That Changed the World* (New York: Random House, 2003), 260.

10. Pastor, *Between Wilson and Lenin*, 64.

11. Gyula Juhász, *Hungarian Foreign Policy 1919–1945* (Budapest: Akadémiai kiadó, 1979), 14. Although members of visiting American and British missions favored active support for the Károlyi regime, the U.S. decision makers remained neutral.

12. When the Transylvanian-Romanian leaders declared for union with Romania they insisted on a guarantee of their traditional rights and privileges, but their demands were not to be fulfilled. For more information, see Stephen Fischer-Galati, *Twentieth Century Rumania* (New York: Columbia University Press, 1970), 27.

13. John C. Swanson, *The Remnants of the Habsburg Monarchy: The Shaping of Modern Austria and Hungary 1918–1933* (New York: Columbia University Press, 2001), 52.

14. French intervention against the Ukraine which started with the landing of 1,800 troops in Odessa December 18, 1918, transformed Romania into an important ally. See Peter Pastor, "French War Aims against Austria-Hungary and the Treaty of Trianon" *20th Century Hungary and the Great Powers,* ed. Ignác Romsics (New York: Columbia University Press, 1995), 39–50.

15. Rezső Peéry, *Requiem egy országrészért* [Requiem for a part of the country] (München: Aurora Kiskönyvek, 1975), 45.

16. Ibid., 27–28.

17. Erzsébet Árvay, interview with the author, Szeged, Hungary. June 2, 1989.

18. Before the war Béla Kun had been a provincial socialist functionary and journalist. As a POW in Russia he had converted to Bolshevism, returned to Hungary on November 16, and went to work to promote the establishment of the dictatorship of the proletariat (Swanson, *Habsburg Monarchy*, 77).

19. Pastor, *Between Wilson and Lenin*, 85.

20. Hajdu, *Károlyi Mihály*, 310.

21. Macmillan, *Paris 1919*, 121. Historian Macmillan commented that, "It has become a commonplace to say that the peace settlements of 1919 were a failure, that they led directly to the Second World War. That is to overestimate their power" (Macmillan, xxx). The Peacemakers' armed forces were shrinking day by day and their taxpayers wanted an end to foreign adventures. More importantly, changes were being made independently on the ground.

22. Zoltán Boross, interview with the author, Debrecen, Hungary, March 22, 1988.

23. Joseph Rothschild, *East Central Europe between the Two World Wars* (Seattle: University of Washington Press, 1988), 78.

24. Macmillan, *Paris 1919*, 121–126; H. Nicolson, *Peacemaking 1919* (New York: Grosset & Dunlap, 1965), 115.

25. Macmillan, *Paris 1919*, 131–132.

26. Macmillan, *Paris 1919*, 127, 131–132; Nicolson, *Peacemaking*, 125–127.

27. The influenza pandemic of 1918–19 killed more people than the Great War; the number is estimated at somewhere between 20 and 40 million people.

28. Zsuzsa L. Nagy, *Magyarország története 1918–1945* [Hungarian history 1918–1945] (Debrecen: Történelmi Figyelő, 1995), 31.

29. Swanson, *Habsburg Monarchy*, 77–78.

30. Men who had reached the age of twenty-one and attended six years of schooling were enfranchised. Women were to be twenty-four and also had to show the ability to read and write.

31. Clemenceau, who ordered transmission of the famous Vix ultimatum, has been faulted for not seeing the potential danger of French policies toward Hungary. In favoring the Romanians, he expected that the Romanian military could salvage the French-led allied intervention in Southern Russia. See Pastor, *Between Wilson and Lenin*, 3.

32. Pastor, *Between Wilson and Lenin*, 120–121; Macmillan, *Paris 1919*, 261–262. Vix believed his orders went against the Belgrade Convention, and he was particularly upset with the orders from General Berthelot, commander of French forces in Romania and southern Russia, which continually favored Romanian advances into Hungary (Pastor, 86).

33. Hajdu, "Revolution, Counterrevolution, Consolidation," in *A History of* Hungary, ed. Peter Sugar (Bloomington: Indiana University Press, 1990), 303; Ignác Romsics, *Magyarország története a XX században* [History of Hungary in the XX century] (Budapest: Osiris, 1999), 121.

34. Swanson, *Habsburg Monarchy*, 123–126.

35. Some historians have argued that Béla Bartók assumed a political role in 1919, but as Nándor Dreisziger points out in his essay, "Béla Bartók: Modern Hungary's Greatest Son," Bartók would never voluntarily have accepted a public let alone a political role. See Nándor Dresiziger, *Hungarians from Ancient Times to 1956: Biographical and Historical Essays* (Ottawa: Legas, 2007), 40.

36. Macmillan, *Paris 1919*, 265; L. Nagy, *Magyarország*, 43.

37. Leslie Laszlo, *Church and State in Hungary 1919–1945*, Published dissertation. Columbia University, Faculty of Political Science, 1973, 108–109.

38. Ignác Romsics, "The peasantry and the age of revolutions: Hungary, 1918–1919." Hungarian Revolution of 1918–1919, International Colloquium, Graz, June 5–9, 1989.

39. L. Nagy, *Magyarország*, 51; Romsics, *Magyarország története*, 123.

40. Macmillan, *Paris 1919*, 263. The belief that Clemenceau was anti-Hungarian because of a Hungarian daughter-in-law appears to be a myth. His son had married and later divorced a Hungarian woman, but Clemenceau had numerous other contacts with Hungary, both personal and political; a play that he had written was actually performed in the Budapest National Theater in 1906. His whole political career indicated that he could rise above personal feelings, and that his primary concern was always what he considered to be the interests of France. See Balázs Ablonczy, "Trianon-legendák" [Trianon legends] in *Mítoszok, legendák, tévhitek a 2000. Századi magyar történelemből*, ed. Ignác Romsics (Budapest: Osiris, 2005), 140–144.

41. Swanson, *Habsburg Monarchy*, 130.

42. Smuts wrote to Lloyd George before his mission: "We cannot be blind to what has just happened in Hungary. Károlyi was favorable to us and endeavouring to work with us but found no encouragement. Rumania and Serbia had to be placated with Hungarian territory. Result: Hungary is now joining hands with bolshevist Russia." See Pastor, *Between Wilson and Lenin*, 147.

43. Nicolson, *Peacemaking*, 304.

44. Juhász, *Hungarian Foreign Policy*, 22.

45. Nicolson, *Peacemaking*, 127.

46. Ibid., 127.

47. Ibid., 328–329.

48. Géza Lakatos, *Ahogy én láttam* [As I Saw It] (Budapest: Európa, 1992), 19. Böhm, a Social Democrat, later immigrated to Stockholm where he helped Hungary contact Allied representatives during World War II.

49. Thomas L. Sakmyster, *Hungary's Admiral on Horseback: Miklós Horthy, 1918– 1944* (Boulder, CO: European Monographs, 1994), 27.

50. Macmillan, *Paris 1919*, 238.

51. Juhász, *Hungarian Foreign Po*licy, 27.

52. For divergent opinions of the White Terror, see Béla Bodó, "Paramilitary Violence in Hungary after the First World War," *East European Quarterly* 38 no. 2 (June 2004); Attila Pók, "Why Was There No Historikerstreit in Hungary after 1989–1990," in *The Holocaust in Hungary: Sixty Years Later*, eds. Randolf L. Braham and Brewster S. Chamberlin (New York: Columbia University Press, 2006).

53. Macmillan, *Paris 1919*, xxviii.

54. For a full account of the activities of the Inter-Allied Military mission, see, *Major General Harry Hill Bandholtz: An Undiplomatic Diary*, ed. Andrew L. Simon (Safety Harbor, Fla.: Simon Publications, 2000).

55. A statue to Bandholtz was erected in 1936 in the center of the park on Szabadság Square with the inscription, "I simply carried out the instructions of my Government, as I understood them, as an officer and a gentleman of the United States Army." Removed in the late 1940s, the statue was replaced at its original location in July 1989. The new inscription on the back reads: "General Harry Hill Bandholtz, head of the American Military Mission, who on October 5, 1919 blocked the removal of the treasures of the National Museum to Romania."

56. Macmillan, *Paris 1919*, 268.

57. Ignác Romsics, *The Dismantling of Historic Hungary: The Peace Treaty of Trianon, 1920* (Wayne, N.J.: Center for Hungarian Studies and Publications, Inc., 2002), 169.

58. Macmillan, *Paris 1919*, 269.

59. L. Nagy, *Magyarország*, 88–89.

60. Magda Ádám, *The Little Entente and Europe 1920–1929* (Budapest: Akadémiai Kiadó, 1993), 63.

61. Since the United States Congress refused to ratify the peace treaties, the United States concluded separate treaties with the defeated countries. The peace treaty with Hungary was signed in Budapest on August 29, 1921.

62. Miklós Zeidler, *A Magyar irredenta kultusz a két világháború között* [The Hungarian irredentist cult between the two world wars] (Budapest: Teleki László Alapítvány, 2002), 20.

63. Macmillan, *Paris 1919*, 269–270.

64. Juhász, *Hungarian Foreign Policy*, 51–52.

65. S. B. Várdy, "The Impact of Trianon upon the Hungarian Mind," in *Hungary in the Age of Total War (1938–1948)*, ed. Nándor Dreisziger (New York: Columbia University Press, 1998), 39.

66. Research on Prime Ministers Teleki, Bethlen, and Gömbös shows that not one of these three most significant politicians represented the demand for total revision. See Ignác Romsics, ed., *Trianon és a Magyar politikai gondolkodás 1920–1953* [Trianon and Hungarian political thinking] (Budapest: Osiris, 1998), 7–8.

67. Those states formed or enlarged from the territory of the Austro-Hungarian monarchy.

68. Deborah S. Cornelius, *In Search of the Nation: The New Generation of Hungarian Youth in Czechoslovakia 1925–1934* (Boulder, Colo.: Social Science Monographs, 1998), 63.

69. The work by József Galántai, *Trianon and the Protection of Minorities* (New York: Columbia University Press, 1992), presents a thorough analysis of the questions raised and procedures developed for the protection of the minority populations.

2. Hungary Between the Wars

1. László Kürti, *The Remote Borderland: Transylvania in the Hungarian Imagination* (Albany: State University of New York Press, 2001), 96.

2. Zeidler, *Magyar irredenta kultusz*, 17–18.

3. Kálmán Molnár in Katalin Sinkó, "Living Historicism," *Budapest Review of Books* 6, no. 1 (1996): 38.

4. Várdy, "The Impact of Trianon," 39.

5. Budapest, composed of Buda on the western bank of the Danube and Pest on the eastern bank, had been officially merged only in 1873, creating the new metropolis of Budapest.

6. Viola Tomori, interview with the author, Velem, Hungary. 26 June 1990.

7. Sociologists and historians have debated the reasons for the startlingly high proportion—about 60 percent—of the politicians of Jewish origin in the revolutionary governing council as well as in the mid-level leadership. For more details see, János Gyurgyák, *A zsidókerdés Magyarországon* [The Jewish question in Hungary] (Budapest: Osiros, 2001), 102–103.

8. Balázs Ablonczy, *Pál Teleki (1874–1941): The Life of a Controversial Hungarian Politician*, trans. Thomas J. and Helen DeKornfeld (New York: Columbia University Press, 2006) 75–76.

9. There was an odd link between anti-Semitism and anti-Feminism. The first draft of the restrictive quota system was directed not against Jews but against women, who had enrolled at the university in larger numbers during the war. See Katalin N. Szegvári, *Numerus Clausus rendelkezések az ellenforradalmi Magyarországon* [Numerus clausus provisions in counter-revolutionary Hungary] (Budapest: Akadémiai Kiadó, 1988), 105–107.

10. Iván Berend, "Inflation, Stabilization and an Independent Financial System," in *Evolution of the Hungarian Economy 1848–1998* by Iván T. Berend and Tamás Csató (Highland Lakes, N.J.: Atlantic Research and Publications, 2001), 163–164.

11. John C. Swanson, "Minority Building in the German Diaspora: the Hungarian-Germans," *Austrian History Yearbook* 36 (2005): 154.

12. Within the framework of the monarchy a division of labor had developed which stimulated Hungarian agriculture but impeded the development of industry (Berend, "The Changed Post-War Conditions," in Berend and Csató, *Evolution*, 146–148).

13. Ibid., 146–148.

14. Géza Lakatos, *Ahogy én láttam*24.

15. Romsics, *Magyarország története*, 137; L. Nagy, *Magyarország*, 87.

16. Sakmyster, *Admiral on Horseback*, 4–9; C. A. Macartney, *October Fifteenth; a History of Modern Hungary, 1929–1945* (Edinburgh: Edinburgh University Press, 1961), 1:52.

17. György Barcza, *Diplomataemlékeim 1911–1945* [My diplomatic memoirs 1911–1945] (Budapest: Európa História, 1994), 1:205; Sakmyster, *Admiral on Horseback*, 21.

18. Barcza, *Diplomataemlékeim*, 1:206–208; L. Nagy, *Magyarország*, 88–89; Sakmyster, *Admiral on Horseback*, 23.

19. Sakmyster, *Admiral on Horseback*, 55–57.

20. John Kosa, "Hungarian Society in the Time of the Regency (1920–1944)," *Journal of Central European Affairs* XVI, no. 3 (October 1956): 254.

21. It was estimated that in 1944 one of every five Hungarians was a nobleman and one of every seventy an aristocrat.

22. L. Nagy, *Magyarország*, 183; Kosa, "Hungarian Society," 257.

23. Kosa, "Hungarian Society," 265.

24. L. Nagy, *Magyarország*, 185.

25. Kosa, "Hungarian Society," 263–265.

26. Olga Gály, *Ördöglakat: Lőrincz Gyula ifjúsága* [The devil's padlock: Gyula Lőrincz's youth] (Bratislava: Madách, 1990), 35.

27. Kosa, "Hungarian Society," 260.

28. Barcza, *Diplomataemlékeim*, 1:182; Macartney, *October Fifteenth*, 1:37, 42.

29. Juhász, *Hungarian Foreign Policy*, 60–63.

30. Ibid., 65–66.

31. Berend, "Inflation, Stabilization and an Independent Financial System," in *Evolution*, 166.

32. András D. Bán, *Illúziók és Csalódások: Nagy-Britannia és Magyarország 1938–1941* [Illusions and disappointments: Great Britain and Hungary 1938–1941] (Budapest: Osiris, 1998), 23.

33. Levente Püski, *A Magyar felsőház története 1927–1945* [The History of the Hungarian upper house] (Budapest: Napvilág kiadó, 2000), 23–31.

34. Precise figures are not available but the census of 1920 shows that the number of people living in truncated Hungary but born in the territories ceded to the successor states added up to 558,154. See István I. Mócsy, *The Effects of World War I. The Uprooted: Hungarian Refugees and Their Impact on Hungary's Domestic Politics, 1918–1921* (New York: Columbia University Press, 1983), 11.

35. The 1924 records of the National Refugee Office list as refugees 15,835 state functionaries, 5,772 municipal and village officials, 3,554 other state employees, and 19,092 railway employees. Refugee students numbered 86,323. See Mócsy, *The Uprooted*, 53.

36. Mocsy, *The Uprooted*, 12.

37. According to the 1930 census figures, 43 percent of judges and public prosecutors were born in the lost territories and 34 percent of state officials. See Mocsy, *The Uprooted*, 188.

38. Sándor Szakály, *A magyar katonai elit 1938–1934* [The Hungarian military elite] (Budapest: Magvető, 1987), 63–66.

39. In 1913–14 students from families of officials or officers constituted about 16 percent of the student body. By 1921–22 students from these families represented about 27.4 percent and a few years later 30 percent. See Mócsy, *The Uprooted*, 192.

40. Tibor Petrusz, interview with the author. Budapest, July 20, 2001.

41. For a full discussion of the Hungarian minority situation in the early 1920s, see Cornelius, *In Search of the Nation*.

42. Cornelius, *In Search of the Nation*, 84–85.

43. Lajos Turczel, *Két kor mezsgyéjén: A magyar irodalom fejlődesi feltételei és problémái Csehszlovákiában 1918 és 1938 között* [On the border between two periods: The development and problems of Hungarian literature in Czechoslovaki between 1918 and 1938] (Bratislava: Madách, 1983), 27–33.

44. Cornelius, *In Search of the Nation*, 142–143.

45. The debate over which people have the right to call Transylvania the birthplace of their nation has filled many volumes and is still bitterly disputed.

46. Many Transylvanian-Romanian leaders feared that Transylvania would be swallowed up by the more backward and conservative old kingdom and favored guarantees of political autonomy.

47. Rothschild, *East Central Europe*, 288.

48. It is estimated that about 222,000 Hungarians left the territories granted to Romania between 1918 to 1920. See Mócsy, *The Uprooted*, 12.

49. Hungarians were largely Catholic or Calvinist, while Székely Hungarians were predominantly Unitarian.

50. By 1929 a few older students had returned to Transylvania while a younger group, educated in the Hungarian denominational schools, entered the Romanian university at Kolozsvár, and a few enrolled in Bucharest.

51. Enikő A. Sajti, "A jugoszláviai magyarok politikai szervezkedésének lehetö-ségei és korlátai (1918–1941)," [Possibilities and limitations of Yugoslav-Hungarian political organization] *REGIO: Kisebbségi Szemle* (1997/2): 3–4; Mócsy, *The Uprooted*, 42–43.

52. Ablonczy, *Pál Teleki*, 128.

53. Agricultural prices had declined even before the depression. More than 50 percent of the arable land was sown with grain, the main export item, and another 20 percent with corn, but the United States and Canada had taken over about 60 percent of the European market. See Ivan T. Berend and György Ránki, *The Hungarian Economy in the Twentieth Century* (New York: St. Martin's Press, 1985), 54–55.

54. Julius Kornis, *Education in Hungary* (New York: Teachers College, Columbia University, 1932), 127.

55. Despite the predominance of the Catholic religion, Hungary had a considerable Protestant population that maintained a strong sense of its separate identity. The peasantry of the Alföld identified the Calvinist church as the church of the Hungarian people against the German Catholics.

56. Bela Erodi-Harrach Jr., "The Tanya World," *Magyar Szemle.* VII, no. 3 (December 1929): 375.

57. Mária Ormos, *Magyaroszág a két világháború korában 1914–1945* [Hungary in the period of the two world wars] (Budapest: Csokonai, 1998), 177.

58. Among the unemployed graduates, 31.5 percent were lawyers and 29.5 percent teachers. See Ferenc Csaplar, *A Szegedi Fiatalok Művészeti Kollegiuma* [The Szeged youth artistic kollegium] (Budapest: Akadémiai Kiadó, 1967), 5.

59. Sándor Kiss, *A magyar demokráciáért* [For Hungarian democracy] (New Brunswick: Bessenyei György Kör, 1983), 10.

60. Juhász, *Hungarian Foreign Policy*, 109; Macartney, *October Fifteenth*, 1:34–35.

61. Macartney, *October Fifteenth*, 1:116.

62. Juhász, *Hungarian Foreign Policy*, 108.

63. By the end of 1936, the Germans already owed Hungary one and one-half billion marks.

64. From 1933–35 the state spent 32.5 million in taking on debt and from 1935–37 75.6 million.

65. Krisztián Ungváry, "Honvédség és külpolitika (1919–1945)," [The Military and foreign policy] in *Magyarország helye a 20. századi Európában* [Hungary's place in

twentieth century Europe], ed. Pál Pritz (Budapest: Magyar Történelmi Társulat, 2002), 93.

66. His attempt to abolish the self-government rights of Budapest gave rise to an Alliance for the Protection of the Constitution, which united not only the parties of the left-wing opposition but also the majority of the Christian-National parties, an informal alliance which was to continue during the war years.

67. István Deák, "Hungary," in *The European Right: A Historical Profile*, eds. Hans Rogger and Eugen Weber (Berkeley: University of California Press, 1965), 380.

68. Ungváry, "Honvédség és külpolitika," 94; Macartney, *October Fifteenth*, 1:129; Deák, "Hungary," 379–380.

69. L. Nagy, *Magyarország*, 178.

70. Laszlo, *Church and State*, 302–304.

71. Ibid., 74.

72. The term *népi* refers to *the people* or *folk*, and has a slightly different connotation than the usual English translation of populist. The *nepi* writers became the most influential group of writers in the Hungarian literary and ideological life of the twentieth century.

73. Deborah S. Cornelius, "The Recreation of the Nation—Origins of the Hungarian Populist Movement," *Hungarian Studies* 6, no. 1 (1990): 29–30.

74. The fifteen members of the Szeged Youth comprised a surprisingly diverse group in Hungary's stratified society: four Jews, including the poet Miklos Radnóti, three women, a Catholic, Gyula Ortutay, later minister of culture, and Ferenc Erdei of Protestant peasant background, minister of the interior in the postwar government. See Deborah S. Cornelius, "Women in the Hungarian Populist Youth Movement: The Szeged Youth." *Nationalities Papers* 25, no. 1 (1997): 123–145.

75. Gyula Illyés, "Pusztulás: Uti jegyzetek," [Destruction: Travel notes] *Nyugat* (September 1933): 192–193.

76. *Kemse: részletek az Elsüllyedt falu a Dunántúlon c.könyvből* [Kemse: Details from the book, a sinking village in Transdanubia] (Budapest: Népművelési intézet, 1986).

77. Zoltán Szabó, *A tardi helyzet—Cifra nyomorúság* [The situation at Tard—fancy poverty] (Budapest: Akadémiai kiadó, 1986), 30.

78. Ibid., 37.

79. Gyula Illyés, *People of the Puszta* (Budapest: Corvina Press, 1967), 8–9.

80. Imre Kovács, *A néma forradalom—A néma forradalom a bíróság és a parlament előtt* [The Silent Revolution—The Silent Revolution before the Court and Parliament] (Budapest: Cserépfalvi, 1989), 139–140.

81. Pál Péter Tóth, "Ötven év után: a Márciusi Frontról" [Fifty years later: the March Front] *Magyarságkutatás: a Magyarságkutató Csoport évkönyve* 1987, ed. Gyula Juhász (Budapest: 1987) 95–107.

82. The twelfth point was opposed by the illegal Communists because of the reference to Pan-Slavism.

83. Imre Kovács, *A Márciusi Front* [The March Front] (New Brunswick, N.J.: Magyar Öregdiák Szövetség, 1980), 55.

84. Kiss, *A magyar demokráciáért*, 18.

85. Kovács, A néma forradalom, 151.

86. Ibid., 153.

87. Ibid., 263–265.

88. Krisztián Ungváry, "Kik azok a nyilasok?" [Who are the Arrow Cross?] *Beszélő* (June 2003): 60.

89. By 1938 only ten out of twenty-seven European countries could be called truly democratic.

90. His *Estado Novo* was based on a selective interpretation of Catholic social doctrine, much like the contemporary regime of Engelbert Dollfuss in Austria.

91. Kiss, *A magyar demokráciáért*, 19–20.

92. As in Fascist Italy and Soviet Russia anti-Semitism was connected with national identity. In Italy there was a campaign to get rid not of Jews but of Jewishness. In the Soviet Union there was a much more intense campaign against Jews.

93. Ungváry, "Who were the Arrow Cross? A socialist mass party," *Rubicon* (November 2004): 9.

3. The Last Year of European Peace

1. Nagy, *Magyarország története*, 152.

2. Quoted in Juhász, *Hungarian Foreign Policy*, 134.

3. On St. Stephen's Day, August 20, the Sacred Dexter, the embalmed right hand of the king, was born through the streets of Budapest; then sent throughout the country by special train.

4. Jenő Gergely, *Eucharisztikus világkongresszus Budapesten 1938* [International Eucharistic Congress Budapest 1938] (Budapest: Kossuth, 1988), 63–67.

5. After becoming Pope, he told György Barcza that at the Eucharistic Congress he had developed an affection for the Hungarians who were chivalrous, freedom-loving, tradition-honoring, religious people. See György Barcza, *A svájci misszió: Diplomata emlékeimből* [Swiss mission: from my diplomatic memoirs] (München: Új Látóhatár, 1983), 9.

6. Sakmyster, *Admiral on Horseback*, 194.

7. Gergely, *Eucharisztikus világkongresszus*, 119–121.

8. 57.4 percent of elementary schools and 57.4 percent of secondary schools were Roman Catholic. Of secondary schools 17.5 percent were Reformed, 7.2 percent Lutheran, and 16.6 percent Jewish. See Kornis, *Education in Hungary*, 284.

9. Gergely, *Eucharisztikus világkongresszus*, 124–129.

10. Ibid., 7–10.

11. Ibid., 135.

12. In historic Hungary in 1913 there had been 2,139 monks and 5,451 nuns. In truncated Hungary the number of monks increased to 3,522 in the 1920s. The number of nuns had increased to 6,667 by 1935, and by 1950 to 8,956.

13. Margit Slachta, the only woman elected to the National Assembly in 1920, founded the Sisters of Social Service, who lived together and carried out charitable and social work, but differed markedly from others in taking part in public affairs and even political activities. See Ilona Mona, *Slachta Margit* (Budapest: Corvinus, 1997), 2:5

14. Gergely, *Eucharisztikus világkongresszus*, 137.

15. Dr. György Farkas, "A KALOT Mozgalom Története," [History of the KALOT Movement], Cultural Institute Archives, NF 3,4.

16. Ibid., NF 6.

17. Margit Balogh, *A KALOT és a Katolikus társadalompolitika 1935–1946* [KALOT and Catholic social policy 1935–1946] (Budapest: MTA Történettudományi Intézete, 1998), 75; Gergely, *Eucharisztikus világkongresszus*, 138.

18. The German government did not officially prohibit participation, but required special permission to travel on the days of the Congress, effectively banning participation. See Gergely, *Eucharisztikus világkongresszus*, 85.

19. On his visit to Berlin in late September of 1937, Mussolini's attitude to Germany and to Hitler had changed. He had been profoundly impressed by the image of German overwhelming strength and of Hitler as a man of destiny. See Gerhard L. Weinberg, *Hitler's Foreign Policy: The Road to World War II 1933–1939* (New York: Enigma Books, 2005), 612–613.

20. Balint Kovács, personal communication with the author, April 20, 1988.

21. Juhász, *Hungarian Foreign Policy*, 134.

22. L. Nagy, *Magyarország története*, 154.

23. In addition to a monthly government subsidy, he gave 10,000 pengő from the prime minister's office for a central club house in Budapest.

24. Stanley G. Payne, *A History of Fascism 1914–1945* (Madison: University of Wisconsin Press, 1995), 267–268.

25. Miklós Lackó, *Arrow-Cross Men, National Socialism 1935–1944* (Budapest: Akademia kiadó, 1969), 41–45.

26. Krisztián Ungváry, "Kik azok a Nyilasok?" [Who are the Arrow Cross?] *Beszélő* June 2003, 60.

27. Hungarian National Archives. 651.f. 7/1938. I kötet 1–86 lap.

28. Ibid.

29. Gyurgyák, *A zsidókerdés*, 137.

30. L. Nagy, *Magyarország története*, 153.

31. Gyurgyák, *A zsidókerdés*, 142.

32. Püski, *Magyar felsőház*, 105.

33. Yehuda Don, "The Economic Dimensions of Antisemitism: Anti-Jewish Legislation in Hungary 1938–1944," *East European Quarterly* 20, no. 4 (January 1987): 448; Gyurgyák, *A zsidókerdés*, 142.

34. Lóránd Dombrády, *A magyar gazdaság es a hadfelszerelés 1938–1944* [The Hungarian economy and instruments of war] (Budapest: Akadémiai, 1981), 11.

35. Ibid, 12.

36. Ibid, 16–17; Péter Gosztonyi, *A Magyar honvédség a második világháborúban* [The Hungarian army in World War II] (Budapest: Európa Kőnyvkiadó, 1992), 14.

37. The census of 1921 records 8,760,937 Czechoslovaks, 3,123,568 Germans, 745,431 Magyars, 461,849 Ruthenians, 180,855 Hebrew and Yiddish, 75,863 Poles, and 25,871 other. Statistics from the State Statistical Office of the Czechoslovak Republic, in Rothschild, East Central Europe, 89.

38. Gergely Sallai, *Az első bécsi döntés* [The first Vienna decision] (Budapest: Osiris, 2002), 39.

39. James Ramon Felak, *"At the Price of the Republic" Hlinka's Slovak People's Party, 1929–1938* (Pittsburgh: University of Pittsburgh Press, 1994), 142–143; Rothschild, *East Central Europe*, 125–126.

40. Imre Molnár, *Esterházy János 1901–1957* (Dunaszerdahely: Nap, 1997), 46.

41. Ibid., 55.

42. Juhász, *Hungarian Foreign Policy*, 138; Sakmyster, *Admiral on Horseback*, 212–213.

43. *Admiral Nicholas Horthy: Memoirs* (Florida: Simon Publications, 2000), 191.

44. Ibid.

45. Shirer points out that, in reality, the parade was put on to impress Britain, France, Russia, and Czechoslovakia with Germany's new military might. When an enormous field gun appeared, "Hitler turned to watch the reaction of the foreign military attachés." See William L. Shirer, *The Nightmare Years 1930–1940* (Toronto: Bantam Books, 1984), 332.

46. Macartney, *October Fifteenth*, 1:242.

47. Ibid.

48. Macartney, *October Fifteenth*, 1:241 (note 1).

49. Sakmyster, *Admiral on Horseback*, 216–217.

50. Juhász, *Hungarian Foreign Policy*, 140.

51. Lakatos, *Ahogy én láttam*, 41.

52. In his final report, Runciman recommended that the Sudeten Germans have the right of self-determination where they were in a large majority, but the Hungarian minority was not even mentioned. See Molnár, *Esterházy János*, 75–79.

53. Molnár, *Esterházy János*, 80.

54. Juhász, *Hungarian Foreign Policy*, 141.

55. Vilmos Nagy Nagybaczoni, who was conducting annual war maneuvers with his troops near the Czechoslovak border, strongly criticized the military leadership's

confusing commands and lack of preparation for mobilization. See Vilmos Nagy Nagybaczoni, *Végzetes esztendők 1938–1945* [Fatal years 1938–1945] (Budapest: Gondolat, 1986), 31–38.

56. International Legislation. VIII. 135, quoted in Edward Chászár, *Decision in Vienna: The Czechoslovak-Hungarian Border Dispute of 1938* (Astor, Fla.: Danubian Press, Inc. 1978), 93.

57. Weinberg, *Hitler's Foreign Policy*, 790. Czechoslovakia had claimed Teschen, originally part of Polish Silesia, for historic, economic, and strategic considerations. Poland received the town of Teschen and eastern part of the region, but the more valuable western areas with major coal, industrial and rail resources went to Czechoslovakia. See Rothschild, *East Central Europe*, 84–85.

58. These included unemployment insurance, public rights for trade unions, the eight-hour work day, state support for building of homes, factory committees, and limitation of work hours for women and children.

59. Péter Hámori, "Kísérlet a visszacsatolt felvidéki területek társadalmi és szociális integrálására" [Attempt to bring about the social integration of the Felvidék], *Századok* no. 2 (1997): 570–571.

60. With the expectation of territorial revision in October the economy of south Slovakia was falling apart. Czech capital was fleeing in panic, factories were closing, workers were laid off, first of all the Hungarian workers. There was significant unemployment in agriculture.

61. Felak, *Hlinka's Slovak People's Party*, 205–208.

62. Sallai, *Az első bécsi döntés*, 82

63. Amnesty for political prisoners and discharging soldiers of Hungarian nationality from the Czech army had been promised.

64. Sallai, *Az első bécsi döntés*, 89.

65. Of the population of 121,000 on the Csallóköz, 117,000 were Hungarians.

66. The population in 1910 numbered 349,026, of whom 341,987 were Hungarians. See Chászár, *Decision in Vienna*, 36–41; Sallai, *Az első bécsi döntés*, 94.

67. Sallai, *Az első bécsi döntés*, 99–100.

68. Ibid., 100–101.

69. Sakmyster, *Admiral on Horseback*, 219; Juhász, *Hungarian Foreign Policy*, 143–144; Macartney, *October Fifteenth*, 1:289–291.

70. Sallai, *Az első bécsi döntés*, 114–117; Chászár, *Decision in Vienna*, 52.

71. Chászár, *Decision in Vienna*, 51.

72. Barcza, *Diplomataemlékeim*, 1:383.

73. Ciano's *Diplomatic Papers*, 239–240.

74. Sallai, *Az első bécsi döntés*, 121–123.

75. L. Nagy, *Magyarország története*, 160; Sakmyster, *Admiral on Horseback*, 220.

76. Molnár, *Esterházy János*, 83. Esterházy's sister, Lujsa, recommended to two Hungarian ministers that they give back Surány and Komjáti in order to keep peace

between the two peoples, but the Hungarians would not give up one centimeter. See Luzja Esterházy, *Szívek az ár ellen* [Hearts against the current], (Budapest: Puski,1991), 95.

77. Quoted in Sallai, *Az első bécsi döntés*, 147.

78. Sakmyster, *Admiral on Horseback*, 220–221.

79. The Czechs had tried to subordinate Slovak culture to Czech culture, which they considered superior. They had also kept the young Slovak intelligentsia from learning Hungarian literature and language which had been a matter of course in the years under Hungarian rule.

80. István Janek, *Rubicon*. 2007, 1–2.

81. Barcza, *Diplomataemlékeim*, 1:401.

82. Péter Sipos, *Imrédy Béla a vádlottak padján* [Béla Imrédy in the prisoner's box] (Budapest: Osiris, 1999), 11.

83. Count István Bethlen, *Hungarian Politics during World War Two: Treatise and Indictment* (München: Dr. Rudolf Trofenik, 1985), 27.

84. Sipos, *Imrédy Béla*, 306. The dopolavoro was a many-faceted leisure-time organization of the fascist regime. See Victoria de Grazia, *The Culture of Consent* (London: Cambridge U. Press), 1981.

85. Ciano's *Diplomatic Papers*, 227.

86. A solution was finally found when cooperative stores, Hangya and Futura, took over the goods and paid into the fund. See Hámori, "Kísérlet," 580.

87. Ibid., 576–583.

88. It is thought that the ensuing rivalry between the two women was the start of bad feelings between Horthy and Imrédy.

89. Hámori, "Kísérlet," 587.

90. Ibid., 595. A number of the community judges from the Komárom and Barsi districts were fired at the end of December.

91. Loránd Tilkovszky, personal communication with the author, November 19, 2001.

92. Hámori, "Kísérlet," 594.

93. Gendarme report on the political situation, December 21, 1938. in Hámori, 593.

94. As the emblem he used the magic stag, representing new Hungarian life in an ancient Hungarian land.

95. L. Nagy, *Magyarország története*, 163.

96. Horthy, *Memoirs*, 210; Sakmyster, *Admiral on Horseback*, 225–226.

97. Sakmyster, *Admiral on Horseback*, 228; Macartney, *October Fifteenth*, 1:328.

4. Clinging to Neutrality

1. Quoted in Tamás Csató, "The War Economy Subservient to Germany," in *Evolution of the Hungarian Economy 1848–1998*, 227.

2. Bán, *Illúziók és Csalódások*, 39/43; Macartney, *October Fifteenth*, 1:353.

3. Teleki was a controversial figure in Hungary during the Communist period for his role as a prominent statesman under Horthy and an aristocrat to boot; in recent times he remains controversial because of his anti-Semitism.

4. According to Ablonczy, from the time the two men traveled together to Belgrade in June 1919, they "found each other very compatible. . . . They were both great hunters, loved automobiles and had traveled enough in exotic places to have much to talk about." See Balázs Ablonczy, *Teleki Pál* (Budapest: Osiris, 2005), 56.

5. In service with the fleet Horthy had met naval officers and diplomats from all over the world, many whom he later received as regent.

6. According to his grandson, Dr. Pál Teleki, the political aspect of Teleki's life is often exaggerated. "My grandfather was a world famous geographer. . . . He concentrated on his scholarly work, founded institutes, taught, and occupied himself with the Scouts." See Dezső Pinter interview with Dr. Pál Teleki: "A Történelem sorsa, hogy meghamisítják," [The fate of history, how it is falsified] *Magyar Hírlap* (March 15, 1991): 8.

7. Ablonczy, *Pál Teleki*, 152; Bán, *Illúziók és Csalódások*, 63.

8. Antal Czettler, *Teleki Pál és a Magyar Külpolitika 1939–1941* [Pál Teleki and Hungarian foreign policy 1939–1941] (Budapest: Magvető, 1997) 26; Loránt Tilkovszky, *Pál Teleki: A Biographical Sketch* (Budapest: Akadémiai, 1974), 44–45.

9. See Map 3, Territorial Increase of Hungary (1938–1941), in Chapter 3.

10. The Czechoslovakia government rationalized the long postponement of autonomy by citing the province's extreme backwardness and poverty, but the true cause was more likely the strong pro-Magyar sentiments of the population. See Rothschild, 83; 121–122.

11. Juhász, *Hungarian Foreign Policy*, 152.

12. The demands presented by Ribbentrop included a return of Danzig to Germany, a road and railway across the Corridor to East Prussia, and, most important to Hitler, adherence to the Anti–Comintern Pact. In return Poland was to receive special rights in Danzig, a German guarantee of her western border, and the extension of the 1934 treaty renouncing the use of force. See Weinberg, *Hitler's Foreign Policy*, 792–793.

13. Gerhard L. Weinberg, *A World at Arms: A Global History of World War II* (New York: Cambridge University Press, 1994), 32–33.

14. Czettler, *Teleki Pál*, 27–28; Hajo Holborn, *A History of Modern Germany 1840–1945* (Princeton: Princeton University Press, 1982), 788–790.

15. Czettler, *Teleki Pál*, 29; Juhász, *Hungarian Foreign Policy*, 153–154.

16. Galeazzo Ciano, *Diary 1937–1943* (New York: Enigma Books, 2002), 200–201

17. Ibid.

18. Weinberg, *Hitler's Foreign Policy*, 844.

19. Quoted in Weinberg, 861.

20. Ablonczy, *Teleki Pál*, 411–412; Juhász, *Hungarian Foreign Policy*, 149; Macartney, *October Fifteenth*, 1:346.

21. Ablonczy, *Teleki Pál*, 412–413; Czettler, *Teleki Pál*, 34; Macartney, *October Fifteenth*, 1:349.

22. A major criticism against Teleki, which has continued into the present, is his anti-Semitism. In 2005 an intense public debate surrounded the plan to erect a statue of Teleki on Castle Hill, and eventually public outcry prevented the plan; the statue was placed at the Balaton on the site where Polish refugees were housed during the war.

23. Gyurgyák, *A zsidókerdés*, 145–146; L. Nagy, *Magyarország története*, 165.

24. Yehuda Don, "Economic Implications of the Anti-Jewish Legislation in Hungary," in *Genocide and Rescue: The Holocaust in Hungary 1944*, ed. David Cesarani (Oxford: Berg, 1997), 56–58; *Statistical Yearbook of Budapest for 1939*, 320.

25. Károlyi, who was unable to get government support for his suggestions, resigned his membership in the upper house. See Püski, *Magyar felsőház*, 113–117.

26. L. Nagy, *Magyarország története*, 196–197.

27. Yehuda Don, "Economic Implications of the Anti-Jewish Legislation in Hungary," *East European Quarterly* XX, no. 4: 457–459.

28. *Horthy Miklós Titkos iratai* [Miklós Horthy's secret papers], ed. Szinai M.and Szücs László (Budapest: Kossuth, 1972), 262.

29. Yehuda Don, "Economic Implications," 457–460.

30. At the time the labor service system was introduced under the Teleki administration it was not exclusively anti-Jewish or even discriminatory in character. For more information on labor issues, see Chapter 5.

31. Yehuda Don, "Economic Implications," 458.

32. Zsuzsa L. Nagy, *Liberális párt-mozgalmak, 1931–1945* [Liberal party movements, 1931–1945] (Budapest: Akadémiai, 1986), 120.

33. Barcza, *Diplomataemlékeim*, 1:434.

34. L. Nagy, *Magyarország története*, 167.

35. Macartney, *October Fifteenth*, 1:351.

36. Ungváry, "Kik azok a nyilasok?" 59.

37. L. Nagy, *Magyarország története*, 173–4.

38. Czettler, *Teleki Pál*, 35; L. Nagy, *Magyarország története*, 168.

39. Balázs Ablonczy, "A magyar parlamentarizmus változásai a harmincas években" [Changes in the Hungarian Parliament in the 1930s] (unpublished article), 4–5; Macartney, *October Fifteenth*, 1:350.

40. Ungváry, "Who were the Arrow Cross?" 5–17.

41. Ablonczy, "A magyar parlamentarizmus," 6. The right was further strengthened by the twenty-six deputies representing the returned territory of the Felvidék who were chosen by Imrédy's followers.

42. In the period from 1932 to 1940 only 279 laws were passed, in contrast to 438 in the period 1921 to 1931, and many laws passed in the second half of the 1930s were without political significance. At the same time the number of edicts multiplied.

43. Ablonczy, "A magyar parlamentarizmus," 8–9.

44. Andor Csizmadia, ed., *Bürokrácia és közigazgatási reformok Magyarhonban* [Bureaucracy and administrative reform in Hungary] (Budapest: Gondolat, 1979), 511.

45. He believed a one-party system would not suit Hungarians, who had an exceptionally strong sense of freedom in contrast to the German population's tendency to obedience. Ibid., 511.

46. Jeremy R. N. King, "Domestic Considerations of Hungarian Policy in Transylvania,1939–1941," November 2, 1988 (unpublished manuscript), 20–21.

47. *Barátok a bajban: Lengyel menekültek Magyarországon 1939–1945* [Friends in need: Polish refugees in Hungary 1939–1945] (Budapest: Európa, 1985), 11.

48. Juhász, *Hungarian Foreign Policy*, 161; Macartney, *October Fifteenth*, 1:358–360.

49. *Barátok a bajban*, 12.

50. Holborn, *A History of Modern Germany*, 792–794; Weinberg, *A World at Arms*, 33–35.

51. Juhász, *Hungarian Foreign Policy*, 162.

52. Czettler, *Teleki Pál*, 55; Macartney, *October Fifteenth*, 1:366–7.

53. Czettler, *Teleki Pál*, 58–59; Juhász *Hungarian Foreign Policy*, 163; Macartney, *October Fifteenth*, 1:366–367.

54. Ciano, *Diary*, September 9, 1939, 274; Czettler, *Teleki Pál*, 59.

55. Horthy, *Memoirs*, 212.

56. On September 11 the minister from Slovakia, now a German protectorate, requested permission for Slovak troops to cross Hungarian territory. Csáky refused the request and told the German minister in Budapest, Erdmannsdorff, that any attempt by the Slovaks to cross would be considered an act of war. See Czettler, *Teleki Pál*, 59–60.

57. Ciano, *Diary*, September 11, 1939, 275.

58. *Barátok a bajban*, 18.

59. *Barátok a bajban*,13; Czettler, *Teleki Pál*, 61; L. Nagy, *Magyarország története*, 169.

60. Ferenc Nagy, *The Struggle behind the Iron Curtain* (New York: Macmillan, 1948), 47–48.

61. *Barátok a bajban*, 23–24.

62. Czettler, *Teleki Pál*, 62.

63. *Barátok a bajban*, 20–21.

64. Norman Davies, *God's Playground: A History of Poland* (New York: Columbia University Press, 1982), 2:324–325.

65. L. Nagy, *Magyarország története*, 170.

66. If the birthplace of parents or grandparents had been included in the study of the top military elite, even more would have been from these areas. See Sándor Szakály, "The Composition of the Higher Military Elite," in *Hungarian Economy and Society During World War II*, ed. György Lengyel (Highland Lakes, N.J.: Atlantic Research and Publication, 1993), 110–111.

67. Lóránd Dombrády, "Financing the Hungarian Rearmament," in Lengyel, *Hungarian Economy*, 82.

68. Dombrády, "Financing the Hungarian Rearmament," 82–83.

69. Juhász, *Hungarian Foreign Policy*, 166; Macartney, *October Fifteenth*, 1:373–374.

70. Macartney, *October Fifteenth*, 1:392.

71. Ciano, *Diary*, March 27, 1940, 335.

72. Bán, *Illúziók és Csalódások*, 94.

73. Ibid., 95.

74. Macartney, *October Fifteenth*, 1:394.

75. Bán, *Illúziók és Csalódások*, 97–98.

76. Ibid., 98.

77. Juhász, *Hungarian Foreign Policy*, 172.

78. To quickly transfer funds to America, Baranyai sent the money in cash with Baron Antal Radvánszky. The money was kept at the Hungarian Legation in Washington in a safe-deposit box; only Horthy, Teleki, or the National Bank president had access to the keys. See Sakmyster, *Admiral on Horseback*, 255.

79. Gyula Rézler, interview with the author, May 22, 2001.

80. Ilona Gyulai, Countess Edelsheim, *Becsület és kötelesség 1, 1918–1944* [Honor and duty] (Budapest: Európa, 2001), 67. Ilona Gyulai was István Horthy's wife.

81. In the Neuilly Peace Treaty in 1919 Bulgaria had lost Southern Dobruja with 20 percent of her cereal production to Romania.

82. L. Balogh Béni. *A Magyar-Román kapcsolatok 1939–1940-ben és a második Bécsi döntés* [Hungarian-Romanian relations 1939–1940 and the second Vienna decision] (Csíkszereda, Romania: Pro-Print könyvkiadó, 2002), 118–120.

83. Rothschild, *East Central Europe*, 314.

84. Irina Livezeanu, *Cultural Politics in Greater Romania: Regionalism, Nation Building & Ethnic Struggle, 1918–1930* (Ithaca, N.Y.: Cornell University Press, 1995), 297.

85. Ibid., 135.

86. See Székely territories on Map 3, Territorial Increase of Hungary (1938–1941), in Chapter 3.

87. Bán, *Illúziók és Csalódások*, 104; Juhasz, *Hungarian Foreign Policy*, 173; Béni, *A második Bécsi döntés*, 124–125.

88. Juhász, *Hungarian Foreign Policy*, 171–174.

89. Béni, *A második Bécsi döntés*, 132–135; Juhász *Hungarian Foreign Policy*, 174.

90. Gerhard L. Weinberg places the actual decision to attack the Soviet Union somewhat earlier, with military planning begun in summer of 1940, and that the decision of July 31 was simply to defer the attack from fall of 1940 to spring of 1941. See *A World at Arms*, 187–188.

91. Juhász, *Hungarian Foreign Policy*, 173–174; L. Nagy, *Magyarország története*, 171.

92. Béni, *A második Bécsi döntés*, 220–225.

93. Juhasz 174; L. Nagy, *Magyarország története*, 171–2.

94. Béni, *A második Bécsi döntés*, 258.

95. Ibid., 271.

96. Béni, *A második Bécsi döntés*, 281; Ciano, *Diary* August 26–28, 378–379.

97. Béni, *A második Bécsi döntés*, 282–283. It is not known why Hitler favored the Hungarians, whereas in the past and in later developments he always favored the Romanians; it does appear that he understood the enormous psychological importance of Transylvania to the Hungarian population.

98. Ciano, *Diary*, 380.

99. Béni, *A második Bécsi döntés*, 294.

100. See Map 3, Territorial Increase of Hungary (1938–1941), in Chapter 3.

101. L. Nagy, *Magyarország története*, 171; Béni, *A második Bécsi döntés,* 299–300; Juhász, *Hungarian Foreign Policy*, 175.

102. That border had been determined by the railroad line that ran south-north to the Ukrainian border which the French had planned to use in their fight against the Bolsheviks.

103. Béla Bethlen, *Észak-Erdély kormánybiztosa voltam* [I was government commissioner of Transylvania] (Budapest: Zrínyi katonai kiadó, 1989), 20.

104. Ibid., 20.

105. L. Nagy, *Magyarország története*, 172.

106. Nagy Vilmos, *Végzetes esztendők*, 59, 63.

107. N. F. Dreisziger, "Civil-Military Relations in Nazi Germany's Shadow: the Case of Hungary, 1939–1941," in *Swords and Covenants, Essays in Honour of the Centennial of the Royal Military College of Canada 1876–1976* (Totowa, N.J.: Rowman and Littlefield, 1976), 229–230.

108. Romsics, *Magyarország története*, 247.

109. A number of peasant immigrants arrived in the eighteenth century from the Swabian regions, and eventually the term came to be used for all German-Hungarians. See Zoltán Ács, "Germans in Hungary," *The New Hungarian Quarterly* 30, no. 116 (Winter 1989): 57.

110. Tilkovszky, *Pál Teleki*, 37.

111. In a similar action to that of Sweden when the Germans demanded rail transport for their invasion of Norway, the Hungarians did not permit German troops to

stop on Hungarian territory or allow German military guards to accompany food shipment for the German troops who regularly passed through starting in winter 1940.

112. Werth had been brought back from retirement and named chief of general staff by the regent on September 29, 1938. Although it has been charged that he was pro-German because of his German origins, it is more probable that he believed cooperation in the presumed German victory would guarantee the lasting possession of the returned territories. See Gyula Borbándi, *Magyar politikai pályaképek 1938–1948* [Careers of Hungarian politicians] (Budapest: Európa könyvkiadó, 1997), 199; Czettler, *Teleki Pál*, 246–247.

113. Macartney, *October Fifteenth*, 1:444.

114. Dreisziger, "Civil-Military Relations in Nazi Germany's Shadow," 230.

115. See Teleki's letter to the regent in *Horthy Miklós titkos Iratai*, 239–252.

116. King, "Domestic Considerations," 27.

117. Ablonczy, *Teleki Pál*, 215.

118. King, "Domestic Considerations," 24.

119. Zsuzsanna Simon, "Erdély köz- és szakigazgatása a második bécsi döntés után" [Transylvanian Administration after the second Vienna Award] *Regio*, no. 4 (1995), 60–82.

120. Váró had been affiliated with the Gusti school of village research and had worked with young apprentices through the IKE/YMCA. See György Váró, Memoirs 1980, 35. (unpublished manuscript).

121. Macartney, *October Fifteenth*, 1:430.

122. Simon, "Transylvanian administration," 75–77; Ablonczy, *Teleki Pál*, 459.

123. Váró, *Memoirs 1980*, 25–26.

124. Ibid.

125. Simon, "Transylvanian administration,"68.

126. Quoted in John Keegan, *The Second World War* (New York: Viking, 1990), 128–129.

127. Ibid., 129.

128. See Keegan, *The Second World War*, 129–130, and Weinberg, *A World at Arms*, 187–188, for somewhat differing accounts of the timing of Hitler's decision to attack Russia.

129. Weinberg, *A World at Arms*, 198–202.

130. Ablonczy, *Teleki Pál*, 493; Czettler, *Teleki Pál*, 240; Macartney, *October Fifteenth*, 1:464–465.

131. Czettler, *Teleki Pál*, 240–244.

132. Barcza, *Diplomataemlékeim*, 1:483.

133. Rothschild, *East Central Europe*, 262–264.

134. Czettler, *Teleki Pál*, 265–6.

135. Colonel William "Wild Bill" Donovan arrived on January 23 and exhorted the leaders to preserve the national honor. Churchill instructed his ambassador to do

Order Number: 79420255

Title: Hungary in World War II: Caught in the Cauldron [Paperback] by

SKU: oxpb12JANjVG-107e-0823233448

Special: AmazonCA/701-5415363-3558614

Recipient: Leslie Majer
Davis Wright Tremaine LLP
1633 Broadway
New YorkNY, US 10019-6708

Shipping Method: standard

Buyer: Leslie Majer, 2b4l7bdgv62g59b@marketplace.amazon.

Quantity: 1

Important Notice to All Customers

Bellwether Books has made every effort to inspect each book prior to shipment to ensure there are no markings and/or inscriptions of an offensive nature in the book you have purchased. However, the majorities of our titles are publisher returns, and while appearing in 'like new' condition, they may have some markings that we did not catch.

If you do find offensive markings in this book, please return the book and upon receipt back to us, we will ship another copy, if available, to you at no additional charge, or credit your account back the full amount (purchase price plus shipping & handling) should this copy be unavailable.

Thanks for purchasing from Bellwether Books, and we hope you enjoy your book!

For any questions or concerns, kindly email us at sales@bellwetherbooks.net everything possible to persuade the Yugoslav government to stay out of the Pact (Keegan, *The Second World War*, 151–152).

136. Ablonczy, *Teleki Pál*, 495; Macartney, *October Fifteenth*, 1:474; Tilkovsky, *Pál Teleki*, 56–57.

137. Sakmyster, *Admiral on Horseback*, 255–256; Tilkovsky, *Pál Teleki*, 60; Macartney, *October Fifteenth*, 1:476–477.

138. Ablonczy, *Teleki Pál*, 496; Tilkovszky, *Pál Teleki*, 61.

139. Ablonczy, *Teleki Pál*, 497; Macartney, *October Fifteenth*, 1:483.

140. Quoted in Ablonczy, *Teleki Pál*, 497.

141. Ablonczy, *Teleki Pál*, 498–500; Tilkovszky, *Pál Teleki*, 63. Bárdossy later told Barcza that the telegram's message caused Teleki's suicide.

142. Ablonczy, *Teleki Pál*, 500.

143. Quoted in Macartney, *October Fifteenth*, 1:488–489.

144. Barcza, *Diplomataemlékeim*, 1:445–447.

145. Macartney, *October Fifteenth*, 2:3.

146. See Map 3, Territorial Increase of Hungary (1938–1941), in Chapter 3.

147. Bán, *Illúziók és Csalódások*, 133; Tilkovszky, *Pál Teleki*, 345.

5. Hungary Enters the War

1. During the difficult early years of the Communist regime, a Hungarian village teacher recalled the first years of World War II as the "The Golden Years" (Personal communication with author by Frigyes Jónás, May 16, 2000).

2. Halder and Brauchitsch thought it better to remain friends with Russia and concentrate on the British; Jodl had doubts early on; Manstein and Guderian were disquieted by the idea of the vast Russian spaces. Bock told Hitler in December that the war with Russia might be difficult even for the *Wehrmacht*. See Keegan, *The Second World War*, 138–140.

3. Between 1937 and 1940, out of an estimated 75,000 to 80,000 officers in the armed forces, Stalin had imprisoned or executed at least 30,000. Another 10,000 officers were dismissed from service in disgrace. Younger men, often lacking experience or training, found themselves thrust into high command. See David M. Glantz and Jonathan M. House, *When Titans Clashed: How the Red Army Stopped Hitler* (University of Kansas Press, 1995), 11–12.

4. Quoted in Keegan, *The Second World War*, 137.

5. Glantz and House, *When Titans Clashed*, 34, 51–52.

6. Péter Szabó, Norbert Számvéber, *A Keleti Hadszíntér és Magyarország 1941–1943* [The eastern war theater and Hungary 1941–1943] (Budapest: Puedlo, 2003), 11.

7. Quoted in Mario Fenyo, *Hitler, Horthy, and Hungary: German–Hungarian Relations 1941–1944* (New Haven, Conn.: Yale University Press, 1972), 21.

8. Another possibility, proposed by Nándor F. Dreisziger, is that the bombing was an error made by raiders in the Soviet Air Force, who mistakenly believed that Kassa

on the Slovak border—one of the cities returned to Hungary in the first Vienna Award—was still a Slovak city. Slovakia had just joined Germany in the war against the Soviet Union and was also a staging area for part of the German war machine. See Dreisziger, "New Twist to an Old Riddle: The Bombing of Kassa (Košice) June 26, 1941," *Journal of Modern History* 44, no. 2 (June 1972): 232–242.

9. Macartney, *October Fifteenth*, 2:25, 26; Sakmyster, *Admiral on Horseback*, 266–267.

10. Sakmyster, *Admiral on Horseback*, 266–267.

11. Macartney, *October Fifteenth*, 2:26; Sakmyster, *Admiral on Horseback*, 266–7.

12. Bárcziházi Bárczy, who had taken the minutes, charged that Bárdossy had falsified the results of the meeting, but since it was known that Bárczy hated the prime minister, his charge has been questioned. Still, differences in the two versions are considerable. Bárdossy's version omits opposition by Radocsay, minister of justice, Dániel Bánffy, minister of agriculture, and József Varga, minister of industry, and gives a false picture of the course of debate. See Pál Pritz, "War-Crimes Trial Hungarian Style: Prime Minister László Bárdossy before the People's Tribunal, 1945," *Hungarian Studies Review* 22, 1 (Spring, 1995): 59–60; Macartney, *October Fifteenth* 2:27–28.

13. Macartney, *October Fifteenth*, 2:28.

14. During the war the United States bombed Schaffhausen in Switzerland, but the Swiss did not declare war.

15. Pál Pritz, *Bárdossy László a népbíróság előtt* [László Bárdossy before the People's Court] (Budapest: Maecenas Könykiadó, 1991), 21; Macartney, *October Fifteenth*, 1:465–467.

16. Az országgyűlés képviselőházának 202 ülési 1941. Évi június hó 27-en pénteken [Minutes of the parliamentary house of representatives, 202 sitting. June 27, 1941. Authentic issue] (Budapest: Athenaeum, 1941). Later the constitutionality of the decision was questioned, but at the time that issue appeared immaterial. Two laws had been passed in 1920; the first did not give Horthy the right to declare war but the addition on August 19, 1920: 1 t-c13 stated that in case of danger to the country the regent could declare war and receive approval from ministers and parliament later.

17. Ibid.

18. Hess archives: Béke előkészitő osztály iratai 1945–47 [Documents of the peace preparation division 1945–47]. XIX-J-a-II-14. 10.d. 194.

19. Tamás Csató, "The War Economy Subservient to Germany," in *Evolution of the Hungarian Economy 1848–1998*, Iván T. Berend and Tamás Csató (Highland Lakes, N.J.: Atlantic Research and Publications, 2001), 226.

20. The total labor force in manufacturing and mining rose 36.6 percent from 1938 to 1943, from 333,048 to 451,032. See Iván T. Berend, "The Composition and Position of the Working Class during the War," in *Hungarian Economy and Society During World War II,* ed. György Lengyel (Highland Lakes, NJ: Atlantic Research and

Publication, 1993), 152–53. The article is part of Berend's unpublished dissertation written over thirty years earlier. The study of workers was neglected during the Communist era, heavily controlled by party ideology.

21. Ibid., 152–154.

22. Sakmyster, *Admiral on Horseback*, 4.

23. Lóránd Dombrády, *A magyar gazdaság*, 29–31.

24. Peter Gosztony, "Hungary's Army in the Second World War," in *Hungarian History/World History*, ed. György Ránki (Budapest: Akadémiai Kiadó, 1984), 225.

25. Quoted in Dombrády, *A magyar gazdaság*, 29.

26. Csató, "The War Economy," 227, footnote 92.

27. Quoted in Lóránd Dombrády, "Financing the Hungarian Rearmament," in Lengyel, *Hungarian Economy and Society*, 80.

28. Berend and Ránki, *The Hungarian Economy*, 158.

29. Dombrady, *A magyar gazdaság*, 33–34.

30. Központi Gazdasági Levéltár, National Worsted Mill, Hüsz. Pk. Order no. 23, cited in Berend, "The Composition and Position of the Working Class," 164.

31. Dombrady, *A magyar gazdaság*, 33–34.

32. Ibid., 21–24.

33. Ferenc Lencsés, *Mezőgazdasági idénymunkások a negyvenes években* [Agricultural seasonal workers in the 1940s] (Budapest: Akadémiai Kiadó, 1982), 130, 135.

34. Ibid., 130–131.

35. Ibid., 131.

36. Ibid., 133–135.

37. Dombrády, *A magyar gazdaság*, 164–165.

38. Károly Szabó and László Virágh, "Controlling the Agriculture and the Producers," in *Hungarian Economy and Society During World War II*, ed. György Lengyel (Highland Lakes, N.J.: Atlantic Research and Publication, 1993), 128.

39. Szabó and Virágh, "Controlling the Agriculture," 132.

40. Péter Gunst, *Magyarország gazdaságtörténete 1914–1989* [Economic History of Hungary] (Budapest: Nemzeti Tankönyvkiadó, 1999), 108.

41. Anna Megyeri, "Az ONCSA (Országos Nép és Családvédelmi Alap) segítő munkája Nagykanizsán 1941–1945 között" [Work of the National Foundation for the Protection of the People and the Family in Nagykanizsa between 1941–1945]. Zalai Múzeum 7 (1997): 177–182; Gyáni, *Magyarország társadalom-története*, 482.

42. Ablonczy, *Teleki Pál*, 432–433; András Hegedüs, *A történelem és a hatalom igézetében* [History and the fascination of power] (Budapest: Kossuth, 1988), 109.

43. There were thirteen hundred Reformed Church congregations and five hundred Lutheran congregations. In 1939/40 thirty winter camps were held, with a total of 3,000 participants from 800 villages.

44. Sándor Jakab, *Visszaemlékezés a népfőiskolás évekre* [Remembrance of the Folk High School Years] (Budapest, 1976). From Népfőiskola files. NF-22, 43.

45. László E. Kovács, *A Sárospataki Népfőiskola 1936–1986*, [The Sárospatak Folk High School 1936–1986] ed. Tóth János, Országos Közművelődési Központ Módszertani Intézete, 83–85.

46. Ferenc Erdei, "Balaton Találkozó" [Balaton Meeting] *Magyar út* (September 1, 1938), 2.

47. Lilly Vigyázó, interview with the author, June 26, 2003.

48. Ibid.

49. Gábor Murányi, "Sorok között, világosan" [Between the lines, clearly] *HVG* (April 2001) 99.

50. Yehuda Don, "Economic Implications," 56–58; *Statistical Yearbook of Budapest for 1939*, 320.

51. Simon Kemény, *Napló 1942–1944* [Diary 1942–1944], 6–9.

52. L. Nagy Zsuzsa, *Liberális párt-mozgalmak 1931–1945*, 91–93.

53. *Náray Antal visszaemlmékezése 1945*, ed. Sándor Szakály (Budapest: Zrínyi, 1988), 12–13.

54. L. Nagy, *Liberális párt-mozgalmak*, 93.

55. Alice Somlai Pók, interview with the author, 6.22. 2008.

56. István Nemeskürty, *Búcsu pillantás: A Magyar Királyság és a Kormánzója 1920–1944* [A farewell glance: the Hungarian Kingdom and the Regent 1920–1944] (Budapest: Szabad tér, 1995), 162.

57. *A százgyökerű szív: Levelek, naplók, visszaemlékezések, Sík Sándor hagyatékából* [Letters, diaries, and memoirs from Sándor Sík's estate], ed. János Szabó (Budapest: Magvető, 1993), 205–206.

58. Converted Jews were among those affected by the change in criteria. They had left the Jewish community but now had lost the Christian community. In the summer of 1939 an organization was established just for their protection —the Magyar Szent Kereszt Egyesület (Hungarian Sacred Christian Society)—with the approval of the Roman Catholic church. See Jenő Gergely, "A Katolikus Püspöki Kar és a Konvertiták Mentése (Dokumentumok)," [The Catholic bench of bishops and rescue of converts] *Történelmi Szemle* 4 (1984): 581.

59. Gábor Támas. Interview with the author. Santa Fe, 10/31/01.

60. Ibid.

61. József Litván, *Ítéletidő* [Time of decision], memoirs written with PPTóth (Budapest: Tekintet könyvek, 1991), 48–49.

62. Sándor Szakály, "A hadsereg és a zsidótörvények az ellenforradalmi Magyarországon," [The army and Jewish laws in counter-revolutionary Hungary] *Valóság* no. 9 (1985): 49–50.

63. Ibid., 57–58.

64. Szombathelyi testified in 1945 that the Jewish Question had a catastrophic effect on the army. See Szakály, "A hadsereg és a zsidótörvények," 62.

65. Szakály, 58.

66. Interestingly, after the German occupation in 1944 the army in many cases saved people from deportation and the Arrow Cross terror by calling them up for labor service.

67. Randolph L. Braham, *The Hungarian Labor Service System 1939–1945* (New York: East European Quarterly, distributed by Columbia University Press, 1977), 9–10.

68. Ibid., 12–13.

69. András Lengyel, "Egy útkereső szociológus a két világ háború közt: Vázlat Reitzer Béláról [A path-seeking sociologist in the interwar period: Sketch of Béla Reitzer], in *Útkeresések: Irodalom-és művelődés története tanulmányok* (Budapest: Magvető, 1990), 323–374.

70. Krisztián Ungváry, *A magyar honvédség a második világháborúban* [The Hungarian Army in World War II] (Budapest: Osiris, 2004), 21–22.

71. Quoted in Ungváry, 22.

72. Keegan, *The Second World War*, 186; Weinberg, *A World at Arms*, 268–269.

73. Szabó and Számvéber, *A Keleti Hadszíntér*, 22.

74. Ibid.

75. Jakab, *Visszaemlékezés a népfőiskolás évekre*, 49.

76. Szabó and Számvéber, *A Keleti Hadszíntér*, 22; Lóránd Dombrády, *A legfelsőbb hadúr és hadserege* [The Supreme Commander and the army] (Budapest: Zrínyi, 1990), 173.

77. Juhász, *Hungarian Foreign Policy*, 272; Sakmyster, *Admiral on Horseback*, 269–270.

78. Dombrády, *A legfelsőbb Hadúr*, 174; Sakmyster, *Admiral on Horseback*, 270.

79. Dombrády, *A legfelsőbb Hadúr*, 177; Sakmyster, *Admiral on Horseback*, 271.

80. Sakmyster, *Admiral on Horseback*, 271; *Szombathelyi Ferenc Visszemlékezései*, ed. Péter Gosztonyi (Washington, D.C.: Occidental Press, 1980), 14.

81. *Szombathelyi Ferenc Visszemlékezései*,14.

82. Along with many other conservative officers, he joined the Hungarian Red Army in 1919 to defend the country against the invading neighbors. After the war in the greatly diminished reorganized Hungarian army he served in the Ministry of Defense and taught history at the Ludovika Academy where he had also been commander from 1933 to 1936.

83. Charles Fenyvesi, *Három összeesküvés* [Three conspiracies] (Budapest: Európa Könyvkiadó, 2007), 235, 302–303.

84. "Bokor Péter interview with Lieszkovszky Pál, Kádár Gyula, and Hüttle Wilhelm" *Magyar Hírlap* (March 19, 1996).

85. Dombrády, *A legfelsőbb Hadúr*, 177–178; Szabó, Számvéber, *A Keleti Hadszíntér*, 22–23; Ungváry, *A magyar honvédség*, 36

86. *Szombathelyi Ferenc Visszemlékezései*, 14–15.

87. Gyula Kádár, *A Ludovikától Sopronkőhidáig* [From the Ludovika to Sopron Stone Bridge] vol. 2 (Budapest: Magvető, 1978), 407–408.

88. Dombrády, *A legfelsőbb Hadúr*, 180–181, Ungváry, *A magyar honvédség*, 35.

89. Jakab, *Visszaemlékezés a népfőiskolás évekre*, 49.

90. Szabó, Számvéber, *A Keleti Hadszíntér*, 23.

91. Simon Kemény, *Napló 1942–1944*, 15–16.

92. Ibid., 15–16.

93. Ibid., 16–17.

94. Juhász, *Magyarország külpolitikája*, 278–279; Macartney, *October Fifteenth*, 2:60–61. Pell closed the legation in Budapest and returned to the United States on January 16, 1942.

95. Juhász, *Magyarország külpolitikája*, 280–281.

96. Quoted in Macartney, *October Fifteenth*, 2:63–64.

97. John Flournoy Montgomery, *Hungary: The Unwilling Satellite* (Morristown, N.J.: Vista Books, 1993), 153.

98. Until this point Roosevelt had tried to have the Hungarians, Romanians, and Bulgarians recall their declarations of war. See Weinberg, *Hitler's Foreign Policy*, 439.

6. Disaster at the Don

1. Richard Overy, *Russia's War* (London: Penguin Books, 1997), 94.

2. Keegan, *The Second World War*, 202–203.

3. Glantz and House, *When Titans Clashed*, 81; Rodric Braithwaite, *Kennan Institute Meeting Report*, vol. XXII, no. 18 (2005).

4. Ian Kershaw, *Hitler, 1936–1945* (New York: Norton, 2000), 412.

5. Quoted in Fenyo, *Hitler, Horthy, and Hungary*, 35.

6. Szombathelyi, *Visszaemlékezései*, 16.

7. Péter Szabó, *Don-kanyar: a magyar királyi 2.honvéd hadsereg története 1942–1943* [The Don-bend: history of the Royal Hungarian Second Army 1942–1943] (Budapest: Corvina, 2001), 12; Fenyo, *Hitler, Horthy, and Hungary*, 37.

8. Bárdossy had promised the entire grain surplus from the Bácska to Germany and Italy. See Dombrády, *A legfelsőbb hadúr*, 183; Szabó, *Don-kanyar*, 12–13.

9. Kemény, *Napló*, 13–14.

10. Ciano, *Diary*, January 15, 1942, 484–485.

11. Szabó, *Don-kanyar*, 17.

12. Szombathelyi, *Visszaemlékezései*, 16–17; Szabó, *Don-kanyar*, 16; Ungváry, *A magyar honvédség*, 35, 157.

13. Overy, *Russia's War*, 156.

14. Baranya, between the rivers Drave and Danube, was the southeastern corner of the Hungarian County of Baranya; Bácska, between the Danube and the Tisza, made up the southern and central portions of the Hungarian County of Bács-Bodrog; the Bánát, on the left bank of the Tisza, was the westernmost third of the area once officially known as Bánát. See C. A. Macartney, *Hungary and Her Successors 1919–1937* (Oxford University Press, 1937), 381.

15. In mid-December Parliament declared formal reannexation of the area.

16. Enikő A. Sajti, *Délvidék 1941–1944: a magyar kormányok délszláv politikája* [Délvidék 1941–1944: the South Slav policy of the Hungarian government] (Budapest: Kossuth Könyvkiadó, 1987), 154–155; Tamás Stark, *Zsidóság a vészkorszakban és a felszabadulás után 1930–1955* [Jews in the time of disaster and after the liberation 1930–1955] (Budapest: MTA Történettudományi Intézet, 1995), 17.

17. Antal Czettler, *A mi kis élethalél kérdéseink: a Magyar külpolitika a hadba lépéstől a német megszállásig* [Our small life-and-death questions: Hungarian foreign policy from the entrance into the war to the German occupation] Budapest: Magvető, 2000), 430; Stark, *Zsidóság a vészkorszakban*, 17.

18. Nicholas Wood and Ivana Sekularac, "Hungarian Is Faced with Evidence of Role in '42 Atrocity," *New York Times*, October 1, 2006.

19. Macartney, *October Fifteenth*, 2:72.

20. Although estimates of the number of victims varied greatly, according to the statistics gathered by the Fifth Army Corps command, the dead numbered 3,340, including 2,550 Serbs, 743 Jews, 11 Hungarians, 13 Russians, 7 Germans, 2 Croats, 1 Slovak, and 13 Ruthenians. Of these 2,102 were male, 792 female, 299 elderly and 147 children. See Sajti, *Délvidék*, 159–160.

21. *Shvoy Kálmán Titkos Naplója és Emlékirata 1918–1945* [Kálmán Shvoy secret diary and memoir 1918–1945] (Budapest: Kossuth Könyvkiadó, 1983), 234–235.

22. Kádár, *A Ludovikától*, 2:643–644.

23. Szombathelyi, *Visszaemlékezései*, 26–27.

24. See chapter 7 for details on the trial of responsible officers.

25. Nicholas Wood and Ivana Sekularac, *New York Times*, October 1, 2006.

26. Szabó, *Don-kanyar*, 62–63.

27. György Molnár, personal communication to the author, March 16, 2005.

28. Quoted in Szabó, *Don-kanyar*, 18.

29. There were sixty-nine worker companies sent with the Second Army to the eastern front in summer of 1942, mainly composed of Jews, approximately seventeen to eighteen thousand people. See Stark, *Zsidóság a vészkorszakban*, 18.

30. Szabó, *Don-kanyar*, 19; Kádár, *A Ludóvikátol*, 2:418.

31. György Váró, *Memoirs 1980 summer*, 57. Váró was one of the young men whom Teleki had selected to represent northern Transylvania in Parliament after the reannexation.

32. Iván Boldizsár, *Don—Buda—Párizs* (Budapest: Magvető Könyvkiadó, 1982), 16, 23.

33. Szabó, *Don-kanyár*, 19–20; György Molnár, personal communication to author. 3/16/05.

34. Szabó, *Don-kanyár*, 22–23, 63; Ungváry, *A magyar honvédség*, 162–164.

35. Szabó, *Don-kanyar*, 20; György Molnár, personal communication to author, June 27, 2008.

36. Rita Péntek, "István Horthy's Election as vice regent in 1942," *Hungarian Studies Review*, vol. XXIII (1996), 18.

37. Gyulai, *Becsület és kötelesség*, 52–54.

38. Péntek, "István Horthy's Election," 18.

39. Gyulai, *Becsület és kötelesség*, 54.

40. Quoted in Péntek, "István Horthy's Election," 20.

41. Ibid., 23–24.

42. Elke Fröhlich, ed., *Die Tagebücher von Joseph Goebbels; Sämtliche Fragmente. Teil II Diktate 1941–1945, Januar bis März 1942*, 345.

43. Gyulai, *Becsület és kötelesség*, 116.

44. Macartney, *October Fifteenth*, 2:83.

45. Ibid.

46. Nicholas Kállay, *Hungarian Premier: A Personal Account of a Nation's Struggle in the Second World War* (New York: Columbia University Press, 1954), 6–7.

47. Ibid.

48. Kállay, *Hungarian Premier*, 8–9, Sakmyster, *Admiral on Horseback*, 283–284.

49. Kállay, *Hungarian Premier*, 12.

50. Sakmyster, *Admiral on Horseback*, 283.

51. Elke Fröhlich, ed., *Die Tagebücher von Joseph Goebbels*, 519–520.

52. Sakmyster, *Admiral on Horseback*, 285, Czettler, *A Magyar külpolitika*, 174–175.

53. Keresztes-Fischer came to be a defender of Jews and the political Left, becoming almost the most-hated figure in Hungary by the Germans and Arrow Cross. See Macartney, *October Fifteenth*, 1:105.

54. Kállay, *Hungarian Premier*, 70–71; Mária Ormos, *Magyaroszág a két világháború korában 1914–1945* [Hungary in the period of the two world wars 1914–1945] (Budapest: Csokonai, 1998), 243–244; Sakmyster, *Admiral on Horseback*, 286.

55. Barcza, *Diplomataemlékeim*, 2:59.

56. In his memoirs Kállay makes no mention of the measures he took against the Left—nor the 180-degree turn he made later. See Ormos, *Magyarország*, 242–243.

57. Sándor Szakály, "A katonai ellenállasi mozgalom Magyarországon a második világháború éveiben," [The Hungarian military resistance movement in World War II] *Honvédségi Szemle* no. 9 (1987): 139.

58. Murányi, "Sorok között, világosan," 97–99.

59. In 1987, at a time when Soviet troops were still in Hungary, a well-dressed older woman asked me to direct her to the Batthány memorial so that she could leave her bouquet of flowers.

60. L. Nagy, *Magyarország története*, 230.

61. Szakály, "A katonai ellenállási mozgalom," 140.

62. Sigray had voted against the Jewish laws and with his American wife had protected Polish and French refugees on their estate. See Borbándi, *Magyar politikai pályaképek* , 389.

63. L. Nagy, *Magyarország története*, 231–232.

64. Macartney, *October Fifteenth*, 1:105; L. Nagy, *Magyarország története*, 232.

65. Szakasits, not knowing what to do with the unwelcome letter, put it in a sealed envelope with a lawyer where it was found by military counterespionage. Kovács had already been caught with his letter. Brought before a military court, Szakasits was released through Kállay's intervention but had to resign secretaryship of the party. Kovács spent time in prison. See Macartney, *October Fifteenth*, 2:106.

66. L. Nagy, *Magyarország története*, 230; Macartney, *October Fifteenth*, 2:104–106.

67. Szabó, *Don-kanyar*, 107; Ungváry, *A magyar honvédség*, 167.

68. Glantz and House, *When Titans Clashed*, 108–110; Keegan, *The Second World War*, 220–222.

69. Glantz and House, *When Titans Clashed*, 116–117.

70. Overy, *Russia's War*, 165.

71. Glantz and House, *When Titans Clashed*, 121; Overy, *Russia's War*, 158–161.

72. Váró was commander of a wagon train used for transport from the last railroad station to the front line. See Váró, *Memoirs*, 58–59.

73. Ungváry, *A magyar honvédség*, 162.

74. Keegan, *The Second World War*, 224.

75. Glantz and House, *When Titans Clashed*, 120.

76. Szabó, *Don-kanyar*, 113–115; Ungváry, *A magyar honvédség*, 169.

77. Szabó and Számvéber, *A Keleti Hadszíntér*, 64; Peter Gosztony, "Hungary's Army in the Second World War," 243.

78. Szabó, *Don-kanyar*, 117–119; Ungváry, *A magyar honvédség*, 170.

79. Szabó, *Don-kanyar*, 125.

80. Ibid.

81. Váró, *Memoirs*, 59.

82. Szabó, *Don-kanyar*, 155–7.

83. Ibid.,161.

84. Lajos Olasz, "Horthy István kormányzóhelyettes halála" [Vice-Regent István Horthy's death] in *Mítoszok, legendák, tévhitek a 20. századi magyar történelemről* (Budapest: Osiris, 2005), 244–246.

85. Stephen in Hungarian is István. It's significant that it was thought István would return on his name's day, which in Hungary is celebrated rather than birthdays.

86. Ibid., 247.

87. Sakmyster, *Admiral on Horseback*, 288–289.

88. Olasz, "Horthy István kormányzóhelyettes halála," 239–242.

89. *Náray Antal visszaemlékezése 1945*, 74.

90. *Horthy István repülő főhadnagy tragikus halála* (Budapest: Auktor, 1992), 9.

91. Szombathelyi, *Visszaemlékezései*, forword by Csicsery-Rónay István, 4.

92. The only product that caught on in Hungarian cuisine, also used after the war, was the so-called *Hitler bacon*—an artificial jam made out of squash.

93. Szabó, *Don-kanyar*, 166; Ungváry, *A magyar honvédség*, 177–179.

94. L. Nagy, *Magyarország története*, 225; Lóránd Dombrády, *A legfelsőbb hadúr és hadserege*, 187.

95. Sakmyster, *Admiral on Horseback*, 292.

96. Váró, *Memoirs*, 59.

97. Vilmos Nagybaczoni Nagy, *Végzetes esztendők 1938–1945* [Fateful years 1938–1945] (Budapest: Gondolat, 1986), 103–104.

98. Géza Lakatos, *Ahogy én láttam*, 31, 56.

99. Nagy, *Végzetes esztendők*, 113, 125–128.

100. Ungváry, *A magyar honvédség*, 180.

101. Nagy, *Végzetes esztendők*, 125.

102. Ibid., 127–129.

103. Keegan, *The Second World War*, 230–231

104. Ibid., 230–234.

105. L. Nagy, *Magyarország története*, 226.

106. Szabó, *Don-kanyar*, 179–174.

107. Ungváry, *A magyar honvédség*,180; Szabó, *Don-kanyar*, 171–172.

108. The *Pester Lloyd* had been founded in 1854 at a time when much of the population of Budapest was German.

109. Iván Boldizsár, *Don—Buda—Párizs*, 61–63.

110. Boldizsár, *Don—Buda—Párizs*, 66–67.

111. In 1972 István Nemeskürty broached the taboo subject of Don losses with his work, *Requiem egy hadseregért* [Requiem for an Army] (Budapest: Magvető, 1972), but the books were immediately confiscated.

112. Frigyes Jónás, personal communication to author May 16, 2000. (Szabó expressed his regret that his study came too late for most of those who had survived the destruction of the Second Army—only a few remained from the Don tragedy who had to remain mute for so many years and were officially scorned and cursed. See *Don-kanyar*, 7.)

113. Sakmyster, *Admiral on Horseback*, 295.

114. Fenyo, *Hitler, Horthy, and Hungary*, 103; Ungváry, *A magyar honvédség*, 184–185.

115. Fenyo, 103–105,

116. Ungváry, *A magyar honvédség*, 196–197.

117. Ibid., 201.

118. Szabó, Számvéber, *A Keleti Hadszíntér*, 92.

119. Ungváry, *A magyar honvédség*, 201.

120. Szabó, Számvéber, *A Keleti Hadszíntér*, 92; Ungváry, *A magyar honvédség*, 197, 200–201.

121. *Gróf Stomm Marcel altábornagy emlékiratok* [Memoirs of Count Marcel Stomm] ed.Gallyas Ferenc (Budapest: Magyar hirláp könyvek, 1990), 117. Stomm had been sent to command the Third Corps in December 1942 after two previous commanders pleaded illness and asked for retirement, as had many high-ranking officers in 1941–1942. Stomm was not happy about his assignment because he was about to be married at the end of November.

122. Ibid., 125.

123. Ibid., 117–133; Szabó, *Don kanyar*, 265–267.

124. Szabó, *Don-kanyar*, 260–271, 346–347; Borbándi, *Magyar politikai pálya-képek,* 399; Ungváry, *A magyar honvédség,* 203.

125. Stomm was released from Soviet prison-of-war camp in 1951, only to be imprisoned again in Hungary as a war criminal. See *Gróf Stomm Marcel altábornagy emlékiratok,* 141–142.

126. Boldizsár, *Don—Buda—Párizs,* 77–79.

127. At one point Dreisziger stole a ride in a German truck heading west. This in itself was a dangerous deed, but it might have saved his life as the truck covered far more distance in a few hours than he could have covered on foot in days. See Nándor Dreisziger, "The nine lives of my dad, Kalman Dreisziger" (unpublished document), 2.

128. During the interview, Szabó, now seriously ill, broke down as he relived the trauma. His daughter reassured him—don't cry, you are safe now. László Szabó and daughter Györgyi Szabó, interview with the author, August 29, 2001.

129. Fenyo, *Hitler, Horthy, and Hungary,* 106.

7. Efforts to Exit the War

1. Sándor Kiss, *A magyar demokráciáért,* 32.

2. The pro-Vichy Admiral François Darlan agreed to turn over the French forces if the Americans agreed to recognize the French military and civilian administration rather than the deGaulle opposition. See Czettler, *A magyar külpolitika,* 185–188.

3. Aladár Szegedy-Maszák, *Az emberősszel visszanéz . . . Egy volt magyar diplo-mata emlékirataiból* [In autumn one looks back . . . Memoirs of a former Hungarian diplomat] (Budapest: Europa, 1996), 2:51.

4. Rezső Peéry, *Requiem egy országrészért,* 70.

5. Gyula Juhász, *A háború és Magyarország 1938–1945* [The war and Hungary 1938–1945] (Budapest: Akadémiai Kiadó, 1986), 300.

6. The Catholics organized separately while a group of Protestant clergy started a movement for closer spiritual cooperation between the churches.

7. Ignác Romsics, *István Bethlen: a Great Conservative Statesman of Hungary* (New York: Columbia University Press, 1995), 366–367; Sakmyster, *Admiral on Horse-back,* 294.

8. Juhász, *Hungarian Foreign Policy,* 218–219; Czettler, *A magyar külpolitika,* 218.

9. Romsics, *István Bethlen,* 366.

10. Czettler, *A magyar külpolitika*, 216–217; Juhász, *A háború és Magyarország*, 301–302.

11. Szombathelyi, *Visszaemlékezései*, 22–23.

12. Czettler, *A magyar külpolitika*, 217; Juhász, *A háború és Magyarország*, 302.

13. Gyula Gueth, *Egy tartalékos tábori lelkész II. világháborús visszaemlékezései 1942–1945* [World War II memoirs of a military pastor 1942–1945] (Kaposvár: Pethő & Társa Nyomdaipari Bt., n.d.), 14.

14. Iván T. Berend, "The Composition and Position of the Working Class during the War," 155, 162; Péter Gunst, *Magyarország gazdaságtörténete, 1914–1989* (Budapest: Nemzeti Tankönyvkiadó, 1999), 108.

15. Károly Szabó and László Virágh, "Controlling the Agriculture," 137–143.

16. Gunst, *Magyarország gazdaságtörténete*, 108–109.

17. In 1942 Kállay had made several initiatives to contact the British and the Americans. A mission of Andor Gellért to Stockholm and contact made by Tibor Eckhardt in the United States, although producing little at the time, remained useful as means to open communications with Allied representatives in the future.

18. Ormos, *Magyaroszág*, 242.

19. Fenyo, *Hitler, Horthy, and Hungary*, 131.

20. Barcza, *Diplomataemlékeim*, 64.

21. Mária Schmidt, *Kollaboráció vagy kooperáció? A Budapesti Zsidó Tanács* [Collaboration or cooperation? The Budapest Jewish Council] (Budapest: Minerva, 1990), 259. Under the German occupation Hain became head of the SS Political Police for the Jewish Division.

22. In his groundbreaking work, *A Magyar felsőház története 1927–1945* [History of the Hungarian upper house 1927–1945] (Budapest: Napvilág kiadó, 2000), Levente Püski, explains the difficulty of conducting his research on the upper house since no records were kept of the closed sessions or private discussions.

23. Romsics, *István Bethlen*, 367.

24. Barcza, *Diplomataemlékeim*, 73–74, 81–83.

25. Barcza, *A svájci misszió: Diplomata emlekeimből*, 5.

26. Ibid., 6.

27. Ibid., 6–8.

28. Ibid., 9. Pope Pius XII's actions during the Holocaust remain controversial; he has been accused of remaining silent when German atrocities were committed. It appears that Pope Pius XII believed that he first needed to preserve Vatican neutrality so that Vatican City could be a refuge for war victims, and secondly, was convinced that he was powerless against Hitler; therefore his best attack against the Nazis was quiet diplomacy and behind-the-scenes action. Barcza felt that the previous pope, Pius XI, whom he had known well, would not have hesitated to condemn Hitler and the Germans.

29. Barcza, *Diplomataemlékeim*, 2:103.

30. Ullein Reviczky had been entrusted by Teleki and Kállay to carry out a unique press policy—supporting the pro-Western opposition papers and attacking the papers of the government party and the Right. The opposition papers, realizing that the "game" was in the national interest, worked out a kind of juggler-show to enable the reader to read between the lines. See Péter Bokor, "Ullein-Reviczky Antal és a 'kiugrási' politika," [Antal Ullein-Reviczky and the 'bail-out' policy] *Magyar Hírlap* May 6, 1993.

31. Tibor Pethő, "Quid nunc?—Hogyan tovább? Ullein-Reviczky Antal emlékiratai," [Quid nunc?—how to go on? Memoirs of Antal Ullein-Reviczky] *Magyar Nemzet* May 29, 1993.

32. Czettler, *A magyar külpolitika*, 229.

33. Ibid., 320–322.

34. Weinberg, *A World at Arms*, 438–440.

35. Kállay, *Hungarian Premier*, 157–158.

36. M. K. Dziewanowski, *War at Any Price: World War II in Europe 1939–1945* (Upper Saddle River, N.J.: Prentice Hall, 1991), 211.

37. Czettler, *A magyar külpolitika*, 323.

38. Szegedy-Maszák, *Az ember ősszel visszanéz*, 2:190–191; Macartney, *October Fifteenth*, 2:144.

39. Paloczi-Horvath returned to Hungary in 1947 on the invitation of the Communist leader Rákosi and joined the Communist Party. He describes his role as an agent of the SOE in the negotiations and his return to Hungary in his autobiography, *The Undefeated* (London: Seeker and Warburg, 1959).

40. Czettler, *A magyar külpolitika*, 227–228; Macartney, *October Fifteenth* 2:142.

41. Initially the committee was to function through three subcommittees, but in April of 1941 it was decided to organize the committee as a single body with two principal functions—to consider the organization of peace and to review the economic plans previously worked out by the Interdepartmental Group. See Harley A. Notter, *Postwar Foreign Policy Preparations 1939–1945*, reprint of the 1949 ed. (Westport, CN: Greenwood Press, 1975), 20–21, 45.

42. Ignác Romsics, "Wartime American Plans for a New Hungary and the Paris Peace Conference, 1941–1947," in *20th Century Hungary and the Great Powers*, ed. Romsics (New York: Columbia University Press, 1995), 157.

43. Romsics, "Wartime American Plans," 160–163; Romsics, *Magyarország Története*, 272–273.

44. Historian Arnold J. Toynbee headed the committee with C. A. Macartney as the sole Hungarian expert.

45. Romsics, *Magyarország*, 273–274.

46. Ibid., 274.

47. Stalin opposed allowing Hungarian POWs to form an anti-Fascist legion like that of the Poles to fight on the side of the Soviets since it would have given them heroic standing in postwar Hungary as resistance fighters.

48. Romsics, *Magyarország,* 274–275.

49. Kállay, *Hungarian Premier,* 216–217; Macartney, *October Fifteenth,* 2:137–138.

50. They focused on industrial development which augmented the German munitions industry and obstructed projects that could have been important to Hungary in peacetime, that is, the establishment of a new metallurgical base in southern Hungary at Mohács, See Tamás Csató, "The War Economy Subservient to Germany," in *Evolution of the Hungarian Economy 1848–1998* vol. I, eds. Iván T. Berend and Tamás Csató, (Highland Lakes, N.J.: Atlantic Research and Publications, 2001), 230.

51. In Clodius' report of December 7, 1943, he seemed satisfied with an agreement on agricultural deliveries even though he mentioned that the Hungarian position on negotiations on agricultural exports had become more rigid. See Czettler, *A magyar külpolitika,* 500–501; Macartney, *October Fifteenth* 2:117–118.

52. Quoted in Tamás Csató, "The War Economy," 232.

53. Ibid., 232.

54. Ibid., 232.

55. Zoltán András Kovács and Norbert Számvéber, *A Waffen-SS Magyarországon* [The Waffen-SS in Hungary] (Budapest: Hadtörténelmi levéltári kiadványok, 2001), 46–48; Valdis O. Lumans, *Himmler's Auxiliaries: The Volksdeutsche Mittelstelle and the German National Minorities of Europe, 1933–1945* (Chapel Hill: University of North Carolina Press, 1993), 224.

56. Loránt Tilkovszky, *Német nemzetiség magyar hazafiság* [German nationality Hungarian patriotism] (Pécs: JPTE, 1997), 238–239.

57. Kovács and Számvéber, *A Waffen-SS Magyarországon,* 54, 57–59.

58. Ibid., 61–62.

59. Lumans, *Himmler's Auxiliaries,* 225.

60. Kovács and Számvéber, *A Waffen-SS Magyarországon,* 62–63; Tilkovszky, *Német nemzetiség,* 243. After the Germans occupied Hungary, a third SS recruiting agreement allowed for the recruiting of ethnic Germans but was in fact forced enlistment. At least another 60,000 ethnic Germans were enlisted in the summer of 1944. They did not lose their Hungarian citizenship, and those who had earlier lost it had it restored.

61. Hungary repatriated more than 400 Jewish families from German occupied countries to prevent their deportation by the Germans (ftnt.78, from Jenő Lévai, *Black Book on the Martyrdom of the Hungarian Jewry* in Fenyo, *Hitler, Horthy, and Hungary,* 3).

62. Sakmyster, *Admiral on Horseback,* 292; Fenyo, *Hitler, Horthy, and Hungary,* 74.

63. Czettler, *A magyar külpolitika,* 169; Fenyo, *Hitler, Horthy, and Hungary,* 92; Sakmyster, *Admiral on Horseback,* 287.

64. Kállay, *Hungarian Premier,* 116–117; Sakmyster, *Admiral on Horseback,* 293; Fenyo, *Hitler, Horthy, and Hungary,* 72–74; L. Nagy, *Magyarság története,* 233.

65. Kállay, *Hungarian Premier,* 121–122; Czettler, *A magyar külpolitika,*164.

66. "Jagow Budapesti Követ Távirata Ribbentrop Külügyminiszternek, Budapest, 1943, April 10" [Telegram of Budapest ambassador Jagow to foreign minister Ribbentrop], *A Wilhelmstrasse és Magyarország: Német diplomáciai iratok Magyarországról 1933–1944* [Wilhelmstrasse and Hungary: German diplomatic documents on Hungary 1933–1944] (Budapest: Kossuth, 1968), 714.

67. Ibid.

68. *Die Tagebücher von Joseph Goebbels*, 124.

69. Horthy, *Memoirs*, 247–248.

70. Horthy, *Memoirs*, 248; Fenyo, *Hitler, Horthy, and Hungary*, 126–127; Sakmyster, *Admiral on Horseback*, 303–304.

71. Sakmyster, *Admiral on Horseback*, 288–290.

72. Horthy, *Memoirs*, 248.

73. Sakmyster, *Admiral on Horseback*, 306.

74. Ibid., 307.

75. Ibid., 307.

76. Ibid., 308.

77. Horthy, *Memoirs*, 249; Sakmyster, *Admiral on Horseback*, 309.

78. *Horthy Miklós Titkos iratai*, 391–396.

79. Quoted in Sakmyster, *Admiral on Horseback*, 311.

80. Ibid., 311.

81. "Veesenmayer Jelentése Magyarország Politikai Helyzetéről és Javaslatai Új Kormány Kinevezésére" [Veesenmayer report on the political situation in Hungary and suggestions on the appointment of a new government], *A Wilhelmstrasse és Magyarország*, 743–751.

82. Kállay had visited Italy in 1938 to study the Italian irrigation system. See Kállay, *Hungarian Premier*, 146.

83. Ibid., 155.

84. Kállay, *Hungarian Premier*, 146–161; Juhász, *Hungarian Foreign Policy*, 227.

85. Czettler, *A magyar külpolitika*, 251–255; Juhasz, *Hungarian Foreign Policy*, 227.

86. Czettler, *A magyar külpolitika*, 270. Kállay eventually found it necessary to ask Nagy to resign. He had compromised himself in some business dealings. The regent agreed reluctantly only after Mussolini joined in criticism of Nagy, but the new minister of defense, General Lajos Csatay, was also a Horthy loyalist.

87. They could not know that Mussolini would be reinstalled as a puppet by the Germans in the north of the country, dashing the hopes of those who had hoped the Western Allies would show up soon at Hungary's southern borders.

88. The day after the Italian capitulation the Independent Smallholders party published a declaration of its political principles and the Social Democrats began to convey details of their program.

89. Gyula Juhász, "Concepts in Hungarian Foreign Policy 1943," in *Kiútkeresés 1943* (Budapest: MTA Történettudományi Intézete, 1989), 22; Macartney, *October Fifteenth*, 2:169.

90. *Szárszó 1943: előzményei, jegyzőkönyve és utóélete: dokumentumok* [Szárszó 1943: Antecedents, proceedings and afterlife: documents] (Budapest: Kossuth, 1983), 219.

91. The Comintern had dissolved itself on May 13, 1943, and also dissolved the Hungarian Communist Party. In the newly formed Peace Party the Hungarian Communists could now operate legally.

92. Béla Kovács was to become prime minister in 1946.

93. *Szárszó 1943*, 188–209. Kovács stated later that it was at this time that he began to become estranged from Erdei, who in all their private discussions had never expressed his Marxist stand in such terms. See Tibor Huszár, *Beszélgetések* [Conversations] (Budapest: Magvető Könyvkiadó, 1983), 159.

94. *Szárszó 1943*, 225.

95. *Bibó István (1911–1979) Életút dokumentumomkban* [Career in documents] (Budapest: Osiris-Századvég, 1995), 51–52, 217.

96. *Szárszó 1943*, 214–225.

97. Zoltán K. Kovacs, speech delivered at the Rutgers Itt-Ott Society, November, 7, 1987; Leslie Laszlo, "Hungary: From Cooperation to Resistance 1919–1945," in *Catholics, the State, and the European Radical Right, 1919–1945* (Boulder, CO: Social Science Monographs, 1987), 119–136.

98. The armistice was announced on September 8, but Mussolini was rescued from prison in mid-September and pressured by Hitler to set up a successor Fascist state in the north of the country. The creation of Mussolini's state ensured that growing resistance to German occupation of the north would swell into civil war.

99. Szegedy-Maszák, *Az ember ősszel visszanéz*, 2:190.

100. Szegedy-Maszák, *Az ember ősszel visszanéz*, 2:197–198; Czettler, *A magyar külpolitika*, 325.

101. Szegedy-Maszák, *Az ember ősszel visszanéz*, 2:198–9; Macartney, *October Fifteenth*, 2:176; Juhász, *Hungarian Foreign Policy*, 257–258.

102. Juhász, *Hungarian Foreign Policy*, 264; Szegedi-Maszák, 199–200; Czettler, *A magyar külpolitika*, 327–329.

103. Quoted in Juhász, *Hungarian Foreign Policy*, 264.

104. Juhász, *Hungarian Foreign Policy*, 266.

105. Hess Archives. XIX-J-1-a. Béke előkészitő osztály iratai 1945–47. Box 10, Magyar ellenállási mozgalom dokumentumai [Documents of the Hungarian resistance movement].

106. Kállay: *Hungarian Premier*, 373–374; Szegedy-Maszák, *Az ember ősszel visszanéz*, 2:200–201.

107. Hess Archives. XIX-J-1-a. Béke előkészitő osztály iratai 1945–47, box 10, Magyar ellenállási mozgalom dokumentumai [Documents of the Hungarian resistance movement].

108. Szegedy-Maszák, *Az ember ősszel visszanéz*, 2:201.

109. Macartney, *October Fifteenth*, 2:186; Czettler, *A magyar külpolitika*, 332–333; Kállay, *Hungarian Premier*, 374.

110. Allied agents may have been eager for this to happen, calculating it would provoke resistance from democratic elements, hamper production, and tie down appreciable German forces, none of which was to happen after the German's occupied Hungary.

111. Hess Archives. XIX-J-1-a. Béke előkészitő osztály iratai 1945–47, box 10, doboz, Magyar ellenállási mozgalom dokumentumai.

112. Szombathelyi and the director of military intelligence, Colonel Gyula Kádár, both knew Hatz well; he often met military attachés from other governments, but above all they considered him a true patriot. See Gyula Kádár, *A Ludovikától*, 2:602.

113. The OSS members explained that they could not commit to any kind of political or other favor but that active cooperation with the Allies in military or political intelligence would mean that Hungary would be regarded favorably by the United States. See Charles Fenyvesi, *Three Conspiracies: Field Marshal Rundstedt, Admiral Canaris, and the Jewish Engineer who Could Have Saved Europe* (unpublished manuscript), chap. 6, 9, from OSS files in NARA RG 226, entry 214, box 6.

114. Kádár, *A Ludovikától*, 2:603.

115. Fenyvesi, *Three Conspiracies*, chap. 6, 11, from NARA RG 226, entry 210, box 447.

116. Kádár, *A Ludovikától*, 603–605.

117. Kádár's memoir was heavily censored and abridged by the Communist regime and the original copy is still not available, not even to Kádár's son.

118. According to an unwritten rule there were two counts of indictment where a central-European officer could deny telling the truth; in the case of intelligence work or of marital infidelity.

119. Fenyvesi, *Three Conspiracies*, chap. 7, 6 from NARA RG226, entry 210, box 81.

120. Ibid., chap. 7, 6–8 from NARA RG, entry 16, box 713. "Intelligence Reports." #59206.

121. OSS files in NARA RG 226 at U.S. National Archives.

122. Hatz's role is still debated by historians. Although he gave information to the Germans, it appears that he did not implicate Szombathelyi or Kállay, or his immediate superior Kádár, and reports delivered to Alan Dulles in Bern by the German Foreign Ministry official Fritz Kolbe show that Hatz was less than truthful with Wagner.

123. Horthy's grandson, István Horthy Jr., believed that it was Admiral Canaris, who initially encouraged Regent Horthy to seek the American contact in Istanbul (Fenyvesi, chap. 12, 17).

124. Czettler, *A magyar külpolitika*, 509.

125. Kádár, *A Ludovikától*, 2:605–606.

126. Despite the provision in the "Secret Intelligence Field Manual" of the Office of Strategic Services stating that "if agents get into trouble as a result of their SI

[secret Intelligence] activities they and their families should be given every aid possible within the bounds of security," the OSS failed to act when Szombathelyi was arrested by the Americans and delivered back to Hungary as a war criminal.

127. Lt. Col. Abram Gilmore Flues of the OSS, commander of the Budapest City Unit, recalled that as early as the summer of 1944 he and his OSS specialists were ready to take off from Italy on two-hour notice and "hit the ground running at a Hungarian airfield." As late as January 1945 on a visit to the OSS camp in Caserta, Italy, OSS head Donovan told the head of the OSS in Caserta, Colonel Howard Chapin, that "a small advance group of fifteen" of the Budapest City Unit should enter the Hungarian capital at the earliest possible opportunity, ..." Fenyvesi, *Three Conspiracies*, chap.6, 33 from NARA RG226, entry 210, box 386.

128. Kállay cited general requisitioning measures used by the Romanians that targeted the Hungarians in southern Transylvania; including objects only owned by Hungarians; pillows and eiderdowns. He did not deny the inexcusable things done on the Hungarian side, but justified the Hungarian government by claiming that it investigated every case brought before it and punished offenders. See Kállay, *Hungarian Premier*, 88.

129. The review was conducted by the department in charge of preparation for peace. Béke előkészitő osztály.

130. Hess Archives, Béke előkészitő osztály iratai. XIX-J-1-a-58.d.

131. Szegedy-Maszák, *Az ember ősszel visszanéz*, 2:205.

132. Czettler, *A magyar külpolitika*, 431; Hess Archives, Béke előkészitő osztály iratai. XIX-J-1-a-58.d.

133. *Szombathelyi Ferenc visszaemlékezései*, 29–30.

134. Czettler, *A magyar külpolitika*, 432; Szombathelyi, *Visszaemlékezései*, 28.

135. Czettler, *A Magyar külpolitika*, 432–433; Macartney, *October Fifteenth*, 2:201–202.

136. Szombathelyi, *Visszaemlékezései*, 32. When the Germans occupied Hungary the officers were rehabilitated and regained their positions as Hungarian generals.

137. "Werkmeister Budapesti Ügyvivő Távirata a Külügyminisztériumnak," [Telegram from Werkmeister, Budapest chargé d'affaires, to the foreign ministry] document 565, *A Wilhelmstrasse és Magyarország*, 761–762.

138. "Werkmeister Budapesti Ügyvivő Távirata a Külügyminisztériumnak," documents 566,567, *A Wilhelmstrasse és Magyarország*, 762–763.

139. There was even knowledge of the Katyn massacres in the officer corps and also in the medical community; one of the experts taken to the site was the Hungarian professor of pathology, Dr. Ferenc Orsós.

140. Barcza, *Diplomataemlékeim*, 2:126.

141. István Páva, *Ország a hadak útján: Magyarország és a második világháboru*, [Country on the march: Hungary and World War II] (Budapest: Pannonia, 1996), 229.

142. Fenyo, *Hitler, Horthy, and Hungary*, 99; Macartney, *October Fifteenth*, 2:222.

143. Szombathelyi, *Visszaemlékezései*, 22–23.

144. Fenyo, *Hitler, Horthy, and Hungary*, 155, Géza Lakatos, *Ahogy én láttam*, 74.

145. Major Jon S. Wendell, United States Air Force, "Strategic Deception Behind the Normandy Invasion," CSC 1997. http://www.globalsecurity.org/military/library/report/1997/Wendell.htm (accessed September 1, 2010); Gyula Juhász, "Some Aspects of Relations Between Hungary and Germany During the Second World War," in *Hungarian History/World History*, ed. Gy. Ránkí (Budapest: Akadémiai Kiadó, 1984), 217–218.

146. László Borhi, *Hungary in the Cold War 1945–1956*, 18.

147. Fenyo, *Hitler, Horthy, and Hungary*, 159.

148. Péter Bokor, "A nagy politikai naivitás: Nem számítottak Magyarország megszállására: Bokor interview with Pál Lieszkovszky, Gyula Kádár, and Wilhelm Höttle" [Political naivety: they didn't count on the occupation of Hungary], *Magyar Hírlap*, March 19, 1996. (Although Höttl, who worked for the U.S. Office of Strategic Services (OSS) became known as a notorious liar, his account of how the memo got to Hitler's bedside table is generally accepted by all branches of Hungarian historians, including the eminent historian Gyula Juhász.)

149. Ibid.

150. Péter Bokor, *Végjáték a Duna mentén: Ausztriai beszélgetés* [End game along the Danube: conversation in Austria (with Wilhelm Höttl)] Budapest: RTV-Minerva-Kossuth, 1982, 187.

151. Ibid., 187.

152. Juhász, "Some Aspects of Relations Between Hungary and Germany," 217; István Csicsery-Rónay, "Új tények az ország megszállásáról: 1944. március 19.—ahogy Macartney látta" [New facts on the occupation of the country: March 19, 1944—as Macartney saw it], *Magyar Nemzet*, March 21, 1995. 13.

153. Quoted in Macartney, *October Fifteenth*, 2:221.

154. Macartney, *October Fifteenth*, 2:221.

155. Páva, *Ország a hadak útján*, 236.

156. The mission consisted of commanding officer Colonel F. Duke , Major Alfred M. Suarez, and Captain Guy T. Nunn, who was fluent in French and German. See Florimond Duke, *Name, Rank, and Serial Number* (New York: Meredith Press, 1969), 11–17.

157. Kállay, *Hungarian Premier*, 413.

158. Péter Bokor, "A nagy politikai naivitás," Bokor interview with Pál Lieszkovszky, *Magyar Hírlap*, March 19, 1996.

159. Sakmyster, *Admiral on Horseback*, 325–6; Kállay, *Hungarian Premier*, 414–415.

160. A circumstantial account exists from Ambassador Paul Schmidt, the interpreter dismissed by Horthy. Horthy gave various accounts, first to his Crown Council on his return to Budapest as well as at the Nuremberg trials. He recounted their

conversation several times to the historian, C. A. Macartney, who attempted to reconstruct the interview. See Macartney, *October Fifteenth*, 2:234.

161. Personal statement to C. A. Macartney. Horthy was in Admiral's uniform—no revolver with this uniform. Macartney, *October Fifteenth*, 2:234–5

162. Sakmyster, *Admiral on Horseback*, 329–330.

163. Quoted in Sakmyster, *Admiral on Horseback*, 330.

164. Horthy *Memoirs*, 260.

165. Fenyo, *Hitler, Horthy, and Hungary*, 164–165; Horthy *Memoirs*, 260; Sakmyster, *Admiral on Horseback*, 332.

166. Horthy, *Memoirs*, 261; Sakmyster, *Admiral on Horseback*, 332–333.

167. Andrew C. Janos, *The Politics of Backwardness in Hungary: 1825–1945* (Princeton, N.J.: Princeton University Press, 1982), 306.

168. In the first three months of 1944 before the German occupation, English and American authors published included Willa Cather, Joseph Conrad, Charles Dickens, Aldous Huxley, Sinclair Lewis, Jack London, and Upton Sinclair. See Rezsö Szíj, "Magyar könyvművészet és könyvkiadás 1920–1940/1944 között" [Hungarian typographic art and book publishing between 1920–1940/1944] in *Erővonalak a két világháború közti magyar szellemi életben*, 228.

169. As late as March 1944 the Hungarian press offered a choice among conservative, liberal, socialist, monarchist, Catholic, fascist, and national socialist points of view.

170. Fenyo, *Hitler, Horthy, and Hungary*, 167–171; Sakmyster, *Admiral on Horseback*, 332–333.

8. German Occupation

1. Mrs. László Bakonyi, interview with the author, Budapest, November 6, 2001.

2. Two weeks before the occupation, at the national student meeting to determine how Hungary should leave the war, the final statement read that the country should leave the war honorably, and afterward carry out the long awaited social reforms (Sándor Kiss, *A magyar demokráciáért*, 33).

3. Kállay, Hungarian Premier, 419.

4. Ibid., 419–420.

5. Ibid., 420.

6. Ibid., 422.

7. Ibid., 425.

8. Tibor Petrusz, interview with the author, July 20, 2001.

9. Jenő Major, *Emléktöredékek: Visszaemlékezés az 1944. március és 1945. július közötti háborús eseményekre* [Fragments of a memoir: memoirs of the military events between March 1944 and July 1945] (Budapest: Hadtörténelmi levéltári kiadványok, n.d.), 12–13.

10. Von Weichs diary, quoted in Péter Gosztonyi,"The Hungarian Resistance Movement and Reaction in Mirror of German Writing," in *Magyarország 1944: fejezetek az ellenállás történetéből* [Hungary 1944: chapters from the history of the resistance], ed. M. Kiss Sándor (Budapest: Nemzeti Tankönyvkiadó, 1994), 10–11.

11. Ibid., 11.

12. Péter Bokor interview with Pál Lieszkovszky, *Magyar Hírlap*, March 19, 1996.

13. Kállay, *Hungarian Premier*, 428.

14. Kállay, *Hungarian Premier*, 431–432; Sakmyster, *Admiral on Horseback*, 335–336; Ilona Gyulai, *Becsület és Kötelesség*, 228–229.

15. Sakmyster, *Admiral on Horseback*, 337.

16. Kállay, *Hungarian Premier*, 433.

17. Ibid, 433.

18. Count István Bethlen, *Hungarian Politics during World War Two: Treatise and Indictment*, ed. Countess Ilona Bolza (München: Dr. Dr. Rudolf Trofenik, 1985), 2.

19. Macartney, *October Fifteenth*, 2:248.

20. Mrs. Endré Bajcsy-Zsilinszky [widow of Endré Bajcsy-Zsilinszky], "1944. Március 19-e egy budai lakásban" [March 19, 1944 in a Budapest apartment], *Kortársak Bajcsy-Zsilinszky Endréről*, Budapest: Magvető könyvkiadó, 1984, 413–415.

21. Zsuzsa L. Nagy, *Egy Politikus Polgár Portréja Rassay Károly (1886–1958)* [Portrait of a political citizen Károly Rassay (1886–1958)] Budapest: Napvilág kiadó, 2006, 169.

22. Ilona Gyulai, *Becsület és Kötelesség*, 234–235.

23. Fenyo, *Hitler, Horthy, and Hungary*, 175.

24. Sándor Szakály, ed., *Náray Antal visszaemlékezése 1945* [Antal Náray memoirs 1945] (Budapest: Zrínyi,1988), 97–100.

25. *Hungarian News Survey*, ed. Andrew Révai and Béla Iványi-Grünwald in London (for private circulation only) XIX-J-1-a.II-18–1945–47, box 11.

26. Ilona Gyulai, *Becsület és Kötelesség*, 235.

27. Von Weichs diary, quoted in Gosztonyi, "The Hungarian Resistance Movement," 11.

28. Keegan, *The Second World War*, 478–479.

29. Péter Bokor, interview with Lieszkovszky Pál, *Magyar Hírlap*. March 19, 1996.

30. Döme Sztójay, Prime Minister and also Minister of Foreign Affairs; Jenő Rátz, Deputy Prime Minister without Portfolio; Andor Jaross, Interior; Lajos Csatay, Defense; Reményi-Schneller, Finance; Béla Jurcsek, Supply and Agriculture; Lajos Szász, Industry; Antal Kunder, Commerce and Communications; István Antal, Education and Cults.

31. Quoted in Macartney, *October Fifteenth*, 2:252.

32. Later she saw groups of Jews walking on the road but didn't think much about it, since as students they had to go out to dig trenches. The Yellow Star didn't seem so bad. At first she didn't believe in the Holocaust; thought it was communist propaganda (Dr. Judit Stúr, interview with the author, June 12, 2003).

33. Sakmyster, *Admiral on Horseback*, 339.

34. Sakmyster, *Admiral on Horseback*, 341–342; Fenyo, *Hitler, Horthy, and Hungary*, 180.

35. Considering the circumstances when the peace treaty was signed in early 1947 at the time of the start of the Cold War, it is questionable whether Hungary could have gained any better terms.

36. Ungváry, *The Hungarian Army in World War II*, 230.

37. Gosztonyi, "The Hungarian Resistance Movement," 14, Ungváry, *Hungarian Army*, 232.

38. Sándor Szakály, "Hungarian-German Military Cooperation during World War II" in *20th Century Hungary and the Great Powers*, ed. Ignáz Romsics (New York: Columbia University, 1995), 152.

39. L. Nagy, *Magyarország története*, 240–242.

40. Ibid., 242.

41. The first year enrollment in economics had grown from an average of 300 to 1,311 in 1943/44. Since medical students were especially likely to escape the draft a number of students changed to study medicine. See Pál Petőcz, "Az egyetemi és főiskolai hallgatók második világháborús történetéhez" [On the history of university students and students in higher education during World War II], *Századok*, no. 2 (1986): 303–304.

42. In the fall of 1944 of the 1,836 regular students in law only 253 were soldiers, 13.8 percent. These were almost without exception those who enrolled when older, including some aged 30 (Petőcz, 307).

43. Ibid., 308.

44. Dombrády, *A Magyar gazdaság*, 187.

45. Memorandum by Clodius, June 21, 1943, NA Microcopy T—120, roll 2564, 313284, quoted in Fenyo, *Hitler, Horthy, and Hungary*, 98.

46. Ungváry, *Hungarian Army*, 242.

47. Dombrády, *A magyar gazdaság*, 187–188; Sándor Szakály, "Hungarian-German Military Cooperation," 150.

48. Pál Tóth, interview with the author, August 2, 2002.

49. By the fall of 1944 the discontent had increased so that it convinced the Germans to attempt to dismantle Hungarian industrial equipment and send it to Germany, but they succeeded only partially because of the worker resistance. Despite the terror under the Arrow Cross regime, Hungarian workers saved some of the industrial equipment from the Germans and their Arrow Cross followers. See Dombrády, *A magyar gazdaság*, 291–292.

50. Gyurgyak, *A zsidókérdés magyarországon*, 173; Tamás Stark, *Zsidóság a vészkorszakban*, 20.

51. Gábor Kádár and Zoltán Vági, "The Economic Annihilation of the Hungarian Jews, 1944–1945," in *The Holocaust in Hungary: Sixty Years Later*, eds. Randolf L.

Braham and Brewster S. Chamberlin (New York: Columbia University Press, 2006), 79–80.

52. For the first time in 1849 Buda and Pest were joined by the Szécheny lánchid [Széchenyi Chain Bridge] across the Danube, the first permanent bridge to connect the western and eastern sides of Budapest. In 1873 Budapest became a single city occupying both banks of the Danube, with unification of the right (west) bank, Buda and Óbuda, with the left (east) bank Pest.

53. J. Molnár, "The Foundation and Activities of the Hungarian Jewish Council, March 20–July 7, 1944." Shoah Resource Center. The International School for Holocaust Studies, Yad Vashem Studies, XXX, Jerusalem 2002, 2–3. http://www1.yadvashem.org/odot_pdf/Microsoft%20Word%20-%205417.pdf (accessed August 12, 2010).

54. Samu Stern memoirs, in Maria Schmidt, *Kollaboráció vagy kooperáció? A Budapesti Zsidó Tanács* [Collaboration or cooperation? The Budapest Jewish Council] (Budapest: Minerva, 1990), 57–59.

55. The council was to be faced with the most outrageous demands. Late one afternoon an SS officer barged into their office to demand that 300 mattresses and 600 blankets be delivered to the Royal Hotel in one and a half hours. When told that his request was completely impossible he shouted that in ten minutes it was possible to kill 10,000 Jews; therefore it would be possible to meet his demand in an hour and a half. "So we went to the hospitals, where the doctors and nurses pulled out the mattresses from under the patients and took their blankets." See Stern, 64.

56. J. Molnár, "The Hungarian Jewish Council," 6–7.

57. The provincial Jewish councils functioned for a few weeks or at most a couple of months (Ibid., 19).

58. Ibid., 6–7, 14–15.

59. Gyurgyák, *A zsidókérdés*, 173–174; Fenyo, *Hitler, Horthy, and Hungary*, 182–183.

60. Támas Gábor, interview with the author, Santa Fe, October 31, 2001.

61. Chorin was one of the most significant personages of Hungarian capitalism in the interwar period.

62. "Chorin Ferenc Levele Horthy Miklóshoz a Weiss Manfréd-konszernnek Az SS-sel Kötött Szerződéséről" [Ferenc Chorin letter to Miklós Horthy on the Weiss Manfréd-concern and contract made with the SS] in *Horthy Miklós titkos iratai,* [Miklós Horthy secret papers] 1944. May 17, 441–442.

63. Ibid., 442–443.

64. Tim Cole, "Building and Breaching the Ghetto Boundary: A Brief History of the Ghetto Fence in Körmend, Hungary 1944" *Holocaust and Genocide Studies* 23, no. 1 (Spring 2009): 54–56.

65. Stark, *Zsidóság a vészkorszakban*, 20; Fenyo, *Hitler, Horthy, and Hungary*, 183; Macartney, *October Fifteenth*, 2:281.

66. David S. Wyman, *The Abandonment of the Jews: America and the Holocaust, 1941–1945* (New York: The New Press, 2007), 236.

67. Sakmyster, *Admiral on Horseback*, 343–344.

68. See Macartney, *October Fifteenth*, 2:279–282.

69. Fenyo, *Hitler, Horthy, and Hungary*, 186–187; Macartney, *October Fifteenth*, 2:281.

70. Gyurgyak, *A zsidókérdés*, 180–181; Stark, *Zsidóság a vészkorszakban*, 21; Macartney, *October Fifteenth*, 2:286.

71. Fenyo, *Hitler, Horthy, and Hungary*, 184; Macartney, *October Fifteenth*, 2:275–276.

72. The local Jewish council in Szeged told Jews "to immediately move into the designated apartments." The local Jewish council of Kecskemét stermly reminded the Jewish population that "neither sickness nor the Sabbath could be used as an excuse for failing to move into the ghetto." See Molnár, *Hungarian Jewish Council*, 21, 26.

73. Samu Stern memoirs, in Maria Schmidt, *Kollaboráció vagy kooperáció?*, 60–62.

74. Molnár, *Hungarian Jewish Council*, 10–11.

75. Yehuda Bauer, *American Jewry and the Holocaust: the Amerian Jewish Joint Distribution Committee, 1939–1945* (Detroit: Wayne State University Press, 1981), 388–389.

76. Quoted in Molnár, *Hungarian Jewish Council*, 11.

77. Recollectons on the Holocaust—The world's most extensive testimonial site. http://www.degob.hu/english/index.php?showarticle = 2021 (accessed January 25, 2010).

78. Asher Cohen, *The Halutz Resistance in Hungary 1942–1944* (Social Science Monographs, Columbia University Press, 1986), 78; Randolph L. Braham, "Rescue Operations in Hungary: Myths and Realities," *East European Quarterly*, XXXVIII, no. 2 (June 2004): 179–180.

79. In the last week of the ghetto's existence over one-sixth of the female population were leaving early each morning to do gardening, agricultural work, and leaf collecting. See Cole, "Breaching the Ghetto Boundary," 64.

80. Endre Berecz, "Emlékezés a csornai zsidóság történetére." [Memoir of the Csorna Jews history] http:///www.hontar.hu/hely/berecz.htm, 11; Personal communication with Nandor Dreisziger, son of Kálmán, December 4, 2006.

81. Cole, "Breaching the Ghetto Boundary," 62.

82. Stern memoirs, 66–67.

83. Leslie Laszlo, *Church and State in Hungary 1919–1945*, published dissertation (Columbia University, Faculty of Political Science, 1973), 381.

84. Jenő Gergely, "A magyarországi egyházak és a Holocaust" [Hungarian churches and the holocaust], in Braham and Pók, *The Holocaust in Hungary 50 years later* (New York: Columbia University Press, 1997), 446–47; Laszlo, *Church and State*, 382–383.

85. Gyurgyak, *A zsidókérdés*, 180; Stern memoirs, 70; Sakmyster, *Admiral on Horseback*, 344–345.

86. Laszlo, *Church and State*, 383–384; Sakmyster, *Admiral on Horseback*, 344–346. (The official position was the same. When Dr. Ernő Pető of the Jewish Council went to the Minister of Finance to protest, Reményi-Schneller told him that he had investigated and there were no deportations. See Stern, 70–71.)

87. Perhaps Serédi's caution can be partly explained by his background. In 1927 he was chosen by the Papal seat to succeed the former Archbishop, partially as a reward for the years he had spent codifying the Corpus Juri Canonici. Serédi came from a simple background; his father had been an agrarian worker and he had never aimed for such a high post, but he was trusted implicitly by the Vatican who knew he would hold true to strict dogma and follow the will of the church faithfully. See György Barcza, *Diplomataemlékeim*, 1:217–226; Jenő Gergely, *A Katolikus egyház története Magyarországon*, 61–62.

88. Both Sztójay and Imrédy spoke up in the Council of Ministers against the cruelties. See Laszlo, *Church and State*, 384–386.

89. Paul A. Hanebrink, *In Defense of Christian Hungary: Religion, Nationalism, and Antisemitism, 1890–1944* (Ithaca, N.Y.: Cornell University Press, 2006), 203.

90. His letter was officially addressed to the bishops, but he asked them to convey the message to members of the church of Jewish descent, to inform them by word of mouth of his interest in their protection. See Laszlo, *Church and State*, 389–390.

91. Sakmyster, *Admiral on Horseback*, 347–349; Fenyo, *Hitler, Horthy, and Hungary*, 187–188.

92. *Horthy Miklos titkos iratai*, 450–453.

93. The Nazis had changed previous procedures by building a new railway ramp which provided direct access to the gas chambers and crematoria, allowing for increasingly rapid and efficient mass murder of the hundreds of thousands of victims scheduled to be transported from Hungary. See Rudolf Vrba, "The preparations for the Holocaust in Hungary: an eyewitness account," in *The Nazis' Last Victims. The Holocaust in Hungary*, ed. Braham (Detroit: Wayne State University Press, 1999), 55–57.

94. Recollections on the Holocaust, 11–12; Tsvi Erez, "Hungary Six Days in July 1944." *Holocaust and Genocide Studies* 3, no. 1 (1988): 50.

95. Quoted in Recollections on the Holocaust.

96. Vrba, "The preparations for the Holocaust in Hungary," 56.

97. Stern memoirs, 82.

98. "Bethlen István gróf emlékirata a Sztójay-Kormány leváltásának szükségességéről és a Végrehajtás" [Count István Bethlen's memorandom on the necessity of the replacement of the Sztójay government and its fulfillment] in *Horthy Miklós titkos iratai*, 457–466.

99. Cohen, *The Halutz Resistance*, 131; Sakmyster, *Admiral on Horseback*, 358–359.

100. Cohen, *The Halutz Resistance*, 131; Sakmyster, *Admiral on Horseback*, 351.

101. Sakmyster, *Admiral on Horseback,* 352.

102. Gergely, "A magyarországi egyházak," 448–449; Hanebrink, *In Defense of Christian Hungary,* 208.

103. Hanebrink, *In Defense of Christian Hungary,* 209.

104. Gergely, "A magyarországi egyházak," 448–449; Hanebrink, *In Defense of Christian Hungary,* 209.

105. Cited in Laszlo, *Church and State,* 392.

106. Gergely, "A magyarországi egyházak," 449–450; Hanebrink, *In Defense of Christian Hungary,* 209.

107. Laszlo, *Church and State,* 404.

108. According to Randolph L. Braham, already at the time of his meeting with Hitler at Klessheim in March 1944, Horthy—as well as the top governmental and political leaders of Hungary—was well informed about the realities of Auschwitz. Later, he asserts, "The evidence is overwhelming that Horthy, like the other top leaders of Hungary, was fully informed about the barbaric treatment of the Jews, including their isolation, marking, expropriation, ghettoization, concentration, and deportation. See "Rescue Operations in Hungary: Myths and Realities," *East European Quarterly* XXXVIII, no. 2 (June 2004): 178–180.

109. Thomas Sakmyster gives the date as June 19 or 20; his source is Tsvi Erez, "Hungary. Six Days in July, 1944," (Kibbutz Dvir, Israel) published in 1988.

110. Ilona Gyulai, *Becsület és Kötelesség,* 263.

111. Ibid., 264.

112. For Hungarian historians the main debate regarding the Holocaust is still the question of who was responsible and to what extent—the Germans or the Hungarian government, Horthy, Hungarian society? Personal communication to the author from historian Tamás Stark, November 25, 2009.

113. M. K. Dziewanowski, *War at Any Price: World War II in Europe, 1939–1945* (Upper Saddle River, N.J.: Prentice Hall, 1991), 309.

114. Péter Bokor, "Az elvetélt csendőrpuccs ismeretlen története" [The unknown history of the aborted gendarme putsch], *Magyar Hírlap,* July 5, 1993. The excuse for their being in Budapest was the gendarme training school in Buda, thus circumventing the legal issue.

115. Sakmyster, *Admiral on Horseback,* 352.

116. Ferenc Koszorús, volt M.Kir.Vk.Ezredes—Az 1. Pándélos hadosztály parancsnokának. *Emlékiratai és tanulmányainak gyűteménye* [Ferenc Koszorús, former Hungarian Royal Staff Colonel, commander of the First Armored Division. Memoirs and collected papers], ed. Mrs. István Varsa. (Universe Publishing Company, 1987), 56–58.

117. Quoted in Bokor, "Az elvetélt csendőrpuccs," 9.

118. Bokor, "Az elvetélt csendőrpuccs," 9; Sakmyster, *Admiral on Horseback,* 352–353.

119. Quoted in Sakmyster, *Admiral on Horseback,* 354. According to Randolph L. Braham one can only give Horthy credit for saving most of the Budapest Jews if one

assigns him a significant share of blame for the deportations. See Braham, "Rescue Operations in Hungary," 179.

120. Stern Memoir, 86.

121. István Deák, "A Fatal Compromise? The Debate over Collaboration and Resistance in Hungary," in *The Politics of Retribution in Europe: World War II and Its Afternath*, ed. István Deák, Jan T. Gross, and Tony Judt (Princeton, N.J.: Princeton University Press, 2000), 72, n. 22.

122. Tamás Stark, personal communication to the author, February 5, 2010. Stark deals with the subject in his book, *Zsidóság a vészkorszakban és a felszabadulás után 1939–1955*, as well as in the English version, *Hungarian Jews During the Holocaust and After the Second World War, 1939–1949: A Statistical Review* (Boulder, Colo.: East-European Monographs, 2000).

123. Barcza, *Diplomataemlékeim*, 1:208.

124. In April of 1944 he had wanted to appoint Lakatos chief of staff, but had been pressured by Veesenmayer to appoint Lt. Gen. János Vörös, a careerist, who was appointed over many older and higher ranked officers. Since there was no position open for someone with Lakatos's rank and experience he retired to his wife's estate to wait for the regent's command.

125. When asked why the regent had chosen him, Lakatos supposed that it was partially because of his pure Hungarian origins, but also that during his one year command on the battle field he had gone against the German command, once ordering the weakly armed Seventh Army Corps out of the zone where the Germans wanted to place them against Russian regular troops. See Lakatos testimony at trial of Szálasi, 1946, February 19, in Lakatos, *Ahogyan én láttam*, 361.

126. Quoted in Fenyo, *Hitler, Horthy, and Hungary*, 209.

127. Ibid., 210.

128. Ibid., 210.

129. Macartney, *October Fifteenth*, 2:309.

130. Wyman, *The Ambandonment of the Jews*, 238–240.

131. L. Nagy, *Magyarország Története*, 245; Ungváry, *Battle for Budapest*, 3.

132. Péter Gosztonyi, *Vihar Kelet-Európ Felett* [Storm over Eastern-Europe] (Budapest: Népszava, 1990), 182–190.

133. Keegan, *The Second World War*, 480–481, 503–505.

134. Ministers in the new government: Foreign Minister: Gusztáv Hennyey; Minister of the Interior: Miklós Bonczos; Minister of Defense: Lajos Csatay (minister under Kállay, anti-Nazi); Minister of Justice: Gábor Vladár; Minister of Commerce: Olivér Markos; Minister of Industry: Tibor Gyulay; Religion and Education: Iván Rakovszky; Minister of Finance: Lajos Reményi-Schneller; Agriculture and Public Welfare: Béla Jurcsek.

135. Pál Tóth, personal communication with the author, April 26, 2001.

136. Juhász, *Hungarian Foreign Policy*, 304–305.

137. Lakatos, *Ahogyan én láttam*, 133; Fenyo, *Hitler, Horthy, and Hungary*, 218.

138. Lakatos, *Ahogyan én láttam*, 132–133.

139. Péter Bokor, *Végjáték a Duna mentén: Interjúk egy filmsorozathoz* [End game on the banks of the Danube: interviews for a film series] (Budapest: RTV-Minerva-Kossuth, 1982), 214.

140. Bokor, *Végjáték a Duna mentén*, 216–210; Lakatos, *Ahogyan én* láttam, 364; Sakmyster, *Admiral on* Horseback, 138.

141. Postscript by Sándor Szakály in Lakatos, *Ahogyan én láttam*, 333.

142. Lakatos, *Ahogyan én láttam*, 138; Sakmyster, *Admiral on Horseback*, 365.

143. Quoted in Ilona Gyulai, *Becsület és Kötelesség*, 284.

144. Lakatos, *Ahogyan én láttam*, 139.

145. Ilona Gyulai, *Becsület és Kötelesség*, 284; Sakmyster, *Admiral on Horseback*, 365–366.

146. Separated from Howie he was kept incommunicado while Wilson contacted London, Moscow, and Washington. Howie vouched for Náday but the officers felt the request for a cease-fire was too vague and had come too late; they had expected it with the Italian surrender or latest March 19th with the German occupation. See Hess Archives XIX—J—1—a, Béke előkészitő osztály iratai 1945–47 586/2002 10.d. 41.187/be; Macartney, C. A., *October Fifteenth*, 2:351–352).

147. Quoted in Sakmyster, *Admiral on Horseback*, 150.

148. Bokor, "interview with Ladomér Zichy," *Végjáték a Duna mentén*, 221

149. Ibid., 222–225.

150. Ibid., 225–226.

151. Gyula Rézler, interview with the author, Budapest, May 22, 2001; Ilona Gyulai, *Becsület és Kötelesség*, 282; Sakmyster, *Admiral on Horseback*, 366–367.

152. Juhász, *Hungarian Foreign Policy*, 307.

153. Bokor, *Végjáték a Duna mentén*, 221–234.

154. Julia Zichy, telephone interview with the author, November 9, 2009. [No direct relation of Count Zichy.]

155. Quoted in Juhász, *Hungarian Foreign Policy*, 314–315.

156. Ilona Gyulai, *Becsület és Kötelesség*, 295.

157. Juhász, *Hungarian Foreign Policy*, 315–316.

158. Macartney, *October Fifteenth* 2:352, Ilona Gyulai, *Becsület és Kötelesség*, 295.

159. Juhász, *Hungarian Foreign Policy*, 317; Ilona Gyulai, *Becsület és Kötelesség*, 296.

160. Quoted in Juhász, *Hungarian Foreign Policy*, 318.

161. Ibid., 318–319.

162. Sándor Szakály, "Nyilas-hungarista hatalomátvétel Magyarországon 1944. október 15–16" [Arrow-Cross *hungarista* takeover in Hungary October 15–16, 1944], *Napi Magyarország*, October 15, 1991.

163. Loránt Tilkovszky, *Nemzetiségi politika Magyarországon a 20. Században* [Nationalities policy in 20th century Hungary] (Budapest: Csokonai Kiadó, 1998), 110; Gosztonyi, "The Hungarian Resistance Movement," 22.

164. Macartney, *October Fifteenth*, 2:313–314.

165. L. Nagy, *Magyarország Története*, 245.

166. Macartney, *October Fifteenth*, 2:314.

167. Other representatives included Gyula Kálai and László Rajk, newly out of prison, for the renamed Communist Party, Gyula Dessewffy and Zoltán Pfeiffer, soon to be joined by Tildy, for the Independent Smallholders, Pongrác Kenessey and József Pálffy for the church group, and Imre Kovács for the National Peasant Party.

168. Loránd Tilkovszky, "The Late Interwar Years and World War II," in *A History of Hungary*, ed. Peter F. Sugar (Bloomington: Indiana University Press, 1990), 352.

169. Mihály Hőgye, *Utolsó csatlós? Magyarország sorsa a második világháború végén* [The last satellite? Hungary's fate at the end of World War II] (Budapest: Püski, 1989), 56.

170. Ibid., 56.

171. Sakmyster *Admiral on Horseback*, 371–372; Ilona Gyulai, *Becsület és Kötelesség*, 300.

172. Sándor Szakály, "Nyilas-hungarista hatalomátvétel."

173. Ibid.

174. Juhász, *Hungarian Foreign Policy*, 321; Ilona Gyulai, *Becsület és Kötelesség*, 302.

175. Juhász, *Hungarian Foreign* Policy, 322. Historian Mária Ormos points out that although Horthy has been criticized for believing the army would blindly follow him, his practical steps do not support the criticism. He had wanted the untrustworthy officers to be removed from decision making, and he conferred only with his most trustworthy officers. One can assume that he did believe the commands given by the trustworthy leaders would be obeyed by most of the army, and that this supposition was not unrealistic. See Ormos, *Magyarország*, 258.

176. Ilona Gyulai, *Becsület és Kötelesség*, 308–310; Sakmyster, *Admiral on Horseback*, 373.

177. Ilona Gyulai, *Becsület és Kötelesség*, 310–311; Szakály, "Nyilas-hungarista hatalomátvétel"; Fenyo, *Hitler, Horthy, and Hungary*, 230–231.

178. Sakmyster, *Admiral on Horseback*, 374.

179. Ilona Gyulai, *Becsület és Kötelesség*, 312.

180. Ibid.

181. Juhász, Hungarian Foreign Policy, 324.

182. Sakmyster *Admiral on Horseback*, 375–376.

183. Szakály, "Nyilas-hungarista hatalomátvétel."

184. Sakmyster, *Admiral on Horseback*, 376; Fenyo, *Hitler, Horthy, and Hungary*, 233–234.

185. Sakmyster, *Admiral on Horseback,* 376; Fenyo, *Hitler, Horthy, and Hungary,* 235.

186. László Lengyel Kenyeres, *Ezt láttam Budapesten: egy szemtanú feljegyzései a Magyar főváros pusztulásáról* [I saw it in Budapest: an eyewitness account of the destruction of the Hungarian capital] (Budapest: A Március könyvkiadó kiadása, 1945), 5–12.

187. Sakmyster, *Admiral on Horseback,* 376–377.

188. Ibid., 378.

189. Horthy, *Memoirs,* 291.

190. Macartney, *October Fifteenth,* 2:379–380.

191. Horthy, *Memoirs* 295. Veesenmayer was sentenced to twenty years in prison for war crimes, but in 1951 he was released by the United States High Commissioner in Germany.

9. From Arrow Cross Rule to Soviet Occupation

1. N. F. Dreisziger, "Hungary in 1945," in *Hungarian Studies Review* XXII, no. 1 (Spring 1995): 5.

2. Horthy had been vehemently against naming Szálasi and had dismissed him twice, saying that he would never name him prime minister. After a day of threats to the security of his son and family, however, he finally gave his assent on the October 16.

3. Ungváry, *Battle for Budapest,* 3; Macartney, *October Fifteenth,* 2:444.

4. Macartney, *October Fifteenth,* 2:447–448; L. Nagy, *Magyarország története,* 250; Agnes Rozsnyoi, "Nyilasok—amig a húr elpattant" [Arrow Cross—until the string snaps], *Magyar Hírlap,* October 13, 1984.

5. Major Jenő, *Emléktöredékek,* 8.

6. Macartney, *October Fifteenth,* 2:162.

7. Imrédy had made an attempt to reorganize the state on a corporatist basis (see chapter 3, 29), and Teleki had made plans to introduce a state based on the corporatist model (see chaper 4, 12).

8. Rozsnyoi, "Nyilasok—amig a húr elpattant."

9. Loránd Tilkovszky, "The Late Interwar Years and World War II," in *A History of Hungary,* ed. Peter F. Sugar (Bloomington: Indiana University Press, 1990), 353.

10. In the initial period the disciplined policemen guarded the Jewish houses marked with the star of David which provided genuine refuge for the inhabitants. See László Karsai, "The Last Phase of the Hungarian Holocaust," in *The Nazis' Last Victims. The Holocaust in Hungary,* eds. Randolph L. Braham and Scott Miller (Detroit: Wayne State University Press, 1999), 104–106.

11. L. Nagy, *Magyarország története,* 250; Krisztián Ungváry, "Kik azok a nyilasok?" *Beszélő* (June 2003): 50.

12. Lilly Vigyazo, interview with the author, June 26, 2003.

13. Macartney, *October Fifteenth*, 2:449.

14. The number included even some of those who were supposed to enjoy total or partial exemption, those in mixed marriages and converts to Christianity.

15. Sándor Szakály, "A hadsereg és a zsidótörvények az ellenforradalmi Magyarországon" [The army and the Jewish laws in counter-revolutionary Hungary], *Valóság* no. 9 (1985): 62.

16. Tamás Stark, *Magyarország második világháborús embervesztesége* [Human losses in Hungary during World War II] (Budapest: MTA Történettudományi Intézet áő, 1989), 38–39.

17. Stark, *Magyarország*, 40; Karsai, 108–110.

18. Stark, *Magyarország*, 40.

19. Stark, *Magyarország*, 40; Ungváry, *Battle for Budapest*, 237.

20. The building of the southeast wall continued until March 1945, but in the face of the advancing Red Army the Hungarian Jewish workers were removed to German concentration camps. See Stark, *Magyarország*, 40–41.

21. Ibid., 41.

22. Ibid., 42.

23. *Óbuda ostroma 1944–1945* [The siege of Óbuda 1944–1945], Collective work written by Óbuda inhabitants (Budapest: Óbudai múzeum, 2005), 71.

24. Ibid.

25. Alice Somlai Pók, interview with the author, June 22, 2008.

26. As Papal Nuncio in Budapest from 1944–45, and Dean of the Diplomatic Corps, he contributed to the actions of the Neutral Powers and the International Red Cross Committee in Budapest.

27. Ungváry, *Battle for Budapest*, 243.

28. On January 17, 1945, Wallenberg left Budapest for the Soviet occupation headquarters in Debrecen. He was never heard from again. Taken to the Soviet Union, he died under circumstances that still have not been clarified. An official Soviet statement reported in 1957 that he had died of a heart attack in Russian prison in 1947. Why the Soviets seized him is unclear. It is possible that they considered him an American spy; they had found documents concerning the Katyn forest massacre in his safe. See Sándor M. Kiss, "A lét terei" [The margin of existence], *Magyar Szemle* XVII (April 2008): 46.

29. Lilly Vigyazo, interview with the author, June 26, 2003.

30. In 1942–1943 Slachta had taken action against the deportation of the Slovak Jews and was able to arrange an audience with the Pope on their behalf.

31. Gergely, "A magyarországi egyházak és a Holocaust," 452–453.

32. Ibid., 451–453.

33. Géza Komoróczy, ed., *A zsidó Budapest:Emlékek, szertartások, történelem* [Jewish Budapest: memoirs, observances, history] (Budapest: MTA Judaisztikai Kutatócsoport, 1995), 544–546.

34. "For Remembrance." Bill Glovin interview with Gabor Vermes. *Rutgers Magazine.* (Fall 1997): 18.

35. Gabor Tamás, interview with the author, December 15, 2001.

36. In practice the Red Army did avoid head-on attacks against major cities, and they attached little military importance to the uprising. But, perhaps more importantly they had little reason to attempt to save the tens of thousands of Polish resistance fighters of the Home Army who were loyal to the government in exile in London and hostile to the Soviet Union. See Evan Mawdsley, *Thunder in the East: the Nazi-Soviet War 1941–1945* (London: Hodder Education, 2007), 324, 331–332.

37. Mawdsley, *Thunder in the East,* 349.

38. Dr. György Molnár in personal communication with the author, June 2008; *Magyarország történeti kronológiája III. 1848–1944,* 997.

39. Macartney, *October Fifteenth,* 2:445, 454; Ungváry, *Battle for Budapest,* 2–3.

40. Quoted in Ungváry, *Battle for Budapest,* 4.

41. Macartney, *October Fifteenth,* 2:453.

42. Zoltán Vőlgyesi, "A történelmi elit felbomlása 1944–45 után—a hajdúvárosok példáján" [The dissolution of the historical elite after 1944–1945—the example of the Hajdú cities], in *Tiltott történelmünk 1945–1947,* ed. János Horváth (Budapest: Századvég Kiadó, 2006), 100–104.

43. Ibid., 104.

44. Under the Horthy regime the title of *vitéz* [valor] was awarded to certain ex-servicemen for their service during World War I.

45. Völgyesi, "A történeme elit felbomlása," 104–105.

46. Ungváry, "The Second Stalingrad," 151–152.

47. Szálasi took the royal crown to Austria, as well as the embalmed right hand of Hungary's first king, István, considered a sacred relic.

48. Petőcz, "Az egyetemi és főiskolai hallgatók," 342.

49. Later he was arrested by the Arrow Cross and taken to military prison on the Margit boulevard. See Petőcz, "Az egyetemi és főiskolai hallgatók,", 339.

50. He recalled hearing the bombing during the destruction of Dresden. Béla Zamory, Interview with the author, October 20, 2001.

51. Macartney, *October Fifteenth,* 2:462–463.

52. N. F. Dreisziger, "Hungary in 1945," 5–6; Macartney, *October Fifteenth,* 2:452–453.

53. L. Nagy, Magyarország története, 251.

54. Dr. József Hasznos diary, "Teljes gőzzel" [With full gas], 1:158, 160.

55. Dr. József Hasznos, interview with the author, June 14, 2007; Dr. József Hasznos diary, "Teljes gőzzel," 158–160.

56. Szakály, "A katonai ellenállási mozgalom," 138–156.

57. József Gazsi, "A Felszabadító Bizottság," in *Magyarország 1944: Fejezetek az ellenállás történetéből,* ed. Sándor M. Kiss. (Budapest: Nemzeti Tankönyvkiadó, 1994), 182–183.

58. The Liberation Committee often met in the flat and office of Miklós Makay, a free democrat and anti-Nazi who gave explosive materials to the resistance group.

59. Those present were Gyula Kállai (Communist Party), Imre Kovács (National Peasant party), Géza Soós (Hungarian Independence Movement), Tibor Hám (youth groups), József Dudás (MHSZSZ), Géza Pénzes (SZUBME). The Social Democratic representative was absent for technical reasons.

60. At first the members of the Liberation Committee met every day but then less often. Bajczy-Zsilinszky, because he was so easily recognized, attended the meetings only a few times and Csorba acted in his stead.

61. In 1944 he had worked out plans for the Hungarian military in case of a German occupation.

62. Several officers were already known for their anti-German attitudes. Pál Almásy, officer to the Berlin Hungarian military attache from 1937–1939, had been recalled at German request because of his defense of the Poles. Some had been affected by the Jewish laws of 1938–39. See Ungváry, *Battle for Budapest*, 252–253.

63. Szakály, "A katonai ellenállási mozgalom," 147; Ungváry. *Battle for Budapest*, 253.

64. Imre Kovács, *Magyarország megszállása* (Toronto: Katalizátor, 1990), 67–70.

65. Gazsi, "A Felszabadító Bizottság," 188.

66. Török was a student at the Budapest Technical University and was training a small group planning for armed resistance. The group later became the Technicians Democratic Front, members of the youth resistance central organization, the Hungarian Youth Freedom Front, MDSZF (Gazsi, "A Felszabadító Bizottság" [The Liberation Committee], 192; Ungváry. *Battle for Budapest*, 254).

67. Gazsi, "A Felszabadító Bizottság,"192–194. The Arrow Cross issued warrants for the stolen airplane, and after that the airports were secured more heavily, leading to the arrest of other pilots who might have been recruited for a similar mission.

68. Ibid., 187.

69. Ibid., 200.

70. *A Szálasi Per* [The Szálasi Trial], ed. Péter Lajos Kovács (Budapest: Reform könyvkiadő, 1988), 429.

71. Kóvacs, *Magyarország Megszállása*, 112.

72. In their bitter days in prison they were obsessed with the question of who had betrayed them. The puzzle was only solved in 1946 when Norbert Orendy and Endre Radó at their trial before the People's Court revealed that Captain Tibor Mikulich had betrayed them.

73. Sakmyster, *Admiral on Horseback*, 149, 254; Ungváry, *Battle for Budapest*, 254.

74. Zoltán Nyeste, "Útkeresés—Adalékok a Magyar Ifjúsági Mozgalmak Történetéhez: 1942–1948" [Search for solutions—contributions to the history of the Hungary youth movements: 1942–1948] (unpublished manuscript: received July 1987) 18–19; Ungváry, *Battle for Budapest*, 257.

75. Nyeste, "Útkeresés," 14–17.

76. Ibid., 21.

77. Sándor M. Kiss, *A magyar demokráciáért*, 40.

78. Sándor M. Kiss and Ivan Vitányi, *A Magyar Diák Szabadságfrontja* [The Hungarian Student Independence Front] (Budapest: Az antifasiszta ifjúsági emlékmű szervezőbizottsága, 1983) [The organizing committee of the antifascist youth memorial], 118.

79. Jónás Pállal beszélget Kende Péter [Péter Kende speaks with Pál Jónás], *Vasárnapi Újság: Válogatás a Népszerű Rádióműsor Adásaiból* [Sunday newspaper: selections from the broadcasts of the popular radio program], Budapest: Új Idő Kft, 1989,

80. M. Kiss, *A magyar demokráciáért*, 35–37.

81. M. Kiss, Vitányi, *A Magyar Diák Szabadságfrontja*, 118.

82. Ungváry, Battle for Budapest, 254.

83. Ibid., 255.

84. Ungváry, *Battle for Budapest*, 255–256; Borbándi, *Magyar politikai pályaképek*, 302–303; M. Kiss, Vitányi, *A Magyar Diák Szabadságfrontja*, 285–286.

85. M. Kiss, "A lét terei," 44–46.

86. Nyeste, *Útkeresés*, 33.

87. Bennett Kovrig, *Communism in Hungary: From Kun to Kádár* (Stanford: Hoover Institute, 1979), 153–156; Domonkos Szőke, "1945 szabad választás—szabad választás?" [Free election—free election?]in *Tiltott történelmünk 1945–1947*, [Our forbidden history 1945–1947] ed. János Horváth (Budapest: Századvég Kiadó, 2006), 19.

88. Szőke, "1945 szabad választás," 18; László Kontler. *Millennium in Central Europe: A History of Hungary* (Budapest: Atlantisz, 1999), 392.

89. In 1919 Rákosi had been commander of the Red Guard of the Hungarian Soviet Republic. He was sentenced to life imprisonment in Hungary after returning from exile and was only released to Moscow in 1940 in exchange for the military flags captured by the Russians in 1849.

90. Kovrig, *Communism*, 156.

91. Juhász, *Hungarian Foreign Policy*, 332–333.

92. Kovrig, *Communism*, 159; Szőke, "1945 szabad választás," 21; Macartney, *October Fifteenth*, 2:459.

93. Kovrig, *Communism*, 159–160.

94. Ibid., 159.

95. Ibid., 160.

96. Stephen D. Kertesz, *Between Russia and the West: Hungary and the Illusions of Peacemaking 1945–1947* (Notre Dame: University of Notre Dame Press, 1986), 29; Kovrig, *Communism*, 160.

97. Szőke, "1945 szabad választás," 23. Ferenc Nagy points out that, for example, the leftist town of Orosháza with a population of 30,000 was assigned fourteen representatives, while the city of Pécs with 80,000 inhabitants and surrounding county of

Baranya with 300,000 was only allowed seven. See Ferenc Nagy, *The Struggle behind the Iron Curtain* (New York: Macmillan, 1948), 74.

98. Szőke, "1945 szabad választás," 25.

99. Béla Dálnoki Miklós, prime minister; Ferenc Erdei, Interior; Gábor Faragho, Public Supply; József Gábor, Commerce; János Gyöngyösi, Foreign Minister; Erik Molnár, Social Welfare; Imre Nagy, Agriculture; Ferenc Takács, Industry; Count Géza Teleki, Religion and Education; Ágoston Valentiny, Justice; István Vásáry, Finance; János Vörös, Defense. See Az Ideiglenes nemzetgyűlés es as Ideiglenes Kormány megalakulás, 70. Molnár was actually a Communist, and Erdei from the National Peasant party was a Communist in all but name.

100. Róbert Barta, "Brit követjelentések és a magyar belpolitika: 1945–1946" [British ministerial reports and Hungarian domestic policy: 1945–1946] in *Tiltott történelmünk 1945–1947*, ed. János Horváth (Budapest: Századvég Kiadó, 2006), 81.

101. Kovrig, *Communism*, 161.

102. Nagy, *The Struggle*, 65–66.

103. The Warsaw Uprising was put down in sixty-three days; the blockade of Leningrad lasted almost three years but with no street battles; the battle for Stalingrad lasted four months but much of the civilian population had been evacuated. See Krisztián Ungváry, *Budapest ostroma*, 9.

104. Lilly Vigyazo, interview with the author, June 26, 2003.

105. Colonel-General Heinz Guderian, chief of staff of the German army, denied permission. See Krisztián Ungváry, *Battle for Budapest*, 40; Mawdsley, *Thunder in the East*, 350.

106. Mawdsley, *Thunder in the East*, 350.

107. The Germans ordered firing stopped and escorted Ostapenko and his group as far as the no-man's land. Despite intense shelling Ostapenko insisted on following his orders to return as soon as possible. As they walked through no-man's land there were several explosions and Ostopenko fell. It is still unclear who was responsible for his death. In the intense shelling some Germans were also wounded. The shelling may have come from an uninformed Soviet battery, but could also have been Hungarian anti-aircraft guns in the area. See Ungváry, *Battle for Budapest*, 99–100.

108. L. Nagy, *Magyarország története*, 253.

109. Ungváry, *Battle for Budapest*, 221.

110. Ibid., 221–226.

111. Ibid., 226–230.

112. Ibid., 121–124.

113. Gábor Tamás, interview with the author, December 15, 2001.

114. Nick Molnar, interview with the author, February 28, 2002.

115. From fall 1944 to April 1945 daily discussion at Hitler's Hauptquartier began with the Hungarian theater of war, even when the first Soviet tanks were only sixty kilometers from Berlin. See Krisztían Ungváry, *A magyar honvédség a második világháborúban* [The Hungarian army in World War II] (Budapest: Osiris, 2004), 430–435.

116. Ungváry, *A magyar honvédség*, 442–444.

117. Quoted in Mawdsley, *Thunder in the East*, 350.

118. Pfeffer-Wildenbrook, the commanding general did not leave the protection of the tunnel during the six weeks of the siege. See Ungváry, *Battle for Budapest*, 66.

119. Ungváry, *Battle for Budapest*, 142–150.

120. In 1943 Stalin had prevented Hungarian prisoners of war from forming a Hungarian Legion, claiming that the exile governments of Czechoslovakia and Yugoslavia were against it, but his secret agreement with the Romanian leadership to take their side over the disputed territories may well have been his actual reason. The Hungarian POWs, with the encouragement of communist émigré, Zoltán Vas, had gained the agreement of their two officers, Lt. Gen. Marcel Stomm and Major General László Deseő, to form the Kossuth Army Corps, but Stalin would not allow it. Stomm was later falsely accused of preventing the formation. See Ferenc Gallyas, "Tanúnak Jelentkezem" *Magyar Hirlap melléklet* (n.d.), 7.

121. Ungváry, *Battle for Budapest*, 173–175.

122. Ibid., 210.

123. Quoted in Ungváry, *Battle for Budapest*, 203.

124. Mawdsley, *Thunder in the East*, 351.

125. Rozsnyoi, "Nyilasok—amig a hur elpattant."

126. *Budapest on the Road of Revival: Report on General Conditions in the Year 1946.* Published by Joseph Kővágó, mayor of Budapest. Compiled by the Municipal Statistical Bureau.

127. Ungváry, *Battle for Budapest*, 269.

128. Kontra pointed out that it is hard to explain this to youth today who see the "liberation" as the beginning of the Soviet military occupation; but at the time it was literally being freed from the Germans. See György Kontra, interview with the author, Elte Anthropology Dept. March 16, 1988).

129. Ungváry, *Battle for Budapest*, 279, 283–284; Macartney, *October Fifteenth*, 2:467.

130. Zsuzsa L. Nagy and János Levai, interview with the author, November 13, 2001.

131. Barta, "Brit követjelentések és a magyar belpolitika," 85.

132. Ungváry, *Battle for Budapest*, 280, 283.

133. Sándor Márai, *Memoir of Hungary 1944–1948* (Budapest: Corvina, 1991), 64–65.

134. Ibid., 48.

135. Andrea Pető, "Női emlékezet és ellenállás" [Women's remembrance and opposition] in *Az Elsodort Város: Emlékkötet a Budapestért folytatott harcok 60. évfordulójára 1944/45* [City swept away: memorial volume on the 60th anniversary of the 1944/45 battle of Budapest] (Budapest: PolgART, 2005), 353.

136. Ibid., 356.

137. Ibid., 366.

138. László Borhi, *Hungary in the Cold War 1945–1956* (Budapest: Central European University Press, 2004), 55; Peter Kenez, *Hungary from the Nazis to the Soviet: the Establishment of the Communist Regime in Hungary, 1944–1948*, (New York: Cambridge University Press, 2006), 44–45.

139. Pető, "Női emlékezet és ellenállás," 359–360.

140. Ungváry, *Battle for Budapest*, 299.

141. Soviet representatives had originally demanded $400 million, but the amount was reduced to $300 million at the insistence of the Anglo-American powers (Kenez, *Hungary*, 63).

142. The Western Allies wanted to prevent the expansion of Soviet influence in the strategically important Mediterranean area, and the Allied Control Commission in Italy was placed under the command of U.S. General Dwight D. Eisenhower. The Soviets resented being excluded, even though at the time they were deeply involved in the fighting within the Soviet interior.

143. Kenez, *Hungary*, 61–62; Kontler, *Millennium*, 393.

144. In 1946 the Americans showed increased interest in the condition of the Hungarian economy and requested a detailed presentation which was prepared by the Minister of Finance. When taken to Marshal Voroshilov he declined even to look at the paper; thus the Americans and British were unable to take note of the document. Again in May 1946 the American government suggested it would like to be informed of economic conditions, but the Hungarian government had received strict directives that it might communicate only through the president of the ACC. The then-president, General Sviridov, emphatically rejected the suggestion that they give any information to either the American or British representative. See Ferenc Nagy, *The Struggle*, 220–221.

145. Borhi, *Hungary in the Cold War*, 60.

146. Barta, "Brit követjelentések és a magyar belpolitika," 78.

147. See Kenez, *Hungary*, 74.

148. Ibid., 75.

149. Susan Glanz, "Economic Platforms of the Various Political Parties in the Hungarian Elections of 1945." *Hungarian Studies Review* 22, no.1 (Spring 1995): 31–32.

150. Tamás Stark, *Magyar foglyok a Szovjetunióban* [Hungarian prisoners in the Soviet Union] (Budapest: Lucidus Kiadó, 2006), 16–17.

151. Ibid., 17.

152. Ibid., 252.

153. Of the 400 prisoners taken in Szeged on October 11 only 100–120 were soldiers. In Hajdúböszörmény they took not only men but children as well. People pleaded in vain while soldiers pushed the captives out of the house and into the courtyard with their guns. "We didn't know where they were taking them—they only said 'kicsi robot'—a little work." See Stark, *Magyar foglyok*, 34–36.

154. Ágnes Huszár Várdy, "Forgottten Victims of World War II: Hungarian Women in Soviet Forced Labour Camps," 80.

155. Nagy, *The Struggle*, 59–60.

156. Zoltán Kugyelka, interview with the author, July 9, 2005.

157. Várdy, "Forgottten Victims of World War II," 82.

158. Béla Gyíres, interview with the author, May 21, 2001.

159. Ágnes Huszár Várdy, "Forgotten Victims of World War II," 74.

160. Etelka Schwertner, interview with the author, June 14, 2007.

161. Stark, *Magyar foglyok*, 251–252.

162. For a discussion of recent scholarship on the mass deportation of civilians to Soviet slave labor camps and the relative lack of attention by historians to the subject, see Steven Béla Várdy & Agnes Huszár Várdy, *Stalin's Gulag: The Hungarian Experience* (Napoli, Italia: Università degli Studi di Napoli L'Orinetale, 2007).

10. Postwar Hungary

1. Gyula Juhász, *A Háború és Magyarország 1938–1945* [The war and Hungary 1938–1945] (Budapest: Akadémiai Kiadó, 1986), 7–8.

2. András Hegedüs, *A történelem és a hatalom igézetében* [Under the spell of history and power] (Budapest: Kossuth, 1988), 110.

3. Borhi, *Hungary in the Cold War*, 66; Kovrig, *Communism in Hungary*, 163.

4. Kovács, *Magyarország megszállása*, 223–224.

5. Ferenc Nagy, *The Struggle behind the Iron Curtain* (New York: Macmillan, 1948), 109.

6. Kontler, *Millennium*, 394.

7. Nagy still tried to force several points; one that the state would compensate for land taken from churches so that they could continue their schools and institutions, but this was also voted down. See Nagy, *The Struggle,* 110.

8. Kovács, *Magyarország megszállása*, 235.

9. Ibid., 236.

10. Kenez, *Hungary*, 111–113; Nagy, *The Struggle,* 111.

11. Glanz, "Economic Platforms," 33; Kontler, *Millennium*, 394–395.

12. Mail service hardly functioned, and newspapers were delivered in many places twice a month. In wintertime the dirt roads became seas of mud (Kenez, *Hungary*, 185).

13. György Gyarmati, "Kényszerpályás rendszerváltások Magyarországon, 1945–1949" [Forced regime transformation in Hungary, 1945–1949] Eötvös Loránd University, October 17, 2005, 13.

14. In 1949 the regime launched a massive campaign to force the peasants into cooperatives. Many peasants gave in and joined or left farming altogether (Kontler, *Millennium*, 418–419).

15. See Tony Judt, *Postwar: a History of Europe since 1945* (New York: Penguin Press, 2005), 41–46.

16. The People's Commissariat for Internal Affairs, abbreviated NKVD, was the Soviet public and secret police organization that directly executed the rule of power, including political repression, during the era of Stalin.

17. Kenez, *Hungary*, 53–58; Kovrig, *Communism in Hungary*, 170–171.

18. Kovrig, *Communism in Hungary*, 171.

19. Kenez, *Hungary*, 66; Szöke, "1945 szabad választás," 31.

20. Kenez, *Hungary*, 142–143.

21. Dr. Sándor Szalai, *Itél a magyar nép! A magyar háborús bünperek tanulságai* [The Hungarian people judge! Lessons of the Hungarian state trials!] (Budapest: Athenaeum, 1946), 7–8.

22. Kenez, *Hungary*, 143–146.

23. Kovács, *Magyarország megszállása*, 281–285.

24. Pál Pritz, "War-Crimes Trial Hungarian Style: Prime Minister László Bárdossy Before the People's Tribunal, 1945," in *Hungarian Studies Review* XXII (Spring–Fall 1995): 289–291.

25. Szombathelyi, *Visszaemlékezései*, 60. As noted earlier, Szombathelyi had contributed important information to the American OSS. Generally the OSS attempted to protect its secret wartime partners, but so far no document has been found suggesting any attempt by the OSS to protect Szombathelyi. See Fenyvesi, *Three Conspiracies*, 7, 15.

26. *Magyarország a második világháborúban: Lexikon A–Zs* [Hungary in World War II: Encyclopaedia A-Zs], ed. Péter Sipos (Budapest: Petit Real, 1997), 339; Szalai, *Itél a magyar nép!* 14; Romsics, *Magyarország*, 279–280.

27. Romsics, *Magyarország*, 279–280; *Trezor 3. Az Átmenet évkőnve 2003* [The transitional yearbook 2003] (Budapest: Állambiztonsági Szolgálatok Tőrténeti Levéltára [State Security Historic Archives], 2004), 81.

28. Nagy, *The Struggle*, 213.

29. Budapest on the Road of Revival: Report on General Conditions in the Year 1946, published by Joseph Kővágó, mayor of Budapest.

30. Balint Kovács, interview with author, June 8, 1988.

31. Sándor Kiss, *A magyar demokráciáért*, 37.

32. Linda Dégh, "The Institutional Application of Folklore in Hungary," *Hungarian Studies* 6, 2 (1990): 201–202.

33. Ibid., 202.

34. Barta, "Brit követjelentések," 82.

35. Gábor Bodnár, *Scouting in Hungary* (Cleveland, Ohio: Hungarian Scout Association, 1986), 94; Zoltan Sztaray, *The Crushing of Hungarian Scouting 1945–1948* (Garfield: Hungarian Scout Association in Exile, n.d.), 3.

36. József Ugrin, *Emlékezéseim* [My remembrances] (Budapest: Püski , 1995), 206–208.

37. According to the declaration at the Yalta Conference, all signatories were to assist liberated countries or former satellites of the Axis powers in the formation of democratic interim governments through free elections.

38. Kovrig, *Communism in Hungary*, 175–176

39. Kertesz, *Between Russia and the West*, 31; Kovrig, *Communism in Hungary*, 175–176; Szöke, "1945 szabad választás," 3.

40. Nagy, *The Struggle*, 71. Nagy asserts that the growth of the party came partly through an unscrupulous recruiting campaign. As Soviet soldiers rounded up people for deportation it was discovered that if one possessed a Communist Party membership card the bearer was released (*The Struggle*, 60–61).

41. Kenez, *Hungary*, 46–47; Kontler, *Millennium*, 392–393.

42. Kontler, *Millennium*, 395; Szöke, "1945 szabad választás," 16–17.

43. Glanz, "Economic Platforms," 38–39.

44. When Károly Peyer returned from the German camp at Mauthausen, he was told by Rákosi that he no longer had a major role to play. See Kenez, *Hungary*, 84–85.

45. Kovács, *Magyarország megszállása*, 278; Gyarmati, "Kényszerpályás rendszerváltások," 5.

46. A postwar revival of religion and the opposition of Cardinal József Mindszenty to the Communists undoubtedly affected election results. In his pastoral letter of November 1 he urged the faithful to vote for the candidate who would fight for moral purity, legality and truth against the sad current situation. "Do not be frightened by the threats of the sons of evil. . . ." See Kontler, *Millennium*, 396; Kenez, *Hungary*, 172.

47. Nagy, *The Struggle*, 159–163.

48. Barta, "Brit követjelentések," 84.

49. Kenez, *Hungary*, 105.

50. The Independent Smallholders' first nominee for prime minister, Dezső Sulyok, had been vetoed by Voroshilov, leading to the appointment of the less experienced Nagy. See Kovrig, *Communism in Hungary*, 190.

51. Nagy, *The Struggle*, 228–229.

52. Glanz, "Economic Platforms," 41; Kontler, *Millennium*, 397; Szöke, "1945 szabad választás," 28.

53. Borhi, *Hungary in the Cold War*, 82; Kovrig, *Communism in Hungary*, 188.

54. The problem was partially solved by greatly reducing the armed forces from the armistice limit of 70,000 to 20,000, a number directed by the Soviet head of the ACC. After dismissals, aimed first at the pro-Western officers, untrained but politically reliable recruits were promoted to officer rank. See Kovrig, *Communism in Hungary*, 171.

55. Borhi, *Hungary in the Cold War*, 82; Kovrig, *Communism in Hungary*, 171, 188–189.

56. Gyarmati, "Kényszerpályás rendszerváltások," 14–15; Romsics, *Magyarország*, 304.

57. Kovrig, *Communism in Hungary*, 190.

58. Ibid., 190–191.

59. Kenez, *Hungary*, 133; Nagy, *The Struggle*, 193–196.

60. Kenez, *Hungary*, 125; Kontler, *Millennium*, 395.

61. *Bibó István (1911–1979)*, 304.

62. Kenez, *Hungary*, 131; Kontler, *Millennium*, 397; Romsics, *Magyarország*, 288.

63. *Bibó István (1911–1979)*, 304, 306. At the time Bibó had been recruited by Ferenc Erdei to head the administrative section of the ministry of the interior. He is noted for his penetrating analyses of political and social problems of the mid-century.

64. Ágnes Tóth, *Migrationen in Ungarn 1945–1948: Vertreibung der Ungarndeutschen, Binnenwanderungen und slowakisch-ungarisher Bevölkerungsaustausch* (München: Oldenburg, 2001), 54.

65. Nagy, *The Struggle*, 131–132.

66. Tóth, *Migrationen in Ungarn*, 36–39.

67. Ibid., 50.

68. Ibid., 56–57.

69. Ibid., 177–180. For a succinct English-language treatment of the deportation of Hungary's Swabian population in 1946, see János Angi, "The Expulsion of the Germans from Hungary after World War II," in *Ethnic Cleansing in Twentieth-Century Europe*, ed. S. B. Várdy and T. H. Tooley (New York: East European Monographs/ Columbia University Press, 2003), 373–384.

70. Kenez, *Hungary*, 127.

71. Their plan was never actualized, since a major part of the Peasant Alliance leadership was accused of conspiracy against the nation and imprisoned on the basis of the charge. See Piroska Póth, "A Magyarországi Népfőiskolák 1945 után" [The Hungarian folk high schools after 1945], *Forrás* (December 1984): 20–21.

72. Ibid., 20–22.

73. Romsics, *Magyarország*, 319–323.

74. The Györffy students were active in starting the movement: "They went to the countryside and looked for someone to be the director of a college, and for progressive people to be teachers." See Tibor Hajdú, interview with the author, July 4, 2008.

75. According to historian Tibor Hajdú, a former Nékosz student, the number of students was more likely to have been about 2,500 rather than the 6,067 mentioned in Romsics, *Magyarország*, 321. Since the plan was to create a new generation of the elite, no poor students were admitted (Hajdú interview).

76. In May 1948 the Hungarian Boy Scout Association was incorporated into the state-controlled Pioneer communist youth movement (Bodnár, *Scouting in Hungary*, 94–100).

77. Margit Balogh, "A parasztifjúság katolikus hivatásrendi szervezése a KALOT keretei között," [Organization of Catholic peasant youth within KALOT framework] *CLIO: Fiatal Oktatók Közleményei 2* (Budapest: ELTE Bölcsészettudományi Kar, 1986), 47–53; Kontler, *Millennium,* 397; Romsics, *Magyarország,* 288.

78. Kertesz had studied at Yale and Oxford, 1935–1937, on a Rockefeller Fellowship, and had taken part in peace preparations in the Ministry of Foreign Affairs in 1943–44.

79. At first Gyöngyösi had shown little interest in foreign affairs or the preparations, believing he could handle all such problems with the assistance of a few secretaries, but he soon realized the impossibility of initiating any serious activity in foreign affairs without the knowledge of able advisers and specialists, and found he had to rely increasingly on officials of the previous regime. See Kertesz, *Between Russia and the West,* 78–80.

80. Ibid., 80–81; Kovrig, *Communism in Hungary,* 199–200.

81. See Kertesz, *Between Russia and the West,* 134–160, for a detailed account of the negotiations.

82. Czechoslovakia deported men and women of working age to Bohemia and Moravia, placed Hungarians into internment camps, and deported all those who had arrived after 1938 across the border with only the goods they could carry. The Hungarian minority were deprived of citizenship, all cultural institutions were dissolved, and Hungarian civil servants were fired, including teachers. See Sándor Balogh, *Magyarország és szomszédai, 1945–1947* [Hungary and its neighbors, 1945–1947] (Budapest: História-MTA Történettudományi Intézete, 1995), 8–14; Tóth, *Migrationen in Ungarn,* 185–186.

83. Kertesz, *Between Russia and the West,* 101; Kovrig, *Communism in Hungary,* 200; Nagy, *The Struggle,* 209–214.

84. Kovrig, *Communism in Hungary,* 200; Nagy, *The Struggle,* 218.

85. Kenez, *Hungary,* 204–205; Nagy, *The Struggle,* 226–229.

86. Nagy, *The Struggle,* 232–233.

87. Kenez, *Hungary,* 204–205.

88. Nagy, *The Struggle,* 234–235.

89. Ibid., 235.

90. Kertesz, *Between Russia and the West,* 182–183.

91. For a full discussion of the peace negotiations in Paris between May and October, see István Kertesz, *Between Russia and the West,* 163–224.

92. Although Bratislava's development had never been in the direction of the south bank, it seems that the villages were offered as a compromise for rejecting the resettlement of the minority Hungarians. See Kertesz, *Between Russia and the West,* 212–213.

93. József Galántai, *Trianon and the Protection of Minorities* (New York: Columbia University Press, 1992), 140–141.

94. Kontler, *Millennium*, 401.

95. Borhi, *Hungary in the Cold War,* 116; Kertesz, *Between Russia and the West,* 228.

96. Kovács, *Magyarország megszállása,* 313. Kovács returned to his flat and wrote his letter of resignation to Péter Veres, the president of the National Peasant Party. He left the country soon afterward.

97. Nagy, *The Struggle,* 420–425; Borhi, *Hungary in the Cold War,* 189; Kenez, *Hungary,* 234.

98. Kenez, *Hungary,* 3–4.

99. Romsics, *Magyarország,* 323–324.

100. Father Kerkai had been charged with antidemocratic organization and conduct against the interests of the people. In 1956 he was freed along with other prisoners, but with the Soviet intervention he was arrested again; he was finally released in September 1959, a broken man.

101. Romsics, *Magyarország,* 324–325; Kontler, *Millennium,* 404–405.

102. Kenez, *Hungary,* 284.

103. Kenez, *Hungary,* 270–271; Romsics, *Magyarország,* 309.

104. Póth, "A Magyarországi Népfőiskolák," 22.

105. Kontler, *Millennium,* 405.

106. The former students, who had been told they would be taking over leadership positions, went their different ways. The many talented women students were in the most disadvantaged position; they had no possibilities afterward and many became housewives. See Tibor Hajdú, interview with the author, July 4, 2008.

107. Ivan T. Berend, *Central and Eastern Europe, 1944–1953: Detour from the periphery to the periphery* (Cambridge: Cambridge University Press, 1996), 37; Kontler, *Millennium,* 405.

Bibliography

This bibliography is divided into the following sections:

Archival Sources
Published Documents
Books and articles
Personal Interviews

Archival Sources

Magyar Országos Levéltár [Hungarian National Archives].
Hess Archives, XIX-J-1-a Béke előkészitő osztály iratai 1945–47 [Documents of the Division for Peace Preparation 1945–47].
Népfőiskola iratai [Folk High School Documents].
Országgyülés képviselöházának [Parliamentary Archives].
Statistical Yearbook of Budapest for 1939.
Zsinati levéltár [Archives of the Calvinist Church in Budapest].

Published Documents

A Szálasi Per [The Szálasi trial]. Edited by Elek Karsai and László Karsai. Budapest: Reform, 1988.
A Wilhelmstrasse és Magyarország: Német diplomáciai iratok Magyarországról 1933–1944 [Wilhelmstrasse and Hungary: German diplomatic documents on Hungary 1933–1944]. Edited by György Ránki, et al. Budapest: Kossuth, 1968.
Az Ideiglenes Nemzetgyűles és az Ideiglenes Kormány megalakulása, 1944. December 21–22 [The formation of the provisional national assembly and the provisional government]. Budapest: Kossuth Könyvkiadó, 1984.
Bibó István (1911–1979) Életút dokumentumomkban [Career in documents]. Budapest: Osiris-Századvég, 1995.
Budapest on the Road of Revival: Report on General Conditions in the Year 1946. Published by Joseph Kővágó, mayor of Budapest. Compiled by the Municipal Statistical Bureau.
Ciano, Galeazzo, *Diary 1937–1943*. New York: Enigma Books, 2002.
Ciano's Diplomatic Papers—200 Conversations. London: Odhams Press, 1948.

Die Tagebücher von Joseph Goebbels; Sämtliche Fragmente. Teil II Diktate 1941–1945, Januar bis März 1942; 8 April bis Juni 1943. Edited by Fröhlich Elke. München: K. G. Saur, 1987.

Horthy Miklós Titkos iratai [Miklós Horth's secret documents]. Edited by M. Szinai and László Szücs. Budapest: Kossuth, 1972.

"For Remembrance." Bill Glovin interview with Gabor Vermes. *Rutgers Magazine* (Fall 1997), 18–19.

Szárszó 1943: előzményei, jegyzőkönyve és utóélete: dokumentumok [Szárszó 1943: Antecedents, proceedings and afterlife: documents]. Budapest: Kossuth, 1983.

Trezor 3. Az Átmenet évkőnve 2003 [The transitional yearbook 2003]. Budapest: Állambiztonsági Szolgálatok Tőrténeti Levéltára [State Security Historic Archives], 2004.

Books and Articles

A százgyökerű szív: Levelek, naplók, visszaemlékezések, Sík Sándor hagyatékából [Letters, diaries, and memoirs from Sándor Sík's Estate]. Edited by János Szabó, Budapest: Magvető, 1993.

A. Sajti, Enikő. *Délvidék 1941–1944: A magyar kormányok délszláv politikáka* [The south slav policy of the Hungarian government]. Budapest: Kossuth, 1987.

———. "A jugoszláviai magyarok politikai szervezkedésének lehetőségei és korlátai (1918–1941)" [Possibilities and limitations of Yugoslav-Hungarian political organization] *Regio: Kisebbségi Szemle* (February 1997): 3–31.

Ablonczy, Balázs. "A magyar parlamentarizmus változásai a harmincas években" [Changes in the Hungarian parliament in the 1930s] unpublished article.

———. *Pál Teleki (1874–1941): The Life of a Controversial Hungarian Politician.* Translated by Thomas J. and Helen DeKornfeld. Boulder, Colo.: Social Science Monographs. New York: Columbia University Press, 2006.

———. *Teleki Pál.* Budapest: Osiris, 2005.

Ács, Zoltán. "Germans in Hungary." *The New Hungarian Quarterly* 30, no. 116 (Winter 1989): 57–63.

Ádám Magda. *A kis-antant 1920–1938* [The little entente 1920–1938]. Budapest: Kossuth, 1981.

———. *The Little Entente and Europe (1920–1929).* Budapest: Akadémiai Kiadó, 1993.

Balogh, Margit. *A KALOT és a katolikus társadalompolitika 1935–1946* [KALOT and Catholic social policy 1935–1946]. Budapest: MTA Történettudományi Intézete, 1998.

———. "A parasztifjúság katolikus hivatásrendi szervezése a KALOT keretei között / 1936–1946." [Organization of Catholic peasant youth within the framework of KALOT]. *CLIO: Fiatal Oktatók Közleményei* 2. Budapest: ELTE Bölcsészettudományi Kar (1986).

Balogh, Sándor. "Magyarország és szomszédai, 1945–1947" [Hungary and its neighbors]. Budapest: História-MTA Történettudományi Intézete, 1995.

Bán, D. András. *Illúziók és Csalódások: Nagy-Britannia és Magyarország 1938–1941* [Illusions and disappointments: Great Britain and Hungary 1938–1941]. Budapest: Osiris, 1998.

Barátok a bajban: lengyel menekültek Magyarországon 1939–1945 [Friends in need: Polish refugees in Hungary 1939–1945]. Budapest: Európa, 1985.

Barcza, György. *Diplomataemlékeim* [My diplomatic memoirs]. Edited by András D. Bán. 2 vols. Budapest: Európa História, 1994.

———. "A svájci misszió," *Diplomataemlékeim.* [The Swiss mission, from my diplomatic memoirs]. München: Új Látóhatár, 1983.

Barta, Róbert. "Brit követjelentések és a magyar belpolitika: 1945–1946" [British ministerial reports and Hungarian domestic policy: 1945–1946]. In *Tiltott történelmünk 1945–1947* [Our forbidden history], edited by János Horváth, 77–87. Budapest: Századvég Kiadó, 2006.

Ben-Ghiat, Ruth. *Fascist Modernities: Italy, 1922–1945.* Berkeley: University of California Press, 2001.

Berend, Iván T. *Central and Eastern Europe, 1944–1953: Detour from the periphery to the periphery.* New York: Cambridge University Press, 1996.

———. "The Composition and Position of the Working Class during the War." In *Hungarian Economy and Society During World War II*, edited by György Lengyel, 151–168. Highland Lakes, N.J.: Atlantic Research and Publication, 1993.

Berend, Iván T., and György Ránki. *The Hungarian Economy in the Twentieth Century.* New York: St. Martin's Press, 1985.

Berend, Iván T., and Tamás Csató. *Evolution of the Hungarian Economy 1848–1998.* Highland Lakes, N.J.: Atlantic Research and Publications, Inc., 2001.

Bethlen, Béla. *Észak-Erdély kormánybiztosa voltam* [I was government commissioner of northern Transylvania]. Edited by Ignác Romsics. Budapest: Zrínyi katonai kiadó, 1989.

Bethlen, Count István. *Hungarian Politics during World War Two: Treatise and Indictment.* Edited by Countess Ilona Bolza. München: Dr. Rudolf Trofenik, 1985.

Bodnár, Gábor. *Scouting in Hungary.* Cleveland, Ohio: Hungarian Scout Association, 1986.

Bodó, Béla, "Paramilitary Violence in Hungary after the First World War." *East European Quarterly* 38, no. 2 (June 2004): 129–172.

Bokor, Péter. "Az elvetélt csendőrpuccs ismeretlen története" [The unknown history of the aborted gendarme putsch]. *Magyar Hírlap* (July 5, 1993): 9.

———. "A nagy politikai naivitás: Nem számítottak Magyarország megszállására" [Surprising political naiveté: they didn't count on the occupation of Hungary]. *Magyar Hírlap* (March 19, 1996).

———. "Ullein-Reviczky Antal és a 'kiugrási' politika"[Antal Ullein-Reviczky and the 'bail-out' policy]. *Magyar Hírlap* (May 6, 1993): 11.

———. *Végjáték a Duna mentén: Interjúk egy filmsorozathoz* [End game on the banks of the Danube: interviews for a film series].Budapest: RTV-Minerva-Kossuth, 1982.

Boldizsár, Iván. *Don—Buda—Párizs.* Budapest: Magvető Könyvkiadó, 1982.

Borbándi, Gyula. *Magyar politikai pályaképek 1938–1948* [Careers of Hungarian Politicians]. Budapest: Európa könyvkiadó, 1997.

Borhi, László. *Hungary in the Cold War 1945–1956.* Budapest: Central European University Press, 2004.

Braham, Randolph L. *The Hungarian Labor Service System 1939–1945.* New York: East European Quarterly, distributed by Columbia University Press, 1977.

Braham, Randolph L., and Attila Pók, eds. *The Holocaust in Hungary: Fifty Years Later.* New York: Columbia University Press, 1997.

Braham, Randolph L, and Brewster S. Chamberlin, eds. *The Holocaust in Hungary: Sixty Years Later.* New York: Columbia University Press, 2006.

Braham, Randolph L., and Scott Miller, eds. *The Nazis' Last Victims. The Holocaust in Hungary.* Detroit: Wayne State University Press, 1999.

Braithwaite, Rodric. *Moscow 1941: A City and Its People at War.* New York: Alfred A. Knopf, 2006.

Chászár, Edward. *Decision in Vienna: The Czechoslovak-Hungarian Border Dispute of 1938.* Astor, Fla.: Danubian Press, Inc. 1978.

Cornelius, Deborah S. *In Search of the Nation: The New Generation of Hungarian Youth in Czechoslovakia, 1925–1934.* Boulder, Colo.: Social Science Monographs, 1998.

———. "The Recreation of the Nation-Origins of the Hungarian Populist Movement." *Hungarian Studies* 6, no. 1 (1990): 29–40.

———. "Women in the Hungarian Populist Youth Movement: The Szeged Youth." *Nationalities Papers* 25, no. 1 (1997): 123–145.

Csaplar, Ferenc. *A Szegedi Fiatalok Műveszeti Kollegiuma* [The Szeged youth artistic kollegium]. Budapest: Akadémiai Kiadó, 1967.

Csató, Tamás. "The War Economy Subservient to Germany." In *Evolution of the Hungarian Economy 1848–1998 Vol I,* ed. Iván T. Berend and Tamás Csató, 225–232. Highland Lakes, NJ: Atlantic Research and Publications, 2001.

Csicsery-Rónay, István, "Új tények az ország megszállásáról: 1944. március 19.— ahogy Macartney látta" [New facts on the occupation of the country: March 19, 1944—as Macartney saw it]. *Magyar Nemzet.* March 21, 1995.

Csizmadia, Andor, ed. *Bürokrácia és közigazgatási reformok Magyarhonban* [Bureaucracy and administrative reform in Hungary]. Budapest: Gondolat, 1979.

Czettler, Antal. *A mi kis élethalél kérdéseink: A magyar külpolitika a hadba lépéstől a német megszállásig* [Our small life-and-death questions: Hungarian foreign policy from the entrance into the war to the German occupation]. Budapest: Magvető, 2000.

———. *Teleki Pál és a Magyar külpolitika 1939–1941* [Pál Teleki and Hungarian foreign policy 1939–1941]. Budapest: Magvető, 1997.

Davies, Norman. *God's Playground: A History of Poland.* New York: Columbia University Press, 1982

Deák, István. "Hungary." In *The European Right: A Historical Profile,* ed. Hans Rogger and Eugen Weber, 364–407. Berkeley: University of California, 1965.

Dégh, Linda. "The Institutional Application of Folklore in Hungary." *Hungarian Studies* 6, no. 2 (1990): 196–216.

Dombrády, Lóránd, "Financing the Hungarian Rearmament," in *Hungarian Economy and Society During World War II,* ed. György Lengyel, 77–101. Boulder, Colo./New York: Columbia University Press, 1993.

———. *A legfelsőbb hadúr és hadserege* [The Supreme Commander and the Army]. Budapest: Zrínyi, 1990.

———. *A magyar gazdaság és a hadfelszerelés 1938–1944* [The Hungarian economy and instruments of war]. Budapest: Akadémiai, 1981.

Don, Yehuda. "The Economic Dimensions of Antisemitism: Anti-Jewish Legislation in Hungary 1938–1944." *East European Quarterly* 20, no. 4 (January 1987): 447–465.

———. "Economic Implications of the Anti-Jewish Legislation in Hungary." In *Genocide and Rescue: The Holocaust in Hungary 1944,* ed. David Cesarani, 56–58. Oxford: Berg, 1997.

Dreisziger, Nándor F. "Civil-Military Relations in Nazi Germany's Shadow: the Case of Hungary, 1939–1941." In *Swords and Covenants: Essays in Honour of the Centennial of the Royal Military College of Canada 1876–1976,* ed. Adrian Preston and Peter Dennis, 216–247. Totowa, N.J.: Rowman and Littlefield, 1976.

———. *Hungarians from Ancient Times to 1956: Biographical and Historical Essays.* Ottawa: Legas, 2007.

———. "Hungary in 1945." *Hungarian Studies Review* 22, no. 1 (Spring 1995): 5–11.

———, ed. *Hungary in the Age of Total War (1938–1948).* East European Monographs, New York: Columbia University Press, 1998.

———. "New Twist to an Old Riddle: The Bombing of Kassa (Košice) June 26, 1941." *Journal of Modern History* 44, no. 2 (June 1972): 232–242.

———. "The nine lives of my dad, Kalman Dreisziger." Unpublished document.

Duke, Florimond. *Name, Rank, and Serial Number.* New York: Meredith Press, 1969.

Dziewanowski, M. K. *War at Any Price: World War II in Europe 1939-1945.* Upper Saddle River, N.J.: Prentice Hall, 1991.

Esterházy, Luzja. *Szívek az ár ellen* [Hearts against the current]. Budapest: Puski, 1991.

Fein, Helen. *Accounting for Genocide: National Responses and Jewish Victimization during the Holocaust.* Chicago: University of Chicago Press, 1979.

Felak, James Ramon. *"At the Price of the Republic" Hlinka's Slovak People's Party, 1929–1938.* Pittsburgh: University of Pittsburgh Press, 1994.

Fenyo, Mario. *Hitler, Horthy, and Hungary: German-Hungarian Relations 1941–1944.* New Haven: Yale University Press, 1972.

Fenyvesi, Charles. *Három összeesküvés: Rundstedt Tábornagy, Canaris Tengernagy és a Zsidó Mernök, aki megmenthette volna Európát* [Three conspiracies: Field Marshal Rundstedt, Admiral Canaris, and the Jewish engineer who could have saved Europe]. Translated by Dr. György Molnár. Budapest: Európa Könyvkiadó, 2007.

———. *Three Conspiracies: Field Marshal Rundstedt, Admiral Canaris, and the Jewish Engineer Who Could Have Saved Europe.* Unpublished manuscript.

Fischer-Galati, Stephen. *Twentieth Century Rumania.* New York: Columbia University Press, 1970.

Galántai, József. *Trianon and the Protection of Minorities.* New York: Columbia University Press, 1992.

Gály, Olga. *Ördöglakat: Lőrincz Gyula ifjúsága* [The devil's padlock: Gyula Lorincz's youth]. Bratislava: Madách, 1990.

Gazsi, József. "A Felszabadító Bizottság" [The Liberation Committee]. In *Magyarország 1944: Fejezetek az ellenállás történetéből* [Hungary 1944: chapters from the history of the resistance], ed. Sándor M. Kiss, 182–214. Budapest: Nemzeti Tankönyvkiadó, 1994.

Gergely, Jenő. *Eucharisztikus világkongresszus Budapesten, 1938* [International Eucharistic Congress Budapest 1938]. Budapest: Kossuth, 1988.

———. *A Katolikus egyház története Magyarországon 1919–1945* [The history of the Catholic church in Hungary 1919–1945]. Budapest: Pannonica, 1999.

———. "A Katolikus Püspöki Kar és a Konvertiták Mentése (Dokumentumok)" [The Catholic bench of bishops and rescue of converts (documents)]. *Történelmi Szemle* (April 1984): 580–616.

———. "A magyarországi egyházak és a Holocaust" [The Hungarian churches and the Holocaust]. In *The Holocaust in Hungary 50 Years Later*, ed. Randolph L. Braham and Attila Pók, 441–456. Boulder, Colo./New York: Columbia University Press, 1997.

Glantz, David M., and Jonathan M. House. *When Titans Clashed: How the Red Army Stopped Hitler.* Lawrence: University Press of Kansas, 1995.

Glanz, Susan. "Economic Platforms of the Various Political Parties in the Hungarian Elections of 1945." *Hungarian Studies Review* 22, no. 1 (Spring 1995): 31–45.

Gosztonyi, Péter. "A magyar ellenállási mozgalom és visszhangja a német iratok tükrében" [The Hungarian resistance movement and reaction in mirror of German writing]. In *Magyarország 1944: fejezetek az ellenállás történetéből*, ed. Sándor M. Kiss, 9–32. Budapest: Nemzeti Tankönyvkiadó, 1994.

———. *A Magyar honvédség a második világháborúban* [The Hungarian army in World War II]. Budapest: Európa Kőnyvkiadó, 1992.

———. *Vihar Kelet-Európ Felett* [Storm over eastern Europe]. Budapest: Népszava, 1990.

Gróf Stomm Marcel altábornagy emlékiratok. Edited by Ferenc Gallyas. Budapest: Magyar hirláp könyvek, 1990.

Gueth, Gyula. *Egy tartalékos tábori lelkész II. világháborús visszaemlékezései 1942–1945* [World War II memoirs of a military reserve clergyman]. Kaposvár: Pethő & Társa Nyomdaipari Bt., n.d.

Gunst, Péter. *Magyarország gazdaságtörténete (1914–1989)* [Economic History of Hungary]. Budapest: Nemzeti Tankönyvkiadó, 1999.

Gyáni, Gábor, and György Kövér. *Magyarország társadalom-története: a reformkortól a második világháborúig* [Social history of Hungary: from the reform period to World War II]. Budapest: Osiris, 1998.

Gyarmati, György: "Kényszerpályás rendszerváltások Magyarországon, 1945–1949" [Forced regime transformation in Hungary, 1945–1949] (lecture, Eötvös Loránd University. October 17, 2005).

Gyulai, Ilona, Countess Edelsheim. Horthy István kormányzóhelyettes özsvegye [Vice-regent István Horthy's widow]. *Becsület és kötelesség 1, 1918–1944* [Honor and duty 1, 1918–1944]. Budapest: Európa, 2001.

Gyurgyák, János. *A zsidókerdés Magyarországon* [The Jewish question in Hungary]. Budapest: Osiros, 2001.

Hőgye, Mihály. *Utolsó csatlós? Magyarország sorsa a második világháború végén* [The last satellite? Hungary's fate at the end of World War II]. Budapest: Püski, 1989.

Hajdu, Tibor. "The Hungarian Revolution—Conjunctures, Conjectures, Generalizations." Hungarian Revolution of 1918–1919: International Colloquium, Graz (June 5–9, 1989).

———. *Károlyi Mihály: Politikai életrajz* [Mihály Károlyi: political biography]. Budapest: Kossuth könyvkiadó, 1978.

Hámori, Péter. "Kísérlet a visszacsatolt felvidéki területek társadalmi és szociális integrálására"[Attempt to bring about the social integration of the Felvidék]. *Századok* 131, no. 2 (1997): 565–610.

Hanebrink, Paul A. *In Defense of Christian Hungary: Religion, Nationalism, and Anti-semitism, 1890–1944.* Ithaca, N.Y.: Cornell University Press, 2006.

Hegedüs, András. *A történelem és a hatalom igézetében* [History and the fascination of power]. Budapest: Kossuth, 1988.

Holborn, Hajo. *A History of Modern Germany 1840–1945.* Princeton, N.J.: Princeton University Press, 1982.

Horthy István repülő főhadnagy tragikus halála [Flying officer István Horthy's tragic death]. Budapest: Auktor Könyvkiadó, 1992.

Horthy, Miklos. *Admiral Nicholas Horthy: Memoirs.* Florida: Simon Publications, 2000.

Horváth, János, ed. *Tiltott történelmünk 1945–1947* [Our forbidden history 1945–1947]. Budapest: Századvég Kiadó, 2006.

Huszár, Tibor. *Beszélgetések* [Conversations]. Budapest: Magvető Könyvkiadó, 1983.

Illyés, Gyula. *People of the Puszta.* Translated by G. F. Cushing. Budapest: Corvina Press, 1967.

———. "Pusztulás: Uti jegyzetek" [Destruction: Travel Notes]. *Nyugat* (September 1933): 189–205.

Jakab, Sándor. "A nép főiskolája" [The people's folk high school]. In *A Sárospataki Népfőiskola (1936–1986)*, ed. Sándor Jakab and Csaba Varga, 85–88. OKK Módszertani Intézetének házi nyomdájában, n.d.

———. *Visszaemlékezés a népfőiskolás évekre* [Remembrances of the folk high school years]. Népfőiskola Archives NF-22. Budapest, 1976.

Janos, Andrew C. *The Politics of Backwardness in Hungary: 1825–1945*. Princeton, N.J.: Princeton University Press, 1982.

Jónás, Pállal beszélget Kende Péter [Péter Kende speaks with Pál Jónás], *Vasárnapi Újság: Válogatás a Népszerá Rádiómásor Adásaiból* [Sunday newspaper: selections from the broadcasts of the popular radio program]. Új Idő, 1989.

Judt, Tony. *Postwar: a History of Europe since 1945*. New York: Penguin Press, 2005.

Juhász, Gyula. *A Háború és Magyarország 1938–1945* [The war and Hungary 1938–1945]. Budapest: Akadémiai Kiadó, 1986.

———. *Hungarian Foreign Policy, 1919–1945*. Budapest: Akadémiai Kiadó, 1979.

———. *Magyarország kulpolitikája 1919–1945* [Hungary's foreign policy 1919–1945]. Budapest: Akadémiai Kiadó, 1988. Third edition.

———. "Some Aspects of Relations Between Hungary and Germany during the Second World War." In *Hungarian History-World History*, ed. Gy Ránkí, 209–220. Budapest: Akadémiai Kiadó, 1984.

Kádár, Gyula. *A Ludovikától Sopronkőhidáig* [From the Ludovika to Sopron Stone Bridge], vol. 2. Budapest: Magvető, 1978.

Kállay, Nicholas. *Hungarian Premier: A Personal Account of a Nation's Struggle in the Second World War*. New York: Columbia University Press, 1954.

Keegan, John. *The Second World War*. New York: Viking, 1990.

Kemény, Simon. *Napló 1942–1944* [Diary 1942–1944]. Budapest : Magvető, 1987.

Kemse: részletek az Elsüllyedt falu a Dunántúlon c.könyvből [Kemse: Details from a sinking village in Transdanubia]. Budapest: Népmüvelési intézet, 1986.

Kenez, Peter. *Hungary from the Nazis to the Soviet: the Establishment of the Communist Regime in Hungary, 1944–1948*. New York: Cambridge University Press, 2006.

Kenyeres, Lengyel László dr. *Ezt láttam Budapesten: egy szemtanú feljegyzései a Magyar főváros pusztulásáról* [I saw it in Budapest: an eyewitness account of the destruction of the Hungarian capital]. Budapest: A Március könyvkiadó , 1945.

Kershaw, Ian. *Hitler, 1936–1945: Nemesis*. New York: Norton, 2000.

Kertesz, Stephen D. *Between Russia and the West: Hungary and the Illusions of Peacemaking 1945–1947*. Notre Dame: University of Notre Dame Press, 1986.

King, Jeremy R.N. "Domestic Considerations of Hungarian Policy in Transylvania, 1939–1941." November 2, 1988 (unpublished manuscript).

Kirk, Tim, and Anthony McElligott, eds. *Opposing Fascism: Community, Authority and Resistance in Europe*. Cambridge: Cambridge University Press, 1999.

Komoróczy, Géza, ed. *A zsidó Budapest:Emlékek, szertartások, történelem* [Jewish Budapest: memoirs, observances, history]. Budapest: MTA Judaisztikai Kutatócsoport, 1995.

Kontler, László. *Millennium in Central Europe: A History of Hungary.* Budapest: Atlantisz, 1999.

Kornis, Julius. *Education in Hungary.* New York: Teachers College, Columbia University, 1932.

Kosa, John. "Hungarian Society in the Time of the Regency (1920–1944)." *Journal of Central European Affairs* 16, no. 3 (October 1956): 253–265.

Koszorús, Ferenc, volt M.Kir.Vk.Ezredes—Az 1. Pándélos hadosztály parancsnokának. [Ferenc Koszorús, former Hungarian Royal Staff Colonel, commander of the First Armored Division]. *Emlékiratai és tanulmányainak gyáteménye.* [Memoirs and collected papers]. Edited by Varsa Istvánné. Universe Publishing Company, 1987.

Kovács, Imre. *Magyarország megszállása* [The occupation of Hungary]. Toronto: Katalizátor, 1990.

———. *A Márciusi Front* [The march front]. New Brunswick, N.J.: Magyar Öregdiák Szövetség, 1980.

———. *A néma forradalom—A néma forradalom a bíroság és a parlament előtt* [The silent revolution—the silent revolution before the court and parliament]. Budapest: Cserépfalvi, 1989.

Kovács, Zoltán András, and Számvéber Norbert. *A Waffen-SS Magyarországon* [The Waffen-SS in Hungary]. Budapest: Hadtörténelmi levéltári kiadványok, Paktum Nyomdaipari Társaság, 2001.

Kovrig, Bennett. *Communism in Hungary from Kun to Kádár.* Stanford, Calif.: Hoover Institute, 1979.

Kürti, László. *The Remote Borderland: Transylvania in the Hungarian Imagination.* Albany: State University of New York Press, 2001.

L. Balogh, Béni. *A Magyar-Román kapcsolatok 1939–1940-ben és a második Bécsi döntés.* Csíkszereda, Pro-Print könyvkiadó, 2002.

L. Nagy, Zsuzsa. *Egy Politikus Polgár Portréja Rassay Károly (1886–1958)* [Portrait of a political citizen Károly Rassay (1886–1958)]. Budapest: Napvilág Kiadó, 2006.

———. *Liberális pártmozgalmak 1931–1945* [Liberal party movements, 1931–1945]. Budapest: Akadémiai, 1986.

———. *Magyarország története 1918–1945* [History of Hungary 1918–1945]. Debrecen: Történelmi Figyelő, 1995.

L. Nagy, Zsuzsa, and Kornélia Burucs, eds. *Kiútkeresés 1943.* Budapest: MTA Történettudományi Intézete, 1989.

Lackó, Miklós. *Arrow Cross Men, National Socialists 1935–1944.* Budapest, Akademia kiadó, 1969.

Lakatos, Géza. *Ahogy én láttam* [As I saw it]. Budapest: Európa, 1992.

László, E. Kovács. "A nép főiskolája" [The people's folk high school]. In *A Sárospataki Népfőiskola (1936–1986)*, ed. Sándor Jakab and Csaba Varga, 83–85. OKK Módszertani Intézetének házi nyomdájában, n.d.

Laszlo, Leszlie. *Church and State in Hungary 1919–1945.* Published dissertation. Columbia University, Faculty of Political Science, 1973.

———. "Hungary: From Cooperation to Resistance,1919–1945." In *Catholics, the State, and the European Radical Right, 1919–1945*, ed. Richard J. Wolff and Jörg K. Hoensch, 119–136. Boulder, Colo.: Social Science Monographs, 1987.

Lencsés, Ferenc. *Mezőgazdasági idénymunkások a negyvenes években* [Seasonal workers in Agriculture during the 1940s]. Budapest: Akadémiai Kiadó, 1982.

Lengyel, András. "Egy útkereső szociológus a két világháború közt: Vázlat Reitzer Béláról" [A Path-seeking sociologist in the interwar period: sketch of Béla Reitzer]. In *Útkeresések: Irodalom-és mávelődéstörténete tanulmányok.* Budapest: Magvető, 1990.

Lengyel, György, ed. *Hungarian Economy and Society During World War II.* Highland Lakes, N.J.: Atlantic Research and Publication, 1993.

Litván, József. *Ítéletidő*, memoirs written with P. P. Tóth. Budapest: Tekintet könyvek, 1991.

Livezeanu, Irina. *Cultural Politics in Greater Romania: Regionalism, Nation Building & Ethnic Struggle, 1918–1930.* Ithaca, N.Y.: Cornell University Press, 1995.

Lumans, Valdis O. *Himmler's Auxiliaries: The Volksdeutsche Mittelstelle and the German National Minorities of Europe, 1933–1945.* Chapel Hill: University of North Carolina Press, 1993.

Major Jenő vezérezredes. *Emléktöredékek: Visszaemlékezés az 1944. március és 1945. július közötti háborús eseményekre* [Fragments of a memoir: memoirs of the military events between March 1944 and July 1945]. Hadtörténelmi levéltári kiadványok, Petit Real, n.d.

M. Kiss, Sándor. "A lét terei" [The margin of existence], *Magyar Szemle.* 17. Budapest (2008).

———. *A magyar demokráciáért* [For Hungarian democracy]. New Brunswick: Bessenyei György Kör, 1983.

M. Kiss, Sándor, and Ivan Vitányi. *A Magyar Diák Szabadságfrontja* [The Hungarian students' independence front]. Budapest: Az antifasiszta ifjúsági emlékmá szervezőbizottsága, 1983.

Macartney, C. A. *Hungary and Her Successors 1919–1937.* London: Oxford University Press, 1937.

———. *October Fifteenth: A History of Modern Hungary, 1929–1945.* Second edition. 2 vols. Edinburgh: Edinburgh University Press, 1961.

Macmillan, Margaret. *Paris 1919: Six Months That Changed the World.* New York: Random House, 2003.

Magyarország 1944: Fejezetek az ellenállás történetéből [Hungary 1944: chapters from the history of the resistance]. Edited by Sándor M. Kiss. Budapest: Nemzeti Tankönyvkiadó, 1994.

Magyarország a második világháborúban: Lexikon A–Zs [Hungary in World War II: Encyclopaedia A–Zs]. Edited by Péter Sipos. Budapest: Petit Real, 1997.

Major General Harry Hill Bandholtz: An Undiplomatic Diary. Edited by Andrew L. Simon. Florida: Simon Publications, 2000.

Márai, Sándor. *Memoir of Hungary 1944–1948.* Budapest: Corvina, 1991.

Mawdsley, Evan. *Thunder in the East: The Nazi-Soviet War 1941–1945.* London: Hodder Education, 2007.

Megyeri, Anna. "Az ONCSA (Országos Nép és Családvédelmi Alap) segitő munkája Nagykanizsán 1941–1945 kózótt" [National foundation work for the protection of the people and the family in Nagykanizsa between 1941–1945]. *Zalai Múzeum* 7 (1997): 177–182.

Mócsy, István I. *The Effects of World War I. The Uprooted: Hungarian Refugees and Their Impact on Hungary's Domestic Politics, 1918–1921.* New York: Columbia University Press, 1983.

Molnár, Imre. *Esterházy János 1901–1957* [János Esterházy 1901–1957]. Dunaszerdahely: Nap, 1997.

Mona, Ilona. *Slachta Margit* [Margit Slachta]. Budapest: Corvinus, 1997.

Montgomery, John Flourney. *Hungary, the Unwilling Satellite.* Morristown: Vista, 1993. Original published by Devin-Adair Company, 1947.

N. Szegvári, Katalin. *Numerus Clausus Rendelkezések az Ellenforradalmi Magyarországon* [Numerus clausus provisions in counter-revolutionary Hungary]. Budapest: Akadémiai Kiadó, 1988.

Nagy, Ferenc. *The Struggle behind the Iron Curtain.* New York: Macmillan, 1948.

Nagybaczoni, Nagy Vilmos. *Végzetes esztendők 1938–1945* [Fatal years 1938–1945]. Budapest: Gondolat, 1986.

Náray Antal visszaemlékezése 1945. Edited by Sándor Szakály. Budapest: Zrínyi, 1988.

Nemeskürty, István. *Búcsúpillantás: A Magyar Királyság és Kormánzija 1920–1944* [A farewell glance: the Hungarian Kingdom and the Regent 1920–1944]. Budapest: Szabad tér, 1995.

Nicolson, Harold. *Peacemaking 1919.* New York: Grosset & Dunlap, 1965.

Notter, Harley A. *Postwar Foreign Policy Preparations 1939–1945.* Reprint of the 1949 ed. Westport, Conn.: Greenwood Press, 1975.

Nyeste, Zoltán. "Útkeresés—Adalékok a Magyar Ifjúsági Mozgalmak Történetéhez: 1942–1948." [Search for solutions—contributions to the history of the Hungarian youth movements: 1942–1948] (unpublished manuscript). Received July 1987.

Óbuda ostroma 1944–1945. Budapest: Óbudai múzeum, 2005.

Ormos, Mária. *Magyaroszág a két világháború korában 1914–1945* [Hungary in the period of the two world wars]. Budapest: Csokonai, 1998.

Overy, Richard. *Russia's War*. London: Penguin Books, 1997.

Özv, Bajcsy-Zsilinszky Endréné. "1944. Március 19-e egy budai lakásban." *In Kortársak Bajcsy-Zsilinszky Endréről*, ed. Károly Vigh, 413–415. Budapest: Magvető könyvkiadó, 1984.

Pastor, Péter. *Hungary between Wilson and Lenin: The Hungarian Revolution of 1918–1919 and the Big Three*. New York: Columbia University Press, 1976.

Páva, István. *Ország a hadak útján: Magyarország és a második világháboru* [Country on the march: Hungary and World War II]. Budapest: Pannonia, 1996.

Payne, Stanley G. *A History of Fascism 1914–1945*. Madison: University of Wisconsin Press, 1995.

Peéry, Rezso. *Requiem egy országreszert* [Requiem for a part of the country]. München: Aurora Kiskönyvek, 1975.

Péntek, Rita. "István Horthy's Election as Vice-Regent in 1942." *Hungarian Studies Review* 23 (1996): 17–28.

Pető, Andrea. "Női emlékezet és ellenállás" [Women's remembrance and opposition]. In *Az Elsodort Város: Emlékkötet a Budapestért folytatott harcok 60. évfordulójára 1944/45*. 351–379. Budapest: PolgART, 2005.

Petőcz, Pál. "Az egyetemi és főiskolai hallgatók második világháborús történetéhez"[On the history of university students and students in higher education during World War II]. *Századok*. 120 évf. 2 sz. (1986): 301–342.

Pethő, Tibor. "Quid nunc?—Hogyan tovább? Ullein-Reviczky Antal emlékiratai" [Quid nunc?—How to go on? Memoirs of Antal Ullein-Reviczky]. *Magyar Nemzet*. Saturday, May 29,1993.

Pók, Attila. "Why Was There No Historikerstreit in Hungary after 1989–1990." In *The Holocaust in Hungary: Sixty Years Later*, 241–256. New York: Columbia University Press, 2006.

Póth, Piroska. "A Magyarországi Népfőiskolák 1945 után." *Forrás* (December 1984), 20–23.

Pritz, Pál. *Bárdossy László a népbirosagelőtt* [László Bárdossy before the people's court] Budapest: Maecenas Könykiadó, 1991.

———. "War-Crimes Trial Hungarian Style: Prime Minister László Bárdossy Before the People's Tribunal 1945." *Hungarian Studies Review* 22, nos. 1–2 (Spring–Fall, 1995): 47–70

Püski, Levente. *A Magyar felsőház története 1927–1945* [The History of the Hungarian Upper House]. Budapest: Napvilág kiadó, 2000.

Rogger, Hans, and Eugen Weber, eds. *The European Right: A Historical Profile*. Berkeley: University of California Press, 1965.

Romsics, Ignác, ed. *20th Century Hungary and the Great Powers*. New York: Columbia University Press, 1995.

———. *The Dismantling of Historic Hungary: The Peace Treaty of Trianon, 1920*. Wayne, N.J.: Center for Hungarian Studies and Publications, Inc., 2002.

————. *István Bethlen: A Great Conservative Statesman of Hungary, 1874–1946*. Social Science Monographs, Boulder, Colo./New York: Columbia University Press, 1995

————. *Magyarország története a XX. Században* [History of Hungary in the XX century]. Budapest: Osiris, 1999.

————, ed. *Mítoszok, legendák, tévhitek a 20. Századi magyar történelemről* [Myths,legends, delusions of twentieth century Hungarian history]. Budapest: Osiris, 2005.

————. "The peasantry and the age of revolutions: Hungary, 1918–1919." Hungarian Revolution of 1918–1919: International Colloquium, Graz June 5–9, 1989.

————, ed. *Trianon és a Magyar politikai gondolkodás 1920–1953* [Trianon and Hungarian political thinking]. Budapest: Osiris, 1998.

Rothschild, Joseph. *East Central Europe between the Two World Wars*. Seattle: University of Washington Press, 1988.

Rozsnyoi, Agnes. "Nyilasok—amig a húr elpattant" [Arrow Cross—until the string snaps]. *Magyar Hirlap* (October 13, 1984).

Sakmyster, Thomas. *Hungary, the Great Powers and the Danubian Crisis, 1936–1939*. Athens: University of Georgia, 1980.

————. *Hungary's Admiral on Horseback: Miklós Horthy, 1918–1944*. Boulder, Colo.: European Monographs, 1994.

Sallai, Gergely. *Az első bécsi döntés* [The first Vienna decision]. Budapest: Osiris, 2002.

Schmidt, Mária. *Kollaboráció vagy kooperáció? A Budapesti Zsidó Tanács* [Collaboration or cooperation? The Budapest Jewish Council]. Budapest: Minerva, 1990.

Shirer, William L. *The Nightmare Years 1930–1940*. Toronto: Bantam Books, 1984.

Shvoy Kálmán, titkos naplója és emlékirata 1918–1945 [Kálmán Shvoy secret diary and memoir 1918–1945]. Budapest: Kossuth Könyvkiadó, 1983.

Simon, Zsuzsanna. "Erdély köz- és szakigazgatása a második bécsi döntés után" [Transylvanian administration after the second Vienna decision]. *REGIO Kisebbségi Szemle* 4 (1995): 60–82.

Sipos, Péter. *Imrédy Béla a vádlottak padján* [Béla Imrédy in the prisoner's box]. Budapest: Osiris, 1999.

Stark, Tamás. *Magyar foglyok a Szovjetunióban* [Hungarian prisoners in the Soviet Union]. Budapest: Lucidus Kiadó, 2006.

————. *Magyarország Második Világháborús Embervesztesége*[Human losses in Hungary during World War II]. Budapest: társadalom- és mávelődéstörténeti tanulmányok, 1989.

Sugar, Peter F., ed. *A History of Hungary*. Bloomington: Indiana University Press, 1990.

Swanson, John C. "Minority Building in the German Diaspora: the Hungarian-Germans." *Austrian History Yearbook* 36 (2005).

————. *The Remnants of the Habsburg Monarchy: The Shaping of Modern Austria and Hungary 1918–1933*. New York: Columbia University Press, 2001.

Szőke, Domonkos. "1945 szabad választás—szabad választás?" [Free election—free election?]. In *Tiltott történelmünk 1945–1947* [Our forbidden history 1945–1947], ed. János Horváth, 15–43. Budapest: Századvég Kiadó, 2006.

Szabó, Károly, and László Virágh. "Controlling the Agriculture and the Producers." In *Hungarian Economy and Society During World War II*, ed. György Lengyel, 127–149. Highland Lakes, NJ: Atlantic Research and Publication, 1993.

Szabó, Péter. *Don-kanyar: a magyar királyi 2.honvéd hadsereg története (1942–1943)* [The Don-bend: History of the Royal Hungarian Second Army 1942–1943]. Budapest: Corvina, 2001.

Szabó, Péter, and Norbert Számvéber. *A Keleti Hadszíntér és Magyarorszag 1941–1943* [The eastern war theater and Hungary 1941–1943]. Budapest: Puedlo, 2003.

Szabó, Zoltán. *A tardi helyzet—Cifra nyomorúság* [The situation at Tard—fancy misery]. Budapest: Akadémiai kiadó, 1986.

Szakály, Sándor. "The Composition of the Higher Military Elite." In *Hungarian Economy and Society During World War II*, ed. György Lengyel, 103–125. Highland Lakes, NJ: Atlantic Research and Publication, 1993.

———. "A hadsereg és a zsidótörvények az ellenforradalmi Magyarországon" [The army and the Jewish laws in counter-revolutionary Hungary]. *Valóság* (1985 9.szám): 49–65.

———. "Hungarian-German Military Cooperation during World War II." In *20th Century Hungary and the Great Powers*, ed. Ignác Romsics, 141–152. New York: Columbia University Press, 1995.

———. "A katonai ellenállási mozgalom Magyarországon a második világháború éveiben" [The Hungarian military resistance movement in World War II]. *Honvédségi Szemle* (1987 9.szám): 138–156.

———. *A magyar katonai elit 1938–1934* [The Hungarian military elite]. Budapest: Magvető, 1987.

———. "Nyilas-hungarista hatalomátvétel Magyarországon 1944" [Arrow-Cross Hungarista takeover in Hungary October 15–16, 1944]. *Nápi Magyarszát* (October 15,1999).

Szalai, Sándor. *Itél a magyar nép! A magyar háborús bűnperek tanulságai* [The Hungarian people judge! Lessons of the Hungarian state trials!]. Budapest: Athenaeum, 1946.

Szegedy-Maszák, Aladár. *Az ember ősszel visszanéz . . . Egy volt magyar diplomata emlékirataiból* [In autumn one looks back . . . Memoirs of a former Hungarian diplomat]. Budapest: Európa, 1996.

Szombathelyi, Ferenc. *Visszaemlékezései 1945* [Remembrances 1945]. Edited by Péter Gosztonyi. Washington, D.C.: Occidental Press, 1980.

Sztaray, Zoltan. *The Crushing of Hungarian Scouting 1945–1948*. Pamphlet. Garfield: Hungarian Scout Association in Exile, n.d.

Tilkovszky, Loránd. "The Late Interwar Years and World War II." In *A History of Hungary*, ed. Peter F. Sugar, 339–355. Bloomington: Indiana University Press, 1990.

Tilkovszky, Loránt. "The Confrontation between the Policy toward National Minorites and the German Ethnic Group Policy in Hungary during the Second World War." *Danubian Historical Studies* 1, no. 4 (1987): 33–49.

———. *Német nemzetiség magyar hazafiság* [German nationality Hungarian patriotism]. Pécs: JPTE, 1997.

———. *Nemzetiségi politika Magyarországon a 20. Században* [Nationalities policy in twentieth century Hungary]. Budapest: Csokonai Kiadó, 1998.

———. *Pál Teleki (1879–1941). A Biographical Sketch*. Budapest: Akadémiai, 1974.

Tiltott történelmünk 1945–1947 [Our forbidden history 1945–1947]. Edited by János Horváth. Budapest: Századvég Kiadó, 2006.

Tóth, Ágnes. *Migrationen in Ungarn 1945–1948: Vertreibung der Ungarndeutschen, Binnenwanderungen und slowakisch-ungarisher Bevölkerungsaustausch*. München: Oldenburg, 2001.

Tóth, János, ed. *A Sárospataki Népfőiskola 1936–1986* [The Sárospatak folk high school 1936–1948]. Országos Közművelődési Központ Módszertani Intézete, n.d.

Tóth, Pál Péter. "Ötven év után: a Márciusi Frontról" [Forty years after: the March Front]. *Magyarságkutatás: a Magyarságkutató Csoport évkőnvye*. Budapest (1987): 95–107.

Turczel, Lajos. *Két kor mezsgyéjén: A magyar irodalom fejlődesi feltételei és problémái Csehszlovákiában 1918 és 1938 között* [Border between two periods: the development and problems of Hungarian literature in Czechoslovakia between 1918 and 1938]. Bratislava: Madách, 1983.

Ugrin, József. *Emlékezéseim* [My remembrances].Budapest: Púski -Magyar Népfőiskolai Társaság, 1995.

Ungváry, Krisztián. *Battle for Budapest: 100 Days in World War II*. London: I. B.Tauris, 2003.

———. *Budapest Ostroma* [The siege of Budapest]. Budapest: Corvina, 1998. 3rd ed.

———. "Honvédség és külpolitika (1919–1945)" [The military aud foreign policy]. In *Magyarorsáq helye a 20. századi Európában*, 93–106. Budapest: Magyar Történelmi Társulat, 2002.

———. "Kik azok a nyilasok?" [Who are the Arrow Cross?] *Beszélő* (2003 június): 58–67.

———. *A magyar honvédség a második világháborüban* [The Hungarian army in World War II]. Budapest: Osiris, 2004.

———. "The 'Second Stalingrad': The Destruction of Axis Forces at Budapest (February, 1945)." In *Hungary in the Age of Total War (1938–1948)*, ed. Nándor Dreisziger, 151–168. New York: East European Monographs, 1998.

———. "Who were the Arrow Cross? A socialist mass party." *Rubicon* (November 2004): 5–17.

Várdy, Ágnes Huszár. "Forgottten Victims of World War II: Hungarian Women in Soviet Forced Labour Camps." *Hungarian Studies Review* 24, no. 1–2 (2002): 77–91.

Várdy, Steven Béla, and Agnes Huszár Várdy. *Stalin's Gulag: The Hungarian Experience*. Napoli, Italia: Universitã degli Studi di Napoli L'Orientale, 2007.

Váró, György. *Memoirs 1980 nyara*. Unpublished manuscript, edited by Váróné Tomori Viola.

Völgyesi, Zoltán. "A történelmi elit felbomlása 1944–45 után—a hajdúvárosok példáján" [The dissolution of the historical elite after 1944–1945—the example of the Hajdú cities]. In *Tiltott történelmünk 1945–1947*, ed. János Horváth, 100–113. Budapest: Századvég Kiadó, 2006.

Warriner, Doreen. *Economics of Peasant Farming*. London: Oxford University Press, 1939.

Weinberg, Gerhard L. *A World at Arms: A Global History of World War II*. New York: Cambridge University Press, 1994.

———. *Hitler's Foreign Policy: The Road to World War II 1933–1939*. New York: Enigma Books, 2005.

Wyman, David S. *The Abandonment of the Jews: America and the Holocaust, 1941–1945*. New York: The New Press, 2007.

Zeidler, Miklós. *A Magyar irredenta kultusz a két világháború között* [The Hungarian irredentist cult between the two world wars]. Budapest: Teleki László Alapítvány. 2002.

Personal Interviews

Árvay, Erzsébet. Szeged, Hungary. June 2, 1989.

Bakonyi, László (Mrs.). Budapest. June 11, 2001.

Boross, Zoltan. Debrecen, Hungary. March 22, 1988.

Dr. Hajdú, Tibor. Hungarian Institute of History, Budapest. July 4, 2008.

Dr. Hasznos, József. Hofkirchen, Austria. June 14, 2007.

Dr. Kontra, György. ELTE Anthropology Department. March 3,1988; March 16,1988.

Dr. Kovács, Bálint. Zsinati Archives. Budapest. June 8, 1988.

Dr. L. Nagy, Zsuzsa and János Levai. Budapest. November 13, 2001.

Molnar, Nicholas. Santa Fe, NM. February 28, 2002.

Petrusz, Tibor. Budapest. July 20, 2001.

Pók Somlai, Alice. Budapest. June 22, 2008; June 7, 2009.

Dr. Rézler, Gyula. Budapest. May 22, 2001.

Dr. Stúr, Judit. Budapest. June 12, 2003.

Szabó, László, retired First Lt. and daughter Györgyi Szabó. Budapest. August 29, 2001.

Támas, Gábor, [Pseudo]. Santa Fe, NM. October 31, 2001; December 15, 2001; February19, 2002.

Tomori, Viola. Velem, Hungary. June 26, 1990.

Dr. Tóth, Pál Péter. Budapest. 2 August 2002.

Vigyazo, Lilly. Budapest. June 26, 2003; August 1, 2003.

Zamory, Béla. Telephone interview. New Brunswick, NJ. October 20, 2001.

Zichy, Julia, countess. Telephone interview. September 11, 2009.

Index